Be inspired !

Jeffrey Riley

Further praise for Cutting Edge Internal Auditing

"Cutting Edge Internal Auditing *is compiled from Professor Ridley's personal and intimate knowledge of the development of the profession since he entered it over half a century ago. It is an insightful and thought-provoking read.*"
—Professor Georges Selim, Professor of Internal Audit, Head of the Faculty of Management, Cass Business School, London

"*Refreshingly different, this book is for the thinking internal auditor, provoking innovation and thoughtful leadership. It seeks to grow the auditor beyond current practices and the imagination of management. If management has the tendency to manage with hindsight, then the auditor needs to be the auditor of the future – at the cutting edge – today.*"
—Vicky Kubitcheck, Head of Risk and Compliance, AEGON

"*This book is a motivational read for those with the imagination to apply themselves to be more than a good internal auditor. A great bringing together of themes to be dipped into at moments when we find we need a framework to hang our best ideas on and help achieve our ambitions for ourselves and our profession.*"
—Kelsey Walker, Director, Kelsey Walker Associates

"Cutting Edge Internal Auditing *convincingly presents many varied aspects of internal auditing practice. The work contrasts a highly interesting and very readable discussion of the key milestones in the development of the internal auditing profession with insightful views of the current governance environment and future prospects. The author's personal perspective on issues important to internal auditing makes this volume a 'must read' for internal auditors.*"
—Dr. Curtis C. Verschoor, CIA, CPA, CFE, CMA, L & Q Research Professor, School of Accountancy and MIS, and Wicklander Research Fellow, Institute for Business and Professional Ethics, DePaul University, Chicago

"*Professor Ridley has provided a comprehensive survey of the characteristics, dynamics and processes of setting 'cutting edge' standards, and an examination of the contributions of internal auditing research in solving problems in this context. The orientation he has outlined is not institutional, but rather an attempt to increase the understanding of the internal auditing processes and its special characteristics from a global perspective.*"
—Ronald Lackland CIA, CCSA, CGAP, CFE, MIRM, Acting Head of the Centre for Internal Audit, Risk and Governance, Birmingham City University Business School

Cutting Edge Internal Auditing

Cutting Edge Internal Auditing

Jeffrey Ridley

John Wiley & Sons, Ltd

Copyright © 2008 Jeffrey Ridley

Published by   John Wiley & Sons Ltd, The Atrium, Southern Gate, Chichester,
                  West Sussex PO19 8SQ, England

                  Telephone   (+44) 1243 779777

Email (for orders and customer service enquiries): cs-books@wiley.co.uk
Visit our Home Page on www.wiley.com

Other Wiley Editorial Offices

John Wiley & Sons Inc., 111 River Street, Hoboken, NJ 07030, USA

Jossey-Bass, 989 Market Street, San Francisco, CA 94103-1741, USA

Wiley-VCH Verlag GmbH, Boschstr. 12, D-69469 Weinheim, Germany

John Wiley & Sons Australia Ltd, 42 McDougall Street, Milton, Queensland 4064, Australia

John Wiley & Sons (Asia) Pte Ltd, 2 Clementi Loop #02-01, Jin Xing Distripark, Singapore 129809

John Wiley & Sons Canada Ltd, 6045 Freemont Blvd, Mississauga, ONT, L5R 4J3, Canada

Wiley also publishes its books in a variety of electronic formats. Some content that appears in print may not be
available in electronic books.

Library of Congress Cataloging in Publication Data

Ridley, Jeffrey.
   Cutting edge internal auditing / Jeffrey Ridley.
      p.   cm.
   Includes bibliographical references and index.
   ISBN 978-0-470-51039-1 (cloth)
   1. Auditing, Internal.   I. Title
   HF5668.25.R527 2008
   657 ′ .458—dc22
                        2008007632

British Library Cataloguing in Publication Data

A catalogue record for this book is available from the British Library

ISBN 978-0-470-51039-1 (H/B)

Typeset in 10/12pt Times by Integra Software Services Pvt. Ltd, Pondicherry, India
Printed and bound in Great Britain by CPI Antony Rowe, Chippenham, Wiltshire

To my parents and their encouragement for me to continuously learn.

To my wife Angela, without whose support and patience, along many audit trails, this book would not have been written.

To our children, Christine and Neil and their families. And most importantly, for our grandchildren Crystal, Lucy, Daisy, Jed and Josh: each, in their own way, is pioneering, with lots of imagination and a will to continuously learn. The future is theirs.

Contents

11   Cutting Edge Internal Auditing Is Creative   273

*'... if internal auditors wish to hold themselves
out as problem-solving partners to management,
they had better become aware of their innate
creativity or learn about creativity and put it to use.'*

12   Cutting Edge Internal Auditing Asks The Right Questions   287

*'I shot an arrow into the air,
It fell to earth I know not where ...'*

> *'To be successful we must be sensitive to the problems of each
> day. All can have an impact on our professional activities far
> beyond the changes we may foresee at the present time.'*

List Of Figures And Training Slides

LIST OF TRAINING SLIDES

Chapter

List Of Cutting Edge Case Studies
Which Appear On The CD ROM

About The Author

Jeffrey Ridley started his auditing career in Her Majesty's Colonial Audit Service in 1953, working in Nigeria, West Africa, as a government and local authority external auditor. In 1963 he left Nigeria to return to the United Kingdom. At that time he joined Vauxhall Motors Limited, England, a subsidiary of General Motors, as a senior auditor. In 1965 he moved, as a senior auditor, to Kodak Limited, England, a subsidiary of Eastman Kodak. He was appointed internal audit manager in 1971 and served in that position until his retirement from Kodak in 1993.

At Kodak he developed internal auditing practices; managed the company's graduate accountant training scheme; and, in the mid-1980s served for some years on the company's Quality Council. In 1977 the Kodak graduate accountant-training scheme won the first prestigious annual Chartered Institute of Management Accounting national award for best training practice. In 1992 he registered his internal audit department to the international quality standard ISO 9001.

In 1966 he joined, and is still a member of, the Institute of Internal Auditors: over many years he has served on committees in the United Kingdom and internationally, including research, quality and education. In 1975–76 he was elected first president of the newly formed United Kingdom Chapter, which subsequently became the IIA – UK and Ireland, an affiliated National Institute of The Institute of Internal Auditors Inc.

In 1991, he accepted a position as visiting professor of auditing at the then South Bank Polytechnic, teaching an internal auditing unit at undergraduate level. After retirement from Kodak, he increased his teaching time and research at the now London South Bank University. He currently facilitates student research and teaches corporate governance at postgraduate level at that university. In 2006, he also accepted a similar position at the Birmingham City University, England.

In 1998, he co-authored with Professor Andrew Chambers *Leading Edge Internal Auditing*, published by ICSA Publishing Limited. He has written and researched widely and internationally on internal auditing and governance topics. In 1996, the Institute of Internal Auditors Research Foundation published his international research into ISO 9000 – *International Quality Standards: Implications for Internal Auditing*. His most recent research papers are 'Quality and Internal Audit – A Survey of Theory and Practice' (2005),[1] 'Continuous Improvement in Internal Audit Services' (2006),[2] 'Internal Auditing's

---

[1] *Proceedings of the 2nd European Academic Conference on Internal Audit & Corporate Governance 2004* (May 2005), ISBN 0-9550137-0-4, London, England.
[2] *Proceedings of the 4th European Academic Conference on Internal Audit & Corporate Governance 2006*, London, England.

International Contribution to Governance' (2007)[3] and 'Innovative Practices in Today's Internal Auditing[4]: the latter three papers co-authored with Dr Kenneth D'Silva, London South Bank University.

He is a fellow of the Institute of Chartered Secretaries and Administrators, a fellow of the Institute of Internal Auditors – United Kingdom and Ireland, and a Certified Internal Auditor.

---

[3] Published also in *The International Journal of Business Governance and Ethics*, Vol. 3, No. 2, 2007, pp. 113–126, Interscience Enterprises Ltd.
[4] *Proceedings of the 5th European Academic Conference on Internal Audit & Governance 2007*, Pisa, Italy.

Preface

'The world can only be grasped by action not by contemplation
... The hand is the cutting edge of the mind.'

Jacob Bronowski 1973[1]

This is not a textbook of internal auditing practices. It is a book about the imagination that has created those practices – practices that have continuously improved internal auditing during the more than fifty years I have audited, advised, taught and researched risk management, control and governance. There are already many excellent books worldwide on techniques for best practice internal auditing that will continue to be revised, and others published, in the future. There are excellent national and international standards and guidelines for risk management, control, governance and auditing, representing best practices in all countries: these will continue to be improved. This book will reference into many of these, and I hope it will encourage the reader to research them and view this book as a supplement to the knowledge and guidance they contain.

The primary referencing is into material and practices in the United Kingdom, and many of these references and practices have been influenced by international activities and events. Countries throughout the world have placed their own interpretations on the influences that globalization has made to risk management, control and governance in their environments. It will be the reader's task to relate the United Kingdom references to more appropriate guidelines in his or her own country.

The title of the book is deliberately chosen to challenge and focus on change in internal auditing in the past, present and future. Cutting edge will always mean different things to different people at different times, nationally and across the world. These differences have been shaped by culture, language, experiences, knowledge and enthusiasm for change.

The Oxford English Dictionary defines cutting edge as a noun '... *the latest or most advanced stage; the forefront* ...' and as an adjective '... *innovative; pioneering*'. In this book it is used as both a noun and an adjective. What does cutting edge really mean in practice? It is a term that has been (still is and always will be) used by many across the world to describe different activities, from strategy to operations, with outputs including both products and services. It has many synonyms – progressive, advanced, forward-looking,

---

radical, even revolutionary: rarely evolutionary. Two other synonyms often used are 'leading edge' and 'best practice'.

Cutting edge is frequently used to promote innovation and motivate customer interest. In this book it applies to all activities pioneering and developing new paths in professional internal auditing services – not just in today's and tomorrow's activities but throughout the history of professional internal auditing, from the early 1960s to the present.

Cutting edge is continuous. What was cutting edge in the past can still be cutting edge today and tomorrow. This book contains a collection of cutting edge internal auditing activities I have experienced and researched as an internal auditor and teacher. Each is updated to reflect the current internal auditing needs. Each is supported by principles and case study examples of how cutting edge is being marketed and practised in internal auditing. I am grateful to the many internal auditors and others worldwide who have given me permission to discuss their cutting edge resources and practices. For those not mentioned I apologize, they would have been, included had I known of their cutting edge internal auditing.

As I write this book my imagination is indebted to David Scott, the US astronaut, for a phrase used in his recent book[2] on the exploration of space in the 1960s, and the cutting edge processes that took men to the Moon and brought them back safely to Earth at that time:

> You can be taught to become a good pilot, but you cannot be taught to become the best pilot. This depends to a great extent on your coordination, how quickly you react to situations and, perhaps more importantly of all, how sensitive you are to the slightest movement of the plane you are flying.

Key to space exploration is the political and strategic commitment, imagination and teamwork of those who worked to enter space, and who eventually stood on the Moon's surface. In many ways I have always seen internal auditors, individually and as teams, following a similar strategic path of commitment, imagination and teamwork in the exploration of each audit engagement. They start with organization and auditing strategies and step along a path that is not familiar, with an achievement in mind. They do this with teamwork. They are trained to do this. They are taught to be good auditors: but they cannot be taught to be the best auditor. That depends on their commitment and imagination: how they can coordinate their work with others; how quickly they can react to the situations in which they find themselves; how innovative they can be in their practices: how sensitive they are to their environment. They may not be aiming for the Moon, but at the beginning of every engagement they are stepping into the unknown.

This view may be criticized as too imaginative and pioneering, but it is one I have always held about the challenges and opportunities facing internal auditors. It is what Lawrence Sawyer[3] believed throughout his internal auditing career, and one he taught me and many other internal auditors through his published material and words:

> Modern internal auditing, to be successful, must be grounded on management support and acceptance and on an imaginative service.

---

[2] David Scott, US astronaut, in his co-authored book with Alex Leonov, Soviet Cosmonaut, *Two Sides of the Moon* (2004: p. 28), Simon & Schuster UK Ltd, London, England.
[3] *The Practice of Modern Internal Auditing* (1973: p. 23), Lawrence B. Sawyer, The IIA. [In the Preface to another more recent IIA Inc. publication, *Sawyer's Words of Wisdom* (2004), a collection of articles by Lawrence Sawyer between the years 1979 to 1998, William Bishop III, former President of The IIA Inc. wrote: *'In the history of the internal auditing profession, no practitioner has ever rivaled Larry Sawyer's prophetic, visionary, and seemingly timeless contribution to internal auditing . . . .'*

This book is alive with ideas for the future of professional internal auditing. Some from my own experiences; many from the experiences of others. Imagination is its theme. I hope internal auditors will continue to act on the messages each chapter contains as the future of professional internal auditing is theirs, not mine.

Jeffrey Ridley
2008

Foreword

This is a remarkable book. There are so many internal auditing books around that it is very refreshing indeed to find one that breaks all the moulds, that comes across as a unique contribution and not just another technical tome. It should be consulted by all those who desire an insightful and inspired appreciation of the development of internal auditing throughout the second half of the 20th century and into the 21st century.

In sketching out the historical panoply of internal auditing, the author is particularly successful in showing how latest developments often have had their roots in the past, and his citations from the past provide novel insights into the present and future.

There is a lot of very good, 'cutting edge' technical advice within it but it is not merely a technical 'how to do it best' work. It is also an odyssey of the development of the art and profession of internal auditing over the years – by someone who has been in the thick of it at a senior level almost from the start of the modern internal auditing movement. Further, it is a highly inspirational work – enthusiasm for internal auditing, and the author's drive to take internal auditing to greater heights, shines through almost every page. Then there is the philosophical positioning and repositioning of internal audit, which the author handles so well. Woven through the book is a particular dedication to, and focus upon, quality. Finally, there is an implicit autobiographical backdrop. The book is quite anecdotal and this author is almost uniquely positioned to make such fine use of appropriate anecdotes.

The style is fresh and the author's use of quotations is apposite. It is not a heavy read at all; fundamentally, it is enjoyable. The book should be purchased by serious internal auditors. Some will be those who are strongly committed to the profession and who will appreciate the opportunity to share with the author the profession's development. Others will be those who wish to take their internal auditing functions to new heights – for whom the book will suggest many progressive ideas. Others will be young internal auditors and students of internal auditing, particularly keen to learn where they fit into the development of the profession and about the next stages in its development.

The book is very well referenced and supported by excellent case studies, written by leading contributors to the development of professional internal auditing and organizations at the cutting edge of corporate governance across all sectors. This, in itself, will be of value to users of the book.

Professor Andrew Chambers
ProfADC@aol.com

Acknowledgements

I would like to acknowledge the experience and wisdom I have gained from:

F.R.M De Paula, for his principles of auditing. These were the basis of my audit training for the Colonial Audit Service in 1953. They have stood me in good stead, and have been with me ever since as an auditor. Though much more complex today, in ever-changing accounting and auditing standards, they are still basic guidance for the quality of all auditing.

The Director of Audit and audit staff in Kaduna, Nigeria, who started and guided me on my first adventures and challenges in auditing.

The dentist in Nigeria, who was my first colonial auditee. He taught me the importance of understanding customer needs during my audit: both his needs as a dentist and my own needs because of my toothache, just before the audit started. I learned then the importance of auditors and auditees seeing themselves as being satisfied as both customers and suppliers in every audit engagement.

The government Resident of the first Nigerian Province in which I carried out audits, who taught me the importance of recognizing the many difficulties faced by those I was auditing. These difficulties exist in every audit engagement, but are not always recognized by the auditor, or auditee.

My first auditee when neither of us spoke the same language. Later on I was to learn communication can be an issue in every audit engagement, even when both auditor and auditee speak the same language.

The first fraudster I met, who demonstrated how easy it had been to circumvent controls and commit fraud. And the management who believed that it could not happen. Little has changed today.

Those members of my audit team in Ibadan, Nigeria, who introduced me to the importance of team building and lateral thinking. Lessons I carried forward in my career.

The audit staff at General Motors, whose well-researched and cutting edge internal audit programmes and questionnaires started me on the path to being a modern internal auditor.

The production manager in my first manufacturing audit, who taught me the importance of quality control in all operations. This led to my interest and research into quality as a risk and opportunity, and its management as a vision and control for all products and services.

The cost accountant, who taught me the importance of control in cost accounting and financial accounting, when these systems operated separately. Later such systems integrated through the use of computers and strengthened the reliability and accuracy of the data being reported. But the reconciliation of both is still as important today.

The production manager, who taught me that control of by-products and waste in manufacturing processes is as important as control over the products being manufactured. This is a principle that applies equally, if not more so, in all the environmental issues that affect the world today.

The Finance Director, who supported my approach to modern internal auditing and its development into a professional assurance, consulting and teaching service.

The Information Systems Director, who encouraged me to enter the world of systems development as an auditor and taught me the importance of this for the implementation of all computer systems and their operation.

The General Auditors of Eastman Kodak Company, who over many years encouraged me to have a vision to be at the cutting edge of internal auditing.

The directors at Kodak Limited who encouraged me to contribute in their quality initiatives, which eventually led to the registration of my internal audit activity to the international quality standard ISO 9001.

All I have worked with over many years in The Institute of Internal Auditors globally and in the United Kingdom from 1967 until now. Not all are here today. I learned from them all and continue to do so.

All the academic staff I have had the good fortune to meet and work with since 1991. I learned from them all and continue to do so.

All my students since 1961. There are too many to mention, but I have had the privilege to teach and supervise their studies and at the same time learn, and am still learning, from them.

All the articles referenced to issues of *Internal Auditor*, the questions from the Certified Internal Auditor Examinations and other material published by The Institute of Internal Auditors, Inc., 247 Maitland Avenue, Altamonte Springs, Florida 32701, USA (www.theiia.org) are reprinted with permission.

Professor Andrew Chambers for the opportunity to use the cartoons in the book, all designed by The Rev. Hugh Pruen and copyright of Management Audit LLP.

All the staff at John Wiley & Sons who have guided me in the preparation of the manuscript for this book. They have been very patient and helpful.

Most importantly, I owe a debt of gratitude to the many contributors to this book in case study form (see CD ROM) who are all named at the end of their case study and listed below in chapter order. Their knowledge and experience form an important part of cutting edge internal auditing today and the future development of internal auditing as a profession. I have also been fortunate to count many of them as friends and colleagues over a long period.

Chapter 3:   Roland de Meulder; David O'Regan; Angelina Chin.

Chapter 4:   Christopher Strong; Dr Kenneth D'Silva (also Chapters 9 and 10); Professor Georges Selim; Dr Sally Woodward; Don Brunton; David Reynolds; Shari Casey.

Chapter 5:   Gillian Bolton; Andrew Robinson; Professor Leen Paape; Tracey Hassell.

Chapter 6:   K.H. Spencer Pickett; Kastuv Ray; Peter Tickner.

Chapter 7:   Professor Andrew D. Chambers (also Chapters 12 and 13); Joyce Drummond-Hill.

Chapter 8:   A.J. Hans Spoel; Patricia Pinel; Florence Bergeret.

Chapter 10:   Professor John S. Oakland; Stan Farmer.

Chapter 11:   William E. Greishober; Vicky Kubitscheck; Professor Jane Henry; Professor Gerard Puccio.

Chapter 12:   Jim Kaplan.

Chapter 13:   Keith Labbett; Jenny Rayner; Hans Nieuwlands; Philippa Foster Back OBE.

Chapter 14:   Richard Gossage; Kelsey Walker; Gerald Cox.

Chapter 15:   Ronald Lackland.

Chapter 16:   Lal Balkaran; Richard Nelson; Iain R. Brown.

And lastly my thanks to the following organizations, presented in alphabetic order, for their contributed case studies and permission to use other material:

Association of Chartered and Certified Accounts, UK; Audit Commission, UK; BG Group plc, UK; Birmingham City University; Business in the Community, UK; Charity Finance, UK; Charities Internal Audit Network, UK; Chartered Institute of Public Finance and Accountancy, UK; Committee on Standards in Public Life, UK; European Confederation of Institutes of Internal Auditing, Belgium; Committee of Sponsoring Organizations, USA; Department of Business Enterprise and Regulatory Reform, UK; Eurocode Working Group, UK; Financial Reporting Council, UK; GoodCorporation; Health and Safety Executive, UK; HM Treasury, UK; Housing Association Internal Audit Forum,UK; Institute of Business Ethics, UK; Institute of Directors, UK; ICSA Publishing Limited, UK; IIA – UK & Ireland South West District; International Chamber of Commerce, Paris; Institute of Chartered Secretaries and Administrators, UK; Institute of Internal Auditors – UK & Ireland; London South Bank University, UK; Nordea AB, Norway; Office of Public Management, UK; Protiviti Inc., USA; Robert Half International Inc., USA; Royal Bank of Scotland, UK; The HR Chally Group, USA; The Institute of Internal Auditors Inc., USA; The IIA Research Foundation, USA; Tomorrow's Company, UK; United Nations.

I apologize if I have missed any person or organization from the above who should have been mentioned. I am indebted to so many for the knowledge, experiences and enjoyment I have had from my careers as an external auditor, internal auditor and academic over many years and adventures, including the writing and compilation of this book.

Introduction

'Science does not know its debt to imagination.'

Ralph Waldo Emerson (1803–1882)[1]

Cutting Edge Internal Auditing Model 1992

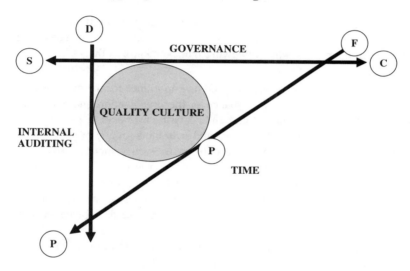

CUTTING EDGE INTERNAL AUDITING BEFORE 1994

In the early 1980s I experimented with developing a framework for managing internal auditing focused on how an organization is governed and the responsibilities of internal auditors. I based the framework on The IIA Standards at that time. This used a similar model to Slide 1, the one above but showed:

- The *horizontal* line as 'Scope of Work' – Standard 300, 'Scope of Work'.
- The *vertical* line as 'Depth' of audit penetration into the company's operations – Standard 400, 'Performance of Audit Work'.
- The *diagonal* line as 'Time' representing past, present and future.
- The *circle* as 'Management of Internal Audit' – Standards 100, 'Independence'; 200, 'Professional Proficiency'; 500, 'Management of Internal Auditing Department'.

My experiences in quality management in the late 1980s encouraged me to change the framework to demonstrate the importance of quality principles in internal auditing:

- The *horizontal* line became 'Control' without the word 'internal'. This emphasized the importance of control across supply chains (both internal and external to the organization). Represented by **S** and **C**.
- The *vertical* line became 'Image'. This brought in the importance of internal auditing selling its products and services to customers, rather than imposing these with management support.
- The *diagonal* line became 'Change'. This recognized the increasing changes occurring in most organizations as they continued to introduce more advanced information technology, outsource and downsize their operations.
- The *circle* became 'Total Quality Management'. This demonstrated the importance of quality assurance and continuous improvement in all internal audit processes

The intention of the framework as it was further developed into the above graphic was to provide training for internal audit staff in how their function was managed and what they should look for in their work when reviewing management by others.

- The *horizontal* line became governance and its importance for the management of internal auditing. It also demonstrated governance in the organization and across all its supply chains, starting with suppliers **(S)** and ending with customers **(C)** – although this is too simplistic. External and internal suppliers and customers for any organization are complex relationships with many different levels for each: even sometimes being both supplier and customer at the same time. These relations can also vary from stand-off to closer ownership, parental, subsidiary, partner and collaboration links.
- The *vertical* line became the standards with which internal auditors should comply to examine deeply in every engagement – the **D** – and use as a benchmark against their services.
- The *diagonal* line introduced the concept of time – past **(P)** present **(P)** and future **(F)** – in internal auditing and every operation in an organization.
- The *circle* became quality in internal audit work and quality in all an organization's management and processes. How its principles are understood and implemented: how it is measured and its cost. This now more correctly represents how all performance is measured in every operation in an organization.

This interaction of the lines and circle showed how all the elements in the graphic interrelated with the others. None stands out alone; each supports the others. The two outward-pointing arrows at the horizontal level demonstrated the importance of always thinking laterally about every operation. The vertical line pointing down demonstrated the importance of depth and detail in the performance of all work, through good planning and competence. The two outward-pointing arrows on the diagonal demonstrated the need to examine the past, present and future in each engagement.

This book continues to develop this cutting edge internal auditing model to represent the interactions between governance in an organization today and tomorrow, the growing professionalism of internal auditing services, changes that are continuous and the never-ending road to better quality: interactions that exist in the operations in every organization. These are interactions that all internal auditors have to imagine in every engagement they start, from the planning stages, setting of objectives, risk assessment, review of control and governance to communication of findings: interactions that require creative thinking and innovation. Creative thinking and innovation are key to the success of internal auditing. They are key to the success of every organization. They require imagination.

Peter Drucker (1955)[2] described the setting of innovative objectives in organizations in two parts: '. . . *one looking a short time ahead and projecting fairly concrete developments which, in effect, only carry out innovations already made; another looking a long time ahead and aiming at what might be.*' Of his five innovation goals for an organization, the fifth is:

> Innovations and improvements in all major areas of activity – in accounting or design, office management or labour relations – so as to keep up with the advances in knowledge and skills.

No mention of internal auditing but the message applies: '. . . *to keep up with the advances in knowledge and skills*' or, better still, to manage that knowledge well and be ahead of the advances!

Later, Drucker (1967)[3] wrote:

> In all matters of true uncertainty such as the executive deals with – whether his sphere is political, economic, social or military – one needs creative solutions which create a new situation. And this means that one needs imagination – a new and different way of perceiving and understanding. Imagination of the first order is, I admit, not in abundant supply. But neither is it as scarce as is commonly believed. Imagination needs to be challenged and stimulated, however, or else it remains latent and unused. Disagreement, especially if forced to be reasoned, thought through, documented, is the most effective stimulus we know.

Challenges from disagreement, whether within internal auditing or from its many different suppliers and customers, are still the best stimulus for imagination and cutting edge practices.

Professor Andrew Chambers (1981)[4] discussed tomorrow's internal auditing with some foresight as to what was to happen in the future:

> There is also now emerging some understanding that exclusive dedication to operational efficiency means that the internal auditor is in danger, amongst other things, of overlooking certain other elements, which may have a much greater bearing upon the long-term health of the organization. These elements are corporate attitudes – for example, attitude to risk, attitude to innovation, attitude to conserving resources, attitude to work, attitude to staff development and so on. While *attitude audits* are not currently generally regarded as legitimate internal audit interest, they may become so in the future.

For corporate attitudes read corporate culture. For corporate culture also read internal auditing culture.

Little is written about the cutting edge of innovation and internal auditing prior to 1994. Then the terms used most to describe best internal auditing were, and still are, modern, world class, first class, leading edge and best in class. Cutting edge and innovation are now relatively new terms used to promote and market internal auditing services and its products and services in risk management, control and governance processes.

Article:
Professional Internal Auditors Are Talented People[5] (1994)

The education and training of professional internal auditors starts at the recruitment interview and continues through their experience of internal auditing into career development paths within and outside the internal audit department. Professional internal auditors develop a variety of roles in their organizations as they provide and develop their professional services. They move from policeman to consultant to teacher in every audit and between professional and technical positions, as they promote their services and careers. Any list of their collective knowledge and skills includes, but is not restricted to, accounting, finance statistics, electronic data processing, engineering, taxation and law.

> *'Professional internal auditors are experts in governance and skilled in the strategic, tactical and operational aspects of risk assessment and audit planning.'*

Professional internal auditors are experts in governance and skilled in the strategic, tactical and operational aspects of risk assessment and audit planning. They are able to adapt their service to the effects of change on structures and procedures and facilitate change to improve control in the future.

They understand how quality is designed and customers are delighted with the products and services they buy. This understanding is built into every audit.

They are good communicators, sensitive to the needs of their customers. They have the ability to develop satisfactory relationships with those they serve. They are committed professionals, dedicated to the marketing of their service.

They continue their education through training programmes linked to their own, their service and their organization's objectives. They participate in their professional institute's activities.

They are successful. They are real!

Research into internal auditing practices always shows that many professional internal auditors are very successful in their careers. They are seen as members of their management teams, receiving rewards and reinforcement equal to, if not better than, many other service functions. They have a high profile in their organizations and their advice is respected. They are talented people.

CUTTING EDGE INTERNAL AUDITING IS ALL ABOUT IMAGINATION

Imagination is the key to excellent internal auditing by talented internal auditors. The aim of this book is to demonstrate this importance, whatever the role acted by an internal auditor, be it assurance, consulting, teaching, facilitation, or other. Internal auditors have many explorations in the pursuit of an engagement's objectives – explorations where there are organization maps to understand; trails to follow, often without structure and signposts; bridges to cross; gaps of information to confuse the pursuit; supply chains stretching across the globe; walls that often block communications; and, new, sometimes unproven, technology. Perhaps the comparisons are a little extreme but they fit many of the engagements in my career as an internal auditor.

Auditing engagements are adventures at all times, not only with obstacles, but also relationships developing along the trails they follow: relationships that can be friendly and participative;[6] relationships that can create dislike and distrust; relationships that can even be aggressive. Imagination plays an important part in every engagement. It is also essential in developing overall audit strategy, policies, processes, style[7] and creating successful end-results for each engagement.

Jean-Pierre Garitte,[8] Chairman of The IIA in 1998, caught the imagination of participative relationships in internal auditing, promoting a theme of *'building bridges'*:

> We internal auditors traverse our organizations; but, as we migrate from one area to another, and another, we haven't always thought about how helpful it might be to promote and enhance connectedness. We haven't always thought of ourselves as bridge builders, or even as partners with the potential to link multifarious elements.

Exploring every engagement with the intention of building bridges can enhance the image of internal auditing, and be cutting edge. Garitte ends his paper with:

> When we work with operating management and others in an ambiance of support and helpfulness, we erect scaffolds for connections, and we tear down walls that divide us.

Imagination is not mentioned in The IIA definition of internal auditing[9] or its supporting standards and guidance, yet its effect can be seen in the present status and promotion of professional internal auditing. Consider whether the definition of internal auditing would have been improved if 'imaginative' had been included:

> Internal auditing is an independent, objective assurance and consulting activity designed to add value and improve an organization's operations. It helps an organization to accomplish its objectives by bringing a systematic, disciplined *[and imaginative]* approach to evaluate and improve the effectiveness of risk management, control and governance processes.

At its heart, cutting edge in science is always about innovation and pioneering change. Often not just 'nudges' but 'paradigm shifts': shifts to improve directions, operations, products, services, achievements and satisfaction; shifts to improve the way life is lived and work is performed. Cutting edge internal auditing is all of these things. It is about creating practices that meet the needs of its customers, but most of all it is about the imagination to create and innovate. Imagination to know which structures, operations and methods need to be created: and innovation to action the best ways to do this.

What is cutting edge today may well be traditional tomorrow, or it may remain cutting edge for some time. There is no better evidence for this than in tools and technology. The hammer was cutting edge at one time, so was the desktop computer. The hammer is now the traditional method of applying instant pressure to a nail, possessed and used by many – though some may now use more cutting edge technology based on air pressure, or even alternatives to nails.

The desktop computer was cutting edge when introduced in businesses in the 1960s and for some it is still cutting edge, but for many it is now traditional, a piece of hardware in all types of business and many homes. Yet, cutting edge devices continuously change its software and accessories, and this will continue. Today, traditional desktop hardware is now being replaced by cutting edge technology, in the form of wireless laptops and more recently in the form of wireless handheld devices. More cutting edge technology changes will happen, and at a faster pace.

What is true of tools and technology applies equally to strategies, policies, processes, techniques and even attitudes. Resource availability, knowledge management, competition and customer needs all drive change. Leading edge organizations recognize this and adapt their products and services accordingly. What changes leading edge into cutting edge is competition, invention and an understanding of customer needs in the immediate future and horizon.

Letter:
We Should Have A Vision To Be Innovators[10] (1998)

After 50 years as a profession we should now have a vision to be innovators! With the formation of the Institute of Internal Auditors (The IIA) in North America in 1941, internal auditors in the 1940s promoted the development of professional internal auditing. The IIA introduced in 1942 a worldwide image for internal auditing ... as an 'added value' professional service, using the challenging statement:

> 'Creativity, innovation and experimentation are now key to our professional success. They must be the vision of all internal auditing functions.'

> Today's happenings pose new and perhaps perplexing problems to internal auditors. The requests and regulations of the several branches and agencies of Government demand a complete knowledge by internal auditors of their effect on the normal units of the companies they represent. The scope of internal audit requirements has increased tremendously

Shortly after this, chapters of The IIA were established across North America and worldwide, including the UK. In 1975, growing membership in the UK resulted in a merger of the five chapters, into the first IIA affiliated national institute. I was proud and honoured to be elected its first president. The IIA–UK is now one of the foremost leaders in the development of internal auditing at national and international levels. No small achievement for a young professional body, its members and staff.

The vision we set ourselves in 1975 was '... to be a profession for the future.' Since then, many IIA developments have contributed to our claim to international status: international standards and a code of ethics, professional examinations based on an international common body of knowledge, global research into control and auditing, international quality assurance reviews, all have played their parts in our growth. However, our vision for tomorrow must be even higher than just being a profession. We also need to be seen as innovators in the world of regulation, control and auditing.

Creativity, innovation and experimentation are now key to our professional success. They must be the vision of all internal auditing functions. This means improving old and developing new products and services for delighting our customers, with a focus on their objectives. This means being at the leading edge in all the markets in which we sell our internal auditing services. This means beating our competitors and knowing who these are. This means having the imagination, and foresight of what our organizations will require from us, not just in 2000, but also beyond.

In this 50th year celebration of our national institute's past and present teamwork, all IIA–UK members should continue to set their sights on being inventors of an improved and new internal auditing, to delight all their customers . . . and increase its status as a profession.

LEADING EDGE INTERNAL AUDITING IN 1998

In 1998, for my book[11] with Professor Andrew Chambers on leading edge internal auditing practices at that time, I included a spectrum of traditional, new and leading edge internal auditing resources and practices, developed by research in 1996 (see Figure 1.1).

In the same book I wrote:

> The recent benchmarking service provided by The IIA has identified in its questionnaire and results the following emerging best and successful internal auditing practices, many of which can be seen in Figure 1.1 as new and leading edge activities:

- develop a partnering role with audit clients;
- participate in corporate task forces;
- align corporate goals, department plans and performance evaluations;
- educate management on their internal control responsibilities;
- carry out customer satisfaction surveys;
- utilize self-directed, integrated work teams;
- provide training to audit committee members;
- utilize integrated auditing;
- external quality assurance reviews of internal auditing practices;
- emphasize TQM principles and apply aggressively;
- utilize computer assisted techniques;
- include audits of environment, health and safety;
- develop a formal risk assessment system involving management;
- empower staff to experiment with a variety of approaches in developing innovative solutions to problems;
- and, provide internal consulting services, such as focus on problem solving rather than problem finding;

> All these trends are encouraging internal audit experiment and development of leading edge practices.

CHARACTERISTICS	TRADITIONAL	NEW	LEADING EDGE
Why internal audit?:	Management Owner	Regulator Governing body	Mandatory Public
Provided by:	In-house Parent body	Audit firm Agency Consortium	
Reporting lines:	Finance External audit	Audit committee Chief executive	Chairman Stakeholders
Objectivity/independence:	Charter	Partnerships External	Regulated
Professionalism:	Accounting	Internal audit Computing	Management Specialists
Scope of work:	Accounting Financial Compliance	Risk assessment Business objectives Consultancy	Risk management Quality management Environmental
Management:	Stock check Computers Systems	Conduct/ethics	Whistleblowing
Skills:	Written Oral Behavioural	Computing Teamwork	Expert systems Virtual reality
Performance:	Critic Detector Protector Checker	Assurer Comforter Assessor Assistant Teacher Partner	Change agent Innovator Leader Value adder
Management structure:	Hierarchical	Empowered team	Visionary
Auditor coordination:	External	Environmental	Integrated Quality Regulator
Other audits:	Operational Management VFM Systems Computer	Self-assessment	Quality Environmental Health and safety Due diligence Joint ventures

Figure 1.1   Model Spectrum For Internal Audit In The United Kingdom 1998
Source: J. Ridley and Dr Kenneth D'Silva, cited in *Leading Edge Internal Auditing* (1998).

There is ample evidence of this experiment and development over the past 10 years in research by The IIA; its statements and standards on professionalism; the syllabi of its professional internal auditing examinations; its internal auditing seminars, training courses and conferences; research by many others; text books on internal auditing; and, many academic courses internationally at both graduate, postgraduate and doctorate levels In this book you will find references to this experiment and development in the articles I have written since 1998. These include many leading and cutting edge practices and more, including discussion on how they have evolved and what has influenced this. Many are still influencing the cutting edge resources and practices of today and will continue to do so tomorrow.

TODAY'S CUTTING EDGE INTERNAL AUDITING VISION

Since its foundation, The IIA and its members have been at the forefront of introducing cutting edge into the services provided by internal auditors. The IIA *Certificate of Incorporation* (1941)[12] states as the purposes of the institute:

> To cultivate, promote and disseminate knowledge and information concerning internal auditing and subjects related thereto, to establish and maintain high standards of integrity, honour and character among internal auditors; to furnish information regarding internal auditing and the practice and methods thereof to its members, and to other persons interested, and to the general public; to cause the publication of articles, relating to internal auditing and practices and methods thereof; to establish and maintain a library and reading rooms, meeting rooms and social rooms for the use of its members; and to do any and all things which shall be lawful and appropriate in furtherance of any of the purposes hereinbefore expressed.

Perhaps it is traditional today, but at the time this was cutting edge thinking, certainly for internal auditing. Compare this statement of purposes with The IIA Vision and Mission[13] in 2007:

Vision

The IIA will be the global voice of the internal audit profession: advocating its value, promoting best practice, and providing exceptional service to its members.

Mission

The mission of The Institute of Internal Auditors is to provide dynamic leadership for the global profession of internal auditing. Activities in support of this mission will include, but will not be limited to:

- advocating and promoting the value that internal audit professionals add to their organization;
- providing comprehensive professional educational and development opportunities; standards and other professional practice guidance; and certification programmes;
- researching, disseminating, and promoting to practitioners and stakeholders knowledge concerning internal auditing and its appropriate role in control, risk management and governance;
- educating practitioners and other relevant audiences on best practices in internal auditing; and
- bringing together internal auditors from all countries to share information and experiences.

All of the above can be seen in The IIA global operations today. They are also seen in many internal auditing resources and practices worldwide. Each of the missions has its own traditional, leading edge and cutting edge activities, which will be discussed in more detail in the following chapters. So, too, will the internal auditing principles on which they are based.

The vision statement is key to the mission of the Institute: it is also a key to cutting edge practices. Richard Whitely (1991)[14] inspired me at the time with his writings on vision statements with the following quotes:

> A good vision leads to competitive advantage.

> One way to define vision is . . . a vivid picture of an ambitious, desirable state that is connected to the customer and better in some important way than the current state.

How does this vision represent the interests of our customers and values that are important to us?

A vision has two vital functions, and they're more important today than ever before. One is to serve as a source of inspiration. The other is to guide decision making, aligning all the organization's parts so that they work together

If your vision is not an impetus to excellence, then it has failed.

When a company clearly declares what it stands for and its people share this vision, a powerful network is created – people seeking related goals.

Constantly communicate your vision for your organization to those who work with you and for you. Don't let a day go by without talking about it.

In 1992 Dr Colin Coulson-Thomas[15] inspired me also on vision statements when he wrote on leadership and transformation, drawing on a series of 1991 surveys of large organizations, highlighting the need for clear vision and sustained top management commitment for change:

The three 1991 surveys we have examined suggest there is some consensus concerning what is important, and what needs to be done to bridge the gap between expectation and achievement that is found in many companies:

- A compelling vision is essential for both differentiation and transformation. Clear vision and strategy, and top management commitment are of crucial importance in the management of change. If either is lacking, a change programme is likely to be built upon foundations of sand.
- The vision and commitment need to be sustained. This requires an effective board composed of competent directors.
- The vision must be shared, the purpose of change communicated, and employee involvement and commitment secured.
- People need to be equipped to manage change. Changes of attitude, approach and perspective are required.
- The ability to communicate is an essential management quality. Successful communication and sharing of a vision requires integrity and a relationship of trust.

As true today as in 1992.

The IIA has always recognized innovation in its promotion of professional internal auditing. In their research Glen Gray and Maryann Gray[16] (1996) prefaced their results with:

The internal auditing environment is facing many challenges, such as spreading technology, new staffing needs, flattening organizational structures, expanding scope of services, increasing competition, and globalization. Many of the 54,000+ IIA members are developing and implementing innovations to meet these challenges. Some of these innovations include major changes to the structure of internal auditing departments or the scope of services provided to their enterprises. Other innovations focus on one specific aspect of the traditional auditing processes.

Their synthesis of developed case studies showed the following common motivations and goals for innovation and categories in internal audit activities:

Motivations

1. Progress within the field of professional internal auditing.
2. Increasing competition leading to pressures to reduce costs and increase efficiency.

3. New challenges, such as increasing internal control risks due to staff reductions and restructuring.
4. Opportunities to increase efficiency and quality as a result of technological advances.
5. Changes in corporate management practices and philosophies, such as Total Quality Management, re-engineering, continuous quality improvement, or related approaches

Goals

1. Improvement of the quality of internal auditing services.
2. Improve efficiency.
3. Expansion of services to increase the value added of internal auditing.
4. Boost staff skills, performance and morale.

Categories

1. Changes in the way that internal auditors interact with the rest of their enterprises.
2. Internal restructuring and changes in the organization and management of internal auditing.
3. Creation of new audit services and methods.
4. Changes in the use of technology.

These results have stood the test of time well. They will be addressed in the summary of each chapter to consider whether cutting edge internal auditing has, or is today, creating new motivations, goals or categories. Look for your own additional or changed motivations, goals and categories as you read each chapter.

In *Leading Edge Internal Auditing* (1998: p. 115) I wrote about vision statements as follows:

Create a Vision of Future Internal Auditing

Imagination needs direction – not in a controlled sense but in a creative sense. It is the art of forming mental images and constructively channelling these into visions for the future. It is not easy to find examples of internal auditing vision statements. Not all internal auditors are committed to the value of vision statements. Yet, in their organizations they are often prominent as management statements or team statements, and always associated with their organization's products and services. So why not for internal audit? Vision statements now generally aim to promote '. . . *a vivid picture of an ambitious, desirable state that is connected to the customer and better in some important way than the current state'*. Vision statements need to be exciting, even emotional. They need a total commitment to succeed. They need to be measured and updated as time improves the vision. They need to be short and simple.

Bill Bishop, Past President of The IIA, summed up in June 2003 the Institute's contribution to cutting edge in the following paragraph in a foreword[17] to an article 'Internal Auditing: *Where are we Now and Where are we Heading?*' by Sridhar Ramamoorie, then chairman of The IIA Academic Relations Committee: part of a publication recognizing the 10th anniversary of the postgraduate programme in internal/operational auditing at Erasmus Universiteit, Rotterdam:

Auditors today must understand the relevant risks, challenges, and opportunities, and The IIA will continue to stand at the forefront of providing research, guidance, and education to ensure internal auditors stay on the cutting edge of the profession.

In his article Sridhar Ramamoorie ends with an appropriate message on the importance of research leading to innovation in internal auditing practices:

> In conclusion, the 21st century presents much promise and unprecedented growth opportunities for the internal auditing profession. However, developments in practice must be carefully studied so that a body of knowledge is systematically built up, and transmitted to future generations of internal auditing professionals. The extant of knowledge should not only be critiqued, and constantly refined to reflect the current state of the art, but should also encourage and stimulate, through research, leading edge thinking that so often produces innovations in practice.

Such research into leading edge thinking and innovation should not just be by academics, but by every internal audit activity. There is evidence in this book that this is happening today in many internal auditing practices across the globe. A 2005 study[18] on innovative practices in the US explored whether there is a pattern today underlying innovation in organizations of diverse sizes and industries. It formed the conclusion:

> This study continues to advance the notion that there are in fact patterns for success. Although the companies in this study are from diverse industries – such as consumer packaged goods, medical services, and industrial equipment – the principles behind their innovation approaches are surprisingly consistent. They all look beyond the walls of their companies to find good ideas. They all follow a structured approach to innovation. They all back their words with action, making innovation a central part of everything the firm does. There are definite nuances and differences, but the commonality of the patterns is an encouraging sign.

I hope this book will challenge your pattern of internal auditing success, now and in the future. That pattern must include the values of professionalism and '. . . *a structured approach to innovation*'. backed with action, if internal auditing is to be seen as a valued profession by all its customers and stakeholders. The number of stakeholders are increasing as organizations become more regulated, not just nationally but also globally.

Article:
Celebrating Professionalism[19] (2004)

Internal auditing is moving into an era of increased regulation, and this indeed is cause for cel-standards – both mandated by regulators – are helping tus of our profes- ebration. Higher self-imposed and external regula- to elevate the sta- sion and enabling

> '. . . *professionalism – like quality – hinges on adherence to a set of core principles and values.*'

practitioners to gain a more influential role in their organizations. One of the most recent examples of regulatory activity comes from the New York Stock Exchange, which now requires all of its listed companies to have an internal audit function. But this requirement and others like it fall short in one key area – specifying a standard of professionalism. Despite what we celebrate today, internal auditors still need to promote and establish the regulation of internal audit professionalism.

How should the internal audit profession be regulated? Achieving professionalism is like achieving quality. The process requires management leadership, standards for the manner in which services are provided, measurement of achievement, input from customers, and a total commitment to excellence by all involved. But above all, professionalism – like quality – hinges on adherence to a set of core principles and values. All other aspects of professionalism stem from this commitment.

Specifically, the set of principles to which a profession adheres is typically defined in its code of ethics. For internal auditors, The Institute of Internal Auditors (IIA) has established its own code that covers principles and rules governing integrity, objectivity, confidentiality, and competency. That code should be understood by all internal auditors and explained to those who rely on the profession's services. Questions all internal auditors should ask themselves are – 'Does my professional conduct meet the requirements of The IIA code?' and 'Does The IIA code match or improve the ethical cultures required by my organization, regulators, governments and other professional bodies?' Knowing the answers to these questions is key to measuring their own professionalism, and the conduct they should expect to see in others. But compliance with a set of principles at a given point in time is only part of the picture. Professionalism also requires commitment to continuous improvement.

Quality assurance and continuous improvement are fundamental to achieving high levels of quality in all products and services, and programmes aimed at achieving this result typically require both internal and external assessments. The same applies to internal audit professionalism – implementation of principles and standards needs to be monitored on an ongoing basis to ensure adequate performance. Yet how many internal audit activities have such a programme up and running? How many report the results of such programmes to their management and board of directors? Research shows that many fall short in this area.

Professionalism is essential to the achievement of high standards in internal auditing. Like quality, it is not a destination but a road that should be followed – one that calls for a customer-focused vision and requires passion and commitment to continuous improvement. Although hazards may exist along the way, these can be overcome with integrity, objectivity, confidentiality, and competency. Internal auditors should certainly take the opportunity to celebrate advances made by the profession thus far, but we should not let this progress serve as an excuse to become complacent.

INTRODUCTION TO THE FOLLOWING CHAPTERS

Each chapter, except the last, is structured as follows:

Introduction to a Cutting Edge Theme for Internal Auditing

This will discuss events/issues related to the theme prior to and around the times of publication/preparation of my articles/research reproduced.

Internal Auditing Today and in the Future

This will discuss relevant events/issues related to the theme since the publication/development of the article/research. It will also attempt to predict how the theme will impact cutting edge internal auditing in the immediate future and beyond the horizon.

Chapter Summary

This will summarize the chapter discussion and consider how it impacts the Gray and Gray (1996) innovation motivations, goals and categories.

Internal Auditing Principia 1998[20] and 2008

This will list internal auditing principia related to the theme, developed and published by me in 1998. It will revise these principia for 2008 to reflect the importance of the cutting edge discussion in the chapter.

A Vision for the Theme

A suggested vision statement from the chapter discussion that will '. . . *promote a vivid picture of an ambitious, desirable state that is connected to the customer'*.

Synopses of Cutting Edge Case Studies Relevant to the Theme

Cases studies have been selected to demonstrate situations and issues discussed in the chapter. They can sometimes go beyond, into other chapters. A few of the case studies are my own, but most have been developed and written by other contributors: their contribution is acknowledged at the beginning of the book and end of their case. Each case study is introduced with a synopsis in the chapter, followed by questions to be considered by the reader. The synopses and questions are my summaries of each case and questions I ask myself after reading the case. **The full case studies are included on the CD ROM inside the back cover**. Readers should read the full case study before considering the questions. I am sure there will be other questions that readers will ask, based on their internal auditing experience and situation, and I encouraged readers to do this. Preferably, the cases should be discussed in groups. Group discussion creates more learning opportunities for the development of cutting edge internal auditing resources and practices. Not all in a group will agree with the issues and challenges in a case, or the cutting edge resources and practices internal auditing now needs to continuously improve. This is good. Remember Peter Drucker's writings on imagination quoted at the beginning of this chapter: *'Disagreement, especially if forced to be reasoned, thought through, documented, is the most effective stimulus we know.'* The cases included in my book are not the end of a learning period but just part of a continuing process. There are now, and will be in the future, many more case studies for internal auditing to learn from and develop best practices. Readers are encouraged to create their own library of case studies and considerations, learn from them and pioneer new resources and practices. That is what cutting edge internal auditing is all about.

Self-Assessment Questions

Readers will be asked questions to answer on their own, or preferably as members of a group, so that they can measure their understanding of what has been discussed. Answers to the questions can be found in the chapter, or in the reader's organization, or are shown in Appendix C.

Notes and References

Annotations in each reproduced article are shown as footnotes. Superscript figures in the text are explained at the end of each chapter in a 'Notes and References', section that provides bibliographic detail and supports statements made in the discussion. A recommended bibliography of cutting edge knowledge that should be on all internal audit activity bookshelves is shown at the end of the book. There are many references in the book to *The IIA International Standards*[21] and supporting Practice Advisories, but little of the detail provided. This is intentional because it will change over time. It will be the reader's challenge to keep the references up to date. Many other references to and sources for best practices are discussed in each chapter. There will be others not mentioned, but recognized and used by the imaginative internal auditor. Time and place change best practices. That is why benchmarking for these is a continuous process worldwide and not just a one-off exercise. Nevertheless those discussed in the book should generate sufficient interest to enable the reader to explore for others. That is the excitement of benchmarking.

The future will see many cutting edge activities in internal auditing: some will develop from documented traditional and leading edge activities today. Others will be created from new knowledge and experiences. Such change is what cutting edge is all about. The address for all references into The Institute of Internal Auditors Inc. (The IIA) and The IIA Research Foundation publications is 247 Maitland Avenue, Altamonte Springs, Florida 32701-4201, USA (www.theiia.org): the address for all Institute of Internal Auditors – United Kingdom & Ireland (IIA–UK & Ireland) publications is 13 Abberville Mews, 88 Clapham Park Road, London SW4 7BX, England (www.iia.org.uk). Because of the many references into publications by these two organizations, these addresses are not repeated in annotations.

FRAMEWORK OF THE CHAPTERS IN CUTTING EDGE

There are many cutting edge links between the chapters. As a framework the titles provide a direction for the development of cutting edge resources and practices in all internal auditing activities worldwide. Yet each chapter is a lecture and seminar on its own. It can be used as part of an education programme or a training course, either in-house or external. For these purposes training slides used at the beginning of some of the chapters and in the middle of the last chapter can also be downloaded from the CD ROM inside the back cover.

My articles and material reproduced in each chapter mainly relate to the chapter's theme, though other important issues may be mentioned. This is inevitable because none of the themes discussed separately applies in isolation from the others, either in theory or practice. Inevitably, because of the reproduced articles and other research, there is some repetition at times of important statements in chapters. I hope the reader will recognize this repetition as emphasizing the importance of the messages these statements contain. Risk management, control and governance are integrated processes influencing change and performance at all levels – strategic, objective setting, implementation of policies, procedures, systems and in all day-to-day operations, reporting and compliance – and, most importantly, across all of an organization's supply chains and in collaborations with others. At least that is what should be, but it is not always so!

There is exploration and adventure in every chapter for the imaginative internal auditor, committed to being at the cutting edge of internal auditing today and tomorrow. Best practice internal auditing owes a significant debt to that imagination and all those who have developed, and continue to develop professionalism in internal auditing.

NOTES AND REFERENCES

1. Cited in *Wisdom of the Ages* (1936: p. 188), The St Catherine Press Ltd, London, England.
2. *The Practice of Management* (1955) (2006 reissue: p. 66), Peter F. Drucker, Butterworth–Heinemann, Oxford, England.
3. *The Effective Executive* (1967) (2006 reissue: p. 127), Peter F. Drucker, Butterworth–Heinemann, Oxford, England.
4. *Internal Auditing* (1981), Andrew D. Chambers, Pitman Books Limited, London, England.
5. Published in *Internal Auditing* (June 1994: p. 10), IIA–UK & Ireland.
6. *Behavioural Patterns in Internal Audit Relationships* (1973), Mints, Dr Frederick E., The IIA. Dr Mints found at the time that *'many auditees still harbour feelings of dislike and distrust towards auditors'*. His research supported the participative approach in audit engagements *'. . . - the teamwork approach, the problem solving partnership may well be the light at the end of a dreary tunnel.'*
7. The 5th edition of Sawyer's *Internal Auditing* (2003), The IIA recognizes in dealing with people that *'imaginative internal audit work, in and of itself, is not enough to ensure improvement in operations. Clients must want to implement audit recommendations. So audit style may be as important as technical competence.'*
8. Jean-Pierre Garritte, 'Building bridges', *Internal Auditor* (August 1998: pp. 26–31), The IIA.
9. This is the current definition of internal auditing published by The IIA in 1999. The previous definition was: *'Internal auditing is an independent appraisal function established within an organization to examine and evaluate its activities as a service to the organization. The objective of internal auditing is to assist members of the organization in the effective discharge of their responsibilities. To this end, internal auditing furnishes them with analyses, appraisals, recommendations, counsel, and information concerning the activities reviewed. The audit objective includes promoting effective control at reasonable cost.'*
10. Published in *Internal Auditing* (March 1998: p. 12), on the celebration of The IIA – UK 50th year, IIA – UK & Ireland.
11. *Leading Edge Internal Auditing* (1998: p. 10), Jeffrey Ridley and Andrew Chambers, ICSA Publishing Limited, London, England [first published in paperback 2007].
12. Cited in *Foundations for Unlimited Horizons – The Institute of Internal Auditors 1941–1976* (1977: Appendix C), Victor Z. Brink (1977), The IIA.
13. www.theiia.org/index.cfm?doc_id=267 visited 4 August 2006.
14. *The Customer-Driven Company* (1991: pp. 21, 26–28, 32, 37), Richard C. Whitely, Business Books Limited, London, England.
15. *Leadership and Corporate Transformation*, Dr Colin J. Coulson-Thomas, *Administrator*, April 1992, Institute of Chartered Secretaries and Administrators, London, England. Professor Coulson-Thomas still researches and writes on management practices. Details of his current *Winning Companies: Winning People* research programme were recently discussed in the ICAEW *Accountancy* magazine (March 2007: pp. 56–57).
16. *Enhancing Internal Auditing Through Innovative Practices* (1996), Glen L. Gray and Maryann Jacobi Gray, The IIA Research Foundation.
17. *Internal/Operational Auditing; bjdragen aan governance & control*, Chapter 1. *Foreword* by William G. Bishop III to *'Internal Auditing: Where are we Now and Where are we Heading?'*,

authored by Sridhar Ramamoortie (2003: p. 20), Editors: Ronald de Korte, Leen Paape and Willem Verhoog, NIVRA, Amsterdam, ISBN 9075103409.

18. *Innovation: Putting Ideas into Action* (2005: p. 7), American Productivity & Quality Control Association (APQC), Houston, Texas, USA. www.apqc.org visited 16 October 2006.
19. Published in *Internal Auditor* (April 2004), The IIA.
20. *Leading Edge Internal Auditing* (1998: Appendix H, p. 385, 'Principia for Leading Edge Internal Auditing'), Jeffrey Ridley and Andrew D. Chambers, ICSA Publishing, London.
21. Recently described in detail in *Implementing The Professional Practices Framework* (2006), Urton Anderson and Andrew J. Dahie, The IIA Research Foundation.

2
Cutting Edge Internal Auditing Looks Into The Future

'The future is purchased by the present.'

Samuel Johnson (1709–1784)[1]

Management Of Internal Audit

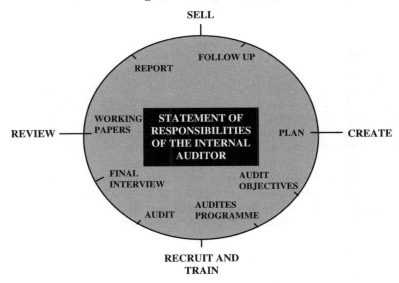

THE FUTURE IN 1975

In the early 1970s responsibility for internal audit management included creating the function; establishing its scope of work and reporting lines; audit planning; recruiting and training staff; developing audit plans and programmes; auditing; reviewing working papers; reporting; following up actions by senior management; and, at all times, selling internal auditing. This slide started a 1972 slide-tape training role-play, developed and acted by the staff in my internal audit activity at that time. Its introduction started as:

> The management of internal audit involves a variety of work, which to most internal auditors is its attraction as a career. This variety can take internal auditors through all the responsibilities delegated to a manager: planning; the setting of objectives and programmes of work; reviews of performance; interviewing people; and, writing reports. During all these aspects of their work internal auditors are selling their professional auditing services to management.

This role-play summed up much of what the science and art of internal auditing was at the time – and in many internal audit activities today is still an important part of their role. Note the reference to management practices, which are fundamental to all internal auditing and its development.

All the practices in the slide had been, and were being influenced in many organizations by The IIA (1971) *Statement of Responsibilities*, Third Version:

Nature

Internal auditing is an independent appraisal activity within an organization for the review of operations as a service to management. It is a managerial control which functions by measuring and evaluating the effectiveness of other controls.

Objective and Scope

The objective of internal auditing is to assist all members of management in the effective discharge of their responsibilities by furnishing them with analyses, appraisals, recommendations, and pertinent comments concerning the activities reviewed. The internal auditor is concerned with any phase of business activity where he may be of service to management. This involves going beyond the accounting and financial records to obtain a full understanding of the operations under review. The attainment of this overall objective involves such activities as:

* Reviewing and appraising the soundness, adequacy, and application of accounting, financial, and other operating controls and promoting effective control at reasonable cost.
* Ascertaining the extent of compliance with established policies, plans, and procedures.
* Ascertaining the extent to which company assets are accounted for and safeguarded from losses of all kinds.
* Ascertaining the reliability of management data developed within the organization.
* Appraising the quality of performance in carrying out assigned responsibilities.
* Recommending operating improvements.

Each of the above statements at the time was stimulating cutting edge internal auditing activities across many organizations, not least the appraisal of performance quality in carrying out assigned responsibilities – even cutting edge today at senior management and board levels.

Future IIA responsibility statements from 1981 onwards defined internal auditing as '... *a service to the organization* ...' not a '... *service to management* ...', promoting internal auditing's developing role across all levels in the organization, including the board: a role that was already emerging as cutting edge in some internal auditing in the 1960s and early 1970s.

How internal auditors, their management, senior organizational management and external auditors developed internal auditing across all industry sectors in 1975 was shaping the development of professional internal auditing in the immediate years that followed. The imagination of all these players can still be seen in much of professional internal auditing today. Their present was buying the future: the present always does.

There was already published material on cutting edge internal auditing. Research and textbooks on internal auditing practices were mainly from the United States, although at least two authors in the United Kingdom had published work on internal auditing: one in the early 1930s and one in the early 1950s. Rose (1932)[2] wrote a paper on management auditing as a means to improve the efficiency and effectiveness of industrial management in a competitive world. He advocated an internal audit of management, as a supplement to the external audit of financial statements, reporting to and supporting the managing director, with such an audit covering all the functions in an organization and employing experienced and mature staff. This was a view well ahead of its time. Smith (1953),[3] a chartered accountant, published a guidance on internal auditing that was mainly focused on traditional compliance auditing. This was possibly the first book published in the United Kingdom devoted solely to internal auditing.

The book that impressed me most in the 1970s was Lawrence Sawyer's (1973) *The Practice of Modern Internal Auditing*. Now in its 5th edition (2003), with authors Lawrence Sawyer, Mortimer Dittenhofer and James Scheiner, this text is still recommended reading by The IIA for its professional examinations. Other textbooks on internal auditing had also been published: Victor Brink and Herbert Witt (1973), *Modern Internal Auditing*, is now in its 6th edition (2005), authored by Robert Moelle. It was, however, Sawyer's approach to modern internal auditing that impressed me most at the time. His foresight and imaginative approach took a giant step forward from Rose's recommendations in the 1930s, which can be seen clearly in Sawyer's (1973) quotes:

> It has been said that modern internal auditing differs from the classical compliance auditing in that it requires a different stance and a different state of mind – but that it is still basically auditing, for does it not function by evaluating internal control systems and testing transactions? True. But the different stance and the different state of mind call for new techniques and different methods to accomplish the auditor's [new] objectives. (pp. vii/viii)

> Successful internal auditing is constructed on a foundation of technical excellence. But the structure must be firmly buttressed – on the one side by demonstrated acceptance and support at the highest levels in the enterprise; on the other by *continued, imaginative service to management*. Each of the two buttresses is an integral member of the structure. Let one weaken and the structure may tilt, ready to fall at the first hard blow from the winds of retrenchment and cost reduction. (p. 21; my italic)

The IIA and many of its members took Sawyer's messages to heart. The Institute had now established itself globally[4] as a professional body, with more than 10,000 members and 100 chapters. In 1974, The IIA 33rd Annual International Conference was held in London, the first time this conference had been held outside North America, with 27 countries being represented. The globalization of the institute was well under way. The programme for the conference included the following topics:

- Opening address by International President Howard L. Aikin with the theme *Horizons Unlimited*
- A motion on the traditional/modern view of internal audit's proper role

- Selling internal audit – what does it have to offer?
- Setting-up an internal audit department
- Selection and training of internal auditors
- Planning and scheduling audits
- Interviewing techniques
- Managing the internal audit department
- Social audit
- Relationship with external auditors
- Techniques and tools of operational auditing
- How can audit findings be financially evaluated?
- Presentation of audit findings
- Operational audit
- Computers – the internal auditor's friend
- EDP security and fraud
- Practical aspects of inflation accounting
- Behavioural sciences
- Business opportunities in Europe.

Two of the speakers were Larry Sawyer and Professor Mints, both of whom will feature in later chapters. If we compare these topics with today's internal auditing conferences and training programmes, many topics are similar.

Consider the foresight of the following topics:

Horizons Unlimited
Traditional/modern view of internal audit's proper role
Selling internal audit – what does it have to offer?
Social audit
Relationship with external auditors
Operational audit
Computers – the internal auditor's friend
EDP security and fraud
Behavioural sciences.

Now compare the 1974 topics with the following topics and workshop themes in The IIA 2006 International Conference in Houston, USA:

Corporate governance: A call for character and integrity
Economics of ethics
Magic of profiling
Enterprise Risk Management
Experiencing the art of possibility
Audit management
Fraud
Regulatory issues and compliance
Information technology
Emerging issues (including:

    Global internal auditing resources;
    Natural disasters;
    Changing environments;
    Government auditing;
    Global quality assessment activities;
    Measuring and proving effectiveness;

    Multinational workforces;
    Maximizing audit performance)

Corporate governance
Risk management
Professional development.

Note how some of the topics and themes relate to the 1974 conference topics. Note also the inclusion in 2006 of the words *integrity, ethics, art, regulatory, emerging, governance, risk, development, disasters, changing, quality, effectiveness,* and *performance.* As I write this book The IIA 2007 International Conference has just been held. Its topics include many of the above, but also have new focuses:

Sustainability
Social responsibility
Terrorism
Reputation
Whistleblowers
Key stakeholders
Success.

All the words italicized above from these conferences will appear in this book as part of, or the focus for, cutting edge resources and practices in internal auditing today and tomorrow. Do they appear in your internal auditing resources and practices?

What was really significant in the late 1960s had been publication of the Institute's Code of Ethics . . . *recognizing that ethics are an important consideration in the practice of internal auditing . . .* What an achievement – an international code of ethics. What foresight, at a time when few if any other professional institute's worldwide had such an international statement. It contained a number of ethical clauses but the one that fixed in my mind at the time was – *A member shall strive for continuous improvement in the proficiency and effectiveness of his* [now also her] *service.* [Later, in future revisions this clause included the words *quality* after *proficiency.* Today this clause[5] has become: *Shall continually improve their proficiency and the effectiveness and quality of their services.* This requirement will form the main theme in many of the chapters in this text.]

In November 1975, just after my presidential address (included in full in this chapter) the United Kingdom Chapter promoted a free exhibition of internal auditing practices in the then Greater London Council County Hall. This promotion of professional internal auditing created considerable interest from internal auditors and professional institutes in the United Kingdom, increasing the chapter's membership significantly. The exhibition was reported later in the chapter's newsletter as:

We Made an Exhibition of Ourselves

Fifteen members and their organizations created an exhibition of their internal auditing services. A full day of free seminars arranged around the exhibition hall, attracted 1,500 visitors to see how professional internal auditing had developed and was being used in the GLC, British Gas, Kodak, American Express, Rolls Royce, Water Authorities, London Transport and others.

Representatives from professional bodies and government were invited and escorted around the exhibition by members. We were one of the first professional bodies to use a free exhibition to promote our services to management. We were at the leading edge of professional promotion.

Such innovation and exhibition was at the cutting edge of promoting professional services at that time. Many of the practices on display were revolutionary in internal auditing thinking and promoted much of the development of cutting edge internal auditing in future years. That promotion also predated much of the thinking about marketing internal auditing that has followed – marketing to the public, in industry sectors and organizations.

Note, in the slide at the beginning of the chapter the emphasis on selling internal audit circling all its practices. Sawyer (1973: p. viii) saw the need and importance of marketing internal auditing: *'It is axiomatic that internal auditing is not bought by management. It must be sold to management . . . '* This will be discussed further, in a later chapter, on cutting edge marketing to promote professional internal auditing.

Article:
The Future Is Ours[6] (1975)

One of the main purposes of any professional institute is to provide for all members a professional identity with high standards of conduct and common objectives. The Institute of Internal Auditors with its Statement of Responsibilities and Code of Ethics provides these. In the past, Chapters in the United Kingdom have developed this identity in their regions, with close ties with each other and the Institute headquarters. Indeed, the history of each Chapter is a record of which we can all be very proud.

> 'We have not stopped growing by our merger but are on the threshold of a new period of development and growth. It is now our responsibility to see the opportunities that surround us are not lost.'

We live in times of high economic risk and important social and business decisions. Every day we are reminded at work, in newspapers and by television of the opportunities that can be taken to develop ourselves and the profession we have chosen. The apparent insoluble problems of the present economic situation; the controversial discussions caused by exposure drafts and new accounting practices; involvement in the European Community; a new awareness of social responsibilities; higher health and safety standards; the now clearly recognized need for more efficient manpower planning and training; the urgency of energy saving; the complexity of advanced computer technology are all changes that management cannot ignore, and neither can we as internal auditors. To be successful we must be sensitive to the problems of each day. All can have an impact on our professional activities far beyond the changes we may foresee at the present time.

- An education programme has already been prepared by the London Chapter for 1975–76 and this will be adopted by the United Kingdom Chapter.

- Courses and seminars have been arranged with The Graduate Business Centre of The City University[a] and two London Polytechnics.[b]
- The previous London Chapter's programme of research will continue.
- The newly formed EDP Auditing Sub-Committee of the research committee will be working closely with the Stanford Research Institute, assisting in the Institute's recently announced international research project into EDP auditing. This sub-committee has as its members a group of the most experienced EDP auditors in the United Kingdom.
- We have concluded an agreement with the Open University to carry out joint research into attitudes to the development of modern internal auditing. It is hoped that the results of this research will be published and be of assistance to all organizations establishing internal audit departments for the first time.
- Three member surveys are planned – one into internal audit as it is practised in the United Kingdom today, one into the recruitment of graduates into internal audit and in this international year for women, one into the recruitment of women in internal auditing.
- In February 1976 the Research Committee will be associated with the City University in the presentation of an international two-day conference on audit research. This is yet another example of the importance which will be given to the Institute's continuous search for knowledge and understanding of attitudes to audit and audit techniques.

These are exciting projects. Their results will be of considerable interest to all members and The Institute.

Three new committees are planned to meet members' needs. One will develop our drive for membership, particularly from organizations not yet represented in the Chapter. It will also establish rules for a student membership class to encourage interest from trainee internal auditors. Another will develop our social responsibilities by providing a free advisory service on the use of modern internal auditing in governmental and public affairs activities. The third will develop long-term plans for the growth of the Chapter and internal auditing in the future.

A strong professional identity needs the support of members who are committed to its development. One of the major obstacles we have to overcome in our development is the temporary nature of many of our members' commitment to internal auditing as a career. I believe there is evidence that this is changing. There are now an increasing number of internal auditors who see a career development in internal auditing, either over a period or returning to internal audit after seeking experience in other areas. This is evidence of our growing strength as a professional Institute and can be attributed to the:

- increased reporting by internal auditors to higher levels of management;
- increasing numbers of organizations using modern internal auditing;

---

[a] Now the Cass Business School, The City University, London, which today still teaches and researches internal auditing in its Centre for Internal Auditing.
[b] One of these is now the London South Bank University, which still teaches and researches internal auditing in its Business, Computing & Information Management Faculty.

- encouragement given for disciplines other than accountancy to take positions in internal audit;
- increased use of the internal auditor as a consultant because of his *[and certainly now her]* experiences and knowledge of control techniques; and,
- increased use of internal auditors as teachers, participating in management training schemes.

All these developments are evidence of the growing importance of modern internal auditing in all types of organizations and the work of Institute members during past years. I personally believe that if we are to be truly professional we need to continue to encourage more dedication to internal audit as a career. Such a change in attitude could be one of the significant developments we will see in our profession during the next decade.

'Progress through Sharing' is our slogan of integrity, trust and help, which from its beginning[c] has represented the attitude of the Institute to a future of growth, a future of service to members and a future of strength. As a profession in the United Kingdom we have grown tall in our first 25 years. Our integrity and professional standards are high and we are respected by management for the service we offer. We have not stopped growing by our merger[d] but are on the threshold of a new period of development and growth. It is now our responsibility to see the opportunities that surround us are not lost.

THE FUTURE THAT FOLLOWED

In the years that followed many changes have occurred globally and in organizations. The provision of internal auditing services is not the same. Yet most, if not all, the statements in my presidential address remain true. Consider again the environment in which they were made:

> We live in times of high economic risk and important social and business decisions. Every day we are reminded at work, in newspapers and by television of the opportunities that can be taken to develop ourselves and the profession we have chosen. The apparent insoluble problems of the present economic situation; the controversial discussions caused by exposure drafts and new accounting practices; involvement in the European Community; a new awareness of social responsibilities; higher health and safety standards; the now clearly recognized need for more efficient manpower planning and training; the urgency of energy saving; the complexity of advanced computer technology are all changes that management cannot ignore, and neither can we as internal auditors. To be successful we must be sensitive to the problems of each day. All can have an impact on our professional activities far beyond the changes we may foresee at the present time.

---

[c] This was Raymond E. Noonan's presidential theme when 13th international president of The IIA in 1953. In May 1955 it was formally adopted as the Institute's theme and added to its corporate seal. It remains the Institute's theme to today and is promoted globally now by all its 94 country affiliates and 154 North American Chapters, representing a membership in 2005 of more than 100,000 members.
[d] At the time of the merger the IIA membership in the United Kingdom was 1000 in its annual report for 2006/07 membership is reported now as 8000.

Do you recognize similarities with today's environment? The importance of some of the issues has changed, but all still apply today, more now on a global rather than just national scale. And, change is much faster. Computer technology is much more distributed, not just in organizations but across education and in homes. The digital age has arrived, creating easier global communications having a significant impact on management and internal auditors. Social and energy issues are now more at the top of the decision-making process in government and business.

What was the future for the following issues raised in my address?

- Education programmes
- Student membership
- Courses and seminars
- Research
- Surveys
- EDP auditing
- Social responsibilities
- Growth
- Reporting by internal auditors to higher levels of management
- Internal auditing careers
- Women in internal auditing.
- More organizations using modern internal auditing methods
- Disciplines other than accountancy in internal audit
- Internal auditor as a consultant
- Internal auditors as teachers.

There has been significant change for the better in all these issues: many will continue to achieve more successes in the future. These successes have been far beyond what we could have imagined in 1975, and it is all due to the many thousands of IIA volunteers across the globe, and staff supporting its headquarters and affiliated institutes and chapters. Many of the successes will be discussed in the course of the book, and as you read the chapters you should recognize them. Link back to the list of 1975 issues above and tick them off. They should all be ticked.

But what of the issues for internal auditing in the immediate future? There are still many more that can be added to the above. Reference to the IIA Research Foundation Website[7] pages will identify many of them:

Research published in 2006

- Role of Internal Audit in Sensitive Situations
- Managing Strategic Alliance: Survey Evidence of Control Practices in Collaborative Inter-organizational Settings
- Sustainability and Internal Auditing.

Research in progress

- Common Body of Knowledge
- Sarbanes–Oxley
- COSO Enterprise Risk Management

- Behavioural aspect of internal auditing
- Corporate Governance relationships
- Fraud
- Managing effective government performance.

Proposals awaiting funding

- More on ERM, Corporate Governance, Sarbanes–Oxley, Fraud
- Quality Assurance
- Information technology

Add these to the missions of the IIA and you have a good start for your future list. Then consider your own national and industry sector regulations and needs and your list of issues will start to become an aim for your personal career growth and the cutting edge of your internal audit activity.

Article:
No Exceptions Allowed – All Internal Audit Activities Should Be Regulated[8] (2003)

More than 10 years ago, at my professorial inaugural address at the South Bank University in Lon-don, I spoke of the future of inter-nal audit. At the time I saw one of the changes most likely to happen being increased regulation and self-regulation in the professional practice of inter-nal audit. Such regulation was already taking place in internal audit activities in some sectors and industries.

> *Today there is more awareness of the need for effective internal audit as part of good corporate governance.'*

Yet still too many internal auditors remained untouched, either by self-regulation, or regulation from outside their organizations. This was despite the fact that all the organizations they were serving and most professions had seen a significant increase in regulation, by laws, standards and principles. In some cases such regulation was mandatory for the organizations and professionals, imposing restriction and penalty. In others, it could be voluntary, but still mean loss of reputation and business if products and services did not meet customer, government and public satisfaction.

At the time most boards relied only on external audit for an external assessment of the effectiveness of internal audit, this being reported mainly through the financial audit. The focus of such assessments normally related to the financial audit and not the performance of any wider operational responsibilities of internal audit, nor its professionalism.

Since my address much has happened to promote professional internal audit, in the private, public and voluntary sectors. Today there is more awareness of the need for effective internal audit as part of good corporate governance practices. Despite this there is still too little attention being given to regulation of internal audit practices, either by those who require internal audit or by those who practise the services it provides.

Quality Assurance and Improvement

The Institute of Internal Auditors (IIA), both here in the UK and Ireland and elsewhere across the world, has improved its regulation by now making it mandatory for internal audit activities using its standard to *'develop and maintain a quality assurance and improvement programme that covers all aspects of the internal audit activity and continuously monitors its effectiveness.'* Such programmes require both internal and external regulation with *'. . . the results of external assessments of performance (communicated) to the board'.*

In my view this quality and improvement programme is still too loose for best practice in any international profession. Many internal audit activities will have introduced such programmes. Many more will not have done so, whether they use The *IIA Professional Practices Framework* or not. And is communicating with the board sufficient? Surely the owners of organizations and other stakeholders should also be told how effective internal audit is and how this is regulated. I have seen many published annual reports that mention the existence of internal audit but none that states how effective it is and how this is assessed and regulated. I recognize that there are some external regulators taking an interest in the effectiveness of internal audit and such a statement, but these are still few and, in my view, not demanding enough.

Corporate Governance

Most of the reviews of corporate governance in the past ten years have mentioned and recommended internal audit as a practice, but none has mentioned how its effectiveness should be assessed and regulated. Even the well-publicized Turnbull report did not comment on the regulation of internal audit in its recommendations for assessing the effectiveness of risk and control processes, only a comment that *'. . . an adequately resourced internal audit function may provide . . . assurance and advice'.* Compare this with the focus across the world on the external regulation of external auditors and the effectiveness and quality of their work. At least this exists and is being actively debated, even if it is not yet best practice. Or even the lesser-publicized regulation of environmental, safety and quality auditors, all of whom have imposed standards and regulation external to the organizations in which they work.

The recent Smith report, *Audit Committees: Combined Code Guidance: 2003*, recommends that the audit committee should *'monitor and review the effectiveness of the company's internal audit function'* without stating how. Although it does suggest that the audit committee *'should ensure that the function . . . is equipped to perform in accordance with appropriate professional standards for internal auditors'.* How many audit committees today do just that? Or ask how the activity is regulated and report the results to their boards?

What will happen to regulation of internal audit in the future? Clearly, there have been improvements in the professionalism of internal audit and many more internal auditors do self-regulate their work and seek external assessments in formal quality assurance and improvement programmes. All evidence today points to this continuing, driven by the profession, its members and those it serves.

But there has still been too little achieved in how the profession is externally regulated, if you benchmark it against other auditing and the needs of all stakeholders, including the public at large. I believe all boards (and the equivalent in government organizations) should be required to publish annually to all their stakeholders how they regulate the effectiveness of internal audit and the internal audit professionals they employ, whether internal audit in their organizations is mandatory or not. I also believe that all industry and government regulators should monitor the absence and effectiveness of internal audit in their sectors. This will require regulators to understand what makes professional internal audit effective and its important role in governance. When all this happens the regulation prediction of my address in 1992 will be established.

Internal Audit Role as a Profession

I also predicted in 1992 that internal auditors should promote their role as consultants and teachers in risk management and control. I still have these opinions too. Consultancy, risk management and control are now well embedded in most internal audit planning. I believe teaching will follow, if it is not already there. I am pleased to see this is now formally recognized by IIA Inc. in its new Professional Practices Framework. In its recently published Practice Advisory (PA) on internal audit relationships with the audit committee, one of the activity examples given for internal audit is *'to inquire from the audit committee if any educational or informational sessions or presentations would be helpful, such as training new committee members on risk and controls'*. Its current exposure draft on governance has a similar guideline regarding changes and trends in the business and regulatory environment. This is a start. Let us all hope that more formal recognition by the profession's global body of the educational role for internal auditors will follow and this will be seen in practice.

Professional bodies will continue to be challenged on the responsibilities they have to their members and society. A current project by The Royal Society of Arts (RSA) is exploring professional values in the 21st century (www.thersa.org). This is addressing many issues and questions that apply to the development of our own emerging profession and the roles we are creating. The anticipated outcomes will eventually provide a new definition of a model profession. Whatever this defines it will always need to be regulated and we will need to benchmark ourselves against it.

I will continue to watch the evolution of my predictions for internal audit, its regulation, professionalism and roles. I am confident that these predictions will add significant value for everyone – the organization, its stakeholders and all professional internal auditors. I hope that the internal audit profession and many internal auditors, consultants and teachers will make sure that they happen.

THE PRESENT WILL ALWAYS BUY THE FUTURE OF INTERNAL AUDITING

There is a scene in Walter Disney's film *The Lion King* when Timon, the outcast meerkat, after leaving his family, meets Rafiki, the wise mandrill. Timon is looking for somewhere safe and secure to live. Rafiki advises a puzzled Timon to '... *look beyond what he can see*'. Timon continues his journey, little the wiser, but eventually does realize what the mandrill meant – sometimes to find what you are seeking you must look beyond the horizon.

The United Kingdom government, HM Treasury (2004) published guidance on the management of risk in the public sector, recognizing a concept of horizon scanning in risk management '*Increasingly both in the public and private sectors the importance of looking over the horizon in managing upcoming risk [and opportunity] is now recognized*'. Its guidance goes on to describe how this is achieved:

> Some organizations use systematic assessment schemes and information search technologies; other organizations will rely almost entirely on informal networks of contact, and good judgement.

Judgement and some luck are the methods used by Timon, with help from Pumbaa, his wart-hog friend – perhaps not far removed from some risk assessments!

What is beyond the horizon for internal auditing? Each chapter in this book will attempt to address that question and encourage readers to do the same.

CHAPTER SUMMARY

The future of internal auditing will always be influenced by the services it provides in the present and the environments in which it operates. Keeping these services up to date and professional is essential if internal auditors are to meet the needs of all their customers. An understanding of the environments in which they operate – local, national and global – and how they are changing and might change, provides indicators for further improvement. Continuous improvement is always needed to sell internal auditing as an added value service.

Looking into the future role of internal auditing is served well by using the following Gray and Gray (1997) five innovation motivational themes, four innovation goals and four innovation categories discussed in the Introduction:

Motivations

1. Progress within the field of professional internal auditing.
2. Increasing competition leading to pressures to reduce costs and increase efficiency.
3. New challenges, such as increasing internal control risks due to staff reductions and restructuring.
4. Opportunities to increase efficiency and quality as a result of technological advances.
5. Changes in corporate management practices and philosophies, such as Total Quality Management, re-engineering, continuous quality improvement, or related approaches

Goals

1. Improvement of the quality of internal auditing services.
2. Improve efficiency.
3. Expansion of services to increase the value added of internal auditing.
4. Boost staff skills, performance and morale.

Categories

1. Changes in the way that internal auditors interact with the rest of their enterprises.
2. Internal restructuring and changes in the organization and management of internal auditing.
3. Creation of new audit services and methods.
4. Changes in the use of technology.

A sixth and seventh motivational theme can be seen today in the flatter and smaller world we live in, with its regulation, social, environmental and cultural issues – all of which are having significant impacts on change in organizations.

6. **Challenges and opportunities of global issues and developments.**
7. **Social and environmental issues impacting all organizations.**

Perhaps also a fifth goal could be added:

5. **Sell internal auditing as future focused.**

And a change could be made to Category 1:

1. Changes in the way that internal auditors interact with the rest of their enterprises **and all those with a stakeholder interest.**

A VISION FOR FUTURE INTERNAL AUDITING

> *To be seen as a professional service adding significant value with our high quality, independent and objective services*

SYNOPSIS OF CASE STUDY

Case 2.1   Do Your Audits Report Plaudits?

Synopsis

Quality programmes and continuous improvement require a vision statement of where you want to be in the future that can be measured: a challenge for any organization, including its internal auditing. Today's internal auditing is changing from assurance to adviser in the planning and development of its facilitation and consulting roles. That trend will require new vision statements with significant changes in direction, driving more positive and cutting edge internal auditing observations in the future. A vision of more plaudits from the internal auditing assurance role is a must.

Based on an article published by the author in Internal Auditing August 2001, p.11, The IIA–UK & Ireland, London, England.

After Reading the Case Study Consider:

1. Does your own internal auditing vision require a paradigm shift?
2. Does it satisfy the direction of the new definition of internal auditing?
3. Does it require changes to your practices?
4. Will it drive continuous improvement?

SELF-ASSESSMENT QUESTIONS

2.1

What words/terms would you expect to see supporting internal auditing cutting edge resources and practices in your organization today and tomorrow?

(List your words/terms and keep as a bookmark: tick each of your words/terms as and when they appear in the book. Add to your list when you read words/terms mentioned that you think should be in your list. At the end of the book I should have mentioned all your words/terms. You will have added others. Keep this final list of words/terms as a reminder of what you should be using to support your cutting edge resources and practices planning, development, implementation and monitoring.)

2.2

What techniques are suggested in the chapter for *'looking beyond the horizon'*?

NOTES AND REFERENCES

1. Cited in *Wisdom of the Ages* (1936: p. 144), The St Catherine Press Ltd, London, England.
2. T.G. Rose (1932), 'The Management Audit', a paper read at a meeting of the Institute of Industrial Administration on 15 March 1932, Gee & Company Ltd, London England.
3. Clark Smith (1953), *Internal Auditing*, publisher unknown. Smith was probably better known as the author of a number of books published in the 1950s featuring Nicky Mahoun, . . . *a tough, cross grained investigating accountant* . . . in a series of adventures, arising from his work examining issues and problems in organizations, published by Hammond, Hammond & Co. and Penguin Books, Harmondsworth, Middlesex, England. An entertaining portrayal of the mysteries and risks that can sometimes be involved in internal audit examinations.
4. *Foundations for Unlimited Horizons*, Victor Z. Brink (1977: p. 64), The IIA, reported 8,000 membership and just under 100 chapters in 1971: these figures rose to 14,000 and 125 in 1977.
5. The Institute of internal Auditors *Code of Ethics*, adopted by The IIA Board of Directors, 17 June 2000. An important part of the Institute's current Professional Practices Framework.

6. This paper was written and presented by me in 1975 as my presidential address, on the integration of the five separate United Kingdom Chapters of The Institute of Internal Auditors into the one United Kingdom Chapter. It was then published in the Chapter Audit Newsletter in the same year.
7. www.theiia.org/?doc_id=503 and id=248/249, visited 29/10/2006.
8. Published in *Internal Auditing & Business Risk* (May 2003: pp. 26–27), IIA – UK & Ireland, London, England.

3

Cutting Edge Internal Auditing Is World-Class

World-Class Internal Auditing

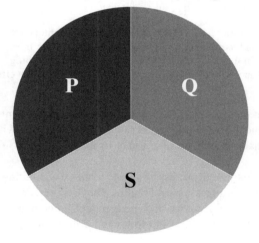

WORLD-CLASS INTERNAL AUDITING BEFORE 1990

Being the best is not a new ambition. Competition will always drive visions of being distinguished above the rest. Many years ago in the early 1990s I had the experience of being a member of an external quality assessment team assembled by The IIA quality assurance service, using the first edition of its *Quality Assessment Manual*. At dinner one evening with Donald Nelson, then head of The IIA service and Roland de Meulder (currently chair of The IIA Standards Committee), the other member of the team, we saw standing in the centre of the restaurant table a card with the words *'We Think We Are The Best In Town – Do You?'* and an invitation to assess the meal as it was served and eaten. This was a challenge before the start and during our meal! I commented at the time that all internal auditors should make this statement to their customers at the beginning and during every engagement, not just at the end. Being best in town during every internal audit engagement is what this chapter is about.

Being distinguished above the rest in today's flat world is better than being best in town. It is being world-class. World-class internal auditing as a mission started the day The IIA was established in 1941. From that day three mainstream international developments began in internal auditing:

Professionalism in the services it provides
Quality measures in its work
Standards to be developed and met.

I have used these three developments and their integration over many years as the framework for world-class internal auditing. They have grown in strength and importance, using many worldwide initiatives and best practices. They have grown not only in the USA, but also across the world, in countries and organizations of all sizes – and are still growing using many cutting edge resources and practices. At their very best professionalism, quality and standards beat all competition and delight all customers.

Professionalism of internal auditing started well before The IIA was established, although it varied greatly across organizations and countries:

> In many organizations [prior to 1941], however, internal auditors were being given high-level organizational status and were being used to analyse and appraise more substantive financial and operational activities. In these situations, internal auditors were reaching out in a very professional manner to make the most of their opportunities and to serve more effectively the interests of management.[2]

Many of the then internal auditors and their managers came into internal auditing through a professional and ethical accounting background. They brought with them a standard of professional service that can still be seen today in the framework of The IIA professional guidance.

Wood et al. (1989) explored professionalism in internal auditing, recognizing it to be separate from internal auditing as a profession. They saw clear evidence of professional practices such as integrity, objectivity and independent judgement but questioned whether internal auditing at the time met all of the following criteria of a profession:

- General systematic knowledge.
- Authority over clients.
- Community interest rather than self-interest (related to symbolic rather than monetary rewards).
- Self-control through occupational associations, training in occupational schools, and existence of a 'sponsor' system rather than external control.
- Public and legal recognition as a profession.
- A distinctive culture.

One of the first developments to satisfy these criteria for a profession came with the approval of The IIA first Code of Ethics in 1968. Its Introduction stated:

> Recognizing that ethics are an important consideration in the practice of internal auditing and that the moral principles followed by members of The Institute of Internal Auditors Inc., should be formalized, adopted the following resolution:

- *Whereas* the members of *The Institute of Internal Auditors Inc.* represent the profession of internal auditing; and
- *Whereas* managements rely on the profession of internal auditing to assist in the fulfillment of their management stewardship; and
- *Whereas* said members must maintain high standards of conduct, honour, and character in order to carry on proper and meaningful internal auditing practices;
- *Therefore be it resolved* that a Code of Ethics be now set forth, outlining the standards of professional behaviour for the guidance of each member of *The Institute of Internal Auditors Inc.*

The framework of the code contained several articles covering:

Honesty; Objectivity; Diligence; Trust; Loyalty; Illegality; Conflict; Gifts; Prudence; Care; Improvement; Competence; Morality; Dignity.

And abide by the bylaws and uphold the objectives of *The Institute of Internal Auditors Inc.*

A tall order for an international professional service in a wide variety of organizations across many countries; but an excellent step down the road of professionalism, and becoming a profession. Later revisions of the *Code of Ethics* up to 1998 included a forfeiture of membership for violation of the code, and in the articles (now Standards of Conduct) to strive for quality as well as '. . . *improvement in their proficiency, and in their effectiveness of their service*'. A good encouragement and jumping-off board for cutting edge internal auditing!

Following the *Code of Ethics*, The IIA standards were born from the structure of its first *Statement of Responsibilities* in 1971. This first statement set a framework for the professional standard developments that were to follow:

Nature [of internal auditing]
Objective and Scope
Responsibility and Authority
Independence.

These four key elements of professionalism remained in the framework of The IIA *Standards for the Professional Practice of Internal Auditing*, published in the 1970s, and subsequent revisions up to the fifth in 1998:

Independence
Professional Proficiency
Scope of Work
Performance of Audit Work
Management of the Internal Auditing Department.

Note the separate emphasis now on professional proficiency. It is worth exploring this further. In 1998 this section was prefaced with '*Internal Audits should be performed with proficiency and due professional care*', and included the following standards:

The Internal Audit Department
  Staffing
  Knowledge, Skills, and Disciplines
  Supervision

The Internal Auditor
  Compliance with Standards of Conduct
  Knowledge, Skills, and Disciplines
  Human Relations and Communications
  Continuing Education
  Due Professional Care.

Compliance with standards and the code of ethics required conformance with The IIA *Code of Ethics*.

The requirements of these standards created new professional challenges and benchmarks for heads of internal audit and internal auditors. The IIA rose to these challenges: with its global affiliates and chapters, developing appropriate (and cutting edge) training courses, research, education and certification programmes, and networking opportunities. In 1990, I wrote of a link between commitment to quality and professional internal auditing as a prerequisite to its achieving world-class status.

Article:
Internal Audit Opportunities In The TQM Environment Can Lead To World-Class Auditing[3] (1990)

'Getting to Grips with Quality' is the title of a recently published booklet produced by the Depart- ment of Trade and Industry for its *'Man-aging into the '90s'*programme part of the DTI's Enterprise Ini-tiative – details are available by telephoning free on 0800 500 200. The programme is supported by

> *'The enthusiasm a commitment to quality generates can lead to the highest accolades of excellence and the achievement of WORLD-CLASS status . . . '*

literature, practical advice and an excellent selection of videos on free loan, dealing with quality improvement policies, ISO 9000 – Quality Systems and the concept of Total Quality Management (TQM).

The DTI estimates that about one third of all effort expended in British businesses (not just industry!) is wasted on correction, rectification and rework: TQM is defined as a *way* of managing to improve the effectiveness, flexibility and competitiveness of a business operation or function. Reading and viewing this material provides a guide to how everyone in an organization should be controlling their processes, to be efficient, effective and economic. It is essential reading for all professional internal auditors carrying out 'full scope' audits! A knowledge and experience of TQM, even if only within the internal audit department, can only improve the audit service and enrich all the internal audit staff, both by job satisfaction and career development.

The TQM concept requires all SUPPLIER and OPERATING PROCESS relationships to create excellent products and services that satisfy all customers' needs. Developing supplier partnerships and knowing customer needs become paramount in the quality environment of team-building and continuous improvement, which develop between groups within the organization and between other organizations. Identifying the 'customer' is not that easy, particularly in large and international organizations.

In TQM everyone is involved, in every way, in everything they do – the involvement is TOTAL, all management and all staff. The *internal* supplier and customer become just as important as the *external* supplier and customer. It is the excellence of these working relationships and all the processes that guarantees the high quality of the product or service and satisfies the customer. Reliance is not placed on quality checks after the service has been completed or product made. The TQM environment develops teams and monitoring activities that are always 'customer' orientated. *THE CUSTOMER BECOMES PARAMOUNT.*

Many organizations already provide internal TQM training and all internal audit managers should take advantage of this for themselves and their staff. If your organization does not do so in whatever sector – then ask why. Do not wait for your organization to adopt TQM, seek the training and use the knowledge gained in the scope of all your audits.

What are some of the gains to be achieved?

- Recognition of the SUPPLIER–PROCESS–CUSTOMER CHAIN for the audit process drives the audit programme into the heart of business activity and highlights the key controls needed for business success.
- Establishing who are the customer and CUSTOMER NEEDS helps to focus audit tests into the most important areas and issues.
- The concept of AUDITOR/AUDITEE teamwork during the audit process is achieved and 'participative auditing' becomes a reality.
- AUDIT RESULTS and RECOMMENDATIONS concentrate on prevention rather than detection, looking to the control of quality in the future, rather than the past.
- QUALITY ASSURANCE requirements to meet IIA Standards take on a wider meaning, linking the quality aims of the internal audit department into those of the organization.
- Emphasis on CONTINUOUS IMPROVEMENT in the TQM environment encourages internal audit staff 'to continually seek improvements in the audit process'.
- TQM requires QUALITY MEASURES in all processes, to monitor quality and highlight non-conformance with standards.
- The audit process becomes a QUALITY SYSTEM, which can lead to recognition under the national accreditation standard BS 5750 (ISO 9000).
- QUALITY SUCCESSES are more easily recognized and rewarded at team and individual levels.

TOTAL QUALITY MANAGEMENT in an organization (even if only in the Internal Audit Department) requires the total commitment of management. However, it is not a journey's end, just the beginning. It is the start of a road that requires a continuing quality commitment by everyone, every day, in every way, in everything. The enthusiasm a commitment to quality generates can lead to the highest accolades of excellence and the achievement of WORLD-CLASS status but that is the subject of a future article!

WORLD-CLASS INTERNAL AUDITING 1990 TO 2000

In October 1991, in response to an article by Roger Carolus,[4] I had published the following letter in The IIA *Internal Auditor* journal:

> Roger Carolus' article reminded me of the 1970s when the Standards were being developed with input from across the world. I believe the Standards have influenced the practice of internal auditing and its acceptance as a profession more than any other development by IIA members.
>
> But we cannot stand still. Our Standards must reflect current trends on management theory and the expectations of our customers. I would like to suggest the following additions to Roger's list of needed changes:
>
> - **Relationships with other auditors.** Over the past five years there has been a growth in auditing activities, both within and outside organizations. Quality auditing, environmental auditing, security and compliance reviews from external groups have increased the need for Standard 550 – External Auditors, to be broadened, so that it covers not only external financial audits, but all other auditing activities.
> - **Due professional care.** Standard 280 is not linked into 580, although it is fundamental to any quality assurance programme. As organizations adopt Total Quality Management (TQM) cultures and practices, the commitment of everyone to excellence becomes the main drive for quality. Currently our quality assurance review elements link more to management monitoring theory than to leadership, team building, and personal contribution.
> - **Quality measurements.** The guidelines in Standard 560 identify potential quality measurement criteria (quality characteristics in the TQM environment), but do not go on to say or recommend how these measures should be made. Such 'qualitative measures' are essential for the measurement of quality. This is in an area where more research and advice is needed
>
> I am sure other more experienced internal auditors will have their own suggested additions to the Standards. Little is heard about the work going on to improve our Standards and keep them at the 'leading edge', but the future of our profession depends on this work.

Strategies recommended by the Office of the Auditor General of Canada (OAGC) (1992)[5] to achieve the shift towards *'more proactive, preventive auditing rather than after-the-fact detective auditing. The intention is to identify risks, trends or breakdowns before problems occur'*, were:

> greater use of technology in carrying out audits;
> audit involvement at the design and implementation stages of systems and programs;
> attention to trend and risk analysis in planning, carrying audits and reporting.

These strategies came from research by the OAGC into internal auditing in organizations in North America, guided by The IIA. *'Although our sample was not developed "scientifically", i.e. not randomly or on any hard statistical basis, we think it valid to assume that we have identified some of the best practices being followed by internal audit groups in Canada and the United States.'* All apply today and will go on being important in the future. You will probably have others not listed above. Would your internal auditing activity meet the choice requirements of The IIA and needs of the OAGC today?

In 1998, I wrote[6] and published the following after research into world-class practices in internal auditing at that time:

Internal audit is now seen by many as a highly professional and skilled unit. While there have been influences on the growth of internal auditing in organizations, much of this development has occurred primarily as an extension of management's responsibility for control. This responsibility is still with all managers, but is now, more than ever before, also associated with all staff in an organization, and many outside the organization with interests in its success. Quality programmes, environmental issues and codes of good conduct now place more and more responsibilities for control on everyone in an organization, and all those associated with its products and services, including its suppliers and customers.

There is ample literature evidence to show that governments, regulators, professional institutes and accounting firms have also been playing an active part in recent years to shape internal audit services in organizations. There is also evidence that other stake-holders are becoming more aware of the value of internal audit through management communications, both inside the organization and to the public. There is also a continuing catalogue of organization failures and litigation highlighting the presence, alertness and sometimes absence of an effective internal audit unit.

Over recent years the Big Six accounting firms have all been addressing values of current and future internal audit practices in the UK and internationally. Arthur Andersen UK (1994)[7] published consensus results from a series of symposiums with 100 senior internal auditors, representing internal audit units in the UK, across all sectors. The results created a vision of internal audit for the year 2000 and identified ten attributes to be key to the internal audit unit of the next century. These are shown as follows, ranked in order of perceived performance:

1. Professional
2. Close to the business
3. Provides solutions
4. Independent
5. High profile
6. Change agents
7. Customer focused
8. Expert in controls
9. Cost effective
10. Multi-skilled

This list and its ranking reveals an interesting perception of internal auditing by internal auditors at that time. Compare this list today with the world-class internal auditing focus on its assurance and consulting roles in organizational governance principles and practices, including risk management and risk-based internal auditing. Note the absence of any understanding of fraud prevention and detection or quality management.

The year 1999 saw significant changes in promotion of internal auditing across the world. Following international research The IIA published a new definition of internal auditing and a new professional competency framework.[8] This built on the previous definitions and framework but approached the task on a much more global scale. The competency framework was designed to sketch '. . . *the landscape of internal auditing in the future'*. What followed the framework in 2000 was a landmark: a new Professional Practices Framework.

In writing of world-class internal auditing as the 21st century approached I focused on the need for internal auditing to recognize competition in the services it provides. Such self-assessments are now an important part of all internal auditing practices as internal audit activities continuously strive to improve their services – hopefully aiming always for world-class status.

Article:
A New Internal Auditor For A New Century[9] (2000)

Internal auditing is an independent, objective, assurance and consulting activity designed to add value and improve an organization's operations. It helps an organization accomplish its objectives by bringing a systematic, disciplined approach to evaluate and improve effectiveness of risk management, control, and governance processes.[a]

The IIA launched earlier this year its new definition of internal auditing for the 21st-century's internal auditor. It should internal auditors and new internal auditing that requires new objectives and plan-definition, the ser- has been growing in

> *'In a competitive market place you also need to be a quality champion. Self-assess the value of your quality initiatives and measure your customers' satisfaction.'*

professional inter-lead and guide all their customers into a service. A service knowledge, skills, ning. Although a new vice image it contains many organizations across the world over a long period. If it is to achieve the recognition it deserves, all internal auditors need to study, understand and ACT its implications.

In the early 70s I designed an 'AUDITOR/CONSULTANT/TEACHER' logo[b] for my recruitment and training of internal audit staff. Each of three equal segments of a pie chart represented the potential roles for an internal auditor in my organization – if not every organization. Together, they provided a proACTive plan for improving the professionalism of internal auditing. Not all internal auditors will learn to be expert in each role. But all internal auditors should recognize the services that they can and should provide in each role.

This logo aptly represents the challenges and opportunities in the new definition. It clearly addresses the AUDITOR (some may call this ASSURER but I still prefer the traditional auditor) and CONSULTANT roles. However, in the new definition the TEACHING segment is still not as clear as it should be! Yet there is ample evidence from both internal auditors and their customers that internal auditing provides a teaching service. Why does this teaching role still receive less recognition than it should? Teaching and its associated continuous learning lie at the heart of the new definition's key words 'accomplish' and 'improvement'. Consider the learning and teaching implications of the dictionary explanations of each of the following words used in the new definition:

---

[a] Approved by The IIA Inc. Board, 1999.
[b] *Leading Edge Internal Auditing*, Ridley and Chambers (1998), ICSA Publishing Ltd, London, England.

Accomplish – *to complete; to fulfill; to achieve; to equip; to finish off, complete, in culture and acquirements – adjective* ***accomplished*** *complete, finished or highly skilled; expert; polished.*

Improvement – *the act of improving; a change for the better; a thing changed, or introduced in changing, for the better; a better thing substituted for, or following, one not so good.*

Why do internal auditors not sell a higher profile for their teaching skills? Is the answer reflected in a low interest in internal auditing learning and certification? Despite the large membership of The IIA worldwide, there are still too few internal auditors studying 21st-century internal auditing at undergraduate and postgraduate levels. Even the professional bodies associated with accountancy and management include little on new internal auditing in their professional examinations.

Some place the low interest in internal auditing learning and certification on the transitory nature of many internal auditing careers. Yet the body of internal auditing knowledge and learning programmes can improve and make all managers more accomplished. Worldwide, there are board members and senior operation managers with an internal auditing background, training and certification in many organizations. The IIA certification programme recognizes this:

> Whether you are a long-term internal auditor or a future manager gaining exposure and expertise in organizational risk management, the CIA (Certified Internal Auditor) will serve you throughout your entire career.[c]

Internal auditors must be experts in how organizations are controlled. This requires a study of control concepts, the primary objectives of control (see The IIA general standard 300/1983) and the characteristics of control (see the COSO report/1992, cited by the ICAEW Turner Internal Control Consultative Draft/1999 in its risk-based approach to control). Current requirements for reporting on control continue to mix the terms 'control' and 'internal control'. Recent studies are no exception. In 1983 The IIA considered 'control' and 'internal control' to be synonymous (Guideline 300.06.3). In the 21st century we should stop referring to 'internal control' and its implied 'within the organization' restriction. Management's control responsibilities span all an organization's supply chains. This includes many relationships with others (owners, partners, alliances, contractors, suppliers, customers, regulators, inspectors, communities, etc.). Consider your own organization's supply chains and many external control requirements. These should all be subject to review and report by management, and independent appraisal. The new IIA definition of internal auditing refers to 'control'. Let us hope the revised IIA professional standards will drop the use of 'internal', and others will follow. Design 'control' not 'internal control' into all your internal auditing. Encourage your board, management and accountants to do likewise for their control responsibilities.

---

[c] *Introduction to the Certified Internal Auditor*® *Programme* (1968), John J. Fernandes, CIA Vice President IIA Learning Centre, The IIA.

Earlier this year I was invited to participate in an internal audit conference at a leading building society. My theme was *Internal Auditing in 2005* . For this I used as an acronym the key word CONTROLS. Each letter representing an imperative for the new internal auditor of the 21st century. The whole word representing the overriding feature for all internal auditing roles – Auditor, Consultant and Teacher.

The acronym and each of the words it represents speak for themselves. Together they offer many opportunities and challenges for the new internal auditing service of the 21st century. Test your own services against each. Create a definition for each that is appropriate for your organization and the customers you serve. Research the implications of your definitions and redefine each year. As a start consider the following suggestions for your definitions:

Competition

For all auditing (and assurance) services it will increase. Study the marketing of services by all professional firms – not just auditing! Learn from their 'selling' skills. Market your internal auditing services as a business. Improve your auditing market share. The IIA's 1994[d] recommended response to outsourcing requires internal auditing to be proactive, innovative, focused, motivated, and *'with information systems integrated and designed to support auditing and management processes'*. In a competitive market place you also need to be a quality champion. Self-assess the value of your quality initiatives and measure your customers' satisfaction.

Objectives

Have a clear sense of internal auditing purpose and values that everyone understands. Create commitment to an exciting vision of the internal auditing services you believe your customers will need in five years' time. Make sure all your current internal auditing objectives link into this vision, your organization's objectives, and span all your organization's supply chains – suppliers, processes and customers.

New business

Keep up to date with research into internal auditing practices and use this knowledge to experiment, develop and market your future services (also products). Products are the most underdeveloped part of internal auditing services. Focusing on products requires you to address specifications, processes and packaging. It also draws your attention to by-products, often resulting in new business. Plan for growth. Particularly focus on your organization's strategies and contribute to their development and implementation. This is the most neglected part of internal auditing.

---

[d] *Perspective on Outsourcing Internal Auditing – A professional briefing for chief executives*, (1994), The IIA.

Technology

Up-to-date technology will be the key to all internal auditing best practices in the future. Use information technology as a means to improve your knowledge management. Internal auditing knowledge spans all organization operations at all levels. Organize and manage this knowledge properly and it will lead you to your organization's most significant risks. Sell your information technology and knowledge management skills as part of the internal auditing services you provide.

Regulation

New inspectors and regulators are being established by government and industries across all sectors. Some are being merged with stronger teeth. Some have established guidance for governance, control and internal auditing. Others will follow. Understand the authority, responsibilities and activities of inspectors and regulators in your own sector, and that of your suppliers and customers. Use this knowledge in the planning and quality of your internal auditing services.

Outstanding

Do not just be 'best' or 'excellent', be 'outstanding'. Recognize achievements and celebrate. In your organization openly reinforce outstanding internal auditing by appropriate rewards, at individual and team levels. Be recognized by your management and peers as leading the development of professional internal auditing services. Build this commitment into your internal auditing vision and objectives. Benchmark your leading edge practices with others and published research.

Learning

Be part of the new learning age.[e] Your working environment must be a learning environment. Carry out a continuous skills audit of your knowledge and abilities. Identify your strengths and weaknesses. Plan to improve both. Master a critical understanding of the concepts and principles needed to understand how organizations should be managed and controlled today and tomorrow. This is essential for all the roles you provide as an internal auditor.

Standards

Search for relevant and appropriate external standards and codes of conduct for all the operations you audit. Test against these standards and codes. Publicize your own standards and codes. Benchmark the services you provide with relevant international standards – professional, accounting, auditing, quality, environmental, training, data, technology, etc. Use the results to add power and value to your services and your reporting to management and at board level.

---

[e] *The Learning Age: a Renaissance for a New Britain*, Department for Education and Employment, 1998.

Finally, as you start the new century as a new internal auditor, focus on the ethics of your service. Remember always that *'Members and CIAs shall continually strive for improvements in their proficiency, and in the effectiveness and quality of the services they provide'.*[f]

Good striving (and luck). Enjoy your part of the 21st century.

WORLD-CLASS INTERNAL AUDITING 2000 TO 2002

Professor Parveen Gupta (2001)[10] in his research into internal audit re-engineering recognized a world-class role for internal auditing in the processes of re-engineering taking place in organizations across the world:

> Since the world-class organizations consider the internal audit function a key aspect of their overall management control and governance process, it is implied that internal auditing has a role to play in creating a value enterprise by becoming a value-added partner in the organization along with others in their organization's value chain. This expectation has led many internal auditing departments in such organizations to chart their course in unprecedented ways to becoming a world-class internal audit function. In this process of transforming themselves to become value-added partners, such internal audit functions have engaged in an extensive search to find ways and means to 're-optimize, re-engineering, or re-relevance' their audit vision, mission, role, departmental structure, and various internal audit processes.
>
> Undoubtedly, the world-class internal audit functions are truly 'thinking outside the box' to become process-oriented organizations. These internal auditing functions are now developing and offering innovative products and services for the changing business models of their organizations as well as taking leadership positions in becoming change agents in their organizations. Even though over the years such internal auditing functions have grown in absolute numbers, the entire internal auditing profession is still a long way from completely reinventing itself. Certainly the process of reinvention is accelerating almost on a daily basis. With The Institute of Internal Auditors as a powerful enabler, the term 'internal auditing' will become synonymous with 'value' in every organization aspiring to become a value-added enterprise.

These were the years for the worldwide introduction of The IIA's new Professional Practices Framework and its International Standards and supporting Practice Advisories, not only through its affiliated institutes and chapters but also in its certification examination programmes. These years also saw a growth in The IIA's advocacy for its professionalism, quality and standards, linked to increased regulation of organizations and sectors, not just in North America but also across the world. It also saw The IIA organization itself becoming more global in its vision, missions and structure: a world-class leader among other international professions. My passion for linking quality aims to The IIA standards and professionalism continued during this period resulting in the following article focused on quality and due professional care.

---

[f] The IIA *Code of Ethics*, first published in 1968.

Article:
Overcoming Complexity In Internal Auditing[11] (2002)

Recent events in a number of global organizations have once again highlighted the complexities met in modern internal audit-ing. Complexity in auditing is not new. It is a part of every audit of risk, control and governance. It is found in all accounting practices, regu-lations, relation-ships, systems and operations. Understanding and overcoming complexity with a quality assured internal auditing activity is a continuous challenge for all boards, audit committees and internal auditors.

> '*All internal auditing policies and procedures should clearly state responsibility for due professional care, not just in internal auditing practices but also how the quality of the service is practiced and assessed.*'

Recent research by The IIA[g] into the effectiveness of audit committees places an understanding of significant accounting principles as a must for all audit committees – '. . . *those (principles) mandated by accounting and regulatory rules and those made at management's discretion. . .* '. In addition to the review of financial statements the research also recognizes that most audit committees '. . . *have responsibility for overseeing the financial reporting process, monitoring compliance with laws and regulations and the corporate code of conduct. . .* '. All audit committee terms of reference should require this understanding and be resourced accordingly.

Experience now tells us that it is also important that audit committees understand the relationships at the heart of significant contracts, strategic alliances and financial transactions. Not just those that can impact earnings, but also the triple bottom-line – economic, social and environmental. This includes risks and controls in the processes of all types of investment and financial instruments. Such as investment strategies, validation of title and value, custody of documentation and management of transactions and income. Particularly possible conflicts of interest between those who manage and those who have custody of documentation.

If internal auditors are also to be effective they too must understand all the complexities facing their audit committee. Due professional care in the services they provide requires they are aware of all risks and these are flagged appropriately in their audit planning and audit surveys. Either by assessing the risks themselves or by using other resources to do so. Any weaknesses in their, or their audit committee's understanding of the complexities of risk, control and governance must be recognized and discussed at board level. Following recent events this may take place more often in the future!

In the 1960s, publications by The Institute of Internal Auditors advised a full understanding of the language of computer operations as a requirement for all internal auditors. The principle behind this advice has followed me throughout my

---

[g] *Audit Committee Effectiveness – What Works Best* (2000), The IIA Research Foundation.

internal auditing career. I learned through many audits that an understanding of the language used in operations being audited is an essential part of due professional care.

I also believe that due professional care, like quality, is '... a road not a destination...'. It is continuously travelled and being improved. It is a commitment and way of life for all professions. For internal auditing due professional care now starts with being aware of the requirements of The IIA *Professional Practices Framework*.[h] This is a must for all boards, audit committees and internal auditors. Is this true in your organization? The framework recognizes due professional care as '... the responsibility of the chief audit executive and each internal auditor'. Followed by they should '... ensure that persons assigned to each engagement collectively possess the necessary knowledge, skills, and other competencies to conduct the engagement properly'.[i]

The IIA old *Standards* and new *Professional Practices Framework* contain many comments on complexity in internal auditing. Included in the new framework are mandatory requirements and guidance for actions by all boards, audit committees and internal auditors. Actions that should ensure all internal auditing engagements are carried out with due professional care. Attribute Standards require internal auditors to exercise due professional care in both assurance and consulting engagements by considering '... relative complexity, materiality, or significance of matters...'. Performance Standards require internal auditing staffing to be based on '... an evaluation of the nature and complexity of each engagement...'.

All internal auditing policies and procedures should clearly state responsibility for due professional care, not just in internal auditing practices but also how the quality of the service is practised and assessed. For every internal auditing activity this road starts with 10 steps. A road that should be understood by all boards, audit committees and internal auditors. These steps are:

1. Approval of a charter.
2. Engaging the best internal auditing resources.
3. Continuing professional development.
4. Assessment of organization risks.
5. Establishing coordination and cooperation with other auditors.
6. Planning engagement coverage.
7. Agreeing engagement objectives and developing appropriate programmes
8. Communicating engagement results.
9. Following up findings and recommendations.
10. Establishing and maintaining a quality assurance and improvement programme for all internal auditing activities.

In how many of these steps do you satisfy your board, audit committee and customers that complexity has been addressed and causes no problems concerning your due professional care? How many of these steps are fully understood by your

[h] *Standards for the Professional Practice of Internal Auditing* (2002), The IIA.
[i] Practice Advisory 1200-1: *Proficiency and Due Professional Care* (2002), The IIA.

board, audit committee and customers? Consider each carefully and be certain that you meet the following criteria:

1. **Approval of a charter**
   Does your internal auditing charter mention complexity? Does it give you access to the special knowledge, skills and experience you may need in your internal auditing engagements? Skills and experience such as '. . . *actuaries, accountants, appraisers, environmental specialists, fraud investigators, lawyers, engineers, geologists, security specialists, statisticians, information technology specialists, external auditors. . .* ',[j] and so on. This is not a definitive list. All organizations have their own special knowledge, skills and experience needs.

2. **Engaging the best internal auditing resources**
   '*Staffing plans and financial budgets, including the number of auditors and the knowledge, skills, and other competencies required to perform their work, should be determined from engagement work schedules, administrative activities, education and training requirements, and audit research and development efforts.*'[k] Investing in the right people for internal auditing requires a detailed analysis of an organization's risk, control and governance processes, and a full understanding of the professional nature of internal auditing work.

3. **Continuing professional development**
   '*Internal auditors are responsible for continuing their education in order to maintain their proficiency. They should keep informed about improvements and current developments in internal auditing standards, procedures and techniques.*'[l] The IIA–UK & Ireland's continuing professional development programme[m] is an excellent competency benchmark for all internal auditors. Following its guidance should be a requirement by all boards and audit committees for all internal auditors.

4. **Assessment of organization risks**
   '*Internal auditors evaluate the whole management process of planning, organizing, and directing to determine whether reasonable assurance exists that objectives and goals will be achieved. Internal auditors should be alert to actual or potential changes in internal and external conditions that affect the ability to provide assurance from a forward-looking perspective. In those cases, internal auditors should address the risk that performance may deteriorate.*'[n] Does your internal auditing activity have the resources to focus on all risk management, control and governance systems in the present and future? Has this been assessed?

5. **Establishing coordination and cooperation with other auditors**
   '*In exercising its oversight role, the board may request the chief audit executive to assess the performance of external auditors.*'[o] Should this apply to only external financial auditors? Why not also all other external auditors and other internal

---

[j] Extracted from the Glossary definition of External Service Provider, supporting The IIA new Professional Practices Framework, 2002.
[k] Practice Advisory 2030-1: *Resource Management* (2002), The IIA.
[l] Practice Advisory 1230-1: *Continuing Professional Development* (2002), The IIA.
[m] *Learning for the Longer Term* (2000), The IIA–UK & Ireland.
[n] Practice Advisory 2100-1: *Nature of Work* (2002), The IIA.
[o] Practice Advisory 2050-1: *Coordination* (2002), The IIA.

auditors? Coordination of all audit efforts is an important part of the monitoring processes in all organizations. Internal auditing should have a principal role in this process.

6. **Planning engagement coverage**

   'Staffing should be based on an evaluation of the nature and complexity of each engagement, time constraints and available resources.'[p] Determining the resources necessary is an essential part of internal auditing engagement planning and training. It should be formal and commented on in all annual activity reports to senior management, the board and audit committee.

7. **Agreeing engagement objectives and developing appropriate programmes**

   All internal auditors should be skilled in using analytical auditing procedures. Such procedures are *'. . . useful in identifying, among other things:*

   - *Differences that are not expected.*
   - *The absence of differences when they are expected.*
   - *Potential errors.*
   - *Potential irregularities or illegal acts.*
   - *Other unusual or nonrecurring transactions or events.'*[q]

8. **Communicating engagement results**

   'The chief audit executive should, at least annually, prepare a statement of the adequacy of internal controls to mitigate risks. This statement should also comment on the significance of unmitigated risk and management's acceptance of such risk.'[r] Included in this communication should be a statement on the adequacy of internal auditing resources for current and future audit planning and engagements.

9. **Following up findings and recommendations**

   'Follow-up by internal auditors is defined as a process by which they determine the adequacy, effectiveness, and timeliness of actions taken by management on reported engagement observations and recommendations, including those made by external auditors and others.' [s] Reviewing management action on internal auditing findings requires persistent monitoring.

10. **Establishing and maintaining a quality assurance and improvement programme for all internal auditing activities**

    'Conformity with applicable standards is more than simply complying with established policies and procedures. It includes performance of the internal audit activity at a high level of efficiency and effectiveness, Quality is essential to achieving such performance, as well as to maintaining the internal audit activity's credibility with those it serves.' [t] Quality in internal auditing is also about the commitment of all internal auditors to continuous improvement in the services

---

[p] Practice Advisory 2230-1: *Engagement Resource Allocation* (2002), The IIA.
[q] Practice Advisory 2320-1: *Analysis and Evaluation* (2002), The IIA.
[r] Practice Advisory 2010-2: *Linking the Audit Plan to Risk and Exposures* (2002), The IIA.
[s] Practice Advisory 2500.A1-1: *Follow-up Process* (2002), The IIA.
[t] Practice Advisory 1310-1: *Quality Programme Assessment* (2002), The IIA.

they provide. It is not a final step, but the beginning for all processes supporting the other steps.

Assessing the right levels of competence and quality to overcome complexity in internal auditing should always address the above 10 steps for achieving due professional care.

CUTTING EDGE INTERNAL AUDITING IS WORLD-CLASS TODAY AND IN THE FUTURE

Consider again the ten key attributes of world-class internal auditing researched in 1994 and discussed in the article:

Professional
Close to the business
Provides solutions
Independent
High profile
Change agents
Customer focused
Expert in controls
Cost effective
Multi-skills.

World-class internal auditing today and tomorrow needs a more up-to-date benchmark than these 10 key attributes. The HR Chally Group,[12] in the executive summary of its 2007 *The World Class Sales Excellence Research Report*, identifies a shifting emphasis and new benchmarks for world-class status:

As the demands on salespeople have changed over the last 14 years, so have the agendas of the sales executives who must invest wisely to ensure that their sales forces are in tune with their customers' needs, and 2006 was no exception. In the four years since our last research effort, sales executives have not only shifted emphasis among their existing benchmark agenda items, new benchmarks have emerged as top priorities of the leading sales forces. The areas of focus we observed in this year's class of World Class Sales Benchmark winners were:

1. Creating a Customer-Driven Culture
2. Recruiting and Selecting the Right Sales Talent
3. Training and Developing for the Right Set of Skills
4. Segmenting Markets in Meaningful Way
5. Implementing Formal Sales Processes (New)
6. Developing Enabling Information Technology
7. Integrating Other Business Functions with Sales (New).

It is no surprise that creating a *Customer-Driven Culture* continues to lead the agenda for sales forces that are considered the best of the best by their customers. As the customers' needs have shifted over the years, these companies have remained in sync with their customers by uncovering and adapting to the new demands on their salespeople. This focus on customer needs and expectations will probably never fall from the list, because it is so fundamental to the success of a sales force. Without it, companies become internally focused and tend to impose their own needs on customers, rather than imposing the customers' needs on their salespeople. What is evolving, though, are the methods that sales executives are employing to drive this philosophy into the heads of their sellers. As you will see, world-class sales forces are experts at connecting customer strategies to selling reality.

For some internal auditing activities this may appear a 'world' away from the reality of their status and services they provide. Yet there are many messages here for internal auditing wanting to sell itself as world-class. Can you see these? Start with the following and develop each into best practice benchmarks for your internal auditing services:

1. Customer-driven at all levels in the organization and across all supply chains.
2. Recruiting the right resources for the all the services needed.
3. Continuous training and development of all resources.
4. Scope of work, risk-based audit planning.
5. Promoting quality and continuous improvement in professional internal auditing.
6. Computer-Assisted Audit Techniques.
7. Partnering with management and collaboration with other auditors.

Consider how The IIA[13] defines benchmarks 2 and 3 in its best practice 2007 revision of guidance for evaluating internal audit resources:

> The skills, capabilities and technical knowledge of the internal audit resources must be appropriate for the planned activities. The CAE should conduct a periodic skills assessment or inventory to determine the specific skills required to perform the internal audit activities. The skills assessment should be based on and consider the various needs identified in the risk assessment and audit plan. The CAE should then determine and assign resources that possess the skills, knowledge and competences identified by the skills assessment. This may include assessments of technical skills, language skills, business knowledge, fraud detection and prevention, accounting and auditing expertise. The CAE must ensure that the skills assessment is driven by the needs of the audit coverage and that this coverage is not being determined primarily by the capabilities present within the internal audit organization. Recognizing the dynamic nature of risk, the CAE should periodically update the skills assessment.
>
> Based on these updates, the CAE may consider needs to increase the skills, capabilities and knowledge of the existing staff. The extent and formality of the skills assessment should be appropriate for the size and complexity of the internal audit function.

Do you see how this relates to the other five benchmarks? Now seek internal auditing best practices for these. They are all discussed in other chapters in this book. Keep looking for the links all seven have to each other. Achieve and maintain best practice in all seven and you have world-class status for your internal auditing.

Few, if any, of those who provide outsourced internal auditing services see themselves as anything less than world leaders, world beaters and world class. The promotion of their products and services state this and will continue to do so. All internal auditing activities have to join their ranks. This message comes over clearly in all the attributes associated with world-class status.

At The IIA 2006 International Conference discussed in Chapter 2, Carmen Rossiter, Managing Director, Protiviti Inc., made a presentation titled 'Top Priorities for Internal

Auditing in the Face of a Changing Environment'. In that presentation she listed the following top priorities for internal auditing:

1. **Raise** the bar – Live up to heightened expectations
2. **Revisit** charter and reporting relationship – Validate purpose and position
3. **Rebalance** internal audit activities – Focus on risk and stakeholder expectations
4. **Communicate** – Sharpen dialogue with senior management and the audit committee
5. **Act** as a change agent – Facilitate positive change
6. **Drive** efficiency – Work smart
7. **Build** talent – Attract, develop and retain the best
8. **Participate** in the profession – Embrace The IIA Standards
9. **Strengthen** quality processes – Focus on continuous improvement
10. **Measure** performance – Add value.

For the internal auditing activity that aims to be world class, these are strong and important missions. See my **PQS** in priorities 7 and 8. As I write this book, The IIA[14] is progressing and publishing preliminary results from its global study into a new body of knowledge for internal auditing. This reports that:

> At the core of the study results: a majority (82%) of internal auditors are following (at least partly, if not entirely) the *International Standards for the Professional Practice of Internal Auditing (Standards)*; . . .

It is only those internal auditors who can be at, or are progressing to, the cutting edge of internal auditing resources and practices. Regulators are starting to recognize the importance of this in internal auditing in the organizations they regulate. This recognition and requirement will grow in the future: even to the possibility that for certain countries/sectors/industries the attributes of world-class internal auditing will become a legal requirement.

CHAPTER SUMMARY

There can be few that will disagree that professionalism, quality and standards have been key to the success of internal auditing as a service in organizations of all sizes, sectors, industries and countries. They may have different interpretations by different internal auditors but their key meaning of being best in any product or service cannot be argued – or at least should not be. They will continue to be so in the future in internal auditing, pioneered by many cutting edge resources and practices – not just by The IIA but also internal auditors and internal audit activities across the world. This chapter has discussed what these terms have meant to internal auditors in the past and how they are, and can be, promoted today, leading the profession forward in its world-class status.

The 10 steps selected in my article of 2003 are worth repeating, in **bold**:

1. **Approval of a charter.**
2. **Engaging the best internal auditing resources.**
3. **Continuing professional development.**
4. **Assessment of organization risks.**
5. **Establishing coordination and cooperation with other auditors.**
6. **Planning engagement coverage.**

7. **Agreeing engagement objectives and developing appropriate programmes.**
8. **Communicating engagement results.**
9. **Following up findings and recommendations.**
10. **Establishing and maintaining a quality assurance and improvement programme for all internal auditing activities.**

World-class internal auditing is served well by using the Gray and Gray (1997) five innovation motivational themes, four innovation goals and four innovation categories discussed in the Introduction, and the additions and changes in Chapter 2:

Motivations

1. Progress within the field of professional internal auditing.
2. Increasing competition leading to pressures to reduce costs and increase efficiency.
3. New challenges, such as increasing internal control risks due to staff reductions and restructuring.
4. Opportunities to increase efficiency and quality as a result of technological advances.
5. Changes in corporate management practices and philosophies, such as Total Quality Management, re-engineering, continuous quality improvement, or related approaches.
6. **Challenges and opportunities of global issues and developments.**
7. **Social and environmental issues impacting all organizations.**

Goals

1. Improvement of the quality of internal auditing services.
2. Improve efficiency.
3. Expansion of services to increase the value-added of internal auditing.
4. Boost staff skills, performance and morale.
5. **Sell internal auditing as future focused.**

Categories

1. Changes in the way that internal auditors interact with the rest of their enterprises **and all those with a stakeholder interest.**
2. Internal restructuring and changes in the organization and management of internal auditing.
3. Creation of new audit services and methods.
4. Changes in the use of technology.

A new Motivation could be:

8. **Recognition that professionalism, quality and standards are essential attributes for world-class status in any internal auditing activity.**

Recognizing the importance of internal auditing managing its knowledge, the changing skills required in internal auditing teams and using both to pioneer cutting edge resources and practices, we could add a new Category today:

5. **Improved knowledge and skills in the teams of staff who carry out internal auditing engagements.**

WORLD-CLASS INTERNAL AUDITING PRINCIPIA
1998 AND 2008

My 1998 principia for internal auditing included the following related to its world-class status (see Appendix A):

1. Understanding the history and development of internal auditing is the foundation for creating a vision for its future.
23. Internal auditing vision and mission statements must be exciting.
26. Internal audit charters must be based on professional standards and ethics.
32. Look for features of excellence in internal audit teamwork.

These are now changed to reflect the world-class status of internal auditing in 2008 and the future:

1. World-class status for internal auditing requires a vision for its professionalism, quality and standards that meets the needs of all its customers, at all levels, both in the organization it serves and outside the organization.
2. All internal audit teams should strive for a world-class status in their engagements and be appropriately rewarded when this is achieved.

A VISION FOR WORLD-CLASS INTERNAL AUDITING

We provide a service seen by all our customers and stakeholders as world-class.

SYNOPSES OF CASE STUDIES

Case 3.1: Internal Auditing can be World-Class

Synopsis

There are three interdependent requirements for an internal auditing to become a world-class player – effective relationships with the board – innovative forward-thinking practices – meeting the requirements of The IIA *International Professional Practices Framework* for its management and performance. Each of these requirements requires cutting edge resources and practices. Each is developed into guidance in how they can be used to continuously improve internal auditing services in an organization.

Contributed by Roland de Meulder. past-chairman of The IIA Internal Audit Standards Board, March 2007.

After Reading the Case Study Consider:

1. Is The IIA International Professional Practices Framework (IIA PPF) used and complied with in your own organization as a cutting edge tool?

2. Do you promote the internal auditing requirements and guidance in The IIA PPF as world-class professional practices in internal auditing in your organization?
3. Do you maintain an up to date review of changes to The IIA PPF?
4. How are The IIA PPF changes communicated to internal audit staff and the board in your organization?
5. How do changes to The IIA PPF provoke innovation and creativity in your internal auditing?

Case 3.2: World-Class Internal Auditing in the United Nations System

Synopsis

Auditing in organizations that are under intensive external scrutiny, nationally and internationally, opens up new cutting edge challenges for internal auditors – better coordination, more transparency, sharing of knowledge and implementing best practices. The Office of Internal Audit Oversight Services sets the tone for addressing these challenges across the United Nations' organization. Its website is filled with data concerning its authority, compliance to The IIA *International Professional Practices Framework,* overviews of its activities, copies of its annual and oversight reports, invitations to communicate confidential allegations. Using its website in this way places OIOS internal auditing in a world-class status.

Contributed by David O'Regan, currently Internal Auditor in the Office of Internal Oversight at the Organization for the Prohibition of Chemical Weapons in the Hague, Netherlands. A fellow of the Institute of Chartered Accountants in England and Wales, and formerly Chief Internal Auditor at Oxford University Press, he has authored a number of books, including *International Auditing* (John Wiley & Sons Ltd, 2003) and the *Auditor's Dictionary* (John Wiley & Sons Ltd, 2004). He is also a contributing editor for The IIA *Internal Auditing* journal. All views and opinions expressed are the case study author's own and do not necessarily reflect any official UN views.

After Reading the Case Study Consider:

1. How transparent is your world-class internal auditing planning and results, for all internal audit staff, management and your organization's external stakeholders?
2. How does your world-class internal audit function promote and encourage the use of best internal auditing practices?

Case 3.3: General Motors Audit Services (GMAS)

Synopsis

This Charter for a quality award-winning world-class internal auditing function contains Vision and Mission Statements reflecting a commitment to being '. . . *recognized as a leader'.* The General Motors Audit Services Charter sets out its authority, independence, audit scope, professional standards and the frequency in which the Charter is assessed to maintain its status as a cutting edge statement.

Contributed by Angelina Chin, CIA CPA CBA CRP CCSA, General Director, GMAS, General Motors Corporation.

After Reading the Case Study Consider:

1. How do the vision and mission statements of your organization's internal auditing compare with those of GMAS?
2. How does internal auditing in your organization demonstrate a commitment to the quality of its '. . . *internal auditing in the areas of professional excellence, quality of service, and professional outreach'*?
3. How does the charter for your organization's internal auditing compare with the GMAS charter?
4. Is the date of approval of the charter for your organization's internal auditing current?

Case 3.4: Key Attributes, Strategies and Actions for World-Class Internal Auditing

Synopsis

These 1998 researched attributes and strategies of world-class internal auditing provided a vision for internal auditing in the 21st century. They are still cutting edge today. Benchmark your internal auditing against the 12 best practice actions developed by me from this research.

Written by the author and from *Leading Edge Internal Auditing* (1998), Jeffrey Ridley and Andrew D. Chambers.

After Reading the Case Study Consider:

1. How many of the ten key attributes are there in your internal auditing?
2. How many of the nine key strategies are there reflected in your internal auditing vision, mission statement and strategies?
3. How many of the twelve actions do you have as key performance measures in your internal auditing – at both individual and group levels?

Case 3.5: Tomorrow's Company

Synopsis

In 1995 Tomorrow's Company developed a '. . . *shared vision of a company tomorrow . . .*'. In this it introduced the concept of an '. . . *inclusive approach to business success . . .*' covering a company's values, a success model, relationships, stakeholders and reputation. It recognized companies as being bound up in a global complex of systems – environment, social and political, economic. Three specific ways are defined in which a company can '*expand its space*' – redefining its success, embedded values and creating frameworks in which to operate.

Extract from *Tomorrow's Global Company – Challenges and Opportunities* (2007) Contributed with permission from Tomorrow's Company. The full report can be seen on its website www.tomorrowscompany.com

After Reading the Case Study Consider:

1. Does your world-class internal audit planning address all of the case study's global challenges and choices facing organizations today?
2. How proactive is your world-class internal auditing function in contributing to the *'three specific ways'* global companies are taking today to *'expand the space'* of their operations – *'redefining success: embedding values: creating frameworks'*?
3. Is your world-class internal auditing at the cutting edge of adding value to these three specific ways in its services to management and the board?

SELF-ASSESSMENT QUESTIONS

3.1

What attributes are required in an internal audit activity for it to be stated as world-class? Compare your answer with the Arthur Andersen UK key strategies discussed in the chapter.

3.2

What are the *'three main stream international developments'* discussed in the chapter that continue to influence achievement of world-class status for an internal audit activity? Compare your answer with the discussion of these in the chapter.

NOTES AND REFERENCES

1. The *Chambers Dictionary* 10th edition (2006), Chambers Harrap Publishers Ltd, Edinburgh, Scotland.
2. *Foundations for Unlimited Horizons 1941–1976* (1977: p. 3), Victor Z. Brink, The IIA.
3. Published in *Internal Auditing* (1990), IIA–UK & Ireland.
4. *Setting the Standards*, Roger Carolus, *Internal Auditor* (June 1991), The IIA.
5. *Internal Auditing – In A Changing Management Culture* (1992), Office of the Auditor General of Canada, Ottawa, Ontario, Canada.
6. *Leading Edge Internal Auditing* (1998), Ridley and Chambers, ICSA Publishing Ltd, London.
7. *Internal Audit 2000: An overview* (1994), Arthur Andersen UK, London, England.
8. *Competency Framework for Internal Auditing* (CFIA) (1999), Elaine R. McIntosh, The IIA.
9. Published in *Internal Auditing & Business Risk* (January 2000), IIA–UK & Ireland.
10. *Internal Audit Reengineering: Survey, Model, and Best Practices* (2001: p. 190), Professor Parveen P. Gupta, The IIA Research Foundation.
11. Published in *Internal Auditing & Business Risk* (July 2002: p. 24), IIA–UK & Ireland.
12. See The HR Chally Group website, www.chally.com, for details of this research.
13. Practice Advisory 2030-1(2) (2007); *Resource Management*, The IIA.
14. See The IIA Press Release *Groundbreaking Global Study Reveals Internal Audit Standardization and Growing Impact on Organizational Governance*, July 2007.

Cutting Edge Internal Auditing
Wears Many Hats

'... internal auditors often find themselves torn by conflicting forces that pull them
in opposite directions... Their role as problem-solving partners for management ...
often competes with their role as a watchdog ...'

Harold M. Williams 1978[1]

Responsibilities Of Internal Audit Staff

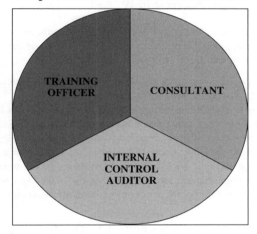

INTERNAL AUDITING HATS BEFORE 2000

My approach to the responsibilities and competency of internal auditors in the 1970s was to recognize the roles of auditor, consultant and trainer, and within those three roles, different levels of competence for each internal auditor. These varied from the two important roles recognized by Harold Williams in 1978 – partner and watchdog – although these could be seen in my training programme. Appropriately the three roles I recognized formed the acronym ACT and when added to PRO[fessional] they formed PROACT – the state in which all professional internal auditing should always be!

Consultancy in internal auditing had been around for a long time. Writers on internal auditing had been promoting this role in research and books since the first statement of responsibilities of the internal auditor was published by The IIA in 1947. Consultancy was never mentioned as such in The IIA statements, but it was implied by its the scope of responsibilities. The best evidence for this is in the '*objective and scope of internal auditing*' in the 1957 statement[2]:

> The overall objective of internal auditing is to assist all members of management in the effective discharge of their responsibilities, by furnishing them with objective analyses, appraisals, recommendations and pertinent comments concerning the activities reviewed. The internal auditor therefore should be concerned with any phase of business activity wherein he can be of service to management. The attainment of this overall objective of service to management should involve such activities as:
>
> – Reviewing and appraising the soundness, adequacy and application of accounting, financial and operating controls.
> – Ascertaining the extent of compliance with established policies, plans and procedures.
> – Ascertaining the extent to which company assets are accounted for, and safeguarded from losses of all kinds.
> – Ascertaining the reliability of accounting and other data developed within the organization.
> – Appraising the quality of performance in carrying out assigned responsibilities.

The final revision of this statement came in 1990 as:

> The scope of internal auditing should encompass the examination and evaluation of the adequacy and effectiveness of the organization's system of internal control and the quality of performance in carrying out assigned responsibilities. Internal auditors should:
>
> – Review the reliability and integrity of financial and operating information and the means used to identify, measure, classify, and report such information.
> – Review the systems established to ensure compliance with those policies, plans, procedures, laws, regulations, and contracts which could have a significant impact on operations and reports, and should determine whether the organization is in compliance.
> – Review the means of safeguarding assets and, as appropriate, verify the existence of such assets.
> – Appraise the economy and efficiency with which resources are employed.
> – Review operations or programmes to ascertain whether results are consistent with established objectives and goals and whether the operations or programmes are being carried out.

Look for the above in the following scope of work in The IIA current Professional Practices Framework (PPF)[3]:

> The comprehensive scope of work of internal auditing should provide reasonable assurance that management's:
>
> – Risk management system is effective.
> – System of internal control is effective and efficient.
> – Governance process is effective by establishing and preserving values, setting goals, monitoring activities and performance, and defining the measures of accountability.

In his predictions for internal auditing in the 1970s, J.G. Brown (1966)[4] recognized all internal audit engagements containing a consultant role:

> For some time there has been a quiet controversy going on in internal auditing about our proper role. One side states that the [internal] auditor is only concerned with control, while the other maintains that the [internal] auditor should be something of an internal management consultant. I suspect that these arguments are, in part, a matter of semantics.

Whenever we audit a given activity, I think we are properly concerned about the *management* of the activity – which is commonly thought to be something more than control. When we conduct an audit of an activity we are concerned about plans (what is its mission, how does this fit into corporate objectives, and how do those in charge of the activity expect to carry out its plans); we're concerned with how the activity is organized, staffed, and directed to accomplish these plans; and finally, we are concerned about the controls that measure and conform progress to the plan. Now, when I speak of evaluating controls, I believe we have in mind the whole process I've just outlined. And, if so, I believe THE INSTITUTE might save some unnecessary controversy by a relatively minor amendment, along these lines, to the Statement of Responsibilities.

Lawrence Sawyer (1979)[5] supported the role of internal auditors as consultants in his writings: drawing vivid pictures of problem-solving internal auditors providing reviews, appraisals, communications and advice on management – '... *the [internal] auditor has a duty to know the functions of management as thoroughly as the manager does'*. He discusses various consulting opportunities for internal auditors in the services they can provide. He also gives recognition to internal auditors as teachers: '*the internal auditor's role as a teacher is little known, insufficiently practised, and generally not believed or accepted.*' He cites Mints' 1972 research (discussed in my 2003 article in this chapter – see p. 70) '*Only 11 percent regarded the internal auditor as teachers. The blame must be laid at the door of the internal auditor... Clearly if a customer won't buy a seller's wares – his ability to teach and counsel – it is not the customer who can be faulted.*'

As The IIA scope statement was being revised, practicing internal auditors were broadening their services by increasing the number of roles they provided in their organizations. Dr James Wilson and Dr Donna Wood (1985)[6] researched the behavioural dynamics of internal auditing, recognizing seven conflicts in the internal auditor's role at that time (conflicts that still exist today):

1. Accountant
2. Policeman
3. Watchdog
4. Teacher
5. Consultant
6. Communicator
7. Future Manager.

They concluded with: '*Obviously, the problems become more complex as additional dimensions are added to the internal auditor's role.*' This research strongly influenced my own role in internal auditing as it developed in later years. Rather than see these conflicts in one role I prefer to see each dimension as a separate role, to be appropriately managed through the internal audit planning and engagement processes – seven hats to be worn at different times. All recognized by the internal audit customer.

The Office of the Auditor General of Canada (1992)[7] published results of a survey it carried out into what was happening in Canadian federal government internal audit units at that time '... *as compared to some of the best units elsewhere'*. Its choice of 'best units elsewhere' included 40 large organizations, some government but mainly commercial corporations, across North America. It reported that most of the organizations studied included some of the following 'other roles' for their internal audit units: some being formalized in mandate or policy statements and others being considered as secondary roles to the main role of auditing:

1. Management trainee
2. Sharer of knowledge
3. Improver
4. Advisor
5. Consultant.

Using the internal audit activity as a training ground for future managers has been practised worldwide, and is still practised by many organizations, whether as a policy decision or because an internal auditor's high reputation leads into a path of promotion into management. The management trainee hat should rest on every internal auditor's head.

At the time of the survey the main driver for improver, advisor and consulting hats in internal auditing was the introduction of new technology in organizations and the changes this required. Other drivers for these hats, such as changing management quality cultures and developments in risk management control and governance processes, were still on the horizon for many internal audit activities, and still are for some even today.

The hat of sharing knowledge is an interesting one because until recently it has had a low profile. Yet, every internal auditor has a knowledge-sharing hat, and every engagement creates, stores, shares and manages knowledge. A formal knowledge-sharing hat can add significant value to an internal auditor's reputation, an internal audit engagement, and an internal audit activity's reporting processes and achievements.

The IIA recognized the importance of knowledge when establishing its first common body of knowledge for internal auditors in 1972[8]:

> One of the important characteristics of a profession is a common body of knowledge. A body of knowledge forms the conceptual foundation of a profession and serves as a basis for education, training, recruiting, and testing the competence of those who wish to enter a professional field. It also provides a framework for dialogue.

This first common body of knowledge shaped the syllabus for The IIA's Certified Internal Auditor (CIA®). Subsequent studies into a common body of knowledge for internal auditing in 1985, 1992[9] and 1999[10] changed the direction of its professionalism to The IIA Professional Practices Framework and CIA syllabus we see today. The knowledge requirements for internal auditing and how these are managed will be further discussed in Chapter 15.

The new definition of internal auditing approved by The IIA in 1999 recognized the two activities/roles for internal auditing '... *assurance and consulting activity*...'. Subsequently the roles of trainer and facilitator have been added to these in some parts of the guidance provided for the implementation of the now *International Standards*. Although all these three roles were seen by many as new roles for internal auditing, they had been evolving for many years. Even my own 1970s use of the roles of auditor, consultant and teacher were developed from the then IIA *Standards*, literature and research.

At the time of the new definition of internal auditing there was some debate, and still is, concerning conflicts of interest that might arise when these three roles are practised by the same internal auditor. This was addressed by Birkett *et al.* (1999: p. 14):

> Internal auditing can add more value when applied earlier in the management process, to anticipate issues rather than react to them. Therefore, internal auditing in the future is likely to move to an anticipatory, if not proactive, mode in addressing an organization's risk and control scenarios.

While independence has been an essential characteristic of internal auditing, it is now suggested that independence may limit effective involvement. It seems that, in future, independence and effective organizational involvement will be weighed in the balance, if not rethought, as mobilizing ideologies.

This is not a concern that will go away. The IIA has addressed, and will continue to address, the issue of role independence in its guidance statements and recommend how this should be best maintained. This debate should not stop the internal auditor from wearing more hats than just assurance.

In the early 1970s Lawrence Sawyer's[11] apt poem on modern internal auditing turned Hubbard's[12] description of the classic auditor as '. . . *a man past middle age*' . . . *'Spare, wrinkled, cold and passive'* into *'He's warm and he's proactive, and commitment is his style. Exchanging ancient wrinkles for the crinkles of a smile.'* Sawyer based his modern description on the changes in internal auditing taking place at the time – changes that have continued to encourage greater participation between internal auditors, their auditees, management and the board. During the 1970s and 1980s more and more internal auditors have been creating new hats for themselves in organization teams, increasing their value to the organizations they served.

All internal auditors, specialists and auditees should be clear about the role of internal auditing in an organization team. This understanding is important if conflict and other concerns are to be minimized or even avoided during teamwork. Later, Lawrence Sawyer (1996)[13] refers to this relationship dilemma as:

> Internal auditors find themselves torn by conflicting forces and faced by duties and responsibilities that may seem completely irreconcilable. They owe a duty to executive management, whose work they appraise and whose pay they accept; they also owe a duty to keep the audit committee of the board of directors informed of serious weaknesses that are detected during their appraisals.
>
> Auditors are admonished to be problem-solving partners of operating managers and help the managers to improve their operation; yet auditors have a duty to be the watchdogs of the enterprise – alert for management inefficiency, ineptitude, and even fraud. They are urged to work together in participative teamwork with operating managers, yet are required to report deficiencies to the managers' superiors.
>
> These operating claims on the auditor's loyalties and responsibilities can create audit schizophrenia. The solutions may not be simple, but solutions will have to be found so auditors can do their jobs with the least possible friction.

More recently Cindy Cosmas[14] researched audit client satisfaction in the mid-1990s, reporting similar approaches in the marketing of internal auditing at that time. Changes seen by Cosmas included:

- Joint agreements between internal auditors and their clients.
- Inclusion of client commendations in audit reporting.
- Internal auditors more like consultants.

Cosmas concluded that:

> Modern internal auditors are rejecting the attitudes of their predecessors which kept auditees at arm's length and encouraged an air of mystery. Auditors are building trust and establishing open lines of communication in an effort to promote confidence and form long-term relationships with their auditees.

Since then and today, there are many published examples of values perceived from internal auditors being partners with management and board teams. Literature and recent revisions to The Institute of Internal Auditors' definition of internal auditing, standards and statements for professional internal auditing, provide useful pointers to where teamwork is in internal auditing today. Not least in the focus on continuous improvement by all professional internal auditors.

The concept of continuous improvement always requires a team approach to continually providing best products and services. This can be seen in all organizations that drive processes to achieve quality and best value. It also applies to both the quality of internal auditing work (the service) and recommendations included in the final audit report (the product). All discussions on the conclusions arising from audit work should be team driven, involving everyone participating in the audit, including those responsible for the controls being reviewed. Observations arising from the performance of internal auditing work should be discussed with appropriate levels of management during the course of an audit and problem-solving methods used to seek best recommendations and agreed action. This will be discussed again in later chapters.

The Institute of Internal Auditors' new 1999 definition of internal auditing[15] describes a service that '... *helps an organization to accomplish its objectives* ... '. There are many opportunities to achieve this helpful state through improved working relationships between internal auditors and those they serve. These opportunities can be found in all parts of The IIA old and new standards.[16] Figure 4.1 lists examples of teamwork that can facilitate compliance with each of the new attribute and performance standards.

The IIA General Standards (2002 edition)	Examples of teamworking
	Attribute standards
Independence and Objectivity	• Lines of reporting • Audit committee • Management • Consultancy • Systems development • Regulation
Proficiency and Due Professional Care	• Networking • Training • Professional
Quality Assurance and Compliance	• Internal audit marketing teams • Quality auditing/reviews • Quality improvement
Managing the Internal Audit Activity	*Performance standards* • Audit activity risk assessment • Development of audit procedures • Recruitment • Training • Internal/other auditing • Performance measurement
Nature of Work	• Organization risk management
Engagement Planning	• Audit planning teams
Engagement Performance	• Audit verification and testing • Audit objectives • Audit interviews

Figure 4.1   Examples Of Internal Audit Teams
Source: J. Ridley (2002)

John Fernandes (2000)[17] describes emerging internal auditing in the 21st century as demanding:

> . . . a greater understanding of the operating environment, creativity, good management skills and, above all, a keen sense of risk awareness, tolerance, and management strategies. The emerging internal auditor is customer driven. He or she is management's partner and consultant.

What is now considered to be the new participative role for internal auditors is not without its critics. Research today shows independence and objectivity are recognized in most organizations as the two most important attributes of internal auditing – and this is also clear from The IIA new definition. Some (there may be many) internal auditors and their customers see participation in consulting work adversely affecting both the independence and objectivity of internal auditing. The IIA new practice advisories for consulting engagements address the importance of maintaining internal auditing independence, objectivity and due professional care in all consulting work. Even if these guidelines are followed there is still some risk that internal auditors might lose their independence and objectivity by building bridges through consulting engagements. There will always have to be a balance between assurance and consulting, with clear lines drawn between each.

Internal auditors always wear an ambassador's hat when they travel through their organizations. Whether local, across their nations or internationally, they need to understand their organization's vision and missions. This hat represents their organization's policies as these are put into practice. It also should be seen at all times as representing the culture of the organization.

Article:
Internal Auditors Are Ambassadors In The Commonwealth . . . Across The European Union, And Internationally Too![18] (2000)

Those internal auditors familiar with paintings on exhibition at the National Gallery will probably be aware of, and have seen, Holbein's 'The Ambassadors'. This painting[a] is considered to be his finest work. On public view for over a century it was recently restored to all its original splendour. I first became aware of its background, and the 'auditing' story it tells, during an afternoon visit to the Gallery, with a friend, in early 1998. At that time the painting was on exhibition in the 'Making and Meaning' series. A series of complex paintings, researched and analysed, to explain their technical, scientific and historical context.

> *'I have always strongly believed that internal auditors are "ambassadors" of good governance conduct and best practices, at all levels in their organizations, and in all their travels.'*

---

[a] The painting and its description can be seen on the website www.wikipedia.org search on The Ambassadors (Holbein).

My interest lay in the exhibition's promotion of 'The Ambassadors,'[b] as a mystery '. . . *most intriguing, with its array of objects, many of them unfamiliar today, and its famous distortion of a skull, which has long puzzled observers. . . '*. The painting contains two portraits, one of Jean de Dinteville, French ambassador to England in 1533, and the other, Georges de Selve, Bishop of Lavaur, a close friend, who visited him in the same year. The story told is that, at the time, Jean de Dinteville had been sent by the French King to the English court to safeguard relations with Henry VIII. Probably a difficult and politically complex task – not unlike internal auditing! *'It was hardly a plum posting, and in this dispiriting process he contrived to grow tired both of London and life.'* The visit of his friend was an important event to be commemorated. Dinterville commissioned Holbein to paint both their portraits.

The painting contains shelves full of apparently unrelated objects, shown in great detail, providing much of the painting's mystery. These include globes, quadrants, a sundial, a torquetum, an arithmetic book, set-square, dividers, a hymnbook and musical instruments. (Perhaps no different to many a travelling internal auditor's briefcase!). Over the centuries there has been much research and speculation into why these objects, some related to time and space, were chosen, and their relationship to each other.

In the foreground is a concealed skull '. . . *using the distortion known as anamorphisosis'*. This is a representation of an object, unrecognizable except when seen from a particular viewpoint. Because of its prominence and distortion, the skull creates much of the painting's interest. Requiring the viewer to see clearly what it is, only from a side view.

During our viewing of the painting I commented to my friend, who is also an internal auditor, that the painting is an example of internal auditing at its best! A political environment, measurement of time and space, technical skills, considerable detail, apparently unrelated objects with unusual relationships, mystery, some distortion and the importance of a right point of view. All part of modern internal auditing. To add to this is the appropriateness of the painting's title.

I have always strongly believed that internal auditors are 'ambassadors' of good governance conduct and best practices, at all levels in their organizations, and in all their travels. I hope I can be forgiven the 'ambassador' analogy because of my early auditing experience. As a member of the Overseas Audit Service (OAS) in the 1950s, I served in Nigeria. OAS was established as Colonial Audit, a branch of the Colonial Office, in 1910. Responsible for the audit of accounts of all British Colonies and Dependencies. During the last century, it established and maintained auditing standards in government and local authorities across the 'Empire', in both developed and undeveloped territories. Although only a small group – around 150 British staff during my time – it managed significant local audit resources across the globe. Much of its influence on the standards of auditing, control and accounting in many governments during the 20th century continues in Commonwealth countries today.

Like all audit work the role of the Colonial Auditor was mostly routine, yet sometimes exciting and very much ambassadorial. A central administrative office in

---

[b] *Making & Meaning – Holbein's Ambassadors* (1997), Susan Foister, Ashok Roy and Martin Wyld, National Gallery Publications, London.

London and a global office - *on which the sun never set* - established the organizational framework. At any one time Colonial Auditors and local audit staff were examining, verifying and signing accounts across the world, frequently in remote places. We were trained as envoys of good accounting, auditing and conduct – much like the role of the present day UK National Audit Office and Audit Commission, merged into one!

My own experiences took me on many travels to remote areas in Nigeria. The audits covered all the services provided by government departments and local authorities, in both rural and urban environments, often spanning many years. (It was not uncommon to be auditing three to five years of financial statements during an audit visit.) A typical tour of audits in the 1950s could last up to six months, living in many isolated locations. Some in difficult and extreme geographical, political and climatic conditions. A portable typewriter, mental arithmetic, 'green' pencil and a local language dictionary, being the only office technology; government manuals of accounting, financial instructions and circulars being the standards of conduct; a copy of F.R.M de Paula's *Principles and Practices of Auditing*, the standards; a camp bed and bath, kerosene lamp, battery radio and 'some refreshments', the only comforts. Faith and a belief in one's invincibility being the only security. Even today, these situations are probably not too uncommon for some internal auditors, in both developed and underdeveloped countries!

I was reminded of Holbein's painting and my Colonial Audit career when I read the recently issued (November 1999) Commonwealth Association for Corporate Governance (CACG) principles for corporate governance.[c] CACG, is a new organization. Established in 1998, in response to the Edinburgh Declaration of the Commonwealth Heads of Government meeting in 1997, to promote excellence in corporate governance in all Commonwealth countries. Its guidelines are intended to promote and facilitate best business practice and behaviour. What an excellent 'flag' for all internal auditors, working and travelling in Commonwealth countries, including the UK!

CACG has developed 15 principles of corporate governance; each aimed at boards of directors of all business enterprises, whether private or state-owned. They represent the good business practice and corporate governance codes already developed by many of the Commonwealth countries (again including the UK). They are seen as a 'living document' applicable to all forms of enterprise. They emphasize the importance of leadership for efficiency and probity. They require responsibilities that are transparent and accountable. Any internal auditor who travels and audits in Commonwealth countries should be aware of their content and use their guidance. The IIA should use the development and use of these principles to fly the flag of our new internal auditing statement of responsibilities, training programmes and standards, across the world.

Principle 10 specifically covers the importance of effective internal systems of control, including implementation of '. . . *a formal internal audit function*'. Unfortunately, like the ICAEW Turnbull[d] report, internal audit is not defined. This is left

---

[c] *Principles for Corporate Governance in the Commonwealth* (1999), Commonwealth Association for Corporate Governance. Website: www.cbc.to
[d] *Internal Control: Guidance for Directors on the Combined Code* (Turnbull Committee Report) September 1999, ICAEW, London.

to those who implement the principles to interpret. Both bodies could follow the example of a recent consultative document published by the European Commission[e], outlining improvements in audit, financial management and control in the Commission. Part of the proposed Action Plan is the creation of a central internal audit service. Internal audit is defined in the plan using the 1999 IIA statement, as *'an independent and objective assurance and consulting activity designed to add value and improve an organization's operations. It helps an organization accomplish its objectives by bringing a systematic, disciplined approach to evaluate and improve effectiveness of risk management, control and governance process.'* A good portrait of an international internal auditor ambassador.

CACG also prevails on professional bodies to focus on corporate governance issues and become involved in these in Commonwealth countries. Its list of professions includes accountants, corporate secretaries, lawyers, directors, etc. It does not specifically mention internal audit – again an unfortunate omission. If they have not already done so, both The IIA and IIA – UK should make CACG aware of the internal auditing profession and its internal auditing statements, standards, research and training.

If, like me, you see your internal audit role as an ambassador of good governance, conduct and best practices, compare the messages in Holbein's painting to your own internal auditing. Both internally and across your organization's supply chains. See what vision the painting tells you. If you see what I see, hang a print of 'The Ambassadors' in your internal audit department as a vision for all your staff. As I write this, I have one in my study – a gift from a good friend who is a good internal auditor, and also a good ambassador for the profession of internal auditing!

INTERNAL AUDITING HATS 2000 TO 2003

Jacqueline Wagner (2000)[19], former General Auditor at General Motors and in her year of office as The IIA chairman, urged *'. . . all internal audit professionals to help in leading their own organizations during these times of significant change'*. She saw internal auditors *'out in front'* in their organizations *'. . . leading our business units from both an overall process and a control perspective and focusing on strategic business objectives'*. This concept of internal auditors wearing a leader's hat in their organizations, and in the profession of internal auditing, is essential for any cutting edge resources and practices in today's changing environment. Wagner saw this and included the following guidance in her article for internal auditors wearing a leader's hat as agents of change:

Internal Auditor's as Change Agents?

From environments of change emerge change agents, those people who make change happen or facilitate change throughout the organization. They have real jobs, do real work – and driving change is built into how they carry out their duties. Creating change is a skill; but getting things done and moving the business are the change agent's passions.

---

[e] *'Reforming the Commission'*, Communication from Mr Neil Kinnock, in agreement with the President and Ms Schreyer, CG3(2000) 1/17, 18 January 2000.

Based on the following key characteristics, I think that internal auditors' most important modern role could be as change agents:

- For change to take hold in an organization, it must be linked explicitly to real performance goals, and it has to be in the hands of people who understand the business first and change second. Change agents ask what the goals of the organization are, and they focus on how reaching their own objectives affect the organization's operation.
- The key to making change happen is to create an environment where people gravitate in the direction you want them to go. The best way to accomplish this is to make people aware of best practices. They'll naturally use a better way if you make one available. Change agents enable change.
- If you're going to get something done, you're going to discomfit people around you. Change agents often interrupt routines, reveal problems, and make more work on the way to making less work.
- A change agent must always be in two places at once: where the organization is and where it's going. They must be equally comfortable dealing with senior management and front-line workers because change agents need the support of both groups.
- Once you begin to work as a change agent, you're automatically subject to a higher level of scrutiny and a tougher standard of judgement – from those both above and below you. People watch change agents even more closely than others to make sure that they measure up.

Wearing a leader's hat can take internal auditing into the roles of a consultant, adviser and mentor. This is happening. In more recent times the hats worn by internal auditing have increased, partly due to its new roles in organizational governance and probably more so to new talents being attracted to internal auditing because of its more prominent role within organizations.

Whatever role the internal auditor has at any one time, it is important that there is agreement in an organization on the roles internal auditors undertake. They must also reflect the purpose, authority and responsibilities of the internal audit activity, as approved by the board/audit committee, and show that these roles meet the needs of internal audit customers, their expectations and satisfaction (if not delight).

Article:
Hat Trick[20] (2003)

My recent research[f] into internal audit practices has resulted in some interesting results concerning the roles internal auditors are perceived to have in their organizations. Respondents were asked to indicate, from a given list, the different roles their charters require them to provide in their organizations, either explicitly or inferred by their authority and scope of work. The list of roles was developed by me from The IIA Professional Practices Framework and research recommendations published by others over past years.

> *It is important that there is agreement in an organization on the roles internal auditors undertake...'*

[f] *Raising the Standard* (2003), J. Ridley, Housing Association Internal Audit Forum, UK. (Details can be found on www.haiaf.org.uk)

Respondents were all in one part of the public sector. They included internal auditors (IAs), their chief executives (CEs) and audit committee chairpersons (ACCs). In 20 organizations all three answered similar questions, including the one on internal audit roles. In each of these organizations there was some consensus among the IA, CE and ACC for the following roles:

Professional
Assurer
Consultant
Risk assessor

This will provide satisfaction for those who researched and developed the latest IIA definition of internal auditing, in which all four roles are seen.

There was little agreement with the roles of *Improver* and *Facilitator* and few indicated *Partner, Team Player, Educator* and *Trainer* as being internal audit roles in their organizations. Yet all are part of the development of professional internal auditing over past years. All can be seen in The IIA current guidance for professional internal auditors.

Early research sponsored by The IIA into internal auditing working relationships (Mints[g] 1972), analysed internal audit relationships into the following three patterns, all of which can still be seen today in the hats worn by internal auditors:

1. **Traditional Audit Approach**
   compliance
   protection
   inspection

2. **Current Moderate Approach**
   constructive
   helpful
   solves problems

3. **Participating Teamwork Approach**
   involves auditee
   develops team spirit
   relates audit aims to auditee's goals.

Mints recommended that the participative teamwork relationship between internal auditors and their clients works best for the development of internal auditing as a profession. However, he did not discard the other two relationships, both of which he believed had their place at times.

Since then, there have been many published examples of values perceived from the roles practised by internal auditors. Including 'improver, facilitator, partner, team player, educator and trainer'. Just look at the vacancy notices for internal

---

[g] *Behavioral Patterns in Internal Audit Relationships* (1972), F. Mints, The IIA.

auditors in most of today's professional journals and newspapers. Many require some, if not all, of these roles.

The purpose of my research was to develop a library of 'best practices' for each of the respondents to use in their benchmarking exercises as they seek improvements in the services they provide. Developing and maintaining such a library is essential for internal auditors in all sectors. Benchmarking has been the hallmark of internal auditing development since the middle of the last century. The IIA motto of 'Progress through Sharing' is as important today as it was when first used so many years ago. According to Roth[h] (2003) in his studies into adding value: '. . . *combining knowledge of current best practices and understanding organization objectives are essential in determining what internal audit practices (and roles) will add the most value to an organization . . .* '.

It is important that there is agreement in an organization on the roles internal auditors undertake and that they reflect the purpose, authority and responsibilities of the internal audit activity, as approved by the board/audit committee. Also, that these roles meet the needs of internal audit customers, their expectations and satisfaction (if not delight). The mixed perceptions for 'improver, facilitator, partner, team player, educator and trainer' show the hats worn by some internal auditors for these roles are not always seen by their customers, or perhaps even worn! Is this the situation in your own organization?

That there were few recognitions and agreements over the hats worn by the 'improver' and 'facilitator' internal auditor should be of concern to all. Can this be a reflection of internal audit modesty? Or is it more likely that few internal auditors are marketing their risk, control and governance services, wearing these hats. If so, why not? These are proactive words that demonstrate much of what internal auditing is all about. Improver is essential to meet the criteria in The IIA new definition for internal auditing. Facilitator is an important part of the role of the internal auditor in risk management processes and recommended as such in its guidance statements, study material and research.

The hats worn by the 'partner' and 'team player' internal auditor require a bridging of the gap between internal auditors and the organizations in which they work. Garitte (1998),[i] when writing at the start of his term of office as chairman of The IIA, used the same theme in his article *Building Bridges:*

> The English poet John Donne reminded us that *'no man is an island'*. In my own mind there is a parallel; internal auditors cannot be islands. We must be pillars and partners in the bridge-building process, and we must find ways to use our bridges to communicate, share, and help our organizations.

Why are not more internal auditors recognized as wearing these hats? Are some internal auditors still living on islands in their organizations? Islands that do not encourage good working relationships with management and other team

---

[h] *Adding Value: Seven Roads to Success* (2003), James Roth, The IIA Research Foundation.
[i] 'Building Bridges', Jean-Pierre Garitte, *Internal Auditor* (August 1998), The IIA.

players? Islands that continue to place barriers between internal auditors and the rest of the organization in which they provide their services? Mints recognized the importance of a participative and team working approach to internal auditing, involving the auditee (now customer). Is this your approach? How many of your customers see themselves as partners and team players in your work engagements?

The hats worn by the 'educator' and 'trainer' internal auditor are new for many internal auditors. Yet some internal auditors in internal auditing practices wear them, even though they may not always be seen as such. New IIA guidance for the relationships between internal audit and the audit committee place the hats for 'educator' and 'trainer' on internal auditors for risk, control and governance teaching. Suggesting that internal auditors '... *inquire from the audit committee if any educational or informational sessions or presentations would be helpful, such as training new committee members on risk and controls (and governance)'*.

(The Institute's survey among heads of internal audit, reported in the [2003] July issue – page 16 – showed that more than half expect more requests from their audit committees for advice on risk, control and governance issues. Yet less than a quarter expects more involvement in training and induction of audit committee members!)

Why not education and training by internal auditors for the whole board, all management, all staff and even all stakeholders? There are many opportunities for internal auditors to pass on their knowledge of risk, control and governance best practices and understanding of their organization's objectives. Current proposed changes by The IIA to the governance section in the *Standards* state that the internal audit activity should *'Serve as an educational resource regarding changes and trends in the business and regulatory environment'*. Teaching hats are well worth wearing with pride by the *'traditional, current and participating'* internal auditor.

But internal auditors must always be wary of wearing too many hats all at the same time. What is now considered to be the new 'participative' role of internal auditors is not without its critics. Research today shows that independence and objectivity are recognized in most organizations as the two most important attributes of internal auditing – this is also clear from all The IIA statements. Some (there may be many) internal auditors and their customers, see the increasing number of hats being worn by internal auditors adversely affecting both their independence and objectivity.

The IIA new practice advisories for consulting engagements address most of these concerns, emphasizing the importance of maintaining internal auditing '... *independence, objectivity and due professional care* ... ' in all consulting work. This may be easier said than done! A 'best practice' for all internal audit hats is to have a feather in each, which is its code of ethics. A feather that is clearly seen by all. The principles and rules of conduct in The IIA Code of Ethics set a high standard and best practice for internal auditors – '*Integrity, Objectivity, Confidentiality and Competency'*. Promoting and achieving each of these is a mark of a true profession. Is this happening in internal auditing today? That must be the subject of another article!

Two challenges for all internal auditors

- How many of the roles mentioned above do you provide in your organization?
- Do you promote those roles with feathers in all of your hats?

INTERNAL AUDITING HATS 2003 TO 2005

Recent events in corporate governance, with its new principles and practices, have increased the number of hats worn by internal auditors and their sizes. The image of internal auditing as a watchdog or bloodhound is not changing but has changed. This could be seen in the following quotes from vacancy notices for internal audit staff, advertised in the IIA – UK & Ireland issue of *Internal Auditing & Business Risk*, August 2003, in which the previous article was published:

> You will undertake a variety of roles, with particular emphasis on operational audits and facilitating control self-assessment (CSA) workshops. We have implemented best practice principles and cutting edge techniques, adopting a risk-based approach to internal auditing . . .

> You will provide a wide variety of audit services.

> You will be responsible for identifying risks and assessing controls in all areas of the supply chain.

> You will plan and direct the work of your team whilst also working on a consultative basis.

> You will work on strategic business reviews within all corporate areas of the business.

> This role will suit someone who is forward thinking and is keen to help organizations improve their business performance . . .

> The ability to be flexible is essential, as you will be required to undertake many different and challenging tasks.

> Driving a risk philosophy throughout the Group.

> You will work on the independent assurance functions throughout the group, undertake special projects and work with complex IT systems in order to gain fast track knowledge of the operations throughout the group.

> . . . you will continue to raise the profile of the function and promote value added reporting and recommendations.

> You will promote and encourage effective internal control, risk management and governance applied to policies, plans and objectives.

> . . . including systems reviews, risk management and support for value for money studies.

> . . . to review all product areas and provide consultancy services for the business.

> You will be involved in reviewing a wide variety of issues . . . .

> You will also support the Director implementing new policies and procedures.

Consider all the hats the holders of these positions will wear in the services they provide.

Article:
Is Internal Auditing's New Image Recognized By Your Organization?[21] (2005)

Last year I met with a group of board members and senior managers from six organizations to discuss the values and principles of internal auditing. The theme for the discussion was 'How do internal audit activities add value and improve an organization's opera-tions?' This gave me an opportunity to explore and consider the wider issues of professionalism in internal auditing. In particular how this has changed to provide a service that helps '*an organization accomplish its objectives*'.

> '*It is not enough to state in an annual report that there is internal audit in an organization – professional or otherwise?*

The statements in italics come from the Institute of Internal Auditors (IIA) new 1999 definition of internal auditing, included in its published Professional Practices Framework[j] for internal auditing. A framework based on international research covering auditing and consultancy practices in risk management, control and governance processes in many organizations. This is the framework that was given a new profile by Sir Robert Smith (2003)[k] in his published guidance for audit committees. That report recommended that the audit committee should question whether internal auditing functions are '*equipped to perform in accordance with appropriate professional standards for internal auditors*'. It further recommended that guidance on appropriate standards '*can be found in The IIA's Code of Ethics and its international standards*'.

The foundation for The IIA professional framework lies in the first IIA *Code of Ethics* for its members, published in 1968. There had been previous IIA statements on the responsibilities of internal auditors, starting from 1948. At the time the first code and its associated responsibility statement were unique in their international application across some 40 countries. Even today there are few international codes binding individuals ethically in countries across the world. There are now 160 countries represented in The IIA membership, all using its framework of professionalism for their internal auditing practices and qualifications. An enormous achievement by The IIA.

The ethic statements in the 1968 published code are still alive today in its current revised code. These have been formalized into four defined principles and rules of integrity, objectivity, confidentiality and competency. Each states clearly the behaviour required from members of The IIA in the performance of their work, and each adds authority and power to their elbows. The UK government and other

---

[j] *International Standards for the Professional Practice of Internal Auditing*, (revised 2004), The IIA .
[k] *Audit Committees Combined Code Guidance*, Submitted to and published by the Financial Reporting Council, London, England

professional institutes have now adopted these principles in their own codes of ethics for internal auditors.

A good question for all audit committee members is to ask whether they or their internal auditors know these principles and rules. The re-branded image of all internal audit activities reflects this code. All involved in assessing its effectiveness should know it. Yet it was not known by those at my discussion. Is this good enough for the re-branded internal audit profession? The Smith report should make audit committee members more aware of The IIA professional framework? But will it? An IIA – UK[1] 2004 publication links its *Standards* to the *UK Combined Code 2003* requirements to make it easier for audit committees to monitor and review the effectiveness of internal audit. Let us hope for all our sakes that this briefing is read, not just by audit committee members, but all stakeholders, in all sectors.

In the early 1970s the internal audit debate on re-branding was on 'participative auditing'. At that time auditing was seen as traditional, current moderate or participative teamwork. Participative auditing involved the clients of internal auditing in the audit team, developing a team spirit and relating audit aims to the organization's objectives. This set the backcloth for much of what has taken place since in the development of today's re-branded internal audit image. Partnering with management is not a new concept.

Later research in the mid-1980s in the USA identified seven aspects of the role internal auditors occupied as – accountant, policeman, watchdog, consultant, teacher, communicator and future manager. Some with conflicts of interest that needed to be well managed if its independence and objectivity were not to be weakened. By the late 1990s some different aspects of the internal auditor's role were identified in new IIA research – assurers of control, risk facilitators, in-house consultants, business analyst, fraud detectors, innovators, quality advocates, advisers on governance. Later research in the UK[m] in 2002 supported these aspects, showing that internal audit in the UK is currently adding value in the following six elements of the governance process, ranked in order of perception by those it serves:

- Assurance that the internal control framework is operating effectively.
- Assurance that major business risks are being managed appropriately.
- Detection and prevention of fraud and irregularities.
- Improving business performance by sharing knowledge of best practices.
- Identification of new business risks.
- Use of knowledge and experience to tackle urgent issues.

The first three are the traditional approaches to internal audit work. Most board members and management recognize these. The last three require a participative teamwork approach and for some internal audit functions are still relatively new services, although in some internal audit activities they have been provided for many years. Today's professional internal auditors should be well trained and competent to add all of these values in their organizations. A measure of their

---

[1] *Internal Auditing Standards – Why they Matter* (2004), The IIA–UK & Ireland.
[m] *The Value Agenda* (2002), Deloitte & Touche and IIA–UK & Ireland.

professionalism is whether they can and do. Board and audit committee members should expect and ensure that all are well provided.

One interesting aspect of the 2002 research mentioned is that few internal audit activities were measuring their performance in all six elements. *'If they are not required to measure or demonstrate that value in anyway, they are less likely to deliver, and be seen to deliver value in the right areas.'* Re-branding does require some measure of its completion and acceptance by the customers of internal audit. Another good question for all board and audit committee members.

A new role in the re-branding of internal audit is its contribution to the review of all governance processes. This requires an understanding of what makes good governance in organizations. This will vary between sector, size of organization and its market place – national, European or international. Governance is about directing and controlling. It is defined by current research into enterprise governance[n] as '. . . *the set of responsibilities and practices exercised by the board and executive management with the goal of providing strategic direction, ensuring that objectives are achieved, ascertaining that risks are managed appropriately and verifying that the organization's resources are used responsibly.'* Some might argue that governance, like quality management, should be exercised by everyone in an organization and not just the board and executive management. True, there has to be a 'tone at the top' that is openly practised, but everyone in an organization is involved in the control of operational processes.

It should not be difficult for internal audit to become involved in monitoring and advising on the controlling part of governance. This includes risk management and all control activities. The directing part is not that easy unless internal audit has a reporting line to the board, not just the audit committee, and preferably the chairman of the board. (It is not uncommon today to see vacancy notices for internal audit staff stating that the role reports to the chairman of the board.) Also that the line allows for all aspects of the internal auditor's role to be discussed and used at strategic level. This is important if an organization is to get best value from its internal audit function.

There has also been a growing interest of late in widening enterprise governance to include responsibilities to all stakeholders, including the communities in which an organization operates. A recent research report on governance in the public sector[o] includes the principle '. . . *good governance means focusing on the organization's purpose and on outcomes for citizens and service users'*. This brings social responsibility into the governance process. This is not a new area for the re-branded internal auditor. There is evidence that some internal auditors are already involved in social responsibility reporting and auditing. The IIA has already issued guidance[p] on this to all its members. The more social responsibility is linked into governance processes the more important it will be for internal audit to become 'participative' in the teamwork involved.

---

[n] *Enterprise Governance – Getting the Balance Right* (2004), Chartered Institute of Management Accountants, UK and International Federation of Accountants, USA.
[o] *The Good Governance Standard for Public Services* (2005), The Independent Commission on Good Governance in Public Services, UK.
[p] *Corporate Ethics and Social Responsibility* (2000), IIA–UK & Ireland.

It is not enough to state in an annual report that there is internal audit in an organization – professional or otherwise. In future, not only audit committees and boards, but also all stakeholders, should be confirming that the internal audit is both professional and effective in all its roles. The re-branded internal auditor will receive more recognition from stakeholders, and this interest will continue to grow. A recent job vacancy in the press for internal audit staff in one organization in the UK states; *'As part of our team you will work with management to develop a robust group audit strategy and ensure the programme is delivered to stakeholder's expectations.'* This is a start.

CUTTING EDGE INTERNAL AUDITING HATS – TODAY AND IN THE FUTURE

The following quotes from vacancy notices for internal audit staff, advertised in the IIA–UK & Ireland issue of *Internal Auditing & Business Risk*, February 2007, provide cutting edge characteristics of their roles of today and tomorrow:

> . . . providing a modern, proactive internal audit service.

> Help develop an innovative approach to internal audit.

> . . . providing internal audit services across a range of Council services. Duties will include systems and regularity audits, special investigations and value for money audits.

> . . . enthusiastic and self-motivated auditor in our ISOI 9001 accredited internal audit section.

> World-class roles

> . . . building cases for change and influencing management in their decision making . . .

> You will have the vision and ability to apply your skills to a range of operational and financial audits . . . .

> You will undertake a broad range of projects covering all aspects of their risk assessment programme, including finance operations and environmental issues.

> . . . providing . . . an expert resource to the business in respect of best practice in corporate governance, risk management and accounting.

> . . . conducting ad hoc investigations and value for money activity.

> . . . supplies internal audit, compliance assurance and ad hoc consultancy services . . .

> . . . wide ranging role . . .

Internationally, similar cutting edge characteristics in internal auditing roles appear in standard job descriptions listed on Protiviti's KnowledgeLeader[22] in March 2007:

> . . . understanding of business strategy . . .

> . . . generating a high degree of respect and trust . . .

... smart, quick, people-oriented, energetic, professionally aggressive ...

... a commitment to excellence.

... design anti-fraud criteria.

... interpret and analyse complex concepts and apply these in innovative ways.

... develop creative approaches and solutions necessary to solve complex problems.

... should be driven to deliver quality results.

... self-reliant and have strong initiative ...

... must be resourceful, strategic ...

... stay abreast of best practices both internally and externally and provide a conduit for introducing those practices to the company.

Be a role model for the company's values ...

Provide high levels of ethical awareness ...

... administer independent investigations of potential ethical problems or conflicts of interest.

... sell ideas and obtain management buy-in for constructive change.

Efficiency and effectiveness in internal auditing are today and tomorrow no longer sufficient characteristics by themselves to be at its cutting edge. They both need to be there, but in addition internal auditing needs to be:

Trusted	Visionary	Creative
Modern	Expert	Problem solver
Proactive	Consultant	Self-reliant
Innovative	Strategist	Initiator
Add value	Respected	Resourceful
Enthusiastic	Smart	Benchmarker
Self-motivated	Aggressive	Role model
World class	Excellent	Salesperson
Driver of change	Designer	

A long list of characteristics applicable for all internal auditing hats: this is necessary if it is to maintain momentum to be recognized as a profession at the cutting edge of its development. Look for the above characteristics in the quotes from the job vacancy notices of 2003 and 2007. What differences do you see? Look for the same characteristics in your own internal auditing job descriptions.

What I have not discussed is the colour of the hats internal auditors should wear. Edward de Bono (1985), the 'lateral thinking' management guru '... *who invented the concept of lateral thinking, now entered in the Oxford English Dictionary as "seeking to solve problems by unorthodox or apparently illogical methods"* '[23] set out in the 1980s his colours for hats,[24] each with its own style of thinking:

White	–	Facts and Figures
Red	–	Emotions and Feelings
Black	–	Cautious and Careful
Yellow	–	Speculative, Positive
Green	–	Creative Thinking
Blue	–	Control of Thinking

These hats have stood the test of time well and are still worn today in many organizations across the world to guide thinking in problem solving. Most internal auditors wear all these colours in their hats at different times in any engagement, mostly without being aware of the colour they are wearing. There is a challenge here for internal auditors. If these coloured hats are worn, would a study and practice of de Bono's concepts for each colour be out of place in internal auditing training? Would such training be innovative and cutting edge?

The 2007[25] research by The IIA Research Foundation into the common body of knowledge for internal auditing mentioned in Chapter 3 is an ongoing research project. Its findings on emerging roles of the internal audit activity are interesting. From a list of functions performed by organizations, respondents (at least 6000+ responding for each function) were asked to indicate those that are included in their scope of work now, or are likely to be in the next three years. The following results reflect a global view on the scope of internal auditing in the future:

Functions	% Currently	% Likely	Total
Risk management	66.6	25.5	92.1
Fraud prevention/detection	69.0	22.9	91.9
Regulatory compliance assessment monitoring	64.0	23.0	87.0
Corporate governance	52.2	31.1	83.3
Develop training and education of organization personnel (e.g. internal controls, risk management, regulatory requirements)	46.6	34.4	81.0
IT management assessment	46.1	32.2	78.3
Project management	39.8	27.6	67.4
Provide training to the audit committee	31.2	34.4	65.6
Benchmarking	28.6	35.7	64.3
Knowledge management systems development review	26.1	38.0	64.1
Strategic frameworks	27.0	36.8	63.8
Evidential issues	39.8	23.9	63.7
Disaster recovery	34.0	26.1	60.1
Alignment of strategy and performance measures (e.g. Balanced Scorecard)	23.1	35.2	58.3
Corporate Social Responsibility	23.6	31.6	55.2
Intellectual property and knowledge assessment	19.2	28.4	47.6

Mergers and acquisitions	18.4	23.7	42.1
Environmental sustainability	14.0	24.7	38.7
Globalization	15.3	21.1	36.4
Emerging markets	11.5	22.5	34.0
Executive compensation	16.0	17.7	33.7

It is not surprising to see the top four functions of risk, fraud, corporate governance and regulation embedded into most internal auditing activity scopes of work, with internal auditors possibly wearing a variety of hats in each. Pleasing to me, and must be to The IIA, is to see *'Develop training and education'* as the fifth most significant function and *'Provide training to the audit committee'* not far behind today and growing in the future. Many internal auditors are now wearing a teacher's hat!

It is unusual in today's technology not to see *'IT management assessment'* in the scope of all internal audit activities, but important to see the likely growth in the future.

It is good to see *'Strategic frameworks'*, *'Alignment of strategy and performance measures (e.g. balanced scorecard)'*, *'Benchmarking'* and *'Knowledge management'* growing significantly in importance. These are definitely functions for the scope of work of internal auditors in the future. But it is disappointing to see *'Corporate Social Responsibility and Environmental sustainability'* ranked low today and tomorrow. However, it's good to see that both functions have been recognized by some internal auditors in their scope of work in the future. Within all of these functions there will be many hats for internal auditors to wear and new cutting edge internal auditing resources and practices.

What is still surprising is to see so few internal audit activities, including *'Disaster recovery'*, in their scope of work now or in the future, particularly with its IT and environmental implications. And, despite the widespread influence of *'Globalization'* in all supply chains impacting most organizations, so few internal audit activities including this as a function in their scope of work.

As for the future, it is worth considering Albrecht *et al.* (1992) again. In addressing future issues at that time they recognized four:

Impact of Technology
The Quality Revolution
Globalization of Business
Increasing Importance of Nontechnical Skills

These are clearly still issues for the future roles that internal auditing will play in their organizations. Perhaps the last needs some explanation – it is described in the research as:

It is interesting to note that three of the top four areas rated as most important were not typical auditing or technical areas. Reasoning, communication, and ethics were amongst the highest rated areas in the survey data. Practitioners suggest that the success of internal auditing in the future will be the ability to be part of the decision-making process. Technical specialists will be needed, but success will come with the ability to analyse, interact with, and communicate audit findings.

Abilities needed for all hats worn by the internal auditor are: auditing, consulting, teaching or other. Albrecht et al. would be pleased to see that The IIA 2007 research into a new common body of knowledge reported that of six ranked choices for top competencies for internal auditors at different responsibility levels, most respondents ranked two out of the following as first or second[26]:

Ability to promote the internal audit activity within the organization
Analytical ability to work through an issue
Communication.

In the 1970s I was forecasting the development of internal auditing into the future and created a set of influences on internal auditing at that time, projecting this into the future. These influences were:

External auditors
Audit committees
Regulators
Shareholders.

There is ample evidence today that the first two have influenced how professional internal auditing has developed and the roles it has played over the past 30 years. Yet even today relationships with these two groups are not always easy for internal auditors. Research among heads of internal audit too often still reveal improvements needed in working relationships with external audit and audit committees. Protiviti (2006),[27] in an internal auditing capabilities and needs survey, showed as a key finding:

Developing Other Board Committee Relationships is the area of **Personal Skills and Capabilities** with the lowest average competency and in greatest need of improvement. *Negotiation, Leadership* (within the internal audit profession), *Presenting* (Public Speaking), *Developing Outside Contacts/Networking, Developing Audit Committee Relationships, Leadership* (within your organization), *Creating a Learning Internal Audit Function* and *Persuasion* are the other areas in greatest need of improvement.

The bold and italics are mine. These are all personal skills and capabilities ready for cutting edge practices.

There is some evidence that regulators in the United Kingdom and across the world have influenced the roles internal auditors have in their organizations, particularly in government and financial sectors. There is less evidence, if any, of influence or interest by shareholders. Yet, as primary stakeholders in an organization, it is surprising that shareholders have not had more influence, or shown greater interest.

Today, it will be the wider group of stakeholders that will start to influence internal auditing professionalism and practices. From that influence new roles may well appear in the governance processes covering conduct, transparency, social and environmental reporting. This is already happening. Some, but not all, internal auditors have already started to wear 'green' hats! Others will follow. It will not be surprising in the future to see green as the colour for all hats worn by internal auditors.

Internal auditors in government departments could be said to have the public as an influence on the hats they wear. This may be more evident when the practice of publishing internal audit reports on government websites becomes more common. At present this is not common in the United Kingdom but is practised by some government departments in North America and global organizations like the United Nations.

CHAPTER SUMMARY

The following quote from my 1972 slide-tape presentation mentioned at the beginning of Chapter 2, reflected on the '... *variety of work, which to most internal auditors is its attraction as a career*':

> The management of internal audit involves a variety of work, which to most internal auditors is its attraction as a career. This variety can take internal auditors through all the responsibilities delegated to a manager: planning; the setting of objectives and programmes of work; reviews of performance; interviewing people; and, writing reports. During all these aspects of their work internal auditors are selling their professional auditing services to management.

This chapter recognizes the importance of variety in the development of cutting edge resources and practices in internal auditing – a variety that is evident from the number and colour of hats an internal auditor can wear in the management and promotion of professional internal auditing. Often many hats are used in every internal audit engagement, and sometimes with feathers. The variety of an internal auditor's work in an organization will always be its attraction for many. For internal auditors this variety still can lead to significant opportunities and challenges to add value, not just to the organization for its stakeholders, but also to their own careers. That variety will continue to grow as the scope of internal auditing widens, the services it provides increase and innovation is encouraged in its resources and practices.

The variety of new hats available to be worn is evident in the Gray and Gray (1997) five innovation motivation themes, four innovation goals and four innovation categories discussed in the Introduction, and the additions and changes made in Chapters 2 and 3:

Motivations

1. Progress within the field of professional internal auditing.
2. Increasing competition leading to pressures to reduce costs and increase efficiency.
3. New challenges, such as increasing internal control risks due to staff reductions and restructuring.
4. Opportunities to increase efficiency and quality as a result of technological advances.
5. Changes in corporate management practices and philosophies, such as Total Quality Management, re-engineering, continuous quality improvement, or related approaches.
6. **Challenges and opportunities of global issues and developments.**
7. **Social and environmental issues impacting all organizations.**
8. **Recognition that professionalism, quality and standards are essential attributes for world-class status in any internal auditing activity.**

Goals

1. Improvement of the quality of internal auditing services.
2. Improve efficiency.
3. Expansion of services to increase the value-added of internal auditing.
4. Boost staff skills, performance and morale.
5. **Sell internal auditing as future focused.**

Categories

1. Changes in the way that internal auditors interact with the rest of their enterprises **and all those with a stakeholder interest.**
2. Internal restructuring and changes in the organization and management of internal auditing.
3. Creation of new audit services and methods.
4. Changes in the use of technology.
5. **Improved knowledge and skills in the teams of staff who carry out internal auditing engagements.**

Today a new motivation exists for internal auditor hats in tomorrow's world:

9. **Importance of organizational governance to meet regulatory and stakeholders' needs.**

INTERNAL AUDITING HATS PRINCIPIA 1998 AND 2008

My 1998 principia for internal auditing included the following related to the hats it was wearing then (see Appendix A):

2. Internal auditing is developing as a spectrum of unrestricted traditional, new and leading edge activities across all organizations of all sizes, in all sectors.

This spectrum of activities still continues today and will always be a part of the development of professional internal auditing. It applies for all hats as item 3 in 2008, and is repeated in one of the case studies that follow, with the one change: 'cutting edge' instead of 'leading edge'. This promotes more clearly the importance of innovation in all internal auditing resources and practices.

A VISION FOR INTERNAL AUDITING WEARING MANY HATS

> *We wear a variety of independent and objective hats to meet all our customers' needs*

SYNOPSES OF CASE STUDIES

Case 4.1: Wanted – A Head of Internal Audit Wearing Many Hats

Synopsis

What cutting edge hats do your vacancy notices ask for in internal auditing? Compare your hats with a recent vacancy notice in the media for a Head of Internal Audit who is a *'creative thinker'*.

Reproduced with permission from Close Brothers Group plc and Michael Page City.

After Reading the Case Study Consider:

1. How many hats do you recognise the Head of Internal Audit wearing, carrying out the responsibilities in the vacancy notice? (See also Self-assessment Question 4.1 at the end of the chapter)

Case 4.2: Hats That Create Internal Audit Value

Synopsis

Research by the author into the perception of internal auditing in 1997 developed a world-wide spectrum of traditional, new and leading edge internal auditing best practices. This spectrum is discussed in the relevance of today's evolving internal auditing resources, practices and services. It reinforces the need for internal auditing to wear many cutting edge hats, including that of innovator.

> Contributed from research into senior management perceptions of values from internal auditing by the author and Dr Kenneth D'Silva, London South Bank University – *Perceptions of Internal Auditing Value* (1997).

After Reading the Case Study Consider:

1. Are the hats in the spectrum of activities in internal auditing in 1997 worn in your own internal audit cutting edge resources and practices?
2. Is the hat of the innovator worn in your internal auditing services and, if so, does it add value in your organization?

Case 4.3: Internal Audit Consulting Provides Cutting Edge Opportunities

Synopsis

Discussed are the findings of research in 2005 into the consulting role in internal auditing. At that time two-thirds of internal auditing respondents had changed their audit charter to reflect the provision of a consulting service. Guidance in this new role is given and two examples of cutting edge internal auditing consultancy presented.

> Contributed by Professor Georges Selim, Dr Sally Woodward and Don Brunton.

After Reading the Case Study Consider:

1. Does the planning and promotion of consulting services in your internal auditing include the words – *'formality, competency, confidence, advice, planned, motivated, clear terms, leadership'*?
2. In your opinion which of the examples is more cutting edge than the other, and why?

Case 4.4: Internal Auditors as Facilitators of Risk Management

Synopsis

Describes how Control and Risk Self Assessment has been implemented in BT plc, facilitated by internal auditing developing a *'. . . toolkit of approaches that the team now feel comfortable using across a range of situations'*, including the cutting edge of *'. . . web based virtual workshops in either real time or over a period of days/weeks'*.

> Contributed by David Reynolds, Director Internal Audit and Regulatory Compliance BT plc (retired 7/07).

After Reading the Case Study Consider:

1. How does internal auditing in your organization tap in to *'culture and attitude'* in their control and risk assessments?
2. How do the BT benefits from CSA *'mirror'* the benefits internal auditing in your organization achieve from its assessments of risk and control?
3. Is CSA used *'flexibly'* by internal auditing in your organization at different stages in its engagement planning and processes?
4. Are CSA and RSA activities in your organization brought *'together'* or do they operate independent of each other?

Case 4.5: The Royal Bank of Scotland Risk Academy

Synopsis

Describes how RBS developed a Risk Academy as a learning programme across its global organization, for all functions and staff. Provides a good cutting edge benchmark for internal auditing in all sectors, as it moves into providing risk management advice, guidance and services.

> The RBS Risk Academy case study is written by Shari Casey, Head of the Risk Academy, February 2007, and published with permission from the Royal Bank of Scotland.

After Reading the Case Study Consider:

1. How does this learning programme for embedding risk management across an organization compare with your own organization's learning programmes for risk management?
2. How many hats do internal auditing wear in risk management learning in your organization?
3. How efficient and effective is your organization's learning risk management programme in its contribution to good corporate governance across your organization and its supply chains?

SELF-ASSESSMENT QUESTIONS

4.1

How many hats did you recognize being worn in Case Study 4.1? I recognized at least 15. (See Appendix C for these.)

4.2

What were the four issues in internal auditing, recognized by Albrecht *et al.* in 1992 and discussed in the chapter, and how have these influenced the wearing of hats by internal auditors in your organization today, and will do tomorrow?

NOTES AND REFERENCES

1. 'The Emerging Responsibility of the Internal Auditor' (1978), Harold M. Williams, *Internal Auditor*, October (1978: pp. 45–52), The IIA. (Cited in *Managing the Behavioral Dynamics of Internal Auditing* (1985: p.5), James A. Wilson and Donna J. Wood, The IIA Research Foundation.)
2. The 1971 revision to this statement changed the fourth activity from accounting to management data, and added a sixth activity – Recommending Operating improvements. In 1981 the statement was further changed to state that internal auditing is a service to the organization, not just to management. This brought the board and all operating levels in the organization into the internal auditing market place.
3. Practice Advisory 2100-1 (8):*Nature of Work* (2001), The IIA.
4. *'Internal Auditing in the 70s'*, J.G. Brown, *Internal Auditor* (Winter 1966: pp. 10–16), The IIA.
5. *The Manager and the Modern Internal Auditor* (1979: pp. 11 and 13), Sawyer, Lawrence B., Amacom – a division of American Management Associations, New York, USA.
6. See note 1, above.
7. *Internal Auditing in a Changing Management Culture* (1992), Office of the Auditor General of Canada, Ottawa, Ontario, Canada.
8. *'The Common Body of Knowledge for Internal Auditors* (CBOK)', Robert E. Gobeil, *Internal Auditor* (November/December 1972: p. 20), The IIA. (Cited in *A Common Body of Professional Knowledge for Internal Auditors* (1985): A Research Study, Michael J. Barrett, Gerald W. Lee, S. Paul Roy and Leticia Verastegui, The IIA Research Foundation.)
9. *A Common Body of Knowledge for the Practice of Internal Auditing* (1992), W. Steve Albrecht, James D. Stice and Kevin D. Stocks, The IIA.
10. *Competency Framework for Internal Auditing* (1999), William P. Birkett, Maria R. Barbera, Barry S. Leithhead and Marian Lower, The IIA Research Foundation.
11. *The International Auditor: Then and Now*, Lawrence B. Sawyer (1971):
    The author Elbert Hubbard, in a moment born of pique,
    Described the classic auditor as something of a freak.
    He dipped his pen in vitriol and opened his Thesaurus,
    And penned a definition of the old-time checker for us.
    The auditor, said Hubbard, is a man past middle age.
    Spare wrinkled, cold and passive, although something of a sage.
    Polite and noncommittal, unresponsive as a post;
    With eyes much like a codfish and the charm of burnt rye toast.
    He's calm and damnably composed, quite like a plaster cast.
    A human perfection that has feldspar for a heart,
    Sans bowels, sans charm, sans passion – and from humans set apart.

But Hubbard had one happy thought that he was pleased to tell:
They never reproduce, he said, and all will go to Hell.
Since Hubbard's time, the auditor *'past middle age'* retired,
But not until he left us with the paragon he sired:
A paragon who's human and who's not a concrete post:
Who raised his sight to find out what his management needs most.
Who's shaken off the shackles that have bound him to 'the books',
Who's altered his perspective and has modernized his looks.
He's warm and he's proactive, and commitment is his style.
Exchanging ancient wrinkles for the crinkles of a smile.
Not petrified but flexible, adjusting to the times –
To broader needs than merely counting pennies, shillings, dimes.
He keeping up the management, with what is good and new:
Statistics, data processing, behavioural science too.
The auditor with the green eyeshade is gone, we hope for good:
A problem-solving analyst emerges where he stood.
And Hubbard notwithstanding, in his eye there is a gleam,
That speaks of brand new paragons for the future management team.

Reprinted in Sawyer's *Words of Wisdom* (2004): A collection of articles by Lawrence B. Sawyer, The IIA Research Foundation.

12. *The Buyer*, Elbert Hubbard (1922), USA.
13. *Sawyer's Internal Auditing* (1996: pp. 1259–1260), Lawrence B. Sawyer and Mortimer A. Dittenhofer, The IIA.
14. *Audit Customer Satisfaction: Marketing Added Value* (1996), Cindy E. Cosmas, The IIA.
15. *'Internal auditing is an independent, objective assurance and consulting activity designed to add value and improve an organization's operations. It helps an organization accomplish its objectives by bringing a systematic, disciplined approach to evaluate and improve the effectiveness of risk management, control and governance processes.'*
16. *Standards for the Professional Practice of Internal Auditing* (1998 and 2002 editions), The IIA.
17. *'Internal Auditing in the Next Millennium'*, John J. Fernandes, *AuditWire*, Volume 22, Number 1, Jan./Feb. 2000, The IIA.
18. Published in *Internal Auditing & Business Risk* (July 2000), IIA–UK & Ireland.
19. *'Leading The Way'*, Jacqueline K. Wagner, *Internal Auditor* (August 2000), The IIA.
20. Published in *Internal Auditing & Business Risk* (August 2003), IIA–UK & Ireland.
21. Published in *Internal Control*, Issue 79 (March 2005), Croner.CCH Group Limited, London, England.
22. These quotes were originally in job descriptions published by Protiviti *KnowledgeLeader* (www.knowledgeleader.com). They are reprinted with permission.
23. *Guide To The Management Gurus – shortcuts to the ideas of leading management thinkers* (1991), Carol Kennedy, Mackays of Chatham plc, Chatham, Kent, England.
24. *Six Thinking Hats*® (1985), Edward de Bono, Penguin Books, Harmondsworth, Middlesex, England.
25. *A Global Summary of the Common Body of Knowledge 2006*, Preview edition (2007: Table 2-13), The IIA Research Foundation.
26. As reported in *Internal Auditing & Business Risk* (September 2007: p.45), *The new gold standard*. IIA–UK & Ireland.
27. *Internal Audit Capabilities and Needs Survey* (2006: p. 8), Protiviti Inc., USA. www.protiviti.com.

Cutting Edge Internal Auditing Knows How To Govern

'The proper function of a government is to make it easy for people to do good, and difficult for them to do evil.'

William Ewat Gladstone 1809–1898[1]

Cutting Edge Internal Auditing Model 2007

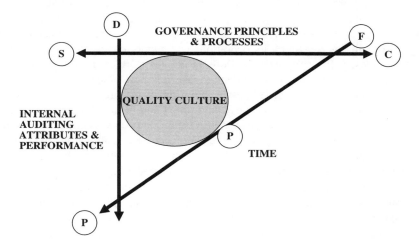

GOVERNANCE BEFORE 1995

For *'a government'* in the quote above read *'governance'*. It is important that governance does not stifle innovation but encourages it to happen for the good of the organization, its performance and the performance of those who are committed to its vision and objectives. It is also important that governance makes it difficult for evil to happen. It is unlikely to stop evil but it can assess the associated risks. Take control to try to prevent them, detect evil when it happens and take appropriate action to investigate it; then restart the cycle of risk assessment and control to prevent, detect and investigate. This cycle of activities fighting evil takes place in every organization every day. Evil covers a wide variety of causes and effects. It can be minor; it can have a strong influence on performance – sometimes the wrong way; it can be disastrous, having significant impact on all stakeholders, communities, nations and internationally; it can mean failure, even death, of the organization and individuals associated with it. It is not nice!

The 'good' in an organization should be seen in its vision and mission statements as well as its ethics and performance. There has to be a direction and commitment at the top of an organization, and at all other levels, for good in resources, practices, ethics and performance. That goodness has to be managed well. There are many hats for internal auditing in the development, promotion and monitoring of organization goodness, but the primary responsibility for this lies with management.

Peter Drucker,[2] in his writings on the practice of management and from as long ago as the 1950s, saw integrity as central to the performance of managers *'The more successfully tomorrow's manager does his work, the greater will be the integrity required of him'* [for *him* also read *her* today and tomorrow]. Integrity and good governance will always need each other. In his book, *The Practice of Management*, Drucker has as his last paragraph:

> No matter what a man's general education or his adult education for management, what will be decisive above all, in the future even more than the past, is neither education nor skill; it is integrity of character.

Governance is more than just risk management, control and internal auditing. Although these are important in every organization – whether the auditing is independent or by management, or both – governance is about direction, how it is implemented across an organization, from top to bottom and across all its operations and supply chains. It offers many choices in how it is imposed, from tightly to loosely, principles to rules. It is applied at all levels in an organization and by many means, strategies, policies, procedures, systems, instructions, visually, verbally; even sometimes by intuition. It requires trust to be implemented successfully. It requires respect from those who direct and those who are directed.

At this time my model for cutting edge interval auditing resources and practices discussed in Chapter 1 was growing in importance as governance and quality principles grew closer together, recognizing that each has some dependence on the other. At the same time developments were taking place in North America and the United Kingdom to improve definitions of risk assessment, control and governance, emphasizing the importance of each for management and auditing. Governments and professional bodies started to take a more active and creative interest in these issues for many reasons, not least because of failures and major fraud in too many organizations across the world. These developments have continued leading to the many frameworks and principles for risk management, control and governance existing today in the United Kingdom, Europe and across the world. All have four things in common:

1. They encourage management in all sectors to address the issues of risk management, control and governance (good and evil) in organizations, providing guidance on how these should be practised and audited.
2. They provide measures for regulators to control the organizations they regulate.
3. They provide benchmarks for governments to use in the enactment of laws and regulations.
4. They create industries of services for their implementation.

Those frameworks and principles that had influenced the development of my model are:

1. The IIA *Statement of Responsibilities of the Internal Auditor* – from its first publication in 1947 to 1968.
2. The IIA *Code of Ethics* – from its first issue in 1968 to today's code.
3. The IIA *Standards for the Professional Practice of Internal Auditing* – from its first publication in 1978 to today's *International Professional Practices Framework*.

4. The United States Report of the National Commission on Fraudulent Financial Reporting (Treadway Commission) in 1987[3] (this report set out clear recommendations for
companies for improving financial reporting, the tone at the top, audit committees,
accounting, internal and external auditing, regulation and education). Its recommendations guided many future commissions across the world, in all industry sectors. They
have been mainly implemented, leading to the Committee of Sponsoring Organization's
(COSO) publications on risk management and control, starting with its Integrated Control
Framework[4] in 1992. Bishop (1991)[5] discussed the exposure draft for this framework
consisting of nine components (sometimes also referred to as elements). Bishop saw three
of these as core, being reviewed on a perpetual basis – Control Procedures, Monitoring, Information Systems. The other six surrounding this core were: Integrity, Ethical
Values, Competence; Control Environment; Objectives; Risk Assessment; Communication; and Managing Change. Bishop saw these as requiring coordination with external
audit:

> Three of COSO's nine components [referred to as the 'Core' by Bishop] would be reviewed
> on a perpetual basis through the continual audit process. An audit department's annual plan for
> operational system and financial auditing would usually include reviews that would cover [these
> three] *Control Procedures, Monitoring and Information Systems* audits to asses the adequacy
> and effectiveness of the design and functioning of these components. The audit plan would
> have to be designed to cover major organizational elements and a significant portion of the
> function (e.g. on a multi-year cycle) for the audit director to know that the five objectives of
> control (as defined by The IIA) are assessed on a continual basis. Full coverage of the core
> might depend upon coordination and reliance with the public accountants. A plan of 'total audit
> coverage' would greatly aid the process of assessing the entity's system of control. In addition to
> assessment of the three specific components mentioned above, the core coverage will naturally
> provide information that is necessary in assessing [the] other components . . .
>
> The remaining six components of the COSO model (*Integrity, Ethical Values and Competence*;
> *Control Environment*; *Communication*; *Risk Assessment*; *Managing Change*; and *Objectives*)
> would have to be specifically assessed each year in order to supplement the 'Core' audits. The
> annual 'supplemental' assessments would be a 'top-down' process that would spread across all
> major elements of the organization.
>
> The assessment of each component would be accomplished through a variety of techniques
> (e.g. interviews, reviews of corporate governance activities such as business and strategic plans
> and code of conduct process, delegations of authority, board minutes, etc.). Because of the
> natural linkage and overlap of the components of control, such a process would have to include
> the recognition of information gathered in the 'Core' audits.
>
> To achieve the overall assessment, the auditor will need to recognize, coordinate and use the
> work of other activities, such as management reviews and the work of the public accountants.
>
> Although the COSO study refers to evaluating the '. . . *effectiveness of controls*', it also
> implies the assessment of the *adequacy* of the system. To meet The IIA *Standards* the auditor
> must evaluate the adequacy and effectiveness of the system and assure that the five objectives
> of control are achieved.

This framework has guided much of the thinking on risk assessment and control in
organizations ever since. The five objectives of control referred to by Bishop in 1991
were those in The IIA *Standards and Guidelines* (Section 300):

- Reliability and integrity of information.
- Compliance with policies, plans, procedures, laws, and regulations.

- Safeguarding assets.
- Economical and efficient use of resources.
- Accomplishment of established objectives and goals for operations or programmes.

These are still fundamental in control requirements and in its professional statements today. Those readers who are familiar with the later publications of COSO on control and risk management will recognize in its 1992 control framework and 2004 enterprise risk management framework the nine components in the 1991 exposure draft. Bishop's comments then on this framework were cutting edge and today are even more so. [See later in this chapter the links between the exposure draft, 1992 framework and COSO's enterprise risk management (ERM) framework.]

5. The United Kingdom Cadbury Report of 1992 set out a code of best practices for companies '. . . *designed to achieve the necessary high standards of corporate behaviour'*, and principles for governance of openness, integrity and accountability. These are principles that have stood the test of time well and since then repeated in many publications on governance. Cadbury also defined corporate governance as '. . . *the system by which companies are directed and controlled'*. This report focused more on the good of 'good behaviour' rather than the evil of 'bad behaviour'. Its linking of good governance to economic performance is often overlooked:

The country's economy depends on the drive and efficiency of its companies. Thus the effectiveness with which their boards discharge their responsibilities determines Britain's competitive position. They must be free to drive their companies forward, but exercise that freedom within a framework of effective accountability. This is the essence of any system of good corporate governance.

6. The Canadian Institute of Chartered Accountants in 1995 published its own criteria of control (CoCo) based on four components: Purpose, Commitment, Capability, and Monitoring and Learning. Text books link the COSO and CoCo models. Sawyer (2003) sees this model as '. . . *more oriented toward internal auditing procedures'*. At the time it was published in 1995 it had little publicity in the United Kingdom, but later on many internal auditors saw it as more useful than COSO in control self-assessment facilitation.

By 1995, I now had a much more attractive model to promote cutting edge professional internal auditing resources and practices. Governance principles for openness, integrity and accountability had become much clearer and were recognized by management and internal auditors across all sectors. The foundation for professional internal auditing was becoming more established and recognized. Its contribution to the fight for 'good' and against 'evil' was being seen in many organizations across the world. The speed of change in organizations was making time more important in every internal audit engagement. The quality culture in all organizations across all sectors had grown in its importance. This model was still relevant for the promotion of cutting edge internal auditing resources and practices.

Article:
Status Of UK Quality Management And Governance[6] (1995)

There are many definitions of quality, internal and external to the organization. Most are estab- lished in organization
visions, missions, strategic plans, key
result areas and per- formance measures.
All have a basic aim, to motivate continuous improvement throughout external
and internal sup- ply chains: regulate
improvement in sup- plier organizations
and achieve customer satisfaction. SEPSU

> **'Quality and governance are now well studied and researched pathways to success or even survival in today's government and business operations.'**

(1994),[a] in explaining its rationale for studying UK quality management, emphasized that:

> . . . quality is self-evidently important in all spheres of human endeavour. In the sphere
> of organized work, quality is now one of the central determinants of competitive survival
> and thus of national prosperity. This leads to a widespread interest in the management of
> quality as a dimension of corporate behaviour. . . .

UK government interest in quality as a driver for change in the private sector
started in the early 80s, National Audit Office (1990)[b] *'A recognition that success
in world markets increasingly depends on quality as well as price led the Government in 1982 to publish the White Paper "Standards: Quality and International Competitiveness" (Cmnd 8621)'.* This White Paper came from research studies by The
Department of Trade and Industry, which ended with promotion of quality standards as a way forward for British industry in international markets. UK government
promotion of BS 5750 – the quality management system standard followed. This
standard, like all standards, was researched by working groups of practitioners and
academics. It was sold as a UK symbol of achievement in the design and implementation of quality systems. This same standard was adopted throughout Europe as
EN 29000 and in 1987 revised by international working groups and adopted across
the world by the International Standards Organization, as ISO 9000. In 1995 all three
standards became the one standard, BS EN ISO 9000. Another quality management
standard was also developed in the UK – BS 7850: 1992 Total Quality Management.
This standard defined TQM as:

> Total Quality Management assures maximum effectiveness and efficiency within an orga-
> nization by putting in place processes and systems which will ensure that every aspect
> of its activity is aligned to satisfy customer needs and all other objectives without waste
> of effort and using the full potential of every person in the organization. This philosophy

---

[a] *UK Quality Management – Policy options* (1994), The Royal Society, London England.
[b] *Promotion of Quality and Standards at Department of Trade and Industry* (1990), National Audit Office, HMSO, London,
England.

recognizes that customer satisfaction, health, safety, environmental considerations and business objectives are mutually dependent. It is applicable within any organization.

The definition link between quality and performance is repeated in the rationale behind SEPSU (1994), '. . . *Quality is self-evidently important, in all spheres of human endeavour. In the sphere of organized work, quality is now one of the central determinants of competitive survival and thus of national prosperity.'* BS 7850 has never become international, although it did start to establish control links between environmental, health and safety objectives and quality management. ISO 14000 will appear soon to manage environmental issues; this new international standard is patterned on ISO 9000 quality principles.

In the late 1980s, the UK government used quality as a mission in its new Citizen's Charter.[c] Change programmes followed in the civil service, under an umbrella of 'Competing for Quality' 1991, requiring, for the first time, competition for many public services – and using 'quality' as an objective and measure of performance and success. In the early 1990s, government and industry sponsored European and national annual competition programmes for quality awards. In the early 1990s, organizations, in the private sector across Europe (European Foundation for Quality Management), researched and created a quality framework, with eight criteria focused on achieving excellent business results – The European Quality Model. In 1992 the British Quality Foundation was set up with the aim of enhancing the '. . . *performance and effectiveness of all types of organizations in the UK through the promotion of Total Quality management'.* It used a quality award process, British Quality Award In 1994; then the UK QUALITY AWARD (based on the European Quality Model), was launched by the President of the Board of Trade. In 1995, the scope of this award was extended to the public and voluntary sectors. The assessment criteria used in these awards measures commitment, culture and control, and how each impacts performance.

Status of UK Governance

In parallel with the European and UK quality revolutions of the 1980s and 1990s, there has been a growing interest by governments and all industry sectors in governance and ethical issues. One of the earliest references to governance as an economic issue was in 1979. The Institute of Chartered Secretaries and Administrators published a series of papers on corporate governance and accountability, by distinguished contributors from industry and academia, introducing these with:

> In recent years, public debate has ranged over industrial democracy, audit committees, the duties and responsibilities of company directors, disclosure of information, accounting standards and other subjects but there has been little new thought about more fundamental aspects – the 'why' and 'how' of corporate governance.

---

[c] Presented to Parliament by the Prime Minister by command of Her Majesty (1991).

Two of the contributors,[d] Sir Arthur Knight and the then Dr K. Midgley, examined boardroom responsibilities, listing the claims of various groups that management need to take into account in their decision making. These lists included most of the groups currently referred to as the organization's 'stakeholders'. In ranking these groups they identified consumers as *'Customers come first; . . . '*. They did not at that time see other groups (stakeholders) as customers! In listing groups with claims on an organization they both predated the current wide definition of 'stakeholder'. Conclusions reached by both contributors placed accountability clearly at the door of directors and profitability, still the most reliable guide to management efficiency.

Corporate concerns and public disenchantment with behaviour in some major businesses worldwide during the 1980s led to a growing demand for improved ethical standards to be adopted publicly by many organizations. These demands have increased, moving into governments and their supporting administrations. Many organizations now publicly declare codes of ethics to their stakeholders, linking these to some, if not all, of their other objectives. The Institute of Business Ethics (1992)[e] included the following statement in its proposed ethics code:

> We will provide products and services of good value and consistent quality, reliability and safety. We will avoid practices which seek to increase sales by any means other than fair merchandising efforts based on quality, design features, productivity, price and product support. We will provide a high standard of service in our efforts to maintain customer satisfaction and cooperation.

Recently, many organizations have been influenced by external stakeholder pressures to reinforce existing governance practices or adopt new ones. Tricker (1994)[f] sees governance not as a separate theory but as a development of both 'stewardship theory' and 'agency theory': emphasizing *'Research in this area has hardly begun . . . '*. He sees governance at present mainly based on two bodies of knowledge *' . . . the legal and the operational perspectives'*. Looking to the future he adds another theoretical focus *'essentially ideological and political'*, deriving *'insights from the worlds of political science, sociology and philosophy'*, leading *'to insights into the importance of values, beliefs and culture . . . '* Cadbury (1992) states *' . . . governance is the system by which companies are directed and controlled'*. Cadbury did not link directors' responsibilities for control over finance with control for quality, but went on to define governance:

> . . . as being the structures, systems and policies in an organization, designed and established to direct and control all operations and relationships on a continuing basis, in an honest and caring manner, taking into account the interests of all stakeholders and compliance with all applicable laws and regulatory requirements.

---

[d] *The Aims And Objectives of Corporate Bodies* (1979), Sir Arthur Knight, and *To Whom Should the Board be Accountable . . . and for What?* (1979), Dr K. Midgley, Institute of Chartered Secretaries and Administrators, London, England.
[e] *Business Ethics and Company Codes* (1992), The Institute of Business Ethics, London, England.
[f] *International Corporate Governance* (1994), R.I. Tricker, Prentice Hall, Singapore.

The principles on which his committee's recommended code of best practice for organizations are based '. . . *are those of openness, integrity and accountability*'. These governance principles and their related best practices are now frequently reported publicly by all sizes of organization across all sectors. Such reports vary in content, but all demonstrate commitment to ethical behaviour. Coopers & Lybrand (1996),[g] in its research into 1996 published accounts, finds that '*compliance with the Cadbury Code of Best Practice has continued to increase in 1995, reaching 97% in FT 100 companies*'. However, '. . . *only a handful of companies are willing to express opinions on the effectiveness of their systems of internal control*'. None of the examples referenced in this research integrates quality objectives or quality programmes into reporting on internal control! However, many do report separately on quality objectives and performance.

The Status of Control Environments

Control is based on its own theories of formality and informality; law and regulation; direction, prevention and detection; monitoring, feedback and correction; punishment and reward. Control has always been seen as an essential management activity. Yet, it applies and is applied across all levels of an organization and integrates many objectives. The US Treadway Commission (1987) researched '. . . *environments in which fraudulent (financial) reporting occurs. . . '.* This research established a demand for control guidance in the USA, which resulted in its – Committee of Sponsoring Organizations (COSO) (1992) developing '. . . *nine interrelated components. . . '* for control theory, which subsequently evolved into six now internationally recognized control elements: '. . . *control environment, objectives and risks, control activities and monitoring; all linked by accurate and timely information systems and communications*'. These elements and their underlying theory are now in worldwide use by management, accountants and auditors, to guide their assessments of reasonableness of control. The most recently researched criteria for control by The Canadian Institute of Chartered Accountants (CICA) (1995), developed concepts based on COSO. Some of these criteria provide the basis of developing a model for this research to measure organization public statements on their internal control frameworks.

A study, by the Institute of Internal Auditors – UK (1994),[h] of these and other worldwide internal control principles and practices, contended that:

> . . . the primary purpose of an internal control system is to enable directors to drive their companies forward with confidence, at an appropriate speed and direction, in both good and bad times; the secondary, but no less important, purpose is to safeguard resources and ensure the adequacy of records and systems of accountability.

Quality and Governance Control Framework Integration

Quality and governance are now well studied and researched pathways to success or even survival in today's government and business operations. There is ample

---

[g] *Cadbury Compliance – A Survey of Published Accounts* (1996), Coopers & Lybrand, London, England.
[h] *Internal Control* (1994), The IIA–UK & Ireland.

research evidence in developed theory and principles that quality is associated with competition, performance and profitability. Yet little evidence that control has been a focus in any of this research. Use of quality as a control is not new. Omachonu/Ross (1994)[i] use '. . . *conformance to requirements*. . .' as a current universal definition of quality; emphasizing the importance of design, deviation and standards. They also recognize control for quality is different to the use of traditional control concepts for financial statements:

> The classical control process will require significant change if TQM is to be successful. Traditionally, control systems have been directed to the end use of preparation of financial statements. Focus has been on the components of the profit-and-loss statement. Quality control has historically followed a three-step process consisting of (1) setting standards, (2) reporting variances and (3) correcting deviations. . . . In an organization that perceives control systems in this way, there is the danger that the system will become the end rather than the means. This is not to say that classical control does not have a place in quality management.

What place classic control has in quality management activities at strategic, tactical and operational levels is explored by the authors, but not as an integrated approach. Nor is classic control defined to include the wider aspects of governance or external controls over an organization's activities.

How organizations are governed and the accountability of those who are governed is not a new issue. Humble (1973),[j] considered social responsibility as an important area in which every business must set objectives and secure results. However, his basic concept for company survival was not only social responsibility, but also profitability:

> Since business is the wealth-producing institution of our society it must be profitable. The greatest social irresponsibility would be to so manage business that wealth was not produced for the community's fabric of schools, homes, roads and so on. This is recognized even in countries where the word 'profit' is not acceptable. 'Surplus' or 'maximum' value added to minimum materials and 'money put in', or similar phrases are preferred. What is done with the profit or surplus is another argument. . . . which can't start if there's nothing to divide. Responsibility and profitability are inseparable.

There is ample evidence in developed theory and principles that governance is associated with control. Yet little evidence that competition, performance and profitability have been a focus in any of this research.

The following model, Figure 5.1 shows the impact of quality and governance on society and in public and commercial environments. It offers many pathways for exploring at strategic, tactical and operational levels the impacts of quality and governance integration.

Each of the six elements in the framework – Society Interests and Values; Stakeholders; Issues; Rules and Regulations; Control; External Monitoring – should be researched in every organization to determine their impact and influence on the

---

[i] *Principles of Total Quality* (1994), V.K. Omachonu, and J.E. Ross, St Lucia Press, Florida, USA.
[j] *Social Responsibility Audit – a management tool for survival* (1973), John Humble, Foundation for Business Responsibilities, London, England.

SOCIETY INTERESTS AND VALUES
STAKEHOLDERS
(primary : secondary : tertiary)

European/International/UK Parliament
Executive Councils/Bodies
Local Authorities
Funding Bodies
Employees
Investors
Employer Associations

Professional Institutions
Universities
Advisory Groups
Religious Bodies
Suppliers
Customers

ISSUES
Ownership – Membership – Independence – Political – Social – Economic

RULES AND REGULATIONS
CHARTERS: AWARDS: CULTURES: CODES: STANDARDS: LAWS: REGULATIONS

RISK & CONTROL
CONTROL ENVIRONMENT: OBJECTIVES AND RISKS: CONTROL ACTIVITIES:
MONITORING INFORMATION: COMMUNICATIONS

SUPPLY CHAIN THEORY
Suppliers – Processes for Products and Services – Customers Complaints

PRINCIPLES OF QUALITY
Customer Focus – Management Leadership – Teamwork
Analytical Approach – Continuous Improvement

PRINCIPLES OF CORPORATE GOVERNANCE
OPENNESS – INTEGRITY – ACCOUNTABILITY

THREE DIMENSIONS OF GOVERNANCE
Organizational Structures and Processes
Financial Reporting and Internal Controls
Standards of Behaviour

GENERAL PRINCIPLES OF CONDUCT
Selflessness – Integrity – Objectivity – Honesty
Accountability – Openness – Leadership

EXTERNAL MONITORING
Police	External Auditors	Inspectors
Regulators	Ombudsmen	Watchdogs
Action Groups	Public Opinion	Media

Figure 5.1 Framework For Quality And Governance 1997
Source: J. Ridley (1995)

organization's approach to governance at strategic, policy and operational levels. Consider the following:

1. Societal interests and values concerns ethics and public attitudes to the organization's existence and performance – not just locally or nationally, but also in relation to the wider impacts an organization might have on global issues.
2. Issues are those theories that cover ownership of an organization and its members and how these interact with society, politics and the economy.
3. Stakeholders are all those interests, financial or otherwise, in an organization's performance. Rarely are these interests exclusive to one type of stakeholder. More often, interests are networked among groups of stakeholders. Some stake-

holders are passive, others can be active, with strong influences on an organization's management, control and governance objectives and processes.

4. Rules and regulations are all the laws and directives that establish mandatory and voluntary behaviour for an organization and all those interested in and associated with its performance. These can be local, national, international.
5. Control concepts are the developed theory and principles underlying all management, risk, control and monitoring activities.
6. External monitoring covers all the independent groups involved in regulation, inspection, review, and investigation of an organization's activities. Some of these groups have contractual relationships with an organization, some have legal status, some are voluntary. Many also have stakeholder interest.

Recent research by Bain and Band (1996)[k] in governance does give some recognition to quality and governance integration:

> We hold the view that corporate governance is very much about adding value. Companies and other enterprises with a professional and positive attitude to governance are stronger and have a greater record of achievement. In fact, some company directors, like Allan Sykes, in his article *'Proposals for Internationally Competitive Corporate Governance in Britain and America'*, suggest that there is an important direct relationship between a country's corporate governance system and its economic success.

GOVERNANCE 1995 TO 2000

By this time the term 'corporate governance' was impacting many of the operations and businesses in the public sector. The Chartered Institute of Public Finance and Accountancy (1995)[7] published its own definitions of corporate governance and the Cadbury (1992) principles as:

Governance

Governance is currently defined as being the structures, systems and policies in an organization, designed and established to direct and control all operations and relationships on a continuing basis, in an honest and caring manner, taking into account the interests of all stakeholders and compliance with all applicable laws and regulatory requirements. Governance is based on the following principles of openness, integrity and accountability:

Openness

Openness is required to ensure that stakeholders can have confidence in the decision-making processes and actions of public service bodies, in the management of their activities, and in the individuals within them. Being open through meaningful consultation with stakeholders and communication of full, accurate and clear information leads to effective and timely action and lends itself to necessary scrutiny.

---

[k] *Winning Ways Through Corporate Governance* (1996), Neville Bain and David Band, Macmillan Business, London, England.

Integrity

Integrity comprises both straightforward dealing and completeness. It is based upon honesty, selflessness and objectivity, and high standards of propriety and probity in the stewardship of public funds and management of a body's affairs. It is dependent on the effectiveness of the control framework and on the personal standards and professionalism of the individuals within the body. It is reflected both in the body's decision-making procedures and in the quality of its financial and performance reporting.

Accountability

Accountability is the process whereby public service bodies, and the individuals within them are responsible for their decisions and actions, including their stewardship of public funds and all aspects of performance, and submit themselves to appropriate scrutiny. It is achieved by all parties having a clear understanding of those responsibilities, and having clearly defined roles through a robust structure.

These are a definition and principles that have stood the test of time well. In the same year Lord Nolan published a report following a study by the government Committee on Standards of Conduct in Public Life. This report recommended a framework of seven principles of public life (shown in Figure 5.2).

This has also stood the test of time well, as is evidenced by future statements on governance in the public sector. CIPFA (1995) interpreted the Cadbury and Nolan reports into a framework of structure, process, financial reporting, internal controls and standards of behaviour as shown in Figure 5.3.

By 2000 a new framework for internal auditing services had started to develop, influenced strongly by The IIA's 1999 new definition of professional internal auditing '. . . *to evaluate and improve the effectiveness of risk management, control and governance processes'*. This was raising many new challenges for internal auditors.

Article:
Risk Management, Control And Governance Challenges And Opportunities For Internal Auditors[8] (2000)

The IIA (1999) strategic directives[l] include '. . . *promoting* the profession and The IIA to foster internal auditing as risk management, and to posi-premiere authority

> **'Internal auditors will have to take the power of risk assessment to their elbows . . . '**

awareness of internal a key function in control and governance. The IIA as the for information and

leading-edge knowledge of the profession'. Compare your own and your organization's definition of internal auditing with The IIA's new definition,[m] developed from international research and consultation:

---

[l] *Strategic Directives* published by The IIA (1999).
[m] *New Definition of Internal Auditing* (1999), The IIA.

SELFLESSNESS

Holders of public office should take decisions solely in terms of the public interest. They should not do so in order to gain financial or other material benefits for themselves, their families, or their friends.

INTEGRITY

Holders of public office should not place themselves under any financial or other obligation to outside individuals or organizations that might influence them in the performance of their official duties.

OBJECTIVITY

In carrying out public business, including making public appointments, awarding contracts, or recommending individuals for rewards and benefits, holders of public office should make choices on merit.

ACCOUNTABILITY

Holders of public office are accountable for their decisions and actions to the public and must submit themselves to whatever scrutiny is appropriate to their office.

OPENNESS

Holders of public office should be as open as possible about all the decisions and actions they take. They should give reasons for their decisions and restrict information only when the wider public interest clearly demands.

HONESTY

Holders of public office have a duty to declare any private interests relating to their public duties and to take steps to resolve any conflicts arising in a way that protects the public interest.

LEADERSHIP

Holders of public office should promote and support these principles by leadership and example.

Figure 5.2   The Seven Principles Of Public Life
Source: First Report of the Committee on Standards in Public Life
Chairman: Lord Nolan
Presented to Parliament by the Prime Minister by Command of Her Majesty, May 1995

Internal Auditing is an independent and objective assurance and consulting activity that is guided by a philosophy of adding value to improve the operations of the organization. It assists an organization in accomplishing its objectives by bringing a systematic and disciplined approach to evaluate and improve the effectiveness of the organization's risk management, control, and governance processes.

The following attempt by The IIA (1999) to define *'risk management, control and governance'* is not yet an authoritative statement. It is still at the consultation stage.

Risk Management processes are put in place by management to identify, evaluate and respond to potential risks that may impact the achievement of the organization's objectives. Control processes are the policies, procedures and activities, which are part of a control framework, designed to ensure that risks are contained within tolerances established by the risk management process. Governance processes deal with the procedures uitilized by the representatives of the organization's stakeholders (shareholders, etc.) to provide oversight of risk and control processes administered by management.

Organizational Structures and Processes

- Statutory accountability
- Accountability for public money
- Communication with stakeholders
- Roles and responsibilities
- Balance of power
- The board
- The chairman
- Non-executive board members
- Executive management

Financial Reporting and Internal Controls

- Annual reporting
- Internal controls
- Risk management
- Internal audit
- Audit committees
- External auditors

Standards of Behaviour

- Leadership
- Codes of conduct
- Selflessness
- Objectivity
- Honesty

Figure 5.3   Standards Of Corporate Governance In The Public Services
Source: *Corporate Governance, UK: A Framework For Public Service Bodies* (1995)

This part of the new definition of internal auditing is worth studying for its impact on the future role of internal auditing. It places the feet of internal auditors firmly alongside the strategic levels of decision making in an organization. A level that most internal auditors are not familiar with, either in their audit work or in their advisory roles. The future of professional internal auditing will depend on how successful internal auditors are in this new level of activity.

My review of a selection of company 1998 annual reports for insurance companies showed a variety of descriptions of the established internal auditing services. Few reflected the involvement of internal auditing in any risk assessment processes. This probably applies to organizations in all industries and sectors for the year 1998. A good example of how internal auditing is now used in other parts of the financial services sector is the following description in the 'corporate governance' section of the 1998 annual accounts and report of a large bank[n]:

Internal Control (extract from)

– Internal audit provides independent and objective assurance to the Audit Committee that processes by which risks are identified, assessed and managed are appropriate and

---

[n] Part of corporate governance statement in financial services organization, Directors' Report and Accounts, 31 December 1998, London, England.

effectively applied, and achieve residual risk exposures consistent with management's risk policy, reporting any material exceptions and following up management responses to ensure effective resolution of issues.

The Auditing Practices Board (APB) (1999)[o] in a recently published practice note for external auditors describes the insurer's control environment as consisting of '. . . *the overall attitude, awareness and actions of directors and management regarding internal controls and their importance in the entity. The control environment encompasses the management style and corporate culture and values shared by all employees. It provides the background against which the various other controls are operated.'* This APB guidance for external auditors relates selected current Statements of Auditing Standards to recognized special needs of insurance companies. Similar recommendations exist for some, but not all, companies in other industries.

The APB goes on to analyse the risk external auditors should recognize in insurance companies as 'inherent risk' and 'control risk'. Factors quoted that may increase the degree of inherent risk in insurance business, include:

– complexity of products . . .
– uncertainty of judgements . . .
– the security of investments . . .
– complex reinsurance contracts . . .
– regulatory risks . . .

Surprisingly, the APB practice note provides no special considerations under SAS 500[p] in insurance companies for the recognition of internal auditing. This is a serious omission that internal auditors in insurance companies and the Financial Services Authority should correct. Other regulators should always consider special needs for SAS 500 when addressing guidance for external auditors.

Risks and key controls exist in all organizations. Those in insurance companies have been strongly influenced by the legal requirements of the Insurance Companies Act 1982 and its definition of *'sound and prudent management'*:

Integrity and skill
due care and professional skill

Direction and management
fit and proper persons

Sound and prudent mannner
adequate accounting, records and control
in the interests of policyholders
supervision of subsidiaries.

These management requirements have received constant monitoring by insurance regulatory staff, boards, and auditors over many years. They relate very

---

[o] Practice Note 20: *The Audit of Insurers in the United Kingdom* (1999), The Auditing Practices Board, London, England.
[p] Statement of Auditing Standards (SAS) 500 – *Considering the Work of Internal Audit* (1996), APB (Auditing Practices Board), London, England.

closely to the principles of risk management, control and governance developed over recent years for all listed companies. All internal auditors should understand how each relates to the other and their own roles and audit planning.

All auditors in their audit planning processes will use risk management techniques to review key controls. Standards[q] for the professional practice of internal auditing have included guidelines for risk assessment in the audit planning process since the early 1980s, *'Risk assessment is crucial to the development of effective audit work schedules. The risk assessment process includes identification of auditable activities, identification of relevant risk factors, and an assessment of their relative significance.'* This requirement received a public profile in North America with the publication of an integrated model for control in organizations, recommended by a committee of professional institutions – COSO (1992),[r] established following publication of the US Foreign Corrupt Practices Act 1987.

The COSO model has revolutionized the way organizations, regulators and auditors look at the control environment. It identifies six key interrelated factors for control – control environment, risk assessment, control activities, monitoring, information systems and communication. Control environment is described as:

> A commitment by directors, management and employees to competence and integrity and the development of an appropriate culture to support these principles.
>
> Communication of appropriate agreed standards of business behaviour and control consciousness to managers and employees (e.g. through written codes of conduct, formal standards of discipline, performance appraisal).
>
> An appropriate organizational structure within which business can be planned, executed, controlled and monitored to achieve the company's objectives.
>
> Allocation of sufficient time and resources by the board, senior management and the company to internal control and risk management issues.
>
> The creation of an environment that promotes learning within the company on risk and control issues, including the provision of relevant training.
>
> Appropriate delegation of authority, with accountability, which has regard to acceptable levels of risk.
>
> A professional approach to the public reporting of matters related to internal control.

Cadbury (1992)[s] studied the financial aspects of corporate governance and recommended a code of best practice for directors, audit committees for all listed companies and board reports on internal control: Rutteman (1994)[t] narrowed internal control to internal financial control, defining this for review and reporting purposes, and providing guidance on how its effectiveness can be measured: Hampel (1998)[u] developed the Cadbury and Rutteman findings into principles of corporate governance, widening the definition of internal control to include

---

[q] *Standards for the Professional Practice of Internal Auditing* (1998), The IIA (first published 1978)
[r] *Internal Control – Integrated Framework* (1992), Committee of Sponsoring Organizations of the Treadway Commission, USA. www.coso.org.
[s] *The Financial Aspects of Corporate Governance* (1992), Gee & Co Ltd, London, England.
[t] *Guidance for Directors on Internal Control* (1994), ICAEW, London, England.
[u] *Report from the Committee on Corporate Governance* (1998), Gee Publishing Ltd, London, England.

operational and compliance controls and risk management. Many organizations not listed on the London Stock Exchange and in the public and voluntary sectors have now also adopted the principles of corporate governance recommended by Cadbury and Hampel.

The London Stock Exchange (1998)[v] accepted Hampel's recommendations and in July 1998 published a Combined Code of Best Practice for Corporate Governance, which it expects listed companies to comply with, and disclose a statement to that effect, in their annual reports published after 31 December 1998. That statement has to include a declaration that the board maintains a sound system of internal control (in its widest sense), and has reviewed its state; also, if it does not have an internal audit function it should regularly review the need to have one.

Turner (1999)[w] studied the Hampel report and combined code, redefining the characteristics of internal control and their link to business risk. His working party claims '. . . *internal controls as one of the primary elements in the management of risk used by a board to achieve the company's objectives'*. It has sought to develop guidance that '. . . *identifies sound business practice, linking control with risk management. . . '*. That guidance includes reference into the criteria recommended in the 1992 COSO model. There can be no doubt that all organizations adopting the Hampel corporate governance principles will be influenced by Turner's recommendations.

Underlying the recommended reviews of a widely defined internal control is a need for all organizations to continually review both control and monitoring activities across all their supply chains. Surprisingly, the implications of control over supply chains external to an organization have received little attention in the reports by Cadbury, Hampel, Rutteman or Turner. Yet their can be few organizations now that are not dependent on external supply chains with links into customers, suppliers, contractors, alliances, associates, joint ventures, etc. Control across external supply chains is as important as internal control and should receive board, management and audit attention.

It is just as important to review the quality of established internal audit functions annually as to review the need to have such a service. In my experience, and that of current researchers, too few organizations have a continuous quality assurance review of their existing internal audit functions. True, the new role of audit committees in organizations now provides a continuous monitoring of internal audit plans and activities. But, quality assurance goes much deeper than this. Designing quality into internal audit structures and processes requires internal auditors to be committed to formal processes and a new culture of professionalism and continuous improvement. That new culture must embrace the principles of quality management. In my book with Chambers[x] (1998) I quote these principles as:

> Many internal audit providers use the quality principles of customer focus, management leadership, teamwork, analytical approach and continuous improvement – to market their

---

[v] *Principles of Good Governance and Code of Best Practice* (The Combined Code) (1998), London Stock Exchange, London, England.
[w] *Internal Control – Guidance for Directors on the Combined Code* (1999), ICAEW, London, England.
[x] *Leading Edge Internal Auditing* (1998), J. Ridley and A.D. Chambers, ICSA Publishing Ltd, London, England.

internal auditing products and services. Some link these principles into other consultancy products and services associated with control, risk and governance.

Boards and management have always assessed risk in their decision-making processes. Risk managers and assessors, both internal and external, have developed and provide professional services to organizations in these decision-making processes. Risk has always been a key factor in the insurance industry, for both the providers of insurance and those who insure. What is now new is the focus on risk in the corporate governance debate. The new integration of risk management, control and governance will change the risk management process in many organizations. New processes are already being created with a new 'risk' language, for boards, management and auditors. It is important that all in the same organization speak a common risk language and use similar risk management processes.

There is now ample evidence to show that many organizations have implemented management control self-assessment programmes as part of their reviews of control. An industry of consultants now provides such services to many organizations. Internal auditors will have to take the power of risk assessment to their elbows, if they are to meet the needs of their organizations. Not all internal auditors have addressed this issue in their service strategies. They will have to do so in the future.

Leech's[y] CARD® *Global Best Practices Scorecard* (1999) includes 20 items for scoring. Check your own scores for the following items related to the above imperatives.

> Use of an entity-wide control and risk management information system with input from work units and all assurance personnel.

> IA service offerings include training, facilitation, control design consulting, direct report audits, fraud vulnerability assessments quality assurance reviews and maintenance of a risk status database.

> IA work is fully integrated with other assurance activities, including external audit, quality, safety, environment, security, risk and insurance, etc.

Kubitscheck[z] (1999) provides an excellent guide to the links between control and risk assessment in an insurance company, '*In my approach, I have sold the "concept of control" as "best management practice" while stressing that controls are not obstacles but ways in which we manage "business risks" to ensure the achievement of "business objectives"'*. Her perception is that financial service organizations have, by and large, been playing the catch-up game in the corporate governance arena. She identifies '. . . *four main driving forces of change over the last two decades*':

---

[y] Details from CARD® published with permission from CARD® decisions Inc., Mississauga, Ontario, Canada, 1999. Visit its website http://www.carddecisions.com.
[z] *Control Self-Assessment* (1999), K. Wade and A. Wynne (Chapter by V. Kubitscheck – CSA in a Financial Services Organizations), John Wiley & Sons, London, England.

- New consumer behaviour
- Technology
- Competition and globalization
- Regulatory and statutory requirements.

Her programme of control and risk self-assessment trains internal auditors as risk facilitators working with appointed divisional or business risk coordinators.

In recent years a growing number of universities worldwide have introduced master's level teaching and learning programmes in corporate governance. This knowledge development has been influenced by the number of national and international studies into corporate governance that have created concepts and theory, leading to principles and recommended practices – inviting critical appraisal. It has also been stimulated by student demands at undergraduate and graduate levels to research corporate governance subjects. Many of the students on these courses are at the leading edge of their professions and are senior managers in their organizations.

Some professional institutes, particularly accounting and internal auditing, are now also requiring such knowledge in their professional examinations and members' continuing development programmes. Other professions are also following suit, including those for managers, company secretaries and lawyers. These influences will continue to grow stronger as the need for good corporate governance increases and its practices evolve across all sectors.

In a recent academic development in London,[aa] the Institute of Chartered Secretaries (ICSA) has collaborated with the London South Bank Business School to validate a new MSc/PGDip Corporate Governance, to be taught full or part time. Entrance requirements are a good first degree or equivalent, with a conversion programme for those without relevant qualifications. Graduation provides the student with exemption from ICSA professional examinations. The skill matrix in this programme covers:

Written communication	Team working
Oral presentation	Planning and organization
Information technology	Researching
Analytical and problem solving	Self-directed study

Knowledge studied includes accounting, auditing, administration, management, finance, law and corporate governance.

Risk management, control and governance across an organization's external supply chains, from supplier to the organization and from the organization to the customer, has already been discussed as a complex issue. This issue has too little coverage in most internal auditing textbooks. Turnbull (1999) uses the term 'internal control' throughout its guidance for directors. External control of suppliers by an organization is just as important and is too often overlooked by management and auditors.

[aa] MSc/PGDip Corporate Governance, South Bank Business School. For further details contact Course Enquiries, London South Bank University, London SE1 0AA, tel: 0171 815 8158, fax: 0171 815 6031, email: registry@sbu.ac.uk

Article:
Weak Links In The Supply Chain[9] (2000)

There can be few in the UK, in or outside internal auditing, that were not impacted by the petrol flow crisis during September this year. There will be many who were not aware of the high risk of such just-in-time (JIT) supply chains in a civilized and highly developed society – politicians, directors, managers, internal auditors and customers. JIT in supply chains can bring significant economic and quality benefits to organizations and stakeholders. It can also be complex, not easy to control and can be the weakest link.

> *'Today and tomorrow's internal auditors must also decorate their risk assessment, audit planning, working papers and audit reports with the many external supply chains in every audit.'*

In October 1999, I wrote in *Internal Auditing* my concerns that the Turnbull report of that year did not comment on the importance of management's control across supply chains. Turnbull uses the accounting term 'internal control' with a focus on the control environment within the organization. There is little or no reference to management's responsibility for ensuring reasonable control across those parts of supply chains external to the organization.

The term 'internal control' is also used by The IIA in its standards and statements. Though in 1983, revisions to the standards placed all variants of the term 'control' into the one definition of:

> Any action taken by management to enhance the likelihood that established objectives and goals will be achieved. Management plans, organizes and directs the performance of sufficient actions to provide reasonable assurance that objectives and goals will be achieved. Thus, control is the result of proper planning, organizing and directing by management. **The IIA Standard 300.06**.

I am pleased to see that in The IIA new definition of internal auditing only the term 'control' is used. It is a pity that the standard definition does not include a reference in its control definition to '. . . *within the organization and across all its external supply chains* . . .'

Control across supply chains is not a new concept. Establishing control over contractors and suppliers has always been fundamental to the direction and management of procurement. Over the years the extent of that control has increased significantly with cost, ownership, quality, technology, environmental, health and safety and conduct requirements. These are familiar control issues for many internal auditors involved in contract audit. There has also been a significant growth of JIT, outsourcing and use of joint venture partnerships for procurement of services and manufacturing. This has increased the importance in risk assessment and control of all external supply chains – primary and secondary (your suppliers' external supply chains). Yet little has been written so far about the auditing implications for internal auditors.

The OECD (2000)[bb] in published guidelines for multinationals includes as one of its general policies: *'Encourage where practicable, business partners, including suppliers and sub-contractors, to apply principles of corporate conduct compatible with the Guidelines.'* This policy clearly recognizes responsibility for the application of corporate governance principles across external supply chains and the importance of using organization rules to improve relationships in supply chains. In some organizations this is already part of the procurement and control agenda. Is it in yours?

Chambers and Rand (1997)[cc] address the implications of JIT for internal auditors: *'Auditors will need to coordinate their approach to operational reviews of JIT systems so as to take into account such diverse aspects as product planning, cost accounting, process design, related information flows, quality issues and relationships with suppliers.'* They list useful actions, from understanding the cultural change to broader control implications and relationships with suppliers.

If nothing else, the petrol crisis this year should have brought home to all internal auditors the importance of addressing JIT and supply chain theory in their risk assessment and auditing processes. Hopefully, gone are the days when internal auditors only matched invoices to purchase orders and receipt notes – though this is still important!

Today and tomorrow's internal auditors must also decorate their risk assessment, audit planning, working papers and audit reports with the many external supply chains in every audit.

GOVERNANCE 2001 TO 2002

Ruud and Bodenmann (2001) designed an interesting model of internal auditing in an organizational governance framework, which placed internal auditing at the heart of governance (see Figure 5.4).

In *Research Opportunities in Internal Auditing*, Chapter 3, T. Flemming Ruud discusses the model (Figure 5.4) as Exhibit 3-1:

As Exhibit 3-1 shows, based on the strategic direction formulated by the top management and the board of directors, the organization develops specific objectives and goals attempting to turn the broad direction into operating, process-oriented, value-creating measures. To ensure these transformation processes, a thorough understanding of the risk threatening the whole organization or elements thereof is needed. Further, different control measures with indicators and signals are installed to measure specific performance, indicate necessary correction, and provide feedback to the operating management as well as to the top management and the board in aggregated form. The controller reports on process performance, the external auditors examine the financial accounting, and the audit committee engages in assuring the provision and reporting of internal and external information. Finally, the organization furnishes its shareholders and stakeholders with financial and

---

[bb] *Guidelines for Multinational Companies* (2000: p. 10), Organization for Economic Cooperation and Development, Paris, France. www.oecd.org
[cc] *The Operational Auditing Handbook* (1997: pp. 450–453), Andrew Chambers and Graham Rand, John Wiley & Sons Ltd, Chichester, England.

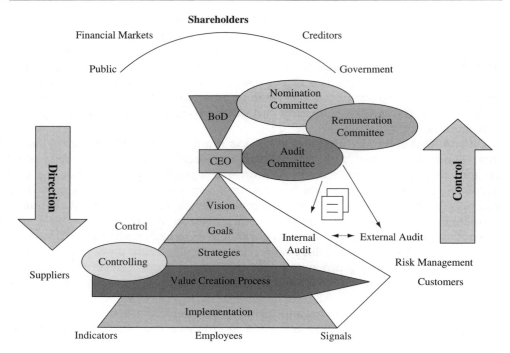

Figure 5.4   Internal Auditing At The Heart Of Governance
Source: Exhibit 3-1 in Ruud and Bodenmann (2001, p. 522). Cited in *Internal Auditing in an
Organizational Framework*, with permission from The IIA Research Foundation
accessed from The IIA website 2007 www.theiia.org

operational information for continued decision-making. Within this direction and control loop, the
internal audit function takes on important roles of organizational governance, integrates several
other governance and control aspects, and stands out as **the** most important, single mechanism for
ensuring adequate and effective organizational governance.

This model shows the internal auditing scope as much wider than just risk management
and control, bringing an organization's direction into its consideration, including vision,
goals and strategies. It also recognizes the importance of governance across an organization's supply chains and into its value-creating processes. Compare this model with the
model at Figure 5.1 discussed earlier in this chapter. Note the similarities though different
shape!

The years 2001 and 2002 saw a number of major incidents in organizations across the world
that were well communicated in the media and have been discussed, diagnosed and dissected
in many books since – in the case of Enron, also told as a film – *Enron: The Smartest Guys
In The Room*.[10] Spencer Pickett (2003),[11] Chambers (2005)[12] and Moeller (2005)[13] cover
many of these incidents very well. These incidents have impacted the way organizations
structure themselves to address corporate governance and implement its processes. They
have influenced revisions to corporate governance principles. Not only that, they have
influenced the way regulators across the world operate and the requirements they impose
on organizations: in some countries they have influenced changes to the law. They have

influenced changes to accounting standards across the world. They have influenced changes to the way external auditors operate and the standards for their work. They have had a significant influence on internal auditing standards, guidance and practices. But have they done enough? Is there more that can be done?

Article:
What Was The Point Of Cadbury – What Should Be The Point Tomorrow?[14] (2002)

It is now 10 years since the Cadbury Committee published its report on the financial aspects of corporate gover-nance. In his preface Adrian Cadbury mittee has become attention than I ever accepted the invita-chairman'.

> *'Today's media still includes too many stories of bad governance in too many organiza-tions ...'*

corporate gover-to that report Sir wrote, '... *the com-the focus of far more envisaged when I tion to become its*

His committee's report and many other subsequent reports, both national and international, have created a wealth of principles of governance. Essential guidance not only at board level, but also for all stakeholders and auditors. Essential, not only for private sector organizations, but also for organ izations in other sectors. Not just for large organizations but all, regardless of size. Good governance has always been a requirement everywhere. Since Cadbury it has been given a new focus in organizations, if not nations, communities and families.

We should continually reflect on what was the point of the Cadbury Committee report, what is its point today and try to influence what it should be tomorrow. Its terms of reference were to consider '... *issues in relation to financial reporting and accountability and to make recommendations on good practice ... '.* Its recommen-dations will not change but continue to have new meaning with wider implications for all organizations. Those recommendations and Code of Best Practice for UK listed companies, span board, audit (internal and external), control and share-holder interests and relationships. The principles, on which the Code is based, '... *openness, integrity and accountability',* have now been adopted universally by many organizations. See evidence of these in The IIA–UK & Ireland new *Code of Ethics* for its members, published in 1999. They should apply in all relationships and transactions. Look for them in all your auditing.

The IIA , from its headquarters and through its many chapters and national insti-tutes, participated in the debate and development of governance principles, both before and after Cadbury. The current worldwide focus on control risk assessment owes much of its early drive to The IIA's involvement in the Committee of Sponsor-ing Organizations (COSO), and integrated internal control model that committee developed in 1991. This model, and its definition of control elements, provide much of the framework for the Turnbull report in 1999 and today's facilitation and use of risk assessment by internal auditors.

I have written in the past about internal auditors as ambassadors of good conduct and practice. This is never truer than today and for the future. The IIA new 1999 definition of internal auditing places internal auditors at the forefront of governance practices in their organizations. Its new 2002 mandatory professional standards and recommended guidelines have written into each that the internal audit activity '. . . should contribute to the organization's governance process . . . ' and '. . . take an active role in support of the organization's ethical culture'. And internal auditors should have 'competence and the capacity to appeal to the enterprise's leaders, managers, and other employees to comply with legal, ethical, and societal responsibilities of the organization'. Are these statements written into your own internal auditing charters and terms of reference of your audit committees? Do all your internal auditors match this level of competence? If not, what was the point of Cadbury?

At a presentation I gave last year to a group of internal audit managers from across all sectors, I asked if their audit committees reviewed and monitored their organization's ethical culture. Few knew if they did and even fewer knew if this was a requirement written into the committee's terms of reference. During some recent research I sought examples in literature of audit committee terms of reference. None included responsibility for monitoring all aspects of governance in the organization, at all levels and across all supply chains. What was the point of Cadbury?

Even though good levels of control are now more frequently required and reported by regulators, boards, management and audit, there are still too many control weaknesses that encourage abuse, nationally and internationally. Today's media still includes too many stories of bad governance in too many organizations – public, private and voluntary. Research shows there is still some way to go for all listed companies to fully comply with governance codes. This situation applies to all organizations.

I believe Cadbury in the future should point to:

- Linking governance codes of practice to social and environmental practices and reporting in all organizations. This is already happening in some organizations. All should also be linked by organizations to the quality of their products and services and economic performance. This is rarely seen today in any published annual reports.
- Audit committees and internal auditing required by their terms of reference to monitor governance practices at board level. This may be happening in some organizations but has little visibility.
- Audit committees and internal auditing monitoring control across all their organization's supply chains and associated business partners, not just internally within their organization. Turnbull should have dropped the use of 'internal' – so should all regulators, boards, management and auditors.
- Audit committees required to report on their activities in their organization's published annual reports. Though recommended by various commissions and

professional bodies for some time, this is not practised at present. It is long overdue.

- Internal auditing including strategy in all its '. . . *assurance and consulting activities'*. This goes beyond the risk assessment process and control criteria to the direction of the organization, its visions and aims. The new IIA standards address this in part with the mandatory requirement that internal auditors should evaluate and improve the process through which *'values and goals are established and communicated . . . '* in their organizations. This is probably the most controversial and difficult step for all today and tomorrow's internal auditors to make.

CUTTING EDGE INTERNAL AUDITING KNOWS HOW TO GOVERN WELL – TODAY AND IN THE FUTURE

Tricker (1994)[15] researched corporate governance practices internationally and wrote:

> The classic paradigm of the corporation, as we have seen throughout our study, is rooted in the power of ownership: he who owns the shares owns the overall right to govern the company. Essentially this is based on an ideological and socio-political view of society. It supports a specific conception of the place of and the relationship between individual, the enterprise and the state. But such belief systems vary around the world and, indeed, can change over time in a given culture.
>
> Despite our study of the differences between corporate governance practices around the world, the real surprise is that, given the widely divergent ideological, political and cultural distinctions even between industrialised societies, the corporate concept has become so widespread.

It is clearly evident today, from government and professional institute statements, academic research, consultant surveys, and books written about corporate governance, that its practices vary in industry sectors and around the world. Few countries, managers, or even internal auditors, can now ignore this fact. In a world that is flatter and migration of trade and populations is greater; most communications are global; supply chains are international networks; and, customers have more choice and power. Although accounting, reporting and auditing standards are now international they can still be interpreted in a variety of ways by countries, influenced by culture, politics and economics.

If governance in an organization is defined as direction and control then to be at the cutting edge today internal auditing must be involved with both: either independently or in partnership with management, serving the owners of an organization, its 'directors' and management. In many respects this is what is taking place in the United Kingdom today and in many countries across the world. This is recommended in The IIA *International Professional Practices Framework*, both directly and implied:

2130 – Governance

The internal audit activity should assess and make appropriate recommendations for improving the governance process in its accomplishment of the following objectives:

- Promoting appropriate ethics and values within the organization.
- Ensuring effective organizational performance management and accountability.

- Effectively communicating risk and control information to appropriate areas of the organization.
- Effectively coordinating the activities of and communicating information among the board, external and internal auditors and management.

Also, more regulators today are requiring internal auditing to be established to meet external standards for the protection of organization owners and other stakeholders with an interest in/claim on an organization. This requirement is not yet by all regulators but it is moving that way, albeit slowly in some sectors. It will draw internal auditing hats into the ownership and direction an organization takes, through involvement in all of the following governance actions:

1. Structure
2. Strategies
3. Behaviour
4. Responsibilities
5. Policies
6. Objectives
7. Risk assessment/response/management
8. Processes – internal and across external supply chains
9. Information and communication
10. Security
11. Performance
12. Feedback
13. Monitoring
14. Developments
15. Change
16. Financial and operating reporting – both internal and external.

This level of internal auditing activity involvement is happening in many organizations today. It will develop in many others tomorrow.

Today there should be no doubt in any regulator's, owner's, director's or manager's mind that internal auditing is involved in the review of control. Many may even see internal auditing as a control, although internal auditors may not view it that way. One of the more recent statements on control came from the Flint (2005)[16] review of the Turnbull (1999) report (although disappointingly for me the statement still uses the word 'internal'):

Elements of a Sound System of Internal Control

19. An internal control system encompasses the policies, processes, tasks, behaviours and other aspects of a company, that taken together:

   - facilitate its effective and efficient operation by enabling it to respond appropriately to significant business, operational, financial, compliance and other risks to achieving the company's objectives. This includes the safeguarding of assets from inappropriate use or from loss and fraud and ensuring that liabilities are identified and managed;
   - help to ensure the quality of internal and external reporting. This requires the maintenance of proper records and processes that generate a flow of timely, relevant and reliable information from within and outside the organization;

- help to ensure compliance with applicable laws and regulations, and also with internal policies with respect to the conduct of the business.

20. A company's system of internal control will reflect its control environment which encompasses its organizational structure. The system will include:

- control activities;
- information and communication processes; and
- processes for monitoring the continuing effectiveness of the system of internal control.

21. The system of internal control should:

- be embedded in the operations of the company and form part of its culture;
- be capable of responding quickly to evolving risks to the business arising from factors within the company and to changes in the business environment; and
- include procedures for reporting immediately to appropriate levels of management any significant control failings or weaknesses that are identified together with details of corrective action being taken.

22. A sound system of internal control reduces, but cannot eliminate, the possibility of poor judgement in decision-making; human error; control processes being deliberately circumvented by employees and others; management overriding controls; and the occurrence of unforeseeable circumstances.

23. A sound system of internal control therefore provides reasonable, but not absolute, assurance that a company will not be hindered in achieving its business objectives, or in the orderly and legitimate conduct of its business, by circumstances which may reasonably be foreseen. A system of internal control cannot, however, provide protection with certainty against a company failing to meet its business objectives or all material errors, losses, fraud, or breaches of laws or regulations.

For 'company' read 'organization', because the above applies to all organizations. Check the five control components in the COSO (1992) integrated control – Control Environment, Risk Assessment, Control Activities, Monitoring, Information and Communications – with the Flint (2005) components. Yes, they are all there in 20 and 21.

Now, check my cycle of 16 governance actions above with the Flint (2005) components of internal control. Note how they are reflected in the components – are they all there? They should be. What about strategies, responsibilities and policies – are these just control activities or should they be given more prominence? What about developments and change? Are these reflected in the first bullet point in 19 and 'unforeseeable circumstances' in 22, or should they not also be given more prominence? It is in developments and change that many weaknesses in control occur. These are good exercises to test the breadth and depth of governance in any organization.

Both the IIA–UK & Ireland and The IIA have published excellent material on risk management, control and governance guidance for internal auditors and management. Details of this guidance are available to download on each of their websites and this will continue to grow. These issues and processes are also examined in their diploma and certification programmes. Internal auditors at the cutting edge of their activities must be experts in risk assessment and the use of risk in their audit planning and reviews. Risk-based internal auditing is not new but as a concept it has recently evolved as a new approach to reviewing risk management in an organization and using the results in audit planning. The IIA–UK & Ireland (2003)[17] explains this as:

Internal auditors might say that they have always focused their efforts on the riskier areas of the organization. However, this approach has historically been directed by internal audit's own assessment of risk. The key distinction with RBIA is that the focus should be to understand and analyse management's assessment of risk and to base audit efforts around that process.

The objective of RBIA is to provide independent assurance to the board that:

- The risk management processes which management has put in place within the organization (covering all risk management processes at corporate, divisional, unit, business process level, etc.) are operating as intended.
- These risk management processes are of sound design.
- The responses which management has made to risks which they wish to treat are both adequate and effective in reducing those risks to a level acceptable to the board.
- And a sound framework of controls is in place to sufficiently mitigate those risks which management wishes to treat.

This approach to risk management is set out in The IIA *International Standards*. Supporting the standards are guidelines[18] stating that the five key objectives of a risk management process are:

1. Risks arising from business strategies and activities are identified and prioritized.
2. Management and the board have determined the level of risks acceptable to the organization, including the acceptance of risks designed to accomplish the organization's strategic plans.
3. Risk mitigation activities are designed and implemented to reduce, or otherwise manage, risks at all levels that were determined to be acceptable to management and the board.
4. Ongoing monitoring activities are conducted to periodically reassess risk and the effectiveness of controls to manage risk.
5. The board and management receive periodic reports of the results of the risk management processes. The corporate governance processes of the organization should provide periodic communication of risks, risk strategies, and controls to stakeholders.

Business strategies in risk management are taken up by COSO (2004)[19] with its Enterprise Risk Management (ERM) model (see Figure 5.5).

This model is based on its 1992 integrated internal control framework, widening risk assessment to risk response, and adding the elements 'objective setting' and 'event identification'. What is more important, it demonstrates the importance of each in the strategic, operations, reporting and compliance decision-making processes. It also demonstrates the importance of all of the elements and processes across the whole enterprise (entity-level), division, business unit and subsidiary. Using the description of each of the elements in the model is a good test for risk management and control in any organization. I still have concerns that the model is too internally focused with no profile for supply chains and other associations/collaborations outside the organization. See Figure 5.6 for the links between the 1991 COSO exposure draft, COSO integrated internal control framework 1992 and the ERM framework.

Cutting edge internal auditors today understand and research the above descriptions of RBIA, risk management objectives, control activities and ERM. They use these not only to evaluate and report on risk management processes, but also to increase the number, sizes

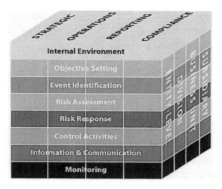

Figure 5.5   Enterprise Risk Management (ERM) Model
Source: COSO (2004)

Internal Control – Integrated Framework components		ERM components 2004
Exposure Draft 1991	Final Report 1992	
1. Integrity, Ethical Values and Competence 2. Control environment	1. Control environment	1. Internal environment
3. Objectives		2. Objective setting
4. Risk assessment 5. Managing change	2. Risk assessment	3. Risk assessment 4. Risk response 5. Event identification
6. Control procedures	3. Control activities	6. Control activities
7. Information systems 8. Communication	4. Information 5. Communication	7. Information 8. Communication
9. Monitoring	6. Monitoring	9. Monitoring

Figure 5.6   Internal Control And Enterprise Risk Management Components
Source: Committee of Sponsoring Organizations (COSO) (1991/1992/2004)

and colours of hats they wear in their organizations. Tomorrow they will need to become more expert in all of these if they are to be world-class and world-leaders in their assurance and consulting roles.

CIMA/IFAC (2004)[20] published a joint research report taking all the concepts of governance and applies these to compliance and performance. This report adopts a definition of enterprise governance as:

> The set of responsibilities and practices exercised by the board and executive management, with the goal of providing strategic direction, ensuring that objectives are achieved, ascertaining that risks are managed appropriately and verifying that the organization's resources are used responsibly.
> (Information Systems Audit and Control Foundation, 2001)

CIMA/IFAC see this as a holistic definition of internal auditing:'. . . *reflecting the dual role of the board of the directors in both monitoring and strategy, and acknowledges the inherent short and long term tensions between governance and value creation.*' In its framework for enterprise governance it embraces both conformance and performance. The importance of this research is its focus on governance as both a model for direction and control leading to compliance and direction and control leading to performance and value creation. Principle findings from the report's case studies shows '. . . *four key corporate governance issues that underpinned both success and failure'*. These are:

- culture and tone at the top;
- the chief executive;
- the board of directors;
- internal controls.

Note the relationships between these key issues and my cycle of 16 governance actions, the Flint (2005) elements of internal control and the COSO (2004) elements in its ERM model. There can be few professional bodies that have not examined the impact of these issues and processes on their members and the services they provide. Almost all major professional accounting firms have researched and published on these issues and processes over recent years. Many coordinating organizations now exist to address these governance processes and issues at national, European and international level. Material from these organizations is available and should be on every internal auditor's bookshelf. A good test of cutting edge internal auditing status is to check whether this is so!

There can be few governments worldwide that have not addressed risk management, control and governance issues and processes in their public and private sectors during recent years: there can be few regulators that have not done so also. The OECD (2004)[21] revised its 1999 principles and in the Foreword stated:

Policy makers are now more aware of the contribution good corporate governance makes to financial market stability, investment and economic growth. Companies better understand how good corporate governance contributes to their competitiveness. Investors – especially collective investment institutions and pension funds acting in a fiduciary capacity – realize they have a role to play in ensuring good corporate governance practices, thereby underpinning the value of their investments. In today's economies, interest in corporate governance goes far beyond that of shareholders in the performance of individual companies. As companies play a pivotal role in our economies and we rely increasingly on private sector institutions to manage personal savings and secure retirement incomes, good corporate governance is important to broad and growing segments of the population.

In the revised version of its principles of corporate governance the OECD use the word 'good' 35 times. It uses the following words in the Cadbury corporate governance principles:

Integrity (or conduct) is used 25 times
Openness (or transparency, disclosure) is used 74 times
Accountability (or responsibility/ies) is used 53 times.

This demonstrates the strong links between all corporate governance statements. Other words used in the OECD principles associated with the above are risk (27 times), control (60 times) and audit (76 times). This analysis demonstrates how important all these words are to the theme of the OECD Foreword: *'Policy makers are now more aware of the contribution good corporate governance makes to financial market stability, investment and economic growth.'* Interestingly the words 'evil' or 'bad' are not in the OECD statement, and the word 'poor' appears only twice.

A good test for internal audit activities is to search for how many times all these words appear in their organization's governance policy statements, procedures and reports, particularly evil, bad or poor. The results could point the way to possible cutting edge changes, in both your organization and its internal auditing.

Although written for companies, the OECD revised principles can be applied and practised across all sectors. In the United Kingdom corporate governance principles and practices have been published for all parts of the public sector, voluntary (third[22]) sector and pension funds. Currently these are:

- *Holding to Account* (2001) – The Review of Audit and Accountability for Central Government, Lord Sharman of Redlynch. HM Treasury, London England.
- *Good Governance Standards for Public Services* (2004) – Sir Alan Langlands, Independent Commission on Good Governance in Public Services (established by the Chartered Institute of Public Finance and Accountancy (CIPFA) and the Office for Public Management (OPM) with funding by the Joseph Rowntree Foundation). CIPFA, London, England.
- *Corporate Governance in Central Government Departments: Code of Good Practice* (2005) – A review by Professor Sir Andrew Likierman. HM Treasury, London, England.
- *Pension Scheme Governance – Fit for the 21st Century?* (2005) – National Association of Pension Funds (NAPF) Discussion Paper. London, England.
- *Good Governance: A Code for the Voluntary and Community Sector* (2005) – Association of Chief Executives of Voluntary Organizations (ACEVO), Institute of Chartered Secretaries and Administrators (ICSA) and National Council for Voluntary Organizations (NCVO). London, England.
- *Delivering Good Governance in Local Government* (2007) – Chartered Institute of Public Finance and Accountancy (CIPFA) and the Society of Local Authority Chief Executives and Senior Managers (SOLACE). London, England.

All the above can be analysed in the same way as the OECD principles and show strong links into the Cadbury (1992) three principles and Lord Nolan's (1995) seven principles of public life, mentioned earlier. All the above see corporate governance from the top of the organization. Lord Sharman gives the most profile to internal auditing:

> Another key element of control is internal audit. Over the years, internal audit in central government has tended to be very broad-based. This has meant that it has covered all operational aspects of a department and not just financial control. Evidence suggests that there has now been a shift back towards internal audit playing a greater role in looking at financial systems. All central government bodies should have access to well-resourced and independent internal audit, reporting to an audit committee.

Was this cutting edge in internal audit in the public sector in 2001? Sir Alan Langlands and Professor Sir Andrew Likierman mention internal audit in its assurance role only, a hint of the black hat[23] perhaps. NCVO does mention internal audit but NAPF does not. Internal auditing should have been in all these statements in a much more cutting edge role. Both The IIA–UK & Ireland (2003)[24] and The IIA Inc. (2006)[25] see such roles and more positive hats for internal auditing in practice.

The IIA–UK propose a 'framework' of corporate governance embedded at all levels in an organization. In this framework it highlights ' . . . *the key roles and responsibilities of its most important parts – the main board of directors, the internal audit function, external auditors and the audit committee'.* In describing what makes a good head of internal audit it lists a combination of the following knowledge, skills and attributes:

- Excellent communication skills. The ability to constructively challenge management, clearly explain and identify findings and persuade management to take action.
- Good interpersonal skills. The ability to work confidently with both the board and management to command their respect.
- Sound judgement and commercial awareness.
- An understanding of the principles and application of good corporate governance, risk management and control processes and procedures.
- The ability to act independently with an objective frame of mind.
- The ability to lead, motivate, manage and develop teams.
- The ability to motivate change programmes and act as a catalyst for organizational change.
- Practical experience of working in internal audit.
- An appropriate professional qualification, such as the Institute of Internal Auditors' MIIA Qualification [now called its Advanced Diploma].

Not mentioned is the ability to recognize evil! What is cutting edge in the description is the ability to motivate change programmes and act as a catalyst for organizational change. Thereby lies innovation and creativity.

The IIA in its overview of organizational governance discusses the black hat role and then, secondly, *'. . . they act as catalysts for change, advising or advocating improvements to enhance the organization's governance structure and practices.'* Possible next steps for the internal auditor to be innovative in an organization's governance processes are seen as *[my comments in brackets]*:

1. Review all the relevant internal and external audit policies, codes, and charter provisions, pertaining to organizational governance. *[Look for the key words and phases about governance, including good and evil.]*
2. Discuss organizational governance with executive management or members of the board. The objectives of these discussions is to ensure that internal auditors have a clear understanding of the governance structure and processes from the perspective of those responsible for them, as well as the maturity of these processes. *[In these discussions relate direction and control in the organization to the achievement of its vision, mission and key objections.]*
3. Discuss options for expanding the role of internal auditors in organizational governance with the board chair, board committee chairs, and executive managers. These discussions could involve explaining the potential actions internal auditors could take and the resources required, as well as the possibility of an assurance gap between the board's assurance requirements and the organization's practices, if internal auditors did not assist in this area. Ensure the internal audit charter is consistent with the expanded role being considered. *[Consider providing education programmes on governance for all board, management and employee training programmes.]*
4. Discuss organizational governance topics with other key stakeholders including external auditors and employees of the organization's departments such as legal, public affairs corporate secretary office, compliance and regulatory affairs. During these discussions, explore their current and future activities as well as how an expanded internal audit role could coordinate with their activities. *[This should also be one of every internal audit engagement's objectives, not only in the organization, but also across all its external relationships.]*
5. Develop a broad framework of the organization's governance structure by identifying potential areas of weakness and concern. *[A real opportunity to be creative in thinking and design.]*

6. Draft a multi-year plan to methodically develop the internal audit role in organization governance areas. [*Another opportunity to be creative.*]
7. Perform a pilot audit in one of the areas noted above. Select a single, well-defined, manageable topic and assess the adequacy of the design and execution of the activities related to the topic. Performing a pilot audit will allow the internal auditor a chance to gauge the organization's response to his or her expanded role and learn how to coordinate more effectively with other stakeholders. [*This should only be the start. It should lead the internal auditor along many paths wearing many hats.*]

The CIPFA/SOLACE (2007) guidance adapts the six core principles developed by Sir Alan Langlands (2004), with '*The principle of leadership has been expanded to emphasize the role of authorities in "leading" their communities . . .*' Also, '*. . . the six core principles have been developed to take a greater account of the political regime in which local authorities operate*'. Detailed guidance is given to local authorities on how to ask and seek answers to questions in the following categories of good governance:

1. Good governance means focusing on the purpose of the authority and on outcomes for the community and creating and implementing a vision for the local area.
2. Good governance means members and officers working together to achieve a common purpose with clearly defined functions and roles.
3. Good governance means promoting values for the authority and demonstrating the values of good governance through upholding high standards of conduct and behaviour.
4. Good governance means taking informed and transparent decisions which are subject to effective scrutiny and managing risk.
5. Good governance means developing the capacity and capability of members and officers to be effective.
6. Good governance means engaging with local people and other stakeholders to ensure robust public accountability.

CIPFA/SOLACE take a wide view of governance for local authorities, not just as compliance but also as a 'best value' process with many benefits for the community. Compare the above categories with my Figure 5.1. Note the similarities.

The importance of my Cutting Edge Internal Auditing Model had not waned over this period. Today and tomorrow the interactions of each part of the framework are still key to managing internal auditing. Some changes to the titles of each part of the framework are needed to bring it more in line with current thinking (see Figure 5.7).

The relationship between internal auditing and the audit committee is now well established in principle and practice across all sectors. Though the practice will vary across organizations, the assurance role by internal auditing as a support service to this committee is well established. Other roles such as consultancy, education and facilitation will vary more but they are developing in many organizations. There will be few audit committees in the future that will not rely on the support of an independent and professional internal auditing service: those who do not will do so at their peril!

A grey area with little or no current research is the relationship between an organization's internal auditing service and the board, including all the other committees with governance responsibilities delegated by the board, e.g. nomination, corporate governance, risk management, environmental, etc. The UK Combined Code 2003, and now 2006, recommends that all boards should self-assess their performance and report annually that they do so, or explain why not:

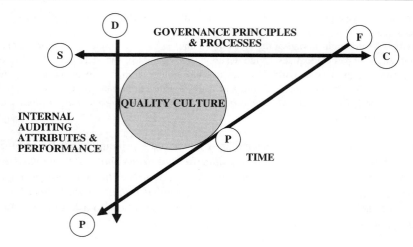

Figure 5.7   Cutting Edge Internal Auditing Model 2007
Source: J. Ridley (2007)

A.6 Performance evaluation – Main Principle
The board should undertake a formal and rigorous annual evaluation of its own performance and that of its committees and individual directors.

Internal auditing providing services direct to the board and all its committees will be at the cutting edge of its professionalism in the future. These services will be discussed in more detail in the chapter on internal auditing assisting the board.

CHAPTER SUMMARY

Governance is about directing and controlling the encouragement of good and discouragement of evil. To be cutting edge in governance principles and practices requires internal auditors to be experts in both – not just in the organizations in which they work, but also across the sectors and countries in which their organizations operate. Not just operate directly, but also through their supply chains, associations and collaborations. The world is flatter today but there are many governance barriers, hills and even mountains to cross in global governance processes. Governance is also about the achievement of all organization objectives – economic, social and environmental. A first step for creative internal auditors is to establish the corporate governance framework in their organization/s and, first, use this to explore its strengths and weaknesses through research and auditing, then use this knowledge to discuss and teach governance in all engagements, at all levels, and in all operations in their organizations.

Understanding governance serves well the following Gray and Gray (1997) five innovation motivational themes, four innovation goals and four innovation categories discussed in the Introduction, and the additions and changes made in Chapters 2 to 4:

Motivations

1. Progress within the field of professional internal auditing.
2. Increasing competition leading to pressures to reduce costs and increase efficiency.
3. New challenges, such as increasing internal control risks due to staff reductions and restructuring.
4. Opportunities to increase efficiency and quality as a result of technological advances.
5. Changes in corporate management practices and philosophies, such as Total Quality Management, re-engineering, continuous quality improvement, or related approaches.
6. **Challenges and opportunities of global issues and developments.**
7. **Social and environmental issues impacting all organizations.**
8. **Recognition that professionalism, quality and standards are essential attributes for world-class status in any internal auditing activity.**
9. **Importance of organizational governance to meet regulatory and stakeholders' needs.**

Goals

1. Improvement of the quality of internal auditing services.
2. Improve efficiency.
3. Expansion of services to increase the value-added of internal auditing.
4. Boost staff skills, performance and morale.
5. **Sell internal auditing as future focused.**

Categories

1. Changes in the way that internal auditors interact with the rest of their enterprises **and all those with a stakeholder interest.**
2. Internal restructuring and changes in the organization and management of internal auditing.
3. Creation of new audit services and methods.
4. Changes in the use of technology.
5. **Improved knowledge and skills in the teams of staff who carry out internal auditing engagements.**

Today there is a new motivation for internal auditors in the governance of organizations:

10. **A continuous search for good and evil in how organizations and all their operations are directed and controlled.**

INTERNAL AUDITING AND GOVERNANCE PRINCIPIA 1998 AND 2008

My 1998 principia for internal auditing included the following related to the governance of organizations (see Appendix A):

6. Professional internal auditors critically understand today's and tomorrow's management principles and practices.
8. Internal auditing objectivity and independence are its most important assets.
9. Coordination of all audit work in an organization strengthens its objectivity and independence.
11. Internal auditors should always be seen as control experts.
12. Planning, organizing, directing and monitoring are essential parts of all control activities.

13. Divisions of responsibilities are a key control mechanism.
14. Financial, social, quality and environmental control objectives are international issues, across all supply chains, in all sectors.
16. Creating integrated control frameworks in an organization provides an understanding of their strengths and weaknesses.
19. Internal auditing should contribute to the reliability and integrity of all management reports and statements on control.
20. Control self-assessment by managers is essential for all aspects of management and auditing.
24. Measures of internal auditing performance must be linked to its customers' and organization's objectives.

These are now changed to reflect in 2008 the importance of risk management, control and governance across all an organization's operations, both internal and external at all levels and with all stakeholders.

4. Good governance is fundamental for all management practices, in all parts of an organization, at all levels and across all its supply chains and operating relationships: this includes the principles of integrity, openness and accountability in all transactions.
5. Governance should be established as a framework of directing and controlling to encourage good performance and discourage evil in the achievement of economic, social and environmental objectives.
6. Internal auditors should be trained and experienced to be able to promote themselves as experts in the practices and coordination of risk management, control and governance processes.
7. Internal auditing performance should always be measured against the status and state of governance in an organization.
8. Internal auditing should encourage and contribute to the self-assessment of risk management, control and governance by all employees at all levels in an organization: this contribution can be by teaching the principles on which these are based.

A VISION FOR INTERNAL AUDITING AND GOVERNANCE

> **We aim to add best value to good governance**

SYNOPSES OF CASE STUDIES

Case 5.1: Internal Audit and Ethics

Synopsis

Organizations need to have a '... *culture of integrity and control, a culture that is set and led right from the very top of the organization'*. Culture needs to be clearly defined. Control is all about assigning responsibilities and accountability. Both must start from the top of an organization. Both are needed for conformance and performance if an organization is to be successful. Internal auditors should provide independent assurance that both exist, are enterprise-wide and well governed. Cutting edge internal auditing should monitor culture, risk and control through education, upholding their own high standards of control and ethics, and providing independent assurance to the audit committee.

> Contributed by Gill Bolton, a freelance consultant operating in the areas of corporate governance, risk management and internal control. She can be contacted on gillbolton@ntlworld.com

After Reading the Case Study Consider:

1. What type of culture does your organization have? Is it one of integrity and control? Is it set and led from the top of the organization?
2. Is conformance and performance linked in your organization's objectives and achievements?
3. How is *'accountability'* implemented in your organization? Is this through clearly defined responsibilities at all levels, timely reporting – both internal and external, and the monitoring of performance – both group and individual?
4. Is your internal auditing function at the cutting edge of monitoring 1, 2 and 3 above?

Case 5.2: Internal Control is Like a Well Lit Christmas Tree

Synopsis

There are four important qualities for a Christmas tree: shape, colour, recognition and a focus for celebration. All are described as qualities for good control. *'Each plays an important part in establishing the "adequate" and "reasonable" levels of control essential if "expected results" are to be achieved.'* Internal auditing should use each to develop cutting edge resources and practices for the services they provide.

> This case study is based on an article published by the author in 1994 and reproduced in *Leading Edge Internal Auditing* (1998).

After Reading the Case Study Consider:

1. Do you see shape, colour, recognition and celebration in your organization's control processes?
2. Do you keep these qualities in mind when you start every internal auditing engagement?

Case 5.3: BG Group Audit Charter

Synopsis

This Internal Auditing Charter starts with The IIA definition of internal auditing and gives a cutting edge responsibility to review the effectiveness of proposed as well as existing controls '... *encompassing the Group's governance, operations and information systems* ...'.

Governance systems are given a wide and detailed definition, covering both tangible and intangible assets. Recognition is also given for the need for each internal audit assignment to be resourced with the right levels of skills and experience – *'In some cases, this resource may be obtained from external providers or from within the business'* – an important cutting edge authority in all charters to ensure that all internal audit teams are appropriately resourced.

Contributed by Andrew Robinson, Head of Group Audit, BG Group plc and with permission from the BG Group plc

---

After Reading the Case Study Consider:

1. Does your internal auditing charter include The IIA definition of internal auditing and recognition of its International *Code of Ethics* and *Standards*?
2. What do you include in your reviews of '... *governance, operations and information systems* ...'?
3. Does your internal auditing charter state it is the responsibility of management for '... *identifying and evaluating risks and designing and implementing effective control*' and '*It has no responsibilities over the operations that it reviews*'?
4. Does your internal auditing charter authorize reviews of proposed controls?
5. Does your internal auditing charter mention controls over the safeguarding of *'intangible'*, as well as *'tangible'* assets?
6. Does your internal auditing charter mention reviewing compliance with '... *relevant legislation...*', as well as '... *policies, plans and procedures* ...'?

Case 5.4: Role of Internal Auditing in Governance

Synopsis

Internal auditing operates in two capacities – providing independent assessments and as catalysts of change. The more mature an organization's governance processes the more internal auditing can focus on the overall process. Internal auditors can '... *assist organizations better by advising the board of directors and executive management on needed improvements and changes in* [governance]*structure and design* ...'. Today's cutting edge internal auditing should be more concerned with governance frameworks, not just compliance with specific parts.

Extract with permission from *Organizational Governance: Guidance for Internal Auditors* (2006). Copyright 2004 by The Institute of Internal Auditors, Inc., 247 Maitland Avenue, Altamonte Springs, Florida 32710-4201 USA. Reprinted with permission.

After Reading the Case Study Consider:

1. Do your internal auditing services operate in the two capacities described – *'independent objective assessments'* and *'catalysts for change'*?

2. Are the qualifications of your internal auditors appropriate for both the capacities described?
3. What is your organization's governance maturity level?
4. Have you identified and assessed the effectiveness of your organization's governance?

Case 5.5: Corporate Governance and Internal Audit

Synopsis

Developing relationships between internal audit and the audit committee in the Netherlands and Europe will drive both closer together creating reporting issues in some organizations and creating cutting edge internal auditing opportunities. This will increase the need for internal auditing to emphasize its quality systems and measures. There is also some convergence between internal auditing and external auditing rules and professional standards worldwide: this will strengthen cooperation between both and each other's positions in the governance processes.

> Contributed with permission from Professor Leen Paape, PhD RA RO CIA, Program Director Internal/Operational Auditing, Erasmus School of Accounting & Assurance and Executive Director, Protiviti Independent Risk Consulting.

After Reading the Case Study Consider:

1. Is your audit committee and internal auditing being '... *driven closer together* ...' in your organization's corporate governance structure and processes?
2. Has your organization's implementation of corporate governance principles affected '... *its relationship with the external auditor and scope of services*'?
3. Has corporate governance increased the need '... *to emphasise quality systems within IA and comparable measures*'?
4. How has the international growth and status of professional internal auditing impacted the status of internal auditing in your organization?
5. Are the COSO 1992 and 2003 internal control and enterprise risk 'models' recognized, as the '... *global standard for risk and control* ...' in your organization?

Case 5.6: Providing an Effective Internal Control System – First Steps to Good Governance in Charities

Synopsis

Senior management in a charity needs to establish an effective framework of control as part of its governance process. *'The voluntary sector is not immune to poor management, fraud or simple breakdowns in controls.'* Responsibility for risk management and control should be clearly understood by all its staff and volunteers. Statements are given as to how a charity can proactively tailor risk management and control for its organization. Cutting edge internal auditing in a charity will always continuously assess its effectiveness as part of the control framework.

Contributed by Tracey Hassell, reproduced from her book *Charities Internal Controls Checklist* (2003), with permission from the publishers Plaza Publishing Limited, London, England.

After Reading the Case Study Consider:

1. How have the recommendations in this case study been impacted by the publications on corporate governance and control published since and discussed in this chapter? [In particular, the Financial Reporting Council statements Internal Control Revised Guidance for Directors on the Combined Code (2005) and The Combined Code (2006), and the ACEVO/ICSA/NCVO Good Governance: A Code for the Voluntary and Community Sector (2005).]
2. *Does the framework of internal control in your organization* '. . . ensure everyone is aware of the contribution that they personally should make to the whole process'?
3. Whether you are a charity, or not, are your internal auditing resources and practices keeping up to date and at the cutting edge of the constantly evolving issues of risk, control and governance in your organization and industrial sector?
4. Have you addressed all the statements on internal control in Figure 5.6.1, including any added or changed by you after considering question 1 above?

SELF-ASSESSMENT QUESTIONS

5.1   Create a Governance Framework For Your Own Organization

A test for expertise in management, control and governance is for an internal auditor to create a framework of how external and internal controls integrate to achieve all their organization's control objectives. Figure 5.1 provided a structure for such a framework. Each of the five elements in the framework can be researched to provide detail of their impact and influence on an organization's management and performance:

1. Societal interests and values concern ethics and public attitudes to the organization's existence and performance. Not just locally or nationally, but wider impacts an organization might have on global issues.
2. Stakeholders are all those interests, financial or otherwise, in an organization's performance. Rarely are these interests only by one type of stakeholder. More often interests are networked amongst groups of stakeholders. Some stakeholders are passive, others can be active, with strong influences on an organization's management, control and governance objectives.
3. Rules and regulations are all the directives which establish mandatory and voluntary directions for an organization's behaviour, and those who are associated with its performance. These can be international, national, local or issued by other bodies with which an organization is associated, through its operations and those participating in its performance.
4. Control concepts are the developed theory and principles underlying all control and monitoring activities.
5. External monitoring covers all the independent groups who are involved in regulation, review and investigation of an organization's activities. Some of these groups have

contractual relationships with an organization, some have legal status, some are voluntary. Many have stakeholder interests.

When you have prepared your organization's governance framework it should be evident that each of the five elements integrate into all the others. Test your framework for this integration with your internal audit team and management.

5.2   Cycle of Governance Actions in an Organization

How many of the 16 governance actions mentioned earlier in the chapter can you remember? List what you can then check your answer with the list shown. How many of these actions do you review and contribute to in your internal auditing services?

NOTES AND REFERENCES

1. Cited in *Wisdom of the Ages* (1948: p. 149), The St Catherine Press Ltd, London, England.
2. *The Practice of Management* (1955) (reprinted and reissued many times, the last in 2007), Peter F. Drucker, Butterworth-Heinemann, Oxford, England.
3. *Report of The National Commission on Fraudulent Financial Reporting* (1987):

   For purposes of this study and report, the Commission defined fraudulent financial reporting as intentional or reckless conduct, whether act or omission, that results in materially misleading financial statements. Fraudulent financial reporting can involve many factors and take many forms. It may entail gross and deliberate distortion of corporate records, such as inventory count tags, or falsified transactions, such as fictitious sales or orders. It may entail the misapplication of accounting principles. Company employees at any level may be involved, from the top to middle management to lower-level personnel.

4. *Internal Control – Integrated Control Framework* (1992), American Institute of Certified Public Accountants, New Jersey, USA.
5. 'Internal Control – What's That?', William G. Bishop III, *Internal Auditor*, June 1991 (50 years celebration issue 1941–1991), The IIA.
6. Extracted from a submission by me through the then South Bank University Research Unit to the United Kingdom Economic and Social Research Council, seeking research funding in 1995.
7. *Corporate Governance: A Framework For Public Service Bodies* (1995), CIPFA, London, England.
8. I based this article on literature research in preparation for a talk to internal auditors employed by insurance companies and related organizations. The talk was presented at a seminar on 10 September 1999, to members of the Insurance Internal Audit Group. The article was published in *Internal Control* (Issue 28, February 2000), abg Professional Information, London, England.
9. Published in *Internal Auditing* (November 2000: pp. 8/9), IIA–UK & Ireland.
10. *Enron: The Smartest Guys In The Room*, © 2005 HDNet Films, Distributed in the UK by Lions Gate Home Entertainment UK Ltd.
11. *The Internal Auditing Handbook* (2003), K.H. Spencer Pickett, John Wiley & Sons Ltd, Chichester, England.
12. *Tottel's Corporate Governance Handbook* 3rd edition (2005), Andrew D. Chambers, Tottel's Publishing, Haywards Heath, England.
13. *Brink's Modern Internal Auditing, Sixth Edition* (2005), Robert Moeller, John Wiley & Sons Ltd, Chichester, England.
14. Published in *Internal Auditing & Business Risk* (March 2002), IIA–UK & Ireland.
15. *International Corporate Governance* (1994), Robert I. Tricker, Prentice Hall, Simon & Schuster (Asia) Pte Ltd, Singapore.

16. *Internal Control: Revised Guidance For Directors On The Combined Code* (Flint Report) (2005), Financial Reporting Council, London, England.
17. *Risk Based Internal Auditing – Position Paper* (2003), The IIA-UK & Ireland.
18. Practice Advisory 2110-1(3): *Assessing the Adequacy of Risk Management Processes* (2004), The IIA.
19. *Enterprise Risk Management – Integrated Framework* (2004), Committee of Sponsoring Organizations of the Treadway Commission (COSO), USA.
20. The Professional Accountants in Business Committee (PAIB) was asked by the International Federation of Accountants (IFAC) to research internationally corporate governance success and failure in organizations. The report *Enterprise Governance – Getting the Balance Right* was published in 1994 and is available from the Chartered Institute of Management Accountants London
21. *OECD Principles of Corporate Governance* (2004 Foreword), Organization for Economic and Cooperation Development, Paris, France.
22. Since 2006 the Third Sector is now a recognized Ministry in the UK government, established in the Cabinet Office. This Ministry is responsible for developing strategic partnerships between government and voluntary organizations, including registered charities. Its recent report *The Future Role of the Third Sector in Social and Economic Regeneration: Final Report*, July 2007, sets out its ten-year plan. This Ministry works closely with the Charities Commission, regulator for registered charities. The increasing links between organizations in the Third Sector and those in government must surely bring closer together the governance guidance and requirements for the Public Sector and Charities.
23. Dr Edward de Bono's hats are discussed in Chapter 4. The black hat is described as:

    Think of a stern judge wearing black robes who comes down heavily on wrongdoers. The black hat is the caution hat. The black hat prevents us from making mistakes, doing silly things which might be illegal. The black hat is for critical judgement. The black hat points out why something cannot be done. The black hat points out why something will not be profitable.' (Cited in *Serious Creativity: Using the Power of Lateral Thinking to Create New Ideas* (1992: p. 79), Dr Edward de Bono, HarperCollins Publishers, London, England.)

24. *The Corporate Governance Framework* (2003), KPMG and The IIA–UK & Ireland.
25. *Organizational Governance: Guidance for Internal Auditors* (2006), The IIA.

6
Cutting Edge Internal Auditing Fights Crime

'History..., is indeed, little more than the register of the crimes,
follies, and misfortunes of mankind.'

Edward Gibbon 1737–94[1]

~ The Expectations Gap ~
Auditors and the detection
of Fraud !

INTERNAL AUDITING FIGHTS CRIME IN ORGANIZATIONS
PRIOR TO 1994

The IIA's position on fraud prevention, detection and investigation has been well established and clear since its first statements on professional internal auditing:

Statement of Responsibilities 1957

The overall objective of internal auditing is to assist all members of management in the effective discharge of their responsibilities . . . the attainment of this overall objective of service to management should involve such activities as:

– Ascertaining the extent to which company assets are accounted for, and safeguarded from losses of all kinds.

This was developed later into its *Standards* as:

280.01   . . . In exercising due professional care, internal auditors should be alert to the possibility of intentional wrongdoing. . . . They should also be alert to those conditions and activities where irregularities are most likely to occur. . . .

300.05   The primary objectives of control are to ensure:

.2 Compliance with . . . laws, regulations, and contracts.
.3 The safeguarding of assets.

This now reads in The IIA *International Standards*:

1210.A2   The internal auditor should have sufficient knowledge to identify the indicators of fraud but is not expected to have the expertise of a person whose primary responsibility is detecting and investigating fraud.

2110.A2   The internal audit activity should evaluate risk exposures relating to the organization's governance, operations, and information systems regarding:

– Safeguarding of assets
– Compliance with laws, regulations, and contracts.

As early as 1983 The IIA modified its 1970s *Standards* for internal auditing with its statement on *Control: Concepts and Responsibilities*. This defined the efficiency and effectiveness objectives of control more clearly for internal auditors and included the following guidance on reasonable assurance.

300 02.5   Reasonable assurance is provided when cost-effective actions are taken to restrict deviations to a tolerable level. This implies, for example, that material errors and improper or illegal acts will be prevented or detected and corrected within a timely period by employees in the normal course of performing their assigned duties. The cost–benefit relationship is considered by management during the design of systems. The potential loss associated with any exposure or risk is weighed against the cost to control it.

Whistleblowing on criminal acts has always been a source of crime detection and in some organizations encouraged/required internally through policy and codes of conduct. Whistleblowing by internal auditors outside the organization has always been a serious step to take with possible significant consequences for the internal auditor. In 1988, The IIA published a position paper[2] on whistleblowing, defining this as *'the unauthorized dissemination by internal auditors of audit results, finding, opinions, or information acquired in the course of performing their duties to anyone outside the organization or to the general public'*. At that time The IIA took the stand that its *Code of Ethics* and *Standards* provided sufficient guidance in organizations when the chief audit executive has a reporting line to the audit committee. Though it recognized that this situation may not apply to all internal audit activities and that in some US states there were whistleblowing statutes.

At The IIA's 50th anniversary Courtney M. Thompson[3] (1991) discussed this position in an article in the *Internal Auditor*, ending with:

> The fraud challenge represents opportunity for internal auditors. Proper response to the fraud challenge sells control recommendations. In the long run, proper response by the internal auditor and the organization may not only build professional credibility, but may also help organizations to sidestep dangers and significant losses. The audit department that chooses to be part of the fraud solution can look forward to continuing professional challenge.

Thompson foresaw at that time fraud risks that are with us today:

> There are additional reasons for the professional internal auditor to be thinking about fraud. The world is moving toward an increasingly computerized, global economy. Organizations will be embarking on new ventures, in new arenas, with new partners and unfamiliar customs. Opportunities for fraud increases whenever managers or auditors are out of their elements. The movement toward an increasingly computerized global economy likely will heighten exposure to fraud. In order to protect themselves organizations must be able to:
>
> Identify wrongdoing early.
> Conduct complete and thorough investigations.
> Take appropriate action based upon investigation results.
> Correct identified weaknesses.

And the roles of internal auditors in the prevention, detection and investigation of fraud as:

> Internal auditors' roles with regard to fraud might be as identifiers, investigators, resident experts, and educators. In many organizations, the internal audit function will be better suited than any other to bring fraud to the surface, conduct or participate in investigations, and raise management awareness about fraud.

He also recognized that '. . . *many internal auditors hesitate to be identified with fraud, apparently because they believe that participating in investigations will somehow damage the image and effectiveness of the internal audit department'*.

Now substitute the word 'fraud' with 'crime' and you are in a wholly new situation. Much more complex. Where does internal auditing stand on fighting crime in an organization, at strategic, risk assessment operational levels, and with assurance, consulting and teaching services? Should internal auditing fight all types of crime? The IIA has covered this issue over many years in a general way through its statements on internal auditing and fraud. But, what about all crime and crooks, (see Figure 6.1)?

My definition of 'crook' is from Chamber's Dictionary: *'a professional swindler, thief or criminal in general. . .'*. This is not meant to imply that an organization would not employ someone in the rehabilitation of persons with a criminal record. There may well be circumstances when this would be an organization's policy. My message is meant to ask the question: Would an organization contract with or employ someone knowing they had criminal intentions? This chapter considers the impact of fraud on organizations, but also argues that internal auditing should be reviewing the possibilities of all types of crime when evaluating their organization's operations. That would be cutting edge.

Would you?

Buy from a crook
Sell to a crook
Employ a crook

Knowingly ?

How do you try to stop this from happening?

Figure 6.1   Questions About Crime
Source: J. Ridley (2000)

Supporting The IIA *International Standards* are guidelines recognizing the importance of an internal audit activity having an appreciation of '... *the fundamentals of subjects such as ... commercial law...*' and '... *should have employees or use outside service providers who are qualified in disciplines such as ... law...*'.[4] In addition there are guidelines for the security and privacy of information and environmental risks.

Article:
Think Like A Criminal[5] (1994)

Preventing fraud is management's responsibility in any organization. Using an integrated con- prevent and detect important part of the manager's activities.

'The risk of fraud is always present'.

trol framework to fraud can be an internal auditor and Understanding what fraud is and how it can be carried out in any organization, at all levels, and from both inside and outside, is key to its prevention and detection. Control and governance as fraud deterrents are essential for the success of all organizations.

The risk of fraud is always present. Approaches to its investigation and disclosure vary. Almost without exception it can impact all of society and an organization's stakeholders. It can cause considerable damage, far beyond the value of its loss, leading sometimes to significant performance failures and even closure of operations, and whole businesses. In the public sector it can lead to political unrest and loss of power.

Harold Russell (1977)[a] studied fraud cases across the world and drew the following conclusions for the internal auditor:

> Fraud in the marketplace, embezzlement in positions of trust, bribery in public life, theft of securities, check kiting, illegal political donations, mail frauds, overloaded expense accounts, manipulation of payrolls, issuance of false financial statements, credit-card swindles, illegal competition, kickbacks and payoffs, bankruptcy frauds, and arson are a few of today's challenges. The outside criminal – the burglar or robber – usually visits

---

[a] *Foozles and Fraud* (1977), Harold F. Russell, The IIA.

his victim but once and leaves telltale evidence of his entry. But the inside criminal is a different story. How is he tracked down? The inside criminal may be the owner, the manager, or the lowest employee. All are in a position to steal on a continuing basis.

Here are four ways by which fraudulent activities are uncovered:

- Reduction of the resource to a noticeable level of depletion
- Accidental discovery of the fraud
- Revelation by an informer
- Diligence of an inquisitive... member of the accounting or internal audit staff who can concentrate on the problems of balances, of checks, and eliminations..., as Brad Cadmus said:

It appears that the internal auditor can make the best contribution to the control of fraud when:

- management clearly assigns the responsibility for handling cases;
- the internal audit program is designed not only for operational audits but also provides for an imaginative approach to the possibilities of controlling fraudulent activity;
- the internal auditor fully understands the legal implication of fraud;
- the auditor acquires the attitude that not every foozle is a fraud and has the keen perception of fraud when he comes in contact with it;
- the auditor gains training and experiences in interrogation of suspects;
- the audit staff recognises that recent disclosures of widespread payola have been made (whether the payola was necessary or not, a serious loss of control over substantial funds occurs when such disbursements are made from off-the-books funds and from laundered money moved from country to country without records);
- the internal auditor is assured by public accountants and outside directors that his responsibility runs to them as well as to management when fraud by top management is suspected, and;
- the auditor does not place unlimited dependence on internal control (the internal control system that can't be penetrated has not yet been invented).

Russell created a fraud checklist for internal auditors, which is as useful today as it was when first designed. See Figure 6.2.

When something does not look right, be persistent in running it down.
To obtain the best results, establish proper relationships with the people you audit.
Recognize improper actions, entries and figures when you see them.
Develop your ability to remember bits of information and, by association, place them in an overall pattern.
Dishonest people are poor liars – listen for their double-talk.
Learn to ask open-ended questions – but only the right kind.
Do not trust an informer's allegations, but never ignore them.
Be alert to the possibility of false documentation.
Do not rely on evidence that cannot be fully supported.
Make sure that audit sampling is not only scientific but also sensible.
Do not be misled by appearances.
Do not be satisfied with unreasonable answers to audit questions.
Do not ignore unrecorded funds for which the organization has a legal or moral responsibility.
Learn as much about the auditees as you possibly can.
Keep audit programmes from becoming too limited or stereotyped.

Figure 6.2   Harold Russell Fraud Checklist
Source: Foozles & Frauds (1977)

CUTTING EDGE INTERNAL AUDITING FIGHTS CRIME TODAY AND IN THE FUTURE

The fight against crime is never ending. There will always be criminals, whether by intention or accident. There will always be people who will identify weaknesses in control and use these for their own benefit and aims, of whatever nature. There will always be broken laws and innocent victims. Internal auditors can have a major role to play in fighting crime in all the services they provide and in all the hats they wear.

The IIA–UK & Ireland[6] published in 2001 its own guidance on whistleblowing, replacing guidance published in 1994. This followed the enactment of the United Kingdom *Public Interest Disclosure Act* 1998, providing qualified protection for some individuals who make external disclosures of information. It recommended that internal auditors should '. . . *use their best endeavours to ensure that the enterprise has appropriate and effective whistle-blowing policies and procedures'*. In any fight against crime in an organization it is a most important first step. This is a difficult issue and one that every cutting edge internal auditor fighting crime should address in their organization. The policy and procedures approved by top management should be clearly defined and known by all its employees. The IIA (2003)[7] includes detailed guidance on this issue supporting its *International Standards*. For any fight against crime, this is important reading and guidance for all internal auditors.

HM Treasury (2003)[8] published its guidance for 'managing the risk of fraud' in the public sector and followed this with a joint National Audit Office[9] publication in 2004 providing guidance on tackling external fraud. In both publications the word 'fight' is only used once. In the first it is a reference into the Fraud Advisory Panel Publication: *Fighting Fraud – A Guide for Small and Medium Sized Enterprises*:

> A fraud policy statement should be simple, focused and easily understood. Its contents may vary from organization to organization but you should consider including references to the organization's determination to:
>
> – take appropriate measures to deter fraud;
> – introduce/maintain necessary procedures to detect fraud;
> – investigate all instances of suspected fraud;
> – report all suspected fraud to the appropriate authorities;
> – assist the police in the investigation and prosecution of suspected fraudsters;
> – recover from fraudsters any assets wrongfully obtained;
> – encourage employees to report any suspicion of fraud.

This is advice appropriate for all organizations worldwide, in all sectors. In the second publication the use is in connection with the fight against tobacco smuggling. In both publications references are made to the roles of internal auditing in managing the risk of fraud.

In the United Kingdom The Fraud Advisory Panel has taken a lead in the fight against fraud, as is evidenced by the publication mentioned above and in its other reports and publications:

> The Fraud Advisory Panel aims to raise awareness of the immense social and economic damage caused by fraud and to help the private and public sectors, and the public at large, to fight back. The Panel works to:
>
> • originate proposals to reform the law and public policy on fraud;
> • develop proposals to enhance the investigation and prosecution of fraud;

- advise business as a whole on fraud prevention, detection and reporting;
- assist in improving fraud-related education and training in business and the professions, and among the general public;
- establish a more accurate picture of the extent, causes and nature of fraud.

Members of the Fraud Advisory Panel include representatives from the law and accountancy professions, industry associations, financial institutions, government agencies, law enforcement, regulatory authorities and academia. The Panel works to encourage a truly multidisciplinary perspective on fraud. No other organization has such a range and depth of knowledge, both of the problem and of the means to combat it.

In the Panel's 2002–03 annual review it states that not all corporate governance statements by businesses highlight the importance of their fraud prevention by mentioning their anti-fraud policy, or any programme to deter and detect fraud. In its latest review in 2007[10] it continues its fight against fraud, identifying seven steps that should be taken following a review by the UK government[11] into fraud, the first of these steps being:

> Recognize that the state has failed to protect the citizen against fraud. The low priority given to the problem leaves even serious frauds uninvestigated, victims floundering and policies uncoordinated. The Government should make fighting financial crime a criminal justice priority.

The UK government review into fraud is introduced by Lord Goldsmith, the Attorney General, with:

> The review is clear that much fraud could be avoided if consumers, businesses, and public sector bodies took elementary precautions and, in appropriate circumstances, exercised sensible scepticism about offers that were obviously too good to be true. Prevention must be the first step we take. But, however strong preventative measures are, they will be insufficient to deal with the major problems created by fraud. The Fraud Review has therefore looked at, and made recommendations on, how we measure fraud, how we record the incidence of fraud, how we use that information holistically, how we investigate fraud, and how fraudulent behaviour might appropriately be prosecuted or otherwise dealt with and punished. Some of the recommendations in the report are challenging. But only by taking a challenging approach to fraud can we hope to provide an effective response to tackle multi-billion pound crime. I hope that a wide range of people will respond to this consultation; and would wish all the recommendations to be considered on their merits and with an open mind.

Interestingly, both the government *Fraud Review* and the Fraud Panel *Annual Review* each use the word 'fight' eight times: though, this is implied still more in the discussion in each review. Little or no mention is made in either publication on the role of internal auditors fighting fraud and no reference is given to any published statements by The IIA or IIA–UK & Ireland on the role of internal auditors in fraud prevention, detection and investigation. Yet these statements have existed for many years.

Considerable advice is published in internal auditing material and text books on the prevention of fraud and the role of internal auditors in contributing to this prevention: including its detection when it happens and investigation. Very little has been published on the role of internal auditors in fighting fraud. The IIA–UK & Ireland *Fraud Position Statement* (2003) discusses the prevention and detection of fraud but not a fight against it. The guidance provided is on the management of fraud as a risk and the role of internal auditing in that management, including whistleblowing.

Corruption is a criminal act in most countries and the fight against it is international. All research and evidence shows that corruption has been growing over the last ten years.

Lal Balkaran (2002),[12] in an article in the *Internal Auditor* journal of The IIA, saw an important role for internal auditing in curbing corruption:

> The impact of corruption on an organization can be devastating. Corrupt practices increase risks and costs to businesses, damage investor confidence, and stifle growth. Eventually, these activities can distort the organization's allocation of resources, undermine its legitimate business practices, and even lead to bankruptcy.
>
> Internal auditors are uniquely qualified to help their organizations to fight corruption. As the eyes and ears of management, auditors are present year-round, they have a broad understanding of business operations, and they are bound by strict standards of performance and ethical conduct. By providing assurance that effective prevention, detection, and correction measures are in place, auditors can play a significant role in the organization's anti-corruption efforts.

All internal auditors should ask themselves the questions –

1. Do I understand what corruption is and what forms its practice can take?
2. Am I '. . . *uniquely qualified*. . . ' to help my organization to fight corruption?
3. How can I contribute to fighting corruption today and tomorrow in my organization's strategies, policies and operations, across all its supply chains and with all its stakeholders?
4. What resources and practices can I employ to be at the cutting edge of fighting corruption?

Balkaran goes on to promote the importance of an organization's ethical environment:

> Specifically, a written code of ethics and business conduct that integrates such values as honesty, trust, and integrity helps to set the tone for the entire company. All employees represent the organization in their relations with others – customers, suppliers, other employees, competitors, governments, investors, or the general public. Whatever the area of activity or degree of responsibility, employees should be expected to act in a way that maintains or enhances the company's reputation.

Included in the article is a list of international anti-corruption resources and practices that can be accessed by internal auditors through the Internet – European Union, Inter-American Development Bank (IADB), International Federation of Accountants, The International Monetary Fund, Organization for Economic Cooperation and Development (OECD), Organization of American States (OAS), Transparency International (TI), United Nations (UN), The World Bank Group and World Trade Organization (WTO). Add to this list many national governments and regulatory bodies around the world. The fight is powerful, but corruption still takes place today across the world, and will tomorrow.

Trace,[13] a US group set up to help companies to fight corruption, has in 2007 launched a Bribery hotline to map bribery worldwide. This, again, is evidence of organizations starting to take more interest in fighting corruption on an international scale. This innovative fight against corruption is evidence of the concerns now being felt by organizations at how widespread this crime is in the world – concerns not just for moral reasons but also for legal reasons and recognition of how bad reported corruption in the media can be for an organization's reputation.

The fight against fraud and corruption is certainly there for internal auditors, but little has been published in internal auditing on internal auditors fighting all other types of crime. Why is this? Today, most, if not all, governments, regulators and employer organizations publish guidance and advice on crime prevention, including a wide range of criminal acts. Is it because, as Thompson said in 1991, the hat of investigator, or even policeman, is not seen as attractive by internal auditors? The role of internal auditing in evaluating and improving '. . . *the effectiveness of risk management, control and governance processes'* can never be far from considering the possibility of all types of criminal act in an organization's operations, if only because of the economic, social and environmental issues such acts can create.

There is evidence that internal auditors have a role to prevent criminal acts that have a fraud or security impact. There can be few who would argue against this. But where is the evidence that this role is a 'fight' and against all criminal acts? There is very little, if anything, in internal auditing textbooks concerning the internal auditor fighting all types of crime against and in the organization and by the organization. And there are many such crimes – too many to list here – that can be and are committed. UK Home Office Statistics[14] in December 2006 use the following recorded crime offence groups:

Violent crime

Violence against the person
Sexual offences
Robbery

Property crime

Domestic burglary
Other burglary
Theft of and from vehicles
Other thefts and handling
Fraud and forgery
Criminal damage

Drug offences
Other offences

These category titles are only a small part of the story of crime and the details they cover. For instance, there are many types of crime in the 'other offences' category that are significant, economically, socially or environmentally. Behind these groups are stories of victims (people, communities and organizations), injuries (minor, serious and death), losses (small and large) and distress among those involved – victim, witness, criminal, and those associated with each. Yet in many cases the crime could have been avoided or deterred with proper risk assessment, controls and good governance before the event.

The US Sarbanes–Oxley Act (2002)[15] is placing a focus on board and management compliance that has changed some internal auditing practices in many USA-listed companies. This Act is a fight against crime. Its influence is not just in the US: many companies in other countries with investment and listing responsibilities in the US will have to comply with the requirements of this Act by 2007. Gray (2004)[16] researched the impact of Sarbanes–Oxley on internal auditing and identified some good and not so good results. Good results include internal auditing receiving a higher profile and more resources in those organizations impacted by the Act. There is also some evidence that relationships between internal and external audit are being strengthened by the Act.

Not so good, at least for some, Gray sees the image of those internal auditors involved in the compliance programme to be shifting away from partner and consultant to that of policeman. The skills needed by internal auditors involved in verifying the effectiveness of internal control to comply with Sarbanes–Oxley requirements being more on compliance and protection and less on operational and consulting skills. There may also be some influence on the independence and objectivity of internal auditing if it becomes too involved in the verification processes.

The IIA (2004)[17] has made it clear that internal auditing's role in Sarbanes–Oxley compliance verifications should be '. . . *compatible with the overall mission and charter of the internal audit function. Regardless of the level and type of involvement selected, it should not impair the objectivity and capabilities of the internal audit function for covering the major risk areas of their organization.*' This involvement will influence the practices of internal auditing in many organizations. It will need to be continuously monitored by The IIA, boards, audit committees and external auditors as experience of Sarbanes–Oxley grows across the world. The challenges for internal auditors will be to use this Act to create new internal auditing practices that add value to the fight against crime and not just compliance with its requirements. That will be cutting edge!

What has not been discussed in this chapter is how modern day fraud is detected and investigated when the fight has been lost. This can involve internal auditing, though in many investigations members of the forensic team need to be independent specialists in the skills needed to interview suspects, witnesses and examine computers and other records. Fraud is always a mixture of fact and fiction: fact in the amounts involved, how the crime/s are perpetrated and by whom; fiction in many of the motives and reasons given for the crimes and the characters who try to hide or explain to the investigator and court what happened. Joe Anastasi[18] (2003) writes fascinating and imaginative stories of such investigations with chapter titles such as:

'Just Move Away From Your Computer Please'
'Its Gonna Be A Raid'
'101 Ways To Cook The Books'
'Hunting The World's Greatest Outlaw'
'Dumbfella's Go Corporate'

He recognizes a commonality in human behaviours driving fraud in the ten years or so before publication of his book. '*Behaviours that led to calamity, and for more than just a few.*' He goes on to say:

I believe it is important for all of us to recognize the elements of this phenomenon, and when we see aspects of it again, in the real world and in the future, to recognize it for what it is. And not succumb to it. The confidence we all wish to be able to place in our financial systems, for all our mutual future benefit, will not be misplaced if the lessons we learn today are remembered, and appropriately acted upon, in the tomorrow.

Even if internal auditors cannot be forensic fraud specialists they can learn lessons from past behaviours, well publicized in the media, and use these lessons to fight future fraud and other crimes with cutting edge resources and practices.

Any discussion on fighting crime must consider information security. In 1967 I addressed this as an internal auditor when auditing computers. Mainframe electronic data processing had brought new control issues into those organizations using computer technology in their accounting and information systems. At that time I developed three approaches in the audit of computers. Firstly, to review information system development documentation and software efficiency and security; secondly, to review how computers were being used to process data, the efficiency and security of their application and operating systems, their location and its security; thirdly, to use computers to assist in the audit of accounting and information systems, through its systems software and the use of audit software. These three approaches are even more important today because of the spread of new computer technology across most organization operations worldwide. This is not just new today but also emerging tomorrow at an ever faster speed. (See Figure 6.3 for the approaches I used in 1967 to promote the auditing of computer security.)

HOW?	WHY?	WHEN?
1	2	3
Systems	**Computers**	**Audit techniques**
Development	Security	Programmes
Recently installed	Control	Messages
Established	Continuity	

Figure 6.3   Three Approaches To Auditing Computers In 1967
Source: J. Ridley (1967)

Whereas the use of computer software by internal auditing to audit has been well developed over many years, the use of audit messages has been low key in most internal auditing textbooks. Recently this has emerged again more technically as 'continuous auditing'. Sawyer (2005) uses The Canadian Institute of Chartered Accountants definition of continuous auditing:

> ... a methodology that enables independent auditors to provide written assurance on a subject matter using a series of auditors' reports issued simultaneously with, or at a short period after, the occurrence of events underlying the subject matter ...

Not dissimilar to the audit checks we embedded into information system software in 1967 to report negative and positive unusual circumstances as 'audit messages' direct to internal auditing. The IIA[19] recognizes that today's and tomorrow's computer technology opens up many new doors for continuous auditing to be used by internal auditors, creating new opportunities for cutting edge resources and practices in its fight against crime.

The IIA Research Foundation's first major publication on IT assurance and control was published in 1977. Since then this has been updated in 1991, 1994 and the last revision, *Systems Assurance and Control* (SAC), in 2002.[20] These publications were landmarks in the knowledge and approaches internal auditing should be taking in meeting the challenges and assessing risks and control in the information technology advances taking place in their organizations. In 2002 these changes were seen in the SAC Executive Summary as:

> Numerous indicators demonstrate the increasing pace of technological change, with concomitant changes in audit practices and supporting techniques. Information technology offers both great opportunity and risk. It no longer just supports organizational strategies; it is integral to them. Some examples of major change include:
>
> – Pervasive use of digital information technologies (communications, visual and audio recording media, embedded processors and sensors, etc.)
> – Rise of network-centric distributed computing
> – Deployment of broadband digital communications

- Rapid growth of wireless communications
- Continuing sharp decline in price per unit of computing performance
- Huge increases in available processing power and data storage capacity
- Maturation of enterprise-wide resource planning (ERP) software packages (such as SAP R/3) and component-based software
- Increasing sophisticated data-mining technologies
- Biometrics
- Geo-positioning telemetry
- Reliance on encryption technologies for key controls
- Natural language interface technologies
- Evolution of technology standards and open systems.

While these changes are dramatic in themselves, their impact on society, governance, economies, competition, markets, organizational structure, even national defence is nothing short of breathtaking. No one can ignore technology. New paradigms such as the rise of the knowledge worker, 'virtulalization' of organizations – manufacturers who own no factories and retailers who have no physical stores – globalization, cyber warfare, and growing concerns regarding personal privacy mean myriad new aspects that internal auditors need to consider.

And that was 2002! What other challenges are there today and will be tomorrow?

Security in and over information technology and its operating and information systems is critical in the fight against crime in every organization. An Institute of Directors (IOD) (2005)[21] *'best practice measures for protecting your business'* explains the context of Information Communication Technology (ICT) in some detail, providing useful guidance by a number of expert contributors. Its Introduction by the Director General IOD strikes a challenge for every internal auditor:

However, there is a bewildering array of new ICT developments such as intranets, extranets, data warehouses and business intelligence systems, all clustered around affordable 'always on' broadband access to the global Internet. As with any set of new processes and tools, these ICT developments offer new vulnerabilities and pitfalls as well as clear top and bottom line benefits. It is imperative that they are treated with care and respect. As a senior police officer once said: *'there are no new crimes, just new ways of committing old crimes'*. The new ICT tools offer all sorts of new ways of subverting old business processes . . .

The cutting edge internal auditor needs each of the three approaches mentioned in Figure 6.3 to fight crime in ICT today and tomorrow. Included in this guide is a security healthcheck developed by the government Department of Trade and Industry. This contains the following 10 questions every organization and internal auditor should ask:

1. Does your organization have an information security policy?
2. Are staff allocated with specific security responsibilities, e.g. locking the building, allocating passwords?
3. Do you know what your organization's main assets are, do you have a list of them, and does this list include information?
4. Are specific personnel measures, such as training users or including security in their job descriptions, taken with respect to security?
5. Does your organization take steps to prevent unauthorized access to your premises?
6. Have you implemented operational controls and procedures to safeguard your information, e.g. use of backups, anti-virus software, firewalls?

 7. Do you control access to information through the effective use of user IDs and passwords, e.g. making sure users don't share passwords, or write their passwords on Post-it notes?
 8. Have steps been taken to ensure that security requirements are defined and incorporated during system development or met by packaged software developers?
 9. Do you have any business continuity plans?
10. Do you ensure that you meet all your legal requirements/obligations, e.g. licensing, copyright, data protection?

All internal auditors at the cutting edge of fighting crime will ask these questions and more in the first two approaches mentioned earlier. In the third approach they will independently verify the answers. To do this they will need at least the Category 1 level of IT knowledge identified by The IIA's International Advanced Technology Committee (2005)[22]:

Category 1 – All Auditors

Category 1 is the knowledge of IT needed by all professional auditors, from new recruits up through the Chief Audit Executive (CAE). Basic IT knowledge encompasses understanding concepts such as the differences in software used in applications, operating systems and systems software, and networks. It includes comprehending basic IT security and control components such as perimeter defences, intrusion detection, authentication, and application system controls. Basic knowledge includes understanding how business controls and assurance objectives can be impacted by vulnerabilities in business operations and the related and supporting systems, networks, and data components. It is fundamentally about ensuring that auditors have sufficient knowledge to focus on understanding IT risks without necessarily possessing significant technical knowledge.

This IIA IT practical guidance goes on to describe a higher level of IT knowledge for audit supervisors (Category 2) and technical IT audit specialists (Category 3). Each of these categories provides useful benchmarks for every internal auditing activity. Each is an important resource for fighting crime in every organization.

CHAPTER SUMMARY

There will always be a fight against crime by people, groups, organizations, communities, nations and internationally. Laws and regulations will continue to be amended and created to help this fight to prevent, catch and punish criminals. Internal auditors need to consider in all their services, and wearing all their hats, how they can contribute to this fight – not just by contributing to its prevention, detection and investigation, but also by understanding all the criminal acts that can take place in and around the organizations they work in, and promoting the fight against them.

This internal auditing fight against all types of crime is not that clear in the following Gray and Gray (1997) five innovation motivation themes, four innovation goals and four innovation categories, or the additions and changes made in Chapters 2 to 5.

Motivations

1. Progress within the field of professional internal auditing.
2. Increasing competition leading to pressures to reduce costs and increase efficiency.
3. New challenges, such as increasing internal control risks due to staff reductions and restructuring.
4. Opportunities to increase efficiency and quality as a result of technological advances.

5. Changes in corporate management practices and philosophies, such as Total Quality Management, re-engineering, continuous quality improvement, or related approaches.
6. **Challenges and opportunities of global issues and developments.**
7. **Social and environmental issues impacting all organizations.**
8. **Recognition that professionalism, quality and standards are essential attributes for world-class status in any internal auditing activity.**
9. **Importance of organizational governance to meet regulatory and stakeholders' needs.**
10. **A continuous search for good and evil in how organizations and all their operations are directed and controlled.**

Goals

1. Improvement of the quality of internal auditing services.
2. Improve efficiency.
3. Expansion of services to increase the value-added of internal auditing.
4. Boost staff skills, performance and morale.
5. **Sell internal auditing as future focused.**

Categories

1. Changes in the way that internal auditors interact with the rest of their enterprises **and all those with a stakeholder interest.**
2. Internal restructuring and changes in the organization and management of internal auditing.
3. Creation of new audit services and methods.
4. Changes in the use of technology.
5. **Improved knowledge and skills in the teams of staff who carry out internal auditing engagements.**

A new motivation, goal and category should be added to channel internal auditing innovative and cutting edge resources and practices into this fight:

Motivation

11. **Recognition that all types of crime in and by an organization should be fought.**

Goal

6. **To reduce the opportunities for all types of crime in an organization.**

Category

6. **New services to fight crime.**

INTERNAL AUDITING FIGHTING CRIME PRINCIPIA 1998 AND 2008

My 1998 principia for internal auditing included only one related to fraud (see Appendix A):

17. Understanding how fraud is perpetrated is key to its prevention and detection.

This is now changed to reflect in 2008 the importance of internal auditing fighting all types of crime:

9. Internal auditing should fight all types of crime at all levels in an organization, across all relationships with its stakeholders and the public.

A VISION FOR INTERNAL AUDITING FIGHTING CRIME

Our services include a fight against all types of crime

SYNOPSES OF CASE STUDIES

Case 6.1: Combating Extortion and Bribery: ICC Rules of Conduct and Recommendations

Synopsis

Part 1 of the 2005 edition of the International Chamber of Commerce (ICC) *Rules of Conduct and Recommendations to Combat Extortion and Bribery* contains principles and procedures for voluntary application in all organizations. The success of these rules depends on the 'tone at the top'. They provide a benchmark for all organizations as an excellent anti-corruption policy. Monitoring of the principles underlying these rules is a must for all organizations. It is also a must for internal auditing as part of its cutting edge fight against crime.

Reproduced from the International Chamber of Commerce (ICC) *Rules of Conduct and Recommendations* (2005 edition) with permission from the International Chamber of Commerce, 38, Cours Albert 1er, 75008 Paris, France. www.icccwbo.org

---

After Reading the Case Study Consider:

1. Does your board use these Rules of Conduct to fight corruption?
2. Does your organization provide guidance and training in identifying corruption in its daily business and across all its supply chains?
3. What resources and practices does your internal auditing use to identify transactions that contravene these rules, and weaknesses in control processes that could lead to such contraventions? Are any of these resources and practices at the cutting edge of internal auditing? If not, should they be?

Case 6.2: United Nations Office on Drugs and Crime

Synopsis

This extract from the *UN Anti-Corruption Toolkit* discusses lessons learnt from its Global Programme against Corruption. It provides definitions of corrupt practices '... *and measures for assessing their nature and extent, for deterring, preventing and combating corruption...*'. Strategies for fighting corruption are also discussed. Cutting edge internal auditors should be familiar with the contents of this toolkit and use its knowledge in their own fight against corruption.

The *UN Anti-Corruption Toolkit* 3rd edition (2004) is part of the United Nations Office on Drugs and Crime Global Programme against Corruption. The full toolkit can be downloaded from www.unodc.org/unodc/en/corruption_toolkit.html

---

After Reading the Case Study Consider:

1. How does your organization's recognition and regulation against corruption compare with the case study?
2. Is the building of integrity in your organization similar to that below?

> Combating corruption, building integrity and establishing credibility require time, determination and consistency. When anti-corruption strategies are first instituted, a long-term process begins, during which corrupt values and practices are gradually identified and eliminated. In most cases, a complex process of interrelated elements is involved: reforms to individual institutions take place in stages as problems are identified; countermeasures are developed and implemented; personnel are reoriented and retrained. Often, progress at one stage or in one area cannot be achieved until other elements of the strategy have come into effect. Generally speaking, training personnel to place the long-term interests of integrity before the more immediate benefits of corruption is a longer, more gradual process than direct measures such as criminal prosecutions or specific administrative reforms. (repeated from the case study)

3. Is your organization's definition of corruption as wide as that in the UN Toolkit?
4. Does your organization have an anti-corruption strategy and appropriate policies?
5. Are there well-established auditing and monitoring safeguards in your organization to identify if corruption has taken place?
6. What cutting edge resources and practices are there in internal auditing in your organization to deter, prevent and combat corruption?

Case 6.3: The Stop Light Model

Synopsis

'The Stop Light Model is a way of illustrating a new philosophy for fighting financial crime.' In this model Red are the staff that combat fraud, Yellow are all the other staff in the organization, Green are the career criminals. Using this model as support for risk management workshops and prevention of fraud training can improve staff awareness of the risks of fraud and how these can be reduced. It asks the right questions, promoting a zero tolerance against fraud. It is a cutting edge practice for internal auditing in its fight against crime. All internal auditors must be Red.

Contributed by K.H. Spencer Pickett, with permission. The description of the Stop Light Model is his. More details on the model and its implementation to fight financial crime can be found in his book *Financial Crime Investigation and Control* (2002), published by John Wiley & Sons Inc., New York, USA.

After Reading the Case Study Consider:

1. Who is at Red and Yellow in your organization's fight against financial fraud?
2. What actions, if any, does your organization take to move people from the yellow light to red light? Does this include fraud awareness training?
3. What contribution does your internal auditing make to encourage this to happen? Is any of this activity at the cutting edge of internal auditing? If not, why not?
4. Does your organization have a zero tolerance to fight fraud? If so, how does it compare with the Stop Light Model?
5. Are the fraud awareness questions listed in the case asked and measured regularly in your organization?

Case 6.4: Militate Against Corruption

Synopsis

Every organization needs a *Statement of Values* in its fight against corruption. Such a statement is an essential start to a fight against dishonest practices. It should set a standard of honesty for all to understand and manage. Internal auditing needs to be at the cutting edge of promoting this statement in all its resources and practices.

Adapted with permission from an article by Kastuv Ray, Global Governance Pantheon www.globalgovernance.co.uk published by The Association of Chartered and Certified Accountants, London as *ACCA Internal Audit Bulletin* Issue 22 – November 2005

After Reading the Case Study Consider:

1. How does your organization's *Statement of Values* compare with the statement in the article?
2. How militant is your internal auditing in the fight against corruption?
3. In how many of the recommended militant actions agains corruption is your internal auditing at the cutting edge with its resources and practices?

Case 6.5: Forensic Auditing in the United Kingdom Metropolitan Police Authority

Synopsis

This is the record of one internal auditing function's fight against fraud and how this started. It promotes the lead internal auditing can take in the fight against fraud in every organization.

It discusses the role of a forensic audit unit, development of its resources and reporting. It demonstrates how such a unit can interface with other services provided by internal auditors, using cutting edge practices to improve audit planning and engagements.

Contributed by Peter Tickner, MSc FIIA MIIA, Director of Internal Audit, Metropolitan Police Authority, London, England.

After Reading the Case Study Consider:

1. How does internal auditing in your organizations plan its fight against fraud?
2. How do internal auditors in your organization work with those who investigate fraud?
3. Does your audit committee review fraud in your organization – its risk, prevention, detection and investigation?
4. Does internal auditing in your organization measure its fight against fraud?

SELF-ASSESSMENT QUESTIONS

6.1

How does your organization and internal auditing fight corruption? Compare your answer with the guidance in this chapter.

6.2

As a teaching guide I developed in 2000 the following framework of questions that should be asked at board and internal auditing levels in all organizations. Can you answer these for your organization?

Is your organization's code of conduct:

- required by your regulators and how?
- led from the top – by style and values?
- embedded in all strategies, plans and operations?
- seen in all structures and systems?
- communicated internally to everyone – staff and visitors?
- communicated externally to all stakeholders?
- known across all supply chains?
- included in all review processes?
- independently monitored?

Does it:

- create/reduce wealth?
- improve/reduce the quality of performance?
- increase/decrease the efficiency and effectiveness of all staff?
- increase/decrease customers' satisfaction?
- improve/lower the organization's reputation in society?

– increase/decrease competitive edge?
– consider/ignore all stakeholders' needs?
– encourage/discourage good behaviour

After answering these questions replace 'conduct' with 'fight against crime' and answer the questions again.

Do you have:

– a formal and published code of conduct?
– a formal fraud policy?
– a formal ant-corruption policy?
– a formal security policy for all your resources, material and people?
– a procedure for dealing with all irregularities?
– a whistleblowing procedure?
– practical ethics training for all your staff?
– environmental management policies, audits and reports?
– environmental, social and ethical accounting and audits?

Satisfactory answers to all these questions, benchmarked against the guidance in this chapter, can reveal many weaknesses in an organization's attitude to fighting crime at all levels. You may even add other questions appropriate for your organization!

NOTES AND REFERENCES

1. From the *Decline and Fall of the Roman Empire* (1776–88) ch. 3; cf. Voltaire 797: 18, included in *The Oxford Dictionary of Quotations* (1999), Oxford University Press, Oxford, England.
2. Position Paper on *Whistleblowing* (1988), The IIA.
3. *Fraud: The Challenge Facing Internal Auditors*, Courtney M. Thompson, *Internal Auditor* (June 1991), The IIA.
4. The IIA Practice Advisories 1210-1 and 1210.A1-1: 2004.
5. Published in *Internal Auditing* (March 1994: p. 7), IIA–UK & Ireland.
6. *Whistleblowing and the Internal Auditor – a Position Statement* (2001), IIA–UK & Ireland.
7. Practice Advisory 2440-3: *Communicating Sensitive Information Within and Outside of the Chain of Command* (2003), The IIA.
8. *Managing the Risk of Fraud – A Guide for Managers* (2003) HM Treasury, London, England.
9. *Good Practices: Tackling External Fraud* (2004), HM Treasury and National Audit Office, London, England.
10. *Which Way Now? Evaluating the Government's Fraud Review, Eight Annual Report* 2005-06 (2007), The Fraud Advisory Panel. www.fraudadvisorypanel.org
11. *Fraud Review – Final Report* (2006), UK Government Attorney General's Office. www.attorneygeneral.gov.uk
12. 'Curbing Corruption', Al Balkaran, *Internal Auditor* (February 2002), The IIA.
13. *Trace* is a non-profit membership association of multinational companies committed to the highest standards of transparency, www.traceinternational.org. Its goal is to provide anti-bribery support across all industries and regions. Its new Bribeline is a hotline for anonymous reporting of bribery practices. www.bribeline.org.
14. Home Office Statistical Bulletin, *Crime in England and Wales: Quarterly Update to December 2006* (April 2007), ISBN 978 1 84726 315 5.

15. This US Act sets out a new system of audit regulation and tougher penalties for corporate wrongdoing. *Inter alia*, CEOs and CFOs must certify in each annual report their companies integrity and assessment of the effectiveness of internal controls over financial reporting.
16. *Changing Internal Audit Practices in the New Paradigm: The Sarbanes–Oxley Environment*, (2004), G. Gray, The IIA Research Foundation.
17. Internal Auditing's Role in Sections 302 and 404 of the Sarbanes–Oxley Act (2004), The IIA.
18. *The New Forensics – Investigating Corporate Fraud and the Theft of Intellectual Property* (2003), Joe Anastasi, John Wiley & Sons Inc., Hoboken, New Jersey, USA.
19. Publications by The IIA in recent years promoting continuous auditing are *Continuous Auditing: Potential for Internal Auditors* (2003), J. Donald Warren and Xenia Ley Parker, and *Continuous Auditing: An Operational Model for Internal Auditors* (2005), Mohammad J. Abdolmohammadi and Ahmad Sharbatouglie, both published by The IIA Research Foundation.
20. *Systems Assurance and Control* (2002), The IIA Research Foundation.
21. *Director's Guide: Information Security* (2005), The Institute of Directors, Director Publications Ltd, London, England. www.director.co.uk.
22. *Information Technology Controls* (2005), Global Technology Audit Guide (GTAG), The IIA. This was the first in a series of GTAG publications on information technology challenges. The latest, No. 8, is in 2007.

7

Cutting Edge Internal Auditing
Assists The Board

'The board should undertake a formal and rigorous annual evaluation of its own performance and that of its committees and individual directors.'

A6   Performance evaluation – Main Principle
The Combined Code On Corporate Governance, June 2006

Audit Committee Best Practices

ORGANIZATION   OVERSIGHT

• INDEPENDENCE	• FINANCIAL REPORTING
• MEMBERSHIP	• FINANCIAL STATEMENTS
• KNOWLEDGE	• RISKS
• EXPERIENCE	• CONTROLS
• MEETINGS	• LEGAL/REGULATORY/TAX
• REPORTING	• AUDITING
• ADDITIONAL RESOURCES	• BOARD

INTERNAL AUDITING ASSISTS THE BOARD
BEFORE 1976

The early 1970s saw a growing interest in audit committees in listed companies in North America. In 1972 the US Securities and Exchange Commission recommended audit committees, consisting of non-executive directors. At this time audit committees were established in the majority of listed companies. This recommendation was also promoted by the New York Stock Exchange. In the United Kingdom there was less interest in establishing audit committees politically and encouragement was mainly by professional accounting firms. A proposal by a private member's bill to require them by law received little or no support. This same lack of interest existed in other parts of Europe.

Article:
The Audit Committee[1] (1976)

Recent press statements in this country have shown a new interest developing in the role of non-executive directors and audit committees. Such committees are not new. Many companies have established audit responsibilities at board level, which satisfy some if not all the duties undertaken by formal audit committees. However, there are still many companies that have no formal review of auditing at board level and for these organizations an audit committee can serve a very useful purpose.

> *'The growth of audit committees is a challenge to all internal auditors'*

An audit committee that has an understanding of the needs both of management and the company's auditors can coordinate the effective planning of all auditing so as to fulfil the needs and clarify the expectations of all concerned – directors, shareholders, management, external auditors and internal auditors.

The activities of those audit committees that do exist have developed in various ways, depending on individual organizations and the needs seen by different boards. These needs can include:

- A wide audit scope
- A formal review of audit results
- Effective internal controls
- A formal review of financial information and results.

Membership of the audit committee normally consists of selected directors and, in some cases, representatives of management. In companies where there are non-executive directors, the committee generally includes all or some of these directors. Non-executive directors can make a valuable contribution by bringing an independent and objective approach to the committee's work. They are not involved in the day-to-day affairs of the company and can take a detached view of information and controls. The audit committee can therefore provide an ideal opportunity for the non-executive director to make a formal review of a company's affairs, as part of his board responsibilities.

Observation of the work of audit committees during recent years has shown that they are now working to satisfy some or all of the following objectives:

- That the audited financial statements present fairly the financial position and results of operations and that the auditors have no reservations about them.
- That there are no unresolved issues between management and auditors that could affect the audited financial statements.
- Where there are unsettled issues that do not affect the audited financial statements (e.g. disagreements regarding correction of internal control weaknesses, or the application of accounting principles to proposed transactions), that there is an agreed course of action leading to the resolution of these matters.

- To ensure that there is a good working relationship between management and the auditors.
- To review audit plans and ensure there is full cooperation between internal and external audit.
- That there are adequate procedures for review of interim statements and other financial information prior to distribution to the shareholders.

Professional accounting firms in North America have encouraged the establishment of audit committees for many years. In the United States a position Paper, issued by the Security Exchange Commission (SEC) in 1972, strongly recommended corporate audit committees. This statement is partly responsible for the rapid development of these committees in that country. A recently published survey by the Institute of Internal Auditors reports that 80% of major companies in North America have established audit committees at board level, consisting of all or some of the company's non-executive directors. More recently, the New York Stock Exchange has proposed mandatory rules for each listed company to have an audit committee dominated by non-executive directors and this proposal will probably have been ratified by the time this article appears in print.

In Britain, some accounting firms encourage clients to set up such committees but their development has been slow. A recent survey by the United Kingdom Chapter's Research Committee of the Institute of Internal Auditors shows that, of the companies that replied, only 149 had established audit committees. However, Britain is not alone in Europe in its present low level of audit committee development. A recent report by the EEC, on supervisory duties at board levels in countries in the EEC, makes no reference to the role of the audit committee in Europe even though part of the report covers the role of the non-executive director and recommends his {her} involvement in the formal review of financial information and results!

In parts of Canada, major companies are now required by statute to establish audit committees, and legislation in that country provides specific duties concerning the review of financial information by such committees. A legal requirement for audit committees in this country was recently the subject of discussion at the committee stage of the current Companies Bill (No. 2). Although the proposed amendments requiring audit committees in major companies were not accepted, it is certain that discussion at government level will continue in the future. (A press release on 5 August 1976 announced a proposed Bill, to be introduced by Conservative MP, Sir Brandon Rhys Williams, during October, requiring the formation of audit committees in all major public companies in this country.)

Publicity for audit committees concentrates mainly on their duties and activities linked to the external audit responsibilities and the filling of communication gaps between external auditors, management, directors and shareholders. Experience in North America has shown that the audit committee can also have a significant effect on the role of internal auditing in an organization. By establishing a reporting line from internal audit to the committee, an organization can establish a recognized independence for internal audit for all to see. Such a direct interest by directors in the work of the internal auditor can change the attitude to his work and improve the standards of auditing within a company, by internal auditors and management. Development of audit committees in major companies in this country will certainly be an influence on the growth of the internal auditing profession. It is possible that this influence may be responsible, more than any other, for shaping the internal auditing of the future in the private sector.

There could also be experience to be learned in the public sector from the development of audit committees. Performance review committees in local authorities have received publicity recently and these committees could develop into the 'audit committees' of the public sector. In a speech by Sir Harold Wilson in 1975, when he was Prime Minister and speaking to a conference of Local Government Officers, he recommended the development of performance review committees to act as 'watchdogs' of public expenditure. Recently, the Layfield Committee report supported this recommendation and came out strongly in favour of performance review committees in local authorities. The duties of these committees could develop in a similar way to those of audit committees and their influence on internal auditing in the public sector may be just as great.

The development of audit committees in the private and public sectors in this country is taking place. How these committees will influence the development of internal auditing is not so clear. The duties of audit committees can concentrate attention mainly on the audit of financial information and security of assets. The review of balance sheet accuracy, statements of earnings, accounting principles, fraud detection, possible corruption and dishonest payments all receive a major share of the committee's time. Because of this attention to financial and proprietary auditing, there is a danger that interest by the committee in internal auditing may emphasize too much that part of the internal auditors' work, thus reducing the image of the operational auditor, which has been successfully developed by the internal auditing profession since the 1950s. It would be unfortunate if internal auditors allow their role as internal consultants to lack the attention by audit committees that it deserves. This would be a setback for internal auditing as a profession. It is important, therefore, that management's image of the internal auditor in the future does not return to being only that of the 'policeman' in accounting systems!

The growth of audit committees is a challenge to all internal auditors – they must encourage their audit committee members to look upon and develop internal auditing as a really true professional service, assisting the board, the committee and all levels of management in the discharge of their responsibilities for effective internal control.

INTERNAL AUDITING ASSISTS THE BOARD
BETWEEN 1976 TO 2000

Lawrence Sawyer (1979)[2] wrote in some detail on how internal auditors can be involved with and assist the board of directors in their organizations. His main theme was assistance through the audit committee, though he also recognized the importance of a strong or dotted line direct to the chair of the board:

The internal auditor's involvement with the board of directors is most often through the audit committee of the board. That involvement is getting more prevalent as both the external and internal auditors educate audit committees about the importance of a competent, objective internal audit function as a means of communication and control.

Internal auditors in different environments report organizationally to different levels within the enterprise. Some report directly to the board of directors. That is particularly true in the case of financial institutions. Others report to the head of the accounting function and have no dealings with the board.

Sawyer was discussing events at the time in North America only. Both activities – through the audit committee and reporting to the chair of the board – were cutting edge activities in that part of the world and rarely seen elsewhere, except in subsidiaries of multinational companies based in other countries. I was fortunate to be in that position. Also, at this time much of the assistance given to boards was in their review of control and recommendations for improvement. Few writers, if any, were commenting on internal auditor involvement in the 'direction' part of governance by boards.

Professional internal auditing is a board service. Its statements have always recommended that it report to senior levels of management and its services have grown to support all levels of management. In the 1980s The IIA changed its statement of responsibilities from '. . . *a service to management . . .*' to '. . . *a service to the organization . . .*' to reflect a growing trend for internal auditors to provide services to all levels in an organization, director, manager and operator. This was evidenced at the time by the increasing use of the term and practice of 'operational auditing', and internal auditors reporting direct to the board or a board committee.

When the above article was written and published, F. Clive de Paula and Frank Attwood (1976)[3] recognized common objectives between independent external and internal audit '. . . *hence the existence in some large organizations of an internal audit department, made up of specially assigned staff with a principal accounting objective of assuring management of the efficient and effective design and operation of internal checks within accounting systems*'. This recognition of internal and external common objectives had been around for many years, probably almost from before the formation of The IIA. De Paula and Attwood also recognized that '*the English Institute emphasizes that there are also fundamental differences*': those differences being '. . . *scope, approach and responsibility . . .*'. Reliance on internal audit by external audit at the time was determined by the competence of internal audit staff; the nature and extent of work it undertook; its effectiveness; reports and action taken; and, its authority and reporting lines. These were very reasonable determinations and are practised even today. No recognition was given to internal audit coordinating the planning of all its services with external audit, although, in practice, this was happening in many organizations, including my own.

Well-organized coordination and cooperation between internal audit and external audit can be an important first cutting edge step in the assistance internal audit can give to the board. Seen in that way it becomes an important objective for all heads of internal audit. Not just coordination and cooperation in the audit of internal checks in accounting systems, but across the whole contract that exists between the organization, its owners and external auditors, from legal and professional requirements for external audit to all contracts for consultancy and advisory services. The IIA has always recognized the importance of this relationship with external audit. Its Statement on Internal Auditing Standards No. 5 – Internal

Auditors' Relationships with Independent Outside Auditors, issued June 1987[4] – reflected more up-to-date thinking on this relationship and included a requirement that the head of internal audit should:

1. Ensure coordination of internal and external audit work through periodic meetings; planning; access to each other's audit programmes and working papers; exchange of audit reports and management letters; and, common understanding and use of audit techniques.
2. Seek support from the board for effective coordination of internal and external audit work.
3. Ensure that the work of internal audit can be relied upon by external audit.
4. Ensure that any work performed for external audit meets the provisions of The IIA Standards for the Professional Practice of Internal Auditing.
5. Evaluate the effectiveness of coordination between internal and external audit work, including aggregate audit cost.
6. If requested by the board, assess the performance of external audit, such assessments may address:

    (a) Professional knowledge and experience.
    (b) Knowledge of the organization's industry.
    (c) Independence.
    (d) Availability of specialized services.
    (e) Anticipation of and responsiveness to the needs of the organization.
    (f) Reasonable continuity of key engagement personnel.
    (g) Maintenance of appropriate working relationships.
    (h) Achievement of contract commitments.
    (i) Delivery of overall value to the organization.

Perhaps, or certainly, can be added today the quality of external audit work.

7. Communicate the assessments of coordination and performance to the board and senior management.
8. Contribute to and understand any external audit reporting to the board required by external auditing standards, regulation or law. These matters may include:

    (a) Significant control weaknesses.
    (b) Errors and irregularities.
    (c) Illegal acts.
    (d) Management judgements and accounting estimates.
    (e) Significant audit adjustments.
    (f) Disagreements with management.
    (g) Difficulties encountered in performing the [external] audit.

Each of the above recommended requirements is still important today. They all offer opportunities for cutting edge internal auditing in its assistance role at board and audit committee level.

The Treadway Commission report of 1987 was one of the first reports to review the development of audit committees in North America. Its findings were:

To be effective, audit committees should exercise vigilant and informed oversight of the financial reporting, including the company's internal controls. The board of directors should set forth the committee's duties and responsibilities in a written charter. Among other things, the audit committee should review management's evaluation of the independence of the public accountant and management's plans for engaging the company's independent public accountant to perform management's advisory services.

One of the more contentious recommendations by the Commission that has seen little implementation in the United Kingdom is: *'The Commission also recommends a letter from the chairman of the audit committee that describes the committees activities. . . should appear in the annual report to stockholders.'* The nearest companies have come to adopting this is the annual report statement on an audit committee's existence, membership, scope of work and frequency of meeting.

The Commission recognized the relationship between the audit committee and internal audit:

Moreover, all public companies must have an effective and objective internal audit function. The internal auditor's qualifications, staff, status within the company, reporting lines, and relationship with the audit committee of the board of directors must be adequate to ensure the internal audit function's effectiveness and objectivity. The internal auditor should consider his audit findings in the context of the company's financial statements and should, to the extent appropriate, coordinate his activities with the activities of the independent public accountant.

It also set out, in some detail, benchmarks for the internal audit function including:

- Must have the acknowledged support of top management and the board of directors through its audit committee.
- Its scope of responsibilities should be reviewed by the audit committee and set down in writing.
- Adoption of The IIA's professional standards is encouraged.
- Endorsement of The IIA's quality assurance standards as a test of an internal audit function's effectiveness.
- The internal audit function should have direct and unrestricted access to the chief executive officer and audit committee.
- Appropriate involvement by internal auditors at corporate level

The Commission's *Good Practice Guidelines for the Audit Committee* are set out as a case study at the end of the chapter. Included in these is the guideline

Audit Plans The committee should review with the chief internal auditor and the independent public accountant their annual audit plans, including the degree of coordination of the respective plans. The committee should inquire as to the extent to which the planned audit scope can be relied upon to detect fraud or weaknesses in internal controls.

In its findings the Commission found that:

. . . internal auditors often concentrate on the review of controls at the division, subsidiary or other business component level, rather than at the corporate level. Independent public accountants, on the other hand, generally are responsible for the audit examination at corporate level. Appropriate involvement by the internal auditors at the corporate level, effectively coordinated to avoid duplication of the independent public accountants' efforts, can help and detect fraudulent financial reporting.

This is an invitation for internal auditors to become more involved at corporate/top management level – an invitation for cutting edge internal auditing.

The Treadway Commission guidelines still set a high standard for audit committees: and have since been repeated worldwide by many commissions and governments. *'Only when all audit committees take seriously the importance of benchmarking themselves against worldwide best practices, will their contribution to good governance be at its best.'*

International research in 1993 by Price Waterhouse[5] studied how audit committees were functioning. This study considered the Treadway Commission audit committee guidelines and developed its own similar audit committee charter. One of the more interesting recommendations for cutting edge internal auditing was:

> The internal auditing department can also be helpful to the audit committee by conducting special studies or investigations of matters of interest to the committee. . . . Internal auditing often reviews the company's compliance with laws and regulations and with the company's code of conduct.

If this recommendation is linked to the report's discussion *'. . . of areas that are likely to command more audit committee attention over the next five to eight years',* even more interesting cutting edge activities are opened up for internal auditing. The future areas listed are:

– International operations.
– Joint-venture and partnership operations.
– Environmental matters.
– Improved monitoring of management estimates.
– More involvement with internal controls, including reporting on the adequacy of controls.
– Expanded involvement with computer-related controls.

Events since 1993 in corporate governance guidelines and best practices have added new future areas to this list. PricewaterhouseCoopers (2000)[6] updated this 1993 research with a similar audit committee charter and the following added future and revised areas for audit committees (and internal auditing):

New Areas

- *Risk Management and Internal Control* – managing key risks and control to achieve organization objectives.
- *Faster Communication of Information* – capital markets will continue to expect more and more information. New technologies such as the Internet will continue to accelerate.
- *Expanded Information* – triple line reporting covering social, environmental and financial results will address increasing demands for more transparency in organization performance.
- *Reliance on Others* – audit committees will look increasingly to the internal audit director and other assurance groups to help to carry out their responsibilities.
- *Liability* – there will be an increasing shortage of board members willing to sit on audit committees because of the liabilities this may incur.
- *More Time, More Pay* – compensation for audit committee members will increase.

Issues from 1993 Report

- *International Operations* – signs that international accounting and auditing standards might be forthcoming. Better knowledge of company operations, including newly conceived and globally integrated supply chains, production processes, and marketing and sales channels.
- *Joint Ventures and Partnerships* – global competition and emerging opportunities through joint ventures, alliances, partnerships and other new relationships will make risk management and control more complex.
- *Training Audit Committee Members* – many audit committee members are still not receiving the right training and may even fall further behind.
- *Monitoring Management Estimates* – greater and more sophisticated use of estimates in accounting statements will increase a need for audit committee members to understand new analytical methods and reporting models and how estimates play into them.
- *Reporting on Internal Control* – there will be a growing demand for information reliability and public reporting on internal control effectiveness.
- *Information Technology* – growing importance of computer systems and controls, through interconnectivity, portability, power and speed expanding exponentially. In addition, e-business has emerged. Audit committees are struggling to catch up.
- *Interim Reporting* – the majority of audit committees now embrace interim financial reporting statements.
- *Compliance with Laws and Regulations and Codes of Conduct* – boards now delegate significant oversight responsibility to the audit committee in these areas.

There were many opportunities in this research, and still are, for internal auditing to pioneer assistance developments in its relationships with top management and the board. Most, if not all, internal audit activities will not be providing assistance in all of these areas. If not, why not? Also, review the assistance your internal auditing activity is providing direct to your board or through your audit committee. Is this up to date in its practices and is it future oriented?

The IIA–UK & Ireland (2000)[7] published its own statement on audit committee and internal auditing best practices based on UK and US research and publications. This included two new challenging statements with wide implications for audit committee oversight activities:

Role and Constitution

The Audit Committee has a key oversight role to play in organizational corporate governance, in particular those aspects relating to internal control and risk management.

Reviewing and advising the main board on the content of the corporate governance report in the annual report and accounts.

Corporate governance is direction and control by the board, not the audit committee. If the audit committee is to oversee organizational governance and its reporting to stakeholders, does this mean that the audit committee must review the performance of the board? There is a simple answer to this – 'Yes'. But is this so simple? How many audit committee members in 2000 saw their responsibilities, individually or collectively, as monitors of board performance? How many internal auditors in the same year saw their review of organizational governance as a review of board or audit committee performance? More recent years have seen the profile of board performance as key to organizational governance. (This will be discussed later in the chapter.)

Article:
How Effective Is Your Audit Committee?[8] (2000)

In 1996[a] I wrote on six essential characteristics that exist in the best audit committees (see Figure 7.1).

```
1. Independence
2. Rotation Of Membership
3. Unrestricted Responsibility
4. Monitoring of all Control
5. Provides Advice Only
6. Reports Results of its Work to Full Board and Externally
```

Figure 7.1   Six Steps To Success For All Audit Committees
Source: J. Ridley (1995)

I recommended that these should be measured by governing bodies and audit committees in all organizations. Since then, the worldwide focus on good governance has emphasized and reinforced the importance of such measures. There have also been a number of important national and international studies with recommendations for audit committee practices. Both government and regulators across all sectors now encourage the establishment and development of audit committees at board and governing body levels. Today, such committees are seen by many worldwide as an essential part of good governance in all types of organization, large and small. Their influence on control and conduct will continue to increase.

> '*Only when all audit committees take seriously the importance of benchmarking themselves against worldwide best practices, will their contribution to good governance be at its best.*'

What measures and benchmarks are being used by audit committees to evaluate their performance? How do audit committee members measure their effectiveness? Do they have any measures? These are important questions that all stakeholders should ask. There is little evidence to show that audit committees self-assess their own performance, or even if this is required by their boards. A 1993[b] study by The Institute of Internal Auditor's Research Foundation covered organization of the audit committee, its training and resources, meetings, activities and working relationships with internal auditors, management and external auditors. It reported '*Survey results indicated that 88% of "state-of-the-art" audit committees have conducted self-assessments of performance by comparing their own activities to those recommended by commissions. . . '*

---

[a] 'Six Steps to Success – does your audit committee add up?' Article by J. Ridley, *Internal Auditing* (May 1996), The IIA–UK & Ireland, London.
[b] *Improving Audit Committee Performance: What Works Best,* A research paper by Price Waterhouse, The IIA, USA, 1993.

The IIA study includes an audit committee self-assessment guide with recommendations for its use and review by the full board. At that time the guide included recognized best practices for audit committees across the world. Such an approach to measuring the effectiveness of an audit committee has not been bettered. Self-assessment measures are now characteristic of good governance and good practices in many organizations. Risk management, control, quality, training, health and safety and other management programmes all use self-assessment techniques. Yet, despite the popularity of this type of measure with management, there is little evidence to show today that many boards or audit committees in the UK have implemented regular performance self-assessment processes.

In 1996 I summed up my six steps to success for audit committees with the statement:

> An audit committee's membership should be **independent of executive authority** at board level and **rotate (membership and chair)**, with **unrestricted responsibility** to **review the monitoring of all control activities,** the impact of change on control, **offer advice** and **report results of its work to the full board and externally**.

Each of the six highlighted characteristics in this statement is capable of being self-assessed by all audit committee members and measured by their boards or governing bodies. Over the past four years each has increased in its importance to good governance. That importance will continue to grow well into the future. The learning curves of audit committee members, increasing publicity over weak governance and the influence of regulators (and perhaps some stakeholders?) will make this happen!

The framework of audit committee organization and oversight responsibilities in Figure 7.2 shows key characteristics and responsibilities for an audit committee's activities. This framework can be used to question audit committee members

ORGANIZATION	OVERSIGHT
1. Independence	1. Financial Reporting
2. Membership	2. Financial Statements
3. Knowledge	3. Risks
4. Experience	4. Controls
5. Meetings	5. Legal/Regulatory/Tax
6. Reporting	6. Auditing
	7. Additional Resources

Figure 7.2   Framework Of Audit Committee Responsibilities
Source: J. Ridley (1995)

on their organization and oversight responsibilities. It is based on my own experience, research and research published by others. More recently, that research by others has been mainly in North America.[c] However, since 1996, the following

---

[c] *Committee Report of the Blue Ribbon Committee on Improving the Effectiveness of Corporate Audit Committees* (1999), New York Stock Exchange and National Association of Securities, USA. *Commission Report of the NACD Blue Ribbon Committee* (1999), National Association of Corporate Directors, USA. 'Audit Committees – Improving Effectiveness', Article by Gill Bolton on the recommendations of the USA Blue Ribbon Committee, *Internal Auditing* (January 2000), IIA–UK & Ireland.

three important guides for measuring audit committee performance have been published from studies in the UK:

1. In 1997,[d] The ICAEW Audit Faculty published *Audit Committees – A Framework for Assessment*. This framework provides an excellent set of benchmarks, with many emerging best practices. Although '. . . *deliberately not prescriptive . . .* ' and recommending *'experimentation rather than imposition'*, it provides detailed and far-seeing recommendations for boards and audit committees, from a practical experience in both large and small plcs and other entities. How many regulators, boards or audit committee members have studied this framework and benchmarked their practices with its recommendations? How many managers, internal auditors and external auditors have used its recommendations to evaluate their audit committee working practices? How many stakeholders have used this framework to question boards on their audit committee effectiveness?

2. In 1998,[e] the UK Auditing Practices Board (APB) published an *Audit Briefing Paper*: 'Communication between External Auditors and Audit Committees'. This paper focuses on the nature and matters to be communicated by external auditors and related auditing standards – from appointment, audit planning, through all financial statement and annual report auditing, to findings and actions by management. References are also made to accounting policy/legal changes, associated risk management, reviews of corporate governance/internal control and working relationships with internal audit. How many audit committee members have studied this paper?

3. Also in 1998,[f] the Institute of Chartered Secretaries and Administrators (ICSA) published a guide for those working in and with audit committees: *Best Practice Guide – Terms of Reference: Audit Committee*. This guide focuses on the audit committee's constitution, remit and authority. One important recommendation on audit committee reporting has still to receive the action it deserves: *'We do believe, however, that the Audit Committee should compile a brief report for shareholders which we have suggested be included in the company's annual report although it could equally be produced as a separate statement.'* Not surprisingly, there is little evidence to date of such reports across all sectors. This will change.

Results from a questionnaire I used at a recent conference produced responses confirming the importance of the framework's content. However, there was little positive response to my question concerning the use of formal self-assessment processes for measuring the performance of the audit committee. Only three of the 25 delegates responding to the questionnaire stated that their audit committee members had used such a measure. At workshops during the conference other delegates, who did not respond to the questionnaire, confirmed a conclusion that formal self-assessment by audit committees is not a common practice.

---

[d] *Audit Committees: A Framework for Assessment* (1997), The ICAEW – Audit Faculty, London, England.
[e] 'Communication between external auditors and audit committees' (1998), *Audit Briefing Paper*, The Auditing Practices Board, London, England.
[f] *Best Practice Guide – Terms of Reference: Audit Committee* (1998), The Institute of Chartered Secretaries and Administrators, London, England.

There are many questions that all audit committee members should ask in an assessment of their organization and oversight responsibilities. Using the above framework they could start with the following:

Organization

1. Have they any executive or other responsibilities and relationships that could weaken the independence of their oversight responsibilities?
2. Is their membership and the chair rotated regularly to bring new thinking into their reviews?
3. Have they sufficient knowledge for all the control, audit and governance issues they are required to oversee?
4. Is their experience of the business plans and operations sufficient?
5. Do they meet the right people regularly and at the right time, to consider both planning and results?
6. Is the reporting of audit committee responsibilities and oversight results known to all stakeholders?

Oversight

7. Do they review all financial reporting throughout the year – both accounting and related operating information?
8. Do they review both the preparation and content of all financial statements published externally?
9. Do they review the adequacy of risk assessment by the board, management and auditors?
10. Do they review the control environment and impact of change, across the organization and all its supply chains, not just within the organization?
11. Do they consider legal/regulatory/tax issues when reviewing management's responsibilities for good governance?
12. Do they require the coordination of all auditing and inspection at the planning, audit, reporting and follow-up stages?
13. Have they the opportunity to call on additional resources to carry out their responsibilities?

Every audit committee member should independently consider the importance and implications of each of the questions in the framework and report their understanding of the best practices and levels of implementation at committee level. Such discussion should be facilitated by external advisers to ensure the best benchmarks are selected for measurement. Benchmarks are available from the studies mentioned above and, in some sectors, statements by regulators. A formal consideration of the self-assessment and its facilitation should be reviewed by the full board. Action for improvement and decisions for future performance measures should be taken.

All stakeholders should be interested in the performance of their audit committees. Only when all audit committees take seriously the importance of benchmarking themselves against worldwide best practices, will their contribution to good governance be at its best.

CUTTING EDGE INTERNAL AUDITING ASSISTS THE BOARD – TODAY AND IN THE FUTURE

Spencer Pickett (2003)[9] cites Sawyer (1996), listing the following wide range of benefits from a good internal audit team:

> Monitoring activities top management cannot itself monitor.
> Identifying and minimizing risks.
> Validating reports to senior management.
> Protecting senior management in technical analysis beyond its ken.
> Providing information for the decision-making process.
> Reviewing for the future as well as for the past.
> Helping line managers manage by pointing to violation of procedures and management principles.

Compare the above with a similar list in Sawyer (2003)[10] [shown in bold are where the differences are seven years later]:

> Monitoring activities top management cannot itself monitor.
> Identifying and minimizing risks.
> Validating reports to senior management.
> **Protecting management in technical fields.**
> **Helping in the decision-making process.**
> **Reviewing for the future – not just the past.**
> **Helping managers manage.**

Apart from the semantics, study the changes in bold. What you see are changes that reflect the new hats internal auditors are wearing today in their assurance, consulting and education roles. Within each of the above the attributes and performance of internal auditing can add a cutting edge to direction, control and performance at board level.

Chambers (2005)[11] developed interesting 'principia' for good corporate governance at board level:

1. Stakeholder control of the business.
2. Maximum and reliable public reporting.
3. Avoidance of excessive power at the top of the business.
4. A balanced board composition.
5. A strong, involved board of directors.
6. A strong, independent element on the board.
7. Effective monitoring of management by the board.
8. Competence and commitment.
9. Risk assessment and control.
10. A strong audit process.

No one would question internal auditing's interest in Principia 9 and 10. Should internal auditing assist the board in the implementation of any or all of Principia 1 to 8? Would any internal audit charter approved by an audit committee include any or all of these in the scope of internal auditing? This would be cutting edge. Yet, I suggest that there are internal audit departments in the world who touch on many of the issues in 1 to 8, certainly 7, during their engagements. There are many opportunities in all organizations for internal auditing to develop innovative practices to assist the board in all of these Principia, either directly or through an audit committee.

All the comments in this chapter have been focused on boards and audit committees in companies. Corporate governance developments in the United Kingdom have spread the practice of cooperation between internal and external audit and audit committee oversight in the public sector, with guidelines developed by Her Majesty's Treasury.[12] The most recent of these, guidelines relevant to this chapter and all organizations, are set out below. Each of these guidance statements adds direction and support for internal auditing to assist the board in many cutting edge ways:

Cooperation Between Internal and External Auditors: A Good Practice Guide

Foreword

The drive for achievement of value for money and effectiveness in public services has never been greater. Both internal and external auditors have distinctive and important contributions to make to this.

As part of this, they should endeavour to offer value for money and effectiveness in the delivery of audit services whenever opportunity presents itself. This guide offers guidance on ways in which that can be achieved while respecting the distinctive functions and professional requirements of both internal and external auditors.

We commend this guide to all concerned with the audit of central government bodies. We encourage both managers in these bodies and those responsible for the leadership of internal and external audit teams to consider it carefully and to use it as a tool to help with the achievement of effective cooperation between auditors.

Andrew Likierman
Director of Financial Management

Martin Sinclair
Assistant Auditor general
National Audit Office

Including:

5.1   Effective cooperation between internal and external audit leads to a range of benefits for both parties, and the clients they serve. While their respective roles are different, cooperation helps both parties to achieve their objectives and also helps them to provide a better service to the bodies they work with and ultimately to Parliament and the public.

5.2   To help with the assessment of cooperation, Annex C provides a checklist. This can be used to identify both the areas where satisfactory cooperation is already happening, and those in which greater benefits from cooperation could still be gained.

Audit Committee Handbook 2007 (first published 2003)

Foreword

The constitution and role of Audit Committees in central government has developed significantly in recent years. There has also been an ongoing initiative to embed effective risk management at all levels of the management of government organizations, which increases the need for explicit assurance about risk, control and governance in the organization. Consequently the value that Accounting Officers and Boards place on the work of Audit Committees has increased.

This edition of the *Audit Committee Handbook* provides updated good practice guidance which:

- supports Audit Committees (and in turn, their Boards) in achieving the principles and provisions of 'Corporate governance in central government departments: Code of Good Practice';
- reflects the increasing availability of good practice experience for Audit Committees in central government; and
- reflects the increasing significance of risk management, and associated assurance needs, in the governance of government organizations.

The guidance in this handbook sets out five fundamental principles, with explanatory good practice notes. It should help with review of the appropriateness and fitness for purpose of the constitution, membership and activity of any particular Audit Committee.

    The content of the Handbook has been developed with the help and support of a wide range of stakeholders. HM Treasury is indebted to those who have helped with this revision, and confident that their assistance has helped to provide a Handbook that promotes challenging but achievable good practice which will support the continuing quest to improve risk management, internal control and governance in government.

Mary Keegan
Head of Government Finance Profession

Including:

6.5   The role of the Audit Committee in relation to Internal Audit should include advising the Board and Accounting Officer on:

- The Audit Strategy and periodic Audit Plans, forming a view on how well they support the Head of Internal Audit's responsibility to provide an annual opinion on the overall adequacy and effectiveness of the organization's risk management, control and governance processes.

    Two board-related activities that will include cutting edge internal auditing in the next few years are:

1. *Strategy and planning processes at board level.* Without exception all corporate governance principles relate to both strategic and operational processes. Can internal auditing services ever be truly effective unless they evaluate the strategic and operational processes in an organization? Consider The IIA *International Standard* requirements on governance and their implications for both strategy and operations:

Governance

2130   The internal audit activity should assess and make appropriate recommendations for improving the governance process in its accomplishment of the following objectives:

- Promoting appropriate ethics and values within the organization.
- Ensuring effective organizational performance management and accountability.
- Effectively communicating risk and control information to appropriate areas of the organization.
- Effectively coordinating the activities of and communicating information among the board, external and internal auditors and management.

There are 25 uses of the word 'strategy' or 'strategic' in The IIA's Position Paper, *Organizational Governance Guidance for Internal Auditors* (2006), including:

A key role of the board and management is the establishment of the organization's strategy. Internal auditors typically do not challenge these key strategic elements or whether the primary organization's strategy is appropriate for the key organization stakeholders. However, this does not mean the internal auditor must remain silent on all items related to strategy. It could be beneficial to the organization for internal auditors to make observations on major issues related to strategy implementation, key risks not adequately addressed by the strategy, conflicts among various strategy elements, or the impact of the strategy on the organization or its stakeholders.

2. *Evaluation of board performance.* This is already happening in some organizations, encouraged by the reporting lines some internal auditing activities have established direct to the board and audit committee. Those internal auditing activities that have recognition of their compliance to The IIA *International Standards* at board level can only find this of assistance when proposing such internal auditing engagements. The Combined Code (2006) requirements for board evaluations of their performance, mentioned as a quote at the beginning of this chapter, is also part of the Professor Sir Andrew Likierman (2005) corporate governance requirements for public sector:

2.13   The board should undertake an annual evaluation of its performance. At least every two years, it should formally consider its remit, constitution and operating procedures.

This report references into another government report by Lynton Barker[13] (2004) into building board effectiveness, recommending that such evaluations *'. . . can be taken forward by the audit committee. The department could report annually on how this appraisal has been done, and there could be external validation.'* The Barker report offers a practical framework for the evaluation of board performance in the public sector appropriate for boards in all sectors:

1.6   The three crucial elements underlying high performing boards which I have used as the basis for the model used in this report are:

- Ensuring that the **structures and functions** of the organization and its board, and the relationships between the board, the organization, the organization's sponsor department and its key stakeholders are clear and fit for purpose.
- The **actions and behaviours** of the board and its key stakeholders are constructive and cooperative, working in the best interest of the public to deliver policy outcomes.
- **Performance evaluation** is objective and constructive, used as a tool to drive through real performance improvements.

The IIA position paper (2000) mentioned above contains 74 occasions when the word 'board' is used, including:

Specific Activities of Organizational Governance

Internal auditors can perform specific tasks that assist organizations in regard to governance structure and processes, and should consider assisting management and the board by assessing the following areas:

Board Structure, Objectives, and Dynamics. The board and its committees should be appropriately structured and chartered to operate effectively. There should be healthy board and management interaction; adequate board meeting time devoted to open discussion; a full range of issues considered at board meetings; appropriate board composition (e.g., number of board members, absence of conflicts of interest, capabilities of board members); sufficient frequency of meetings; and meetings in private executive sessions. A board should devote sufficient attention to risks, the organization's risk appetite, and risk management practices. It is not commonplace for internal auditors to evaluate these topics. However, organizations and their boards should consider whether internal audit involvement would be beneficial and accepted.

CHAPTER SUMMARY

To be at the cutting edge of internal auditing at board level internal auditors need to be involved in its direction, control and performance. *Direction* through development of its strategies, and policies; *control* through the implementation of its risk and control activities; *performance* through its ability to govern well all of its operations for the good of all its stakeholders. Internal auditors with direct lines of reporting to the board and audit committee and complying with The IIA *International Standards* are in a better position to assist boards in all sectors. Such internal auditors, wearing many hats, can and do provide value added independent and objective services to boards today. They will continue to do so tomorrow and these services will continue to develop and grow through innovative practices. Very few would question internal auditing's roles in control by the board and its monitoring of organization performance. Many may question internal auditing's roles in direction by the board and the board's monitoring of its own performance. Yet, these are key governance processes. Any discussion of internal auditing's roles in the governance of an organization must raise this involvement as an issue.

Internal auditing assisting the board is clearly covered in many of the following Gray and Gray (1997) five innovation motivation themes, four innovation goals and four innovation categories, and the additions and changes made in Chapters 2 to 6.

Motivations

1. Progress within the field of professional internal auditing.
2. Increasing competition leading to pressures to reduce costs and increase efficiency.
3. New challenges, such as increasing internal control risks due to staff reductions and restructuring.
4. Opportunities to increase efficiency and quality as a result of technological advances.
5. Changes in corporate management practices and philosophies, such as Total Quality Management, re-engineering, continuous quality improvement, or related approaches.
6. **Challenges and opportunities of global issues and developments.**
7. **Social and environmental issues impacting all organizations.**
8. **Recognition that professionalism, quality and standards are essential attributes for world-class status in any internal auditing activity.**
9. **Importance of organizational governance to meet regulatory and stakeholders' needs.**
10. **A continuous search for good and evil in how organizations and all their operations are directed and controlled.**
11. **Recognition that all types of crime in and by an organization should be fought.**

Goals

1. Improvement of the quality of interval auditing services.
2. Improve efficiency.

3. Expansion of services to increase the value-added of internal auditing.
4. Boost staff skills, performance and morale.
5. **Sell internal auditing as future focused.**
6. **To reduce the opportunities for all types of crime in an organization.**

Categories

1. Changes in the way that internal auditors interact with the rest of their enterprises **and all those with a stakeholder interest.**
2. Internal restructuring and changes in the organization and management of internal auditing.
3. Creation of new audit services and methods.
4. Changes in the use of technology.
5. **Improved knowledge and skills in the teams of staff who carry out internal auditing engagements.**
6. **New services to fight crime.**

A new category should be added to give more focus to internal auditing assisting in the evaluation of board performance:

7. **Assistance in evaluation of the board's performance.**

INTERNAL AUDITING ASSISTS THE BOARD PRINCIPIA 1998 AND 2008

My 1998 principia for internal auditing included the following related to assisting the board (numbers refer to the list in Appendix A):

25. Audit committees should strengthen internal auditing objectivity and independence.

This is now changed to reflect the importance of internal auditing assisting the board in 2008 and the future:

1. The primary role of internal auditing is to assist board performance in the achievement of the organization's vision and objectives, within a well-governed, regulated and legitimate environment.

A VISION FOR INTERNAL AUDITING ASSISTING THE BOARD

> *Our independence, resources and professional practices assist board performance*

SYNOPSES OF CASE STUDIES

Case 7.1: Corporate Governance Practices in the Context of the Combined Code 2006

Synopsis

This checklist provides a cutting edge tool for all boards and internal auditors to use when evaluating performance against the requirements of the Combined Code 2006. Each question is critical to board effectiveness in today and tomorrow's corporate governance structure, whether in the private, public or voluntary sectors.

This Checklist has been developed by Professor Andrew Chambers, Management Audit LLP and is currently included in the context of the Combined Code 2003 in Chapter A6 of Tottel's *Corporate Governance Handbook*, 3rd edition (2005). It will be included in the 4th edition (2008), ISBN 978 184766 0534. It is reproduced with permission from the publisher, Tottel Publishing, Haywards Heath, England.

After Reading the Case Study Consider:

1. How can internal auditing assist the board to evaluate its performance in each of the sections of the checklist?
2. In how many of the sections is your internal auditing assisting the board through its planning, engagements and reporting?

Case 7.2: Review of Corporate Governance at Board Level in the United Kingdom Prison Service

Synopsis

Based on an interview with the Head of Internal Audit at Her Majesty's Prison Service in the United Kingdom, published in the October 2005 issue of The IIA *Internal Auditor* this is the second review of corporate governance processes at board level in the Prison Service carried out by its Head of Internal Audit in 2005. The scope and objectives of the review are cutting edge examples of the service internal auditing should be providing when reviewing governance processes in their organizations – from top down. As a result of the review, the Head of Internal Audit now chairs a group comprising representatives of all relevant audit and inspection bodies, which includes HM Inspector of Prisons, Board of Visitors, Adult Learning Inspectorate, National Audit Office (both the financial and value for money sections) and Standards Audit Unit.

Contributed by Joyce Drummond-Hill, Head of Internal Audit in the Prison Service, with permission from the Prison Service Management Board. Joyce qualified as an MIIA in 1986 and became a fellow of the Institute of Internal Auditors–UK & Ireland in 1996. She is also Certified Internal Auditor (CIA), Certification in Control Self-Assessment (CCSA) and Certified Government Auditing Professional (CGAP) qualified. She is a member of the Institute of Internal Auditors and was President of the Institute in 1999. She has served on a number of International Committees – she was a member of The IIA Board of Regents and went on to become a member of its Ethics Committee and has chaired that for the past three years. She became Chair of The IIA Government Relations Committee in 2007.

After Reading the Case Study Consider:

1. How do you plan the scope and objectives for the audit of governance processes at board level in your organization?

2. How does your approach compare with the top-down approach in the Prison Service?
3. Would any of the findings apply in your organization?

Case 7.3: Good Practice Guidelines for the Audit Committee 1987

Synopsis

These guidelines, developed and published by the US Treadway Commission in 1987, still provide an excellent benchmark for all boards, audit committees and internal auditing. Many of the guidelines discuss issues and situations that should and have motivated innovation and cutting edge resources and practices in internal auditing.

From the *Report of the National Commission on Fraudulent Financial Reporting* (1987, Appendix I, pp. 179-181) [The Treadway Commission], with permission from Committee of Sponsoring Organizations, New York, USA. www.coso.org

After Reading the Case Study Consider:

1. How do the above 1987 guidelines benchmark with the terms of reference for your own organization's audit committee?
2. How are these guidelines implemented in your own audit committee's monitoring activities?
3. Are there other practices today in your audit committee's activities not mentioned above?
4. Has your internal auditing used these guidelines to improve the services it provides to your board and audit committee?

Case 7.4: Specimen Terms of Reference for an Audit Committee 2003

Synopsis

These guidelines were developed by a committee chaired by Sir Robert Smith and published by the UK Financial Reporting Council in 2003, They provide excellent reinforcement and an up to date perception of the guidelines in Case Study 7.3. A comparison of each should lead you in your creative thinking towards cutting edge resources and practices internal auditing can and should develop to assist today and tomorrow's board and audit committee.

Appendix 1 of *Audit Committees Combined Code Guidance*, a report and proposed guidance by an FRC-appointed group chaired by Sir Robert Smith in December 2002 and published in January 2003. [© Auditing Practices Board Ltd (APB). Adapted and reproduced with the kind permission of the Financial Reporting Council. All rights reserved.] For further information please call + 44 20 7492 2300 or visit www.frc.org.uk

After Reading the Case Study Consider:

1. Compare this case study with the Treadway Commission (1987) guidelines and note the differences.

2. What other differences would you have expected to see in the 17 years between each?
3. How appropriate are these guidelines for your own organization's audit committee and your own assistance to that committee and the board?
4. What changes would you have liked to have seen?

Case 7.5: Key Questions for an Audit Committee 2007

Synopsis

Although written for the public sector these key questions apply to all audit committees and internal auditing. They provide a *'prompt'* for all board members, audit committee members and internal auditors. Many of these questions should lead internal auditing in every organization into new and cutting edge resources and practices in the services they provide.

Reproduced with permission from HM Treasury *Audit Committee Handbook – Key Questions For An Audit Committee To Ask* (2007). www.hm-treasury.gov.uk

---

After Reading the Case Study Consider:

1. How does your internal auditing assist your audit committee in seeking satisfactory answers to these questions?
2. Are there any other questions you would add after reading the previous four case studies?
3. Are you assisting your audit committee members to answer the understandings listed at the end?

SELF-ASSESSMENT QUESTIONS

7.1 Internal Audit Role in the External Aspects of Corporate Governance

[Question contributed with permission from Professor Andrew Chambers, Management Audit LLP]

'Corporate governance' as a term also includes the accountability of the Board to the owners (and perhaps also to other stakeholders) so that the shareholders and others can exercise effective external control over their stakes in the business. For some parties, these *external* aspects of corporate governance are as important, or even more important, than the *internal* governance processes.

Internal audit findings often relate to issues which may impact the reliability of financial statements that will be published – and this is not new: internal audit may draw the attention of the audit committee to inadequate accounting which impacts upon the reliability of financial statements. Internal audit may assist the external audit in the statutory audit of the published financial statements. Internal audit is now assisting the board and the audit committee in formulating its public report on internal control and risk management. More generally, internal auditing is giving assurances to the board on other operational published analyses, especially those not subject to other independent attestation. Internal audit sometimes also now has direct relationships with regulators.

Are internal auditors key players in the *external* aspects of corporate governance, or only in the *internal* aspects of corporate governance? *Should* internal auditors be key players in the *external* aspects of corporate governance, and in what ways?

Do you consider that internal auditors may contribute to the *external* side of corporate governance, in the following ways? Tick each box that applies. Can you suggest other ways?

☐ Assisting the board in formulating their published reports on internal control under the UK Turnbull guidance, and similar guidance elsewhere.

☐ Under the Sarbanes–Oxley Act (Section 302), assisting CEOs and CFOs in their groundwork to be able to certify that each annual or quarterly report does not contain any untrue statement of a material fact or omit to state a material fact necessary in order to make the statements made, in light of the circumstances in which such statements were made, not misleading – i.e. *internal control over disclosures.*

☐ Under the Sarbanes–Oxley Act (Section 404), assisting CEOs and CFOs in the groundwork necessary to certification of the effectiveness of *internal control over financial reporting.*

☐ Contributing to the reliability of financial statements through some of the routine work that internal auditors do.

☐ Contributing to the reliability of financial statements through the results of fraud investigations undertaken by the internal audit activity.

☐ Involvement in environmental/sustainability audit and reporting.

☐ Assurances to the board on other published operational analyses, especially those not subject to other independent attestation.

☐ Advising the audit committee on the quality of external audit.

☐ Providing secretarial services to the audit committee.

☐ Other. List and address in the same context as above.

For those boxes that you tick do you have any cutting edge internal auditing resources and practices in your organization to provide these services? If not, why not?

7.2

Without looking back at the opening graphic, list the seven criteria an audit committee should address efficiently and effectively, as a cornerstone of its organization's good governance. Then list the seven issues that an audit committee should oversee successfully? Check your answers with the graphic. Does your internal auditing contribute to any on either list with cutting edge resources and practices? If not, ask why not?

NOTES AND REFERENCES

1. Published in *Certified Accountant* (October 1976), The Journal of the Association of Chartered Certified Accountants, London, England. Also in the United Kingdom Chapter of the IIA in its Audit Newsletter, March 1977.
2. *The Practice of Modern Internal Auditing* (1979), Lawrence B. Sawyer, The IIA.
3. *Auditing Principles and Practice,* 15th edition (1976: pp. 41–42), F. Clive de Paula and F.A. Attwood, Pitman Publishing Ltd, London, England. (In 1953, I was taught the fundamental principles of auditing using a much earlier edition of this book by F.R.M. de Paula CBE FCA, a significant contributor of original thought to the development of auditing worldwide.)

4. *Statements on Internal Auditing Standards* (SIAS) were first published in 1983 by The IIA to reflect developments in internal auditing. These were later used to modify its standards at future revisions.

5. *Improved Audit Committee Performance – What Works Best* (1993), Price Waterhouse, The IIA Research Foundation, Altamonte Springs, Florida, USA.

6. *Audit Committee Effectiveness – What Works Best,* 2nd edition (2000), PricewaterhouseCoopers, The IIA Research Foundation.

7. *Audit Committees and Internal Auditors – A Position Statement* (2000), IIA–UK & Ireland. (More recent advice for internal audit and the audit committee has been published by the IIA–UK & Ireland, *Meeting higher expectations* (2007))

8. Published in *Internal Auditing & Business Risk* (December 2000: p. 30), The IIA–UK & Ireland.

9. *The Internal Auditing Handbook* (2003), 2nd edition, K.H. Spencer Pickett, John Wiley & Sons Ltd, Chichester, England.

10. *Sawyer's Internal Auditing* (2003), 5th edition, The IIA.

11. Tottel's *Corporate Governance Handbook*, 3rd edition (2005: p. 173), Andrew Chambers, Tottel Publishing Haywards Heath, England.

12. Both of the guidance statements quoted can be downloaded from www.hm-treasury.gov.uk

13. *Building Effective Boards: Enhancing the Effectiveness of Independent Boards in executive Non-Departmental Public Bodies* (2004), Lynton Barker, HM Treasury, London, England. This can be downloaded from www.hm-treasury.gov.uk

8

Cutting Edge Internal Auditing Is Committed To Quality

*'As internal auditors adjust to the rigours of functioning in a
total quality environment, their focus will be external, or
toward the customer. Their mission will be one of quality
service to the organization to help management attain
its goal of Total Quality Management.'*

Elaine McIntosh 1992[1]

**Quality & Internal Audit
TQM Framework**

QUALITY PRINCIPLES

CUSTOMER FOCUS

LEADERSHIP

TEAMWORK

ANALYTICAL APPROACH

CONTINUOUS IMPROVEMENT

**SUPPLY CHAIN THEORY (INTERNAL + EXTERNAL)
INPUT........PROCESS.......OUTPUT**

QUALITY IN INTERNAL AUDITING BEFORE 1997

Quality as a measure for products and services has been around for a long time: more so as a measure by customers and less so until recently as a total commitment by those who provide products and services. Lawrence Sawyer (1973: p. 279) discussed the importance of measuring quality in any operations during field work by internal auditors: *'The auditor's measurements will normally be directed to three aspects of an operation: quality, cost and schedule.'* Despite its then simplicity, this statement is still very true today and tomorrow, although the three words quality, cost and schedule have taken on much wider definitions in organizations and operations.

My first contact with quality as a control was in the early 1960s in England when, as an internal auditor in manufacturing, I reviewed inspection processes in production, called then 'quality control' operations. These quality control operations were based on standards – material, labour, design – and inspection. At no time did I see 'quality control' processes in areas outside of production, e.g. accounting, finance, marketing, distribution, etc. Rarely was the word 'quality' mentioned or seen in the operations in these areas – though in marketing it was used in the promotion of products, but little seen in the promotion of services. And never seen in the promotion of internal auditing.

The quality focus in the early 1960s in manufacturing organizations in most countries was to find faults and errors by inspection: then to rectify or waste poor-quality products – processes that were rarely measured in organizations as a total quality cost performance. Measuring cost of rectification and waste was not used at this time as part of a total quality cost key performance indicator in operations. In some organizations it is still not today.

I did see supervision and correction processes outside of manufacturing. These existed in auditing, but in a role of inspection, similar to that in manufacturing quality control. Mainly these were informal, irregular and subjective, and did not verify compliance with any standards. At the time, I frequently commented in my audits that 'quality' and 'control' were two words rarely seen outside of production areas! All that was to change.

Any study into quality management in the 1950s and 1960s had to include an understanding of the work of Phil Crosby, Bill Conway, Dr W. Edwards Deming and Joe Juran. All seen then, and still today, as American experts/gurus/pioneers in quality principles. Oakland (1989: pp. 281–305)[2] discusses their contribution to quality principles in some detail: this is well worth reading and understanding by every internal auditor. All focused their principles on the needs of the customer: actions to satisfy these needs first time; measurements to monitor that this happens; and corrections to continuously improve.

My own quality experience in Kodak was with the Conway six tools[3] for quality improvement:

1. *Human relations skills* – the responsibility of management to create at every level, among all employees, the motivation and training to make the necessary improvements in the organization.
2. *Statistical surveys* – the gathering of data about customers (internal as well as external) employees, technology, and equipment, to be used as a measure for future progress and to identify what needs to be done.
3. *Simple statistical techniques* – clear charts and diagrams that help to identify problems, track work flow, gauge progress, and indicate solutions.
4. *Statistical process control* – the statistical charting of a process, whether manufacturing or non-manufacturing, to help to identify ands reduce variation.
5. *Imagineering* – a key concept in problem solving. Involves the visualization of a process, procedure, or operation with all waste eliminated.
6. *Industrial engineering* – common techniques of pacing, work simplification, methods analysis, plant layout, and material handling to achieve improvements.

Oakland likens the concept of 'imagineering' to the power of a vision statement '. . . *which is based on images of the desired future being used to shape thoughts and guide actions. The power of the method lies in its ability to generate creativity and energy and extend the problem-solving framework.*' How close this is to the theme of innovation and creativity in this book!

Oakland's analysis of Total Quality Management requirements in the early 1990s was structured around the following 12 words:

Understanding	Planning	Control
Commitment	Design	Teamwork
Organization	System	Training
Measurement	Capability	Implementation

Words such as customer, continuous, improvement may well be given a higher profile today, but each was included in Oakland's discussion of the words above.

The 1980s saw a growing interest in quality principles in the United Kingdom, starting with the publication of the quality standard BS 5750: 1979, which later became the international quality management standard ISO 9000: 1987. At the time many saw these standards as *'conformance to requirements'* rules rather than the foundation for quality management systems. In parallel to these standards many organizations were also turning to a total commitment to quality in their products and services to better satisfy their customers, reduce costs and beat competition. These organizations were being led in their quality culture changes by many consultants and academics.[4]

At this early stage in development of Total Quality Management (TQM) in organizations in the United Kingdom there was still a high focus on quality inspection and rejection processes. The concept of stopping quality inspection and relying on quality management systems to achieve high levels of quality first time was still in its early stages in many organizations. This is the main purpose of TQM – a total commitment to 'right first time'.

The UK led the world in development of its national quality standard BS 5750: 1979. This established standards for design, manufacture, inspection and testing, and came about through requirements in government procurement programmes. Government departments required suppliers to register their manufacturing processes to the standard as a demonstration of their commitment to quality. Interest in the standard grew across all industry sectors and it became appropriate for both service and manufacturing operations.

The International Standards Organization (ISO) (1987) published its own ISO 9000 series of quality management standards for manufacturing and service operations, based on BS 5750. Since that date various international working parties associated with ISO have revised the ISO 9000 series to the family of standards that it is today, all of which now relate much more clearly to the quality principles mentioned earlier and TQM.

In late 1980s[5] the IIA–UK & Ireland conducted research into quality methods used by internal auditing activities. Responses were few; those that participated ranked the methods they were using in their functions to achieve a high level of quality, as shown in Figure 8.1. A customer focus and auditing methods ranked high for the achievement of quality, though customer feedback was lower. While a commitment to train and involve all internal audit staff in rules for a TQM culture, ranked low, an external quality assessment did not rank at all! Many of these methods to achieve quality in internal auditing are still in use today and will be tomorrow.

Further research into the key measures of audit quality in the United Kingdom by John Bevan (1990: p. 2) reported:

... in the use and definition of [quality] measures considerable variation was found between participants, making inter-organizational comparisons difficult, if not impossible. Whilst value was often claimed for the use of measures within any one organization, a few significant shortcomings were also noted, especially in the completeness of what was measured. . . .

Ranked by most used first

1. Audit charter/objectives/policies.
2. Clear understanding of audit objectives between auditor and auditee.
3. Supervisory reviews of audit working papers.
4. Housekeeping/administration in work areas and files.
5. Responses to recommendations and follow-ups with auditees.
6. Training for all internal audit staff in auditing and personal skills.
7. Communication and significance of audit results.
8. Job descriptions for all levels of internal audit staff.
9. Working relationships with other audit groups.
10. Audit time measures.
11. Computer technology in internal auditing.
12. Reviews of internal auditing work by audit committee.
13. Audit manual to direct internal auditing.
14. Feedback from customers.
15. Recognition of good audit and staff performance.
16. Risk analysis techniques to select audits.
17. Working relationships with other management support groups.
18. Quality management standards as a benchmark
19. Laws and regulations as benchmarks.
20. Internal peer reviews of internal auditing engagements.
21. IIA Standards/Code of Ethics/Statements as benchmarks.
22. Working involvement with an organization's quality activities.
23. Training for all internal audit staff in techniques for quality improvement.
24. Quality statement by internal auditing and/or organization.
25. Use of quality teams to focus on improvements.
26. External reviews by staff outside the internal auditing function.

Figure 8.1   Internal Auditing Quality Methods In Late 1980s
Source: Quality Assurance in the Internal Audit Department (1991)

Only one measurement method, that of customer satisfaction surveys, attempts to assess the overall value of internal audit work with any success. Despite the obvious difficulties inherent in conducting any survey of opinion, and despite the caution advised in much of the literature, these measures were thought to be very useful by most if not all participants.

Internal audit activities adopting a TQM culture in the early 1990s – and using this to promote quality cultures in their organizations – were at the cutting edge of internal auditing at the time. This was discussed earlier in my article on world-class internal auditing, published in 1990, included in Chapter 3, and repeated here:

What are some of the gains to be achieved?

- Recognition of the SUPPLIER–PROCESS–CUSTOMER CHAIN for the audit process, drives the audit programme into the heart of business activity and highlights the key controls needed for business success.
- Establishing who are the customer and CUSTOMER NEEDS helps to focus audit tests into the most important areas and issues.
- The concept of AUDITOR/AUDITEE teamwork during the audit process is achieved and 'participative auditing' becomes a reality.
- AUDIT RESULTS and RECOMMENDATIONS concentrate on prevention rather than detection, looking to the control of quality in the future, rather than the past.

- QUALITY ASSURANCE requirements to meet IIA Standards take on a wider meaning, linking the quality aims of the internal audit department into those of the organization.
- Emphasis on CONTINUOUS IMPROVEMENT in the TQM environment encourages internal audit staff 'to continually seek improvements' in the audit process.
- TQM requires QUALITY MEASURES in all processes, to monitor quality and highlight non-conformance with standards.
- The audit process becomes a QUALITY SYSTEM, which can lead to recognition under the national accreditation standard BS 5750 (ISO 9000).
- QUALITY SUCCESSES are more easily recognized and rewarded at team and individual levels.

My first contact with quality as an ethic for internal auditors was in The IIA revised *Code of Ethics* (1988):

X. Members and CIA's [Certified Internal Auditors] shall continually strive for improvement in their proficiency, and in the effectiveness and quality of their service.

Note the commitment *'strive'* and relationships between *'proficiency'*, *'effectiveness'* and *'quality'*. This was a significant step by The IIA in recognizing the importance of the individual in any quality commitment process.

Supporting this ethic was the requirement in The IIA *Standards* of the day:

560   Quality Assurance: The director of internal auditing should establish a quality assurance programme to evaluate the operations of the internal auditing department.

This requirement patterned a similar quality requirement for external auditors at that time. Recommended structures and processes for this quality assurance programme were (and still are today) supervision, internal reviews and external reviews. Together, the ethic and *Standard* took an important step towards the professionalism of internal auditing. They are both essential today in all professions, and all organizations.

Although most references to TQM discuss quality commitment in an organization, it is important to recognize that by organization is meant also all an organization's relations with its suppliers, as well as customers. The UK National Audit Office (1990) stated: *'A recognition that success in world markets increasingly depends on quality as well as price.'* This led the UK government in 1982 to publish a White Paper: *Standards: Quality and International Competitiveness* (Cmnd 8621).

A British Standards Institution quality management standard was developed in the UK – BS 7850: 1992 *Total Quality Management*. This standard defined TQM as:

Total quality management assures maximum effectiveness and efficiency within an organization by putting in place processes and systems which will ensure that every aspect of its activity is aligned to satisfy customer needs and all other objectives without waste of effort and using the full potential of every person in the organization. This philosophy recognizes that customer satisfaction, health, safety, environmental considerations and business objectives are mutually dependent. It is applicable within any organization.

This definition of TQM brought in the importance of TQM for issues other than quality – health, safety, environment. This was an important inclusion evidenced today in the promotion of ISO 9000, as we will see later.

Elaine McIntosh's manual on TQM, published in 1992, came about five years after I had started down the quality road. In the quote mentioned above, she recognized that achieving quality in internal auditing demands a commitment to standards; a focus on customers; and assistance by internal auditing for all levels of management in the achievement of an organization's quality aims. Quality in internal audit work is never an end in itself. It should always be seen as a means for adding better value to management and the whole organization.

The IIA publication in 1992 recognized that:

> (p. 3) Many organizations worldwide have found that by following a TQM philosophy they can provide goods and services that better meet their customers' needs. As a consequence, these organizations achieve greater revenue, contain costs, and surpass competitors that try to increase profit without proper regard for customer requirements.

and

> (p. 7) As internal auditors provide their service to management, they evaluate their own internal audit processes to make their functions more effective.

SEPSU (1994),[6] in explaining its rationale for studying UK quality management, emphasized that:

> . . . quality is self-evidently important in all spheres of human endeavour. In the sphere of organized work, quality is now one of the central determinants of competitive survival and thus of national prosperity. This leads to a widespread interest in the management of quality as a dimension of corporate behaviour . . . .

Quality cultures were now (and are still today) frequently stated publicly in advertisements and other communications by all sizes of organization across all sectors. This, however, is mainly to impress stakeholders, sell products and services and increase market share. Organizations use many definitions of quality, most of which are established in organization visions, missions, strategic plans, key result areas and performance measures. All have a basic aim: to motivate continuous improvement throughout internal and external supply chains; to encourage and regulate improvement in supplier organizations; and to achieve customer satisfaction, if not also delight. The framework in Figure 8.2 shows how Total Quality Management is embedded in an organization from quality policy to a commitment for world-class status, across all supply chains, inside and across an organization, from suppliers (internal and external) to customers (internal and external). Use this framework to assess your own organization's commitment to quality.

The 1990s provide ample evidence that organizations across the world were using quality initiatives to control and promote their products and services, and drive improved performance. The ISO 9000 of the day was being focused on both quality management and

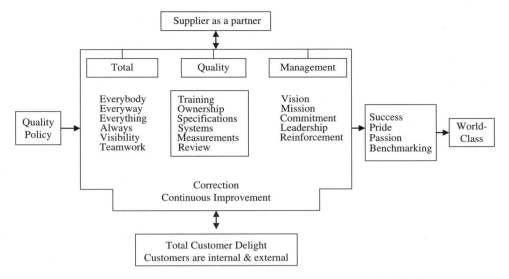

Figure 8.2   TQM Framework: Total Commitment Across The Supply Chain
Source: J. Ridley, *Leading Edge Internal Auditing* (1998)

continuous improvement. Its established quality requirements formed an important foundation for the introduction of TQM.

Article:
Embracing ISO[7] (1997)

The number of ISO 9000 certificates issued by the end of 1995 totalled more than 127,000 most recent Mobil tificates World-more have been Such widespread affects all aspects environment, internal audit function.

> *'Recent global research conducted for The IIA Research Foundation documents the growing interest in ISO 9000 and the resulting impact on the internal audit function.'*

according to the Survey of ISO Cer-wide. Hundreds awarded since. allegiance to ISO of the business including the

Recent global research conducted for The IIA Research Foundation documents the growing interest in ISO 9000 and the resulting impact on the internal audit function. Almost half the internal auditors responding to the survey indicated that their companies have acquired or are planning to acquire ISO 9000 registrations (see Figure 8.3). Quality auditing, the control environment, and quality improvement in internal audit functions appear to be the three primary areas to be impacted by ISO 9000 initiatives.

Industry	Total respondents	Number who have implemented or are planning ISO 9000
Agriculture, Forestry, Fisheries	4	2
Mining	5	3
Contract Construction	2	1
Manufacturing	62	46
Transport, Communications, Utilities	37	14
Wholesale and Retail Trade	7	1
Financial, Insurance and Real Estate	48	10
Services	19	7
Government	27	8
Non-classified	2	1
Total	213	93

Figure 8.3   ISO 9000 Involvement 1996

Source: International Quality Standards: Implications For Internal Auditing (1996)

Quality Auditing

Across the globe, quality auditors are growing in number and professionalism. Quality auditing is seen by many as an important part of business process re-engineering and total quality management. Many quality auditors no longer focus on compliance as their only objectives, but go on to address continuous improvement and follow up their audit recommendations with management.

At present there is little evidence of coordination and liaison between quality and other types of auditing; but in many organizations the integration of quality auditing with other internal audit services at strategic, tactical, and operational levels will soon be a reality. Already, there are signs that audit work performed by quality auditors overlaps the work of internal or external auditors. If for no other reason, the cost of auditing will drive management and audit committees to review how all auditors communicate and interact with each other.

When survey participants were asked how they see their interaction with quality auditors developing during the next five years, most predicted an increased coordination and liaison. However, only a small percentage believes there will be more joint auditing, or that internal and quality auditing will become one function. Respondents whose organizations are ISO registered were asked to denote which of nine audit types could be improved by coordination and liaison with quality auditing. Most noted that compliance auditing would be improved, while half named operational auditing. Few saw any added value to their financial auditing. Surprisingly few saw reduced total audit costs as a benefit of increased coordination. In reality, however, links between quality and other types of auditing appear to be essential if an organization is to achieve maximum benefit from its monitoring and total auditing costs.

Control and ISO 9000

In organizations registered to ISO 9000 standards, the impact on control systems is significant, although often overlooked. For example, survey respondents were asked to consider the objectives of internal control, as stated in The IIA *Standards*, and to indicate which objectives could be influenced by Total Quality Management (TQM) or ISO 9000. Most respondents stated that ISO and TQM could have an impact on *'compliance with laws and regulations'* and the *'accomplishment of objectives'*, however, few perceived any influence on the *'safeguarding of assets'* (see Figure 8.4).

Control objectives	% of Internal audit functions considering ISO 9000 that perceive impact of TQM or ISO on the Objective		% of functions not considering ISO 9000 that perceive impact of TQM or ISO on the objective	
	TQM	ISO	TQM	ISO
Reliability and Integrity	65	65	55	46
Compliance	54	81	46	63
Safeguarding of Assets	33	31	36	31
Economy and Efficiency	69	35	74	38
Accomplishment of Objectives	79	54	81	46

Figure 8.4   Perceived Influence Of TQM And ISO On Control Objectives
Source: International Quality Standards: Implications For Internal Auditing (1996)

The failure to recognize any influence of TQM and ISO 9000 on the safe-guarding of assets indicates that most respondents do not see the connection between quality and physical security over buildings, material, and cash. Yet TQM can reduce levels of control through its change environment, empowerment, and teamwork; and ISO 9000 focuses strongly on inspection and checking activities.

Such weak perceptions of the link between quality and the control environment can also be found in internal auditing literature. Few organizations or previous researchers have attempted to relate quality to governance and regulation or to link the objectives of each in common mission and policy statements. An appendage to the Canadian Institute of Chartered Accountants' Criteria of Control Board (CoCo) guide does relate its control criteria to the Malcolm Baldrige quality award criteria, demonstrating a clear link between each. However, the guide makes no reference to quality standards or ISO 9000.

Yet, it is not difficult to see the quality requirements in ISO 9000 in the accepted control frameworks. Building a frame of reference between both can be an excellent learning exercise for every internal auditor.

Linking ISO 9000 to Control

Each of ISO 9000's quality requirements can influence all the elements of control identified in *Internal Control – Integrated Framework*, published by the Committee of Sponsoring Organizations (COSO) of The Treadway Commission (1992). Comparing the ISO 9000 quality requirements with the COSO control elements shows important links between the two (see Figure 8.5).

ISO 9000 Quality Requirements

Management Responsibility

Quality System

Contract Review

Design Control

Document and Data Control

Purchasing

Control of Customer-supplied Product

Product Identification and Traceability

Process Control

Inspection and Testing

COSO Control Elements

Control Environment
Risk Assessment
Control Activities
Monitoring
Information Systems
Communication

Control of Inspection, Measuring, and Test Equipment

Inspection and Test Status

Control of Nonconforming Product

Corrective and Preventive Action

Handling, Storage, Packaging, Preservation and Delivery

Control of Quality Records

Internal Quality Audits

Training

Servicing

Statistical Techniques

Figure 8.5   ISO 9000 And COSO. Integrated Control Framework
Source: 'Embracing ISO 9000', J. Ridley, *Internal Auditor*, August 1999, The IIA

Many of ISO 9000's quality requirements echo the elements of a good internal control system as defined by COSO. For example, the quality principles of customer focus, leadership, teamwork, analysis, and continuous improvement can also be applied to each of the COSO elements. Quality, although not specifically mentioned in COSO, is an important requirement of the COSO control objectives assuring the effectiveness and efficiency of operations, the reliability of financial reporting, and compliance with applicable laws and regulations.

Quality requirements are also present in the control framework and criteria of control defined by CoCo. According to CoCo, control involves purpose, commitment, capability, monitoring, and learning. The following CoCo description of a properly controlled environment could apply equally to a quality system:

> A person performs a task, guided by an understanding of its purpose (the objective to be achieved) and supported by capability (information, resources, supplies, and skills). The person will need a sense of commitment to perform the task well over time. The person will monitor his or her performance and the external environment to learn about how to do the task better and about changes to be made. The same is true of any team or work group. In any organization of people, the essence of control is purpose, commitment, capability and monitoring and learning.

Still, little practical evidence exists that organizations see how forging a connection between quality and control is essential for success, and even for survival. Despite the fact that both COSO and CoCo link control requirements to quality requirements, there is still a lag between theory and practice.

Quality as Control

Any risk analysis focused on an organization's vision and mission must consider the risk of poor quality and dissatisfied external customers and stakeholders. Any study of internal control frameworks in organizations will always show clear links between the control requirements of efficiency, effectiveness, and economy, and the quality requirements of ISO 9000. When visions for excellence and quality missions are married to control environments for governance, both are more successful: both can and do drive improvement in each other.

In the near future, many organizations are expected to make public statements on their environmental management and assessment systems. All internal auditors should review how their organization relates quality, risk management, governance and environmental management in its control framework and statements to stakeholders. As evidenced by The IIA's recent involvement in these issues, internal auditors may find it advantageous to lead the debate and practice in these emerging relationships.

Immediate Impacts

Internal audit functions are not only affected by ISO 9000 through the emergence of quality auditing and new approaches to internal control: some internal audit functions have gone so far as to register their own services to the standard, training staff as quality auditors and providing quality management advice as part of their service. Almost 25% of the respondents said they have considered registering some or all of their internal auditing services to ISO 9000, of these, 60% actually pursued assessment and became ISO 9000 registered (see Figure 8.6).

Staff size	Considering ISO 9000	Registered to ISO 9000
Less than 5	3	2
5–9	12	8
10–14	5	2
15–25	10	5
26–50	6	5
51 or more	11	5
Size unknown	5	4
Total functions	52	31

Figure 8.6   Number Of Internal Audit Functions Pursuing ISO 9000 In 1996
Source: International Quality Standards: Implications for Internal Auditing (1996)

Why Register?

The research findings revealed some surprising attitudes regarding the benefits of registering the internal audit function. Survey respondents ranked nine organizational attributes that might be improved as a result of ISO 9000 registration. The highest ratings went to image, consistency, efficiency, teamwork and communication. Surprisingly, training, flexibility, and risk received lower rankings. The low ranking of risk is of particular concern, because the ISO 9000 requirements for a quality system can have a significant impact on control levels throughout the organization. Both internal auditors and managers should be concerned about the lack of recognition of the link between risk management and quality [management].

Case Studies

Eight internal audit functions that were registered or planning to register their services to ISO 9000 were selected for an in-depth study of the impact on their practices (see Figure 8.7).

Industry	Base of parent Company	Staff size	Date of registration
Manufacturing	USA	6	ISO 9001 – 1992
Audit Agency	UK	30	ISO 9002 – 1992
Communications	UK	100	ISO 9002 – 1993
Government	UK	58	ISO 9002 – 1993
Manufacturing	UK	21	ISO 9001 – 1994
Retail Trade	UK	57	ISO 9001 – 1994
Utilities	Ireland	25	ISO 9001 – 1994
Banking	USA	42	Planned – 1995

Each internal audit function varied in staff size and length of ISO 9000 experience. All of the functions had been established for some time and had some form of internal auditing charter, procedures, and a wide scope of audit work before they considered ISO 9000. All had some form of quality assurance designed into their processes, but only a few had previously experienced any formal external review. Those external reviews were mainly by professional accounting firms. One function had been reviewed in 1991 by The IIA's Quality Assurance Review service.

Figure 8.7   Internal Audit Functions Registered To ISO 9000 In 1996
Source: International Quality Standards: Implications for Internal Auditing (1996)

Several reasons, which varied in order of importance among the group, were given for pursuing registration:

- *Procedural needs:* such as the desire to update and improve procedures; to motivate internal auditing staff to comply with procedures; and to develop more uniform practices.
- *Strategic needs:* such as being required by the organization to pursue ISO 9000 or to demonstrate quality in services provided.
- *Organizational needs:* such as the desire to change the structure of global or national service and to improve supervision and team building.
- *Marketing needs:* such as using ISO registration as part of a programme to market test the internal auditing service in competition with other bids and to market internal auditing services within the organization.

The mix of reasons changed as the process of registration proceeded and the ISO 9000 experience increased. For example, most initial intentions were not to seek improvements in professional practices, but to document the current practices more clearly and uniformly. However, addressing ISO 9000 quality requirements focused attention on the structure needed to achieve and maintain a quality management system and organization. This focus emphasized responsibilities for quality at all levels. In addition, continuous cycles of monitoring and correction, driven by the quality system and its required audits, encouraged staff to strive for new methods and responsibilities.

Study participants found that actually going through the registration process afforded several benefits, mainly in the areas of quality vision and mission. Management leadership, teamwork, and good communication were necessary to mould the existing internal auditing practices into compliance with ISO 9000. These changes required training and a writing and re-writing of audit procedures.

Overall, participants perceived four main benefits of ISO 9000 registration:

1. *Development of a quality policy*: Like The IIA *Standards*, ISO 9000 requires a declaration of quality purpose. For ISOI 9000, this declaration involves publication of a quality policy. Each of the internal auditing functions had incorporated such a statement in its charter.

2. *Established standard of conduct*: The IIA *Standards* require internal auditors to take due professional care in their audit work. Compliance to ISO 9000 quality requirements promoted diligence in audit work and established an environment that embraced many of the principles in The IIA *Code of Ethics*.

3. *Improved documentation*: The IIA *Standards* require written policies and procedures for all audit work. The importance of such written documentation was reinforced by the ISO 9000 quality requirements for controlled documentation and records.

4. *Procedures for quality assurance*: The IIA *Standards* require evidence of supervision and quality assurance in all audit work. The ISO 9000 quality assurance and quality audit requirements provide a framework for the supervision, management, and external review of all internal auditing practices.

According to the response of the [case study] group, using ISO 9000 to develop and register audit documentation, records, and auditing systems had the most significant impact on their functions. In all cases the process of registration required changes and improvements to satisfy the ISO Standards 20 quality requirements. Some are using ISO 9000 as a framework for implementing The IIA quality assurance requirements into their internal auditing practices. Some used their certification to promote quality consulting and auditing as an internal auditing service.

Continuing Impact

In the June 1995 issue of *Internal Auditor* the article 'ISO's Impact' by David Sherick reported the experiences of one internal audit function's registration to ISO 9000. The author reported a positive outcome and stated that by staying out of the ISO 9000 arena '. . . *internal auditors may be missing an opportunity to contribute significantly to their organization's quality commitment and competitive potential in the global environment'*.

The current research corroborates Sherick's theory. Internal auditors can use ISO 9000 to:

- support and strengthen compliance with The IIA *Standards*;
- promote quality in internal audit work;
- establish quality assurance in internal auditing functions;

- establish quality as a leading edge in the internal audit market place;
- require quality learning programmes for internal auditors;
- improve links with quality auditors;
- forge coordination between quality objectives and governance;
- sell quality consulting by internal auditors.

Registrations to ISO 9000 are growing, and its influence over quality and control practices is being felt in many organizations across the world. Internal auditors need to be among the leaders in this movement.

QUALITY IN INTERNAL AUDITING 1997 TO 2001

Interest in quality management grew between these years in all sectors in the United Kingdom and across the world. Registrations to ISO 9000 increased significantly fuelled by the growth of global business and changes to the standard to relate it more to the quality principles of continuous improvement. In the public sector there was an increased interest in quality awards and best value programmes to meet public interest in improved services and competition with the private sector. The importance of quality in internal auditing and the services it provides increased.

Article:
Quality Schemes And Best Value In The 21st Century[8] (2001)

Challenges of Quality

There can be few suppliers and customers that do not recognize the importance of quality. It chal- lenges all prod- ucts and services.

> *'A successful internal auditing role requires all internal auditors to understand how quality schemes contribute to success.'*

The use of quality schemes to meet these challenges is evident in most countries. Quality schemes change strategies, struc- tures, processes and people. Gov- ernments and managing bodies in all sectors have learnt to lead, develop and monitor them, often for survival. The challenges of doing so have been difficult for many. The consequences of not doing so have been disastrous for many.

Every day, internal auditors meet these same challenges and recognize the same consequences in their own work and the work of others. A successful internal auditing role as '. . . *an independent, objective, assurance and consulting activity, designed to add value and improve an organization's operations.*[a]', requires all

---

[a] New definition of internal auditing (1999), The IIA.

internal auditors to understand how quality schemes contribute to success. Their knowledge and experience of control is a good starting point.

Consider all the elements in the now well-used COSO[b] integrated control model – *Control Environment, Risk Assessment, Control Activities, Monitoring, Information and Communication.* The descriptions of each of these elements (see Figure 8.8) have direct links to all quality principles. Look for these elements in your own and your organization's quality schemes. Require them in all your suppliers' quality schemes. Integrated they can meet all the challenges of achieving quality in everything you do.

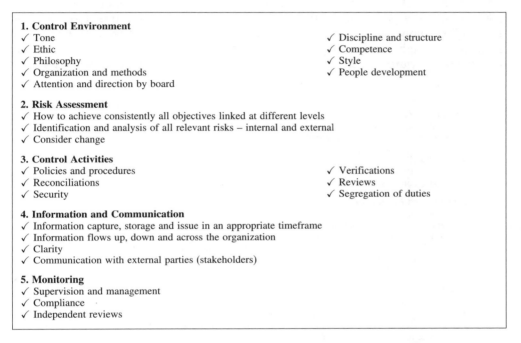

1. Control Environment
✓ Tone
✓ Ethic
✓ Philosophy
✓ Organization and methods
✓ Attention and direction by board

✓ Discipline and structure
✓ Competence
✓ Style
✓ People development

2. Risk Assessment
✓ How to achieve consistently all objectives linked at different levels
✓ Identification and analysis of all relevant risks – internal and external
✓ Consider change

3. Control Activities
✓ Policies and procedures
✓ Reconciliations
✓ Security

✓ Verifications
✓ Reviews
✓ Segregation of duties

4. Information and Communication
✓ Information capture, storage and issue in an appropriate timeframe
✓ Information flows up, down and across the organization
✓ Clarity
✓ Communication with external parties (stakeholders)

5. Monitoring
✓ Supervision and management
✓ Compliance
✓ Independent reviews

Figure 8.8 Five Components Of The COSO Control Model (1992)
Source: COSO *Internal Control – Integrated Framework* (1992)

Principles of Quality

The 1980s and 1990s saw a worldwide increase in the teaching and implementation of quality schemes. Most of these programmes focused on economics and customer satisfaction, with controlled processes, feedback mechanisms and appropriate measures. Most motivated those involved with the need for continuous improvement. All required total commitment. Many evolved from existing quality control and assurance functions. Many were new, established because of regulatory, competitive or cost pressures.

---

[b] *Internal Control – Integrated Framework* (1992), Committee of Sponsoring Organizations of the Treadway Commission, New York, USA.

During this period 'quality objectives' in business and public sector organizations moved into all levels of direction and management decision making. Strategic plans embraced the need for quality and customer satisfaction, *if not delight*. Directors of Quality appeared on many boards. The results could be seen in a growth of quality cultures and quality system standards, fuelled by many governments and consultants. Competitive national and international quality awards were created to stimulate the development of these cultures. These awards still attract many organizations to quality self-assessment programmes and external quality audits.

When quality programmes are created by a *'total commitment'* to quality in all strategies, structures and systems, then total quality management (TQM) is implemented. Quality gurus across the world have created exciting quality principles, motivating many organizations to adopt TQM practices. Often with significant benefits – not just for the organization, but also for their customers, suppliers and employees. Figure 8.9 shows the five key principles in TQM. One of the most

---

1. **Customer Focus**
   - All customers are different, their satisfaction is paramount
   - Focus on both internal and external customers, primary and secondary
   - View all customers as partners in your supply chains
   - Understand all your customers' needs
   - Aim for customer delight at all times, not just satisfaction
   - Do not ignore customer complaints

2. **Management Leadership**
   - Organize for quality
   - Establish a clear and motivating vision understood by everyone
   - Identify your key success factors and build these into a clear mission statement
   - Provide the right structures, methods and resources for quality achievement
   - Communicate well at all levels, both in clarity and timeliness
   - Give high visibility to your quality policy

3. **Teamwork**
   - Recognize and encourage the power of teams
   - Develop teams across the whole supply chain, internal and external
   - Interlock all teams at operation, function and cross function levels
   - Reinforce and reward teams for success
   - Teach teams to focus on your vision and mission statements
   - Delegate responsibility to teams to take action

4. **Measurement**
   - If it cannot be measured, it cannot be improved
   - Measure by statistics – do not inspect.
   - Establish measures in all processes, across all supply chains, with high visibility
   - Relate all measures to your vision and mission statements
   - Focus measures on customers, both internal and external
   - Take prompt corrective action on all measurements

5. **Total Commitment to Continuous Improvement**
   - Look for problems, develop solutions and train
   - Create a learning organization with a constant commitment to improve
   - Encourage a constant and continuous search for excellence
   - Be creative – look for paradigm shifts
   - Benchmark – internally and externally
   - Verify the success of change

Figure 8.9   Quality Principles
Source: Leading Edge Internal Auditing (1998)

important principles is the satisfaction of quality across all supply chains – which is essential for all of the principles.

Oakland[c] describes quality (now referred to by many as supply) chain theory as a continuous chain of meeting customer requirements across processes, both external and internal to the organization:

> Throughout and beyond all organizations, whether they be manufacturing concerns, banks, retail stores, universities, or hotels, there is a series of quality chains which may be broken at any point by any one person or piece of equipment not meeting the requirements of the customer, internal or external.

An understanding of this simple definition of the supply chain is fundamental to the achievement of quality.

> **TQM** is therefore all the internal and external chains of **Supplier, Process and Customer**, directed by **Quality Strategies** and measured by the achievement of **Quality Objectives**, with a **Total Commitment** to all the **Quality Principles** in Figure 8.2.

Benchmark this statement with your own interpretation and commitment to TQM.

Development of Quality Schemes

Research in the 1990s showed that there were different levels of quality commitment in organizations, usually recognized by the types of schemes used. Quality assurance was and still is the basic level, characterized by agreed specifications, supervision, inspection and rectification. Next came ad hoc quality improvement projects, using staff in motivated teams with performance targets focused on customer satisfaction. Then came TQM systems satisfying the quality principles already mentioned. At the same time international quality standards (ISO 9000) were developed and promoted. These require external registration of quality systems to international quality requirements and a quality manual with operating procedures – all subject to independent internal and external quality audit.

After TQM and ISO 9000 came national and international quality awards by external assessment, e.g. Business Excellence Model, Quality Charters, Investors in People, ISO 9000, etc. These awards have developed with a wider stakeholder focus on results and impacts on society as a whole. All these quality levels do not stand in isolation from each other; they can all be linked, even integrated, under an umbrella of *quality schemes*. That they are not in many organizations weakens their impact, on both the organization and its stakeholders.

More recently the use of quality schemes in organizations in Europe resulted in a 1999 cross-border quality charter, agreed for all countries in the European Union.[d] The European Quality Charter was launched by quality representative

---

[c] *Total Quality Management* (1989), John S. Oakland, Butterworth-Heinemann, Oxford, England.
[d] European Organization for Quality (EOQ) Switzerland website www.eoq.org

organizations in Europe as an advantage for Europe in international competition. Its opening statement summarizes the aims of quality as an *organizational excellence objective, a methodology and a way of promoting people's active participation based on involvement and responsibility of each individual.* Ten significant challenges[e] in this new charter for all organizations and internal auditors are:

1. Quality is the key to *competitiveness.*
2. Quality is an excellence *objective.*
3. Quality is a way of *participation.*
4. Quality implies *motivation.*
5. Quality is based on *initiative.*
6. Quality is a concern for the *customer.*
7. Quality is a measure of *efficiency.*
8. Quality must be a *priority.*
9. Quality is inseparable from *solidarity.*
10. Quality *chains link all economic and social players.*

Relate these charter challenges to the COSO control elements and quality principles mentioned earlier.

Quality Schemes and ISO 9000

There have been many debates over the years as to whether a quality system registered to ISO 9000 is TQM. Those that agree that it is, usually base their opinion on the detailed requirements of ISO 9000 and its supporting guidelines (9004-1: 1994). These guidelines do not form part of the registration process, however they are advisory for the development of a quality system and clearly written in a TQM context. They require quality systems to meet and satisfy both customer and organization needs and expectations:

(a) *The customer's needs and expectations*
    For the customer, there is a need for confidence in the ability of the organization to deliver the desired quality as well as the consistent maintenance of that quality.

(a) *The organization's needs and interests*
    For the organization, there is a business need to attain and to maintain the desired quality at an optimum cost; the fulfilment of this aspect is related to the planned and efficient utilization of the technological, human and material resources available to the organization.

Those that do not agree usually base their opinion on the detailed documentation required for registration of a quality system and the compliance nature of quality auditing. Many also believe that there is not sufficient focus on customer satisfaction and continuous improvement in ISO 9000, even though both are referred to in the guidelines. This debate is reflected in the current revisions to ISO 9000: 1994, which will consolidate the family of ISO 9000 standards into four primary

---

[e] 'Ten Quality Challenges for Internal Auditors' (1999), Jeffrey Ridley, *Internal Auditing & Business Risk*, September 1999, IIA–UK & Ireland.

standards 9000, 9001, 9004 and 10011 (Guideline for auditing quality systems). The 1998 introduction to the final draft of ISO 9000: 2000 gives '*customer needs*' as the main force driving the revision. It also introduces a revised guidelines ISO 9004: 2000, developed to be consistent with the new ISO 9001: 2000:

> Whereas the revised ISO 9001 more clearly addresses the quality management system requirements for an organization to demonstrate its capability to meet customer requirements, the revised ISO 9004 is intended to lead beyond ISO 9001 towards the development of a comprehensive quality management system. In particular, the revised ISO 9004 will not be an implementation guide to the revised ISO 9001. The revised ISO 9004 is based on eight quality management principles: customer focus, leadership, involvement of people, process approach, system approach to management, continual improvement, factual approach to decision making, and mutually beneficial supplier relationships.

There is evidence that ISO 9000 has been used by organizations to achieve other awards leading to marks of excellence, e.g. Business Excellence Model, Investor in People Award, charters, supplier awards, productivity awards, training awards, etc. This wide variety of relationships was recognized by the British Standards Institute in its 1996 annual report:

> *Our (ISO 9000) clients have enjoyed considerable success in the UK Quality Awards, the Wales Quality Awards, the European Quality Awards and the Construction Industry Awards.*

Quality Schemes and Best Value

The recently introduced UK government Best Value Review (BVR) concept for local government is defined[f] '. . . *as a duty to deliver services to clear standards (covering both cost and quality) by the most economic, efficient and effective means available.*' From this year, all local authorities must have a Best Value Performance Plan (BVPP) that includes a programme of BVRs, applying the government's four best value principles (4Cs) of:

Challenge	why, how and by whom a service is being given.
Comparison	with the performance of others across a range of relevant indicators, taking into account the views of both service-users and potential suppliers.
Consultation	with local tax-payers, service users, partners and the wider business community in setting new performance targets.
Competition	fair and open wherever practicable as a means of securing efficient and effective services.

---

[f] *Modernising Government: White Paper* (Cm 4310, 91999), Cabinet Office Website: www.cabinet-office.gov.uk/moderngov/1999/whitepaper/index.htm

Its guidance on Best Value published in 2000[g] recognizes that quality schemes *'... will not in themselves guarantee Best Value. However, if used properly they can provide considerable help in achieving Best Value ...'.* The guide references into a number of schemes in support of Best Value:

Business Excellence Model[h]
Investors in People[i]
Charter Mark[j]
ISO 9000[k]
Local Government Improvement Plan[l]

In 1999,[m] the UK government established a task force to consider how these quality tools can be used and linked together to help the public sector meet its challenges ahead. It is not difficult to identify theoretical relationships between each of the schemes and Best Value. Developing these relationships in practice has been more difficult as they are too often driven with uncoordinated quality strategies.

Both these studies only covered the public sector but the results have some important messages for organizations across all sectors. Not least, that quality and best value need to be managed with coordinated strategies, if each is to support the other. Figure 8.10 shows how the task force matched its chosen quality tools.

Business excellence model	ISO 9000	Charter Mark	Investors in People
Enablers			
Leadership	X	X	X
Policy & Strategy	XX	XX	XX
People Management	X	XX	XXX
Resources	XX	XX	X
Processes	XXX	X	X
Results			
Customer Satisfaction	XX	XXX	X
People Satisfaction	X	X	XXX
Impact on Society			
Business Results	XX	XX	XX
XXX = critical impact	XX = secondary impact	X = indirect impact	

Figure 8.10   How Business Excellence Model Criteria Match Other Quality Systems
Source: A Guide to Quality Schemes for the Public Sector (2000)

---

[g] *Guide to Quality Schemes and Best Value* (2000), Department of the Environment, Transport and the regions, London, England. (www.detr.gov.uk) and its Improvement and Development Agency – www.idea.gov.uk
[h] *Business Excellence Model*, The British Quality Foundation. www.quality-foundation.co.uk; EFQM Excellence Model, European Foundation for Quality Management. www.efqm.org
[i] Investors in People – UK, London, 020 7467 1900
[j] Charter Mark, www.servicefirst.gov.uk
[k] British Standards Institute, www.bsi.org.uk
[l] Local Government Improvement Programme, The Improvement and Development Agency, London. E-mail: Igip@idea.gov.uk
[m] *A Guide To Quality Schemes For The Public Sector* (2000), Cabinet Office, United Kingdom Government, London, England.

[It should be noted here that the Business Excellence Model and ISO 9000 have been revised since this table was prepared.]

Quality Schemes and Good Governance

The 1996, research by Bain and Band[n] into governance, demonstrates some recognition of quality and governance integration:

> We hold the view that corporate governance is very much about adding value. Companies and other enterprises with a professional and positive attitude to governance are stronger and have a greater record of achievement. In fact, some company directors . . . suggest that there is an important direct relationship between a country's corporate governance system and its economic success.

In 1998, these links were explored by me[o] with little success:

> There is ample evidence in developed theory and principles that quality is associated with competition, performance and profitability; yet there is little evidence that control and governance has been a focus in any of this research.

At that time only a few researchers had linked control and governance into achieving quality in products and services. In practice, few organizations were reporting these links and there are still few today. Yet, as already demonstrated earlier, control is an essential part of all quality schemes and governance can be related to many of the principles driving quality. Why is it that too few organizations see quality and governance as bedfellows? This is a question that all should ask in every organization.

More recent publications have started to link governance to effectiveness. Sir Adrian Cadbury, in his foreword to *A Strategic Approach to Corporate Governance*,[p] states:

> The essential point is that good governance is an aid to effectiveness. It is not there to shackle enterprise, but to harness it in the achievement of its goals.

International organizations, such as the Commonwealth Association for Corporate Governance (CACG)[q] and Organization for Economic Cooperation and Development (OECD)[r] recognize the synergy between governance and economics. Both the CCAG and OECD have published international principles that link economic objectives and long-term success with good governance. Although it may take some time, these principles will revolutionize the way business and government is conducted in many countries across the world.

---

[n] *Winning Ways Through Corporate Governance* (1996), Neville Bain and David Band, Macmillan Business, London, England.
[o] *Leading Edge Internal Auditing* (1998), Ridley and Chambers, ICSA Publishing Ltd, London, England.
[p] *A Strategic Approach to Corporate Governance* (1999), Adrian Davies, Gower, Aldershot, Hampshire, England.
[q] Commonwealth Association for Corporate Governance, www.cbc.to/governance/finalver/cacg.htm
[r] Organization for Economic Cooperation and Development, website www.oecd.org/daf/governnance/principles.htm

Quality Challenges for Internal Auditing

In 1978, The IIA standards for the professional practice of internal auditing recognized the importance of quality assurance. These professional guidelines recommend four steps to achieving quality in internal auditing work – *due professional care, supervision, internal reviews and external reviews*. This is still part of the standards. However, most research shows that many internal auditing functions do not have formal quality assurance programmes. Contrast this with the recently revised UK Auditing Practices Board – *Quality Control for Audit Work*,[s] which establishes basic principles for quality in external auditing. This statement balances the quality drivers of ownership, control responsibilities, policies, procedures and monitoring, in a framework of quality requirements for all external auditing functions. Non-compliance with this statement can have serious consequences for external auditors.

In 1992, both The IIA and IIA–UK & Ireland published statements on internal auditing and TQM. The IIA[t] promoted internal auditors as '*agents of change*':

> In this role, (internal) auditors can actively participate in helping management achieve their [quality] objectives and still maintain independence and objectivity.

Interviews with a number of North American organizations had shown that TQM was being used to improve internal auditing processes as well as a means of contributing to improving control environments, risk assessment, control activities and monitoring. Internal auditing benefits from involvement in TQM were seen to come from improved training, teamwork, measurement techniques and benchmarking.

The IIA–UK started its Professional Briefing Notes series in 1992 with a definition of TQM[u] and an exploration of the following options for internal auditors to explore:

1. The internal audit appraisal of departmental TQM activities.
2. The relationship between 'internal audit' and 'quality audit'.
3. The extent to which heads of internal audit may seek to gain ISO 9000 registration for their audit departments.

In the 1990s, some internal auditing functions registered to ISO 9000. This required all their processes to comply with the standard's quality requirements. The IIA–UK & Ireland published an example of such a registration in 1993.[v] This internal auditing interest in ISO 9000 continues today.

Research into internal auditing registrations[w] prior to 1993 identified the reasons listed in Figure 8.11. Not all had the same reasons. In most, the initial intentions were not to seek improvements in professional practices but to document

---

[s] Statement of Auditing Standards 240 – *Quality Control for Audit Work*, Auditing Practices Board, London, 2000.
[t] *Internal Auditing in a Total Quality Environment – A Reference Manual* (1992), Elaine McIntosh, The IIA.
[u] *Total Quality Management: The Implications for Internal Audit Departments, PBN One* (1992), IIA–UK & Ireland.
[v] *A Quality System Manual for Internal Auditing* (1993), Jeffrey Ridley, IIA–UK & Ireland.
[w] *International Quality Standards: Implications for Internal Auditing* (1996), Jeffrey Ridley and Krystyna Stephens, The IIA Research Foundation.

PROCEDURAL
- Need to update procedures
- Need to improve procedures
- Need to motivate internal auditing staff to comply with procedures
- Need for more uniform procedures

STRATEGIC
- Requirement by organization to pursue ISO 9000
- Requirement by organization to demonstrate quality in services provided

ORGANIZATIONAL
- Need to change structure of global/national service
- Need to improve supervision
- Improve team building

MARKETING
- Part of programme to market test the internal auditing service in competition with other bids
- Part of a programme to market internal auditing services within the organization

---

Figure 8.11   Internal Auditing: Reasons For Registration To ISO 9000
Source: *International Quality Standards: Implications for Internal Auditing* (1996)

current practices more clearly and uniformly. However, addressing ISO 9000 quality requirements focused attention on the structure needed to achieve and maintain a quality organization and system. This changed responsibilities for quality at all levels. The continuous cycle of monitoring and correction, driven by the quality system and its required internal auditing, also encouraged staff to be innovative in new and better methods – sometimes with paradigm shifts!

The same research showed the benefits from registration as listed at Figure 8.12. These were mainly in the quality vision and mission, which required management

---

Quality Policy
Like The IIA standards, ISO 9000 requires a declaration of quality purpose. For ISO 9000 this is the publication of a quality policy. Each of the internal auditing functions had incorporated such a statement in its charter.

Standard of Conduct
The IIA standards require internal auditors to take due professional care in their audit work. Compliance to ISO 9000 quality requirements promoted diligence in audit work and established an environment, which embraced many of the principles in The IIA Code of Ethics.

Documentation
The IIA standards require written policies and procedures for all audit work. Such evidence was reinforced by the ISO 9000 quality requirements for controlled documentation and records.

Quality Assurance
The IIA standards require evidence of supervision and quality assurance in all audit work. The ISO 9000 quality assurance and quality audits requirements provided a framework for the supervision and management of all internal auditing practices.

Figure 8.12   Internal Auditing: Benefits From Registration To ISO 9000
Source: *International Quality Standards: Implications for Internal Auditing* (1996)

leadership, teamwork and good communication, to mould existing internal auditing practices into compliance with ISO 9000 quality requirements. Changes also required training and a writing or rewriting of audit procedures.

Whatever the options internal auditing follow to achieve quality, it is clear that the challenge of quality schemes cannot be left out of audit planning and risk assessment. Today's and tomorrow's drive for quality and best value across all organizations requires all internal auditors to add the following to the IIA–UK & Ireland's 1992 list of options:

- Provide advice on all quality scheme/Best Value planning and implementation.
- Link all quality schemes and Best Value Reviews to all risk assessments.
- Relate quality and Best Value policies to the implementation, monitoring and reporting of good governance practices.

CUTTING EDGE INTERNAL AUDITING COMMITMENT TO QUALITY TODAY AND THE FUTURE

One of the most significant statistics, demonstrating global interest in quality management, is the latest ISO survey of certifications to ISO 9001: 2000. At the end of 2005 these registrations were reported by the ISO[9] as 776,608. (Note the increase from the reported 126,000 in 1994, mentioned earlier.) Notably the country with the largest number of registrations was China, 143,823, followed by Italy, 98,028. In its report of these figures in 2006, ISO stated:

> ISO 9001: 2000 is now firmly established as the globally accepted standard for providing assurance about quality of goods and services in supplier–customer relations. Up to the end of December 2005, at least 776,608 ISO 9001: 2000 certificates had been issued in 161 countries and economies, an increase of 18% over 2004.

The report goes on to confirm a rising importance of services in the global economy borne out by 33% of these certificates being awarded to organizations in the service sectors.

There is also ample evidence, both from research[10] and literature, that the quality principles underlying TQM are being practised in many organizations today, across all sectors and worldwide. There can be few organizations that do not use some or all of these principles to achieve their objectives and compete with other organizations. The use of quality principles in all professions as part of the regulation of their members is now universal. Governments and most regulators also seek quality assurances from the organizations they control. As customers we all look for quality in the products and services we buy. Often, without realizing it, we are all suppliers of products and services and are being measured for quality by our customers.

What are the quality principles on which TQM is based today? The UK Department of Trade and Industry[11] state:

> The core of TQM is the **customer–supplier interfaces**, both externally and internally, and at each interface lie a number of processes. This core must be surrounded by **commitment to quality**, **communication of the quality message**, and recognition of the **need to change the culture** of the

organization to create total quality. These are the foundations of TQM, and they are supported by the key management functions of **people**, **processes** and **systems** in the organization.

The DTI[12] sees quality as the pathway to excellence:

> Managing quality to achieve excellence means managing an organization, business or unit so that every job, every process, is carried out right, first time, every time. To be successful this must be viewed as a holistic approach that affects, and involves, all stakeholders – employees, customers, suppliers, shareholders and society.

Those quality gurus that have developed quality principles over past years would still see other important principles prominent in a TQM foundation. Principles[13] such as:

- Quality costs are high, often largely unquantified and need to be controlled.
- The pursuit of quality within an organization has a philosophical basis
- Technical tools to achieve quality in products and services are important.

Most of the above quality principles and theories are seen in the The IIA *International Professional Practices Framework*; its new definition of internal auditing; its *International Standards for the Professional Practice of Internal Auditing*; and its *Code of Ethics*. Its *Practice Advisories* and supporting development and practice aids provide quality assurance and continuous improvement guidance for all internal audit assurance and consultancy engagements by:

- focusing on customers' needs to '. . . *accomplish [their] objectives* . . .';
- the use of '. . . *a systematic and disciplined approach* . . .' for all internal auditing processes;
- the emphasis on internal auditing improving both '. . . *an organization's operations* . . .' and the '. . . *effectiveness of risk management, control and governance processes*';
- the mandatory requirement for '. . . *a quality assurance and improvement programme* . . .' in the internal audit activity;
- the '. . . *exercise of due professional care and skill* . . .' by competent staff;
- the importance of '. . . *continuing professional development* . . .' for all internal auditors,

These professional links to quality principles and theory add significant strength to the practical importance of the *International Professional Practices Framework* for all internal audit activities and the organizations they serve.

An overall framework developed by Professor John Oakland[14] that provides guidance on what actually needs to be implemented to achieve TQM is shown in Figure 8.13. It offers a practical blueprint for achieving organizational excellence and pulls together all the concepts used to establish TQM, Key Performance Indicators (KPIs) and achieve excellence.

Note the feedback cycle linking these concepts to an organization's vision, goals and strategies in a continuous measurement cycle. Note also the prominence given to benchmarking and continuous improvement. All these concepts[15] are still influencing and measuring the implementation of TQM in many organizations today and will continue to do so in the future. That some are still not well established in some organizations, or even internal audit activities, should be of continuing concern to all internal auditors and management of the organizations in which they work.

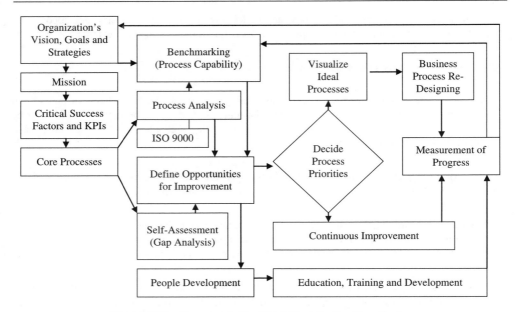

Figure 8.13 Framework For Total Organization Excellence
Source: Professor John S. Oakland, *Total Quality Excellence – Achieving World-Class Performance* (1999)

Pursuing excellence in organizations has increased awareness of and interest in the achievement of external quality awards – such as the EFQM Excellence Model.[16] This model explains how the nine criteria of *Customer Results, People Results* and *Society Results* are achieved through *Leadership* driving *Policy and Strategy, Management of People, Partnerships and Resources and Processes*, leading to excellence in Key Performance Results. (Note the links to the TQM principles discussed earlier.) The model can be used both as a self-assessment programme and through external assessment for the achievement of a quality award. The Cabinet Office's Public Sector Excellence Programme promotes the benefits of the model to public bodies and encourages self-assessments.[17] Other awards are:

- *Charter Mark*[18] – This quality improvement scheme is run by the Cabinet Office. It focuses on customer service, encouraging excellence and continuous improvement. Applicants for Charter Mark are assessed externally against set criteria that drive customer-focused quality improvement programmes.
- *Investors in People*[19] – This national standard sets a level of good practice for improving an organization's performance through its people. It requires commitment to developing people through learning and training programmes aimed at achieving organization objectives. Applicants for this award are externally assessed and re-assessed to maintain this recognition.

All of the above quality schemes, except Charter Mark, are also used by many organizations in the private and voluntary sectors. Current and past internal auditing literature and research has shown that some internal audit activities across all sectors have been impacted by these schemes through their use within the activity and/or by involvement in the registration and monitoring processes associated with the schemes.

Other quality assurance and continuous improvement schemes use TQM principles. The life and pensions industry established its own quality mark *'Raising Standards'*. Launched in 2001 by the Association of British Insurers (ABI),[20] its focus is on customer service and measured satisfaction. It requires clarity in communications and documentation in all transactions. The principles underlying its foundation can be linked into and supported by the other quality schemes.

In the voluntary sector the National Council for Voluntary Organizations (NCVO)[21] provides advice on quality management. Its research and publications have provided guidance to all types and sizes of voluntary organizations based on its own quality principles requiring a voluntary quality organization to:

- strive for continuous improvement;
- use recognized standards or models as a means to continuous improvement and not as an end;
- agree requirements with stakeholders and endeavour to meet or exceed these first time and every time;
- promote equality of opportunity through its internal and external conduct;
- add value to its end users and beneficiaries.

The NCVO Quality Standards Task Group has published guidance on the use of the Excellence Model in voluntary organizations (its current research indicates use of this model in some voluntary organizations). It also monitors use of Investors in People, ISO 9000, Charter Mark and other specific quality award processes for the voluntary sector.

Annual surveys of quality initiatives in local government authorities were carried out by the Local Government Quality Group until 1998 when its parent body, The Local Government Board, ceased to exist. At that time almost all local authorities were involved in one or more quality initiatives, which included all those mentioned above as well as Best Value.[22] Best Value requires local authorities, including fire and police (LAs), to review and reform the way they deliver all their services to secure continuous improvement. LAs are expected to demonstrate that they have addressed the 4Cs of *challenge, comparison, consult,* and *competition* through the development of a published Best Value Performance Plan. There are clear links between the tools used for Best Value Reviews and those used for other quality schemes, such as customer focus, benchmarking and performance measures, such as in the Excellence Model mentioned above. An Improvement and Development Agency (I&DeA) survey[23] of local authorities in 2001 shows a high level of use of the Excellence Model linked to Best Value in local authorities.

The Audit Commission[24] recommends internal audit as a source of Best Value assurance for local authorities, because of its *'. . . independence and objectivity, technical skills, authority-wide knowledge and comprehensive review methodology'*. It recognizes that internal audit currently provides assurance on *'. . . overall management and financial probity; compliance with statutory requirements; reliability and performance; and the effective use of resources'*.

Both The IIA new definition of internal auditing and its *International Professional Practices Framework* require internal auditors to identify, evaluate and improve the effectiveness of their organization's risk management and control processes. How this is implemented through assurance and consultancy engagements varies across internal audit activities. A pattern of internal auditing involvement in risk management processes is now emerging across all sectors. This involvement includes internal auditor participation in organization risk management processes and the use of information from these processes to develop audit plans and objectives. This involvement must include risk to quality in products and services.

The IIA–UK & Ireland's recently published statement *Risk Based Internal Auditing* (RBIA)[25] describes how internal auditors can and are becoming involved in risk assessment in their organizations as part of the services they provide. RBIA starts with an organization's objectives '*. . . and then focuses on those risks that have been identified by management that may hinder their achievement*'. There can be no higher risk to the achievement of an organization's objectives than that it provides poor quality with related costs and dissatisfies its customers. Quality must always be a key objective in all risk assessments – at both strategic and operational levels. Internal auditors, conversant with TQM principles and experienced in implementing quality schemes have an important role to play in advising management on quality strategies and objectives during the assessment and evaluation of risk.

The COSO[26] integrated control framework, discussed in previous chapters, has provided risk and control guidance to internal auditors and management since it was developed and published in 1992. Its five elements of "*. . . control environment, risk assessment, control activities, monitoring and information and communications. . . *" are basic requirements in all quality schemes and quality programmes. Its definition of control as a process "*. . . designed to provide reasonable assurance regarding the achievement of [effectiveness and efficiency of operations] objectives. . . *" is critical to all processes designed to achieve quality and excellence. The importance of the COSO control elements and key concepts is significant in all quality schemes. This is even more evident today as organizations embed risk management in all processes, from strategy setting to the achievement of objectives in every level and unit. The embedding of its Enterprise Risk Management (ERM) framework in an organization is also important for the achievement of quality assurance and continuous improvement objectives.

The impact of quality objectives and requirements of quality schemes on governance processes is rarely discussed in research or literature. Nor is it communicated by organizations to their stakeholders. Yet there are many aspects of quality schemes and quality programmes that require good governance to achieve customer satisfaction. Research by Bain and Band[27] into governance, previously quoted, demonstrates some recognition of quality and governance integration:

> We hold the view that corporate governance is very much about adding value. Companies and other enterprises with a professional and positive attitude to governance are stronger and have a greater record of achievement. In fact, some company directors . . . suggest that there is an important direct relationship between a country's corporate governance system and its economic success.

Few researchers have linked the achievement of quality with good governance and economic success, although, governance principles can be related to many of the risks and controls influencing economic success. Why is it that so few see and report on how quality schemes and governance each strengthen the other in all supply chains, internal and external? Internal auditors have an opportunity in their engagements to seek answers to this question.

More recent publications have started to link governance to effectiveness. Sir Adrian Cadbury, in his foreword to *A Strategic Approach to Corporate Governance*,[28] also previously quoted, states:

> The essential point is that good governance is an aid to effectiveness. It is not there to shackle enterprise, but to harness it in the achievement of its goals.

International organizations, such as the Commonwealth Association for Corporate Governance (CACG)[29] and Organization for Economic Cooperation and Development (OECD)[30] recognize the synergy between governance and economics. Both the CCAG and the OECD have published international governance principles that link economic objectives and long-term success with good governance. Although it may take some time, these principles will change the way business and government are conducted in many countries across the world.

Monitoring the implementation of TQM requires continuous use of quality measures linked to a quality strategy. Quality measures in TQM do not stand-alone from all other measures used to monitor total performance. As mentioned earlier, the cost of quality is an important part of any organization's financial performance revenue and expenditure – revenue through lost sales, expenditure through high quality costs:

> Quality-related costs are those incurred in the design, implementation, operation and maintenance of an organization's quality management system, the cost of resources committed to the process of continuous improvement, plus the costs of systems and/or product [and services] failures [inspection, rectification and waste].[31]

Quality measures may be quantitative, qualitative or a mixture of both. They need to be timely, accurate and reported openly to all staff and management for appropriate corrective action. Quality measures should be established for input, process and output activities. They need to be linked to strategic planning, customer satisfaction and total performance.

Gupta and Ray (1995)[32] show that '. . . *internal auditors can leverage their knowledge of business processes and play an active role in the development and implementation of [the] Total Quality Improvement process. . .*'. Their research describes the complete range of quality management tools and techniques used by organizations to implement and measure quality improvement programmes: showing how a knowledge of these and experience in their use can improve an internal audit activity's services and processes. Their research identifies seven steps (Table 4-22, p. 104) to be undertaken in internal auditing to implement TQM:

1. Development of Mission and Vision Statements and establishing internal audit department objectives.
2. Establishment and implementation of performance measures for various stages of the internal auditing process.
3. Identification of customers of internal auditing department.
4. Development and implementation of internal auditing customer satisfaction surveys and feedback systems.
5. Benchmarking with other internal auditing departments.
6. Introspective self-analysis
7. TQM training and education of the internal auditing staff.

Today, I would add:

8. Identification of suppliers and detailed specifications of what is agreed to be delivered from them, when and at what cost and quality.

Remember, quality objectives cross all supply chains, not just between an organization and its customers.

Kaplan and Norton[33] in the development of their concept the *Balanced Scorecard* recommend a measurement framework that includes the essential dimensions '*customer expectations and satisfaction, continuous improvement, efficiency and organizational learning'* – dimensions that need to be all balanced with financial performance. They also see the integration of all these measures as an important part of implementing strategy and the measurement of total performance.

Mark Frigo[34] researched how the *Balanced Scorecard* concept and framework can be used by an internal audit activity, explaining four recent trends impacting the way performance should be measured within an internal audit activity:

1. The IIA new 1999 definition of internal auditing.
2. Changing expectations of internal audit customers.
3. The increasing focus on value-added services.
4. The increasing use of benchmarking processes.

These trends can also be seen in the implementation of TQM, quality schemes and quality programmes in internal audit activities. Frigo's use of measurements shows how strategy maps can be used to link performance to all internal auditing and organization objectives. His recommendations have application to the linking of quality strategies through quality measures to total performance of an internal audit activity

At least one example of the use of strategic mapping and the balanced scorecard in an internal audit activity was presented at The IIA International Conference in Amsterdam, July 2007. Frank Alvern, Head of Business Support in Group Internal Audit (GIA), Nordea Bank AB, Norway, discussed its group internal audit strategy map themes and use of a balanced scorecard for their achievement:

GIA Ambition: Highly Valued – Providing Audit Excellence

Theme 1: *Improve communication*
Improve assurance and periodic reports
Increase perception and knowledge of GIA
Improve interaction with management and risk functions.

Theme 2: *Ensure professionalism*
Perform audits efficiently
Provide value adding, high quality and timely audit results
Ensure alignment with GIA's governance system.

Theme 3: *Attract, develop and retain highly motivated, competent and performance-oriented employees*
Improve leadership, including executive capabilities
Be a preferred employer
Attract and develop performance-oriented employees.

Each of the above themes have been further developed by GIA into key performance indicators (KPIs) in the balanced scorecard framework of:

Financial Perspective
Customer Perspective
Internal Process Perspective
Learning Perspective.

And most importantly linked into the Nordea organization balanced scorecard strategic themes and KPIs.

Figure 8.14   Quality Measures For The Internal Audit Function
Source: J. Ridley, *Leading Edge Internal Auditing* (1998)

Figure 8.14 is an example of a quality measurement framework for an internal audit activity. I designed this in 1992. Its vision and mission create the charter for internal auditing approved by the board. Key result areas (KRAs) are identified – sometimes referred to as key performance indicators. Then, using trained quality teams, the activities that need to be measured, and the methods, are agreed.

Monitoring of KRA performance requires appropriate input, process and output measures linked to benchmarking for continuous improvement.

Note that, in TQM, all quality measures should relate back to the vision and mission, focusing at the same time on customer needs and satisfaction. Also, when implementing such a framework in an internal audit activity it is essential to address all the quality principles mentioned in the DTI definition of TQM discussed earlier:

- customer–supplier interfaces, both externally and internally
- a commitment to quality
- communication of the quality message
- the organization's culture
- performance measurements for all the people, processes and systems involved.

The IIA's new '*. . . quality assurance and improvement . . .*' mandatory requirement is an essential programme in all internal audit activities, whatever the size of resource, or whether it is provided by in-house staff, outsourced, or a mixture of both. The elements of such a programme include '*due professional care*' by each internal auditor, formal processes with quality objectives, proper supervision, internal assessments of quality and an external quality assessment. How each of these elements is evaluated is of importance to everyone in the internal audit activity – its customers, the organization's management and governing body (and audit committee).

In its *Practice Advisory* for the assessment of quality in an internal audit activity, The IIA recommends the following should be evaluated:

- Compliance with the *International Standards* and *Code of Ethics*;
- Adequacy of the internal audit activity's charter, goals objectives, policies, and procedures;
- Contribution to the organization's risk management, control and governance processes;
- Compliance with applicable laws, regulations and government or industry standards;
- Effectiveness of continuous improvement activities and adoption of best practices;
- Whether the auditing activity adds value and improves the organization's operations.

The IIA[35] published its first quality assurance review manual in 1984, followed by revisions leading to its latest 5th edition, published in 2006. This is a structured guide for internal and external quality assessments of an internal audit activity, including preparation and fieldwork, using the requirements of its *Professional Practices Framework*. The manual contains examples of review questionnaires and programmes with interview modules. Many internal audit activities across the world have used this manual to self-assess their operations. It is also used by The IIA Quality Auditing Services[36] and other external consultants. Guidance in the *Practice Advisories* recommends that external assessments should be carried out by a competent person or team well versed in the best practices of the internal auditing profession, with current knowledge of its *International Professional Practices Framework*.

Internal audit activities in government departments[37] have prepared their own quality assurance assessment questionnaires in accordance with Government Internal Auditing Standard (GIAS) 10: Quality Assurance. These questionnaires are for both internal and external assessments. They contain a set of compliance questions related to all the GIAS standards and what is considered good practice support to the achievement of compliance. Both the Excellence Model and ISO 9000 are considered to support good practice and enhance assurance about the quality of internal audit work in government departments.

Across all sectors there are many examples of internal auditors and internal audit activities using TQM principles to achieve quality assurance, continuous improvement and excellence in the services they provide: sometimes through pursuit of the quality schemes mentioned earlier; sometimes by just implementing quality objectives in their planning, by controlling for quality in their performance and continuously improving the services they provide; and sometimes by contributing to their organization's quality and improvement objectives in all their work engagements.

The importance of the following five quality principles discussed at the beginning of the chapter has not changed today. Each is an essential part of commitment to quality in any organization. What has changed is how each is now being applied today across organization supply chains.

1. **Customers** are now not just receivers of a product or service, but in many organizations seen as partners. Customer focus is not just supported by customer feedback; it has developed its own science in the form of Customer Relationship Management (CRM). Bain & Company (2005)[38] places CRM just behind Strategic Planning in usage as a management tool across the organizations in its annual survey. Bain & Company defines CRM as:

> Companies use CRM to better understand customers in order to acquire, retain, and grow accounts with those most profitable. Data collected through CRM enables firms to differentially serve target segments, including tailoring products to include features valued by these segments, and exclude

features that add cost but fail to significantly influence target customer purchases. CRM provides data to educate employees, align their incentives. And position a company strategically to profit from evolving market needs.

With a few changes of the words this statement could also be written for the public and voluntary sectors, as well as for functions within an organization, including the internal audit activity. CRM is about collecting and analysing data about customers to understand their needs, and using that data to understand the customer, tailor products and services, and educate and reward employees. It requires the information technology that is now available today in every organization. It can and should have a significant influence on strategic planning. It can be used for customers in any supply chain, whether internal or external to the organization. The aim of CRM is not to satisfy customers but to anticipate their needs and delight them.

In most organizations customer complaints are now given a high priority. Return warranties and after-sales servicing have as high a focus as quality, and many organizations use these policies in their marketing. The importance of customers can never be overstated in any organization and process. Statements showing this can start with *'our customers' satisfaction is paramount'*, through to *'we delight our customers'*. These are often seen associated with organization advertisements in the press: like that of the German motor manufacturer Audi,[39] in its March 2007 advertisement in the *Financial Times*:

> We continued our success story in 2006 by posting record figures for sales, revenue and earnings. New, emotion-inspiring products of the premium quality expected of the brand captivate our customers all over the world. We are setting the trends of the future with our innovative and customer-oriented developments of today.

Consider all the quality messages in this statement and how they can be applied to internal auditing today and in the future.

2. **Leadership** in organizations and internal audit activities that have adopted a TQM culture is now at all levels, by every employee. All lead if they are committed. Vision statements are still being used by many organizations to create clear directions for all stakeholders. Strategic planning requires the establishment of key missions to control a vision's achievement. Quality and Excellence initiatives, such as the Business Excellence Model provide frameworks for self-assessment and creation of the right structures, methods and resources for quality achievement. Information technology in the form of the Internet and Intranet has opened up new methods of communicating quality messages and motivating total commitment in quality cultures. They also add to the high visibility needed to lead these messages to all stakeholders.

3. **Teamwork**. The best quality teams are those that are inter-functional, using resources and skills across the organization and not just within a function, and empowered to take action. They should have clear terms of reference and the resources to carry these out. TQM cultures encourage this. Mints (1972)[40] analysed behaviours between auditors and their customers, recommending the participative teamwork approach, involving the customer, developing team spirit and relating the audit engagement to the customer's aims. This is the thinking behind internal audit teamwork in most internal auditing textbooks today and guidance in The IIA *International Professional Practices Framework*. It is also fundamental to any team in an organization.

4. **Analytical Approach**. The IIA definition of internal auditing requires internal auditing to be *'systematic'* and *'disciplined'*. These are essential attributes for all auditing and analysis and measurement of quality. Quality measures must flow from an organization's vision, through its missions to the actions being taken at operating levels. Measures alone are not sufficient. Their results should drive correction, action and improvement. An interesting, yet too little discussed, impact of quality supply chains is that the internal audit activity is in many supply chains during the services it provides, both as a supplier and a customer. As a supplier much has been written about the activity measuring its customers' satisfaction and addressing any complaints through continuous improvement. Yet the internal audit activity is also a customer in all the services it provides. As a customer its administration, communication, planning and engagement processes constantly request information and material from a variety of suppliers, including its customers. That request is the start of a supply chain. Too little has been written about how inefficient and ineffective such requests can be through wrong specifications, timing and poor communication. As customers, internal audit activities should measure this quality, just as much as the quality of services provided to the customers that receive its services.

5. **Continuous Improvement**. Today and tomorrow, the increasing speed of change must be part of every organization's strategic planning. Change not just for change sake, but also to meet global competition in almost every product and service supplied in every sector. Continuous improvement in every organization and its function parts should start with innovation as a strategy and policy, implemented through drive and encouragement at all levels. There is ample evidence of this across the globe, in all sectors and professional bodies: It is a requirement of The IIA *International Standards for the Professional Practice of Internal Auditing*. To be at its best, continuous improvement needs each of the previous four quality principles practised successfully if it is to delight customers and meet the needs of those who provide products and services. It must have feedback from customers; drive by leadership through learning and a continuous search for excellence; integrated teams of suppliers and customers; and, timely verification and analysis of results. It needs to continuously delight customers in the short and long term. That delight will mark out the best and its absence will result in failure.

CHAPTER SUMMARY

The readers of this chapter should be in no doubt total commitment to quality aims and customer satisfaction in any organization (and in any internal audit activity) is essential for its success, if not survival. How such aims are achieved can vary across organizations and internal audit activities, but an understanding and practice of quality principles and TQM are fundamental to this achievement. A high level of quality in any product or service is a road and never a destination: the journey never ends. Customers' needs, people, circumstances and events continuously change, requiring new operating procedures and work instructions, and new products and services. The quality achieved along the road needs to be continuously measured, improved, adapted and rewarded to meet all these changes.

Establishing a quality commitment in an internal audit activity is served well by using the Gray and Gray (1997) five innovation motivational themes, four innovation goals and four innovation categories discussed in the Introduction, and the additions and changes made in Chapters 2 to 7.

Motivations

1. Progress within the field of professional internal auditing.
2. Increasing competition leading to pressures to reduce costs and increase efficiency.
3. New challenges, such as increasing internal control risks due to staff reductions and restructuring.
4. Opportunities to increase efficiency and quality as a result of technological advances.
5. Changes in corporate management practices and philosophies, such as Total Quality Management, re-engineering, continuous quality improvement, or related approaches.
6. **Challenges and opportunities of global issues and developments.**
7. **Social and environmental issues impacting all organizations.**
8. **Recognition that professionalism, quality and standards are essential attributes for world-class status in any internal auditing activity.**
9. **Importance of organizational governance to meet regulatory and stakeholders' needs.**
10. **A continuous search for good and evil in how organizations and all their operations are directed and controlled.**
11. **Recognition that all types of crime in and by an organization should be fought.**

Goals

1. Improvement of the quality of internal auditing services.
2. Improve efficiency.
3. Expansion of services to increase the value-added of internal auditing.
4. Boost staff skills, performance and morale.
5. **Sell internal auditing as future focused.**
6. **To reduce the opportunities for all types of crime in an organization.**

Categories

1. Changes in the way that internal auditors interact with the rest of their enterprises **and all those with a stakeholder interest.**
2. Internal restructuring and changes in the organization and management of internal auditing.
3. Creation of new audit services and methods.
4. Changes in the use of technology.
5. **Improved knowledge and skills in the teams of staff who carry out internal auditing engagements.**
6. **New services to fight crime.**
7. **Assistance in evaluation of the board's performance.**

A new goal and category should be added to recognize the importance of the internal audit customers:

Goal

7. Increase satisfaction from all our customers.

Category

8. Improved satisfaction from all our customers.

INTERNAL AUDITING COMMITMENT TO QUALITY PRINCIPIA 1998 AND 2008

My 1998 principia for internal auditing included the following related to its world-class status (see Appendix A):

28. Internal auditing procedures and documents are an essential part of marketing internal auditing quality.
34. Learn to recognize, applaud and reward achievement by internal audit teams.

These are now changed to reflect the importance of internal audit being committed to quality in 2008 and the future:

11. A total commitment to and understanding of quality principles, practices in an internal audit activity and the services it provides is essential for its success, if not survival.

A VISION FOR COMMITMENT TO QUALITY IN INTERNAL AUDITING

> ***Our quality delights all our customers***

SYNOPSES OF CASE STUDIES

Case 8.1: Certification of the Internal Audit Function under ISO 9001: 2000

ISO 9000 is the international standard for quality management. For some internal auditing functions it is also the standard used to establish quality assurance in the services they provide. Alcatel Group Audit Services (GAS) registered its services to this standard in 2001. For this it established a set of best practices developed by consensus from its entire world-wide internal audit staff. *'It certainly brought consistency and homogeneity to GAS's audit practices and audit products, which in turn, impacts customer satisfaction.'* Since its introduction it has developed into a *'continuous quality improvement process'* creating*'. . . something in which we all take pride'* and continues to encourage cutting edge practices.

> Contributed by A.J. Hans Spoel, Global Corporate Executive Director and Patricia Pinel, Senior Audit Coordinator Communications & CRSA.

After Reading the Case Study Consider:

1. Does the motivation and commitment to quality in the process of registration to ISO 9000 and its maintenance offer any of the benefits in the case study for your internal auditing?

2. Do you carry out any risk assessment in your internal auditing processes to identify quality risks and opportunities for improvement in the achievement of your Key Performance Indicators?

3. Do you report to your board and senior management on the standard of quality in the services you provide and compliance to The IIA *International Standards*? If not, why not?

4. Is your internal auditing sufficiently knowledgeable and experienced to provide quality assurance and consulting services in your organization's quality policy?

Case 8.2: After Registration to ISO 9000 – a Quality Manual

Synopsis

Registration to ISO 9000 requires formal operating procedures and supporting work instructions to be developed, approved and included in a Quality Manual. The process of preparing these statements creates new opportunities for the implementation of cutting edge resources and practices.

> Extract from the Introduction to *A Quality System Manual for Internal Auditing*, based on registration by the author and his internal auditing team in Kodak Limited, England, to ISO 9001. Published in 1993 by The Institute of Internal Auditors – United Kingdom & Ireland, London, England.

After Reading the Case Study Consider:

1. How do the operating procedures and work instructions compare with those in your own internal auditing?

2. How do the quality measures in your internal auditing benchmark with the measures in the case study?

3. Which of the quality measures do you think are the most important to encourage continuous improvement in the registered quality system?

4. What quality measures are missing from the above and in your own internal auditing to ensure audit time is prioritized to review the governance processes discussed in Chapter 5?

Case 8.3: A Unique Approach for External Quality Assessments

Synopsis

The IFACI (*Institut Français de l'Audit et du Contrôle Internes*), the French Institute of Internal Auditors, external *Quality Certification* process is discussed. Established in 2004 it has already operated in countries outside France. It goes beyond the quality assurance requirements of The IIA *International Standards* with other key benefits. It recognizes where improvements are needed from non-conformances and promotes cutting edge best practices.

Contributed by: Florence Bergeret, CIA, Manager, IFACI Certification, Graduate from High Management School. Florence Bergeret started her career at Deloitte Touche Tohmatsu then at KPMG. She has joined IFACI, the French Institute of Internal Auditors, in 2000 as the Research Director, responsible for running and coordinating the work of taskforces composed of internal audit professionals. She directly contributed to the writing of booklets, position paper and articles, as well as the French translation of the *Standards*. Since 2004, she has been involved in the certification activity, first of all as a member of the steering team, charged with the designing and development of the certification of internal audit departments, then as a team leader on certification mission. Up to now, she has performed more than 20 certification engagements and supervises the certification teams.

After Reading the Case Study Consider:

1. Do the seven best practices identified by the IFACI Certification exist in your internal auditing?
2. Do the seven most frequent non-compliances identified by the IFACI exist in your internal auditing?
3. Are the nine key benefits achieved through certification in your internal auditing?

Case 8.4: Internal Auditors Too Can Be Quality Champions

Synopsis

Research findings show that internal auditors can be at the cutting edge of quality by championing knowledge and experience of Total Quality Management (TQM) in their engagements, as well as using TQM tools and techniques in their own internal auditing. Such a contribution to an organization's quality programmes can be through various roles – as a systems developer, as a systems auditor, as a compliance auditor – and adopting *'quality characteristics'* recognized in TQM principles.

Extracted from The IIA Research Foundation report *Total Quality Improvement Process and The Internal Auditing Function* (1995), Professor Parveen P. Gupta and Professor Manash R. Ray. Copyright 1995 by The Institute of Internal Auditors Research Foundation, 247 Maitland Avenue, Altamonte Springs, Florida 32710-4201, USA. Reprinted with permission.

After Reading the Case Study Consider:

1. How do attitudes to quality management in your own organization compare with those discussed in the case?
2. Can you identify examples of internal audit involvement in your organization's quality programmes? Are your examples by design or driven by your organization's quality policies?
3. Are any of the following quality characteristics used by you to achieve quality in your audit work and other services you provide:

   • Use of feedback from auditees.
   • A working involvement with your organization's quality auditors.

- Issue of a quality statement by internal audit.
- Clear understanding of audit objectives between auditor and auditee.
- Supervisory reviews of audit working papers.
- Use of quality teams to focus on activities that need to be improved.
- Training of internal audit staff in techniques for quality improvement.
- Use of quality measures.
- Reviews of selected audit work by internal audit staff independent of audit.
- Reviews of selected audit work by staff outside of the internal audit department.
- Use of internal audit standards/code of ethics/statements of responsibilities.
- Use of any other quality management standards, laws, regulations as a benchmark.

Case 8.5: Collecting Performance Data

Synopsis

Measuring quality performance in internal auditing requires a framework that balances all the measures needed across a wide spectrum of activities. Developing such a framework and appropriate key performance measures can be a cutting edge process.

After Reading the Case Study Consider:

1. What quality issues do you see for Carlton to solve?
2. What *'key performance indicators'* should Carlton consider for his balanced scorecard strategy?
3. How can Carlton use the new key performance indicators to achieve his mission to implement a *'... formal quality assurance and improvement programme within the department'*?

SELF-ASSESSMENT QUESTIONS

8/1   You are my Customer – You are also my supplier

(A question still relevant to today and tomorrow, asked first in an article written by the author in 1995.[41])

The theories and practices of quality management and quality systems are all based on the supply chain. Understanding the supply chain is an important part of performing any internal audit. Supply chains link all activities and relationships in the transformation of materials and information into a product and service: they are a complex web of control activities, internal, external to the organization and mixtures of both. They have many owners. They can be the whole organization or the smallest part of a process. They are dynamic, ever changing and snap at the weak points, causing many failures.

Most, if not all supply chain theories separate supplier from customer. This is a mistake. Recognizing the supplier as a customer and the customer as a supplier can have a significant impact on product and service development. Developing the right specifications for both supplier and customer interfaces are the keys to quality. Recognizing that these should be developed at the same time with the same person is fundamental to high-quality achievement.

Most internal auditors will recognize the persons they audit as either primary or secondary customers. Primary, if they are the first priority and have direct control over whether internal audit stays in business; secondary, if they are receiving an internal auditing product or service and have only an indirect control over whether internal audit stays in business. Primary can be the audit committee and senior management; secondary can be operating management and the workforce being audited.

How many internal auditors see their primary and secondary customers also as suppliers? Yet, they provide time, information, materials and sometimes processes which can add significant value to internal auditing performance. Recognizing this contribution as a supply switches the internal auditor's mind set into a different quality relationship with the auditee. It is now the turn of the internal auditor to set the quality specifications, establish a contract and measure cost, delivery and reliability. It is now the internal auditor's role to be delighted or dissatisfied. Are you satisfied with your customers' roles as suppliers?

(a) Do your auditees see you as a customer?
(b) Do you measure the performance of your customers as suppliers?

8/2   Implementing TQM In Internal Auditing

What are Gupta and Ray's seven steps that internal auditing should undertake to implement TQM within an internal auditing function? What is the eighth step added to these by the author? How many of these steps have you implemented in your internal auditing function? If you have implemented and are monitoring all eight you are at the cutting edge with your commitment to quality.

NOTES AND REFERENCES

1. *Internal Auditing in a Total Quality Environment: A Reference Manual* (1992: p. 29), Elaine McIntosh, The IIA.
2. *Total Quality Management* (1989), John S. Oakland, Butterworth Heinemann Ltd, Oxford, England.
3. Cited in Oakland's *Total Quality Management*.
4. The UK Department of Trade Industry, *The Quality Gurus – What Can They Do For You?* A contribution to its 'Managing into the 90s' series. This booklet discusses the roles of W. Edwards Deming, Joseph M. Juran, Shigeo Shingo, Philip B. Crosby, Armand V. Feigenbaum, Dr Kaoru Ishikawa, but there were many other quality consultants and academics across the world working in the field of quality cultures at that time.
5. The date was around 1988, at a time when the IIA–UK carried out a survey into the practice of quality assurance in internal audit functions.
6. *UK Quality Management – Policy Options* (1994), Science and Engineering Policy Studies (SEPSU), The Royal Society and The Royal Academy of Engineering, London, England.
7. 'Embracing ISO 9000' appeared as an article in The IIA *Internal Auditor*, August 1997, following the author's research into the impact of ISO 9000 on internal auditing in 1996/97. The author registered his own internal audit function to ISO 9001 in 1992, following a period of involvement

in his organization's implementation of a Total Quality Management programme, and registration of many of its operation's to ISO 9000.

8. 'Quality Schemes and Best Value in the 21st Century – Challenges for Many Organizations and Internal Auditing', *Internal Control*, Issue 38 February 2001, abg Professional Information, part of the CCH group, Institute of Chartered Accountants in England & Wales, London, England.

9. International Organization for Standardization Press Release Ref.: 1020, 3 August 2006 – The ISO Survey sheds light on roles of management system standards in globalization (see www.iso.org).

10. Research by SEPSU into UK quality management options in the early part of 1990s showed that TQM had penetrated some businesses in the UK "*. . . though companies that were small, public sector or service organizations were least likely to be involved in TQM*". Recommendations from the research suggested that successful implementation demanded "*. . . close attention to company culture – both internal arrangements and external relations – and is likely to lead to changes in company cultures. Agents for cultural change include role models, quality awards, systematic self-assessment, benchmarking and partnership sourcing. Attention to human factors is crucial. So, too, is an ungrudging commitment of time and other resources.*"

11. Visit its website www.dti.gov.uk/quality/tqm

12. *From Quality to Excellence* (2000), DTI publication that supports its website www.dti.gov.uk/quality

13. *Bendell's 14 Pointers, The Quality Gurus*, one of a series of '*Managing into the 90s*' publications, by the DTI, England. Prepared by Professor Tony Bendell this publication placed into context the varying methodologies propounded by various major quality gurus for the needs of British companies.

14. *Total Organizational Excellence – Achieving World-Class Performance* (1999), John S. Oakland, Butterworth-Heinemann, Oxford, England. Figure 8.13 is based on many years of research, education and advisory work in the European Centre for Business Excellence, the research division of Oakland Consulting plc – www.oaklandconsulting.com

15. The IIA operates its own benchmarking service Global Auditing Information Network (GAIN). For more information see its website or contact gain@theiia.org. Results of many of its surveys can be seen on its own website www.gain2.org

16. Developed by the European Foundation for Quality Management (EFQM) this 1999 revised model is widely used as a framework for continuous improvement initiative by private, public and voluntary sector organizations of all sizes.

17. Self-assessment data can be benchmarked with organizations across the public sector using a database run by the Centre for Management and Policy Studies (CMPS) – www.cmps.gov.uk

18. Charter Mark is very much a government scheme, the responsibility of the Charter Mark Policy and Marketing Team at the Cabinet Office.

19. General information about Investors in People can be obtained from Investors in People UK. www.iipuk.co.uk

20. A new independent body, the Pensions Protection and Investment Accreditation Board (PPIAB) has been set up to assess companies who wish to apply for accreditation – see website www.raisingstandards.net for details.

21. Established in 1998 from National Lottery funding the NCVO's Quality Standards Task Group (QSTG) has researched and published principles and other quality recommendations for voluntary organizations. More information on its current activities can be found on the National Council for Voluntary Organizations (NCVO) website, www.ncvo-vol.org.uk

22. The Local Government Act of 1999 places a duty on all local authorities to make arrangements to secure continuous improvement in the way in which their functions are exercised, having regard to a combination of economy, efficiency and effectiveness. The Department of the Environment, Transport and the Regions (DETR) in 2000 published its own *Guide to Quality Schemes and Best Value*, which explores the interrelationships between quality schemes and Best Value.

23. The Improvement and Development Agency was established by and for local government in 1999 to support improvement in LAs from within. Its publication *Made to Measure – Best Value* and the EFQM Excellence Model, 2001, provides guidance to LAs on the implementation of quality initiatives. See its website www.idea.gov.uk

24. The Audit Commission Management Paper (2000) 'An Inside Job' considered the work of the internal auditor as fundamental to a LAs approach to Best Value. Internal auditors are seen as important contributors to Best Value Reviews (BVR).

25. The new Position Statement: *Risk Based Internal Auditing* published by the IIA–UK & Ireland in August 2003, provides useful guidance for internal auditors involved in risk management processes. It is an approach '. . . *that focuses (internal auditors) on the issues that matter to the organization'*. Quality must always be one of those issues.

26. *Internal Control – Integrated Framework* (1992). Committee of Sponsoring Organizations of the Treadway Commission. A new COSO Enterprise Risk Management (ERM) framework was published in 2004. This framework breaks organizational objectives into four categories: 1, strategic; 2, operational; 3, reporting; and 4, compliance. Each of these categories is key to the implementation of TQM and the achievement of excellence.

27. *Winning Ways Through Corporate Governance* (1996), Neville Bain and David Band, Macmillan Business, London, England.

28. *A Strategic Approach to Corporate Governance* (1999), Adrian Davies, Gower, Aldershot, England.

29. Commonwealth Association for Corporate Governance. www.cbc.to/governance/finalver/cacg

30. OECD. www.oecd.org/daf/governance/principles

31. *The Case for Costing Quality* (1992), 'Managing in the 90s' series, Department of Trade and Industry, London, United Kingdom.

32. *Total Quality Improvement Process and The Internal Audit Function* (1995), The IIA Research Foundation.

33. *The Balanced Scorecard: Translating Strategy into Action*, Robert S. Kaplan and David P. Norton, 1996, Harvard Business School Press, USA.

34. *A Balanced Scorecard Framework for Internal Auditing Departments* (2002), Mark L. Frigo, The IIA Research Foundation.

35. *Quality Assessment Manual*, 4th edition (2002), The IIA. This edition represents an update and expansion of the *Business Focused Quality Assurance Review Manual*, 3rd edition, published in 1996. *It continues to be the principal guidance and set of practical tools to assess conformity to the International Standards for the Professional Practice of Internal Auditing, and to reveal opportunities for enhancing the effectiveness and value of internal audit activities.* There is now a 5th edition (2006) *Quality Assessment Manual* responding to '. . . *issuance of the revised International Standards and Practice Advisories, related changes in the internal auditing profession and the increasingly demanding business environments in which the profession operates'*. Also, read the IIA–UK & Ireland Professional guidance for internal auditors. *Quality assurance and improvement programmes* (2007).

36. Over the past 17 years The IIA has conducted a wide variety of quality assessments for organizations both large and small across the world. For details visit its website or contact qar@theiia.org

37. *Government Internal Audit Standards – Quality Assurance Questionnaires* (2002), Audit Policy and Advice (APA) HM Treasury, London, England.

38. This position remains the same in its 2006 survey published in *Management Tools and Trends* (2007), Darrell Rigby and Barbara Bilodeau, Bain & Company, USA. www.bain.com

39. Advertisement *'2006 – Best year in the company's history'* – Annual Report www.audi.com, *Financial Times*, Thursday 1 March 2007, p. 7.

40. *Behavioural Patterns in Internal Audit* (1972), Frederick E. Mints, The IIA.

41. 'You Are My Customer – You Are Also My Supplier', Jeffrey Ridley, *Internal Auditing* (October 1995), IIA–UK & Ireland.

9

Cutting Edge Internal Auditing
Continuously Benchmarks

*'Always to be the best,
and to be distinguished above the rest.'*

Homer: 8th century BC[1]

~ Benchmarking ~

INTERNAL AUDITING CONTINUOUSLY BENCHMARKING
BEFORE 1998

Commitment to quality requires best practice benchmarking. I was inspired to write my article on benchmarking in 2000 by this cartoon. Not that it fully represents best practice benchmarking. Rarely are there only two participants in a competitive benchmarking process: nor is there only one measure, or one product or service. But it does demonstrate the importance of promoting the quality and class of your product and service. The purpose of my article at that time was to emphasize the importance of continuous benchmarking.

At the time, benchmarking was not a new tool. In the past and on a less formal basis it has been called 'comparing'. Comparisons have always been made in auditing, and still are made, formally and informally. At the time of the article, benchmarking, as a comparison, had developed into a more formal management tool to identify where improvements should take place to achieve excellence, and monitor its implementation. It was then, and still is, a continuous process by many organizations and functions, including internal auditing. The skill of benchmarking is a tool all internal auditors should possess. Mark Frigo (1997)[2] recognized this in his research for The IIA Research Foundation:

> Internal auditors have the opportunity to participate in the process of benchmarking and help organizations to identify and innovatively adapt the 'best of the best' methods and practices.

The IIA, through its adopted theme *Progress through Sharing*,[3] has always developed and published statements and standards on internal auditing from benchmarking best practices across its membership, and externally with other professions and organizations. Since 1993, its GAIN programme has been promoting benchmarking through member questionnaires and 'flash surveys'. In 1997 its Research Foundation sponsored Frigo's research into internal auditing activities providing benchmarking services for their clients. This research promoted the use of benchmarking in internal auditing, and as a service in the organization. It defined benchmarking as '... *a process of identifying and disseminating best practices* ... '.

The IIA–UK & Ireland has always supported active District Societies in regions across the United Kingdom and Ireland, providing forums for discussion, training programmes and informal network benchmarking. It has also encouraged and supported a variety of industry Discussion Groups for its members, with similar activities.

The United Kingdom civil service has its own internal audit advisory group in HM Treasury, the Assurance, Control and Risk Team (ACRT). ACRT has promoted and organized networking of internal auditing across government departments. Its standards and guidelines, developed closely with the IIA–UK & Ireland, established internal auditing consistency and uniformity: introducing best practice training and qualifications for government internal audit staff.

The United Kingdom Chartered Institute of Public Finance and Accountancy (CIPFA), through its Audit Panel, has researched and networked internal auditing in local government: promoting professional internal auditing in its publications. In 1997 its *Perceptions of Audit Quality*[4] demonstrated '... *the existence of a* [public services]*quality expectations gap between auditors and auditees*'. The survey did not mention benchmarking as a management or internal auditing tool but did recommend that '*Auditors need to acquire and "sell" skills in value for money assessments to meet the expectations of their customers who are facing competitive and financial pressures*'. All value for money assessments are based on benchmarking practices.

Macdonald and Tanner (1996)[5] published their guide to understanding benchmarking with the introduction:

> Benchmarking is changing the perspectives of executives and managers around the world. It is showing them how good, bad or mediocre their company is in aspects of their own business as compared with world class companies. Benchmarking continuously challenges the best practices of modern management. The principles of benchmarking apply equally to manufacturing or service industries [public services could have been included here], and to large or small organizations.

At this time, most quality programmes recognized that improvement can always be made: be it strategic, procedural, operational or the competency of people: be it input into a process, the process itself or output in the form of products or services: be it within an organization or across all its supply chains and partnerships: be it risk management, control or governance. Benchmarking was recognized as one of the tools to make such improvements happen. The Business Excellence Model developed by the European Foundation for Quality Management (EFQM),[6] discussed in Chapter 8, was a tool being used by many organizations '. . . *as a way to benchmark with other organizations'*. The model's framework of nine criteria '. . . *against which to assess an organization's progress towards excellence . . .* ' had been promoted by the United Kingdom government[7] for use in the public sector.

The Chartered Institute of Public Finance and Accountancy (CIPFA) launched Benchmarking Clubs in 1998 to promote comparisons of costs in UK local authorities. In 1999 the UK Local Government Act established 'best value' criteria for local authorities, defining best value as a duty to deliver services to clear standards – covering both cost and quality – by the most economic, efficient and effective means available. Best value requires robust reviews using four principles of challenge, comparison, consultation and competition. These principles have become fundamental to the provision of services by all local authorities and form the basis of their benchmarking practices.

Article:
Have A 'Best Value' Christmas And Prosperous 'Learning' New Year[8] (1998)

Two announcements this year by the UK government will significantly influence many of our future working lives. These are the policy of 'best value' in the public sector and national preparations for the 'learning age'. Both based on principles of improved proficiency, effectiveness and quality. Both are interdependent. Both will have a significant impact on internal auditing services during 1999 and after. Both offer ways of achieving changed attitudes and prosperity for internal auditors across all sectors. They are in my Christmas message and should be desired achievements in all our New Year resolutions.

> *'Understanding and experience of best practice benchmarking is the key to best value.'*

Do you Add Value by Best Value?

Best value is the continuous search to improve quality, efficiency and effectiveness of all activities. Such a search starts with an agreed vision. It requires a framework of activities, including review, assessment, comparison, learning, change, target-setting and public reporting of results. Its development and recognition will spread across all branches of the public sector during the next few years. It has already been introduced in many local government authorities and government departments and will impact all public sector suppliers and customers. It is spreading into non-government departments. It will impact internal auditing, both in how it is provided and what is reviewed. It will be subject to independent external monitoring.

Understanding and experience of 'best practice' benchmarking (BPB) is the key to best value. BPB is a continuous discovery process. It means continuously comparing practices to seek the best and improve. BPB is not a new technique. What is new is the way that many organizations worldwide, across all sectors, have adopted BPB to drive continuous improvement. Benchmarks can be internal and external to the organization. They can be structures, practices, technology, equipment and people: they can be a mixture of any or all of these. They can be standards, codes of practice, regulations and even the law. They can be social, environmental, economic, financial and religious.

Benchmarks should be what customers see as being best for them at a given time. They are created by innovation, research, development and above all competition. They are constantly changing, because competition drives improvement and customers change their needs.

The UK Department of Trade and Industry[a] defined what is involved in benchmarking as:

- Establishing what makes the difference, in customers' eyes, between an ordinary supplier and an excellent supplier.
- Setting standards in each of those things, according to the best practice that can be found.
- Finding out how the best companies meet their challenging standards.
- Applying other people's experience to meet new standards, and exceed them.

Some years ago The IIA established an internal auditing benchmarking service called GAIN – Global Auditing Information Network. It has been successfully marketed across the world as:

- A tool for reassuring priorities and direction.
- A benchmark for comparing best practices.
- An instrument for evaluating auditing issues.
- A window for viewing auditing practices of successful organizations.

GAIN offers global, national and industry group benchmarks. Its methods are based on benchmarking practices, which now exist in most organizations. Those internal auditing functions that have not yet benchmarked their services with best practice should start doing so now before it is too late. Competition to provide internal auditing services will continue to grow as the prosperity of the assurance market place continues to increase.

---

[a] *Best Practice Benchmarking* (1990), Department of Trade and Industry, London, England.

Do You Have an Agreed Vision for Internal Auditing in Your Organization?

An agreed vision is essential for best value. It provides the framework and pathway for all the benchmarking activities that follow. How many internal audit functions have an agreed vision? Research[b] this year into the marketing of internal auditing in housing associations shows only a few had developed a vision for their services, as a part of their strategic planning. I believe this situation exists in internal audit functions in most industry sectors.

Understanding what a vision is must be the first step. Vision statements were defined for this research as

'... a vivid picture of an ambitious, desirable state that is connected to your customers and better in some important way than your current state. It is a short statement, which establishes the strategic direction of the internal auditing mission and key objectives. It can and does change as internal and external influences dictate. Both the vision statement and changes to it are team agreements.'

There are many good examples of visions published by organizations every day. They surround all activities and are there to motivate both the provider and customer. A good example is:

'Altogether Better Internal Auditing Business', our aim is:

- to provide benefits for all our customers across the widest possible range of services;
- to maintain quality, value and integrity in all our business dealings.

This vision statement is proactive, innovative, focused, integrated and motivating. The key word **'altogether'** establishes a teamworking environment, embracing all staff, their suppliers and customers: it implies that the products and services being provided meet the needs of all. The key word **'better'** creates an environment of continuous improvement: it implies a constant search for best practices through benchmarking. The key word **'business'** provides a focus on all operations to achieve the organization's objectives. The **'aim'** focuses on customer satisfaction, expansion and high ethical and professional standards.

All internal auditors should have a vision that links into the vision statements of the organizations they serve and their audit scope and planning.

How Can We, Together, Realize a New Learning Age?

'Learning is the key to prosperity – for each of us as individuals, as well as for the nation as a whole.' This is the introduction to the UK government's[c] current marketing of a national debate about how we can, together, realize a new Learning Age. It starts the debate by stating '... this is the first time that a comprehensive policy paper has been produced which encompasses the range of possibilities in developing

---

[b] Benchmarking Regulation Audit Control Excellence (BRACE 3) – Best Practice Marketing in Internal Audit in Housing Associations (1998), Housing Association Internal Audit Forum, www.haiaf.org.uk
[c] The Learning Age – a renaissance for a new Britain (1998), Department for Education and Employment, London, England.

education and skills from post-school to post-retirement.' This vision of a Learning Age is based on a foundation of principles, which includes:

Achieving world-class (learning) standards and value for money by:

- better management, target-setting and improved quality assurance; and
- making sure that learning meets the highest professional standards.

Has The IIA established world-class learning for internal auditors? What do you think?

This month will see The IIA's publication of a new competency framework for internal auditing (CFIA).[d] The CFIA had its grand unveiling at The IIA's International Conference in July this year. This new study, by a global research team, builds on The IIA's researched common body of knowledge (CBOK),[e] published in 1992. CBOK comprised 334 individual competencies in 20 different discipline areas, ranking reasoning, communications, auditing, ethics and organizations as the five most important disciplines – in that order.

Internal auditing leaders, trainers and educators across the world have used CBOK to design degree and postgraduate education, skill courses and professional qualification programmes. The success of these programmes comes from their international status, and a growing recognition by internal auditors and their employers. There is also a growing recognition by governments, regulators and other professional institutions. Yet, much has still to be achieved if the learning programmes we see today for internal auditors are to be seen by all internal auditors and their employers as the peak of their profession.

CBOK has directed and guided the learning of thousands of internal auditors across the world, contributing significantly to the development and improvement of professional internal auditing. Both The IIA and IIA–UK used CBOK to design the syllabi for their professional qualifications. The IIA with its international Certified Internal Auditor (CIA) programme and the IIA–UK with its Practitioner (PIIA) and Membership of Institute Internal Auditors (MIIA).

From November 1998 The IIA has introduced changes to the CIA syllabi[f] that reflect some of the CFIA findings: *'. . . the Board of Regents used many of the study's findings to increase its international scope.'* Based on the research results the following competency-based definition of internal auditing has been developed:

Those organizational processes instituted to provide assurance that risk exposures are understood and managed appropriately, in the midst of ongoing and dynamic change.

This new definition of today and tomorrow's internal auditing focuses internal auditors on assuring management that all risks are being managed appropriately. It offers new opportunities for internal auditors to build bridges across management and all assurance activities. It promotes internal auditing as a facilitator of

---

[d] 'Will CFIA Transform Internal Auditing?', *The IIA Today*, May/June 1998, The IIA.
[e] *A Common Body of Knowledge for the Practice of Internal Auditing* (1992), Albrecht, Stice and Stocks, The IIA.
[f] 'CIA Exam Undergoes Changes', *The IIA Today*, September/October 1998, The IIA.

assurance. It sets exciting challenges for internal auditors to be part of a new learning age, built on the foundation of CBOK with an even wider scope in the control environment. It offers increased reward. It should lead internal auditors into making new resolutions for the continuous improvement of their proficiency, and in the effectiveness and quality of their service. It should encourage more internal auditors to seek and promote internal auditing professional qualifications.

What recognition do you give to these world-class internal auditing learning programmes and how they are being developed? Will they be part of your learning age? Are they recognized and rewarded in your organization? Improving the status and recognition of our internal auditing professional qualifications with governments, regulators and our customers should be a priority of The IIA and all its members, in 1999 and beyond.

Have You Made any Predictions for Internal Auditing in the 21st Century?

Accurate predictions made by the CBOK researchers in the early 1990s have become real issues in today's internal auditing. These predictions are listed as:

Impact of Technology
'. . . as computer technology continues to develop, internal auditing practice will change its focus more toward analysis and interpretation of data.'

The Quality Revolution
'. . . this area will have a significant impact on internal auditing in the future.'

Globalization of Business
'. . . auditing multinational organizations may require additional skills. . . '

Increasing Importance of Nontechnical Skills
'. . . technical specialists will be needed, but success will come with the ability to analyse, interact with, and communicate audit findings.'

The new CFIA research studied internal auditing practices around four questions:

1. What is internal auditing today and what will it be in the future?
2. What are the attributes of a competent internal auditing function from a best practice perspective?
3. What capabilities should be required by those in a competent internal audit function?
4. How is the competency internal auditors and an internal audit function best assessed?

What accurate predictions can you associate with these questions?

This Christmas and New Year Ask Yourself the Following Ten Questions:

1. Do you have a continuous programme to seek best value for your internal audit function and organization?
2. Does this programme include best practice benchmarking?

3. Have you an agreed vision statement for your internal audit function that links into your organization's vision statement?
4. Do you relate your vision statement to your audit scope and objectives?
5. Have you considered all the learning opportunities needed to be an educated and skilful professional internal auditor?
6. Do you, your customers and organization know what these opportunities are?
7. Have you a learning programme for yourself and staff that includes both education and skill training?
8. Is your learning programme well managed, and monitored by target setting, and improved quality assurance?
9. Does your learning include the best practice professional standards established by The IIA?
10. Do your predictions for internal auditing in the 21st century include those of The IIA?

Action the answers in your New Year resolutions!

The Audit Commission, UK local authority external auditor, became the auditor of best value performance, and in 2000 published guidelines[9] for local authority internal auditors to contribute to best value planning and practices, not least in demonstrating '. . . *that its own performance satisfies the principles of best value'*. This principle applies to all internal audit activities in every sector. Not only should best practice benchmarking in internal audit be part of its services, it should also be shouted to all its customers.

Article:
Shout How Best You Are In All Your Internal Auditing Market Places[10] (2001)

In 1996 The IIA in its research publications recognized the following emerging best internal auditing practices[g]:

- Development of partnering roles with audit clients.
- Participating in corporate task forces.
- Aligning corporate goals, audit department plans and performance evaluations.
- Educating management on their internal control responsibilities.
- Carrying out customer satisfaction surveys.
- Providing training to audit committee members.
- External quality assurance reviews of internal auditing practices.
- Involvement in TQM practices.
- Using computer-assisted techniques.
- Including audits of environment, health and safety.
- Development of formal risk assessment system involving management.

[g] *Leading Edge Internal Auditing* (1998), J. Ridley, and A.D. Chambers, ICSA Publishing, London, England.

- Empowerment of staff to experiment with a variety of approaches in developing innovative solutions to problems.
- Providing internal consulting services that focus on problem solving rather than problem finding.

These internal auditing practices have been adopted by many internal auditing functions in a variety of ways. Evidence for this promotion of inter-in-house internal the marketing of

> **When best practice is achieved it should be shouted to all customers**

can be found in the nal auditing by auditing functions; internal auditing services by professional accounting firms and consultants; the developing syllabi of professional certificates for internal auditors; training programmes provided by The IIA and other institutes; programmes for internal auditing and risk assessment conferences and their speakers' presentations.

Much of this improvement in internal auditing services has been developed through formal benchmarking processes carried out or influenced by The IIA and its worldwide affiliated National Institutes and Chapters. Those working in internal auditing, both in-house and outsourced, have also been shouting their best practices to each other: formal research by The IIA has recommended internal auditing and control best practices: involvement of internal auditors in national commissions and working parties has influenced significant changes in attitudes to governance, control and internal auditing.

Internal benchmarking has involved internal auditors in comparing their practices with those of other services in their organizations. External benchmarking has involved internal auditors looking outside their organizations comparing their practices with all the sources of best practice mentioned in the previous paragraph. Recognizing the key external benchmarks is an important part of the process. For all internal auditors it is important that they study and understand the following list of ten past and current external benchmarks:

Benchmark 1

1977: The IIA[h] publication of **international statements** and standards for professional practices in internal auditing, continuously improved with supporting guidelines and revisions. Publication of a revised international definition for professional internal auditing and code of ethics[i] in 1999 has widened the role of internal auditing into risk assessment and consultancy. This has been followed by a consultative document[j] **containing revised standards to be introduced in 2002.** These statements and standards will become even more

---

[h] *Standards for the Professional Practice of Internal Auditing* (1977) (latest update 1998), The IIA.
[i] The Institute of Internal Auditors definition of internal auditing (1999) *"Internal auditing is an independent, objective assurance and consulting activity designed to add value and improve an organization's operations. It helps an organization accomplish its objectives by bringing a systematic, disciplined approach to evaluate and improve the effectiveness of risk management, control and governance processes."*
[j] 'New Standards Bring Professional Practices Framework to Life', *Internal Auditor Journal* (February 2001), The IIA.

important as more and more audit committees require internal auditors to define their roles and challenge them to meet high standards of professionalism and methodology.

Benchmark 2

1982: First development of **a common body of knowledge for internal auditors**,[k] followed by research reports published by The IIA in **1988**,[l] **1992**[m] **and a new competency framework for internal auditors in 1999**.[n] This body of knowledge supports the framework of knowledge on which **The IIA professional examinations have been based since the mid 70s.**

Benchmark 3

1987: USA publication of the Treadway[o] report on **fraudulent financial reporting**, including recommendations on internal auditing and audit committee practices, followed by the **COSO**[p] **integrated internal control framework in 1992.** This framework has been used worldwide to assess control levels in organizations of all sizes and in all sectors. It was the first definition of control that required an assessment of risk linked to an organization's objectives before control activities are established.

Benchmark 4

1987: Publication of an international standard for **quality management systems and auditing** (ISO 9000), based on the UK standard BSI 5750, **revised in 1994 and completely re-written in 2000.** The following quality principles and requirements on which the re-written standard is based are essential for the assurance of quality in all internal auditing services:

- Customer focused organization
- Leadership
- Involvement of people
- Process approach
- System approach to management
- Continual improvement
- Factual approach to decision-making
- Mutually beneficial supplier relationship

---

[k] 'The Common Body of Knowledge for Internal Auditors', Gobiel, R.E., *Internal Auditor Journal* (November/December 1982), The IIA.
[l] *A Common Body of Professional Knowledge for Internal Auditors (CBOK)* (1985), Barrett, M.J. *et al.*, The IIA.
[m] *A Common Body of Knowledge for the Practice of Internal Auditing (CBOK)* (1992), Albrecht, W.S. *et al.*, The IIA Research Foundation.
[n] *Competency Framework for Internal Auditing (CFIA)* (1999), McIntosh, Elaine R., The IIA Research Foundation.
[o] *Report of the National Commission on Fraudulent Financial Reporting* (1987), Treadway Commission, Sponsored by American Institute of Certified Public Accountants, American Accounting Association, Financial Executives Institute, The Institute of Internal Auditors and National Association of Accountants, American Institute of Certified Public Accountants, New Jersey, USA.
[p] *Internal Control – Integrated Framework* (1992), Committee of Sponsoring Organizations of Treadway Commission (COSO), American Institute of Certified Public Accountants, New Jersey, USA.

Benchmark 5

1991: The IIA[q] publication of guidance for the auditing of **information technology (updated in 1994)**. This guidance has not dated. At the time of its publication it was in advance of its time. For some internal auditors it still is.

Benchmark 6

1992: UK Cadbury[r] report on **corporate governance** (reviewed by **Hampel**[s] **in 1998** and followed by the **Turnbull**[t] **report in 1999**, introducing risk-based control techniques linked to the COSO recommendations of 1992). These reports all link internal auditing into satisfying the needs of their audit committees and boards. Risk assessment is now firmly placed in internal audit planning and as a service internal auditors can facilitate and add value to in their organizations.

Benchmark 7

1996: Publication of an international standard for **environmental management systems and auditing** (ISO 14001), based on the UK standard BSI 7750. This standard has been well received across the world. It provides internal auditors with a best practice benchmark for the management of all environmental issues. Its auditing practices provide guidance for all environmental audits, whether carried out by internal auditors or environmental auditors.

Benchmark 8

1998: The IIA[u] model for improving the internal audit service to the organization through **risk management techniques**. This model demonstrates clearly the links between risk assessment for internal audit planning and risk assessment by management for the achievement of their objectives.

Benchmark 9

1999: USA Blue Ribbon Committee[v] report on improving the **effectiveness of audit committees**. This committee's ten recommendations are focused on financial reporting and audit committee oversight processes. This 'next step' in the effectiveness of audit committees in North America will influence many audit

---

[q] *Systems Auditability and Control® (SAC)* (1991) – revised (1994), The IIA Research Foundation.
[r] *Committee on the Financial Aspects of Corporate Governance* (1992), chaired by Sir Adrian Cadbury, Gee Publishing Limited, London, England.
[s] *Committee on Corporate Governance Final Report of the Committee on Corporate Governance* (1998), chaired by Sir Ronald Hampel, Gee Publishing Limited, London, England.
[t] *Internal Control – Guidance for Directors on the Combined Code* (1999), Turnbull report, Institute of Chartered Accountants in England and Wales, London, England.
[u] *Risk Management: Changing the Internal Auditor's Paradigm* (1998), George M. Selim and David MacNamee, The IIA Research Foundation.
[v] *Improving the Effectiveness of Corporate Audit Committees* (1999), The Blue Ribbon Committee, New York Stock Exchange and National Association of Securities Dealers, New York, USA.

committee terms of reference worldwide. It is important that internal auditing keeps up to date with how audit committees are achieving best practice and how this impacts its assurance role.

Benchmark 10

1999: UK Institute of Social and Ethical Accountability[w] publication of a foundation **standard in social and ethical accounting, auditing and reporting** (AA1000). Followed by a guidance statement[x] for internal auditors, published by the IIA–UK & Ireland. In recent years social and ethical responsibilities have become increasingly important at board, management and staff levels in all organizations. The involvement of internal auditing as an adviser and assessor in these issues has started in some organizations. Others will follow. This involvement will grow.

These benchmarks have had and will have a significant influence on how internal auditing best practices evolve. Some are just starting to influence internal auditing. Their improvement will continue to have a significant impact on how internal auditing services develop. Each will influence how control and corporate governance is measured and monitored. It is important all internal auditors should be aware of their content and the best practices they promote. Other new benchmarks will follow in the future, improving on past statements and adding new best practices. Benchmarking internal auditing never ends!

The IIA benchmarking process is called GAIN – Global Auditing Information Network. It markets its service as:

- A tool for reassessing priorities and direction.
- A benchmark for comparing best practices.
- An instrument for evaluating auditing issues.
- A window for viewing the internal auditing practices of successful organizations.

GAIN offers global, national and industry group benchmarks. Its database has been developed since the mid-1990s with input from internal auditing organizations across the world. For those using its services all input starts with a questionnaire requiring details of the internal auditing services being provided. The 2001 questionnaire has been updated to now include:

- Details of any external quality assurance reviews in the last three years.
- Internal auditing relationships with audit committees.
- Audit committee implementation of the Blue-Ribbon committee recommendations.
- The amount of IT auditing outsourced.
- A listing of recent successful internal auditing practices.

---

[w] *Accountability 1000 (AA1000), A Foundation Standard in Social and Ethical Accounting, Auditing and Reporting* (1999), Institute of Social and Ethical Accountability, London, England UK, www.AccountAbility.org.uk
[x] *Ethics and Social Responsibility*, Professional Briefing Note Fifteen (1999), IIA–UK & Ireland.

The questionnaire is now on-line: web-based data submission provides clients with electronic delivery of reports via e-mail.

The IIA–UK & Ireland has its own benchmarking research, published annually, the latest is based on a survey of 200 internal audit functions. Reported in its journal[y] in June 2001, the survey covers a wide range of sectors in the UK and Ireland, providing excellent data for benchmarking internal auditing practices today. Included is data on numbers of internal auditors in organizations, reporting lines, composition of risk committees, annual opinions on assurance, outsourcing, staff professional backgrounds, department budget analyses and performance indicators used to measure the effectiveness of internal auditing.

But shouting is not enough when benchmarking practices or products. Differences have to be analysed and measured. Best Practice Benchmarking (BPB) is a formal management tool for seeking and achieving the best. It is a discovery process requiring continuous comparisons to make change happen. The UK Department of Trade and Industry, in its publication *Best Practice Benchmarking*, part of its 'Managing into the '90s' series, defined what is involved as:

- Establishing what makes the difference, in customers' eyes, between an ordinary supplier and an excellent supplier.
- Setting standards in each of those things, according to the best practice that can be found.
- Finding out how the best companies meet their challenging standards.
- Applying other people's experience to meet new standards, and exceed them.

BPB is not a new technique. What is new, is the way that many organizations worldwide, across all sectors, have adopted BPB to drive continuous improvement, as they structure to meet competition, with excellent products and services. The importance of customers during BPB is paramount. The DTI statement above emphasizes this importance. Customers think that the kite marks excellence and superiority. Leading customers to that belief is an essential part of promoting products and services as best.

Benchmarks can be internal and external to the organization. They can be structures, practices, technology, equipment and people. They can be a mixture of any or all of these. They can be standards, codes of practice, regulations and laws. They can be social, environmental, economic, financial and religious. They are what people, as customers, see as being best for them at a given time. Culture, innovation, research, development and, above all, competition create them. They are constantly changing, because competition drives improvement.

A good approach to benchmarking is to establish a team from those with interest and/or responsibility for internal audit in an organization. The team should include at least one main internal audit customer. Then take the following seven steps:

1. Determine the features of your internal audit unit to be benchmarked. Do not choose too many. No more than five at first.
2. Agree what influences there are on your features. Consider both internal and external influences. Use these influences to establish your benchmarks.

---

[y] *Benchmarking Survey 2000*, IIA–UK & Ireland.

(Before proceeding create a framework to identify what you need to measure. Select the key features you wish to benchmark: these are the most important actions you believe you and your organization need to develop, to improve regulation, audit, control and excellence in your organization. Having agreed the features, identify the internal and external influences that impact how they perform: see these influences as levels, which can and do interact one with the other. Study how these levels impact your organization's control and your internal audit service. Agree measures for each of your benchmarks. The right measures are important. Test how appropriate they are by trying to link them into your team's vision of excellent internal audit. If the link is not strong, change your measure.)

3. Use your measures to identify and agree 'current gaps' between your practices and benchmarks.
4. Analyse your 'current gaps'. Look for causes why you do not already meet your benchmark's level of service. Consider structure, processes, delegated responsibilities, competencies, resources, etc. Agree what actions need to be taken to achieve best practice; over what time span and how they will be measured.
5. Continuously follow-up achievement of your benchmarks. Celebrate success.
6. Shout your best practices and products to all of your customers.
7. Continuously improve all your benchmarks and add others.

Benchmarking is not just the domain of internal auditors. All organizations, particularly those in competitive market places, continuously benchmark their strategies, structures, processes, products and services. Internal auditors can often help in this process, through their reviews, as consultants and as educators. The IIA[z] 1997 research into benchmarking services provided by internal auditors in their organizations found some evidence in the USA of internal auditors providing benchmarking services, either in their normal audit planning or in consultancy services. The report makes the following six recommendations:

1. Internal auditors should consider how benchmarking can be incorporated into each internal auditing engagement.
2. Internal auditors should target specific areas for benchmarking.
3. Internal auditors should incorporate benchmarking into their departmental plans to identify where benchmarking would be most valuable to the organization and consistent with departmental skills and resources.
4. Internal auditors should develop benchmarking skills. This can be done through training or working with internal or external benchmarking experts.
5. Internal auditing departments should be positioned as a major source of internal benchmarking information.
6. Internal auditors should combine external benchmarking with internal benchmarking where appropriate.

Not all internal auditors will agree with each recommendation, though many will agree with some. Consider how such a benchmarking service could be part of your internal auditing consultancy service.

---

[z] *Providing Benchmarking Services for Internal Auditing Clients* (1997), Mark L. Frigo, The IIA Research Foundation.

It is not enough for internal auditors to benchmark their services internally and externally against what are perceived to be best practices elsewhere. The results must be measured and continuously reviewed for improvement. When best practice is achieved it should be shouted to all customers. Not just to say that the internal auditing practices are best, but also to demonstrate that internal auditors are good at benchmarking – a service they can provide during their audits and when asked to do so by their customers.

CUTTING EDGE INTERNAL AUDITING CONTINUOUSLY BENCHMARKS TODAY AND IN THE FUTURE

Many organizations worldwide, across all sectors, continue to use benchmarking as a tool to identify best practice and drive continuous improvement at a cutting edge. A search of the Internet reveals many organizations promoting benchmarking with codes of practice for the exchange of information. Bain & Company,[11] a global business-consulting firm, in its annual review of management tools recognizes a continuing high use and satisfaction from benchmarking to improve performance in organizations. There can be few organizations and internal auditing activities that do not now benchmark, whether formally or informally.

Oakland (2002),[12] in his concept of world-class performance, defines a benchmark as a '. . . *reference or measurement standard used for comparison* . . .' and benchmarking as '. . . *the continuous process of identifying, understanding and adapting best practice and processes that will lead to superior performance*'. He sees the purpose of benchmarking to be:

Change the perspectives of executives and managers
Compare business practices with those of world class organizations
Challenge current practices and processes
Create improved goals and practices for the organization.

This is very good guidance for all organizations and internal auditors when benchmarking.

Sawyer's *Internal Auditing* (2003)[13] discusses benchmarking as a tool to be used '. . . *to enhance all levels of the internal auditing function*':

> It can be applied to the basic philosophy of internal auditing's relationship to the organization; to the organization of the auditing function; to the planning process, including risk assessment and self-evaluation processes; to field work, including methods of examination and evaluation; to the reporting processes; and to relationships with external auditors and boards of directors. The important thing is that change be made not just to use new methods, but also to result in substantial improvements in the audit operation.

O'Regan (2004)[14] defines 'benchmarking' in his dictionary of auditor's language:

> The comparison of data or operations against those of similar organizations. Benchmarking, whether 'quantitative' or 'qualitative', is often performed with the intention of seeking ways to improve an organization's operations. Auditors also frequently use benchmarking as part of their analytical review procedures. For example, an industry average of payroll cost per employee is a common benchmark to assess the reasonableness of payroll costs in a specific organization.

His inclusion of benchmarking in 'analytical review procedures' highlights the importance of this process in auditing. The practice of comparing in analytical auditing procedures is rarely referred to as benchmarking yet the principles are similar – making comparisons, analysing differences, reviewing the reasons and recommending improvements.

How to benchmark has changed little since 2000. The process and 7 steps in my article are the same today (see Figure 9.1).

> 1. Determine the features
> 2. Agree what influences there are on your features.
> 3. Use your measures to identify and agree 'current gaps'
> 4. Analyse your 'current gaps'.
> 5. Continuously follow-up achievement
> 6. Shout your best practices and products
> 7. Continuously improve

Figure 9.1   Seven Benchmarking Steps
Source: J. Ridley (2000)

Improvements for my article's ten Benchmarks today and tomorrow are discussed in the following chapters:

Chapter 3   Cutting Edge Internal Auditing is World-Class
              Benchmarks 1, 2 and 6
Chapter 5   Cutting Edge Internal Auditing Knows How to Govern
              Benchmarks 3, 8 and 9

Chapter 8   Cutting Edge Internal Auditing is Committed to Quality
              Benchmark 4

Chapter 14   Cutting Edge Internal Auditing Manages Knowledge Well
              Benchmark 5

Chapter 13   Cutting Edge Internal Auditing Contributes to Good Reputation
              Benchmarks 7 and 10

The IIA still recognizes the essential need for benchmarking professional internal auditing principles and practices through its sharing of knowledge, conferences, examination programmes, networking, research projects, publications and developed *International Professional Practices Framework*. Its current Information Network (InfoNet) has been developed from its Global Audit Information Network (GAIN). Today InfoNet provides one-off and continuous benchmarking services through an annual updated questionnaire, flash survey facilities, and the networking opportunities these offer participants. It promotes its services as a global forum providing:

Learning from the challenges and solutions of your peers.
Gaining best internal audit practices from top organizations.
Enhancing your operational effectiveness and efficiency.

Its 2006 Questionnaire section on *'Successful Internal Auditing Practices'* includes questions on practices developed over many years of surveying internal audit activities. Many of the questions in this section, if answered YES, could represent current cutting edge internal auditing, such as the following 10 examples:

- Education of operation management on their internal control responsibilities.
- Maintain an ethical issues hotline.
- Develop a formal risk assessment system involving management.
- Audit disaster recovery plans and tests.
- Utilize continuous control monitoring.
- Emphasize Total Quality Management (TQM) principles and apply aggressively.
- Include audits of environment, health and safety.
- Include regulatory audits.
- Provide training to the Audit Committee.
- Review electronic commerce applications.

The mission of InfoNet is to share, compare and validate data through:[15]

- **Gaining best internal audit practices** from top organizations.
- **Sharing knowledge** with internal and external customers to improve their operational efficiency and effectiveness.
- **Providing networking opportunities** that organizations can learn from the challenges and solutions of their peers.

InfoNet's mission assists its customers to find the knowledge they need to be effective and efficient in the professional services they provide. Its global service feeds in to management of knowledge in internal auditing. It is an important contributor to the development of cutting edge internal auditing across the world.

The IIA–UK & Ireland has now introduced an open Discussion Forum[16] on its website '. . . *to debate internal auditing issues in depth . . . to seek input on specific work challenges, and for the experienced internal auditors to share their knowledge with others.*' Many of the topics listed on the website offer opportunities for benchmarking internal audit responsibilities and practices.

CIPFA's Benchmarking Clubs, established by its subsidiary The Institute of Public Finance Ltd (IPF), have grown into a large and important network of comparisons of costs and quality across many functions in UK local authorities. Interest in these Clubs is shared by the Fédération des Experts Comptables Européens (FEE) (2001). A CIPFA (2001) discussion paper[17] promoted such Clubs in the United Kingdom, encouraging development of international comparisons. IPF describes each CIPFA Benchmarking Club operating along systematic and disciplined lines creating a benchmarking culture in local authorities. Although the primary scope of such Clubs has been to compare costs CIPFA recognizes:

2.9 Benchmarking can help both to measure and achieve improvements in quality and impact through the very detailed analysis of activity. Benchmarking should not therefore be used solely to focus on reducing costs, but also to improve the quality and impact of services.

5.16 Benchmarking can help to change the culture of the organization, as part of a continuous process of performance improvements. It can motivate staff to provide a better service, with greater job satisfaction.

The IPF website shows internal auditing as a Benchmarking Club. It provides details of measures used in the benchmarking of audit customer satisfaction. Like The IIA InfoNet

2006 questionnaire, these include a number of measures representing cutting edge practices, such as the following 10 examples.

Advice and guidance on policies/procedures
Internal control reviews
Value for Money reviews.
Audit of IT systems and controls.
Facilitating the risk management process.
Investigation of allegations.
Ability to establish positive rapport.
Audits focus on significant risks.
The degree of interaction with auditees.
Fostering of service department participation.

Note similarities between The IIA InfoNet questionnaire measures and the measures used by IPF's benchmarking of audit customer satisfaction. Although different terms are used there is much the same in risk management, control, ethics and relationships with audit customers and other services in the organization.

For more general benchmarking in the UK public service the Public Sector Benchmarking Service (PSBS)[18] was launched in 2000 as a partnership between the Cabinet Office and HM Revenue & Customs, with the aim of promoting effective benchmarking and sharing good practices. Its website contains the European Benchmarking Code of Conduct (this is shown in full in Chapter 9, Case 9.3, on the CD ROM) and a link into the American Productivity & Quality Control Center (APQC). APQC provides benchmarking and best practices for organizations worldwide. Its website[19] is a mine of information on benchmarking studies, including a useful Glossary of benchmarking terms.

Benchmarking is about seeking best practices in a search for excellence, whether as a one-off tool or a continuous process. It can be internal in an organization or external. It can be part of other review programmes or a programme on its own.

In all measuring of what is excellent it is useful to develop a qualitative scale with extremes, such as 'awful' and 'superior'. Using such a scale an interesting model can be developed as a qualitative measure for most input/process/output benchmarking. Consider using the following scale:

Awful
Poor
Adequate
Good
Excellent
Superior

All internal auditors will have their personal definitions for these or their own similar terms, and be able to apply them in benchmarking. In my early auditing days 'awful' was replaced by the official term 'not susceptible to audit'. Such terms can also be used in audit fieldwork to measure operations under review. Placing 'awful' before 'poor' classes it as the extreme, which should rarely be encountered, but unfortunately is. Placing 'superior' after 'excellent' demonstrates that there can be situations when even 'excellent' is not sufficient to beat competition: an organization's performance has to be better than any other, it has to be superior. In all operations there will be different interpretations and perceptions for each level of performance, but there will always be levels. Seeking some consensus for levels and their definitions can be an interesting exercise in the management of internal audit and internal audit engagements, if not all management.

IPF uses such qualitative levels in benchmarking performance scores:

Poor
Weak
Less than adequate
Adequate
Good
Excellent

However, qualitative measures are rarely sufficient in benchmarking. The skill of benchmarking is to develop detailed analytical analysis using quantitative measures that will support the qualitative judgements. The cutting edge internal auditor will be the one that can master the art of benchmarking to measure both qualitatively and quantitatively to achieve not just excellence, but superiority.

Benchmarking is an important part of improvements in governance. Not just across industry sectors and nations but internationally as well. There are now a number of organizations, nationally and internationally, using benchmarking to promote good governance practices in organizations, developing governance models and principles, and promoting governance measures. Among these in the United Kingdom are industry models developed by government departments, e.g. schools, hospitals, etc., Business in the Community, Business in the Environment, the Financial Times Corporate Responsibility Index, Good Corporation, CSR Academy. Internationally there is the OECD, World Bank, Transparency International. All of these, and many others, have in common a mission to promote excellence in governance using developed benchmark frameworks and models to measure and rank organizations/countries.

A recent good example of this type of national public benchmarking is the United Kingdom National Consumer Council's (NCC) testing of supermarkets on four chosen environmental indicators. The NCC measured and rated shops from A for excellent to E for poor (note the comments above on qualitative benchmarking levels). Why not the use of 'awful' and 'superior' levels? Such levels would describe more vivid environmental pictures and provide a more competitive 'best practice' benchmark. The importance of benchmarks in governance processes are discussed in other chapters in the book.

Those emerging best internal auditing practices recognized in The IIA research publications in 1996, listed at the beginning of my article in 2000, have grown in importance and value in all internal auditing services. All mentioned will continue to develop in the immediate future, and beyond the horizon. They are all recognized by current research and thinking in internal auditing as being significant practices that have spawned numerous cutting edge activities. There will be more, identified by research and practice in the future. Keep looking for best practices in internal auditing in:

– coordination of all auditing;
– reviews of other auditors;
– relationships with audit committees and the board;
– relationships with stakeholders, including regulators;

- involvement in social and environmental reporting;
- involvement in external reporting of internal control;
- involvement in risk management across an organization;
- involvement in development of ethical cultures and whistleblowing;
- involvement in business continuity processes;
- involvement in data protection;
- contributing to knowledge management;
- adding forensic investigations into the services it provides;
- focusing on the prevention of fraud.

Research has already started to show that some of these practices are beginning to be more formal in internal auditing activities, innovated by internal auditors, required/recommended by The IIA in its professional guidance, and requested by management.

Whatever else happens there will be more information: it will be created more quickly; it will require more, wider and deeper knowledge; and it will be more freely available. There will also be more change and this will spur more benchmarking. Bill Gates (1999) in his book *Business and the Speed of Thought* starts his Introduction to today's digital age with *'Business is going to change more in the next ten years than it has in the last fifty'*. And it is doing so. For 'business' read all types of organizations, across all sectors. Such change will require creativity, innovation and above all imagination by all internal auditors.

The wider and more sophisticated use of technology in benchmarking practices across and between organizations will certainly increase. It has already done so since my article was written. Websites and search engines will grow in their number, size and shape: their design and search facilities will become more user friendly, though many are that now. Access to knowledge and experience on websites will become commonplace in all internal auditing activities and engagements, particularly at the early stages. Better knowledge management by organizations and internal auditors will both encourage and improve the use of benchmarking for planning and objective setting.

Despite, or perhaps because of, such changes it is useful to remind ourselves of benchmarking guidance published by the UK Department of Trade and Industry in 1993.[20] Its relevance is just as appropriate for today's future, as it was when published. It also sums up well the benchmarking recommendations in this chapter and the theme of my book – imagination:

How do they do it? BPB [Best Practice Benchmarking] comes in many forms, but essentially it will always involve:

- Establishing what makes the difference, in their customers' eyes, between an ordinary supplier and an excellent supplier.
- Setting standards in each of those things, according to the best practice they find.
- Finding out how the best companies meet those challenging standards.
- Applying both other people's experience and their own ideas to meet the new standards – and, if possible, to exceed them.

It is not about aiming to clone the success of other companies, or indulging in industrial spying. The real goal is to build on the success of others to improve future performance. By benchmarking on a continuous basis, you are always researching current best practice, not dated ideas. Benchmarking is always carried out with the goal of putting improvements into action.

CHAPTER SUMMARY

There are many examples in sectors, industries, nationally and internationally of good practice and quality models being developed as benchmarks. Benchmarking is used by many organizations to make significant change happen and to meet new challenging objectives. Benchmarking is an exploration into practices within an organization and those outside the organization, not always in organizations with similar objectives. It can be an adventure with many surprises: opening up new networks and starting changes that lead to many improvements in performance. Macdonald and Tanner (1998: p. 5) summed this up well in their one-week published teaching of benchmarking, concluding with:

> This week we have seen that benchmarking requires a strong degree of commitment – from management and from all others involved. It takes time and resources. It needs a disciplined and systematic approach. In short, it is not easy and it is not for the faint-hearted.
> But then who has the right to believe that *aiming to be the best* should ever be easy?

And, who better to be the best than an internal auditor. Benchmarking is more than just comparing. It is a management tool with well-established formal processes used by many managers and internal auditors. It is fundamental in the achievement of quality and superiority in all products and services. Both The IIA and IIA–UK & Ireland include a requirement for knowledge and practices of benchmarking in their professional examinations. In the future this will become an even more important part of their syllabi as an audit tool, a measure in quality assurance, and as the demand for consulting services in internal auditing continues to grow. The steps in formal benchmarking as set out in Figure 9.1 need to be a skill for every internal auditor.

Establishing a quality commitment in an internal audit activity is served well by using the Gray and Gray (1997) five innovation motivational themes, four innovation goals and four innovation categories discussed in the Introduction, and the additions and changes made in Chapters 2 to 8.

Motivations

1. Progress within the field of professional internal auditing.
2. Increasing competition leading to pressures to reduce costs and increase efficiency.
3. New challenges, such as increasing internal control risks due to staff reductions and restructuring.
4. Opportunities to increase efficiency and quality as a result of technological advances.
5. Changes in corporate management practices and philosophies, such as Total Quality Management, re-engineering, continuous quality improvement, or related approaches.
6. **Challenges and opportunities of global issues and developments.**
7. **Social and environmental issues impacting all organizations.**
8. **Recognition that professionalism, quality and standards are essential attributes for world-class status in any internal auditing activity.**
9. **Importance of organizational governance to meet regulatory and stakeholders' needs.**
10. **A continuous search for good and evil in how organizations and all their operations are directed and controlled.**
11. **Recognition that all types of crime in and by an organization should be fought.**

Goals

1. Improvement of the quality of internal auditing services.
2. Improve efficiency.
3. Expansion of services to increase the value-added of internal auditing.
4. Boost staff skills, performance and morale.
5. **Sell internal auditing as future focused.**
6. **To reduce the opportunities for all types of crime in an organization.**
7. **Increase satisfaction from all our customers.**

Categories

1. Changes in the way that internal auditors interact with the rest of their enterprises **and all those with a stakeholder interest.**
2. Internal restructuring and changes in the organization and management of internal auditing.
3. Creation of new audit services and methods.
4. Changes in the use of technology.
5. **Improved knowledge and skills in the teams of staff who carry out internal auditing engagements.**
6. **New services to fight crime.**
7. **Assistance in evaluation of the board's performance.**
8. **Improved satisfaction from all our customers.**

Goal 2 could be improved by changing to the following:

2. **Achieve best practice by continuously benchmarking.**

INTERNAL AUDITING CONTINUOUSLY BENCHMARKING PRINCIPIA 1998 AND 2008

The principia for internal auditing that I developed in 1998, included the following related to benchmarking practices:

3. Best practice internal auditing and good management practices use the same quality measures of planning, doing, checking and action.
29. Benchmark internal audit marketing with the marketing of other services within and outside the organization it serves.

Consider the following new principia for cutting edge internal auditing:

12. Knowledge and experience of benchmarking are essential for internal auditing in the management of its performance, in the auditing/review processes in all its engagements, and the assurance/consulting services it provides.
13. The focus of internal audit benchmarking should always be on the needs of its customers and stakeholders of the organizations it serves.
14. Benchmarking should never be a 'one-off' activity. It is a continuous process for improvement.

A VISION FOR INTERNAL AUDITING CONTINUOUSLY BENCHMARKING

> ***To continue to be the best supplier of professional internal auditing services***

SYNOPSES OF CASE STUDIES

Case 9.1: Internal Auditing According to Treadway Commission 1987

Synopsis

This definition of the nature of internal auditing and how it operates in an organization was cutting edge at the time it was written and for many is still cutting edge today. It predates much of the development of professional internal auditing since it was published and still provides an excellent benchmark for today and tomorrow.

> Extract from the *Report of the National Commission on Fraudulent Financial Reporting* (1987), American Institute of Certified Public Accountants, New York, USA, with permission from the Committee of Sponsoring Organizations (COSO).

After Reading the Case Study Consider:

1. Benchmark your own internal auditing with the Commission's statement. Note current gaps, measure these, consider what needs to be improved and plan for improvement.

Case 9.2: Use a Delphi Study to Develop Best Practice Internal Auditing

Synopsis

This Delphi study was undertaken in 1997. At the time it used the knowledge and experience of a number of experienced internal auditors and academics to predict the development of professional internal auditing, using signposts from the past and then present. From the predictions made five cutting edge Benchmarks were developed based on the then framework of The IIA *Standards for the Professional Practice of Internal Auditing* – Independence: Professional Proficiency: Scope of Work: Performance of Audit Work: Management of the Internal Auditing Department,

> Contributed by the author and Dr Kenneth D'Silva, Centre for Research in Accounting, Finance & Governance, Department of Accounting & Finance, Faculty of Business, Computing & Information Management, London South Bank University, London, England.

After Reading the Case Study Consider:

1. How do the Benchmarks developed in the 1997 Delphi study compare with your own internal auditing today?
2. What changes would you make to the benchmarks to promote today's cutting edge internal auditing resources and practices?

Case 9.3: The European Benchmarking Code of Conduct

Synopsis

This European Code of Conduct for benchmarking has been developed by an independent group to advance the professionalism of benchmarking in Europe. Its principles are at the cutting edge of benchmarking. They provide useful guidance for any person or organization using benchmarking to seek improvements in their performance.

Ownership

This document has open ownership, and may be freely reproduced and distributed to further the cause of good benchmarking practice. If you reproduce the Code of Conduct, print it in its entirety, giving credit to the members of the Eurocode working group who contributed their time and expertise without cost. Anyone requiring further information or wishing to participate in the Eurocode Working Group should contact:

Robin Walker, European Centre for Business Excellence, 33 Park Square, Leeds, LS1 2PF, UK. Tel: +44 (0) 113 244 9434 Mobile: +44 (0) 7974919175 Email: robinwalker@ecforbe.com

---

After Reading the Case Study Consider:

1. Does your organization/internal auditing have a code of conduct when benchmarking? If it has, then benchmark it against the above looking for gaps and improvements. If it has not, consider the importance of implementing such a code.

SELF-ASSESSMENT QUESTIONS

9.1   Are You Ready for Benchmarking in Your Organization?[21]

Study the statements below and tick one box for each to reflect the level to which the statement is true for your organization.

	Most	*Some*	*Few*	*None*
Processes have been documented with measures to understand performance.	☐	☐	☐	☐
Employees understand the processes that are related to their own work.	☐	☐	☐	☐
Direct customer interactions, feedback or studies about customers influence decisions about products and services.	☐	☐	☐	☐

Problems are solved by teams.	□	□	□	□
Employees demonstrate by words and deeds that they understand the organization's mission, vision and values.	□	□	□	□
Senior executives sponsor and actively support quality improvement projects.	□	□	□	□
The organization demonstrates by words and by deeds that continuous improvement is part of the culture.	□	□	□	□
Commitment to change is articulated in the organization's strategic plan.	□	□	□	□
Add the columns	□	□	□	□
Multiply by the factor	×6 =	×4 =	×2 =	0
What is the grand total?	□	□	□	□

9.2   Are You Ready for Benchmarking in Your Internal Auditing Activity?

1. Now repeat the same questionnaire but this time answering for your internal audit activity. What score did you obtain using the same scale as previously?
2. Assess both your scores in Appendix C.

NOTES AND REFERENCES

1. *The Iliad*, bk 6, l. 208, quotation from *The Oxford Dictionary of Quotations* (1999: p. 382), Oxford University Press, Oxford, England.
2. *Providing Benchmarking Services for Internal Auditing Clients* (1997: p. vii), Mark L. Frigo, The IIA Research Foundation.
3. *Foundations for Unlimited Horizons* (1977), Victor Z. Brink, The IIA. The presidential theme of Raymond E. Noonan,1953/54, was 'Progress Through Sharing Internal Auditing Knowledge'. The theme *Progress Through Sharing* was formally adopted and added to the Institute's seal in 1955. Since then this theme has been the drive for much of the Institute's development worldwide.
4. *Perceptions of Audit Quality* (1997), Chartered Institute of Public Finance and Accountancy, London, England.
5. *Understanding Benchmarking* (1998), John Macdonald and Steve Tanner, The Institute of Management, Corby, Northamptonshire, England.
6. *EFQM Excellence Model* (1999), European Foundation for Quality Management, www.efqm.org [EFQM is a membership-based organization '. . . *created in 1988 by fourteen leading European businesses, with a Mission to be the Driving Force for Sustainable Excellence in Europe and a Vision of a world in which European organizations excel. By January 1999, membership had grown to over 750 members, from most European countries and most sectors of activity.*']
7. *A Guide to Quality Schemes for the Public Sector* (1999), Service First Unit, Cabinet Office, London, England: *Getting it together – A Guide to Quality Schemes and the Delivery of Public Services* (2001), Quality Schemes Team, Cabinet Office, London, England. Both promote public body continuous self-assessment against the EFM model.

8. Published in *Internal Auditing & Business Risk* (December 1998), The IIA–UK & Ireland.
9. *An Inside Job – Internal Audit and Best Value* (2000), Audit Commission, London, England.
10. 'Shout How Best You Are In All Your Internal Auditing Market Places', *Internal Control Journal* (September 2001), Jeffrey Ridley, Accountancy Books, London, England.
11. *Management Tools* (2005), Bain & Company, Boston, USA. *'Benchmarking improves performance by identifying and applying best demonstrated practices to operations and sales. . . . The object of Benchmarking is to find examples of superior performance and to understand the processes and practices driving that performance.'* www.bain.com visited 30 September 2006. In its latest *Management Tools and Trends* (2007) results from surveys in 2006, Benchmarking is still ranked in the top four of tools used by organizations.
12. *Total Organizational Excellence – Achieving world-class performance* (2002), John S. Oakland, Butterworth-Heinemann, Oxford, England.
13. *Sawyer's Internal Auditing – The Practice of Modern Internal Auditing*, 5th edition (2003), Lawrence B. Sawyer, Mortimer A. Dittenhofer, James H. Scheiner, The IIA.
14. *Auditor's Dictionary – Terms, Concepts, Processes and Regulations* (2004), David O'Regan, John Wiley & Sons, Hoboken, New Jersey, USA.
15. From InfoNet's Business Plan with permission to quote from Donna M. Batten, Director, Information Network, The IIA. www.theiia.org
16. www.iia.org.uk/knowledgecentre/q&a/discussion.cfm?PrintPage=1 visited 29 September 2006
17. *The Use of Benchmarking as a Management Tool in the Public Sector to Improve Performance: A Discussion Paper* (2001), Chartered Institute of Public Finance and Accountancy,
18. www.benchmarking.gov.uk visited 16 October 2006.
19. www.apqc.org visited 16 October 2006.
20. *Best Practice Benchmarking – Managing Into The 90's* (1993: p. 1), Department of Trade and Industry, London, England.
21. This questionnaire has been used with permission from Professor John Oakland. It is used in his *Total Organizational Excellence* (2002), Chapter 8, Benchmarking, pp. 120–121.

10

Cutting Edge Internal Auditing
Continuously Improves

'Every day, in every way, I am getting better and better.'

Émile Coué 1857–1926[1]

Quality Leadership Process

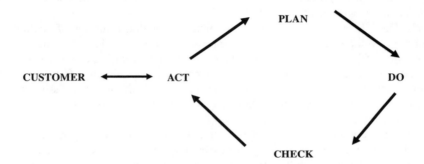

CONTINUOUS IMPROVEMENT IN INTERNAL AUDITING
BEFORE 1994

A wish to be continuously better at internal auditing is not new. It started before the incorporation of The IIA in 1941. It has been with internal auditing for a long time. Sometimes caused by necessity, sometimes just motivated by self-will to be better '... *every day, in every way...* '. Towards the end of the last century competition for many internal auditors changed this self-will to a commitment to being best: a commitment by the individual, teams and internal audit activities. The pace of change forced this to happen. Change not just in technology but change in all the events that take place in and around the organizations in which internal auditors work. A constant change: requiring quality and continuous improvement. Fundamental to this continuous improvement is the 'Deming' PDCA Cycle, discussed later in this chapter.

Our predecessors in internal auditing recognized this commitment to continuous improvement when they wrote the purpose of The IIA in its Certificate of Incorporation:[2]

To cultivate, promote and disseminate knowledge and information concerning internal auditing and subjects related thereto; to establish and maintain high standard of integrity, honour and character among internal auditors; to furnish information regarding internal auditing and the practice and methods thereof to its members, and to other persons interested therein, and to the general public; to cause the publication of articles, relating to internal auditing and practices and methods thereof; to establish and maintain a library and reading rooms, meeting rooms and social rooms for the use of its members; to promote social; intercourse among its members; and to do any and all things which shall be lawful and appropriate in furtherance of any of the purposes hereinbefore expressed

Note the word 'cultivate', and one of its meanings being *'to improve or develop something usually by study or education'*. Continuous improvement is a more recent term, associated with research and practices, quality initiatives and innovative policies. The IIA recognized this concept in its first approved *Code of Ethics* for members in 1968.

'Members shall continually strive for improvement in the proficiency and effectiveness of their service.'

Subsequently the requirements in this code were included in its Certified Internal Auditor (CIA) examination programme for all registered CIAs, whether members or not. The first CIA examinations were held in 1974.

In 1976 The IIA established its Research Foundation with the mission of facilitating guidance for the development of internal auditing. Its reputation as a leader in the development and promotion of improvements in professional internal auditing quickly grew to the important global status it has today. Any study of its catalogue of published funded research and educational activities is impressive. There can be few, if any, internal audit activities and internal audit education providers worldwide that do not have one or more of its publications on their bookshelves.

Benefits from continuous improvement in the TQM environments were discussed in my article of 1990, reproduced in Chapter 3 discussing the world-class status for internal auditing. These are repeated below with the other benefits to emphasize continuous improvement does not stand alone, but is part of other actions in an internal audit department:

What are some of the gains to be achieved?

- Recognition of the SUPPLIER–PROCESS–CUSTOMER CHAIN for the audit process, drives the audit programme into the heart of business activity and highlights the key controls needed for business success.
- Establishing who are the customer and CUSTOMER NEEDS helps to focus audit tests into the most important areas and issues.
- The concept of AUDITOR/AUDITEE teamwork during the audit process is achieved and 'participative auditing' becomes a reality.
- AUDIT RESULTS and RECOMMENDATIONS concentrate on prevention rather than detection, looking to the control of quality in the future, rather than the past.
- QUALITY ASSURANCE requirements to meet IIA *Standards* take on a wider meaning, linking the quality aims of the internal audit department into those of the organization.
- Emphasis on CONTINUOUS IMPROVEMENT in the TQM environment encourages internal audit staff 'to continually seek improvements in the audit process'.
- TQM requires QUALITY MEASURES in all processes, to monitor quality and highlight nonconformance with standards.
- The audit process becomes a QUALITY SYSTEM, which can lead to recognition under the national accreditation standard BS 5750 (ISO 9000).
- QUALITY SUCCESSES are more easily recognized and rewarded at team and individual levels.

At its best continuous improvement should be a focus from an organization's vision to its customer needs. It should be planned, measured and its implementation monitored. It should also relate to events surrounding and influencing the improvement. Too many 'so-called' improvements are not planned, measured and monitored. Adopting the benchmarking process discussed in Chapter 9 is a must for any 'continuous improvement' strategy. Teamwork is also important for any continuous improvement programme.

Article:
If You Have A Good Audit Recommendation – Look For A Better One[3] (1994)

The concept of continuous improvement is a process-oriented team approach to continually providing the best product and service. It applies to both the quality of audit work and the recommendations included in the final report. Findings arising from the performance of audit work should be discussed with appropriate levels of management during the course of an audit and problem-solving methods used to seek the best recommendations.

> '*The concept of continuous improvement is a process-oriented team approach to continually providing the best product and service.*'

All of the discussions arising from the audit work should be team driven, involving everyone participating in the audit, including those responsible for the controls being reviewed. The internal auditor should ensure that all findings and recommendations are based on a full and clear understanding of the following:

- What standards, measures and expectations have been used in making the audit conclusions?
- The clear evidence of what exists.
- The reasons for the difference between expected and actual conditions.
- The risks being taken.

This methodical approach to the process of establishing the cause and effect underlying audit conclusions ensures a continuous improvement in the development of audit recommendations.

Remember, audit recommendations are best when:

- They can be clearly linked to agreed desirable results.
- They correct the cause of a problem and not just the effect.
- They are accepted by management and implemented.

(Based on IIA Standard and Guideline 430.04: 1994.)

As mentioned earlier, continuous improvement should not be an accidental process but part of a programme linked into an organization's vision and strategic objectives. This applies to all parts of an organization, including its internal audit activity, and all its operations. At times such improvement may only be slow and evolutionary. At other times it will involve re-engineering complete operations with paradigm shifts at strategic and operating levels. Such improvement can hurt.

Article:
What Is Success?[4] (1997)

Success should not be the aim.
The aim should be to improve.
Improvement requires controlled change.
Change is best controlled when it is seen as a continuous process
    of selection, education and development opportunities.

Processes should always start with commitment to a vision.
A vision that must be right for the time.
Visions require measured strategies and tactics.
The achievements of strategies and tactics depend on the control of people.

People in the supply chain depend on each other for success.
To succeed as individuals is not enough.
All people in the supply chain need to belong to successful teams.
All people in the supply chain need the reinforcement of successful lives.

The role of all managers is to control.
Control requires an understanding of its objectives.
Each control objective impacts and influences success in people.
It is the way people succeed that controls the successful organization.

Managers in the Best Organizations Select, Educate and Develop the Best People and Teams

The aim of every organization should be to improve. This means not only the structure and processes, that make up the organa- people who surround part of its supply the community that it generates success.

> '*Improvement does not happen by accident, it has to be controlled as a process of change.*'

not only the people nization, but also the the organization, as chains. It also means serves. Improvement Improvement does not happen by accident, it has to be controlled as a process of change. Continuous improvement is now a way of life in organizations across the world. It knows no national boundaries. The quality it creates is the way of business and government everywhere. It thrives on benchmarking and the search for best practices. It recognizes change as a continuous cycle of selection, education and development.

The cycle of selection, education and development is at the heart of all human activity. It always has been and always will be. Best management of that cycle in others requires an understanding of how the cycle works for you. We all learn, from the day we are born, to the day we die. At first, the selection stage is mainly by others – we are fully controlled.. We soon move into our own selection process and from thereon life is a mixture of choices by ourselves, and others. Each and every day, each and every moment we are making and being subjected to a selection process. The choices we make forge our destiny. They create the opportunities and emotions we experience all our lives. They contribute to our failures and successes.

In any organization, it is management's role to communicate clearly the choices people have and the results expected from those choices. Some may call this control, others opportunity. Perhaps, it is always a mixture of both. Selection is best if it is communicated as opportunity. The art of management is to be a good communicator: to communicate the importance of selection in the minds of people: to help choice.

But selection is not the end. Selection starts the education process. Being taught and teaching oneself are everyday experiences. This activity is often seen as the learning curve. In an organization it starts the day people are employed and continues until the day of leaving. It is at its best when motivated by a feeling of self-selection. I choose to learn is better than 'you will learn'. The good manager will encourage education self-selection. It drives the best understanding. A search for knowledge through education stimulates innovation.

'How, What, Why, When Where, Who' are the six honest workingmen of Rudyard Kipling's Just So Stories. They are as true today as they always have been. They are fundamental to invention and progress. They are the questions all people should ask as they learn. But education is not the end. Education by itself is not sufficient for success. Education requires development. And, development does not come by accident; it needs to be planned. Planned development is a skill in itself. All tasks require a period of training. For some tasks and people this training is brief: for other tasks and people it is a long and sometimes continuous process. Recognizing the time needed for development is an important part of good management, in oneself and in others.

Committing time for development in oneself and others is not always easy. Pressure and stress, even in controlled change can reduce the time available for development. We have all experienced reduction of staff and training costs: what follows can too often be a reduction of time spent on development, both at work and at home. Yet, development is the key to success. It always will be the key to successful change. Good managers recognize this. Those that train recognize this. Professions recognize this. Governments recognize this. Why is it then that development receives such a low priority with some managers and some people? To know the answer to this is the key to success.

But good managers and good people do not stop at development. The cycle of selection, education and development starts all over again. It is a continuous process and because of this needs direction. It needs vision. A vision is a forecast of a future desired state at a point in time, which is attractive to the beholder. All people have visions. Visions change: they need to be appropriate to their time. Not all people use their visions to select, educate and develop themselves or others. Good managers create visions for organizations and, through the cycle of selection, education and development establish commitment for the future state.

Commitment not just by people but also by teams of people. Once the vision is agreed, key strategies and tactics must follow, linked and measured to the required future state. A wish for success is part of everyone's vision, though the measure may be different for each person. Personal visions need to be built into team and group visions. All visions should stretch people and teams to improve. All visions should demand change for the better. All visions should aim for success. The art of good management is to establish and achieve visions by the cycles of selection, education and development of people and teams. Creating the wish to succeed in people makes success happen.

Establishing visions and commitment is not easy. Using measures for each strategy involves all people in the process. That involvement can be made easier and more quickly if managers follow the selection, education and development cycle for everyone participating in the associated supply chains. This means considering people who are employed by suppliers and customers. The good manager helps people in both suppliers and customers to succeed. The good manager builds suppliers and customers into their teams. This means that suppliers and customers must also help their people to select, educate and develop. Good managers recognize this.

But is success by people in an organization sufficient reward and reinforcement for others to follow? All research and evidence shows that this is not so. People need to be successful in all parts of their lives, or at least feel success. This is a tall order! How can managers help people to succeed in their lives outside the workplace? Such a question is not irrelevant. Many organizations and managers have recognized the importance of opportunities for their people to be successful in activities other than work. Provision of resources and time to select, educate and develop in families, hobbies, sports and pastimes is not new. What is new is the reduction of these facilities in times of change. Yet such reduction takes away opportunities for people to be successful, which is not what an organization wants. Too often managers are seen to be short sighted in the opportunities they provide for selection, education and development both inside and outside the workplace. Yet the key to their own success lies in such opportunities.

The continuous cycles of selection, education and development in and around any organization and supply chain, need to be managed. This means they need to be controlled. Many will say that they are controlled in the best organizations. But are they? Linking each of the processes to the primary objectives of control provides managers with a useful framework to test how successful they are. The objectives of control can be analysed as:

- reliability
- compliance
- security
- economy
- efficiency

- effectiveness
- environmental
- ethics
- equality

None of the above needs explanation to any manager. They are all part of the decision making process in every organization, whether by people or the teams they form. Some are more recent as objectives than others. All are changing shape and definition as we move into the 21st century. Without exception each is becoming more demanding: each is becoming a requirement, not only of the organization, but also of the community, nation and world. Yet few managers approach success in their people through the achievement of each. Any success that does not recognize all these control objectives, fails to make the most of people.

All control activities should require each of the nine objectives to be achieved. Every vision, strategy and tactic in an organization can be influenced by the quality of performance of each. Penalty for failure to achieve any one can make the difference between success or failure, survival or demise. Good managers realize this and use control objectives to influence the cycles of selection, education and development in the people they manage. Corporate history is full of organizations that ignored these relationships: full of the managers who did not link success in people to the management of control and change.

In the same way that visions and success are a moment in time, so is control. Each requires consideration of past and present when planning the future. The framework for controlling the cycles of selection, education and development takes on a multidimensional model. It is a clear understanding by managers of this fundamental law of success and control, which helps most people to succeed. Success is the key motivation for change: controlled success breeds successful change.

Success, best, better, good, excellent and delight are the hallmarks of customer satisfaction. Each has an association with success – in organizations, their products, services and the people they employ. We all recognize these associations but few analyse the controls that influence each, or award success the applause it so often deserves. Control is the key to success. Applause should be seen as an accolade, not an embarrassment.

How should performance in people be applauded? Is applause seen by people to be more an embarrassment than a reward? Are managers well trained to recognize success, reinforce its achievement or punish failure? There are clearly mixed good and bad reinforcement and punishment practices within and between all organizations. Few recognize the importance of relating such best practices to the control of selection, education and development. If it were otherwise the number of people succeeding would increase many times. There would be no need for training awards and the focus on helping people to succeed would have a high profile in every organization. Good reinforcement and punishment administered through the process of change is at the heart of all success.

Helping people to succeed through their cycles of selection, education and development is the only future for any organization. It is also the only future for any community, nation or the world. Linking that help into personal and group visions is essential. Linking that help into the objectives of control in an organization. ensures success, both for the organization and the people it employs and serves.

CONTINUOUS IMPROVEMENT IN INTERNAL AUDITING
1997 TO 2006

Continuous improvement has always been an important part of the benchmarking process. This was discussed in the previous chapter on benchmarking. Professor John Oakland (1999) devotes a full chapter, seeing this as '... *probably the most powerful concept to guide management*', but also commenting: '*It is a term not well understood in many organizations.*' It has a high profile in Oakland's diagram in Chapter 8, Figure 8.13: 'The Framework For Total Organizational Excellence'.

Research by the author and D'Silva (1997)[5] showed perceptions, by chief executive officers (CEOs) and chief finance officers (CFOs), of internal auditing attributes from a list of best practices identified from literature and research at that time. Each was asked to score the importance of the attributes from 1 to 5. Figure 10.1 shows the ranking of their mean scores, which are interestingly similar, although none of the attributes had a high mean score.

	CEO	CFO
Quality of Audit Work	3.7	3.9
Competence	3.6	3.5
Technical Skills	3.4	3.5
Follow-Up of Results	3.4	3.5
Experience	3.3	3.4
Working Relationships	3.2	3.2
Low Audit Cost	2.9	2.8
Innovation	2.8	2.8
Staff Continuity	2.6	2.5

Figure 10.1 List Of Internal Auditing Best Attributes Ranked By Perceptions Of Value
Source: Research by J. Ridley and Dr Kenneth D'Silva (1997)

The scores focus attention on areas where many internal audit functions needed to improve promotion of the requirements in The IIA *Standards*. Quality of audit work and competence are the two most important features of internal audit professionalism, and innovation is fundamental to continuous improvement. North American research at the time recognized a growing interest by internal audit and its management, in innovative roles for internal auditors and innovation in internal audit work. Fewer in management in the UK saw value from innovation in internal audit work. The researchers predicted that in all sectors of the economy it is likely that innovation and quality would be important for all operations and organizations.

A sample of press job advertisements for internal audit staff taken during the research, included superlatives describing internal audit staff requirements as: innovative, proactive, creative, self-starter and outstanding! Similar superlatives can be seen today in internal audit vacancy notices. The same superlatives can be seen in most quality initiatives.

Article:
What Does Continuous Improvement Imply And How Has It Evolved?[6] (2006)

Continuous improvement is an essential ingredient of all quality programmes. Omachhonu and Ross (1994)[a] recognized this in their defi-nition of the concept of Total Quality Man-agement (TQM). It has been an important prin-ciple in quality theory devel-oped during the 1950-60s and still is today. The continuous improvement cycle developed by Deming (1982)[b] – see Figure 10.2 – continues to be used by many consultants, academics and organizations internationally.

> '... *continuous improvement being only one part of a wider vision and mission programme, aimed at achieving quality...*'

PLAN	Know what the customer wants and needs.
	Develop a plan for improvement.
	Define problems and searching for solutions.
	Recommend action.
DO	Implement the plan.
CHECK	Analyse what has been done to determine if objectives achieved
ACT	Based on results at the CHECK stage standardise best practices.
	PLAN again (from above).

Figure 10.2   Deming Continuous Improvement Cycle
Source: W. Edwards Deming

In development of their concept '*balanced scorecard*', Kaplan and Norton (1996)[c] recommend a measurement framework that includes the essential dimensions of '*customer expectations and satisfaction, continuous improvement, efficiency and organizational learning*'. These dimensions need to be balanced with financial per-formance. They also regard the integration of all these dimensions as an important part of implementing strategy and the measurement of total performance. Thus, the

---

[a] See *Principles of Total Quality*, St Lucia Press, 1994, p. 5.
[b] W. Edwards Deming is attributed with developing this PDCA as a model circle balanced on a line of never-ending improvement.
[c] Kaplan and Norton's inclusion of continuous improvement as a dimension in their scorecard and its relationship with the customer, efficiency and learning dimensions is an important recognition of the context in which continuous improvement should always be placed.

balanced scorecard is not just a measurement system, but also a strategic management system that clarifies an organization's vision and strategies: and, turns these into actions. Arveson (1998)[d] quotes Kaplan and Norton:

> The balanced scorecard retains traditional financial measures. But financial measures tell the story of past events, an adequate story for the industrial age companies for which investments in long-term capabilities and customer relationships were not critical for success. These financial measures are inadequate, however, for guiding and evaluating the journey that information age companies must make to create future value through investment in customers, service users, suppliers, employees, processes, technology and innovation.

The balanced scorecard suggests that an organization is viewed from four perspectives, all focused on an organization's vision and strategy, balanced between external measures for shareholders and customers and internal measures for business processes, innovation and growth:

- Customer Perspective
- Financial Perspective
- Business Processes Perspective
- Learning and Growth Perspective.

For each perspective there needs to be objectives, measures, targets and initiatives. Each perspective also has a relationship with the other three. Key to its implementation is the feedback systems that are introduced so that management can determine the causes for variation and take appropriate continuous improvement actions.

Oakland (2001: pp. 227–228)[e] considers continuous improvement as '. . . *probably the most powerful concept to guide management'*. And goes on to state it is still not a well understood term in many organizations. He also contrasts its relationship to business process re-engineering. His analysis of activities associated with continuous improvement includes a systematic approach to planning, providing and operating processes; evaluating and examining outputs; modifying the processes and their inputs. All '. . . *firmly tied to a continuous assessment of customer needs, and depends on a flow of ideas on how to make improvements, reduce variation, and generate greater customer satisfaction'*. Note the similarity with the Deming cycle of activities, recognized in his discussion, but with more emphasis on all activities being 'customer needs' focused and dependence on 'ideas'. Oakland (2001) sees continuous improvement as being a ' - *way of life – that permeates the whole organization.'* with three basic principles:

1. Focusing on the customer.
2. Understanding the process.
3. Commitment from the employees

---

[d] *What is the Balanced Scorecard* (1998) Paul Arveson, www.balancedscorecard.org/basic/bsc1.html retrieved 20/09/06.
[e] *Total Organizational Excellence* (2001), Professor John S. Oakland, Butterworth-Heinemann, Oxford, England.

These three principles are basic to all continuous improvement models. They have been developed and promoted by many as part of a variety of management tools, including Total Quality Management, Business Process Re-engineering, Benchmarking, Balanced Scorecard, Customer Relationship Management, Supply Chain Management. They are also fundamental to internal auditing and can be seen in the development and current requirements of the IIA *International Standards.*

Oakland (2001) describes each as:

- Focusing on the customer – '. . . *an organization must recognize, throughout its ranks, that the purpose of all work and all efforts to make improvements is to serve the customers better.'*
- Understanding the process – '. . . *intense focus on the design and control of the inputs, working closely with suppliers, and understanding process flows to eliminate bottlenecks and reduce waste.'*
- Commitment from employees – *'Everyone in the organization, from top to bottom, from offices to technical service, from headquarters to local sites, must play their part.'*

Oakland (2001) sees the structured approach to continuous improvement requiring teamwork across the organization from top to bottom and across all supply chains, both internal and external.

Oakland (2001) cites Hammer and Champey[f] (1993) analysis of re-engineering '. . . *the fundamental re-think and radical re-design of a business process, its structure, and associated management systems, to deliver major or step improvements in performance (which may be in process, customer or business performance terms)'.* He goes on to say that *'BPR then challenges managers to rethink their traditional methods of doing work and to commit to customer-focused processes'.* Today BPR[g] is described as:

> Business Process Re-engineering involves the radical re-design of core business processes to achieve dramatic improvements in productivity, cycle times and quality. In BPR, companies start with a blank sheet of paper and rethink existing processes to deliver more value to the customer. They typically adopt a new value system that places increased emphasis on customer needs.

The links between continuous improvement, the balanced scorecard and business process re-engineering are important in all quality management programmes and the rules on which they are based. Ridley and Chambers[h] (1998) include continuous improvement as one rule in the criteria for achieving quality for products and services. This is developed by them into a framework of five rules, shown in Figure 10.3, all of which need to be integrated with each other.

---

[f] *Re-Engineering the Corporation – A Manifesto for Business Revolution*, Hammer M. and Champey J. (1993). [Omanchonu and Ross, whose work on the principles of total quality was referred to earlier, also cites an article on re-engineering by Hammer in the *Harvard Business Review* (1990).]
[g] See http://www.bain.com/management_tools/tools_business_process.asp?groupCode=2 retrieved 25/10/2005.
[h] The author's study of important criteria in quality initiatives worldwide is discussed in *Leading Edge Internal Auditing* (1998), ICSA Publishing Limited. It is also cited in the author's paper *Quality and Internal Audit – a survey of theory and practice*, presented at the 2nd European Academic Conference on Internal Audit and Corporate Governance (2004), Cass Business School, London.

> 1. Customer Focus – all customers are different, their satisfaction is paramount
> 2. Management Leadership – organize for quality
> 3. Teamwork – recognize and encourage the power of teams
> 4. Analytical Approach – if it cannot be measured, it cannot be improved
> 5. Continuous Improvement – look for problems, develop solutions and train

Figure 10.3   Rules For Promoting Quality
Source: *Leading Edge Internal Auditing* (1998)

The view of continuous improvement being only one part of a wider vision and mission programme, aimed at achieving quality, is repeated across most of today's thinking and research into quality management programmes. Continuous improvement in practice is now recognized by many as only one part of the quality framework. Evidence of this is seen in the European Foundation for Quality Management (EFQM) Business Excellence Model (1999)[i]. This model is currently developed from eight fundamental quality concepts, shown in Figure 10.4. These concepts can also be seen in the Oakland principles of continuous improvement and Ridley's rules of quality discussed earlier.

> **Enablers**
> 1. Results Orientation
> 2. Customer Focus
> 3. Leadership and Constancy of Purpose
> 4. Management by Processes and Facts
>
> **Results**
> 5. People Development and Involvement
> 6. Continuous Learning, Innovation and Improvement
> 7. Partnership Development
> 8. Public Responsibility

Figure 10.4   EFQM Eight Fundamental Quality Concepts In Excellence Model
Source: *European Forum for Quality Management* (1998)

The EFQM eight fundamental quality concepts can all be seen in the five 'soft' variables in organizing for excellence, researched by Peters and Waterman (1982)[j]

---

[i] EFQM was established in 1988 by 14 leading European businesses, with a mission to be the driving force for sustainable excellence in Europe and a vision of a world in which European organizations excel. There are now hundreds of European organizations, across all sectors – private, public and voluntary who are members of EFQM. In addition to being owner of the Excellence Model and a European Quality Award process, it also provides a portfolio of services for its members. The model was last revised in 1999 with changed Enabler criteria – Leadership: People: Policy and Strategy: Partnerships and Resources: Processes and changed Results criteria – People Results: Customer Results: Society Results and Key Performance Results. The diagram representing these criteria shows '. . . *innovation and learning helping to improve enablers that in turn lead to improved results*' and is used as both a self-assessment and external assessment process for measuring progress towards excellence in an organization. The comments in the article apply equally to the new model.

[j] The Peters and Waterman research for their book *In Search of Excellence* (1982) included discussion on their 7S Framework, a framework they developed earlier when working for McKinsey and Company. This research was the first to popularize the use of the term 'excellence' as an achievement by organizations.

and known as the McKinsey 7S Framework. This framework recognizes Strategy and Structure as the 'hardware' in an organization and Style, Systems, Staff (people), Skills and Shared Values as the 'software'. Peters and Waterman (1982) saw each of these seven S's as variables to be managed for excellence, each integrating with the others. The two 'hard' variables of Strategy and Structure can also be seen in the EFQM Excellence Model. This linking of quality concepts to the McKinsey Framework supports the importance of understanding each of their researched variables in any continuous improvement programme.

The International Standards Organization (ISO) (1987) published its own ISO 9000 series of quality management standards for manufacturing and service operations, based on the UK BS 5750. Since that date various international working parties associated with the ISO have revised the ISO 9000 series to the family of standards that it is today, which now relate much more clearly to all the quality rules mentioned in Figure 10.3. The revised ISO 9000: 2000 quality management interprets the four steps for the achievement of quality in the Deming Cycle discussed earlier, as:

Plan – Establish the objectives and processes necessary to deliver results in accordance with customer requirements and the organization's policies.

Do – Implement the processes.

Check – Monitor and measure processes and product against policies, objectives and requirements for the product and report the result.

Act – Take actions to continually improve process performance.

This quality standard is now firmly linked to continuous improvement. It is based on the following eight quality principles, all of which can also be seen in the EFQM fundamental quality concepts in Figure 10.4:

1. Customer focused organization
2. Leadership
3. Involvement of people
4. Process approach
5. System approach to management
6. Continual improvement
7. Factual approach to decision making
8. Mutually beneficial supplier relationship

Each of the principles is described in some detail. The principle 'continuous improvement' is stated to lead to:

- Employing a consistent organization-wide approach to continual improvement of the organization's performance.
- Providing people with training in the methods and tools of continual improvement.
- Making continual improvement of products, processes and systems an objective for every individual in the organization.
- Establishing goals to guide, and measures to track, continual improvement.
- Recognizing and acknowledging improvements.

Measurement of Continuous Improvement

Deming (1982), Oakland (2001), Ridley (1998), and EFQM (1999) each emphasize the importance of measuring both quality and continuous improvement. This is not surprising because all quality consultants and practitioners recognize this importance. Performance measures are an essential, part of any quality programme, including continuous improvement. An important message and advice for all quality processes has always been *'if it cannot be measured it cannot be improved'*.[k]

Oakland (2001) recommends all excellence measurements should focus on what is expected by the customer. Such measures should also identify opportunities for improvements and compare performances, both internal and external to the organization:

> Traditionally, performance measures and indicators have been derived only from cost-accounting information, often based on outdated and arbitrary principles. These provide little motivation to support attempts to improve performance and, in some cases, actually inhibit continuous improvement because they are unable to map process performance. In the organization that is to succeed over the long term, performance must begin to be measured by the improvements seen by the customer. In the cycle of never-ending improvement, measurement plays an important role in:

- tracking progress against organizational goals
- identifying opportunities for improvement
- comparing performance against internal standards
- comparing performance against external standards

Criticisms of performance measurement systems by Oakland are:

> Traditionally, the measures used have not been linked to the processes where the value-adding activities take place. What has been missing is a performance measurement framework that provides (timely) feedback to people in all areas of business operations and stresses the need to fulfil customer needs.

Developing and implementing an appropriate performance measurement framework that provides timely feedback for corrections and improvements in all quality processes is an essential principle in all the rules for quality included in Figure 10.3. This principle can also be seen clearly in the EFQM Excellence Model criteria for customer results, people results, and society results. Each has guidance on customer, people and society perception measures and performance indicators that should be established in processes by any organization striving for excellence.

Oakland (2001) describes four levels for a performance measurements framework:

Level 1: Strategy development and goal deployment leading to mission/vision, critical success factors and key performance indicators.

---

[k] Frequently quoted in texts on quality, source unknown by authors, but could probably be from a quote by Lord Kelvin, Scientist, 1824–1907, in his lecture to the Institution of Civil Engineers, 3 May 1883, *'When you can measure what you are speaking about and express it in numbers, you know something about it.'* Source: *The Oxford Dictionary of Quotations*, Fifth Edition (1999), p. 432.

Level 2: Process management and process performance measurement (including input, in-process and output measures, management of internal and external customer–supplier relationships and the use of management control systems).

Level 3: Individual performance management and performance appraisal.

Level 4: Review performance (including internal and external benchmarking, self-assessment against quality award criteria and quality costing).

Within Level 2 there are many tools that can be used as quality measures. Research by Gupta and Ray (1995), describes 14 such tools. Seven traditional quality control tools referred to as statistical process control, often called *Ishikawa* tools because they were popularized by Dr Kaoru Ishikawa in Japan: and, seven new tools promulgated in Japan in 1979 to focus measurement on quality management.

Continuous Improvement and Innovation

Quality circles first gained acceptance in Japan in the late 1940s as part of its drive to improve levels of productivity and quality. The reason for Japanese management support for the concept of quality circles, as described by Perry (1984)[1], was to provide '. . . *opportunity, encouragement and support for individual work group volunteers to meet with their supervisors to discuss and analyse work-related problems and to develop alternative solutions and plans for improving the way work gets done.*' As such, they were a success in Japan, though it was not until the late 1970s that the concept emerged in organizations in the USA and other countries. Since then the concept has seen a number of different faces and names but is still used to focus on innovation for improvements to productivity and quality.

Encouraging innovative ideas into work practices to achieve wider objectives than just productivity and quality is an extension of the quality circle concept. Innovation is about managing improvement for an advantage, whether it be for productivity and quality or other objectives such as 'beating the competition', expanding or supporting a range of products or services being provided, satisfying customers, introducing new technology, adding new skills or knowledge to a work group, etc. Drucker (1973)[m] (cited in Omachonu and Ross, 1994) saw this when he said '. . . *a company has but one objective: to create a customer*'. Following this statement he identified eight key areas for his concept of management by objectives:

1. Marketing
2. Innovation
3. Human organization
4. Financial resources
5. Physical resources
6. Productivity
7. Social responsibility
8. Profit requirements

---

[1] *Improving Audit Productivity* (1984), William E. Perry, John Wiley & Sons, New York, USA.
[m] This statement by Peter Drucker is cited in *Principles of Total Quality* (1994), Vincent K. Omachonu and Joel E. Ross, in their chapter 'Strategic Quality Planning,' p. 71.

This early recognition of innovation as a key objective and responsibility of management is important. It is recognized in all quality programmes.

The link between continuous improvement and innovation is a strong one. Whiteley (1991)[n] at the time describes old and new innovation in organizations. Old innovation ways have many barriers in the processes caused by unclear delegation of responsibilities, little or no feedback from organization functions or integration of efforts. New innovation ways include a much more organized teamwork (quality circles) and an ongoing analysis of each of the following processes:

- learning customers' needs
- keeping up with technology outside the firm
- maintaining basic technical strengths
- discovering new technology that will be useful in products (and services)
- neutralizing competitors' basic technical strengths
- keeping the organization as a whole informed about discoveries.

These ways are still objectives in innovation today. Note the importance placed on what is taking place in technology outside the organization. Probably more important than events inside in today's flatter world and global market places.

Whiteley (1991) is based on a five-year series of research projects by The Forum Corporation, USA, resulting in recognition of seven imperatives that '... *work together to produce a well-integrated organization that can deliver high quality in both product and service'* and were then '... *the game plans of today's and tomorrow's winners'*.

1. Create a customer-keeping vision
2. Saturate your company with the voice of the customer
3. Go to school on the winners
4. Liberate your customer champions
5. Smash the barriers to customer-winning performance
6. Measure, measure, measure
7. Walk the talk

Whiteley (1991) developed a customer-focused toolkit explaining how the above essentials can be planned and achieved. These essentials can also all be seen in The Deming Cycle, Oakland's principles of continuous improvement, Ridley's rules of quality, the EFQM concepts of excellence and innovation.

In Figure 10.5 we show how the previously discussed Deming Cycle, Kaplan and Norton balanced scorecard, Oakland principles, Ridley rules and EFQM fundamental concepts are reflected in the ISO 9000: 2000 principles. This is subjective but in a study of each it is not difficult to find all the previous statements on quality and continuous improvement in the detail of the ISO 9000: 2000 principles for quality management, and in particular the detail of continuous improvement.

---

[n] *The Customer Driven Company: moving from talk to action* (1991), Richard C. Whitely, Business Books Limited was one of the first management books '... *dedicated to helping organizations improve customer service. . . '.*

ISO Principles	D	K&N	O	R	EFQM
1. Customer-focused organization	√	√	√	√	√
2. Leadership	√	√	√	√	√
3. Involvement of people	√	√	√	√	√
4. Process approach	√	√	√	√	√
5. System approach to management	√	√	√	√	√
6. Continual improvement					
Consistent approach	√	√	√	√	√
People training	√	√	√	√	√
Personal objective	√	√	√	√	√
Goals and measures	√	√	√	√	√
Recognizing improvements	√	√	√	√	√
7. Factual approach to decision making	√	√	√	√	√
8. Supplier relationships	√	√	√	√	√

D. = Deming   R = Ridley
K&N = Kaplan and Norton   EFQM = European Foundation for Quality Management
O = Oakland

Figure 10.5   ISO 9000 Continuous Improvement Principles Related To
Other Quality Principles, Rules And Concepts
Source: Research arrangement, J. Ridley and Dr Kenneth D'Silva (2006)

In its guidelines[o] for the assessment of quality in an internal audit activity The
IIA recommends the following should be evaluated:

(i)   Compliance with the *International Standards* and *Code of Ethics*;
(ii) Adequacy of the internal audit activity's charter, goals objectives, policies, and procedures;
(iii) Contribution to the organization's risk management, control; and governance processes;
(iv) Compliance with applicable laws, regulations and government or industry standards;
(v) Effectiveness of continuous improvement activities and adoption of best practices;
(vi) Whether the auditing activity adds value and improves the organization's operations.

The same guidance under the title 'Continuous improvement' recommends that
'. . . *all quality assessment and improvement efforts should include appropriate timely
modification of resources, technology, processes, and procedures as indicated by the
monitoring and assessment activities'*. Quality assessments are seen by the IIA as a
driver for continuous improvement.
    Quality assessments can be both internal and external. Internal assessments are
by staff within the organization and can be ongoing or one-off exercises. External

---

[o] Practice Advisory 1310-1(3): *Quality Programme Assessments*. There is currently a proposal by the IIA under consultation to revise 1312 requiring the chief audit executive to discuss with the board any potential need for '. . . *more
frequent external assessments as well as the qualifications and independence of the external examiner or review team,
including any potential conflict of interest'*. This latter requirement emphasizes the need to address at board level the
importance of the issue of quality assessment processes for internal auditing (and, the importance of demonstrating
quality and continuous improvement in all internal audit work at all levels.)

assessments are required by The IIA '. . . *at least once every five years by a qualified independent reviewer or review team from outside the organization'.*[p]

Internal audit activities in UK government departments have prepared their own quality assurance assessment questionnaires in accordance with Government Internal Auditing Standard (GIAS) 10: *Quality Assurance.* These questionnaires are for both internal and external assessments. They contain a set of compliance questions related to all the GIAS standards, including what is considered good practice for the achievement of compliance. Both the Excellence Model and ISO 9000 are stated to be good practice and enhance quality of internal audit work in government departments.

The IIA in North America has marketed its own quality assurance services since the 1980s using its own framework of assessment processes. Other quality assurance services are being developed by some of The IIA's affiliate organizations across the world and by many consultants. The IIA published the first edition of its own *Quality Assurance Manual* in 1984, the second in 1990, third in 1996 the fourth in 2002, and the latest fifth edition in 2006. The IIA website states the rationale for the new edition is the '. . . *increasing focus (of internal auditing) on business risk, closer alignment of its activities with management strategies and accountabilities, and its strong emphasis on assisting management through the advisory and consulting services, while continuing to provide traditional assurance services'.* Each one of these reasons could be a paradigm shift for many internal audit activities.

This manual continues to be the principal guidance and set of practical tools by The IIA to assess conformity to its *International Standards.* The assessment programmes covered include, self-assessment, internal assessment by third parties and external assessments by independent reviewer/s from outside the organization.

Continuous improvement is mentioned in the manual as a process to be reviewed but it is not defined or related to other change programmes and little detail is given as to how it is to be reviewed on an ongoing basis. This is in contrast to the EFQM (1999, sections 3.3 and 3.4) required assessment of its Excellence Model. The concept underlying this assessment is called RADAR, being the initial letters of – **R**esults, **A**pproach, **D**eployment, **A**ssessment and **R**eview[q] – the elements to be assessed to determine what an organization has to do to achieve excellence in each of the criteria in the model. The Assessment and Review element covers:

. . . what an organization does to assess and review both the approach and the deployment of the approach. In an excellent organization the approach, and deployment of it, will be subject to regular **measurement**, **learning** activities will be undertaken, and the output from both will be used to identify, prioritize, plan and implement **improvement**.

---

[p] *IIA International Attribute Standard* (2004): 1312.
[q] The EFQM RADAR concept is not unlike and similar to the Deming Improvement Cycle of Plan, Do, Check Act mentioned at the beginning of the paper.

The RADAR Scoring Matrix (section 4.2) assesses each of *'measurement, learning activities and improvement'* as:

0 %   No evidence or anecdotal
25 %   Some evidence
50%   Evidence
75%   Clear evidence
100%   Comprehensive evidence

Reporting Continuous Improvement to Internal Auditing's Customers

The IIA has always recommended the results of internal and external quality assessments of internal audit activities should be communicated to senior management and the board, to support an internal audit activities professionalism. Such guidance has been included in its standards since the mid-1980s. From the publication of its new *International Standards* in 2000 this guidance has *'. . . included the effectiveness of continuous improvement programmes and adoption of best practices'.*[r]

As mentioned earlier, Cosmas (1996) recommended involving an internal auditing activity's customers in a systematic approach to continuous improvement as part of marketing the activities added value. This should require a total commitment to continuous improvement by an internal audit activity and reporting of the results to all its customers.

National and international guidance for audit committees now includes statements that such committees should monitor and evaluate the performance of their internal audit activities as part of their overall monitoring and review responsibilities. Smith (2003: p. 8) recommends *'Where the audit committee's monitoring and review activities reveal cause for concern or scope for improvement, it should make recommendations to the board on action needed to address the issue or make improvements.'* An extension of this reporting could be confirmation from an internal audit activity that a quality assessment and continuous improvement programme is in place and the results are presented to the audit committee.

Smith (2003: p. 14) does recommend that the audit committee should ensure that its internal, audit activity *'. . . is equipped to perform in accordance with appropriate professional standards for internal auditors.'* IIA–UK & Ireland (2004: p. 4) published an audit committee briefing developing this recommendation, describing the *International Standards*. This mentions the development and maintenance of a *'. . . quality assurance and improvement programme in an internal audit activity that covers all aspects of the internal audit activity and continuously monitors its effectiveness.'* Audit committee members are advised to examine an internal audit activity's attributes and performance, including questioning the existence of a quality assurance programme and the results. No mention is made of questioning the existence of a continuous improvement programme and the results!

---

[r] Practice Advisory 1310-1(3): *Quality Programme Assessments.*

PricewaterhouseCoopers (2005)[s] interviewed 49 audit committee chairmen, predominantly from the FTSE 100. The results from questions on how they measure the effectiveness of internal audit did not identify continuous improvement. Nor did it identify for many the IIA requirement for an external evaluation once every five years.

Continuous Improvement Systematic Approach

Cosmas (1996) researched marketing internal audit to achieve audit customer satisfaction, deducing that at that time this concept in internal auditing was virtually unexplored. Her study, based on experience and much of the thinking at that time of Peter Drucker[t] and Lawrence Sawyer and Mortimer Dittenhofer,[u] included discussion on performance measurement in internal auditing and the importance of using a systematic approach to continuous improvement to market internal audit services. She developed 12 basic steps to implementing continuous improvement. Each of these steps can be related to the Oakland principles of continuous improvement, Ridley rules of quality and EFQM fundamental principles of excellence, all discussed earlier (see Figure 10.6).

Linked to previous discussion on the Deming improvement cycle = D				
Oakland basic principles of continuous improvement discussed in this article = O				
Ridley rules of quality Figure 10.3 = R				
EFQM fundamental principles of excellence, Figure 10.4 = E				

D	O	R	E	Cosmas Steps
PLAN	3	2	3	1. Identify processes and their associated criticality
	3	2	3	2. Select process for improvement and define ownership
	1	1	1/2	3. Define customer requirements
	3	3/5	5/7	4. Organize an improvement team
	2	4	4	5. Develop an improvement plan
DO	2	4	4	6. Review the current process
	2	4	4	7. Establish measures of performance
	2	4	4	8. Analyse process and identify improvements
	3	5	6	9. Implement the process change
CHECK	3	5	6	10. Validate process improvement effectiveness
ACT	2	4	4	11. Establish and maintain controls
	3	5	6	12. Continuously improve

Figure 10.6   Cosmas Twelve Steps To Implementing Continuous Improvement
Source: Audit Customer Satisfaction: Marketing Added Value
(1996) Research arrangement, J. Ridley and Dr Kenneth D'Silva (2006)

---

[s] *In control – views of audit committee chairman on the effectiveness of Internal Audit* (2005), PricewaterhouseCoopers, London, England.

[t] *Management: Tasks, Responsibilities, Practices* (1974), Peter F. Drucker, Harper & Row, New York.

[u] Cosmas frequently refers to *Internal Auditing: The Practice of Modern Internal Auditing* (1996), Lawrence B. Sawyer and Mortimer A. Dittenhofer, The IIA. This textbook was first published in 1973 and the latest 5th edition, published in 2003, contains general guidance on quality management. It continues to be recommended reading for candidates sitting the IIA CIA professional examinations in 2006.

This linking together of the various concepts and principles for continuous improvement, quality and excellence demonstrates the importance of understanding each in any systematic approach to continuous improvement.

CUTTING EDGE IN INTERNAL AUDITING CONTINUOUSLY IMPROVES TODAY AND IN THE FUTURE

Note how even today The IIA Certificate of Incorporation of 1941 and its 2007 Mission Statements are similar, and link into the index in its website:

Certificate of Incorporation 1941

To cultivate, promote and disseminate knowledge and information concerning internal auditing and subjects related thereto; to establish and maintain high standard of integrity, honour and character among internal auditors; to furnish information regarding internal auditing and the practice and methods thereof to its members, and to other persons interested therein, and to the general public; to cause the publication of articles, relating to internal auditing and practices and methods thereof; to establish and maintain a library and reading rooms, meeting rooms and social rooms for the use of its members; to promote social intercourse among its members; and to do any and all things which shall be lawful and appropriate in furtherance of any of the purposes hereinbefore expressed

Mission Statement 2007

The mission of The Institute of Internal Auditors is to provide dynamic leadership for the global profession of internal auditing. Activities in support of this mission will include, but will not be limited to:

– Advocating and promoting the value that internal audit professionals add to their organization;
– Providing comprehensive professional educational and development opportunities; standards and other professional practice guidance; and certification programmes;
– Researching, disseminating, and promoting to practitioners and stakeholders knowledge concerning internal auditing and its appropriate role in control, risk management and governance;
– Educating practitioners and other relevant audiences on best practices in internal auditing; and
– Bringing together internal auditors from all countries to share information and experiences.

Website www.theiia.org

Standard and Practices
Quality
Information Technologies
Benchmarking
Academic relations
Discussion Groups

Where do you look for continuous improvement in internal auditing today but in these statements? They provide the direction for future professional internal auditing.

So much has already been written about the processes for continuous improvement, be it formal or informal. One important point to remember is that continuous improvement needs direction and management. It should not be left to chance. The first direction should be in the internal auditing charter: this should be benchmarked against best practice and the needs of the organization – at least annually. Research in the past has frequently shown that not all internal audit activities review and update their charters annually with their organization at board, audit committee and senior management levels. The other main direction is the needs of their customers, whoever they may be and at whatever level. It is their needs that continuous improvements should always address, and this should include internal audit staff as customers as well as suppliers!

The IIA publishes on its website 'hot topics' for the internal auditing profession. The IIA Communications Advisory Committee, staff, readers, editorial reviewers and members of The IIA Advanced Technology Committee and Communications Advisory Committee develop these. It is worth keeping all these topics under review when planning continuous improvement, to see the direction others believe the internal auditing profession should go. Consider the following 'hot topics' available to me at the time of writing this book, reprinted with permission from The IIA. All will continuously improve and involve internal auditing.

Hot Topics – March 2007

Governance

– The changing relationship between audit committees and chief audit executives.
– How has emphasis on financial reporting impacted internal auditing and the organizations they serve? Has excessive focus resulted in lapses in governance, controls? Has financial reporting improved since Sarbanes–Oxley?
– Improving audit committee performance – is internal auditing stepping up to the plate?
– Governance structures of foreign companies with US subsidiaries.
– The Sarbanes–Oxley journey – is it migrating from 'project to process'?

Fraud

– What is internal auditing's level of involvement in the organization's fraud-related efforts?
– Whistleblowing – a comparison of approaches used in different countries.
– What are organizations doing to protect customer data, in light of recent incidents of customer data loss?
– Forensic auditing.
– Working relationships between in-house legal counsel and internal audit departments.
– Lessons learned/best practices in auditing the US Foreign Corrupt Practices Act globally.

Risk

– What are the leading causes of financial statement restatements?
– Case study article on ERM implementation.
– Comparison of risk management approaches in several countries.
– Effective reporting of risk assessment results (leading practices).

Technology

– Business continuity planning.
– Identity management.
– IT controls.
– Privacy.
– IT security vulnerability.
– Emerging technologies.

Ethics

- Case studies of audits involving the organization's moral principles, rules, standards, or tone at the top.
- Merging of compliance and ethics departments.

Internal Control

- Auditing entity-level controls.
- Internal control assessments – how much is enough?

Other Topics

- Self-assessment with independent validation – are you getting your money's worth?
- Disaster recovery planning.
- Relationship with the external auditor.
- Value-add audits (non Sarbanes–Oxley areas of focus).
- Issues pertaining to internal auditors in the public sector.
- Doing more with less.
- Industry-specific case studies – utilities, gaming, health care, etc.

Audit and Control

- Website management.
- Web-enabled systems.
- Computer networks.
- Internal control assessments.
- Business continuity and contingency planning.
- Document and electronic imaging.
- Distributed databases.
- Enterprise resource planning.
- Project management.
- Systems development life cycle.

Audit Tools

- Continuous monitoring.
- Internal control tools.
- Risk analysis tools.
- File interrogation systems.
- Audit planning tools.
- Fraud detection and computer forensics.
- Security vulnerability tools.
- Using the Internet for audits.

Emerging Issues

- Laws and regulations.
- Guidance, frameworks, and standards.
- Business impact of new technologies.
- IT audit research findings.
- Privacy.

New IT Auditor

– How to get started on IT audit projects.
– Beginning IT audit techniques.
– How to audit various systems and technologies.
– Training and certification.

Risk Management

– Enterprise risk management.
– Application development risk.
– Project risks.
– Information security risk metrics and assessments.

Security

– Intrusion detection and prevention.
– Physical and logical security.
– Website security.
– Authentication.
– Wireless network security.
– Data encryption.
– Data theft.

Technology

– Radio frequency identification.
– Grid computing.
– E-mail and instant messaging.
– Wireless communications devices.
– Portable devices.
– Voice over Internet Protocol.
– Web services.
– Single sign-on.

CHAPTER SUMMARY

There will always be a need for improvement. This need is continuous for success. A commitment to continuous improvement should be built into every organization at all levels and in all operations, including internal auditing. It never ends. The speed of change today and tomorrow will always dictate this. Improvements do not stand-alone: they should be part of and encouraged by all management practices. They must always reflect the needs of suppliers and customers. They are at their best when they have direction from a vision statement and key objectives, which are current and forward looking. They need to be continuously planned, implemented, measured, monitored and re-evaluated (PDCA).

A commitment to continuous improvement is an essential part of innovation and the Gray and Gray (1997) five innovation motivational themes, four innovation goals and four innovation categories discussed in the Introduction, and the additions and changes made in Chapters 2 to 9.

Motivations

1. Progress within the field of professional internal auditing.
2. Increasing competition leading to pressures to reduce costs and increase efficiency.
3. New challenges, such as increasing internal control risks due to staff reductions and restructuring.
4. Opportunities to increase efficiency and quality as a result of technological advances.
5. Changes in corporate management practices and philosophies, such as Total Quality Management, re-engineering, continuous quality improvement, or related approaches.
6. **Challenges and opportunities of global issues and developments.**
7. **Social and environmental issues impacting all organizations.**
8. **Recognition that professionalism, quality and standards are essential attributes for world-class status in any internal auditing activity.**
9. **Importance of organizational governance to meet regulatory and stakeholders' needs.**
10. **A continuous search for good and evil in how organizations and all their operations are directed and controlled.**
11. **Recognition that all types of crime in and by an organization should be fought.**

Goals

1. Improvement of the quality of internal auditing services.
2. **Achieve best practice by continuously benchmarking.**
3. Expansion of services to increase the value-added of internal auditing.
4. Boost staff skills, performance and morale.
5. **Sell internal auditing as future focused.**
6. **To reduce the opportunities for all types of crime in an organization.**
7. **Increase satisfaction from all our customers.**

Categories

1. Changes in the way that internal auditors interact with the rest of their enterprises **and all those with a stakeholder interest.**
2. Internal restructuring and changes in the organization and management of internal auditing.
3. Creation of new audit services and methods.
4. Changes in the use of technology.
5. **Improved knowledge and skills in the teams of staff who carry out internal auditing engagements.**
6. **New services to fight crime.**
7. **Assistance in evaluation of the board's performance.**
8. **Improved satisfaction from all our customers.**

Goal 1 and Category 8 could be changed to add the word '**Continuous**' at the beginning of the sentences and Category 5 changed to '**Continuously improve . . .** '

CONTINUOUS IMPROVEMENT IN INTERNAL AUDITING PRINCIPIA 1998 AND 2008

My 1998 principia for internal auditing included the following related to a commitment for continuous improvement:

5. Seeking best practice internal auditing is a continuous learning process.

33. Use team concepts to encourage change, quality and innovation in the internal audit unit and organization it serves.

These are now changed to reflect the importance of a commitment to continuous improvement today:

15. A commitment to continuous improvement in all the services provided by internal auditing is essential if the needs of all its customers and suppliers are to be satisfied now and in the future.

A VISION FOR CONTINUOUS IMPROVEMENT IN INTERNAL AUDITING

We are committed to continuously improve

SYNOPSES OF CASE STUDIES

Case 10.1: Quality Assurance and Improvement – The IIA Guidance 2007

Synopsis

This guidance sets out a cutting edge framework for the development of best practice quality assurance and improvement in an internal auditing. It addresses ownership for quality, the nature and scope of the programme and its key elements.

Practice Advisory 1300-1 (2004): *Quality Assurance and Improvement Program* Interpretation of Standard 1300 from *The International Standards for the Professional Practice of Internal Auditing*. Copyright 2004 by The Institute of Internal Auditors, Inc., 247 Maitland Avenue, Altamonte Springs, Florida 32710-4201, USA. Reprinted with permission.

After Reading the Case Study Consider:

1. Who is responsible for implementing the quality assurance and improvement programme in your internal auditing?
2. How does your programme compare with the guidelines in the Practice Advisory.
3. How many of the key elements in the Practice Advisory are in your quality assurance and improvement programme?

Case 10.2: Continuous Improvement in Internal Auditing is a Must not a Luxury

Synopsis

An update on the impact of quality programmes, including ISO 9000, on continuous improvement in organizations and internal auditing. Discussed are ISO 9000: 2000, *Principle 6,*

Continual Improvement and the European Organization for Quality vision for quality in Europe – *'Those who do not constantly improve will not only stand still, but fall behind.'* Both support and encourage a continuous need for cutting edge to be seen in all quality programmes.

Based on an article by the author, published in the European Confederation of Institutes of Internal Auditing, December 2005 Newsletter, www.eciia.org

After Reading the Case Study Consider:

1. What are the implications for continuous improvement in your organization's internal auditing *'All organizations worldwide now operate in global "e-commerce" market places with new customer quality requirements and demands'*?
2. How are you balancing your continuous improvement needs in internal auditing: *'Those that want to compete successfully in the future... have to balance all stakeholders' expectations and continually improve internal efficiency and anticipate future trends'* ?

Case 10.3: Implementing Teamwork for Continuous Improvement – the 'Drive' Model

Synopsis

The continuous improvement model DRIVE is introduced – a mnemonic for a structured approach to continuous improvement in teams – **D**efine: **R**eview: **I**nvestigate: **V**erify: **E**xecute. Each stage is discussed in some detail. Each stage offers opportunities to contribute to the development of cutting edge resources and practices in internal auditing.

From *Total Organizational Excellence – Achieving World-class Performance* (2002), Professor John S. Oakland, Butterworth-Heinemann, Oxford, England. Contributed with permission from Professor John Oakland, Oakland Consulting plc. www.oaklandsconsulting.com

After Reading the Case Study Consider:

1. Do you DRIVE your continuous improvement teams?
2. How structured is your continuous programme?
3. How does it compare with the DRIVE model?

Case 10.4: Innovative Practices in Today's Internal Auditing

Synopsis

'... all professions and their members must continually innovate their relevant knowledge and skill sets'. The results of research in 2007 into innovative practices in internal auditing are discussed, both theoretically and empirically. These support the view *'... that there are perceptions of innovative resources and practices in internal auditing in the United Kingdom*

today'. A pattern emerges showing a greater focus on cutting edge resources and practices in quality and efficiency with '*. . . less attention being devoted to the expansion of services and the boosting of staff skills and performance'*.

Extract from 2007 research by the author and Dr Kenneth D'Silva, Centre for Research in Accounting, Finance & Governance, Department of Accounting & Finance, Faculty of Business, Computing & Information Management, London South Bank University, London, England, presented as a paper at the ECIIA research conference, University of Pisa, Italy, 19–20 April 2007.

After Reading the Case Study Consider:

1. How do the innovative resources and practices discussed in the research findings compare with those in your internal auditing?
2. Are there any implications from these research findings and recommendations for future internal auditing in your organization?

Case 10.5: Performance Measurement and Innovation in Internal Auditing

Synopsis

Discussed are seven different forces that motivate innovation to happen in an organization and internal auditing – Competition; Organizational; Customer Needs; Activities of Others; Resources; Motivation of Staff; Performance. Questioned is the need for innovation for its own sake or as a response to risks, threats or opportunism. Four different scenarios are considered. A model of innovation is developed, designed '*. . . to stimulate thought and debate. . . '*.

Contributed by Stan Farmer, Head of Corporate Assurance at English Partnerships, the National Regeneration Agency. He is a CIPFA qualified Accountant, and an Affiliate member of The IIA. He is currently Chairman of the Smaller Government Bodies, Head of Internal Auditing Forum, and active in the group established to set up an External Quality Assurance Service for Central Government Bodies. Stan completed his MSc in Auditing Management and Consultancy at the University of Central England in 2005, with a dissertation on Performance Measurement in Internal Auditing. As a result of this work Stan was co-opted onto an IIA working group to develop guidance on this subject. Stan and others on that group have now given numerous presentations on this topic, but combining innovation and performance in this presentation provided an opportunity to extend the thinking in this area, and to perhaps provide an opportunity for others to take on further research on the topic.

After Reading the Case Study Consider:

1. How are you responding to the seven forces that can drive innovation in your internal auditing?
2. Do your current internal auditing performance measures '*. . . only stimulate modest, incremental or transactional innovation'*?

3. Do any of your internal auditing performance measures drive *'revolutionary'* innovation?
4. Do you recognize any of the four scenarios mentioned in the case (revolution, evolution, growth and maintenance) in your internal auditing and are any of these influencing innovation in the services you provide?

SELF-ASSESSMENT QUESTIONS

10.1 Hot Topics

How many of The IIA 2007 'hot topics' are currently part of your continuous improvement direction and planning? What cutting edge internal auditing resources or practices do you have in the 'hot topics' you have listed? You must have some if you are to improve.

10.2 Success

In the cycle of *'selection, education and development'* for the achievement of success, discussed in the chapter, what are the nine control objectives that need to be continuously inproved? Can you add others?

NOTES AND REFERENCES

1. Cited in *The Oxford Dictionary of Quotations*, Fifth Edition (1999) *To be said 15 to 20 times, morning and evening, De le suggestion et de ses applications* (1915).
2. Cited in *Foundations For Unlimited Horizons: The Institute of Internal Auditors 1941–1976*, Victor Z. Brink, The IIA.
3. Published in *Internal Auditing* (April 1994: p. 6), IIA–UK & Ireland.
4. Published in *Internal Auditing* (April 1997: pp. 22–23), IIA–UK & Ireland, and as a case study in *Leading Edge Internal Auditing* (1998: pp. 172–176), Jeffrey Ridley and Andrew Chambers, ICSA Publishing, London, England.
5. 'Perceptions of Internal Audit Value' (1997: p. 16), *Internal Auditing Journal*, June Issue, IIA–UK & Ireland. (Article based on research paper presented on 25 March 1997 at the Annual BAA National Conference, Birmingham Conference Centre, Birmingham, England.)
6. Extract from *Continuous Improvement in Internal Audit Services,* a joint research paper by Professor Jeffrey Ridley and Dr Kenneth D'Silva, delivered at Cass Business School, London, England, Fourth European Academic Conference, April 2006.

11

Cutting Edge Internal Auditing Is Creative

'. . . if internal auditors wish to hold themselves out as problem-solving partners to management, they had better become aware of their innate creativity or learn about creativity and put it to use.'

Lawrence B. Sawyer 1992[1]

WILL YOU WALK A LITTLE FASTER?"
SAID THE WHITING TO THE SNAIL,
"THERE'S A PORPOISE CLOSE behind
US, AND HE'S treading ON MY
TAIL !"

CREATIVITY IN INTERNAL AUDITING BEFORE 1995

Imagination is '. . . *the faculty or action of forming ideas or mental images . . . the ability of the mind to be creative . . .'.*[2] Creativity has applied to all activities since time began. Creativity leads all cutting edge developments. It makes you 'walk faster' than those around you, both in thought and action. Creativity applies in all operations in an organization at all levels: just as much to all internal auditors as its does to all managers. Lawrence Sawyer recognized this in his explorations into and teaching of internal auditing practices.

There are many books written and learning programmes taught on creativity for those who wish to study its theories in depth. Suffice for me to say that creativity has been seen as part of the development of all professions since their beginnings, and will continue to be so into their futures: internal auditing is no exception to this. Many pioneers of professional internal auditing, as we know it today, recognized this.

Harold Russell (1968)[3] saw creativity in the photographer internal auditor and wrote of this when describing the use of photographs for communicating observations during and at the end of an audit assignment:

> Yesterday's internal auditor is gone forever . . . today's auditor is using today's tools and communicating with greater speed and comprehension than ever before. His role in the company is changing rapidly from just another name at the end of a long report to a personality with a point of view. He is speaking directly to management and getting action when and where he wants it. . . . He is doing what I feel we all must do – projecting a new image of himself and his profession.

Equally applicable to today, both in the environment it describes and the image of the internal auditor – now definitely he and she.

Wilson and Wood (1985), whose research into managing behaviour in internal auditing was discussed in Chapter 4, questioned in their findings *'what makes a good [internal] auditor'*:

> Our respondents felt that a creative, broad-based approach to auditing allowed them 'to get quickly to the second and third levels' – to perceive higher order abstractions, to 'sense' problems underlying the initial tests and observations, as in detective work or abstract analytical reasoning, and to decipher the implications of findings.

Roger Carolus (1991)[4] when directing development of the first of The IIA *Standards for the Professional Practice of Internal Auditing* set out to establish internal auditing as an art, which required rules:

> All of us believed internal auditing is an art; consequently, internal auditors are artists. Like musicians with their notes, painters with their colours, and writers with their arrangements of words, there are time-honoured rules within which the artist has learned to excel. The five general standards and 25 specific standards represent the rules of our artistry.

Lawrence Sawyer (1992) expressed his own views on the difficulty of creativity in internal auditing:

> Creativity is not reserved for the arts and sciences. It is needed in our profession as well. But it will never be tapped [in internal auditing] if we do not develop a divine discontent with what we see and if we fail to search for new ways of solving the problems which we identify or which management present to us. We can offer a new presence to the business community – as creative problem-solving partners to managers at all levels.

Creativity is also part of management. Professor Jane Henry (1991)[5] wrote of creativity in management, defining it as:

> Creativity is about the quality of originality that leads to new ways of seeing and novel ideas. It is a thinking process associated with **imagination**, **insight**, **invention**, **innovation**, **ingenuity**, **intuition**, **inspiration**, and **illumination**. However, creativity is not just about novelty: for an idea to be truly creative, it must be appropriate and useful.

A message equally true for internal auditors: particularly the eight i's (my bold) for all internal auditing cutting edge resources and practices.

At the time Carolus was writing his comments on internal auditors as artists, we made the decision in my internal audit activity to register our internal auditing processes as a quality system using the international quality system standard ISO 9000: 1987. This required much brainstorming and development of ideas from conception to practice. It challenged our imaginations and made us think creatively about new ways of achieving our objectives and meeting the rules and guidance in The IIA *Standards* at that time. Everyone in the audit team was involved. Everyone in the internal audit team had to be an artist as the picture of our quality system was being painted. The result was a registered quality manual, including a set of operating procedures and working instructions that complied with both the ISO 9000/1 standard requirements, and The IIA *Standards*.

Article:
Creativity And Inspiration Are Essential Requirements For The Artist Auditor[6] (1995)

There can be little creativity for internal auditors from the statement that '*internal auditing is an independent appraisal function established within an organization to examine and evaluate its activities as a service to the organization.*' (The IIA Statement of Responsibilities of Internal Auditing.) Important as this statement is, it does not inspire!

> '*Inspiration and creativity are not reserved for the arts and sciences. They are needed in internal auditing as well.*'

Inspiration and creativity are not reserved for the arts and sciences. They are needed in internal auditing as well. Creativity will never be tapped in internal auditing, says Lawrence Sawyer in *Internal Auditor,* December 1992, '*if we do not develop a divine discontent with what we see and if we fail to search for new ways of solving problems which we identify, or which management present to us.*' What Sawyer was expressing is the secret of excellent auditing. The ability to create from a structured and disciplined approach to facts, an attractive picture, which delights the observer and communicates truth as seen by the 'artist' internal auditor.

Roger Carolus, when directing the development of the IIA *Standards* in 1975, set out to establish internal auditing as an art, which requires rules. He believed that internal auditors *are* artists. '*Like musicians with their notes, painters with their colours and writers with their arrangement of words, there are time-honoured rules within which the artist has learnt to excel.' The five general standards were written to represent the rules of internal auditing artistry.*'

Both Sawyer and Carolus expressed what many internal audit managers feel about their professional service. But how would the artist [painter] relate to these same feelings and what artistic techniques best represent the work of the internal auditor? The skills of picture making are **Line**, **Tone**, **Colour**, **Perspective**, **Scale** and **Composition**. Each can guide the creative internal auditor.

- **Line**   Line starts with the audit survey. A time when the internal auditor can be fluent and expressive. A time of high imagination. Background information about the activities to be audited starts the drawing process and links loose lines into a pattern of audit objectives to achieve the audit scope. Lines establish plans.
- **Tone**   All objects are intrinsically light and dark. There are many tones between white and black. Knowledge is the internal auditor's tone. Once the survey lines of the audit are planned, the levels of knowledge required for the audit must be set. Knowledge provides atmosphere and interest. Like tone the right levels of knowledge in the audit team will attract those being served by the audit.
- **Colour**   There is no colour without light. Colour is closely linked to tone. The internal auditor's choice of audit tests establishes the colour palette for the picture audit. Creative skill is needed in mixing the tests so that they focus light into all of the audit objectives and complement each other. Just as it is very easy to end up with a muddy colour palette, it is also very easy to end an audit with 'muddy' objectives if the mix of tests is not right.
- **Scale**   Objects in themselves have no scale – they can only be small or large scale in relation to something else. Audit scale is size in relation to the risks for the organization as a whole and not just for the activities being audited. Risk assessment provides scale for the audit. To be creative during risk assessment requires the process to continue from the organization level through the audit objectives to the selection of audit tests and review of the results.
- **Perspective**   Perspective is the three-dimensional reality of the world created by leading lines to viewing points. Each line in the audit must lead to a viewing point. Not all viewing points are within the activities being audited. The creative internal auditor looks for viewing points in other parts of the organization and frequently leads lines to viewing points outside the organization.
- **Composition**   The arrangement of an audit has to attract those it is serving. A picture with poor composition will fail to find a buyer. The composition of the audit report must [like a painting] lead the customer's eyes into its subject matter and keep interest throughout the viewing.

Encouraging creative internal auditing using the artist's rules improves the performance of internal audit work. It develops a divine discontent with what is seen and opens new paths for problem solving.

Together with Dr Kenneth D'Silva I researched perceptions of internal audit value in the private and public sectors in 1996/97, including attitudes to innovation in internal audit activities. Part of that research catalogued internal auditing practices into traditional, new and leading edge. It also sought and reported on perceptions of innovation in internal auditing. Our research report was submitted to the sponsor for the research, the Audit Faculty of the Institute of Chartered Accountants in England and Wales. The following article was then published.

Research:
A Question Of Values[7] (1997)

Organizations and control environments are changing. Within all sectors of the economy it is likely that tomor-row's organiza- rows will pro-mote the scope and quality of their internal audit activities to their stake- holders and the public at large. At present, most chief finance officers see values from internal audit reviews of compliance, accuracy and security of assets. However, fewer see values deriving from internal audit reviews of economy and efficiency. Even fewer see values from reviews of effectiveness.

> '... tomorrow's internal auditors will promote innovation in the scope and quality of their work.'

Most chief executive officers and chief finance officers perceive values from a list of best internal audit attributes identified from literature and audit codes of best practice. Each was asked to score the importance of these attributes. The following ranking of mean scores by chief executive officers (A) and chief finance officers (B) is similar. Not all attributes have a high mean score:

	A	B		A	B
Quality of Audit Work	3.7	3.9	Working Relationships	3.2	3.2
Competence	3.6	3.5	Low Audit Cost	2.9	2.8
Technical Skills	3.4	3.5	Innovation	2.8	2.8
Follow-Up of Results	3.4	3.5	Staff Continuity	2.6	2.5
Experience	3.3	3.4			

These scores focus attention on areas where many internal audit functions need to improve. Quality of audit work and competence are seen as providing the two most important features of internal audit excellence. This ranking probably results from recent increased interest by senior management in quality programmes and benchmarking.

At present, few in senior management see or seek innovation from internal audit practices. Recent North American research[a] recognizes a growing interest by internal audit and its management, in innovative roles for internal auditors and innovation in internal audit work. Within all sectors of the economy it is likely that tomorrow's internal auditors will promote innovation in the scope and quality of their work. The North American research concludes with the following statement:

> Whether or not they recognize it, each day internal auditors choose to be reactive or proactive towards the forces for change occurring around them. Those who choose to be reactive are endangering their careers, their organizations or both. Financial executives

---

[a] *Internal Audit and Innovation* (1995: p. 2), James A.F. Stoner and Frank M. Werner, Financial Executives Research Foundation, Morristown, New Jersey, USA.

must encourage their internal audit functions to seize the opportunities for new roles, greater contributions, and more satisfying work. These new opportunities to contribute to corporate competitiveness are too important to leave to chance.

CREATIVITY IN INTERNAL AUDITING 1997 TO 2002

On the occasion of the fifty-year celebration of the establishment of The IIA Chapters in the United Kingdom, in 1998 I wrote an article[8] that included the following message:

We need to be seen as innovators in the world of regulation, control and auditing. Creativity, innovation and experimentation are now key to our professional success. They must be the vision of all internal auditing functions. This means improving old, and developing new, products and services for delighted customers, with a focus on their objectives. This means being at the leading edge in all the markets in which we sell our internal auditing services. This means beating our competitors and knowing who these are. This means having the imagination, and foresight into what our organizations will require from us, not just in the year 2000, but also in 2005 and beyond.

In this 50th year celebration of our national institute's past and present teamwork, all IIA–UK [and Ireland] members should continue to set their sights on being inventors of an improved and new internal auditing, to delight all their customers . . . and increase its status as an international profession.

I offer no apologies for my focus once again on imagination as the key to the success of professional internal auditing. Imagination, not just in the resources and practices it uses, but also in the review and evaluation of an organization's policies and structures, from board level to all its operations, through the many processes and people it uses to achieve its objectives. People, not just in the organization, but also across all its supply chains and partnerships.

Article:
Walk Faster This Year[9] (2002)

In early 1999 an internal auditing job vacancy notice in the UK press called for applicants that would 'hit the ground run-ning'. The speed of movement impressed me, as I am sure it did the appli-cants. The notice described the person they were seeking as:

> *'One of the superlatives that must describe internal auditors of the future must be imaginative.'*

. . . a dynamic professional who will 'hit the ground running' and play a lead role in control systems evaluations, audit programme development and special reviews. The audit team is seen as having a very positive mission to continually improve the business.

Those that recruit internal audit staff in the job market place frequently use superlatives to attract the best experienced and qualified staff. This enhances the value of internal audit, not just for the applicants but also for their employing organizations. There are also benefits for the profession of internal auditing. All marketing of internal auditing as a profession has an impact on those who work in the profession and those who are served by it. An impact that is often wider than apparent at the time.

Today, the most frequently used superlatives describing internal auditors in job vacancy notices are **rigorous, astute, self starter, innovative, outstanding,** and **leader.** Widen this list by looking up each in any thesaurus and you have a range of attractive and positive, if not some conflicting, descriptive images of today's successful internal auditor. A good exercise for all internal auditing conferences! Try it at your next group meeting and measure the reaction to each image.

Elbert Hubbard and Larry Sawyer both described the auditor in their different ways. Hubbard in the 1930s with his now well-known '. . . *spare wrinkled cold and passive . . . a human perfection that has feldspar for a heart . . . polite and non-committal, unresponsive as a post . . . '*: Sawyer with his 1990s poem dedicated to the international auditor *'not petrified but flexible, adjusting to the times . . . warm and proactive . . . keeping up with management . . . a problem solving analyst. . . '.*

But is *'keeping up with management'* sufficient for the international or national internal auditor in the year 2002? I think not. Hitting the ground running in 1999 may have been ahead of the recruitment game then, but now there has to be a commitment by internal auditors to outpace the runner. To be ahead of management. One of the superlatives that must describe internal auditors of the future must be **imaginative**. Imagination, not so much in the fanciful sense but in a disciplined and professional approach to future events and needs. Essential for the internal auditing new roles in risk assessment and consultancy. Closely linked to imaginative is **innovative**. This has been used in recent years to describe internal auditors, particularly those in changing environments. Innovation is key to continuous improvement and the satisfaction of customer needs. Both imagination and innovation will increase in their importance in the future. Internal auditors without these characteristics will not be running as they hit the ground.

Gray and Gray (1996)[b] research in North America recognized a growing interest by internal audit and its clients in innovative roles for internal auditors and innovation in internal audit functions. At the time common needs for innovation were seen in most internal audit units. These needs included quality improvement, increased efficiency, expanded services, increased value and improved staff skills, performance and morale. Do any or all of these needs for innovation exist today in your internal auditing function?

Studying the IIA–UK's[c] analysis of leading edge internal audit functions is a good start for those that want to be imaginative and innovative. In its introduction it identifies management's '. . . *need to know what (internal auditing) can do for them, and . . . need to believe that they have the best or a function that can be developed into the best'.* For people, it questions whether internal auditing has the right people to

[b] *Enhancing Internal Auditing Through Innovative Practices*, G. Gray and M. Gray, 1996, The IIA .
[c] 'Is Your Internal Audit Function Leading Edge?', *Professional Issues Bulletin*, Number 1: 2000, The IIA–UK & Ireland.

achieve its objectives, understand the core competencies needed and is creating future managers with '. . . *an unequalled knowledge of your organization*'.

Competitors in the internal auditing market place will always be seeking to be at leading edge in the services they can provide. They have to, to stay in business. They will always be looking for those that are not walking fast enough so that they can provide the right level of professional service with the right people.

Make sure you are always walking fast. . .

CUTTING EDGE INTERNAL AUDITING IS CREATIVE TODAY AND IN THE FUTURE

Imagination and innovation have always been passwords for creativity. Today the need for organizations across all sectors to innovate is seen by governments to be important for both competition and survival. Competition because of the flatter world[10] we live in: survival because of that competition. The United Kingdom government Department of Trade and Industry, has its own Office of Science and Innovation, promoting success through innovation. In a publication[11] issued at the time this book is being written, it summarizes its education on innovative practices as:

- Businesses must be highly aware of the environment in which they operate and the wider changes taking place.
- Innovation is an essential business strategy to add value, and can take many forms. It is the only way to meet and stay ahead of the competition.
- Innovation will not take place without inspirational leadership and powerful motivation.
- An innovative organization will have awareness of customer opportunities, ambitious and entrepreneurial leadership, the ability to generate and develop new ideas, and the availability of the necessary resources to achieve success.
- Innovation is a key business process and can be managed using a pipeline/funnel model, encompassing four basic stages. Movement down the pipeline is governed by evaluation at each interface or gate.
- There are risks to innovation, and these must be evaluated and considered against the potential reward. However, there are ways to manage and reduce them. There are also significant amounts of advice and help available, to those who seek it.

The above statement is good innovation learning for organizations, in all sectors, not just those with profit aims: also, good learning for innovation in all internal auditing activities.

Sawyer (2003) repeats his guidance on creativity for internal auditors by restating from his 1992 article:

Creativity is not reserved to scientists and artists. It is employed in the business world all, the time. It is sorely needed and can be developed. The days when internal auditors pointed to a problem and then walked away are gone. Now they are expected to be part of the solution. And they are fully capable of applying creativity to their daily tasks. Creativity can be fostered by:

Scepticism
Refusing to accept existing practices as the ultimate and always searching for something better.

Analysis
Analysing activities and operations to determine their components and dynamics.

Amalgamation
Combining information to transform separate concepts into something new and better

I like the last 'amalgamation'. I have always seen the best internal auditing coming out of an internal auditor's imagination to relate the apparently unrelated, and to arrive at recommendations for improvement.

CHAPTER SUMMARY

This chapter is about imagination and the continuous drive everywhere to create new and exciting products and services for the benefit of everyone. Creativity has always been about open-ended thinking, not just thinking within boundaries. Professional internal auditing, as we see it today and predict it for tomorrow, is about sharing knowledge and ideas across organization and national frontiers. Future creativity will need more sharing across supply chains and other collaborations if it is to be global. This means more trust in the using of other people's thinking to develop best practices. Internal auditors will have a role to play in making this happen: assessing the risks and evaluating the controls – not just in the profession of internal auditing, but also in national and international governmental processes and the communities in which they live and work. The need for innovation at all levels in society, for its well-being and standards of living and work, will always be there.

Creativity is an essential part of innovation. It should drive all of the Gray and Gray (1997) five innovation motivational themes, help to achieve their four innovation goals and support each of their four innovation categories discussed in the Introduction and the additions and changes made in Chapters 2 to 10.

Motivations

1. Progress within the field of professional internal auditing.
2. Increasing competition leading to pressures to reduce costs and increase efficiency.
3. New challenges, such as increasing internal control risks due to staff reductions and restructuring.
4. Opportunities to increase efficiency and quality as a result of technological advances.
5. Changes in corporate management practices and philosophies, such as Total Quality Management, re-engineering, continuous quality improvement, or related approaches.
6. **Challenges and opportunities of global issues and developments.**
7. **Social and environmental issues impacting all organizations.**
8. **Recognition that professionalism, quality and standards are essential attributes for world-class status in any internal auditing activity.**
9. **Importance of organizational governance to meet regulatory and stakeholders' needs.**
10. **A continuous search for good and evil in how organizations and all their operations are directed and controlled.**
11. **Recognition that all types of crime in and by an organization should be fought.**

Goals

1. **Continuous** Improvement of the quality of internal auditing services.
2. **Achieve best practice by continuously benchmarking.**
3. Expansion of services to increase the value-added of internal auditing.
4. Boost staff skills, performance and morale.
5. **Sell internal auditing as future focused.**
6. **To reduce the opportunities for all types of crime in an organization.**
7. **Increase satisfaction from all our customers.**

Categories

1. Changes in the way that internal auditors interact with the rest of their enterprises **and all those with a stakeholder interest.**
2. Internal restructuring and changes in the organization and management of internal auditing.
3. Creation of new audit services and methods.
4. Changes in the use of technology.
5. **Continuously improve knowledge and skills in the teams of staff who carry out internal auditing engagements.**
6. **New services to fight crime.**
7. **Assistance in evaluation of the board's performance.**
8. **Continuous improved satisfaction from all our customers.**

One more important motivation could be added:

12. **Encouragement to think creatively.**

CREATIVITY IN INTERNAL AUDITING PRINCIPIA 1998 AND 2008

My 1998 principia for internal auditing included the following related to creativity. (see Appendix A):

10. Imagination and confidence are the keys to innovative internal auditing.

   This is now changed in 2008 to reflect the importance of creativity for all organizations and internal auditing:

16. Creative thinking in internal auditing is essential and should be encouraged by experiment and development to support continuous improvement in all its resources and practices.
17. Internal auditing should use its engagements to evaluate creative thinking and processes in all the operations it reviews.

A VISION FOR CONTINUOUS CREATIVITY IN INTERNAL AUDITING

> *We have no boundaries in our thinking*

SYNOPSES OF CASE STUDIES

Case 11.1: Creative Problem Solving for Internal Auditors

Synopsis

Internal auditors must think creatively. Creative thinking is a method. Brainstorming sessions are a creative method: they are a *'structured methodology'* with rules that should be followed.

There are techniques and tools to improve Brainstorming sessions. These should be used by internal auditors to improve their creative thinking.

Contributed by William E. Grieshober M.Ed., M.S., CIA, CPA, adviser in the School of Professions at Buffalo State College in Buffalo, New York for the past seven years. Prior to this he has been a Chief Executive Officer, a VP of Finance and a Corporate Controller as well as an Internal Auditor. He has served for over 25 years as an adjunct faculty member with the Institute of Internal Auditors and has presented business subjects all over the world. Bill received a Master of Science in Creative Studies, Creativity and Change Leadership from Buffalo State College – State University of NY. He helped to develop the Institute of Internal Auditor's training course 'Maximizing Your Potential: Creative Problem-Solving Techniques for Auditors'.

After Reading the Case Study Consider:

1. How does your approach to brainstorming compare with the case study approach?
2. Do you approach *'complicated and simple problems'* in your organization using brainstorming techniques? If not, why not try next time to do so using the above approach?

Case 11.2: Succeeding Through Innovation

Synopsis

This guide *'. . . focuses on the key business process of innovation, the exploitation of new ideas, and the factors most relevant to this'*. The promotion of innovation as an output is seen as a coupling of *'. . . creativity, calculated risk, and entrepreneurial spirit. . . '* all attributes for cutting edge resources and practices in internal auditing.

From *Succeeding Through Innovation* (2006), authored by Dr John Beacham and published by UK Department of Trade and Industry, London, England. The full report can be obtained from the UK Department for Business Enterprise & Regulatory Reform. www.berr.gov.uk

---

After Reading the Case Study Consider:

1. How does your own leadership of innovation compare with the guidance in the case study?
2. Does your creativity and innovation interact with your customers' environments and recognize their potential needs?

Case 11.3: Principles-Based Regulation Requires Creative Thinking in Financial Services

Synopsis

'The principles-based approach to regulation in the United Kingdom financial services creates many opportunities for innovation and competition for firms and internal auditors.' Customer-driven principles established by the Financial Services Authority (FSA) challenge all aspects of the business. Professional internal auditing with its *International Professional*

Practices Framework is also principles-based. Comparison of both principles shows close relationships and opportunities for creative thinking in internal auditing. Cutting edge internal auditing resources and practices are discussed in three main areas of financial services organizations.

Contributed by Vicky Kubitscheck, Head of Audit, Risk and Compliance at AEGON UK. She leads the internal audit, risk and compliance groups across AEGON UK, providing services that support the organization's corporate governance, risk and compliance frameworks. Her work is centred on developing integrated risk and control management, and raising the profile of internal audit, risk management and compliance in the business. She led the implementation of an enterprise risk management approach within AEGON UK and previously at AXA, developing techniques that are focused on gaining management accountability and embedding sound risk management that is aligned with the ambitions of the business. Vicky is a member of the ABI Chief Risk Officer Forum, and as a Fellow of the Institute of Internal Auditors, she is also active in promoting the internal audit profession. Vicky chairs the Insurance Internal Audit Group, which has over 100 corporate members, and has served on various IIA District Committees, including currently the Scottish District Committee.

After Reading the Case Study Consider:

1. What customer-focused high-level principles are there in the regulation of your organization that should influence innovation in your internal auditing?
2. Do any of the three main areas discussed influence innovation in your internal auditing?

Case 11.4: Creativity, Innovation and Change

Synopsis

'How can you develop a more creative approach in yourself and a more creative climate in your organization?' The Open University Business School's course *Creativity, Innovation and Change* provides development and learning in how to develop their'. . . *creative skills, develop ideas with their team, sustain a creative climate at work, manage innovation and develop partnerships across organizational boundaries'*. All '. . . *tools, procedures and behaviours. . .'* necessary for the development of cutting edge internal auditing resources and practices.

Accessed from The Open University, Milton Keynes, England website www.open.ac.uk June 2007. The description is of its postgraduate degree course B822: Creativity, Innovation and Change – 2007. It is included as a case study with permission.

After Reading the Case Study Consider:

1. How do you develop your '. . . *creative climate at work,* [and] *manage innovation. . .'*?
2. Does the training for creativity, problem solving and managing change in your organization and internal auditing cover the knowledge base and learning in the Open University Business School course?

Case 11.5: Why Study Creativity? – Here are Twelve Solid Reasons

Synopsis

'The scientific study of creativity has enjoyed a more than fifty-year history.' Here are 12 reasons why this field of study has drawn the attention of researchers, practitioners and teachers. Good reasons also for creativity in cutting edge internal auditing resources and practices.

Contributed by Professor Gerard J. Puccio, PhD, Chair, International Center for Studies in Creativity, Buffalo State University of New York www.buffalostate.edu/centers/creativity

From 'Why Study Creativity?' (1995), Professor G.J. Puccio, in *Introduction to Creativity: An Anthology for College Courses on Creativity* which provides historical and current thinking from interdisciplinary perspectives (pp. 49–56). Copley Publishers, Acton, MA, USA.

After Reading the Case Study Consider:

1. How does your organization and internal auditing *'. . . nurture the creative potential of its human resources'*?
2. Are you using creative thinking skills to enhance your internal auditing *'. . . knowledge base'*?
3. Do you have any learning on creativity, which adds to your understanding of how to *'. . . instill creativity throughout the organization'*?

SELF-ASSESSMENT QUESTIONS

11.1

How many of the eight 'i's in Professor Jane Henry's creativity in management can you remember? How many are seen in your internal auditing resources and practices?

11.2

What three actions did Lawrence Sawyer say fostered creativity? Do these foster creativity in your internal auditing resources and practices?

NOTES AND REFERENCES

1. 'The Creative Side of Internal Auditing', Lawrence B. Sawyer, *Internal Auditor*, December 1992: pp. 57–62, The IIA. [Reprinted in *Sawyer's Words of Wisdom* (2004), A Collection of Articles by Lawrence B. Sawyer, The IIA Research Foundation.]
2. Definition in the *Concise Oxford Dictionary*, Eleventh Edition (2004), Oxford University Press, Oxford, England.
3. The Projection of Your Image, The IIA *Internal Auditor*, September/October 1968, pp. 41–47.
4. Roger Carolus, commenting on his committee's 1975 development of the first IIA *Standards*, when writing in the Fifty Years anniversary issue of *Internal Auditor*, June 1991, The IIA.

5. Creative Management (1991, 1st edition, ISBN 0 8039 8491, p. xi. © The Open University, 2007) Professor Jane Henry, SAGE Publications Ltd, London, England.
6. Published in *Internal Auditing*, March 1995: p. 12, IIA–UK & Ireland.
7. Published in *Internal Auditing*, 1997 June: p. 16, IIA–UK & Ireland.
8. 'IIA–UK Celebrates 50th', *Internal Auditing*, March 1998, IIA–UK & Ireland.
9. 'Walk Faster This Year', *Internal Auditing & Business Risk*, January 2002, IIA–UK & Ireland.
10. The challenges and opportunities of the flattening world of the 21st century is very well discussed and debated by Thomas Friedman in his book *The World is Flat* (2005), Penguin Group, London, England. Friedman argues for a *'whole new age of globalization'* equalizing the field for competitors.
11. *Succeeding Through Innovation: 60 Minute Guide To Innovation – Turning Ideas Into Profit* (2006), Department of Trade and Industry, London, England. www.dti.gove.uk/innovation (details of the pipeline/funnel model mentioned in the Summary can be found in this guide). Since accessing this site the DTI name has now been changed to Department for Business, Enterprise and Regulatory Reform. www.berr.gov.uk. Also, see the promotion of innovation in UK organizations by the UK government's recent White Paper *Innovation Nation – Unlocking talent*, Cm 7345 March 2008, published by the new Department for Innovation, Universities & Skills. This paper starts in its executive summary with an important message for all organizations and the profession of internal auditing, underlying the cutting edge theme for this chapter:

> Innovation is essential to the UK's future economic prosperity and quality of life. To raise productivity, foster competitive businesses, meet the challenges of globalisation and to live within our environmental and demographic limits, the UK must excel at all types of innovation. This will mean harnessing ideas from the public and private sectors, users and professionals to create more effective products, services, processes and methods of public service delivery. The UK must unlock the talent of all of its people and become an Innovation Nation.

Cutting Edge Internal Auditing
Asks The Right Questions

'I shot an arrow into the air,
It fell to earth I know not where...'

Henry Wadsworth Longfellow 1807–82[1]

Time & Change

GOAL	PAST	PRESENT	FUTURE	BTH
EFFICIENCY				
EFFECTIVENESS		GOVERNANCE PROCESSES		
ECONOMY				
OTHER E's +				

INTERNAL AUDITING ASKS THE RIGHT QUESTIONS PRIOR TO 2001

Asking the right questions is often like shooting an arrow into the air. Like archery, with skill, the aim to the target can be improved. Modern internal auditing has been built on the three 'E's of **Efficiency, Effectiveness, Economy** as targets, developed as objectives into audit planning; reviewed and tested during audit work; reported on and followed up. Value for money auditing adopted the same 'E's in the public sector. These three 'E's can be found in The IIA *Standards*, as part of the primary objectives of internal control. When placed in the context of time, they create an interesting matrix of nine question 'boxes'. Each has past, present and future implications in all organizations. The cutting edge internal auditor will always ask questions about the four phases of time: the past, present and future . . . and also 'beyond the horizon' (BTH) – making twelve question 'boxes'.

More 'E's can be added as organization and control environment needs change. Consider **Ethics** and **Environmental** issues. They raise important questions that can reveal significant control strengths and weaknesses. Include questions on **Empowerment** and **Enlightenment**. Each impacts the control environment. Empowerment as part of process re-engineering and quality management: enlightenment through technology and a growing pursuit of knowledge and innovation, by both organizations and the people they employ. **Equality** is also now an important issue in objectives.

These eight 'E's now make 32 question 'boxes' spanning the four phases of time – all to be addressed during audit planning and audit work. Shooting arrows into all these boxes needs the right questions for accuracy! Asking such questions is sometimes like shooting an arrow into the air, not knowing whether it is addressed to the right person, if it is the right question, or the right direction. Asking the right questions is not always an easy skill for internal auditors to acquire.

Lawrence Sawyer (1973)[2] approached the skill of questioning as one of the six forms of fieldwork:

Observing
Questioning
Analysing
Verifiying
Investigating
Evaluating

He saw the first five '... *as part of the measurement process. The last – evaluation – gives meaning to the information that the auditor has gathered.*' It is questioning as part of the fieldwork that this chapter is about: questioning as a measurement to determine what other form/s of fieldwork should be undertaken. It is the most important part of fieldwork and probably the most difficult to get right – first time. Sawyer saw this as '... *the most pervasive technique of the auditor...*'

> Oral questions are usually the most common, yet probably the most difficult to pose. Obtaining information orally can be raised to the level of an art. To get to the truth and to do so without upsetting the auditee is sometimes not an easy task. If the auditee detects an inquisitional tone or perceives a cross-questioning attitude...

So, oral questioning is one part of other forms of fieldwork, a measurement process, and an art, which can be changed by tone. Another style of more formal questioning can be through written questionnaires, either as a guide for the internal auditor to ask orally, or as a communication for the auditee to answer.

For many years the questions auditors should ask were listed clearly in questionnaires printed in auditing textbooks. In some organizations these were further developed into questionnaire manuals, both general and specific for departments and operations. Many auditors have been trained in their careers to use such questionnaires and questionnaire manuals. I was one of them. Yet, even with all the questionnaires I have used there has never been one that was complete and did not need some questions changed and others added. Sawyer saw the development of a questionnaire essential at the preliminary survey stage of every audit: '... *but let haste not interfere with the orderly listing of questions; for without a methodical guide, the conversation will ramble, the manager's time will be wasted [if not also the auditor's], and the first impression the manager receives will be one of disorganization.*'

A useful start to development of any questionnaire is the drawing of flowcharts – '. . . *a combination of science and art'*. Flowcharting is an excellent creative process, developed by questioning. It can be informal, or formal using standardized templates and instructions. Flowcharts take time to produce and deserve a place in all working paper files. They are evidence of an understanding of the operations being audited. My early audit training through de Paula's guidance taught me *'Flowcharts probably represent the most satisfactory method of recording systems, consistent with a disciplined approach to systems audits'*. They also lead to developing the right questions.

Standard questionnaires provide a base to be developed to fit the scope (S), knowledge (K), understanding (U), objectives (O), programme (P) and time (T) of the audit engagement – SKUOPT. This is their value. An important formal resource in every engagement and for all working papers supporting an internal audit engagement: from my experience one that is not always used as frequently as it should be, and by every auditor. Consider each of the engagements attributes just mentioned:

- *Scope* – These are the terms of reference for an engagement. It covers all the responsibilities of the operation being reviewed and how these relate to the organization's vision and mission. Scope is not just within the organization but also any that exists across all its supply chains and relationships with all stakeholders. It also needs to take into account the responsibilities of the internal audit activity as shown in its charter and professional standards.
- *Knowledge* – This is the appropriate knowledge needed to complete the engagement. This must be available to the internal auditing as its own resource, or in partnership with management or other functions, including the auditee, or bought-in from outside the organization.
- *Understanding* – Knowledge is not enough. This is the ability to apply the appropriate knowledge to complete the engagement.
- *Objectives* – These are the aims of the engagement as agreed by the internal auditor with its customers. These can change during an engagement as a result of asking the right questions.
- *Programme* – This starts with risk assessment, audit planning, a preliminary survey, setting of objectives, fieldwork processes, findings, communication of results to management, follow-up and reporting to the board or audit committee.
- *Time* – This spans the past, present, future and 'beyond the horizon': not as four separate stages, but as a continuum looking into the short term and beyond.

There is also the importance of what type of question to ask. This will vary at different stages of the audit. It can also depend on the confidence of the questioner. The more knowledge an auditor has of the process being audited the more 'right' can be the question. This demonstrates the importance of a preliminary survey in every audit engagement.

There is also the importance of the professional language to use and how the person to whom it is addressed understands this. During my first auditing of computer operations and related systems development in the early 1960s one of my audit staff drew the analogy between the Rosetta Stone and knowledge needed to ask the right questions to computer operators, systems development staff and management. The Rosetta Stone was found in Egypt, and is now exhibited at, the British Museum in London. Its significance lies in its writings in three languages, Egyptian hieroglyphic, demotic, and Greek. These allowed scholars to interpret the hieroglyphic language for the first time. To be able to ask the right questions when auditing computer operations it is sometimes necessary to understand three languages – computer, systems and operations

My approach was not entirely original. Many writers at the time were exploring how computers could assist internal auditing and how internal auditors should audit computers. The 1966 publications of the *Internal Auditor*, journal of the Institute of Internal Auditors, included eight articles on Electronic Data Processing (EDP) auditing. One, in the winter publication, written by J.N. Isaacs,[3] offered similar guidance to my own thoughts:

> ... the auditor, however, must avoid fuzzy thinking. He [she] must be fully aware that basically three generic aspect of EDP merit his [her] attention:
>
> 1. The efficiency of the EDP operation, including both machines and personnel.
> 2. Factors relating to the reliability of EDP processing.
> 3. Use of the machines as tools to assist in performing audits.

Isaacs concludes his article with:

> Auditors should be characterized by a willingness to confront the new and use it to their advantage. A whole new approach to auditing may some day become necessary because of the advent of EDP. That day has not yet arrived.
>
> For the time being, however, the auditor will do well to seek out ways to use the capabilities of EDP to his [her] advantage, to check on its work by using his [her] own techniques, and to audit those charged with the responsibilities of EDP operations in his company. By doing so, he [she] will serve to develop any new techniques required for meeting the changes of electronic data processing, educating himself [herself] for the new era.

From the early 1970s the internal auditor was being encouraged to be involved with and to audit computer operations. Sawyer (1973)[4] devoted a chapter to computer auditing, introducing it with:

> The expanding universe of electronic data processing is gradually surrounding the internal auditor's entire world. It is a changing, unending universe; and it cannot be ignored. The old ways are going or gone. The new ways are here and now and are getting even more difficult to deal with in an accustomed manner
>
> Some auditors have plunged eagerly into the exploration of this new world. Some have timidly refrained, still standing in their accustomed places, fearful of mysteries that are not really all that mysterious. But every auditor is in one way or another affected. And as the computer and its generations proliferate, the internal auditor must become involved or leave the arena to the more venturesome.

Other authors worldwide adopted similar approaches. The knowledge and experience they demonstrated became conference themes and training courses across the world, encouraged by demand and The IIA, its affiliated chapters and many consultants. This knowledge base for the internal auditor's approach to computers became part of the syllabus of professional accounting and internal auditing qualifications. Asking the right questions when auditing computer operations was important then, still is today and will be tomorrow.

In *Leading Edge Internal Auditing* (1998: pp. 134–135) I included my internal auditing vision at that time. In that vision language is mentioned: *'Language skills and knowledge of the local environment. . . deliver quality audit work anywhere in the world.'* The language in questions can be too dull at times, not representing the true situation. When asking questions, consider using more exciting and meaningful words and phases. The results can often provide more accurate answers.

Article:
Mind Your Language[5] (2001)

Last Christmas I was given a book – *The Surgeon of Crowthorne*[a] an insight into the development of the English language as we know it today. It tells of the compilation of the Oxford English Dictionary (OED) during the mid- 19th to early part of the 20th cen- tury. Covering the lives of two men, Dr James Murray, an eminent lex- icographer, and Dr. W.C. Minor, the surgeon subject

> *'Popular words used in 1996 to describe internal auditor qualities were – rigorous, astute, self-starter, innovative, proactive, creative, leader. They are still used today. How do you use these terms in the questions you ask your auditees?'*

of the book, both with widely different personalities, both significant contributors to the OED. But they were not alone. At that time and today there have been and are many other voluntary contributors, from all backgrounds: documenting and defining the old and new words we use in all our communications: influencing how we speak, write and read. So it is also with those that write about internal auditing. Their language is a significant part of its professional development.

I was reminded of the lives of Drs Murray and Minor when I read the September 2000 issue of *Internal Auditing & Business Risk*. Contributors, from many different backgrounds, using old and new words and phrases about internal auditing. The new words and terms are challenging. They bring emotion and superlatives into our too often dull professional language – essential for the marketing of any product or service. Words and terms such as:

flexible CPD
control delusion
good business behaviour
audit approaches that are proactive
holistic and participative
quality people
primary customers
internal audit brand
strategic service
passion for internal audit

---

[a] *Surgeon of Crowthorne* (1999), Simon Winchester, Penguin Books, London, England.

Words and terms familiar to some internal auditors and strange to many. A new language that is already contributing significantly to the development, growth and status of professional internal auditors. One that offers many opportunities and challenges. One with mixed interpretations that need common definitions.

The IIA addressed the need for a common language in professional internal auditing when it published in 1999 its *Glossary of Terms*, with internal auditing meanings as described in the context of its new *International Standards*. A major work with many international contributors: currently being revised with a proposed 2002 reissue: an excellent interpretation of the professionalism of internal auditing. This year the United States marketing literature of The IIA still uses the terms in this Glossary in its promotion of professional internal auditing. Do you use them in the promotion of your internal auditing services? A good test of your professionalism is to benchmark your internal auditing job descriptions, training, auditing and communications against the Glossary's terms and meanings. How many do you use? How many do your staff and customers understand?

During research in 1996 I commented on a new internal auditing image emerging across the world. This image used a mixture of old and new words and terms to describe internal auditing. It could be seen in job vacancy notices, marketing material promoting internal audit services and statements on control responsibilities in organization annual reports. It portrayed internal auditing across all sectors, as an *independent, professional service* with a wide *scope of work*, providing *value-adding* audit and other services. Popular words used in 1996 to describe internal auditor qualities were: *rigorous, astute, self-starter, innovative, proactive, creative, leader*. They are still used today. How do you use these terms in the questions you ask your auditees? Such as, *'How proactive and vigorous are you in finding weaknesses in your controls?'* and *'How creative is your leadership of innovative practices?'* They can improve your image and lead to some interesting answers.

This year watch your language. Create your own dictionary of words and phrases, based on today's internal auditing agenda of *assurance, consultancy* and *training*. One linked to the IIA Glossary and the new image of internal auditing one that all will understand. Use this in your team-building to link all internal auditing processes, from charter, recruitment and training to planning, risk assessment, audit programmes and reporting. Use it to influence all those to whom you report and with whom you coordinate, including your audit committee, external auditing and other auditors. Use it to create the vision for your services and market internal auditing professionalism for 2001 and beyond . . .

CUTTING EDGE INTERNAL AUDITING ASKS THE RIGHT QUESTIONS TODAY AND IN THE FUTURE

Lawrence Sawyer (2003)[6] still sees questioning as only one part of other forms of fieldwork, a measurement process, and an art, which can be changed by tone. Its importance as an accurate measure is even greater today than yesteryear, because of the speed of change in every organization. There can be few internal audit engagements whose scope and objectives do not change during the engagement when looking into the immediate future and 'beyond the horizon'.

Computer generation software is now available in most organizations, either in-house or can be bought in for use by auditors. This has improved the use of flowcharting and provides a more uniform approach for all staff in an internal audit function.

Today there is one important new resource for questioning during every internal audit engagement – the Internet. Opportunities to ask questions into the World Wide Web are almost limitless. Asking the right questions to the web on operational issues, during risk assessments, reviewing control and advising on governance processes can add significant value to an engagement's results: Answers can improve the other five forms of fieldwork – observing, analysing, verifying, investigating and evaluating, and lead to better findings, recommendations and added value.

More than ever before it is important that internal auditors ask the right questions to the right people at the right time during their planning and engagements. The right questions will always be the key to effective internal auditing. So will the right listening!

CHAPTER SUMMARY

The speed of change has made it more important than ever before for internal auditing today to develop and ask the right questions in the right language to the right people at the right time, as part of its planning, preliminary surveys, fieldwork, development of recommendations, and follow-up of findings. Flowcharting can significantly improve this selection. Internal auditing professional qualifications and access to the World Wide Web have opened up many opportunities for internal auditors to increase their knowledge and understanding of the operations they review. Making it much easier to ask the right questions today and in the future.

Asking the right questions is essential for the Gray and Gray (1997) five innovation motivational themes, four innovation goals and four innovation categories discussed in the Introduction, and the additions and changes made in Chapters 2 to 11.

Motivations

1. Progress within the field of professional internal auditing.
2. Increasing competition leading to pressures to reduce costs and increase efficiency.
3. New challenges, such as increasing internal control risks due to staff reductions and restructuring.
4. Opportunities to increase efficiency and quality as a result of technological advances.
5. Changes in corporate management practices and philosophies, such as Total Quality Management, re-engineering, continuous quality improvement, or related approaches.
6. **Challenges and opportunities of global issues and developments**.
7. **Social and environmental issues impacting all organizations**.
8. **Recognition that professionalism, quality and standards are essential attributes for world-class status in any internal auditing activity**.
9. **Importance of organizational governance to meet regulatory and stakeholders' needs**.
10. **A continuous search for good and evil in how organizations and all their operations *are directed and controlled.***
11. **Recognition that all types of crime in and by an organization should be fought**.
12. **Encouragement to think creatively**.

Goals

1. **Continuous** Improvement of the quality of internal auditing services.
2. **Achieve best practice by continuously benchmarking**.

3. Expansion of services to increase the value-added of internal auditing.
4. Boost staff skills, performance and morale.
5. **Sell internal auditing as future focused**.
6. **To reduce the opportunities for all types of crime in an organization**.
7. **Increase satisfaction from all our customers**.

Categories

1. Changes in the way that internal auditors interact with the rest of their enterprises **and all those with a stakeholder interest**.
2. Internal restructuring and changes in the organization and management of internal auditing.
3. Creation of new audit services and methods.
4. Changes in the use of technology.
5. **Continuously improve knowledge and skills in the teams of staff who carry out internal auditing engagements**.
6. **New services to fight crime**.
7. **Assistance in evaluation of the board's performance**.
8. **Continuous improved satisfaction from all our customers**.

Questioning is essential to satisfy all the motivations already listed. It should have a higher profile as a new goal and category:

Goal

8. **Add new skills in the art of questioning**.

and

Category

9. **Changes in the way internal auditing asks questions**.

INTERNAL AUDITING ASKS THE RIGHT QUESTIONS PRINCIPIA 1998 AND 2008

My 1998 principia for internal auditing included the following related to asking the right questions (see Appendix A):

18. The best internal auditors review control in the past and present, and accurately forecast the future.

This is now changed to reflect the importance of internal auditing asking the right questions in 2008 and the future:

18. It is essential for internal auditing to ask the right questions of the past, present, future and 'beyond the horizon', to the right people and from a good knowledge and understanding of risks, controls and governance.

A VISION FOR INTERNAL AUDITING ASKING THE RIGHT QUESTIONS

> ***We understand your business needs and***
> ***ask the right questions***
> ***to help you achieve these***

SYNOPSES OF CASE STUDIES

Case 12.1: Six Honest Working Men

Synopsis

Curiosity and structured questioning are the art of cutting edge internal auditing. Developing this art should be part of all internal auditing. Linking a curious and structured question matrix into risk assessment processes is important in every internal audit engagement.

> Adapted from the author's article. 'I Keep Six Honest Working Men' (1993), published in *Internal Auditing* (December 1993: p. 8), IIA–UK & Ireland.

After Reading the Case Study Consider:

1. Do you measure how curious and structured your questioning is in internal audit engagement?
2. Does your internal auditing always include questions on '... *your organization's objectives and the rules governing the environment in which you are auditing'?*
3. Does your internal auditing always include questions on the past, present and future?

Case 12.2: When Asking Questions be Modern and Confident

Synopsis

Questions need to be asked with confidence. *'An understanding of modern management responsibilities is fundamental to the asking of all questions.'* This understanding includes management principles, tools and the use of technology today and tomorrow. Each has an impact on cutting edge resources and practices in internal auditing and the services it provides.

> Adapted by the author from his Introduction to *Leading Edge Internal Auditing* (1998). (The then current developments have changed little!)

After Reading the Case Study Consider:

4. How well do you understand modern management principles and practices?
5. How well do you understand technology today and its developments for the future?
6. Do your internal auditing engagements include questions on how management is managing today and in the future?
7. Do your internal auditing engagements include questions on the use of technology today and in the future?

Case 12.3: Interviewing Style

Synopsis

Questions vary in style and content. These rules for developing the right questions and avoiding the wrong questions should help all internal auditors to ask cutting edge questions in their engagements.

Source: Tolley's *Internal Auditor's Handbook* (2005: A4.2.30 & A4.2.31, pp. 440–442), by Professor Andrew D. Chambers. Published by LexisNexis Group, Great Britain. Reproduced with permission.

After Reading the Case Study Consider:

1. How do you train internal audit staff in your organization to ask the right types of questions?
2. How do you use and monitor the types of questions in your internal auditing to seek information relevant and important for your engagements' objectives?
3. How do you choose questions in your engagements to be at the cutting edge of internal auditing?

Case 12.4: Asking the Right Questions when Planning for Information Technology

Synopsis

A structured approach to developing control objectives and the right questions when reviewing strategic planning issues. An example is given of how this can be used for information technology strategic planning. Such structures are important cutting edge resources in every internal auditing engagement.

Contributed with permission. *Source*: *The Operational Auditing Handbook* (1997, pp. 334–337), Professor Andrew Chambers and Graham Rand, John Wiley & Sons, Chichester, England.

After Reading the Case Study Consider:

1. How structured are your internal auditing reviews of strategic planning?
2. How many of the IT strategic planning key and detailed issues questions can you ask in your organization with a reasonable knowledge of what they mean and understanding of how they are implemented?
3. Do the control objectives and issues provide you with any ideas for innovative IT questions in your internal auditing services?

Case 12.5: Leverage the Internet

Synopsis

The Internet is and will remain a cutting edge resource for internal auditing in the future. *'Asking the right questions to the Internet can add to the knowledge of the internal auditor and value to all risk assessments, internal audit planning, programmes of work and final recommendations.'* Imagination is the key to successful use of the Internet in every internal audit engagement.

Contributed by Jim Kaplan, CIA, founder and Chief Executive Officer of AuditNet, 2007 recipient of The IIA's Bradford Cadmus Memorial Award, and the author of *Leverage the Internet*, published in The IIA *Internal Auditor* (June 2007).

After Reading the Case Study Consider:

1. How familiar are you with '... *available resources, a grasp of search strategies and language, and the ability to think critically about online content'*?
2. Are you developing a catalogue of Internet websites that can be used by your internal auditing in the development of its cutting edge resources and practices?
3. How imaginative is your use of the Internet in the services you provide in your organization?

SELF-ASSESSMENT QUESTIONS

12.1

What are Sawyer's six forms of fieldwork? Write an open question for each.

12.2

Write one question for each of the following types of question addressed to the chair of your audit committee during an engagement to review the performance of the committee.

Closed
Forced choice
Direct

Open
Probe
Encouraging

Now consider each question in the four phases of time discussed at the beginning of the chapter. You should end up with 24 questions. This is not as easy as it may appear and requires some research.

NOTES AND REFERENCES

1. From *The Arrow and the Song* (1845) by Henry Wadsworth Longfellow.
2. *The Practice of Modern Internal Auditing*, 5th edition (1973: p. 283), Lawrence B. Sawyer, The IIA.
3. '*An Argument for Reason*', *Internal Auditor* (Winter 1966: pp. 54–63), The IIA.
4. *The Practice of Modern Internal Auditing*, 5th edition (1973: pp. 216–273), Lawrence B. Sawyer, The IIA.
5. Published in *Internal Auditing & Business Risk* (January 2001: p. 13). IIA–UK & Ireland.
6. *The Practice of Modern Internal Auditing*, 5th edition (2003), Lawrence B. Sawyer, The IIA.

Cutting Edge Internal Auditing Contributes To Good Reputations

'The best way to gain a good reputation is to endeavour to be what you desire to appear.'

Socrates 469–399 BC[1]

Vision

**'TOGETHER A BETTER
INTERNAL AUDIT BUSINESS'**

**'A VIVID PICTURE OF AN AMBITIOUS, DESIRABLE STATE
THAT IS CONNECTED TO YOUR CUSTOMERS AND BETTER
THAN YOUR CURRENT STATE....'**

INTERNAL AUDITING AND GOOD REPUTATIONS PRIOR TO 1997

The first step to gain a better business is to have a good reputation, then to make sure that a good reputation is desired by all and clearly seen by those that will judge your reputation. This is not a new philosophy; it has been around since Socrates and probably before. For an organization this means; first, building such a desire into its strategic direction (vision, mission statements, code of conduct, all policies) and its management of operations (resources, key objectives, risk management, controls, procedures, knowledge and innovation); then constantly measuring all stakeholder perceptions of its reputation through key performance indicators, taking positive corrective actions if any harmful perceptions are seen, and communicating clearly and honestly to all stakeholders; and, finally teaching the importance of this desire through training at all levels and across all operations. No organization is exempt from the need for a good reputation in every sector, of whatever size, whether local, regional,

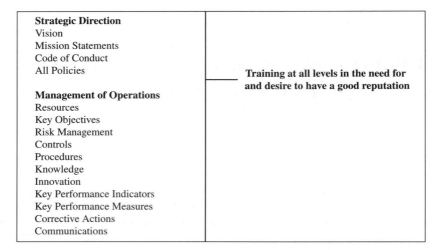

Figure 13.1   Need For And Desire To Have A Good Reputation
Source: J. Ridley (2007)

national or global. That need has to be addressed by a desire for such a reputation in all the actions above, repeated in Figure 13.1.

Do you recognize these actions in your own organization's strategies and management of operations?

All the cutting edge resources and practices discussed in previous chapters support the actions in Figure 13.1: management practices, quality standards and awards; benchmarking; professional standards; codes of ethics; accounting standards; auditing standards; regulations; laws; and, even fighting crime. They all contribute to that important perception by all stakeholders of a good reputation. The more internal auditing is involved in all these resources and practices, the more it is involved in its organization's reputation and at the cutting edge of its profession.

This chapter addresses one part of the reputation perception – the social (including health and safety) and environmental issues surrounding and inside all organizations: sometimes too often neglected in many organizations, at their peril. Today it is more often referred to as corporate responsibility; embracing all governance processes and practices. Before 1997 these issues were not at the top of the agenda in some organizations or in many internal audit activity risk assessments and audit plans. Though this is not to say that there were no organizations addressing these issues as top priorities, and even some internal auditors driving social and environmental auditing in their organizations. There is evidence of this in The IIA's vision, mission statements, activities, journal and position statements. It is also there in regulations, research, textbooks and governance processes, including the implementation of recommended codes of conduct.

It is not my intention to discuss the history of how good social and environmental practices, reporting and auditing in organizations have grown in importance; but to recognize, they are now fundamental to the success of any organization today and important issues for internal auditors. Writing on the social responsibility audit in the 1970s John Humble[2] cites Peter Drucker's key areas in which an organization must set objectives as:

- Business(es)
- Profitability
- Innovation
- Market standing
- Productivity
- Financial and physical resources
- Manager performance and development
- Worker performance and attitude
- Public [Humble preferred 'social'] responsibility

Little has changed! All of these areas are a part of every organization's objectives today. Humble viewed the challenge of social responsibility at that time as '... *one of the critical and difficult management tasks is balancing these objectives at any time, taking into consideration the changing requirements of stockholders, employees, customers and society generally*...' He went on to define social responsibility as one of the key areas of the business '... *typically concerned with the external environment problems of pollution, community and consumer relations, and the internal environment problems of working conditions, minority groups, education and training*'.

Stearn and Impey (1990)[3] discuss health, safety, social and environmental auditing as 'specialist audits' in a book to which I contributed with a chapter on managing the internal audit department. Their inclusion of these risks, with an internal audit assurance involvement, shows a cutting edge approach to internal auditing at that time, and still does today. For health and safety they provide a list of relevant and at the time topical questions, with the proviso:

> To provide this service in the field of health and safety, the internal auditor must become familiar with the policies, procedures, laws and regulation relating to health and safety at work... The auditor should examine statements of policy, accident records, minutes, correspondence and notices... also... make visits to examine working practices, hazardous material stores, fire escapes, alarms, hydrants, entrances and exits, etc.

For social and environmental auditing they follow a similar approach, recognizing the concept is new (despite Humble's writings in the 1970s).

> The concept recognizes that there are social and environmental responsibilities to be satisfied in the pursuit of business or service related objectives. Some of these responsibilities are enforceable by law, others may involve risks of serious personal injury, which could lead to costly claims for damages, while some of the organization's activities may just be socially or environmentally undesirable and even unacceptable.
>
> The management of the organization must of course ensure that all its activities are lawful... However, it is often a matter of subjective judgement to decide whether or not an activity is socially undesirable. It is thus a top management responsibility to establish a social policy for determining how operational decisions are to be influenced by consideration of the social and environmental consequences. An audit is thus appropriate to examine and report on compliance with the social policy.
>
> In this context, social audit may be perceived as a facet of operational auditing. It requires similar skills, employs the same techniques and its effectiveness depends upon a thorough knowledge and a sound understanding of the activities to be audited. Indeed, the concept of internal auditing as a service to management involves examining the entire range of an organization's activities in the

context of the objectives being pursued by management. Since the management objectives need to have social and environmental perspectives, so should the internal audit scope.

The Institute of Business Ethics (IBE), London, addressed many of these issues when it was established in 1986. A history of its activities and catalogue of research and publications are available on its website. They make excellent reading for the student of business ethics and will continue to do so. The IBE report on Current Best Ethical Practices in the United Kingdom, published in 1992, included the following statement in a proposed code of conduct:

> We will provide products and services of good value and consistent quality, reliability and safety.... We will avoid practices which seek to increase sales by any means other than fair merchandising efforts based on quality, design features, productivity, price and product support... We will provide a high standard of service in our efforts to maintain customer satisfaction and cooperation.

Interesting links between quality, safety, fair merchandising, high standards of service and customer satisfaction. The IBE has subsequently gone on to be a leader in promoting codes of business ethics in organizations, their content and implementation.

Cadbury, in 1992, addressed standards of conduct in his committee's report:

> **4.29** It is important that all employees should know what standards of conduct are expected of them. We regard it as good practice for boards of directors to draw up codes of ethics or statements of business practice and to publish them both internally and externally.

Such codes/statements are now recognized in most organizations as being important though research still shows they are not in every organization, or always published externally. Interestingly this recommendation is still not included in the UK Combined Code in 2006, though a similar recommendation is included in today's New York Stock Exchange Listing Standards!

So far I have discussed the private sector before 1997. My comments apply equally to all sectors. In Leading Edge Internal Auditing I included the Citizen's Charter[4] as a case study, published by the UK government in 1991. This charter applied, and still does apply, '... to all public services. These include government departments and agencies, nationalised industries, local authorities, the NHS, the courts, police and emergency services. In the private sector, it covers the key utilities; it does not encompass wider consumer protection law.' It established that every citizen has the right to:

Standards

Explicit standards, published and prominently displayed at the point of delivery. These standards should invariably include courtesy and helpfulness from staff, accuracy in accordance with statutory entitlements, and a commitment to prompt action, which might be expressed in terms of a target response or waiting time. If targets are to be stretched, it may not be possible to guarantee them in every case; minimum, as well as average, standards may be necessary. There should be a clear presumption that standards will be progressively improved as services become more efficient.

Openness

There should be no secrecy about how public services are run, how much they cost, who is in charge, and whether or not they are meeting their standards. Public servants should not be anonymous. Save only where there is a real threat to their safety all those who deal directly with the public should wear name badges and give their name on the telephone and in letters.

Information

Full, accurate information should be readily available, in plain language, about what services are being provided. Targets should be published, together with full and audited information about the results achieved. Wherever possible, information should be in comparable form, so that there is a pressure to emulate the best.

Choice

The public sector should provide choice wherever practicable. The people affected by services should be consulted. Their views about the services they use should be sought regularly and systematically to inform decisions about what services should be provided.

Non-discrimination

Services should be available regardless of race or sex. Leaflets are being printed in minority languages where there is a need. In Wales public bodies are aware of the needs of Welsh speakers.

Accessibility

Services should be run to suit the convenience of customers, not staff. This means flexible opening hours, and telephone inquiry points that direct callers quickly to someone who can help them.

And if things go wrong? At the very least, the citizen is entitled to a good explanation, or an apology. He or she should be told why the train is late, or why the doctor could not keep the appointment. There should be a well-publicized and readily available complaints procedure. If there is a serious problem, it should be put right. And lessons must be learnt so that mistakes are not repeated. Nobody wants to see money diverted from service improvement into large-scale compensation for indifferent services. But the Government intends to introduce new forms of redress where these can be made to stimulate rather than distract from efficiency.

These rights exist today and form an important framework for good reputation for all those providing public services.

In 1995, Lord Nolan's Committee on Standards in Public Life[5] published its first report, setting out seven principles of public life shown in Figure 13.2. These principles are very much alive today in the public sector, built into its current recommended governance principles (discussed later in this chapter). They established a reputation framework *'for all who serve the public in any way'*.

At the same time as these developments in social auditing and standards for ethics were developing in the UK, a new more global interest was taking place in environmental

---

SELFLESSNESS

Holders of public office should take decisions solely in terms of the public interest. They should not do so in order to gain financial or other material benefits for themselves, their families, or their friends.

INTEGRITY

Holders of public office should not place themselves under any financial or other obligation to outside individuals or organizations that might influence them in the performance of their official duties.

OBJECTIVITY

In carrying out public business, including making public appointments, awarding contracts, or recommending individuals for rewards and benefits, holders of public office should make choices on merit.

ACCOUNTABILITY

Holders of public office are accountable for their decisions and actions to the public and must submit themselves to whatever scrutiny is appropriate to their office.

OPENNESS

Holders of public office should be as open as possible about all the decisions and actions they take. They should give reasons for their decisions and restrict information only when the wider public interest clearly demands.

HONESTY

Holders of public office have a duty to declare any private interests relating to their public duties and to take steps to resolve any conflicts arising in a way that protects the public interest.

LEADERSHIP

Holders of public office should promote and support these principles by leadership and example.

Figure 13.2   The Seven Principles Of Public Life
Source: First Report of the Committee on Standards in Public Life Chairman: Lord Nolan
Presented to Parliament by the Prime Minister by Command of Her Majesty, May 1995

management and auditing. The IIA–UK & Ireland[6] published a statement on environmental auditing in 1993:

> **1.1**   The impact which business operations, in the widest sense of the term, have on the environment in which we live has been attracting increasing attention from the legislative and advisory bodies over the last decade or so. In view of this increasing attention it is only right that the Institute provide guidance, to members and others, as to how internal auditors can be involved.

Although not defining in any detail what an environmental audit should be, the statement did recommend that such audits *'can be conducted by an internal audit department'*.

On my bookshelf there is a 1991 book[7] by Ledgerwood, Street and Therivel, two academics and a practitioner in environmental strategic planning, all three writing in some detail on environmental issues at that time. I quote from their chapter on environmental regulation and the consequences for business strategy:

> The origins – economic, political and cultural – of environmental regulation are complex. Environmental audit is a new element in corporate strategy. It is the natural outcome of a growing environmental awareness, which began in the 1960s and has culminated in the 1990s with the understanding that it is the responsibility of every firm and individual to contribute towards the solution of global environmental issues. For these reasons it must be seen as an area of business innovation, requiring the skills of change management as it is being adopted within the corporate setting.

They go on later in their first chapter to write:

> Over the next decade, these changes are likely to have a major effect on the way that organizations manage their plants and products. Companies will be required to take responsibility for the pollution and wastes they cause, and for the future recycling of their products . . .

Their views and predictions at the time are very true of events today. They influenced my own risk-based auditing at the time. They should certainly influence risk-based auditing today, and not just in companies but in every organization.

Similar to the concept of ISO 9000 the British Standard 7750 specification for an environmental management system was first published in 1992. It was subsequently revised in 1994. (Later again it was designed to be compatible with the European Community's Eco-Management and Audit System – EMAS – and also with the International Standard ISO 14001.) Compliance with BS 7750 requirements includes an environmental policy to be in existence fully supported by senior management, outlining the policies to staff and the public. The management part of the system requires objectives, targets, controls, programmes, documentation, records and audits – both internal and external assessments. This standard set a benchmark for environmental management and auditing which still exists today.

Research Paper:
Quality and Environmental Auditing – A Time For Internal Auditors To Be Involved[8] (1997)

[Quality cultures were discussed in some depth in Chapter 8 and are not repeated here. The follow-on environmental tures is an extract paper linking quamental manage-ment cultures from a research lity and environ-ment cultures tog-ether as essential for an organization's reputation.]

> '. . . few internal auditors have become involved in environmental auditing.'

Quality and environmental management cultures and systems now have high profiles in all types and sizes of organizations across the world. The implications of policies and practices for both can be significant, ranging from success to survival; cultures for both require reasonable control frameworks; systems for each need to be formal; controls for each can integrate and strengthen the other; reviews and audits of each require an understanding of the principles underlying best management practice.

Environmental management and auditing has become more public in recent years. Attention has also focused on environmental costs and liabilities. In many cases this focus is caused by the media and environmental groups. Governments and international organizations are now committed to environmental policies, which are having a significant impact on regulation and organization objectives.

Penalties for weak environmental control can be considerable, from fines to lost business, and even imprisonment for staff, managers and directors.

Environmental management is one part of health, safety and environmental (HSE) policies. In many organizations HSE management and policies combine to form common management and auditing systems. Organizations across the world have developed frameworks to guide their HSE management and policies. Internal auditors should know and understand the principles of these in their own organizations.

Environmental auditing is defined by The IIA[a] as '. . . *an integral part of an environmental management system, whereby management determines whether the organization's environmental control systems are adequate to ensure compliance with regulatory requirements and internal policies'*. The IIA–UK[b] adopts the following definition from The International Chamber of Commerce 1989:

A management tool comprising a systematic, documented, periodic and objective evaluation of how well environmental organization, management and equipment are performing with the aim of helping to safeguard the environment by:

- facilitating management control of environmental practices;
- assessing compliance with company policies, which would include meeting regulatory requirements.

Health and safety must be associated with both definitions. Each requires similar programmes of assessment and verification to ensure that all practices satisfy both regulations and an organization's HSE objectives.

As with quality auditing, it is not difficult to link HSE auditing to governance, other control frameworks, and quality management. Yet few internal auditors have become involved in environmental auditing. Wade and Birchall[c] identified only 17% of internal audit units out of a responding sample of 216, with 40% believing they will be involved in the future: this, despite the importance of HSE and its impact on other controls and an organization's success.

The IIA[d] recognizes environmental auditing as a current issue for all internal auditors:

The (environmental) audit team is being asked to evaluate the organization's environmental plan on the front end, rather than after the fact. Therefore, while environmental audit teams will continue to need engineers and scientists, there is a real need for internal auditing's focus on controls, risk assessment, and standards. Most informed observers . . . believe it's time for internal auditors to get involved.

It also examines environmental management regularly in its professional examinations for Certified Internal Auditor (CIA®) status.

The new international standard on environmental management and auditing – ISO 14000 – will forge links between quality and environmental management.

---

[a] *The Role of Internal Auditors in Environmental Issues* (1993), The IIA.
[b] *Professional Briefing Note Two, Environmental Audit* (1993), The IIA–UK & Ireland.
[c] *Environmental Auditing Survey* (1996), K. Wade and D. Birchall, The Henley Research Centre, Henley-on-Thames, England.
[d] *Warming Up to Environmental Auditing*, (March/April 1997) *IIA Today*, The IIA.

To become ISO 14000 registered, an organization must plan and implement an environmental management system. The principles and framework of ISO 14000 pattern those for quality management (ISO 9000), requiring compliance with specified criteria, regular monitoring and independent reviews of performance. In many situations, registration and third party auditing for ISO 14000 will be by the same assessors as for ISO 9000. Understanding both standards will lead to organizations registering to both standards. The IIA and the Environmental Auditing Roundtable (EAR) in the USA have recently formed a joint venture to establish an environmental credential process, with training and a qualification, leading to environmental auditing certification.

The following checklist of 5 questions can help internal auditors, and the management they serve, to measure the levels of internal auditing understanding, practice and involvement in quality management and environmental programmes, in their organizations. Answering YES to each question indicates a high level. Answering NO to any question must be of concern. (Undecided for any question counts as a NO!)

Internal Auditing Understanding, and Involvement in HSE Management – Checklist

1. Has internal audit satisfied itself the worldwide principles underlying best practice HSE management, have been designed into the mission statements and key objectives of the organizations it serves?
2. Does internal audit advise management on implementation of its organization's HSE policies, across all its supply chains?
3. Does internal audit include key HSE objectives in all its risk assessments?
4. Does internal audit training, planning, and reviews, require a full understanding of its organization's key HSE objectives?
5. Does internal audit liaise and coordinate its planning and audits with HSE auditors, internal and external to the organization it serves?

One of the reasons for internal auditing not being involved in HSE audits may be a low interest by audit committees in environmental management and auditing. This is often because other board committees review this type of auditing. Price Waterhouse[e] recognizes this in its research:

> The importance of the contingent liabilities to which many companies are exposed as a result of environmental problems (sometimes arising in the distant past) continues to grow. The accounting for environmental liabilities, specifically the point at which companies recognize a liability for environmental problems in their financial statements, is an evolving area. Environmental matters are so important to some companies that they have established a special oversight committee of the board of directors to monitor compliance with environmental laws and regulations. Even in these companies, audit committees will find themselves devoting increasing attention to the financial implications of these matters.

---

[e] *Improving Audit Committee Performance: What Works Best* (1993), Price Waterhouse, The IIA.

INTERNAL AUDITING AND GOOD REPUTATIONS
1997 TO 2000

Developments in the management, auditing and reporting of social and environmental issues in organizations across the world continued during these years with a growing awareness that internal auditing was not divorced from these, and that they are an important aspect of risk management. The Association of Chartered and Certified Accounts (ACCA) commissioned a report on these issues as they related to the Turnbull guidance for directors on the UK Combined Code 1998. In this report leaders in the field of social, ethical accountability, management and auditing published a variety of papers. They are introduced by:

> Turnbull's guidance is based upon the adoption by a company's board of a risk-based approach to establishing a sound system of internal control, and on reviewing its effectiveness. This should be incorporated by a company within its normal management and governance processes. The span of internal control contemplated by Turnbull stretches wider than financial controls, to encompass social and environmental issues – matters that have recently come to be grouped together under the generic heading of 'reputational risk'.

The IIA established in 1997 a Board of Environmental, Health and Safety Auditor Certifications to develop and promote certifications and standards and enhance the professional practice of health and safety auditing (EH&S). BEAC's vision is to be the recognized global leader in EH&S auditor certification.

Following publication of the Combined Code 1998 the ACCA recognized *'previously marginal accreditation mechanisms such as ISO 14000, SA 8000, AA 1000[9] and the host of industry charters/standards that now exist may have a significant role to play in enabling boards of directors to fulfil their newly enlarged [internal control] responsibilities under the Combined Code'.*

In 1999, The IIA–UK[10] & Ireland published a professional briefing note on ethics and social responsibility raising awareness of these issues, including environmental challenges for the future – global warming, ozone depletion, waste, pollution and sustainability. Its comments on organization reputation are particularly appropriate for this chapter:

> A good corporate reputation can be a very important organizational resource, since it cannot be imitated completely. A good reputation can be linked to any number of factors. It can for instance, be linked to excellent quality or highly innovative products or services, and attention to customer needs. Just as importantly, it may be associated with the way the organization conducts its business: its relationship with shareholders, employees, customers, suppliers, the local community and other stakeholders. The organization's societal relationships are also important, because these will almost certainly influence its business reputation.

The briefing note goes on to discuss the Turnbull report of 1999 and the importance it gave to the ethics and corporate social responsibility in risk management:

> This, however, assumes that systems, processes and audit procedures are in place to enable the risks to be identified and assessed. [If] the systems and processes exist, the crucial factors are:
>
> - are they recognized as essential constituents of ethical and social responsibility management;
> - are they part of the auditing and reporting process;
> - are they institutionalized;

- are they regularly reviewed;
- are they regularly communicated and related to all aspects of the organization's operations, processes, behaviour and conduct?

Article:
Social Responsibility – A Challenge For Organizations And Internal Auditing (2000)[11]

This article discusses the importance of social responsibility for organiza tions and internal auditing. It starts with John Hum-ble's social audit of the 1970s and introduces some of the current developments in social and ethical accounting, audit-ing and reporting. It shows how social responsibility is now being integrated into economic and environmental performance measures; it provides evidence that social responsibility is now an important part of the principles of good corporate governance, requiring both internal and external auditing; and, it challenges internal auditors to take a more proactive role in how social responsibility is being managed and audited. The discussion is based on a presentation by the author at an International Internal Auditing Summer School, organized by Management Audit Ltd in London, during August 2000.

> *'. . . social responsibility is now an important part of the principles of good corporate governance.'*

Management of Social Responsibility

Writing on the social responsibility audit in the 1970s, John Humble[f] cites Drucker's key areas in which an organization must set objectives as:

- Business(es)
- Profitability
- Innovation
- Market standing
- Productivity
- Financial and physical resources
- Manager performance and development
- Worker performance and attitude
- Public (Humble preferred 'social') responsibility

Little has changed! Humble viewed the challenge of social responsibility at that time as '. . . *one of the critical and difficult management tasks is balancing these*

---

[f] *Social Responsibility Audit* (1973), John Humble, Foundation for Business Responsibilities, London, England.

objectives at any time, taking into consideration the changing requirements of stock-holders, employees, customers and society generally'. He goes on to define social responsibility as one of the key areas of the business '. . . *typically concerned with the external environment problems of pollution, community and consumer relations, and the internal environment problems of working conditions, minority groups, education and training'.*

His definition of the social responsibility audit and analysis of its scope spanned both the external and internal environments of an organization – see Figure 13.3.

"Part of the strategic and operational planning process, to examine systematically on an organization-wide basis the existing policies and practices relating to social responsibilities, internal and external to the organization."

It asks the right questions about –

1. **SOCIAL RESPONSIBILITY: STEWARDSHIP**

   • Is the business so organized that it makes the most effective and balanced use of its financial, physical and human resources?
   • Is there a full understanding within the business that long-term profitability, earned within the context of progressive social policies, is essential for all stakeholders . . . including Society at large?

2. **SOCIAL RESPONSIBILITY: POLICY & ORGANIZATION**

   • Does the board/general management team recognize the need to look systematically at Social Responsibility as part of the planning process?
   • What problems/pressures/felt needs exist which would appear to make further studies worthwhile?
   • Which of the existing company policies are relevant to this field? When were they last reviewed and their interrelationship examined in the light of changed circumstance?
   • Recognizing that virtually every department/function is involved, is there, however, a single person/small group at Corporate level with the responsibility for a continuing overall review of developments?
   • If you have a public relations department, is it fully involved in the development and communication of social policies?

It includes:

Internal environment
Physical environment
Working conditions
Minority groups
Organization structure and management style
Communications
Industrial relations
Education and training

External environment
Social responsibilities and new opportunities
Community relations
Consumer relations
Pollution
Packaging
Investment relations
Shareholder relation

Figure 13.3   John Humble's Social Responsibility Audit (1973)
Source: *Social Responsibility Audit* (1973)

In many organizations some, if not all, of Drucker's key areas are now measured against new external standard initiatives, such as quality, environmental and best practice awards. Developing international standards also offer accreditation and auditing processes for quality and environmental management. Many of the requirements in these standards address social responsibility issues. The European Foundation for Quality management (EFQM) Excellence Model[g] is based on eight fundamental concepts, one of which is Public Responsibility (note the link to the Drucker key areas!). This concept states that the '... *long-term interest of the organization and its people are best served by adopting an ethical approach and exceeding the expectations and regulations of the community at large'*. It requires that societal expectations are measured and actioned.

All organizations should review their conduct towards social responsibility issues on a regular basis and as part of their risk management. The questions in Figure 13.4 provide a start. The results from such assessments will always require actions for control, monitoring and improvement.

Is **it:**

- required by your regulators?
- led from the top – by style and values?
- embedded in all strategies, plans and operations?
- seen in all structures and systems?
- communicated internally to everyone – staff and visitors?
- communicated externally to all stakeholders?
- known across all supply chains?
- included in all review processes?
- independently monitored?

Does it:

- create/reduce wealth?
- improve/reduce the quality of performance?
- increase/decrease the efficiency and effectiveness of all staff?
- increase/decrease customers' satisfaction?
- improve/lower the organization's reputation in society?
- increase/decrease competitive edge?
- consider/ignore all stakeholders' needs?
- encourage/discourage good behaviour

Do you have:

- a formal and published code of conduct?
- a procedure for dealing with all irregularities?
- a whistleblowing procedure?
- practical ethics training for all your staff?
- environmental, health and safety policies?
- environmental, social and ethical accounting, auditing and reporting?

Figure 13.4   How Good Is Your Conduct?
Source: J. Ridley (2000)

---

[g] *The EFQM Excellence Mode* (1999), European Foundation for Quality Management, Belgium. www.efqm.org

Many organizations now report on social responsibility in audited annual statements, published with their annual reports or separately. This trend will increase. What is important is that these reports are related to all other objectives in the organization, with clear links showing how the adoption of a high standard of social responsibility is contributing to all other achievements.

Social Responsibility and Corporate Governance

The 1990s has seen an increasing focus on social responsibility, reporting and auditing, reflected in a growing number of governance principles. Most governance guidelines include references to social responsibility as an important part of risk management and control, across organization supply chains. One of the latest of these governance guidelines is that adopted by the OECD[h] for Multinational Enterprises on 27 June 2000. These are international recommendations that provide:

> . . . voluntary principles and standards for responsible business conduct consistent with applicable laws. The Guidelines aim to ensure that the operations of these (multinational) enterprises are in harmony with government policies, to strengthen the basis of mutual confidence between enterprises and the societies in which they operate, to help to improve the foreign investment climate and to enhance the contribution to sustainable development made by multinational enterprises.

Figure 13.5 sets out the policies that multinationals should take fully into account in the countries in which they operate. The first guideline establishes a commitment to contribute to economic, social and environmental progress with a view to achieving sustainable development. This is followed by other social and economic guidelines, including '*Support and uphold good corporate governance principles and develop and apply good corporate governance practices.*' All the guidelines encourage application across multinational supply chains as well as in the organizations they manage. The OECD also recognizes that '*Many enterprises have developed internal programmes, guidance and management systems that underpin their commitment to good corporate citizenship, good practices and good business and employee conduct. . .*' including '*. . . consulting, auditing and certification services. . .*'. There is a reference to the application of '*. . . high quality standards for disclosure, accounting and audit*'. but despite the references to good corporate governance, internal auditing is not mentioned!

Also in June, the Global Reporting Initiative (GRI)[i] published international guidelines for the reporting and verification of sustainability '*Since its inception in 1997, the GRI has worked to design and build acceptance of a common framework for reporting on the linked aspects of sustainability – economic, environmental and social.*' This is a powerful and far-reaching initiative, creating principles that will encourage and drive debate on many governance and control issues related to

---

[h] *Guidelines for Multinational Enterprises* (2000), OECD. www.oecd.org
[i] *Sustainability Reporting: Guidelines on Economic, Environmental and Social Performance* (2000), Global Reporting Initiative. www.globalreporting.org

Multinational enterprises should:

1. Contribute to economic, social and environmental progress with a view to achieving sustainable development.
2. Respect the human rights of those affected by their activities consistent with the host government's international obligations and commitments.
3. Encourage local capacity building through close co-operation with the local community, including business interests, as well as developing the enterprise's activities in domestic and foreign markets, consistent with the need for sound commercial practice.
4. Encourage human capital formation, in particular by creating employment opportunities and facilitating training opportunities for employees.
5. Refrain from seeking or accepting exemptions not contemplated in the statutory or regulatory framework related to environmental, health, safety, labour, taxation, financial incentives, or other issues.
6. Support and uphold good corporate governance principles and develop and apply good corporate governance practices.
7. Develop and apply effective self-regulatory practices and management systems that foster a relationship of confidence and mutual trust between enterprises and the societies in which they operate.
8. Promote employee awareness of, and compliance with, company policies through appropriate dissemination of these policies, including through training programmes.
9. Refrain from discriminatory or disciplinary action against employees who make bona fide reports to management or, as appropriate, to the competent public authorities, on practices that contravene the law, the Guidelines or the enterprise's policies.
10. Encourage, where practicable, business partners, including suppliers and sub-contractors, to apply principles of corporate conduct compatible with the Guidelines.
11. Abstain from any improper involvement in local political activities.

Figure 13.5   OECD General Policies For Multinationals
Source: OECD *Guidelines for Multinational Enterprises* (2000)

sustainability, both as separate elements standing alone, but more and more as the elements are integrated in the practice, verification and reporting of sustainability.

The GRI Guidelines examine much that has been achieved already in the reporting of sustainability, albeit that this varies across organizations and sectors across the world. The GRI hopes that the principles in its Guidelines will encourage development and integration of improved economic, environmental and social performance in future sustainability reporting. Figure 13.6 shows the key GRI performance indicators for sustainability reporting. Compare these with Humble's scope for a social responsibility audit in Figure 13.3.

On the independent verification of sustainability reports the GRI recognizes that the '. . . *quality, usefulness, and credibility . . . can be enhanced in several ways'*, one of which is the *'internal auditing of systems and procedures for measuring, recording and reporting performance data'*. No mention is made of a possible role for internal auditing in advising or teaching organizations how to report on sustainability. Nor is the alignment of governance with the elements of sustainability explored in any great detail. These are clearly aspects that will evolve across sectors, as best practices develop, influencing and being influenced by government and regulatory requirements.

A current development in Europe is the drafting of a charter of fundamental rights of the European Union.[j] This charter will guarantee basic procedural human rights

---

[j] *Draft Charter of Fundamental Rights of the European Union* (2000), The European Council. http://db.consiliumeu.int/df

ECONOMIC	SOCIAL	ENVIRONMENTAL
Profit	Quality of management	Energy
Intangible assets	Health & Safety	Materials
Investments	Wages and benefits	Water
Wages and benefits	Non-discrimination	Emissions, effluents & waste
Labour productivity	Training & education	Transport
Taxes	Child labour	Suppliers
Community development	Forced labour	Products & services
Suppliers	Freedom of association	Land use/bio-diversity
Products & services	Human rights	Compliance
	Indigenous rights	
	Security	
	Suppliers	
	Products & services	

Figure 13.6   Key Global Reporting Initiative Performance Indicators
Source: *Sustainability Reporting Guidelines on Economic, Environmental and Social Performance* (2000)

and freedoms as well as economic and social rights. Much of what it will contain is already established across Europe. However, publication of the charter, and its promotion later this year, will impact strategies and practices in many, if not all, European organizations: increasing the adoption of social and ethical accounting, auditing and reporting policies. A recent UK appointment of a Minister for Corporate Social Responsibility is a sign of this government's interest and intent in social responsibility developments.

Social Responsibility and Internal Auditing

The Institute of Social and Ethical AccountAbility (ISEA),[k] combines the terms 'social' and 'ethical' to refer ' . . . *to the systems and individual behaviour within an organization and to the direct and indirect impact of an organization's activities on stakeholders'*. Its new international standard AccountAbility 1000 (AA1000) has at its core the importance of stakeholder engagement in the social and ethical accounting process. Its framework, incorporates auditing as an essential criteria in the:

(i)   stand-alone implementation of its framework;
(ii) integration of its principles and guidelines into other standards and performance measurements used in organizations;
(iii) accounting and reporting of social and ethical issues.

Auditing guidelines refer ' . . . *to all assessment processes where the social and ethical, accounting, auditing and reporting process, including the social and ethical report(s), are examined by an independent body in order to provide assurance*

---

[k] *Accountability 1000 (AA1000) Framework – Exposure Draft* (1999), Institute of Social and Ethical AccountAbiity (ISEA), London, England. www.AccountAbility.org.uk

to the organization and stakeholders as to the quality of the process and reports'. AA1000 refers to the roles of both internal and external auditing. Internal auditing is recognized as providing '*. . . assurance to the organization as to the quality of the social and ethical accounting, auditing and reporting (SEAAR) process and the organization's social and ethical performance. It also provides support to the process of the external audit'.* External auditing is recognized as providing the same assurance and credibility '*. . . to the organization and its stakeholders . . . '.*

A comparison between the AA1000 auditing principles and guidelines and The Institute of Internal Auditors' Professional Practices Framework is shown in Figure 13.7. This shows strong links between each, both at the conduct and audit engagement levels. Codes of Conduct for both types of auditing are very similar.

AA1000	IIA Professional Practices Framework
Auditing Principles	Code of Ethics Principles
Integrity	Integrity
Objectivity and Independence	Objectivity
Professional Competence	Confidentiality
Professional Behaviour	Competency
Confidentiality	
Due Care	**International Attribute Standards**
	1100 Purpose, Authority and Responsibility
	1200 Proficiency and Due Professional Care
	1300 Quality Assurance and Improvement Programme
Auditing Guidelines	**International Performance Standards**
1 Audit engagement	**2300** Performing the Engagement
2,3 Control environment	**2100** Nature of Work
4,5,6 Audit planning	**2200** Engagement Planning
7 Audit evidence	**2300** Performing the Engagement
8,9 Use of experts	**2000** Managing the Internal Audit Activity
10,11 Audit reporting	**2400** Communicating Results
12,13,	
14,15 Audit documentation	**2300** Performing the Engagement

Figure 13.7   Links Between AA1000 Auditing Principles/Guidelines
And The IIA Professional Practices Framework
Sources: Institute of Social and Ethical Accountability (1999) The IIA (2000)
Arrangement by J. Ridley (2000)

Despite the importance now being given to social responsibility and its significance in good corporate governance there is still little evidence that many internal auditors are taking a proactive role in social responsibility auditing or reporting. Yet, there can be few internal audits that do not touch on social responsibilities.

In a recent revised exposure draft for a new Code of Ethics[1] for professional internal auditors, The IIA sees the code's purpose as '*. . . to promote an ethical culture in the international profession of internal auditing'.* The new code

---

[1] *Revised Code of Ethics – Second Exposure Draft* (2000), The IIA.

revises an existing code, providing guidance principles and rules of conduct for
the proficiency of all IIA members. The IIA–UK & Ireland recently published a
professional briefing note[m] on social and ethical responsibilities. This professional statement sees every corporate decision as having a social impact, for
good or bad. It recognizes economic implications in societal decision making
and the increasing influence of governments looking '. . . *to business to take a
leading role in repairing and improving the basic fabric of society'*. The statement does not '. . . *set out a proscribed role for internal audit in this area but
rather to raise awareness of the issues'*. No attempt is made to recommend how
internal auditors should audit or otherwise become involved in social or ethical
responsibilities.

The ISEA has established an internal auditing learning network for internal auditors employed by its members. This group now meets quarterly to share their social
and ethical responsibility practices and developments. A recent article in the ISEA
journal *AccountAbility*[n] demonstrated how one internal auditing group in the UK
participated in a social accounting and reporting exercise in their organization.
Internal auditing reviewed the systems involved, provided advice during dialogue
with all stakeholders and audited the collection and analysis of data. The resulting assurance and consulting work is stated as adding significant value to the final
reporting.

The importance of social responsibility for good governance will continue to
grow across the world. This is a high priority for most governments and global
organizations and institutions. It is essential that all audit committees recognize this
trend and ensure that their internal auditors include these responsibilities in the
scope of their charters and services they provide. The following actions should be
pursued by all internal auditing functions:

1. Commitment to a code of ethics for all internal auditing staff – one established
   by the organization it serves or The IIA code for professional internal auditing,
   preferably both!
2. Understand what is meant by social responsibility across the supply chains in
   which the organization operates. Create a learning programme for internal audit
   staff for this understanding. Keep it up to date.
3. Establish links between social responsibility and governance principles across
   the organization, at strategic and operational levels. Assess the key risks associated with social responsibility. Ensure these are seen in all risk assessment
   processes and internal auditing scopes of work, audit tests and other services
   being provided to management and the board.
4. Look for ways to assist in the integration of economic, social and environmental
   issues in management, accounting, auditing and reporting activities.
5. Include social, environmental, health and safety policies and practices in every
   audit.
6. Be involved in any external social auditing of the organization.

---

[m] *Ethics and Social Responsibility*, PBN 15 (1999), IIA–UK & Ireland.
[n] 'The Contribution of Internal Audit to Stakeholder Engagement', Ian Birchmore, *AccountAbility Quarterly*, 1st Quarter
2000, ISEA, London, England.

7. **Benchmark internal auditing involvement in social and ethical management, accounting, auditing and reporting across the organization's supply chain sector/s and nationally.**

The IIA in development of its current *International Professional Practices Framework* (PPF) for internal auditors introduced its Practice Advisory 2130-1: *Role of the Internal Audit Activity and Internal Auditor in the Ethical Culture of an Organization* in 2001. The development of this guidance brought into the definition of governance the interests of society and stakeholders:

2. An organization uses various legal forms, structures, strategies, and procedures to ensure that it:
   - Complies with society's legal and regulatory rules.
   - Satisfies the generally accepted business norms, ethical precepts, and social expectations of society.
   - Provides overall benefit to society and enhances the interests of the specific stakeholders in both the long-and short-term.
   - Reports fully and truthfully to its owners, regulators, other stakeholders, and general public to ensure accountability for its decisions, actions, conduct, and performance.

This guidance is still in its PPF and recognizes an active role for internal auditing in the above governance processes:

5. Internal auditors and the internal audit activity should take an active role in support of the organization's ethical culture. They should possess a high level of trust and integrity within the organization and the skills to be effective advocates of ethical conduct. They have the competence and capacity to appeal to the enterprise's leaders, managers, and other employees to comply with the legal, ethical, and societal responsibilities of the organization.

It goes on to recommend that the features internal auditors should look for in an *'enhanced, highly effective ethical culture'*. Of these, regular surveys, of the perceptions of employees/suppliers/customers, to determine the ethical climate in the organization is a key measure of the organization's reputation.

At this stage I have discussed only a little concerning the importance of health and safety in the need and desire for a good reputation. There can be few, if any, activities in any organization that do not impact on the health and safety of some, if not all, of its stakeholders. There is also ample evidence that organizations ignoring this do so at significant risk. Health and safety in an organization and all its products and services should be, and usually is, highly regulated and inspected: it should also be, and usually is, a key objective and performance indicator. The qualifications of 'should be' in both the preceding statements are because this is not always so! Accidents do happen and continue to happen, for whatever reason, whether neglect, inefficiency, ineffectiveness or act of God! And the penalties can be high.

Article:
Skeletons In The Closet[12] (2001)

Organizations need to assess and manage non-conventional risks '... *such as health, safety, envi*ronmental, reputation *and business probity* issues'. This 1999 rec-ommendation by the Turnbull[o] working party has focused many managers, inte-rnal auditors and consultants on an

> '*What can be more important than health, safety and the environment?*'

area I believe to have been neglected in internal audit planning processes in the past. My understanding is that in all these issues too few internal auditing teams (and audit committees) spend enough time assessing the associated risks. Is it that they do not have the right skills and competencies to do so? I do not think so. There are many able internal auditors, consultants and audit committee members with the right knowledge and experience. Is it then because these issues are not seen as important, or as important as other issues?

What can be more important than health, safety and the environment? All are now well covered by legal requirements and formal assessment programmes, both internal and external to an organization. Such programmes are of immense importance to all stakeholders. The societal implications of adverse publicity linked to these issues can result in significant impacts on both an organization's reputation and survival. Not to mention the personal impacts on those that direct, manage and work in the organization. Ask the following question to the internal audit team and audit committee:

> When did you last review the strategies, policies, audit planning and results for these programmes?

The answers may surprise you!

Reputation and business probity auditing is less well defined, both by law and assessment programmes. Some may argue that this auditing is part of every strategy, policy and action in an organization. Certainly, it can be linked to all of the above issues as well as quality, relationships with all stakeholders and brand management. Reputation and probity are fundamental for all good vision statements and related key objectives. Every audit assessment programme should include questions concerning these issues. But is this always so? Test your internal audit assessment programmes and audit committee agendas. When were these issues last assessed and the results reviewed at top management levels?

One of the problems concerning reputation and probity issues is that there is no common standard to benchmark against. Both terms mean different things to different people. They have both narrow and wide definitions. A good attempt to

---

[o] *Internal Control – Guidance to Directors on the Combined Code* (1999), Institute of Chartered Accountants in England and Wales, London, England.

provide guidance to their meaning is in the recently published IIA–UK & Ireland Professional Briefing Note 15 – *Ethics and Social Responsibility*:

> Probity is defined as uprightness, honesty. Does the organization conduct its business in an open, transparent, honest and trustworthy manner? And, does it behave ethically and socially responsibly, not only in its business dealings, but in its attitudes to and, recognition of society's concerns and needs?

> Reputation is defined as what is generally said about a person's or organization's character or standing: the state of being well thought, of distinction, respectability.

Both probity and reputation are influenced by how an organization conducts itself. The perception of its conduct is as important as the conduct itself.

INTERNAL AUDITING AND GOOD REPUTATIONS 2001 TO 2006

The 21st century has seen significant changes in the regulation of requirements by society and focus on health, safety and environmental issues. Not just nationally, but also across the globe. Many of these changes build on previous concerns, some are new, reflecting the dynamic risks associated with all of these issues and their impact on organization reputations. There can be few if any organizations that do not address reputation risk today, although their interpretation of what this means will vary. What should not be argued is that any assessment of reputation risk must contain the interests and issues of society and the environment, not just nationally or regionally but globally, including the health and safety of all the world's citizens. Today, many global organizations are working to make this happen.

The IIA also included in its PPF in 2003 a Practice Advisory 2100-7: *Internal Auditor's Role in Identifying and Reporting Environmental Risks*, introduced by '*Chief Audit executive (CAE) should include the environmental, health, and safety (EH&S) risks in any entity-wide risk management assessment and assess the activities in a balanced manner relative to other types of risk associated with an entity's operations*'. This guidance was based on research into EH&S auditing. Suggestions are made that the CAE should develop close working relationships with those responsible in an organization for environmental management and audit issues, if these do not rest in the internal audit activity. The CAE should also evaluate the reporting of environmental issues at board level. This recognition in the PPF is a further step in recognizing the importance of such reviews and need for cutting edge resources and practices in internal auditing to make them happen.

Jenny Rayner (2001)[13] researched and published best practices in managing reputation risks. Identified were the major sources of such risks which, if managed effectively, can result in reputation being enhanced:

    financial performance and profitability
    corporate governance and quality of management
    social, ethical and environmental performance
    employees and corporate culture
    marketing, innovation and customer relations
    regulatory compliance and litigation
    communications and crisis management

She also listed the following components, as recognized by leaders of reputation risk as being at the heart of their approach to its management:

- a clear vision: 'what we stand for and are prepared to be held responsible for';
- clear values, supported by a code of conduct, setting out expected standards of behaviour;
- policies clearly stating performance expectations and 'risk tolerance' in key areas;
- understanding of stakeholders' expectations, information requirements and perceptions of the organization;
- an open, trusting, supportive culture;
- a robust and dynamic risk management system, which provides early warning of developing issues;
- organizational learning leading to corrective action where necessary;
- reward and recognition systems, which support organizational goals and values;
- extension of vision and values to major partners and suppliers;
- open and honest communications tailored to meet the needs of specific stakeholders.

Cutting edge internal auditing resources and planning should be addressing each of the major drivers of risks to reputation using the above-listed components at the heart of their practices. Are you doing all of this? Compare the listed components with my need for and desire to have a good reputation in Figure 13.1 at the beginning of the chapter.

The IIA–UK & Ireland followed its 1999 Professional Briefing Note Fifteen with a number of statements on social and environmental issues, written by Walter Raven. The first, in May 2002, described triple bottom line reporting; the second, in July 2002, covered assurance on sustainability, environmental and social responsibilities. Neither mentioned an internal auditing role. The third, in March 2003, discussed emerging social responsibility issues such as trust, materiality, brand and internal auditing. This included the following on internal auditing:

> The internal auditor is a vital conduit to the creation of trust. The internal auditor is already contributing to a number of CSR and sustainability issues by keeping management informed on aspects of operational and compliance issues, which is part of their core function, as well as brand management audits and through participation in the stakeholder dialogue process. Also, the increasing importance of CSR and sustainability and its impact on risk management brings additional challenges involving the control environment, including the provision and installation of effective management and reporting systems, which will provide clarity and transparency, and therefore trust.

and:

> The internal auditor . . . has a key role to play in determining the materiality of the content of the CSR and sustainability report. This is a responsibility that can only increase with the burgeoning of CSR and sustainability reports, both in volume and size of content.

The fourth, in May 2003, discussed the AA1000 Assurance Standard, developed and promoted by the Institute of Social and Ethical Accountability. All were published with the intention of keeping these issues at the forefront of internal auditing.

At the time of the fourth report The IIA–UK & Ireland also published a Professional Issues Bulletin – *Ethical and Social Auditing and Reporting – The Challenge for the Internal*

Auditor. This still makes excellent reading today for the internal auditor starting down the path of social and environmental assurance and consulting. It concludes that '... *ethics and social responsibility are not seen as optional add-ons, but as essential constituents of the strategic and long-term planning process.*' Its reference to corporate reputation is of interest in this chapter:

> Corporate reputation is inextricably linked to the management of ethics and social responsibility. Reputation management is equivalent to public trust building, and is a long-term exercise. Organizations must be seen to act proactively to ensure that trust is maintained. A good reputation grows out of good behaviour.

Business in the Community (BITC) introduced its case for corporate responsibility in 2003[14] with the following Foreword from its chairman:

> We live in an increasingly complex and sceptical world. Corporate scandals, stock market downturn, uncertain economy, threat of terrorism – all have diminished trust in the corporate sector and its leaders. Companies have to address this, individually by demonstrating their positive impact on society and collectively by developing comparative meaningful measures by which to report their progress against. Corporate Responsibility is not a fad, but an imperative. Yet even as it becomes more mainstream, stakeholders are becoming more critical, and the standards for meaningful social interaction are rising.
>
> Business in the Community has been in existence for 21 years, but the need for it has never been greater. The need to inspire and engage more companies and the importance of sharing best practice and learning has never been more vital. Therefore, I welcome the opportunity for this joint publication with Arthur D. Little and the simplicity with which it sets out the compelling arguments for companies, large and small, to integrate responsible business practices into the very heart of their operations. In the coming year Business in the Community will use this document and work more intensely to ensure the accurate reporting of corporate impact on society, without which there cannot be sympathetic consideration of the real challenges and dilemmas companies face.

The paper is then introduced by:

> Companies that embrace Corporate Responsibility recognize that their social and environmental impacts have to be managed in just the same way as their economic or commercial performance. But getting started, putting Corporate Responsibility principles into practice, can be difficult and many companies struggle to justify the management of social and environmental affairs in terms of tangible business benefit.
>
> Corporate Responsibility should be seen as a journey rather than a destination, and as society's expectations of business continue to get more demanding, the sooner companies start out the better. In recent years much has been written about the subject and the business imperatives. There are six commonly recognized benefits that can be gained from an effective business-led approach:

Reputation management
Risk management
Employee satisfaction
Innovation and learning
Access to capital
Financial performance

This publication contains excellent key messages for each of the above benefits, including for reputation management:

> Corporate Responsibility offers a means by which companies can manage and influence the attitudes and perceptions of their stakeholders, building their trust and enabling the benefits of positive relationships to deliver business advantage.

Links between corporate responsibility, stakeholder perceptions and business advantage are strong messages throughout the publication as the benefits of good social and environmental performances are discussed.

As mentioned earlier, reputation management in the public sector has also been seen as important by successive United Kingdom governments, since before and after the Citizen's Charter of 1991. Current risk management guidance, published in 2004 by HM Treasury, includes 'Reputation' as a category of risk, describing this as *'Confidence and trust which stakeholders have in the organization'*. It interestingly notes that this risk is not (fully) transferable:

> in particular it is generally not possible to transfer reputational risk even if the delivery of a service is contracted out. The relationship with the third party to which risk is transferred needs to be carefully managed to ensure successful transfer of risk.

This is advice that is well worth listening to in the other sectors as the transfer of manufacturing products and providing services between organizations continues to grow. This can also be extended into suppliers and partners.

The Independent Commission for Good Governance in the Public Services (2004)[15] chaired by Sir Alan Langlands developed governance standards for the public services, including the promotion of values for the organization and demonstrating these through behaviour:

> Good governance flows from a shared ethos or culture, as well as from systems and structures. It cannot be reduced to a set of rules, or achieved fully by compliance with a set of requirements. This spirit or ethos of good governance can be expressed as values and demonstrated in behaviour.

> Good governance builds on the seven principles for the conduct of people in public life that were established by the Committee on Standards in Public Life. Known as the Nolan principles: selflessness, integrity, objectivity, accountability, openness, honesty and leadership. *[As discussed earlier in this chapter]*

This review recommends the six core governance principles in Figure 13.8 for all organizations in the public sector.

CIPFA (2007)[16] revised its 2001 corporate governance framework for use in local government with a new framework introduced by:

> Good governance leads to good management, good performance, good stewardship of public money, good public engagement and ultimately, good outcomes for citizens and service users. Good governance enables an authority to pursue its vision effectively as well as underpinning that vision with mechanisms for control and management of risk. All authorities should aim to meet the standards of the best and governance arrangements should not only be sound but also be seen to be sound.

Its new framework is based on the six core principles recommended in the Langlands (2004) review shown in Figure 13.8, adapted for local government purposes. Supporting

The standard comprises six core principles of good governance, each with its supporting principles.

1. **Good governance means focusing on the organization's purpose and on outcomes for citizens and service users**
   1.1 Being clear about the organization's purpose and its intended outcomes for citizens and service users
   1.2 Making sure that users receive a high quality service
   1.3 Making sure that taxpayers receive value for money

2. **Good governance means performing effectively in clearly defined functions and roles**
   2.1 Being clear about the functions of the governing body
   2.2 Being clear about the responsibilities of non-executives and the executive, and making sure that those responsibilities are carried out
   2.3 Being clear about relationships between governors and the public

3. **Good governance means promoting values for the whole organization and demonstrating the values of good governance through behaviour**
   3.1 Putting organizational values into practice
   3.2 Individual governors behaving in ways that uphold and exemplify effective governance

4. **Good governance means taking informed, transparent decisions and managing risk**
   4.1 Being rigorous and transparent about how decisions are taken
   4.2 Having and using good quality information, advice and support
   4.3 Making sure that an effective risk management system is in operation

5. **Good governance means developing the capacity and capability of the governing body to be effective**
   5.1 Making sure that appointed and elected governors have the skills, knowledge and experience they need to perform well
   5.2 Developing the capability of people with governance responsibilities and evaluating their performance, as individuals and as a group
   5.3 Striking a balance, in the membership of the governing body, between continuity and renewal

6. **Good governance means engaging stakeholders and making accountability real**
   6.1 Understanding formal and informal accountability relationships
   6.2 Taking an active and planned approach to dialogue with and accountability to the public
   6.3 Taking an active and planned approach to responsibility to staff
   6.4 Engaging effectively with institutional stakeholders

Figure 13.8 Principles Of Good Governance For The Public Sector
Source: *Good Governance Standard for Public Services* (2004)

the framework is guidance for how it can be implemented: guidance with many reputation messages for organizations in all sector.

Risk management has always been an important tool for analysing and evaluating risks and opportunities for an organization's reputation, including establishing its risk appetite. COSO (2004)[17] recognizes this in its Enterprise Risk Management (ERM) model:

> Enterprise risk management helps to ensure effective reporting and compliance with laws and regulations, and helps to avoid damage to the entity's reputation and associated consequences. In sum, enterprise risk management helps an entity to get to where it wants to go and avoid pitfalls and surprises along the way.

No attempt is made in this book to discuss the concept of ERM. Others have written much already about this in textbooks, including position papers by The IIA and IIA–UK & Ireland, available on their websites. There have also been many research reports and will be more.

One of the most recent is that by James Roth with Donald Esperen, Daniel Swanson and contributing author Paul Sobel (2007).[18] This explains ERM, and opportunities for its use in Sarbanes–Oxley compliance, detailing four case study approaches to its implementation. Each of these approaches includes many reputation risks.

In 2005 a group of *'voluntary sector infrastructure bodies'*[19] developed and endorsed a good governance code for the voluntary sector, based on Cadbury's three principles of good governance – openness, integrity and accountability. The code also recognizes the Langland's governance standards, the Nolan principles and managing risk and control, including suggesting for larger organizations' audit committees and internal audit services; and uniquely social issues, such as health and safety, equality, diversity, discrimination. Included in managing risks is:

> C9   The board must avoid undertaking activities which might place at undue risk the organization's service users, beneficiaries, volunteers, staff, property, assets or reputation.

Interestingly this governance code, which is voluntary, also brings into internal control requirements a need to consider '. . . *adoption of an appropriate quality assurance system, or other forms of accreditation'*, including references to ISO 9000, the Business Excellence Model, Charter Mark, Investors in People UK and Social Accounting and Auditing. In the introduction to the code the chairman of the UK government Charity Commission (the charity regulator) encourages charities to adopt good governance practices:

> We have worked with our voluntary sector partners to develop this code of governance. It has been produced by the sector, from the sector and for the sector. The code provides a flexible and proportionate framework for charities; there are common standards to which all charities should aspire, with higher expectations of larger charities. We shall watch with interest to see how charities meet the challenge of complying with the code.

Under this code a charity is not required to report compliance but is expected to be *'open and accountable to stakeholders about its own work, and the governance of the organization'*.

Once again the concept of good governance flowing from a culture of the Nolan principles, as well as systems and structures, is seen. Does this point the way for a new skill for the cutting edge internal auditor to develop? That is, the ability to form an opinion on the culture of the organization being reviewed as well as examine systems, structures and documentation against approved strategies, policies and operating procedures. The Citizen's Charter mentioned earlier recognizes culture as fundamental to the reforms it promoted. *'There is a well-spring of talent, energy, care and commitment in our public services.'* Nolan's 1995 seven principles endorsed this, providing a framework for the 'talent, energy, care and commitment', as a culture and Langlands continued this using the seven principles as fundamental to good corporate governance:

> It is perhaps surprising that there is no common code for public service governance to provide guidance across the complex and diverse world of public services, which are provided by the public sector and a range of other agencies. The *Good Governance Standard for Public Services* addresses this issue head on. It builds on the Nolan principles for the conduct of individuals in public life, by setting out six core principles of good governance for public service organizations. It shows how these should be applied if organizations are to live up to the Standard and provides a basis for the public to challenge sub-standard governance.

The six core principles are shown with supporting principles in Figure 13.8. Each can have reputation risks. Currently a review of the reach of this standard across the public sector and internationally is ongoing.

Sustainability is now the reputation issue of the day. Savitz and Weber (2006)[20] describe the growing use today of the term 'sustainability' in association with the way organizations approach social and environmental issues:

> Sustainability has ... become a buzzword for an array of social and environmental causes, and in the business world it denotes a powerful and defining idea: *a sustainable corporation is one that creates profit for its shareholders while protecting the environment and improving the lives of those with whom it interacts.* It operates so that its business interests and the interests of the environment and society intersect.

They see organizations that are sustainable as those that are not only responsible ethically, socially and environmentally but also enjoy benefits from that responsibility. They see sustainability as addressing *'a wide array of business concerns about the natural environment, workers' rights, consumer protection, and corporate governance, as well as the impact of business behaviour on broader social issues, such as hunger, poverty, education, health care, and human rights – and the relationship of all these to profit'.*

The convergence of social, health, safety, environmental, governance and sustainability responsibilities into a broad 'corporate responsibility' umbrella is now being recognized by many researchers and those promoting these responsibilities. This convergence will continue well into the future with a commitment from many global leaders – political and business. More and more governance principles are including all these issues as part of good governance in every organization.

Article:
All Professional Institutes Should Be Involved In Social Responsibility Issues – So Should All Internal Auditors[21] (2006)

In the mid 1970s, when I was president of the IIA United Kingdom Chapter (now the IIA–UK & Ireland), I chose as the theme for my year of office – *The Future is Ours.* This is just as important today for all professional institutes and their members, as they face and shape the opportunities and challenges of today's future. In my presidential address, 30 years ago, I started with the following observation of then current issues:

> *'There are clearly many opportunities for internal auditors to add value to their organization's sustainability ...'*

> We live in times of high economic risk and important social and business decisions. Every day we are reminded at work, in newspapers and by television of the opportunities that can be taken to develop ourselves and the profession we have chosen. The apparent insoluble problems of the present economic situation; the controversial discussions caused by

exposure drafts and new accounting practices; involvement in the European Community; a new awareness of social responsibilities; higher health and safety standards; clearly recognized needs for more efficient manpower planning and training; the urgency of energy saving; the complexity of advanced computer technology. These are all issues management cannot ignore and neither can we, as internal auditors. To be successful we must be sensitive to the problems of each day. All can have an impact on our professional activities far beyond any changes we may foresee at the present time.

These issues are still with us in the 21st century; although they are now more complex and some require urgent solutions. The Institute of Internal Auditors and its affiliated National Institutes, Chapters and many internal auditors have made much happen since my address. Many opportunities have been seized in the shaping of today's professional internal auditing. But there is still much to do, particularly in our approach as institutes and internal auditors to the social responsibilities of the organizations we are members of and serve, and our recognition by governments and the public.

What is social responsibility? Most governments and many organizations now define this widely to include any issues that impact people at organization, community, national and global levels. The Global Reporting Initiative (GRI)[p] defines social responsibility as part of sustainability, and sustainability as '. . . *one of the three ideas that are playing a pivotal role in shaping how business and other organizations operate in the 21st century'*. The other two ideas stated by GRI are accountability and governance. This linking into governance is an important statement for internal auditors. Sustainability developments should be seen as part of every organization's governance in all sectors – private, public and voluntary. They are an integral part of all risk management and control processes, and as important as quality and economic performance, if not more so. Though some may challenge this statement. And many do!

In the GRI reporting principles, sustainability reporting is seen as the placing of economic performance in the context of broader ecological and social issues. The now well-known 'triple-bottom line' reporting of economic, social and environmental performance, promoted by GRI, has been adopted by many organizations as part of their annual reporting to stakeholders. The European Commission and national governments in Europe, if not the world, have been and are continuing to make many of the reporting guidelines promoted by GRI to be recommended requirements (and in some cases legal/regulatory).

Organizations have always been responsible for the impact they have on others and the environment. There is sufficient evidence available to know that this responsibility is not always recognized, or accepted efficiently, effectively and economically. Some organizations today measure, monitor and report this acceptance as part of their public relations and financial reporting. Some do this well, winning awards in the process. But research shows that there are still many organizations that do not measure, monitor and report their sustainability responsibilities.

---

[p] *Sustainability Reporting Guidelines* (2002), Global Reporting Initiative. www.globalreporting.org

Recent research published by McKinsey,[q] studying the role of corporations in society, supports this view for organizations in the private sector. But what of the public and voluntary sectors?

There are clearly many opportunities for internal auditors to add value to their organization's sustainability development performances and reporting. The IIA maintains a useful repository in the 'Guidance' section of its website. Visit www.theiia.org and search for 'sustainable development'. This leads you into a network of other websites related to sustainable issues, including the Board of Environmental, Health and Safety Auditor Certifications (BEAC). BEAC[r] was originally created as an education joint venture with the IIA to promote itself as a worldwide certification board for specialty sustainable auditors. The IIA *International Standards* and supporting guidelines cover aspects of social responsibility and environmental performance. The former as part of the ethics and values needed for good governance, and the latter as part of risk management. The IIA Certified Internal Auditor examination programme examines at proficiency and awareness levels various aspects of sustainability. But is the extent of this covered sufficiently for the 21st century?

The IIA–UK & Ireland has many useful articles on social responsibility on its website pages – www.iia.org.uk It published in 1999 a Professional Briefing Note (PBN Fifteen)[s] for internal auditors' *Ethics and Social Responsibility*. This PBN is referenced into in Bruce Fraser's[t] *Corporate Social Responsibility* cover story in the February 2005 issue of The IIA's *Internal Auditor* journal. Do read this article if you have not done so already.

Laws and guidelines for measuring sustainable developments, monitoring their performance and reporting are evolving across the European Community, if not the world. The latest communication from the European Commission[u] on its Social Agenda states '... *the sustainable development of Europe (is) based on balanced economic growth and price stability, a highly competitive social market economy, aiming at full employment and social progress and a high level protection and improvement of the quality of the environment'*. There can be few that will argue against such a vision.

The European Union Accounts Modernization Directive increases organization-reporting requirements on non-financial comment and analysis, including environmental and employee matters. The UK government has now issued reporting requirements for environmental key performance indicators,

---

[q] *Global Survey of Business Executives: Business and Society* (2006), McKinsey. www.mckinseytquarterly.com

[r] BEAC is an independent, nonprofit corporation established in 1997 to issue professional certifications to environmental, health and safety auditing and other scientific fields. BEAC was originally created as a joint venture between The IIA and the Auditing Roundtable Inc. (Roundtable). www.beac.org

[s] *Ethics and Social Responsibility* discusses these issues concluding with *'There can be no doubt that ethical and social responsible behaviour has become a major management issue. It will remain so. Just as important is the requirement for management to develop the processes and systems for its effective management. This is particularly important in the area of risk management.'*

[t] Bruce Fraser writes: *'There is broad agreement for the future, chief audit executives need to ensure that social responsibility is on the board's agenda of corporate governance issues. They should be aware of existing standards and global initiatives as they relate to CSR and use them as yardsticks against which to measure their organization's performance. Additionally, auditors should advise the board on identified best practices and determine whether their organization's core values and code of conduct still reflect the desired position of the enterprise in today's and tomorrow's world.'*

[u] *Communication on the Social Agenda*, European Commission, 2005. www.europa.eu.int/comm

recognizing '... *that good environmental performance makes good business sense'.* These guidelines include reporting on emissions to air/water/land, resource use, supply chains and products. Other governments in Europe will be addressing the EU modernization directive as appropriate. This directive will change many future reporting requirements for the private sector in the European Union.

Today there is daily discussion in the media concerning government and organization social and environmental responsibilities. As I write this article the confectionery industry in the UK has made a move towards issuing health warnings on packaging for snack foods. Such warnings will not stop but spread across many industries and grow both in volume and importance. Good governance practices will dictate that this will happen.

So, what are governments, organizations, professional institutes and professional internal auditors doing about it? What should we be doing about it? How do you start? The beginning must always be a strategic objective. There should be a vision and measurable missions in all organizations for sustainable developments to be linked into economic performances. This applies equally to governments and professional institutes as it does to organizations in all sectors. Has your National Institute or Chapter such a vision and mission?

The UK government currently supports an academy[v] to develop and promote social responsibility competencies through training and development programmes at business schools and in professional institutes. It has recently launched a measurable framework designed to help organizations to integrate social responsibility into decision making and operations. Other nations in Europe will have developed their own approaches. It is important that each has its own programmes for social responsibility skills and education.

Results from a 2005 worldwide IIA Flash Survey[w] completed by 163 internal audit activities demonstrate some internal audit involvement in sustainable development in their organizations – only one-third of respondents confirming this and two-thirds stating no involvement. The results are not analysed by country; however, many of those responding see a growth of this involvement in the future.

So some internal auditors in Europe may already be contributing to make sustainability development part of their risk-based audit and engagement planning. Will others follow? In recent research in the UK into the governance of social responsibility in a selection of large UK companies – Rewarding Virtue[x] – links are drawn between good governance practices and social responsibility. Results support a need for social responsibility in all organizations '... *to be backed by a powerful system of incentives and sanctions – including laws, regulations, taxes and subsidies, licences and fines, and market-based instruments – that change the shape of markets and create material opportunities and risks for companies'.* All this is happening today and will continue to happen in the future. This research is supported by a number of live case studies. One describes the role of an internal audit activity

---

[v] The CSR Academy aims to promote CSR learning through the first dedicated *CSR Competency Framework*. The Academy is supported by the Department of Trade and Industry. www.csracademy.org.uk
[w] Downloaded from www.theiia.org/gain/sdsum.htm, 12 February 2006.
[x] *Rewarding Virtue – Effective Board Action on Corporate Responsibility* (2005), Business in the Community (BITC), London, England. www.bitc.org.uk

in one organization's social responsibility risk management and assurance processes. A case study with some good messages for internal auditing and a good starting benchmark for all internal audit activities in Europe and worldwide. But only a starting benchmark.

CUTTING EDGE INTERNAL AUDITING CONTRIBUTES TO GOOD REPUTATIONS TODAY AND IN THE FUTURE

The United Nations Global Compact in 2000,[22] challenged business leaders to join a new international initiative to support universal environmental and social principles. Its developed 10 principles in the areas of human rights, labour, the environment and anti-corruption continue to be promoted today and will be tomorrow. Consider how each relates to what has already been discussed in this chapter and preceding chapters; and note the focus on human rights and labour standards as social challenges:

Human Rights
Principle 1: Businesses should support and respect the protection of internationally proclaimed human rights; and
Principle 2: Make sure that they are not complicit in human rights abuses.

Labour Standards
Principle 3: Businesses should uphold the freedom of association and the effective recognition of the right to collective bargaining;
Principle 4: The elimination of all forms of forced and compulsory labour;
Principle 5: The effective abolition of child labour; and
Principle 6: The elimination of discrimination in respect of employment and occupation.

Environment
Principle 7: Businesses should support a precautionary approach to environmental challenges;
Principle 8: Undertake initiatives to promote greater environmental responsibility; and
Principle 9: Encourage the development and diffusion of environmental technologies.

Anti-Corruption
Principle 10: Businesses should work against corruption in all its forms, including extortion and bribery.

In July 2007 its Leaders Summit in Geneva had the following Agenda, reflecting its focus into the future:

- Current megatrends in corporate responsibility
- Advancing the Compact's mission and principles
- Embedding human rights, labour, environmental and anti-corruption principles into business strategies and operations and education
- Climate change.

These are clearly universal issues and challenges, which impact all businesses in the world, and the public sector too, including governments in every nation.

The International Organization for Standardization[23] is developing a new international standard giving guidance on social responsibility (SR) – ISO 26000. Its target date for launch is currently early 2009. A memorandum of Understanding (MoU) has been reached with the United Nations Global Compact Office for cooperation on this project:

> ISO has emphasized since launching its SR initiative that its standard will complement and add value to existing public and private sector initiatives in the field, including declarations and conventions of the United Nations and its constituent organizations. In line with this approach, the MoU will help to ensure consistency between ISO 26000 and the 10 Global Compact principles, which address human rights, labour, the environment and anti-corruption.

The IIA (2006)[24] recognizes the broad 'corporate responsibility' governance umbrella. Its position paper and guidance for internal auditors performing specific governance-related tasks discusses governance outputs as a broad concept:

> **Completeness of Ethics Policies and Codes of Conduct.** Most organizations have ethics policies and codes of conduct that govern acceptable employee behaviour and represent a key part of the organization's governance structure. Internal auditors can assess whether their organization's policies and codes include appropriate subjects and guidance. A number of codes of conduct are available for comparison. Most contain sections addressing conflicts of interest; confidentiality; fair dealing; proper use of organization assets; compliance with laws, rules, and regulations; and reporting of illegal or unethical behaviour.

> **Transparency and Disclosure**. Organizations commonly report financial results and information to key stakeholders and increasingly are reporting more than financial results. Reporting on social responsibility, efforts to preserve the environment, and other social issues are becoming common. Communicating an organization's values regarding stewardship, management practices, employee relations, and other topics often shows an organization's culture and tone. The transparency of financial and non-financial disclosures to stakeholders is a key element of governance.

It recommends that internal auditors *'should consider assisting management and the board'* by assessing a wide definition of governance, including the above. Cutting edge internal auditors will already be doing this and more.

In the UK, Tomorrow's Company (2006)[25] concluded its publication on climate change stating *'. . . businesses which aim to be global leaders into the long-term have a critical role in helping to steer the global community towards sustainability . . . '*. It goes on to say in its conclusions:

> The shape of that role is clear because it is already being demonstrated by progressive global businesses and their leaders. It is to educate consumers, influence suppliers, create strong partnerships, demonstrate low-carbon solutions, and to use the authority that flows from leadership of successful global enterprises to persuade policy-makers to seize the moment and reach an agreement that harnesses the power of business to preserve the world for future generations.

Are internal auditing resources and practices also 'seizing the moment' today in businesses and other sectors to make a contribution to the reputations of the organizations in their preservation of the world for future generations? Any that are including in their risk assessments and audit planning the concepts, principles and codes of best corporate responsibility practices discussed in this chapter, are at the cutting edge of their profession. The IIA *International Standards* and *Code of Ethics* give important support to all internal auditors in any reviews they conduct into health, safety and environmental strategies and practices in their organizations. Their customers should know of these standards and ethical statements and see these as a significant power in the value internal auditors add to their organization's reputation risk and its management.

In 2006, the UK Department for Environment Food and Rural Affairs[26] published its own voluntary guidelines for environmental key performance indicators (KPIs), discussing 22 KPIs relevant for measuring environmental performance in organizations, though recognizing that not all are necessary for every organization. Nevertheless this is a good starting point for all organizations to consider how they measure their environmental impact: if not also for all internal auditors addressing environmental impact in the services they provide, or should be providing. Its executive summary starts with:

> There is an increasing recognition that good environmental performance makes good business sense. Environmental risks and uncertainties impact to some extent on all companies, and affect investment decisions, consumer behaviour and Government policy. Management of energy, natural resources or waste will affect current performance; failure to plan for a future in which environmental factors are likely to be increasingly significant may risk the long-term future of a business.

The UK Health and Safety Executive[27] recently commissioned research into the relationship between occupational health and safety and the broader corporate responsibility umbrella seen today in many organizations. The researchers developed seven best practice principles, recommending these for future discussion. *'In summary, we found the key elements of good practice in OHS Governance are reflected by the seven key principles outlined below'*. The seven principles are shown in Figure 13.9. Note the strong links with all the other governance standards discussed earlier and importance of integrating occupational health and safety into all governance processes. How many audit committees today review their organization's health and safety responsibilities as part of their review of risk management, control and governance? How many internal audit activities do?

The Institute of Directors[28] provides considerable guidance for directors in their responsibilities for health and safety. In 2007, with the United Kingdom Health and Safety Executive its published consultation draft – *Leading Health and Safety at Work – Actions and Good Practice for Board Members* is addressed to board members and their equivalents across all sectors. This guidance develops essential principles for board members to follow to lead and promote health and safety in their organizations. It recognizes the following significant opportunities for better health and safety, including reputation:

- reduced costs and reduced risks – employee absence and turnover rates are lower, accidents are fewer, the threat of legal action is lessened;
- improved standing among suppliers and partners;
- a better reputation for social, responsibility among investors, customers and communities;
- increased productivity – employees are healthier, happier and better motivated.

All in keeping with the good reputation theme of this chapter and the corporate responsibilities discussed. What is excellent are the links it makes with wider corporate governance principles and practices:

Director competence

All directors should have a clear understanding of the key OHS issues for their business and be continually developing their skills and knowledge.

Director roles and responsibilities

All directors should understand their legal responsibilities and their role in governing OHS matters for their business. Their roles should be supported by formal individual terms of reference, covering as a minimum setting OHS policy and strategy development, setting standards, performance monitoring and internal control. At least one nominated director (which could be the Chairman or preferably one of the independent non-executive directors, where they exist) should have the additional role of overseeing and challenging the OHS governance process.

Culture, standards and values

The board of directors should take ownership for key OHS issues and be ambassadors for good OHS performance within the business, upholding core values and standards. They should set the right tone at the top and establish an open culture across the organization with a high level of communication both internally and externally on OHS issues.

Strategic implications

The board should be responsible for driving the OHS agenda, understanding the risks and opportunities associated with OHS matters and any market pressures which might compromise the values and standards, and ultimately establishing a strategy to respond.

Performance management

The board should set out the key objectives and targets for OHS management and create an incentive structure for senior executives which drives good OHS performance, balancing both leading and lagging indicators and capturing both tangible and intangible factors. Non executives (through the Remuneration Committee, where one exists) should be involved in establishing the appropriate incentive schemes.

Internal controls

The board should ensure that OHS risks are managed and controlled adequately and that a framework to ensure compliance with the core standards is established. It is important that the governance structures enable management systems, actions and levels of performance to be challenged. This process should utilise, where possible, existing internal control and audit structures and be reviewed by the audit committee.

Organizational structures

The board should integrate the OHS governance process into the main corporate governance structures within the business, including the activities of the main board and its subcommittees, including risk, remuneration and audit. In some cases, the creation of an additional board sub-committee to consider OHS (and/or Risk/Corporate Responsibility) may be relevant.

Figure 13.9   Best Practice Principles For Occupational Health & Safety (OHS) Governance
Source: Defining Best Practice in Corporate Occupational Health & Safety Governance (2006)

Corporate Governance

For many organizations, health and safety is a corporate governance issue. The board should integrate health and safety into the main corporate governance structures, including board sub-committees, such as risk, remuneration and audit.

The Turnbull guidance in the Combined Code on Corporate Governance requires listed companies to have robust systems of internal control, covering not just 'narrow' financial risks but also risks relating to the environment, business reputation and health and safety.

In 2007, the South West District of the IIA–UK & Ireland presented a cutting edge seminar on the UKs proposed Corporate Manslaughter Bill[29] and its impact on organizations at all levels (see Figure 13.10).

This Bill will have a significant influence on future health and safety policies in all organizations. Its requirements should influence future management of all health and safety risks, and as such internal auditing has a cutting edge contribution to make to ensure that such risks are identified, managed by the board and recognized in its own audit planning.

The Nolan seven principles of public life are still an excellent standard for a good reputation. In its 2006 *Annual Report*[30] the committee responsible for maintaining and promoting these principles reports:

Since its establishment in 1994, the Committee has responded positively to requests from the Foreign Office, other government departments and NGOs, to explain and promote overseas the UK's approach to standards of conduct in public life and, in particular, to the prevention of bribery and corruption. This year, for example, the Chair gave a seminar in Poland on Ethics in Parliamentary Work (which has, in part, led to the adoption in the Polish Parliament of a variant of the Seven Principles of Public Life) and the Secretary to the Committee acted as an expert evaluator for the Council of Europe's Groups of States against Corruption (USA and Turkey). The Committee has found that the UK has a high international reputation in such matters and many other countries wish to learn from our experience.

The annual report goes on to say that currently the committee is reviewing results of research to improve the wording of the principles in today's culture and governance standards. It will be interesting to see what the outcome of this will be. Internal auditing will have new opportunities to contribute to the domestic and international reputation of these principles in the future.

The UK Department of Trade and Industry CSR Academy, mentioned earlier, has been taken over by Business in the Community[31] from 31 March 2007. Launched in 2004 by the DTI, this Academy supports companies to develop the skills and competences to integrate CSR into their business. Its CSR Competency Framework '... *has been designed to be a flexible tool, meeting the needs of companies and organizations of all shapes and sizes'*. The framework '... *consists of six core characteristics that describe the way all managers need to act in order to integrate responsible business decision-making'*. These are:

Understanding society
Building capacity
Questioning business as usual
Stakeholder relations
Strategic view
Harnessing diversity

The Framework is designed for application across the full spectrum of business functions: operations: planning; supply chain; finance; human resources; and marketing. It sets out different levels of attainment for each characteristic, together with detailed behaviour patterns and case study examples. It includes the following scale for measuring the contribution a manager can make to corporate social responsibility in an organization. Which level are you at?

Health & Safety risk – Corporate manslaughter

Wednesday 17 January 2007

"Go to jail: go directly to jail, do not pass go, do not collect £200!"

Do you know the Health & Safety requirements for your organisation?

Are you breaking the law?

Could you be held to account?

What role can internal audit play?

Venue

Westland Conference & Leisure Complex, Westbourne Close, Yeovil BA20 2DD Tel: 01935 848380

See www.westlandonline.co.uk for map and directions

Health and Safety is a crucial area within every organisation, particularly with the growing trend for employees to sue their employers. Ignorance of the law is no excuse. This is an excellent opportunity to hear a variety of perspectives.

Attend this seminar to:

- Gain an understanding of the Health & Safety legal position
- Learn how internal audit can provide assurance that your organisation is on the correct side of the law
- Prepare for the new legislation – before it's too late

Guest speakers:

Derek Woodward
Local Principal Inspector, HSE

Kevin Bridges
Senior Associate, Pinsent Masons, Solicitors

Brian Oldham
H&S Manager, Somerset County Council

Dave Langford
H&S Manager, Lloyds TSB Bank plc

Figure 13.10   Health & Safety Risk – Corporate Manslaughter

Awareness   A broad appreciation of the core CSR characteristics and how they might impinge on business decision-making.

Understanding   A basic knowledge of some of the issues, with the competence to apply this to specific activities.

Application   The ability to supplement this basic knowledge of the issues with the competence to apply it to specific activities.

This seminar will provide you with best practice guidance on relevant aspects of Health & Safety, and enable you to prepare for the new Corporate Manslaughter legislation.

9.15   Registration/networking/coffee

9.45   Introduction
This introductory session will provide the background and basis for the day. It will cover the key elements of Health & Safety and Corporate Manslaughter

10.00   Health & Safety today – A guide to best practice
Derek Woodward is a local principal inspector for the HSE in Bristol. He will highlight key points of the Health & Safety at Work Act 1974, and then explain the practicalities of what these points mean. He will then highlight how we can check for compliance - and the consequences of failing to comply.

11.15   Corporate Manslaughter – the law and practical tips in avoiding prosecution
Kevin Bridges is an associate with Pinsent Masons, Solicitors, based in Bristol. In addition, he is also the current Chairman of the Institution of Occupational Safety & Health for the South West District. Kevin is going to explain the forthcoming legislation and provide some useful advice.

12.30   Lunch
Included in cost. Please let us know (when booking) of any special requirements.

13.45   A public sector example
Brian Oldham is the Health & Safety manager at Somerset County Council. Having followed the progress of the Corporate Manslaughter Bill for the last four years, Brian is perfectly placed to tell us how his council is facing up to the challenge.

15.00   A private sector example
Dave Langford is the Health & Safety Manager at Lloyds TSB Bank plc in Bristol. Dave will describe how such a large organisation is managing the risk of Corporate Manslaughter and what changes have had to be made. He will then look at key Corporate Governance issues and control measures to mitigate the risks of falling foul of the law.

16.15   Wrap up and close
This session will reiterate some of the key points from the day and allow for discussion of any final questions or problems.

Source: Reproduced with permission from the Institute of Internal Auditors UK & Ireland (2007)

Integration   An in-depth understanding of the issues and an expertise in embedding CSR into the business decision-making process.

Leadership   The ability to help managers across the organization to operate in a way that fully integrates CSR in the decision-making process.

Cutting edge internal auditing should be at the Leadership level.

Today, there is no excuse for any organization not recognizing the way it is governed includes an ethics strategy. The reasons for this are many and span an organization's relationships with all its stakeholders. The tone of its ethics has a significant contribution to make to its reputation, sustainability and long-term success. Philippa Foster Back OBE, Director, The Institute of Business Ethics (IBE) UK, at a presentation in 2007 used the message in Figure 13.11 to demonstrate the benefits from a business ethics strategy in every organization.

It is good corporate governance	THE CITIZEN CASE
It helps to develop a sustainable organization	THE ENVIRONMENT CASE
It is essential for risk reduction programmes	THE RISK MANAGEMENT CASE
It sustains a good reputation	THE PR CASE
It can enhance profitability in the long term	THE BUSINESS CASE

Figure 13.11   The Case For A Business Ethics Strategy
Source: The Institute of Business Ethics UK (2007)

In its publication *Living Up To Our Values*[32] the IBE promotes a responsible role for internal auditing in ethical assurance:

Box 13[33]   The Role of Internal Audit in Ethical Assurance

The internal auditor needs systematically to assess the company's climate and control environment as regards ethical policies and issues. Does the company have clear ethical codes, values and policies? Are they appropriate for the company and the ethical issues it faces? Do the board and the employees merely pay lip service to them or do they determine how people think or act? Internal audit needs to confirm that:

- an appropriate ethical culture is set by the board and permeates throughout the company;
- directors (both executive and non-executive) take an inclusive view, and an understanding of the key ethical risks and also opportunities *continued*;
- the company is fully aligned behind up-to-date relevant and appropriate ethical values, policies and codes of conduct, which help to guide behaviour and decision making in all areas of its operations;
- these policies are modified in the light of experience;
- ethical threats and opportunities are properly integrated into the strategic planning process;

and to check how well ethical issues are being identified, assessed and managed.
   This can be addressed by asking:

- Is management's response appropriate?
- Is all information sought and utilized in formulating a response?
- Are there appropriate early warning indicators and embedded monitors in respect of ethical issues and threats?
- How adequate are management's assurances on ethical risk management?
- Are ethical management systems in place, regularly reviewed and updated and subjected to external assessment?

In regard to all ethical issues, internal audit should check for:

- a clear understanding of the nature and extent of the issue;
- an analysis of its impact on the company in financial terms, its corporate and brand reputation and its risk profile;
- clear objectives are set and budgets agreed;
- a strategy and plan put in place;
- responsibilities allocated;
- progress monitored;
- the outcome reviewed and assessed against objectives and budget;

- stakeholder opinion sought and analysed;
- failures investigated
- further action if any agreed.

The internal auditor will play a key and vital role in determining the management processes and putting into place the relevant controls necessary to ensure effective ethical management. This will be combined with the equally important role of monitoring, and possibly auditing the ethical programme. It may also extend to a major participation in ethical reporting.

Professional internal auditing has a responsibility to promote each of these benefits and review the implementation of ethics in the organizations in which it provides services. The IIA recommends this in its *International Standards* and guidance statements.[34] That guidance offers many opportunities for the development of cutting edge internal auditing resources and practices:

6. Internal auditors and the internal audit activity should take an active role in support of the organization's ethical culture. They possess a high level of trust and integrity within the organization and the skills to be effective advocates of ethical conduct. They have the competence and capacity to appeal to the enterprise's leaders, managers, and other employees to comply with the legal, ethical, and societal responsibilities of the organization.

GoodCorporation, working in partnership with the Institute of Business Ethics, revised its *GoodCorporation Standard* in 2007.[35] This standard '... *is based on a core set of principles that define a framework for responsible management in any type of organization'*. The principles in the standard cover policies and procedures for Employees, Customers, Suppliers, Contractors, Community, Environment, Shareholders or equivalent and Management commitment, based on the following precept:

While the organization is accountable to its shareholders (or equivalent for not-for-profit organizations), it takes into account the interests of all its stakeholders including employees, customers and suppliers as well as the community and environment in which it operates. The organization aims to achieve clarity, fairness and effectiveness in the setting of policies and procedures, and it respects human rights as defined by the United Nations Global Compact and the Universal Declaration of Human Rights.

The standard is used by GoodCorporation to provide an independent assessment process looking at the following four levels of evidence for individual practices supporting the implementation of the eight principles.

That a policy exists
That a system is in place to implement the policy
That records exist which show that the system works in practice
That stakeholders, when asked, agree that the system works and is fair

The standard and process of assessment make a good benchmark for the assessment of an organization's management of its responsibilities and reputation in 2008 and beyond.

CHAPTER SUMMARY

The importance of reputation for an organization is critical to its survival. Its value is reflected in all stakeholder relationships. An important aspect of this reputation is its approach to social and environmental issues and challenges, including health and safety. These issues and challenges are now being addressed by many organizations under an umbrella of 'corporate responsibility' including recognition of and compliance with good corporate governance. The many concepts, principles and codes that make up this umbrella are converging and need to be addressed by an organization as a whole and not individually. Internal auditing is in an excellent position to contribute to an organization's good reputation through the independent professional services it provides, including the strength of its *International Standards* and *Code of Ethics*. Such a contribution will need cutting edge resources and practices.

The Gray and Gray (1997) motivational themes, goals and categories for innovation in internal auditing, including the additions and changes already made in Chapters 2 to 12, reflect some of the reputation issues and risks discussed in this chapter:

Motivations

1. Progress within the field of professional internal auditing.
2. Increasing competition leading to pressures to reduce costs and increase efficiency.
3. New challenges, such as increasing internal control risks due to staff reductions and restructuring.
4. Opportunities to increase efficiency and quality as a result of technological advances.
5. Changes in corporate management practices and philosophies, such as Total Quality Management, re-engineering, continuous quality improvement, or related approaches.
6. Challenges and opportunities of global issues and developments.
7. **Social and environmental issues impacting all organizations.**
8. **Recognition that professionalism, quality and standards are essential attributes for world-class status in any internal auditing activity.**
9. **Importance of organizational governance to meet regulatory and stakeholders' needs.**
10. **A continuous search for good and evil in how organizations and all their operations are directed and controlled.**
11. **Recognition that all types of crime in and by an organization should be fought.**
12. **Encouragement to think creatively.**

Goals

1. **Continuous** Improvement of the quality of internal auditing services.
2. **Achieve best practice by continuously benchmarking.**
3. Expansion of services to increase the value-added of internal auditing.
4. Boost staff skills, performance and morale.
5. **Sell internal auditing as future focused.**
6. **To reduce the opportunities for all types of crime in an organization.**
7. **Increase satisfaction from all our customers.**
8. **Add new skills in the art of questioning.**

Categories

1. Changes in the way that internal auditors interact with the rest of their enterprises **and all those with a stakeholder interest.**

2. Internal restructuring and changes in the organization and management of internal auditing.
3. Creation of new audit services and methods.
4. Changes in the use of technology.
5. **Continuously improve knowledge and skills in the teams of staff who carry out internal auditing engagements.**
6. **New services to fight crime.**
7. **Assistance in evaluation of the board's performance.**
8. **Continuous improved satisfaction from all our customers.**
9. **Changes in the way internal auditing asks questions.**

The following improvements that would make that contribution clearer:

Motivation

Add:

7. 'Including health and safety'.

Goals

Add:

9. Sell internal auditing services as a contribution to the organization's good reputation.

Categories

Add:

10. Contributions to the organization's good reputation.

INTERNAL AUDITING CONTRIBUTES TO GOOD REPUTATIONS PRINCIPIA 1998 AND 2008

My 1998 principia for internal auditing included the following related to its contribution to good reputations (see Appendix A):

15. Control embraces all aspects of governance, including ethics, equality, honesty, caring and sustaining.

This is now changed to reflect the importance of all aspect of reputation risk for organizations in 2007 and the future:

19. Internal auditing has a responsibility to contribute to the processes of assessing reputation risks and advising at all levels in their organizations on how reputation can be managed and enhanced through good corporate responsibility practices.

A VISION FOR INTERNAL AUDITING CONTRIBUTING TO GOOD REPUTATIONS

We add value to the organization's good reputation

SYNOPSES OF CASE STUDIES

Case 13.1: Internal Auditing Contributes to Good Reputation in British Waterways

Synopsis

This case study focuses on internal auditing involvement in social and environmental issues. It sets out an emerging new internal auditing role reviewing the way that organizations meet their public and society responsibilities. It discusses the business drivers for such corporate responsibilities and how internal auditing within British Waterways approached these issues through the risk management process and its cutting edge services.

Contributed by Keith Labbett, Head of Audit, British Waterways – April 2007

After Reading the Case Study Consider:

1. Are the potential areas for corporate responsibility consideration in the case study being addressed in your organization?
2. How does the '. . . *logical process* . . . ' for corporate responsibility delivery in the case study compare with your organization's corporate responsibility delivery process?
3. What '. . . *facets within corporate responsibility* . . . ' are being developed as cutting edge internal auditing resources and practices in your organization?

Case 13.2: Risk and Control Issues for Health, Safety and the Environment

Synopsis

Listed are control objectives for both health and safety and environmental issues. Each provides leads into the development of possible cutting edge resources and practices for internal auditing.

Reproduced from *The Operational Auditing Handbook – Auditing Business Processes* (1997, pp. 396–399 and 417–420), John Wiley & Sons, Chichester, England, with permission from Management Audit LLP.

After Reading the Case Study Consider:

1. How many of the control objectives do you include in your internal auditing engagements?
2. How many of the control objectives have led internal auditing in your organization to develop cutting edge resources and practices?

Case 13.3: Reputational Risk the Challenge for Internal Audit

Synopsis

Internal audit must redefine its role and include all areas that *'impact reputation'*. All governance processes in an organization need to address its reputation as well as its operations. Board effectiveness reviews can be used to address reputation issues and cutting edge internal auditing can provide consulting services to assist. To do this internal auditing needs '. . . *people who can think both "in" and "out" of the box; people who are good communicators, are not afraid to drill down when required and ask penetrating questions* . . . '. Such questions need to addressed both internally and externally in all an organization's supply chains and to its customers.

Contributed with permission from Jenny Rayner, Abbey Consulting www.abbeyconsulting.co.uk, extracted from her book *Managing Reputational Risk – curbing threats, leveraging opportunities* (2003: pp. 239–242), published by John Wiley & Sons Ltd, Chichester, England.

After Reading the Case Study Consider:

1. How many of the risk management challenges for internal auditing mentioned in the case study did you recognize as cutting edge resources and practices discussed in this book? There are many.
2. Does your internal auditing have the '. . . *right skill-sets, tools, knowledge, experience and sheer chutzpah* . . . ' to tackle reputation risks?
3. Is your internal auditing at the cutting edge of thinking *'in and out of the box'*?

Case 13.4: Auditing Sustainable Development

Synopsis

'Internal auditors are well-positioned to assist management in implementing a sustainability management system and perform system audits after the implementation phase.' Various roles for internal auditors are discussed, each of which can lead to the development of cutting edge internal auditing resources and practices, leading to the recruitment of '. . . *sustainability specialists'*.

Contributed by Hans Nieuwlands, CIA, CCSA, CGAP, RA, Technical Director Internal Auditing and CSR, at Royal Nivra, Amsterdam, the Netherlands. This case is based on research by the contributor: published as *Sustainability and Internal Auditing* (2006), The IIA Research Foundation (ISBN 0-89413-594-5). It is reprinted from an article with the same title in the April 2007 issue of *Internal Auditor*. Copyright 2007 by The Institute of Internal Auditors, Inc., 247 Maitland Avenue, Altamonte Springs, Florida 32710-4201 U.S.A. Reprinted with permission.

After reading the Case Study consider:

1. How does the Sustainability Management System (SMS) described in the case study compare with the SMS plan in your organization?
2. Is the *'sustainability communication plan'* in your organization reviewed by internal auditing?
3. Do internal auditors *'play'* the roles of auditor, consultant, trainer and coordinator in the implementation of your organization's sustainability policy and strategy?
4. Does your sustainability strategy and policy cross all your supply chains?

Case 13.5: Setting the Tone

Synopsis

Ethical leadership, sometimes addressed as the 'tone at the top', is an essential part of governance in every organization. *'Tone in this context means the qualities and style that characterizes business behaviour.'* That tone needs to cascade down the organization to all levels and across all supply chains – to suppliers, customers, business partnerships and other stakeholders. This case study sets a 'values' theme internal auditing can contribute to through its own ethics and cutting edge resources and practices.

Published summary of report *Setting the Tone – Ethical Business Leadership* (2005), Philippa Foster Back, OBE, Director, The Institute of Business Ethics, London, England. www.ibe.org.uk

---

After Reading the Case Study Consider:

1. How does internal auditing in your organization *'have an effect'* on its ethical leadership, in all its teams and at all levels?
2. Does your organization *'clearly state'* the tone of how it does business, to all its employees and all those with whom it has operating relationships?
3. Does your organization recognize and respond appropriately to all the external influences discussed in the case?

SELF-ASSESSMENT QUESTIONS

13.1   Risk and Control Health and Safety Issues

Key Issues

1.1   How can management be assured that they have identified and adequately addressed all health and safety risks and hazards within the organization?
1.2   Has an authorized and documented health and safety policy been developed and implemented, and is it maintained up-to-date?
1.3   How can management be certain of compliance with all the relevant legislation and regulations?
1.4   What processes ensure that staff are fully aware of workplace risks and how to correctly utilize safety equipment and protect themselves?
1.5   Has sufficient and appropriate safety equipment (i.e. fire extinguishers, protective clothing, etc.) been provided, and what measures ensure that it all remains in working order and effective?
1.6   Have sufficient and effective fire prevention and protection systems been provided, and are they regularly tested?
1.7   Are adequate security measures in place to restrict access to facilities and protect staff and equipment from attack?
1.8   How can management be certain that all incidents and accidents are reported and appropriately dealt with?

1.9   Have adequate first aid and medical facilities (equipment and personnel) been provided, and are supplies replenished when used?

1.10 Are adequate hygiene and cleanliness standards established, and what mechanisms ensure that the required standards are maintained?

1.11 How can management be assured that adequate and appropriate insurance cover is provided and maintained?

1.12 What mechanisms ensure that all the required regulatory inspections are conducted and that the appropriate regulatory certification is obtained?

1.13 How can management be assured that all hazardous materials are safely, correctly and securely stored?

Detailed Issues

2.1   Has management undertaken a risk assessment of health and safety implications throughout the organization in order to identify the risks and ensure that they are addressed?

2.2   Has a health and safety policy been introduced, and have specific responsibilities for safety issues been allocated?

2.3   What mechanisms prevent non-compliance with the prevailing health and safety regulations?

2.4   How can management be sure that they maintain an up-to-date awareness of all the relevant health and safety regulations?

2.5   Are all staff adequately trained in safety matters, including use of equipment and clothing (and how can management be certain that all the relevant staff actually receive the appropriate training)?

2.6   Are staff progressively tested on their level of understanding of safety measures in order to identify further training needs?

2.7   How can management be assured that all the relevant safety equipment is maintained in working order?

2.8   Are all relevant machines fitted with guards, safety cut-outs, etc., to the required standard?

2.9   How can management be sure that all computer equipment conforms to the required standards (i.e. screen radiation levels, etc.)?

2.10 Are building evacuation, fire and security drills regularly conducted and assessed for effectiveness?

2.11 Are adequate fire alarms and security systems installed, tested and maintained (and would faults be promptly detected)?

2.12 How can management be assured that all building environmental systems (i.e. heating, lighting, air conditioning, etc.) are working correctly and to the required legal standards?

2.13 What mechanisms prevent unauthorized access to buildings and facilities?

2.14 Are the relevant staff (i.e. receptionists, door guards, post room staff, etc.) aware of the action required in the event of a bomb alert, an attack on the building, or a suspicious package, etc.?

2.15 What processes ensure that the records of incidents and accidents are fully and correctly maintained in accordance with any regulatory requirements?

2.16 Are sufficient and suitably trained first aid and medical personnel available, and how can they be promptly summoned to an incident?

2.17 In the event of an emergency, how can management be certain that all visitors are accounted for?

2.18 Are transitory safety risks (such as trailing power leads, wet floors due to cleaning, etc.) adequately addressed?

2.19 How can management be certain that the organization has sufficient insurance cover in the event of being sued for negligence with regard to health and safety conditions?

2.20 What processes ensure that insurance cover is renewed, at the appropriate level and current?

2.21 What processes ensure that all the required certificates and licences are obtained to enable the lawful operation of facilities?

2.22 What mechanisms prevent unauthorized access to hazardous materials?

2.23 How is accuracy of data input from other systems (i.e. human resources) confirmed?

2.24 How is the accuracy of data output to other systems (i.e. estates management) confirmed?

Reproduced from *The Operational Auditing Handbook – Auditing Business Processes* (1997: pp. 396–399), John Wiley & Sons, Chichester, England, with permission from Management Audit LLP.

13.2   Risk and Control Environmental Issues

Key Issues

1.1   Has an approved and documented environment policy been established which defines the required approach for business operations?

1.2   What measures ensure that the principals of the environmental policy are complied with, and how would non-compliance be promptly detected?

1.3   Have production processes and other business activities been assessed for their environmental impacts (and how is the necessary corrective action evidenced)?

1.4   How does management ensure that all the relevant environmental legislation and regulations are fully complied with, thus avoiding penalties and adverse effects on the organization's public image?

1.5   How can management be assured that all waste products are correctly and safely treated, discharged or disposed of?

1.6   What measures prevent the pollution and contamination of the environment?

1.7   Are the organization's products assessed for 'environmental friendliness' (i.e. impact during production/use, potential to be recycled, safe disposal at end of product life, restricted use of scarce resources, etc.)?

1.8   Has management actively considered alternative and less environmentally harmful production/business processes?

1.9   Are measures in place which ensure that all environmental impacts are identified, monitored and effectively managed (and what is the evidence for this)?

1.10 Has management established a 'recycling' policy and if so, how is compliance confirmed?

1.11 Have the full costs of adopting an environmental approach to the business been accurately identified, justified and authorized (and are they subject to monitoring and review)?

Detailed Issues

2.1 Is the environmental policy supported by the commitment of senior management and a suitable staff training/awareness programme?

2.2 Are all projects to reduce the impact of business activities on the environment subject to a full feasibility and cost appraisal, before being authorized?

2.3 Is the assessment of environmental impacts kept up-to-date in order that management action is relevant and targeted?

2.4 Where required, have measurements of environmental impact (i.e. water discharge, fume extraction, waste materials, etc.) been established (and are they checked for accuracy)?

2.5 How can management be certain that they remain aware of all the relevant environmental legislation and regulations?

2.6 Has a responsibility for environmental management been defined and allocated?

2.7 What measures ensure that all waste products are identified, assessed for their environmental impact, and appropriately treated/processed?

2.8 Are all discharges of waste products subject to monitoring and permitted within the prevailing regulations (and how would non-compliance be detected)?

2.9 How can management be sure that all waste product treatment processes are operating correctly and efficiently?

2.10 Would management be made aware of all accidental and unintentional spillages of potentially harmful materials?

2.11 Are contingency plans and resources in place to effectively deal with the likely range of environmental accidents?

2.12 How can management be assured that waste disposal sites and operators are appropriately licensed to handle the specific by-products generated by the organization?

2.13 Whenever necessary, are management considering utilizing alternatives to either hazardous or scarce materials as a means of reducing the environmental impacts?

2.14 Are the potential long-term environmental liabilities adequately assessed for both newly acquired sites and those being disposed of?

2.15 Are environmental impact audits regularly conducted by appropriately experienced personnel and are their findings and recommendations effectively followed up?

2.16 Does the design and development of new products take into account the potential environmental impact of production, and what measures ensure that such impacts are minimized and contained?

2.17 Are the operating costs of any 'recycling' programmes monitored, and are such programmes assessed for their effectiveness?

2.18 How does management verify that the adopted environmental approach is justified (on cost or company image grounds)?

2.19 Has management reviewed the type of packaging in use as the basis for adopting alternatives with a reduced environmental impact?

2.20 In the event of an environmental problem, are mechanisms in place to deal effectively with media and public relations, so that the reputation of the organization will be protected?

2.21 How is the accuracy of data input from other systems (e.g. new product development or design) confirmed?

2.22 How is the accuracy of data output to other systems (e.g. industry regulation and compliance) confirmed?

Reproduced from *The Operational Auditing Handbook – Auditing Business Processes* (1997: pp. 417–420), John Wiley & Sons, Chichester, England, with permission from Management Audit LLP.

NOTES AND REFERENCES

1. Cited in *Wisdom of the Ages* (1948), The Saint Catherine's Press Ltd, London, England.
2. *Social Responsibility Audit* (1973), John Humble, Foundation for Business Responsibilities, London, England.
3. *Manual of Internal Audit Practice (1990)*, edited by H.J. Stearn and K.W. Impey, ICSA Publishing Limited, London, England.
4. Presented to the UK Parliament by the Prime Minister by Command of Her Majesty, 1991.
5. *Standards in Public Life*, First Report of the Committee on Standards in Public Life, presented to UK Parliament by the Prime Minister by Command of Her Majesty, 1995.
6. *Professional Briefing Note Two, Environmental Audit* (1993), The IIA–UK & Ireland.
7. *The Environmental Audit and Business Strategy – A Total Quality Approach* (1991), Grant Ledgerwood, Elizabeth Street and Riki Therivel, Financial Times/Pitman Publishing, London, England.
8. *Quality and Environmental Auditing – A Time for Internal Auditors to be Involved.* (A paper based partly on 1996 research by Professor Jeffrey Ridley and Dr Krystyna Stephens, into the impact of quality auditing on the internal auditor, updated by current environmental auditing developments. Presented at the first International Internal Auditing Winter Conference, arranged by The Management Development Centre of the City University Business School, London, England, on 10 December 1997.)
9. AA1000 Assurance Standard, a worldwide corporate accountability standard will be republished as a 2nd edition in 2008. This will follow a *'collaborative web-based co-development process using open-source "wiki" techniques to maximize participation and leverage synergies of collective knowledge'*, starting in October 2007. Details can be obtained from the AccountAbility website www.accountability21.net
10. *Corporate Ethics and Social Responsibility* – Professional Briefing Note Fifteen (1999), The IIA–UK & Ireland.
11. Published in *Internal Control*, Issue 35, October (2000), abg Professional Information, London, England. Reproduced in Tottel's *Corporate Governance Handbook*, 3rd edition (2005: p. 1046), Tottel Publishing, Haywards Heath, England.
12. Published in *Internal Auditing* (April 2001: p. 11) The IIA–UK & Ireland.
13. *Risk Business – Towards Best Practices in Managing Reputation Risk* (2001), Jenny Rayner, Institute of Business Ethics, London, England.
14. *The Business Case for Corporate Responsibility* (2003), Arthur D. Little, Business in the Community, London, England. (BITC values are to inspire companies by sharing and experience to

develop innovative and challenging ways to catalyst for change. It supports and challenges companies to integrate responsible business through their operations in order to have a positive impact on society and therefore be of public benefit – see its website www.bitc.org.uk)

15. *Good Governance Standards for Public Services* (2004), Chaired by Sir Alan Langlands, Chartered Institute of Public Finance and Accountancy and Office for Public Management Ltd. supported by the Joseph Rowntree Foundation, London, England. (see also *Going Forward with Good Governance* (October 2007)). www.opm.co.uk

16. *Delivering Good Governance In Local Government Framework* (2007) and *Delivering Good Governance In Local Government Guidance: Note for English Authorities* (2007), The Chartered Institute of Public Finance and Accountancy, London, England. www.cipfa.org

17. *Enterprise Risk Management – Integrated Framework Executive Summary* (2004), Committee of Sponsoring Organizations of the Treadway Commission, USA. www.coso.org

18. *Four Approaches to Enterprise Risk Management . . . and Opportunities in Sarbanes–Oxley Compliance* (2007), James Roth, Donald Esperen, Daniel Swanson, Paul Sobel, The IIA Research Foundation.

19. *Good Governance – A Code for the Voluntary and Community Sector* (2005). This version developed and endorsed by National Council for Voluntary Organizations (NCVO), Association of Chief Executives of Voluntary Organizations (ACEVO), Charity Trustees Network (CTN) and Institute of Chartered Secretaries and Administrators (ICSA). It has also been endorsed by the Charities Commission and National Hub of Expertise in Governance, which will take responsibility for future work on the Code. Published by NCVO, London, England. www.governancehub.org.uk

20. *The Triple Bottom Line* (2006), Andrew W. Savitz with Karl Weber, John Wiley & Sons Inc., San Francisco, USA.

21. Published in the European Confederation of Institutes of Internal Auditors (ECIIA) *website Newsletter*, May 2006. www.eciia.org

22. For more details of this initiative visit www.unglobalcompact.org

23. Progress on the development of the Social Responsibility international standard ISO 26000 can be found at www.iso.org/sr

24. *Organizational Governance: Guidance for Internal Auditors* (2006), The IIA.

25. *Tomorrow's Global Company – the challenges and choices: Climate change – the role of global companies*, Tomorrow's Company London, England. www.tomorrowscompany.com

26. *Environmental Key Performance Indicators – Reporting Guidelines for UK Businesses* (2006), Department for Environment Food and Rural Affairs, London, England. www.defra.gov.uk

27. This research is available on the Health and Safety Executive website. www.hse/gov.uk/leadership

28. *Leading Health and Safety at Work: Leadership Actions for Directors and Board Members* (2007), Institute of Directors and Health and Safety Executive, London, England. www.iod.com/hsguide.

29. The *Corporate Manslaughter and Corporate Homicide Act* 2007 received Royal Assent on 26 July 2007 and will come into force in 2008. It introduces a new statutory offence of corporate manslaughter in England, Wales and Northern Ireland, and corporate homicide in Scotland. It means that an organization whose gross negligence leads to death can face criminal prosecution for manslaughter.

30. Committee on Standards in Public Life Annual Report, 2006. www.public-standards.gov.uk

31. See Press Release CSR Academy News, 31 March 2007. www.bitc.org.uk

32. *Living Up To Our Values – Developing ethical assurance* (2006), Nicole Dando and Walter Raven, Institute of Business Ethics, London, England.

33. *Source:* Adapted from J. Rayner (2003), *The Crucial Role of Internal Audit: Managing Reputational Risk*, John Wiley & Sons, and *'Ethical and Social Auditing and Reporting – the Challenge for the Internal Auditor'*, The IIA–UK & Ireland, Professional Issues *Bulletin*.

34. Practice Advisory 2130-1(5) (2001): *Role of the Internal Audit Activity and Internal Auditor in the Ethical Culture of an Organization*, The IIA.

35. The GoodCorporation Standard was established in 2001. The standard is reviewed and updated every three years. This is its second revision, which can be downloaded from www.goodcorporation.com

Cutting Edge Internal Auditing
Promotes Itself

'No man is an Island, entire of itself;
every man is a piece of the Continent,
a part of the main . . . '

John Donne 1572–1631[1]

NO MAN IS AN ISLAND

INTERNAL AUDITING PROMOTES ITS SERVICES BEFORE 1997

The IIA has promoted and marketed internal auditing as a profession globally since its formation in New York in 1941. Toronto became a Chapter in 1944, followed by Montreal in 1945: by 1962 there were 25 Chapters outside the United States, five of which were in the United Kingdom (established in 1948). The IIA's commitment to the internal auditing as a global profession has never stopped. This can be seen in its 2007 vision and mission statements discussed in Chapter 1 and repeated again here:

Vision

The IIA will be the global voice of the internal audit profession: advocating its value, promoting best practice, and providing exceptional service to its members.

Mission

The mission of The Institute of Internal Auditors is to provide dynamic leadership for the global profession of internal auditing. Activities in support of this mission will include, but will not be limited to:

- Advocating and promoting the value that internal audit professionals add to their organization;
- Providing comprehensive professional educational and development opportunities; standards and other professional practice guidance; and certification programmes;
- Researching, disseminating, and promoting to practitioners and stakeholders knowledge concerning internal auditing and its appropriate role in control, risk management and governance;
- Educating practitioners and other relevant audiences on best practices in internal auditing; and
- Bringing together internal auditors from all countries to share information and experiences.

In 1990, A.J. Spoel,[2] the first European chairman of the IIA Board, set as his theme *Globalization Through Partnership* to be viewed as a long-range goal – a vision. He recognized a global transformation of business and governments focused on global issues that would be *'complex and risk prone times'*. He promoted and believed in professional internal auditing as a developing global profession in partnership with management, but with some qualifications:

> I believe if internal audit departments are not equipped to meet the prevailing needs of their organizations, a vacuum will occur; and other solutions may seem attractive to management. This may happen even if the internal audit's position is supported by supplemental instruments, such as audit committees. I would submit that internal audit has a chance for significant progress if, among others, the following criteria are met:

- Our place in the organization is close to top management.
- We have a systematic and managerial approach to our jobs.
- Above all, we clearly uphold our independence and objectivity.
- We have an intellectual integration with the business objectives and policies of our organizations.
- We work on broad information bases and close to the event.

On the other hand, our effectiveness will be strongly compromised under the following conditions:

- If we show too little discrimination of critical areas in our corporations.
- If we lack future orientation.
- If we get caught up in the perceived need for ultimate accuracy.
- If we work with highly intelligent, but inexperienced staff.
- If we lack outward-oriented behaviour.

We must be in a position to make the quantum leap into the management of strategy audit. Obviously we cannot neglect our role and responsibility for internal control as the core element in our audit portfolio, but I believe that the business developments taking place as part of the worldwide integration afford us the opportunity to secure the partnership with management upon which we can build our future.

His proposals for The IIA at that time included the adoption of 12 strategic thrusts, shown in Figure 14.1. Read these carefully, at least twice. Consider how they promote the vision of The IIA then, and even today. Read through thrusts 2, 5, 8, 9 and 10 again, replacing 'we' with 'I'. These thrusts should be in your internal auditing activity's business plan and promotion of its services in your organizations. That would still be cutting edge.

The IIA's 12 Strategic Thrusts for the 1990s

1. Through aggressive global membership growth, we must gain a reputation as the association for *all* internal auditors. We must be certain that our membership organization provides centralized service where needed and autonomy when warranted. The structure must be clear and well understood.

2. To promote acceptance for the foundation of our profession on a world-wide basis, we must promote the *Standards for the Professional Practice of Internal Auditing* globally at the government and regulatory levels.

3. To establish the CIA designation as the desired qualification worldwide, we must mobilize significant public relations efforts and adapt our market strategies to local conditions.

4. We must provide professional development programmes tailored to the members' needs at the member's sites, and we must be responsive to emerging issues for internal auditors (such as auditing in an EDI-environment; auditing environmental issues, and auditing social accounts).

5. We must actively exploit the benefit of our status as a truly international organization by promoting our capabilities and actual performance of cross-border analysis of the practice of internal auditing.

6. As a major focus, we must ensure that we meet the technological needs of our members. We must ensure that we are performing significant research, as well as offering professional development programmes in this area.

7. We must promote and assist in the development of programmes in the educational community, so that students are encouraged and given opportunities to prepare themselves for the expanding possibilities of internal auditing careers.

8. To enhance the professional image of internal auditing on a global basis, we must provide support and give major promotional emphasis to our involvement with outside organizations.

9. Through research, professional development programmes and intense public relations activity, we must promote the concept of basic internal controls and the role of internal audit with respect to internal control.

10. Through dissemination of information on the varying roles and responsibilities of audit committees worldwide, we must promote understanding and development of the concepts the audit committee member needs in specific programmes.

11. We must design, develop, and implement a reorganization plan that will enhance our volunteer management structure, with the objective of having the right people involved at the right time in the decision-making process.

12. Through our European member bodies, we must not only stay abreast, but lead, in terms of establishing how the profession will be affected by Europe's move toward economic, political, and monetary union.

Figure 14.1   The IIA's 12 Strategic Thrusts For The 1990s
Source: *'Globalization Through Partnership'*, *Internal Auditor*, October 1990, A.J. Spoel when chairman of The IIA Board, 1990–91

In 1991 the then chairman of The IIA Board, G. Peter Wilson, wrote for the 50 years *Internal Auditor* celebration issue:

> While we might take pride and satisfaction in the reputation we enjoy today, we cannot afford to rest on our laurels. We must work hard to retain the respect we have earned through our contributions to the global community. We must continue to cooperate with other international organizations in the achievement of common goals. We must seek out new ways to make our presence felt and to provide added value to our various constituencies. And last, but not least, we must reach out

to embrace our fellow professionals in the developing world, the emerging market economies of Eastern Europe, and wherever else we can be of service to the internal audit profession.

In the same issue, Hugh A. Parkes from Australia wrote:

> We can be very isolated from our organization and its activities. I once met an auditor who locked himself inside his office each day so that his independence would not be compromised . . . ! We could greatly improve our communications and our image with all segments of our organizations . . . We also have a desperate need to remarket internal audit's contributions in a fresh way. We need to show what we can do – show the audit committee and top management the direct contribution we make, the results we achieve; and the corrective actions taken by those we have audited. . . . We could also use the resources and data available to us in more creative ways. We need to look beyond the obvious and the traditional. . . . We could also place more emphasis on thinking ahead. And do more to prevent problems rather than spending time curing them.

Do you lock yourself in your office to maintain your independence? I doubt it, though the metaphor can apply with some internal auditors who insist on keeping their role totally separate from management responsibilities and close working relationships with staff in other areas. This does not promote the vision of The IIA for professional internal auditing.

The lines from John Donne's writings reinforce the theme in this chapter that no man (or woman) internal auditor is in isolation in their organization. At all times they are promoting themselves and their internal auditing profession in the services they provide. How they do this can, and often does, create innovative experiments and new ways of promotion. Encouraging cutting edge resources and practices to happen. In 1992, during the registration of my internal audit activity to ISO 9000, the internal audit team developed the customer satisfaction survey questionnaire in Figure 14.2.

The team's intention was to manage relationships between the internal auditing service being provided though the customers' satisfaction and needs. For any promotion of products and services this is a must. The survey sought an evaluation of our performance and value of an engagement's findings to the customer. Initially the survey form was given to the customer at the end of an engagement, at the final interview. Shortly after its introduction, and as an improvement to its benefit for both internal auditor and customer, it was decided to introduce the survey at the beginning of an engagement and ask for the form to be completed at the end. This had a much better impact on both the internal auditor and the customer, increasing significantly the response rate and value of the survey for the organization!

Such surveys are an important tool for continuously improving products and services, but only if the importance of the questions is clearly explained to the internal auditor and customer – and results are actioned promptly and fed into the internal auditing activity's future marketing plans. Comments on the content of the survey form will be discussed later in this chapter in the context of today and tomorrow's internal auditing customers' needs.

In 1996, research into perceptions of audit quality in the public sector, by the Chartered Institute of Public Finance and Accountancy[3] in the United Kingdom, raised important issues for all sectors:

> . . . internal audit will need to demonstrate that it enjoys close relationships with all key managers throughout the organization, as anything less must compromise its ability to deliver a quality service. It is only by creating effective communication with the rest of the organization that internal audit can show that it has as its objective common goals with the organization. It can then be seen as facilitating change, not encumbering progress towards organizational goals.

Customer Satisfaction Survey Questionnaire

Please provide your evaluation of the recently completed audit by circling the number that best reflects the manner in which the audit was conducted. We would also be interested in any additional comments you have:

	Poor	Fair	Very Good	Good	Exceptional
1. *Auditor Communication:*					
(a) The objectives of the audit were clearly communicated.	1	2	3	4	5
(b) The auditors asked for your input/concerns.	1	2	3	4	5
(c) Your input/concerns were satisfactorily addressed.	1	2	3	4	5
(d) Significant developments were communicated on a timely basis during the audit.	1	2	3	4	5
(e) Audit findings were clearly communicated and agreed upon at the conclusion of the audit.	1	2	3	4	5
2. *Auditor understanding of your business operations*	1	2	3	4	5
3. *Findings of the audit:*					
(a) Accurate	1	2	3	4	5
(b) Reasonable	1	2	3	4	5
(c) Useful and 'value-adding'	1	2	3	4	5
(d) Significant	1	2	3	4	5

4. *How could internal audit have been more useful to your organization?*

....
....
....
....
....

Figure 14.2 Customer Satisfaction Survey Questionnaire
Source: J. Ridley, *A Quality System Manual for Internal Auditing* (1993)

The findings go on to say '... *In order to establish effective relationships internal audit must identify its key customers and understand how they perceive internal audit.*' To do this internal audit needs to:

- determine who its key customers are (the greatest market risk to internal audit);
- understand its customers' needs by determining exactly what it is that the customers want (this implies a thorough understanding of how customers see internal audit)

- widen the internal audit scope to cover every area of the organization (this implies that internal audit should examine the functioning of the quality systems that underpin strategic planning and decision making); and
- project auditors as advisors marketing imaginative solutions *not* problems.

As well as projecting an imaginative problem-solving image the research identified pro-motion, training and behaviour as three key actions for internal auditors in the marketing of their services in an organization.

Cosmas 1996[4] researched the marketing of internal auditing in organizations in North America, concluding that this first requires some planning and formality, but with significant benefits:

A marketing program, or plan, is essential for every internal auditing department. A well-devised plan will direct internal auditors in their quest to provide valuable services to their organization.

Cosmas goes on to say that such a plan should consist of specific objectives, a well-developed customer base, effective promotional tools, a plan of action, and a way to monitor success: in other words, a business strategy. It is not about internal auditing living on an island in an organization, separated from its customers! She discusses marketing of internal auditing creativity in her chapter on internal auditing participating in management teams: *'Utilizing creative instincts is one of the internal auditor's most powerful marketing tools.'* She recognized at the time the growing participation by internal auditors in team projects across organizations, working closely with operating staff and management. See-ing internal auditing creativity as an important part of the marketing of its professional services:

As a marketing tool, audit participation on project teams has been beneficial overall in winning management's praise and support. Internal auditing brings a unique perspective to project teams through their background and training.

Cosmas also saw the marketing of internal auditing as an important part of its perform-ance measures and continuous improvement programmes – *'The primary purpose of a performance measurement system is to support continuous improvement'* and *'To improve a process we must know how our customer intends to use the process outcome'*. Know-ing what the internal auditing customer wants is fundamental to a good marketing plan.

The key words for marketing internal auditing prior to 1997 from the above literature and discussion are:

Customer Needs	Creativity
Planning	Thinking Ahead
Communication	Measuring
Reputation	Continuous Improvement
Image	Added Value
New (and Fresh) ways	

All are potential for cutting edge resources and practices, then and now.

What the two professional internal auditors referenced into above recognized in 1991 was a need for internal auditors to be more proactive in promoting themselves and their profession: not just in their organizations, but also in their communities, nations and globally. Internal auditors should always remember it is not what *'creative ways'* means to you as an internal auditor, it is what your customer thinks is creative that is important.

Article:
All-Year Greetings From Internal Auditing[5] (1997)

This is the time of year when we all communicate seasonal greetings of best wishes to our fam- colleagues, both the world. Orga- the festive time ings and publicity across all their Many organiza-

> *'There are still too few good examples of internal auditing brochures, selling a leading edge service, linked to professional standards, ethics and delighted customers.'*

ilies, friends and locally and across nizations also use to pass on greet- about their aims, supply chains. tions also use Christmas and New Year communications to market their image, products and services, through diaries and calendars. Christmas messages are quality activities that require assessment, planning, doing and verifying. They are big business.

Traditionally written Christmas and New Year wishes are communicated by letters and cards. Today, new technology has given us video, Internet and intranet. I am sure there will be an increasing number of Christmas and New Year messages by video and across websites, this year and in the future. New technologies will follow – virtual reality Christmas greetings cannot be too far away!

It has occurred to me as I write my internal auditing Christmas message that internal auditors can learn a lot from the colour, design, words and technology used in Christmas and New Year messages. Certainly there are a lot of similarities between Christmas cards and internal auditing brochures – or there should be. Do you have an internal auditing greeting card for every day of the year?

Unfortunately, there are not many good examples of in-house selling of internal auditing greetings. If they exist, many in-house internal auditing brochures are – too long, too cold and uninteresting. Sending out messages of regulation, compliance, discipline and routine. Many lack any strong vision, colour or links into organization objectives. Strong words, but I believe true. Most research into in-house internal auditing shows that only a few internal audit units sell themselves with attractive promotion material, through any form of planned marketing strategy. There are still too few good examples of internal auditing brochures, selling a leading edge service, linked to professional standards, ethics and delighted customers. How many Christmas cards would sell if they had the same appeal as your internal auditing brochure?

When you receive your written Christmas and New Year greetings this year study the characteristics of each. Analyse what appeals to you. Benchmark with your existing or planned internal auditing greetings for 1998. Think about improving your selling of internal auditing through an attractive greetings package!.

Most Christmas and New Year greetings can be categorized by:

- SIZE
- COLOUR
- DESIGN
- GRAPHICS
- PAPER QUALITY
- PRINTING STYLE
- GREETINGS - PRINTED AND WRITTEN

Consider and use each category in the printing of your own internal auditing promotion material:

Size

Not too big – keep it short and small. A useful size is one that fits into a Filofax or other organizer, or can stand on a mantelpiece. Keep all brochures portable.

Colour

Cheerful and friendly. Choose bright colours – adopt or include any organization colours, to establish internal auditing as serving the organization.

Design

Use professional marketing staff to create a design that patterns your vision for internal auditing in the future. If you do not have a vision – create one with your main customers. Emphasize goodwill towards all! Use a slogan that matches your vision. Improve on '. . . *a service to management'*. Use organization styles and logos to emphasize the organization ownership and status of internal auditing.

Graphics

Include drawn models, photographs of internal audit staff and customers. Do not identify individuals as this dates a brochure, particularly if there is a high staff turnover in the internal audit unit. Demonstrate visually the scope of internal auditing, both across organization functions, through organization structures – from top to bottom, and geographical. Make graphics tell a story of professionalism.

Paper Quality

Print on high-quality paper or card, preferably with a gloss finish.

Printing Style

Choose carefully an *appropriate* font. Use font size to emphasize your important messages.

Greetings – Printed and Written

Study your customers to ensure that printed greetings satisfy their needs. Include in each brochure you issue a personal message for the customer. Space should be provided in the brochure for this message to be added after printing.

I recently came across an excellent example of internal auditing greetings in a brochure published by an Executive Agency of the Department of Social Security. The Benefits Agency[a] brochure is one of only a few in-house internal auditing guides that I have seen that sells professional internal auditing, using professional marketing standards. I emphasize 'in-house' because there are many examples of good brochures which market internal auditing services, but these are mainly published by those who contract internal auditing services. Figure 14.3 summarizes the greetings in the Benefits Agency brochure.

But remember, cards are only a part of the festive season. There are many other activities associated with Christmas and New Year. There is also the 'personal touch' to most greetings. In the same way, all internal auditing promotion greetings should be supported by personal contacts and follow-up outside of normal auditing activities, linking greetings to objectives. A 1997 article in Internal Auditor,[b] emphasizes the importance of marketing internal audit by aligning internal auditing objectives with the organization's objectives and promotion. The writer recognizes a brochure as important but not in isolation from other selling of internal auditing. '*Presentations, one-on-one discussions outside of formal audit engagements, a control newsletter, and customized reporting are a few examples of low-cost promotional activities that enlighten customers.*'

Sawyer (1981),[c] on the selling of modern internal auditing to management, concludes: '*[Internal] auditors must mount a continuing campaign to promote their product to executive management, and the product they sell must be of the quality that will capture and keep management's interest.*' On brochures, his 1996 recommendations,[d] define a brochure as seeking '*. . . to remove the mystery from the internal audit function and to prevent any potentially adversarial relationships with auditees*'.

My own recommendations for marketing internal auditing are included in a new book,[e] co-authored by Professor Andrew Chambers and myself, to be published in early 1998:

---

[a] My thanks to Colin Hume of the UK Benefits Agency for permission to publish extracts from his team's 1997 internal auditing brochure – still cutting-edge today.
[b] 'How to Sell Internal Audit', George A. Ewert, *Internal Auditor*, October (1997: pp. 54–57). The IIA.
[c] *The Practice of Modern Internal Auditing* (1981), Lawrence Sawyer, The IIA.
[d] *Internal Auditing* (1996), Lawrence Sawyer, The IIA.
[e] *Leading Edge Internal Auditing* (1998), Jeffrey Ridley and Andrew Chambers, ICSA Publishing Limited, London, England.

Welcome To Our Guide

'Internal audit can help by providing you with an objective review and giving advice on how your procedures can ensure that the objectives are met, financial and other risks are minimised and value for money achieved.'

We are

- providing a professional audit service
- determined to exceed your expectations
- keen to offer support to operational managers
- keen to obtain your opinions of Internal Audit

Our key objectives are

- independence
- appraise controls
- identify opportunities for improvements
- offer advice and guidance on control issues

Our team

- understands your business
- delivers a tailored service
- contributes
- assists

Our staff

- professional excellence
- appropriate audit qualifications
- trained
- motivated and enthusiastic

Our commitment to quality

- competitive
- meet customers' objectives and requirements
- responding to customer feedback
- investing in appropriate resources
- pursuing best practices
- benchmarking with other internal audit suppliers

Figure 14.3   Internal Audit 'Supporting Management'
Source: Best Practice Marketing in Internal Audit in Housing Associations (1998).

Internal auditors should study the promotion programmes of their own organization's products and services, and promotion programmes of other organizations marketing internal auditing services. There are many lessons to be learnt from each. Consider the following promotion criteria common for most products and services:

- focus on specifications that satisfy customer's needs
- excel in leadership
- encourage team learning
- measure for quality
- innovate and improve continuously.

These criteria can be interpreted into the following guidelines for all internal auditing brochures:

- Focus on customer needs
- Demonstrate management's interest in internal auditing

- Emphasize teamwork and auditing coordination
- Explain how internal auditing quality is measured
- State your passion for continuous improvement.

On a recent trip to the dentist I was greeted with a brochure at the reception, which included messages promoting the practice under the following headings:

A WARM WELCOME
CARING
MODERN TECHNOLOGY
THE TEAM
THE INVITATION

If dentists can greet you in such an attractive way, so can internal auditors!

Jean Pierre Garitte (1998),[6] when writing at the start of his term of office as chairman of The IIA, also used the John Donne quotation in his article 'Building Bridges':

> The English poet John Donne reminded us that *'no man is an island'*. In my own mind there is a parallel; internal auditors cannot be islands. We must be pillars and partners in the bridge-building process, and we must find ways to use our bridges to communicate, share, and help our organizations.

This theme introduces a further aspect of marketing internal auditing: its participation with management in the direction and control of objectives to achieve an organization's vision. Not only the organization's vision but also the vision of the internal audit activity, which must be linked in some way. At this time my research across the United Kingdom showed that few internal audit activities had vision statements, or formal marketing plans.

Research:
Marketing Internal Auditing Starts With A Vision[7] (1998)

In 1998, the United Kingdom Housing Association Internal Audit Forum commissioned research into how internal auditors in its marketing their services. The research instruments used are Delphi study and literature in the UK and internationally.

> *'The research showed that only a few internal auditing functions had approached the marketing of their internal auditing using a vision statement and business plan.'*

The results were published in July. The research instruments used are Delphi study and literature review of related and a questionnaire, internationally.

Housing Associations in the UK provide social housing in the community. Many also provide services and care for the elderly. Most are registered charities. An external government regulator requires internal auditing to be established. Published requirements recommend that this internal auditing comply with The IIA framework of standards and ethics. Many Housing Association Internal auditors are members of The IIA. Housing Associations are also required to establish an audit committee at board level. Since 1995 all make statements on governance and internal financial control in their annual reports.

The research was based on the premise that all internal auditors market themselves by their actions and plans. Yet few see these practices as 'marketing'. At the beginning it was known that some of the internal auditing functions in housing associations had created business plans for their services and were actively marketing themselves. Services that had been developed included auditing, internal consultancy, quality, risk assessment and facilitation. The extent of this use of business plans and marketing was not known.

Few internal auditor respondents saw their services including products. Yet, all are working in environments where both audit products and services are being created and promoted. Respondents were asked to list the five most important products and services (not ranked in importance) supplied by their internal audit functions. The term 'products and services' was defined in the questionnaire as the whole range of material and personal contacts supplied by internal auditing staff to their customers, spanning auditing, consultancy and any other work that their internal auditing staff provides. Those most frequently mentioned were:

AUDIT	ADVISE	ASSURE	ASSESS
INVESTIGATE	REVIEW	POLICE	MONITOR
OTHER	CONSULTANCY	TRAIN	FACILITATE
SUPPORT	BENCHMARK	ADD VALUE	

Developing and designing material to support the above products and services is key to successful marketing. Little mention is made by any of the respondents of material supplied to their customers. The only materials mentioned are reports, plans and systems documentation. No mention is made of any of the following as possible products:

Working Papers
Operational Review Programmes
Audit Manuals
Control Self-Assessment Programmes
Risk Assessment Programmes
Computer Audit Programmes
Expert Systems
Quality Audit Programmes
Environmental Audit Programmes
Security Programmes
Health and Safety Programmes

Internal auditor perceptions of marketing concepts

The results and evidence from other research show that many internal auditors, across all industry sectors, do not plan the marketing of their products and services, or even see a need to market themselves in their organizations. For many internal auditors, 'marketing' is still a new world, to be ventured into only if there is a threat from internal and external competitors to provide the same or similar products and services.

The traditional marketing concept of the 1950s saw marketing as a separate functional role, selling products and services to customers with a focus on profit as the objective of the business. Decades later, there have been many changes in sizes of market places and nature of marketing. The supply chains of many, if not most organizations, in all sectors, span the globe, creating new marketing challenges. Organization structures and management styles have changed, with more emphasis on quality management, employee participation, involvement, and supply chain partnering. All these changes can be seen in Housing Associations.

Marketing an organization's external products and services is now seen in many organizations as a total commitment, involving everyone. This concept relates all internal products and services with a primary focus on both internal and external customer satisfaction and loyalty. Webster (1994)[f] describes this meaning and practice as *'market-driven management'* and summarizes this as:

> The new marketing concept is much broader than the old. It is also more pervasive. The old marketing concept encompassed customer orientation, innovation, and profit as the reward for creating a satisfied customer. It looked at the business from the customer's point of view. It was a management philosophy. The new marketing concept is more than a philosophy; it is a way of doing business. It includes customer orientation, market intelligence, the focus on distinctive competences, value delivery, market targeting and the value proposition, customer-defined total quality management, profitability rather than sales volume, relationship management, continuous improvement, and a customer-focused organizational culture. It requires hands-on involvement by management at all levels and in all functions, throughout the complex networks of strategic partnerships, to develop and deliver superior value to customers. It requires that everyone put the customer first.

Webster, integrates the new marketing concept with all phases of corporate strategy, structure and culture, and shows how it should work today. He considers brand equity as a replacement for the older concepts of brand image and brand loyalty. Brand equity recognizes the financial value of a brand name. Many internal and external audit providers worldwide have focused on the 'a brand image' for their auditing services. For those that face competitive situations in and outside their organizations – and these are many – the importance of customer brand loyalty is important, often for survival! As yet, there are no examples of internal or external auditors placing a financial value on the brand of internal auditing they are selling in or outside their organizations.

---

[f] *Market-Driven Management – Using the new marketing concept to create a customer-oriented company* (1994), Frederick E. Webster, Jr, John Wiley & Sons, Inc., New York, USA.

This new marketing concept, and selling of brand image and loyalty, can be seen in the marketing strategies and practices of many Housing Associations and those professional accounting firms that provide external audit and other services to Housing Associations. It is also seen in those professional institutes providing education, training and codes of practice for auditors – both external and internal.

Cosmas (1996)[g] studied marketing practices in internal auditing departments in the USA, identifying many *'market-driven management'* practices. She demonstrates an insight into marketing practices, not only in the USA, but also in many internal audit functions in other countries, including the UK:

> To improve customer satisfaction and continuously add value to the organization, a strategic marketing programme is an essential auditing tool. Internal auditors must devise specific marketing methods to appeal to management's cost and efficiency expectations. Company-wide issues which govern the auditor's marketing plan objectives include cost savings, product quality and customer satisfaction. To add value to the organization's objectives, internal auditing should base their activities on the direction and expectation's of organization leaders. . . .
>
> . . . the bottom line must be this: marketing the internal auditing function is key to successful contribution in the 1990s and beyond. A well-developed marketing programme will enable audit management to chart a strategy, monitor their department's progress, and make appropriate changes.

Definitions of Marketing

At the beginning of the research, definitions of 'marketing' and 'marketing internal auditing' were developed from the literature search. These definitions were distributed for comments to a selected group of internal auditing practitioners, consultants, academics and managers. The group was chosen for the known active involvement of each member, in marketing theory and practice, and/or the promotion of internal audit. Comments from the group were taken into account during the design stage of the research questionnaire.

The definitions are reproduced below, to give all internal auditors an opportunity to form their own views on the content of each. Such an exercise is an important part of understanding where and how marketing of internal audit fits into the strategic plan for their services:

Marketing

Selling any product or service requires knowledge of potential markets, and understanding of potential customers' needs and satisfaction. It requires research and development, a strategic plan, code of conduct, objectives, appropriate resources and processes, and a skilled sales force. It promotes orally and visually a clear vision and mission statements for its products and services, to its total organization and all customers. It motivates everyone involved by perceived high levels of quality, value, continuity and growth. It creates improved and new products and services, at the right prices, for existing and new customers. It continuously monitors results. Establishing and maintaining markets is a continuous learning process.

---

[g] *Audit Customer Satisfaction: Marketing Added Value* (1996), Cindy E. Cosmas, The IIA.

Marketing Internal Auditing

Selling internal auditing services is not an option. It is a necessity for all internal audit staff. It identifies markets within and sometimes outside the organization it serves. It is based on market research that studies its customers' perceptions and identifies what they want and need. It develops products and services, through improvement and innovation, based on appropriate knowledge of the organization it serves. It seeks growth, both in market share and new services. It is flexible and adapts accordingly. It requires agreed team statements on its vision and missions. It demonstrates a high level of understanding of the control environments in which it operates, providing guidance and advice on risk assessment, control activities, monitoring, information systems and communications. It communicates both orally and visually. As such, it is an ambassador of best management practices. It focuses on adding value by providing a professional service, which embraces high standards of auditing independence, objectivity, proficiency, management and a code of conduct. It demonstrates unrestricted scope and rigorous processes. It requires measurement criteria, to monitor the value and quality of its performance. It starts at the recruitment stage and flows through all internal auditing activities. As a continuous learning process, it promotes and develops all internal audit staff, and delights their customers.

Key words in the above definition of marketing internal audit are:

selling	customers	innovation	growth	flexibility
vision	best	professional	conduct	measurement
quality	all	delight	learning	promotes

Clear messages can be learnt by all internal auditors from the new 'market-driven management' concepts, current internal audit literature and comments by many of the respondents. These messages create the following 15 internal audit marketing principles:

Internal Audit Marketing:

- starts with a strategic business plan
- agrees a vision statement for the next three years
- creates a marketing plan for today
- relates all its objectives to organization objectives
- demonstrates commitment to satisfy all its customers
- demonstrates its professionalism and ethics
- demonstrates competence and experience
- covers all its activities and relates these to organization activities
- is supported by quality systems
- demonstrates how it delivers best value to the organization
- is well documented
- is measured to assess its success
- justifies its cost
- is communicated throughout the organization it serves
- is used by organization management to demonstrate commitment to control.

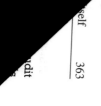

auditing in the future

...ed that only a few internal auditing functions had approached
...heir internal auditing using a vision statement and business
...se with business plans had not developed a vision statement.
...ors demonstrated in their responses that they had learnt from
...'s marketing best practices, or current thinking on marketing
concepts.

The IIA (1994)[h] guidance to internal auditors, when outsourcing of the internal
audit is being considered, includes:

> By marketing professionalism and demonstrating value-added qualities to management,
> internal auditing will further increase its stature within the environment of corporate
> governance . . .

The IIA goes on to recommend that there should be an internal audit vision statement as a prerequisite for the marketing of professionalism. Such a statement to
be based on and linked to the overall organizational vision, and promoting the
following qualities in internal audit:

Proactive	The proactive internal auditing establishes itself as a change agent throughout the organization. It sets its own objectives in line with organizational goals and finds new ways to contribute.
Innovative	The innovative internal auditing department searches out the most valuable use of its resources, questioning the value of routine audits and creating new opportunities to increase the value of the internal auditing function.
Focused	Decisions must be consistent with predetermined objectives. This applies to decisions made by auditing management as individuals.
Integrated	To be efficient, internal auditing information systems should be integrated and designed to support auditing and management processes.
Motivated	A motivated auditing staff has a sense of mission, teamwork, and organizational pride. Internal auditors find personal reward in the success of their organizations and work cooperatively to meet management goals.

A recent job advertisement for a Head of Audit Services in a Housing Association included the requirement '. . . *We need a person with vision and drive
to provide an innovative and comprehensive audit service.'* The importance of a
clear vision for all organizations as they develop products and services, cannot be overestimated. All books and learning on management theory and practice include reference to clear visions as an essential part of strategic planning.

---

[h] *Perspective on Outsourcing Internal Auditing – A professional briefing for chief executives* (1994), The IIA.

As this particular job advertisement states, this applies equally to internal audit.

Vision statements were defined in the research questionnaire as

> . . . a vivid picture of an ambitious, desirable state that is connected to your customers and better in some important way than your current state. It is a short statement which establishes the strategic direction of the internal auditing mission and key objectives. It can and does change as internal and external influences dictate. Both the vision statement and changes to it are team agreements.

There are many good examples of visions published by organizations every day. They provide a motivated direction, both the provider and customer. A good commercial retail example referenced in the research is the vision *'Altogether a Better Business'*, with the following aims:

> . . . to provide benefits for the Society's members, customers and the communities we serve across the widest possible range of services, and to maintain quality, value and integrity in all our business dealings.

This is an excellent vision statement. It is proactive, innovative, focused, integrated and motivated. The key word 'Altogether' establishes a teamworking environment, embracing all staff, their suppliers and customers: it implies that the products and services being provided meet the needs of all. The key word 'Better' creates an environment of continuous improvement: it implies a constant search for best practices through benchmarking. The key word 'Business' provides a focus on all operations to achieve the organization's objectives. The aims focus on benefits for everyone, a wide range of services (and products), quality value and integrity. It also implies an intention to grow. All internal audit functions should use *'Altogether a better internal auditing business'* as their vision!

It is not always necessary to have a slogan for your vision. In recent years the Big Six accounting firms have all created visions for auditing in the 21st century, as part of their strategic planning. Arthur Andersen (1994),[i] published consensus views from a series of symposiums with 100 senior internal auditors, representing internal audit in the UK, across all sectors. The results identified a vision of the following nine key strategies, ranked in order of perceived importance, to be achieved by the year 2000:

1. Recruit and retain good people
2. Establish and communicate a clear vision and strategy
3. Demonstrate the value of internal audit
4. Understand customer needs
5. Focus on risk
6. Improve the communication of results
7. Improve the audit process
8. Educate management on risks and controls
9. Is your organization in a position to monitor internal control?

---

[i] *Internal Audit 2000: An Overview* (1994), Arthur Andersen, London, England.

The skill of vision making is to take these strategies and create a 'vivid picture', linked to an organization's overall vision, which will motivate internal audit staff and their customers to achieve set objectives.

The results of this research apply to all internal auditors worldwide. Every internal auditing team should:

- review all published statements that mention internal audit, and consider how these can be improved to sell professional internal audit;
- encourage their organizations to promote their existence externally;
- be given marketing training – both the concepts and practice;
- study the perceptions and needs of their many customers;
- promote their use of internal audit professional standards and ethics;
- invest time in development of new products and services;
- benchmark their own internal audit brand image with other internal auditors;
- use their audit results to promote their professionalism;
- coordinate all auditing;
- communicate using motivating language;
- use documentation that promotes an internal audit vision;
- focus all documentation on their customers needs;
- be seen as agents of change;
- be proactive, innovative, integrated, focused and motivated;
- set audit objectives linked to their customer's objectives;
- be trained as consultants and facilitators;
- continuously seek new ways to contribute to their organization's success;
- understand the importance and implications of risk management for control:
- be trained to facilitate risk assessment;
- use risk management to promote internal audit;
- develop and maintain a strategic business plan based on the 15 principles of marketing internal audit created by this research.

CUTTING EDGE INTERNAL AUDITING PROMOTES ITS SERVICES TODAY AND IN THE FUTURE

In my 1998 research into marketing internal auditing in Housing Associations, Roy Clark, then Chief Executive and Managing Director, Ano-Coil Limited, gave me the following definition of marketing:

> The definition of marketing could be embroidered forever, and bring in advertising, publicity and promotion. A great difficulty a marketer has is when dealing with a 'one product' company. Competitors edge into the market place . . . in this situation the company has to stay ahead by innovation, quality and efficiency, while creating new edges and constantly looking for new possibilities.

These are still important messages for internal auditing when marketing its services today and in the future. They can be seen in much of the guidance on promoting internal auditing over the past 10 years. Note the emphasis by Roy Clark on staying *ahead by "innovation"*, *"creating new edges"* and *"constantly looking for new possibilities"*.' As true today and in the future in the promotion of all products and services – see the advertisements every day in the media for proof. These quotes underlie most of what is written about cutting edge internal auditing in all the chapters in this book.

In 2000, the IIA–UK & Ireland[8] published its own marketing guidance for internal audit activities. Introducing this with:

> There has never been a more important time for Internal Auditors to market themselves. Within the framework of risk management, corporate governance, best value and the Turnbull guidance in particular, internal auditors have a unique window of opportunity in which to raise the status of the profession of internal auditing and to contribute in an unprecedented way to external communications objectives of the organizations as a whole.

After discussing what an internal auditing activity should address when developing its marketing strategy, the guidance includes the following checklist of questions to assist internal auditors in their market planning:

1. What are the key objectives for internal audit?
2. How, if at all, can we state these in qualitative and quantitative terms?
3. What are our strengths and weaknesses?
4. What opportunities and threats do we have?
5. What are our marketing goals?
6. Who are our stakeholders and what do each of these require from us?
7. What are the products and/or services we are offering and to whom are we offering them?
8. How do our stakeholders perceive the benefits of our competitors' products and services?
9. Are our marketing goals realistic in terms of what the market place will accept?
10. What benefits, both tangible and intangible, do our products and/or services need to have to give us a differential and sustainable advantage over our competitors?
11. What is our stakeholders' perception of value?
12. Where on the attitudinal spectrum (e.g. compliance through to risk based) do we believe our stakeholders lie?
13. What is going to be our vision statement and how will we communicate this to our stakeholders?
14. How are we going to monitor the performance of our marketing activities?

Many of these questions have been asked and addressed in earlier chapters. Question 10 is critical in a competitive market place, and internal auditing is in a competitive market place. Such a question should focus the mind on innovation and creativity in the products and services internal auditing is promoting. Note that I say products and services. Discussion on internal auditing promoting itself too often refers only to its services. In those services there can be many products in the communication and administration of assurance and consultation planning, evaluation and reporting. These products are just as important as the services themselves. They form the structure on which the internal auditing services will be judged, too often just as much as the 'added value' of the services.

There is little current research into how internal audit activities are promoting themselves today – their strategic direction, professional services or performance measures. Mark L. Frigo[9] researched in 2002 the use of a balanced scored card (BSC)[10] as a tool for internal auditing activities to develop a vision, strategy maps and performance measures to measure and communicate its services. The BSC builds on management tools already discussed in this book, including world-class status; quality management; customer and supply chain management; benchmarking; continuous improvement; creativity; asking the right questions, good conduct; and, the following chapter, managing knowledge well. The promotion benefit seen by Frigo in his case studies was to help to shape an internal audit activity's vision statement and missions for its staff (and customers). BSC *'can be an effective tool for refining and implementing departmental strategy and for measuring and managing performance'.*

The BSC performance categories are a must for all promotions of internal auditing as a professional service:

Customer value performance
Financial performance
Internal business process performance
Learning and growth performance.

All need to be linked to vision and strategy statements, missions and key performance indicators; and all need to be to linked to each other. Any promotion of internal auditing needs to address all of the components in some detail. Kaplan, Norton and Frigo provide that detail, some of which has been discussed here and in previous chapters. Frigo recognized that a BSC *'for internal auditing departments can help chief audit executives in:'*

- 'describing and clarifying the departmental strategy and strategic themes' *[based on The IIA Professional Standards Framework]*
- 'communicating departmental strategies and priorities throughout the department' *[and to all internal auditing customers]*
- 'aligning performance measures to departmental and corporate strategy' *[including the department's and corporate vision statements]*
- 'identifying leading indicators that drive outcome performance in internal auditing departments' *[communicating all results to the audit committee and board]*
- 'identifying cause and effect linkages between performance measures' *[quality management]*
- 'enhancing the usefulness of benchmarking performance measures from GAIN' *[and through networking and learning programmes]*
- 'focusing departmental activities on value-added services and other corporate strategies and priorities' *[linking internal audit planning into enterprise risk management]*
- 'using performance measures as a continuous improvement tool' *[creative thinking].*

The words in italics at the end of each benefit are my own additions. I would also add another benefit – *'Developing a marketing strategy, plan and action for all its professional services.'* You may add others – the list can be considered just the beginning: each benefit offers opportunities for cutting edge resources and practices.

Consider *'communicating departmenta strategies. . . '* – in some organizations these are now starting to appear on the Intranet, promoting an internal audit activity's charter, plans and the services it provides. There is now evidence of organization websites on the Internet mentioning existence of an *'independent and objective internal audit'* complying with The IIA *International Standards*. Some organizations are even including in their websites separate internal auditing sites with information that can be downloaded. The United Kingdom government website www.hm-treasury.gov.uk (discussed later in this chapter) is a good example of this with internal auditing, risk management, control and governance guidance applicable to all public services (even, in some cases other industry sectors). This guidance includes:

Government Internal Auditing Standards
Internal Auditing Good Practice Guides
   Audit Strategy
   Consultancy role of internal auditing
   Reporting
   A risk-based approach to internal auditing
   Cooperation between internal and external audit
   Building a cooperative assurance relationship
   Role of internal audit in resources budgeting
   Role of internal auditing – resource based financial systems
Head of Internal Audit Letters
Internal Audit Training and Development Handbook
Fraud

Other globally funded organizations, such as the United Nations, are promoting their internal auditing services through their websites. Some including compliance to The IIA *International Standards*. The Internet will be the promotion vehicle for professional internal auditing in the future – not just by professional institutes and their members, but also by the organizations in which they provide services.

There has been considerable marketing of professional internal auditing to internal auditors in the past 10 years globally and nationally by The IIA, and its network of Audit Clubs, Chapters and National Institutes. *International Standards*, *Code of Ethics*, position papers, journals, research, conferences, seminars, training programmes have all added to this: all linked to the vision and key objectives of professional internal auditing promoted by The IIA. There have also been great strides in promoting professional internal auditing to governments, other associations and commissions, national and international, through proactive position statements and websites, USA (www.theiia.org) and in other websites around the world by its global network.

Examples from this global network are the European Confederation of Institutes of Internal Auditing (ECIIA) website www.eciia.org and IIA–UK & Ireland website www.iia.org.uk, both of which promote professional internal auditing by publications, statement and activity. Two other examples of cutting edge internal auditing promotion in today's websites in the United Kingdom promoting internal auditing are:

1. Housing Association Internal Audit Forum (see Figure 14.4)

Welcome – Our Mission

To be a beacon for best practice in internal auditing in Housing Associations and other non government providers of social housing.

Our Vision

The Housing Association Internal Audit Forum will promote internal audit best practice in risk management, internal controls assurance and governance within Registered Social Landlords by:

- Creating a centre of excellence in social housing internal audit matters
- Helping internal audit professionals develop their skills and knowledge
- Providing a platform for consultation and liaison
- Promoting the role of internal audit and influencing assurance related policy in social housing

The current membership stands at over 200 organizations with members in England, Scotland, Wales and Northern Ireland and, with the help of our external provider members, we represent almost the entire provision of housing in the sector.

Information

Welcome to the Housing Association Internal Audit Forum website, which is your portal to authoritative fact, comment and specialist information about audit issues within the housing sector.

Our website caters for general visitors and HAIAF members who have access to a restricted area of the site. The members' area contains an invaluable library of good practice guides, a discussion forum to share experiences and ideas, and an archive of presentations that contain a wealth of information from past events.

You navigate the site through the menus on the left hand side of the page. You can access various sections within the site by clicking on the lists. Several sections are split into sub sections. Any areas that are restricted to members-only will ask you to enter a username and password if you are not already logged into the website.

Navigation:
Home; About HAIAF; Internal Audit; Latest News; Conferences and Events; Information; Contact Us; Members Home; Discussion Forum; Site Help

---

Figure 14.4   Introduction To Housing Association Internal Audit Forum Website (HAIAF)
Source: www.haiaf.org accessed July 2007

2.   Charities Internal Audit Network (see Figure 14.5)

The (ECCIA)[11] position paper *Internal Auditing in Europe* promotes the position of internal auditing in current governance processes worldwide:

> The Internal Market Directorate of the European Commission has proposed a new Directive on statutory audit (the 8th Directive) and is working to implement its action plan, 'Modernization of Company Law and Enhancement of Corporate Governance in the European Union – A Plan to Move Forward'. The European Confederation of Institutes of Internal Auditing (ECIIA) is taking this opportunity to highlight how the professional practice of internal auditing makes a positive contribution to achieving good corporate governance and effective risk management in organizations based in Europe and beyond. In particular, this position paper describes how internal auditing sits at the heart of these processes, not least by the promotion of the highest ethical standards among ECIIA professionals. The paper also sets out how internal auditors add value to the relationships they have with other participants in the governance process. It is hoped that these comments will be of use to the Commission in its deliberations.

Founded in 1994 CIAN has over 125 members working in a wide range of charities, many of which are household names.

CIAN has the active support of the Charity Commission and the Institute of Internal Auditors UK and Ireland.

The aim of CIAN is to assist its members in the effective discharge of their responsibilities and to promote the profession of internal audit in the voluntary sector, thereby helping charities to achieve their objectives more efficiently. To this end, CIAN provides its members with a forum for the exchange of ideas, information and opportunities for further training.

To achieve this aim CIAN undertakes a range of activities and provides a number of services to its members.

- Quarterly meetings at which expert speakers talk on selected subjects. This is followed by a group discussion and informal networking session.
- Workshops where smaller groups explore topics in greater depth; for example, risk management, audit of charity shops, the application of the Turnbull report.
- The provision of training by and for its members.
- A library of relevant papers and publications, copies of which are available to members.
- A network directory, listing all members and the key details of the charities they work in. This enables members to contact one another and share experience and expertise on matters of mutual interest.
- Passing on examples of fraud and current scams to create awareness of these dangers.

All members of CIAN are aware of and totally endorse the standards required of professional internal auditors as applied by The Institute of Internal Auditors.

Membership is free to all those operating as internal auditors or those with responsibility for internal control in charities.

Information on becoming an internal auditor for a charity [click here]

Navigation:
Home; About Us; Events; Contact Us; Membership; Special Interest Groups; Latest News; Job Vacancies; Membership Area; Survey

Figure 14.5   Introduction To Charities Internal Audit Network Website (CIAN)
Source: www.cianonline.org.uk accessed July 2007

This paper contains in its discussion useful messages to use when promoting internal auditing, though not identified as such. If you search for the word 'promotion' you will find that internal auditing promotes:

- profession of internal auditing;
- highest ethical standards in its services;
- worldwide contribution of best internal auditing practices;
- many different roles internal auditors have in their organizations;
- contribution to good corporate governance;
- highest ethical standards in the organizations;
- public interest in its work;
- quality assurance in its resources and practices;
- continuous improvement;
- added value it achieves for the organizations which it serves; and
- knowledge requirements for internal auditors.

Compare the above with the Contents structure of this book: there are many similarities. The framework for developing professional internal auditing services is now well established. Look for this framework in the internal audit activity in your organization. This is a good framework to address when developing a marketing strategy, plan and action today and tomorrow, and one that is cutting edge. Compare this list with the questions in Figure 14.2, repeated here as Figure 14.6. Only one of the above statements is referred to – added value. Yet the perception of internal auditing customers to all the others is very important for the services internal auditing provides. How many of the statements above are addressed in your internal auditing customer satisfaction survey?

Customer Satisfaction Survey Questionnaire

Please provide your evaluation of the recently completed audit by circling the number that best reflects the manner in which the audit was conducted. We would also be interested in any additional comments you have:

	Poor	Fair	Very Good	Good	Exceptional
1. *Auditor Communication:*					
(a) The objectives of the audit were clearly communicated.	1	2	3	4	5
(b) The auditors asked for your input/concerns.	1	2	3	4	5
(c) Your input/concerns were satisfactorily addressed.	1	2	3	4	5
(d) Significant developments were communicated on a timely basis during the audit.	1	2	3	4	5
(e) Audit findings were clearly communicated and agreed upon at the conclusion of the audit.	1	2	3	4	5
2. *Auditor understanding of your business operations*	1	2	3	4	5
3. *Findings of the audit:*					
(a) Accurate	1	2	3	4	5
(b) Reasonable	1	2	3	4	5
(c) Useful and 'value-adding'	1	2	3	4	5
(d) Significant	1	2	3	4	5

4. *How could internal audit have been more useful to your organization?*

....
....
....
....
....

Figure 14.6   Customer Satisfaction Survey Questionnaire
Source: J. Ridley, *A Quality System Manual for Internal Auditing* (1993)

Another source for benchmarking the marketing of internal auditing services is to study the innovation and creativity in brochures, advertising and websites of firms marketing internal auditing services. Their professional approach to this can be expensive and not within the budgets of most in-house internal auditing activities. But their approach can still be studied and lessons learnt from the customer needs they are aiming to satisfy and the quality of work they are promoting.

At a presentation to the IIA–UK & Ireland Heads of Internal Audit Group in 2007, Kelsey Walker of Just Assured Ltd listed some of the challenging messages she has had to 'sell' in the past few years:

- Risk Management is worth doing well
- Risk-based internal auditing is a great service to the Board and top management team
- Consulting is an important internal audit role that will benefit the organization – here's how . . .
- We really can do something on corporate social responsibility – and our customers will expect us to . . . how about including it in the audit plan.
- People, not systems run organizations
- I need more resources because . . . !

Each applies to all internal audit activities. How do you market these messages? Her following analysis of to whom internal auditing are marketing – *customer versus stakeholder* – is interesting and opens up new challenges for the marketing plan:

Customer: Those with the power to contract or withdraw their custom (or have significant influence over those who do).

Could include:
Audit Committee
Board
Chief Executive
Executive Team

Stakeholder: Those who benefit from or place reliance on the work of internal audit.

Could include:
Department heads and teams
End user of organization's service or products
Shareholders
Regulator / External Audit

This listing of customers and stakeholders is well worth considering when developing the internal auditing marketing plan. Most marketing plans focus on identifying only the customer. Internal stakeholder interest in internal auditing has always been there. External stakeholder interest in internal auditing is growing. It is being promoted both by The IIA and the IIA–UK & Ireland at professional level. Why not also at organization level by internal auditing activities? Today, there are many examples of internal auditing being promoted on organization websites as part of their assurance of good governance. Today, some websites even go further and have separate sites for their internal auditing activities and reporting, particularly in the public sector. This is more common in North America, but must increase more globally in the future if professional internal auditing is to grow in its status in governance structures and processes.

CHAPTER SUMMARY

The IIA and its global network of associations have always promoted themselves through the sharing of knowledge, development of vision and mission statements, professional standards, code of ethics, position statements, journals, education and training programmes, conferences and many other activities, not least its growing membership. But at internal audit activity level in organizations there is little research today to indicate how this promotion is being extended into marketing plans and promotions addressed to internal auditing's customers and stakeholders, both internal and external to the organization. Those organizations providing outsourced internal auditing services have led the way in the promotion of their services. All internal auditing activities should benchmark their own marketing with these. Where evidence exists that in-house internal auditing is promoting itself there is some use of brochures and customer satisfaction surveys: these today need to cover the professional attributes of internal auditing as well as how it is performed. There is also some evidence of the use by internal audit activities of Intranet and website promotion of the services they provide, in some cases including audit planning, findings and recommendations – and this really is cutting edge.

Promotion of internal auditing can have an important influence on the success of the Gray and Gray (1997) motivational themes, goals and categories for innovation, including the additions and changes already made in Chapters 2–13:

Motivations

1. Progress within the field of professional internal auditing.
2. Increasing competition leading to pressures to reduce costs and increase efficiency.
3. New challenges, such as increasing internal control risks due to staff reductions and restructuring.
4. Opportunities to increase efficiency and quality as a result of technological advances.
5. Changes in corporate management practices and philosophies, such as Total Quality Management, re-engineering, continuous quality improvement, or related approaches.
6. Challenges and opportunities of global issues and developments.
7. **Social and environmental issues, including health and safety, impacting all organizations.**
8. **Recognition that professionalism, quality and standards are essential attributes for world-class status in any internal auditing activity.**
9. **Importance of organizational governance to meet regulatory and stakeholders' needs.**
10. **A continuous search for good and evil in how organizations and all their operations are directed and controlled.**
11. **Recognition that all types of crime in and by an organization should be fought.**
12. **Encouragement to think creatively.**

Goals

1. **Continuous** improvement of the quality of internal auditing services.
2. **Achieve best practice by continuously benchmarking.**
3. Expansion of services to increase the value-added of internal auditing.
4. Boost staff skills, performance and morale.
5. **Sell internal auditing as future focused.**
6. **To reduce the opportunities for all types of crime in an organization.**
7. **Increase satisfaction from all our customers.**
8. **Add new skills in the art of questioning.**
9. **Sell internal auditing services as a contribution to the organization's good reputation.**

Categories

1. Changes in the way that internal auditors interact with the rest of their enterprises **and all those with a stakeholder interest.**

  2. Internal restructuring and changes in the organization and management of internal auditing.
  3. Creation of new audit services and methods.
  4. Changes in the use of technology.
  5. **Continuously improve knowledge and skills in the teams of staff who carry out internal auditing engagements.**
  6. **New services to fight crime.**
  7. **Assistance in evaluation of the board's performance.**
  8. **Continuous improved satisfaction from all our customers.**
  9. **Changes in the way internal auditing asks questions.**
  10. **Contributions to the organization's good reputation.**

The most important foundation for a good promotion programme is commitment to a good business plan. The motivation themes would be improved by the addition of:

13. **Commitment to the promotion of a good business plan.**

PROMOTING INTERNAL AUDITING PRINCIPIA 1998 AND 2008

My 1998 principia for internal auditing included the following related to the promotion of its products and services (see Appendix A):

  4. Many of the attributes demonstrated by internal auditors, and valued most by management, are the same attributes recommended in codes of best practice for internal auditors.
  21. Success of internal auditing lies in how it is researched and developed, and then promoted in the organization market place.
  22. Innovation and understanding its customers' needs are the keys to how internal auditing should be sold throughout the audit process.
  27. Use superlatives to reinforce internal audit staff and market their services.
  30. Market internal auditing as a contribution to your organization's quality improvement programme.

These are now changed to reflect the importance of promoting internal audit services today (see Appendix B):

  20. Success of internal auditing lies in how its professional best practices are researched, developed and promoted in its organization market place.
  21. Understanding its customers risk management, control and governance needs are the keys to how internal auditing should be sold throughout the audit process.
  22. Use superlatives to reinforce internal audit staff and promote their services.

A VISION FOR INTERNAL AUDITING PROMOTING ITSELF

> **We promote our professional**
> **values at all times**

SYNOPSES OF CASE STUDIES

Case 14.1: Meeting New Demands

Synopsis

Marketing internal auditing in an organization is a must. *'The success of a marketing programme depends on the auditor's ability to seek and create marketing opportunities for the purpose of making economic contributions to their organization.'* Marketing internal auditing can be a *'... rigorous and profitable journey... '*. After the first marketing plan begins the second step is to improve it to *'... ensure that audit duties are performed while providing quality consulting services to management, and streamline it to make it more economically sound and effective'*. Marketing is always a continuous process requiring creative thinking and the promotion of best practices, if not also cutting edge resources and practices.

From *Audit Customer Satisfaction: Marketing Added Value* (1996), Cindy E. Cosmas. Copyright 1996 by The Institute of Internal Auditors, Inc., 247 Maitland Avenue, Altamonte Springs, Florida 32710-4201, USA. Reprinted with permission.

After Reading the Case Study Consider:

1. How does your current internal auditing planning compare with that in the case study?
2. When did you last reassess your internal auditing plan looking for ways to improve it to meet the challenges of internal auditing as a service in the future?
3. Does your internal auditing plan include the promotion of any cutting edge resources and practices?

Case 14.2: Selling and Marketing are two Different Things

Synopsis

'Selling and marketing are two different things.' The challenge in internal auditing is to communicate key messages to different audiences. Ten words of wisdom for selling and marketing internal auditing introduce new themes for cutting edge resources and practices to sell and market in the future.

Richard Gossage, then Deputy President of the IIA–UK & Ireland contributed these words of wisdom on the selling and marketing of internal auditing in the Housing Association Internal Audit Forum research BRACE 3, discussed in the chapter.

After Reading the Case Study Consider:

1. How does your selling and marketing of internal auditing compare with the definition above?
2. What 'current gaps' exist when you benchmark the 10 words of wisdom with your own internal auditing actions to sell and market internal auditing?

Case 14.3: The Housing Association Internal Audit Forum as a Promoter of Professional Internal Auditing

Synopsis

How one sector of internal auditors sold and marketed themselves with their organizations' regulator and trade bodies, establishing a strong independent forum of experience and knowledge, linked to The IIA, its *International Professional Practices Framework* and other professional bodies. Its research, training programmes, conferences, meetings and new website have demonstrated a cutting edge approach to enhancing the profession of internal auditing for its members, the organizations they serve and the whole sector.

> Contributed by Kelsey Walker, MBA FIIA, an early member and past executive committee postholder of the Forum, with permission from the current Forum Chair.

After Reading the Case Study Consider:

1. How does the promotion of professional internal auditing in your industry sector compare with that of the Forum's voluntary collective approach and its research, training and marketing strategies?
2. Is internal auditing in your industry sector collectively promoting its professionalism to your regulator(s) and trade bodies?

Case 14.4: Internal Auditing is Re-branding Itself

Synopsis

Internal auditing is now marketing its services as *'added value'* through the governance processes being required in many organizations, across all sectors and internationally. Six of the elements of a governance process are discussed: each offering opportunities for innovation and cutting edge resources and practices in internal auditing.

> This case study is based on an article by the author submitted to a national newspaper in 2003, but not printed.

After Reading the Case Study Consider:

1. Have you re-branded your internal auditing for the 21st century and are you promoting this throughout your organization?
2. How many of your customers know about internal auditing *'values and principles'* and are making the most of these?
3. Is your internal auditing *'adding value'* and measuring this in all of the six elements of the governance process identified in the research discussed in the case study?

Case 14.5: South West Audit Partnership, England

Synopsis

How one internal audit manager 'raised the bar' of professional internal auditing in local government by marketing and establishing partnership internal auditing for a group of local government authorities. The aims of this project, how it was established and benefits after two years are discussed. A partnership website page promotes what it does and how it does it, addressing in each a cutting edge approach to all its services.

> Contributed by Gerald Cox, CIA MIIA, Head of Internal Audit, South West Audit Partners, England – an organization that provides internal audit services to a growing number of local authorities in the southwest of England. See its website page on www.southsomerset.gov.uk for more details

After Reading the Case Study Consider:

1. Are there benefits for partnerships in your sector and, if so, how could you promote these?
2. Do you promote The IIA *International Professional Standards* compliance for your services to all your customers and stakeholders?
3. Do you promote your *'protocol'* with your *'... external auditors to ensure that resources are effectively utilised and duplication of effort is minimised'*?
4. Do you promote sharing of best practices during your internal audit engagements?

SELF-ASSESSMENT QUESTIONS

14.1

Ask the following questions in your internal auditing team and to your customers and stakeholders. Compare the answers and start developing your cutting edge marketing plan. (Reproduced with permission from the IIA–UK & Ireland and taken from *Effective Marketing, Guidance on Marketing your Internal Audit Function* (2000).)

1. What are the key objectives for internal audit?
2. How, if at all, can we state these in qualitative and quantitative terms?
3. What are our strengths and weaknesses?
4. What opportunities and threats do we have?
5. What are our marketing goals?
6. Who are our stakeholders and what do each of these require from us?
7. What are the products and/or services we are offering and to whom are we offering them?
8. How do our stakeholders perceive the benefits of our competitors' products and services?
9. Are our marketing goals realistic in terms of what the marketplace will accept?
10. What benefits, both tangible and intangible, do our products and/or services need to have to give us a differential and sustainable advantage over our competitors?
11. What is our stakeholders' perception of value?

12. Where on the attitudinal spectrum (e.g. compliance through to risk based) do we believe our stakeholders lie?
13. What is going to be our vision statement and how will we communicate this to our stakeholders?
14. How are we going to monitor the performance of our marketing activities?

14.2

How many of the following IIA–UK & Ireland (2000) checklist questions can you answer satisfactorily for your internal auditing activity?

1. What are our marketing goals?
2. Who are our stakeholders and what do each of these require from us?
3. What are the products and/or services we are offering and to whom are we offering them?
4. What is going to be our vision statement and how will we communicate this to our stakeholders?
5. How are we going to monitor the performance of our marketing activities?

NOTES AND REFERENCES

1. From *Devotions Upon Emergent Occasions* (1624), Meditation XVII, Cited in *The Oxford Dictionary of Quotations*, 5th edition (2000), Oxford University Press, Oxford, England.
2. Globalization Through Partnership, A.J. Spoel, Internal Auditor (October 1990), The IIA.
3. *Perceptions of Audit Quality – A Survey Analysis* (1996), The Chartered Institute of Public Finance and Accountancy (CIPFA), London, England. www.cipfa.org.uk
4. *Audit Customer Satisfaction: Marketing Added Value* (1996), Cindy E. Cosmas, The IIA.
5. Published in *Internal Auditing* (December 1997), IIA–UK & Ireland.
6. 'Building Bridges', Jean-Pierre Garitte, *Internal Auditor*, (August 1998), The IIA.
7. *BRACE 3 Benchmark – Best Practice Marketing in Internal Audit in Housing Associations* (1998), research by Professor Jeffrey Ridley, Housing Association Internal Audit Forum, www.haiaf.org
8. *Effective Marketing: Guidance on Marketing your Internal Audit Function* (2000), IAA–UK & Ireland.
9. *A Balanced Scorecard and Framework for Internal Auditing Departments* (2002), Mark L. Frigo, The Institute of Internal Auditors Research Foundation, Altamonte Springs, Florida, USA.
10. *The Balanced Scorecard: Translating Strategy into Action* (1996), Robert S. Kaplan, David P. Norton, Harvard Business School Press, Boston, USA.
11. *Position Paper – Internal Auditing in Europe* (2005), ECIIA European Confederation of Institutes of Internal Auditing, Brussels, Belgium. www.eciia.org

Cutting Edge Internal Auditing
Manages Knowledge Well

*'The simple fact is that if you have the right people in the right jobs
and you have teamwork you can achieve anything you want.'*

Errol J. Yates 1990[1]

Scientists know more and more about
less and less ~ until they know
everything about nothing!
And Auditors ......? ....

INTERNAL AUDITING MANAGES KNOWLEDGE
WELL BEFORE 2001

Growing knowledge in an organization is not just about the abilities of individuals, however well these are mastered and the knowledge supporting them continuously improved. It is also about how this knowledge is encouraged, grown in teams and managed by the organization to achieve its vision and objectives – not just teams in the organization, but also teams involving its many different external stakeholders.

In Chapter 11 my 1995 article comparing internal auditing to painting a picture discussed the tone of an internal audit engagement as its level and depth of knowledge:

- **Tone**   All objects are intrinsically light and dark. There are many tones between white and black. Knowledge is the internal auditor's tone. Once the survey lines of the audit are planned, the levels of knowledge required for the audit must be set. Knowledge provides atmosphere and interest. Like tone the right levels of knowledge in the audit team will attract those being served by the audit.

Knowledge is managed by the other painting skills discussed in the article – line, colour, perspective, scale and composition. All make a painting attractive to the viewer. All manage knowledge, not just in an internal audit engagement but also in the organization it serves. These skills make knowledge attractive. These skills manage its knowledge. Knowledge by itself has little value unless it is used to create. Consider this by re-reading the definitions I gave to each of the other painting skills:

- **Line**   Line starts with the audit survey. A time when the internal auditor can be fluent and expressive. A time of high imagination. Background information about the activities to be audited starts the drawing process and links loose lines into a pattern of audit objectives to achieve the audit scope. Lines establish plans.
- **Colour**   There is no colour without light. Colour is closely linked to tone. The internal auditor's choice of audit tests establishes the colour palette for the picture audit. Creative skill is needed in mixing the tests so that they focus light into all of the audit objectives and complement each other. Just as it is very easy to end up with a muddy colour palette, it is also very easy to end an audit with 'muddy' objectives if the mix of tests is not right.
- **Scale**   Objects in themselves have no scale – they can only be small or large scale in relation to something else. Audit scale is size in relation to the risks for the organization as a whole and not just for the activities being audited. Risk assessment provides scale for the audit. To be creative during risk assessment requires the process to continue from the organization level through the audit objectives to the selection of audit tests and review of the results.
- **Perspective**   Perspective is the three-dimensional reality of the world created by leading lines to viewing points. Each line in the audit must lead to a viewing point. Not all viewing points are within the activities being audited. The creative internal auditor looks for viewing points in other parts of the organization and frequently leads lines to viewing points outside the organization.
- **Composition**   The arrangement of an audit has to attract those it is serving. A picture with poor composition will fail to find a buyer. The composition of the audit report must [like a painting] lead the customer's eyes into its subject matter and keep interest throughout the viewing.

The importance of individual learning for all internal auditors, through continuing professional development programmes, is essential in any management of their knowledge as individuals and as team members. Such planned programmes not only address skill needs but also the knowledge individuals need for the services they are providing. The IIA requires internal auditors to '. . . *enhance their knowledge and skills, and other competencies through continuing professional development programmes*'. It also includes in its *Code of Ethics* the following principle and rules:

Principle   Internal auditors apply the knowledge, skills and experience needed in the performance of internal auditing services.

Rules of Conduct

4.1   Shall engage only in those services for which they have the necessary knowledge, skills and experience.
4.2   Shall perform internal auditing services in accordance with the *International Standards for the Professional Practice of Internal Auditing*.
4.3   Shall continually improve their proficiency and the effectiveness and quality of their services.

Both The IIA and the IIA–UK & Ireland support these requirements with learning, training and conference programmes. Other members of The IIA global network do the same. More universities are now supporting internal auditing learning and other colleges, private tuition providers, governments and international organizations such as the World Bank. The knowledge these programmes teach needs to be planned through personal development programmes and evaluation of the results. It is not sufficient to attend learning programmes and obtain certificates. All internal auditor learning should be a planned step to another level of knowledge. Learning programmes need to be planned and results evaluated to determine how well new knowledge is being managed. Managed into the services being provided – as perceived by the internal auditor, audit management and their customers. If carried out formally this process can be cutting edge.

Equally as important The IIA requires *'The internal audit activity collectively should possess or obtain the knowledge, skill, and other competencies needed to perform its responsibilities.'* This team approach to managing knowledge needed for professional internal auditing is essential when planning its services at function and engagement level. Peter Senge's[2] five disciplines of the learning organization are still as relevant today as they were when first published in the early 1990s:

> Today, I believe five new 'component technologies' are gradually converging to innovate learning organizations. Though developed separately, each will, I believe, prove critical to the others' success, just as occurs with any ensemble. Each provides a vital dimension in building organizations that can truly 'learn', that can continually enhance their capacity to realize their highest aspirations.

Senge's five component technologies are *'systems thinking; personal mastery; mental models; building shared vision; team learning'*. Each is a study in their own right but also strongly influence each other. Any management of knowledge needs to address all five. In *Leading Edge Internal Auditing* (1998) I wrote:

> Senge (1990) sees mastering team learning as a need for all organizations in today's working environments:

> This is so because almost all important decisions are now made in teams, either directly or through the need for teams to translate individual decisions into action. Individual learning, at some level, is irrelevant for organizational learning. But if teams learn, they become a microcosm for learning throughout the organization. Insights gained are put into action. Skills developed can propagate to other individuals and to other teams (although there is no guarantee that they will propagate). The team's accomplishments can set the tone and establish a standard for learning together for the whole organization.

Use Technology to Make Teams More Effective

Research by Ernst & Young International[3] in the UK, showed that technology in internal auditing teams is already taking place:

> Internal audit departments operate a structured service delivery approach, most often using small hierarchical teams. The consensus between team leaders was that team building was managed effectively and on the job coaching worked well. Communication within the departments and between teams was considered an issue that needed to be monitored closely. Regular team meetings and annual audit conferences were promoted whilst e-mail systems have proved very successful in keeping staff working at remote locations 'in touch'.

> Advances in communications now mean that for some teams it is not necessary to meet physically. Communication can be by telecommunications, computer networks and video conferencing. These communication advances have increased opportunities for national, and international teamwork.

The facility to create teams across functions and organizations at local, national and international levels has never been better.

Global teamworking is now common place in many organizations. If it does not already exist it is likely that it is being or will be planned in the future. Successful teamworking depends on individuals being motivated to work together, empowered to seek solutions to common problems and being able to communicate with each other. Three developments that have encouraged teambuilding in organizations of all sizes are change, empowerment and technology.

Change and its current speed of implementation in most organizations has encouraged development of teams to innovate and create new structures to achieve organization objectives. Empowered individuals have brought to teambuilding a new dimension of group creativity, encouraged by management and board members. Local issues have been overshadowed by more immediate tasks of achieving corporate goals and visions.

Both change and empowerment have been made more possible by the use and speed of information technology. Not just computers, but also communications networks, both internal and external to an organization. These networks now permit teams to achieve their objectives, often without meeting physically, or just on a few occasions. There can be few readers of this book who are not linked by technology into one or more teams across their organizations, and even outside with other organizations.

Professor John Oakland (1999)[4] devotes a chapter of his book on organizational excellence to people, their development and teamwork, the '... *only efficient way to tackle process improvement or complex problems...*'. He cites the value of John Adair's[5] 1960's model for teamwork for measuring a team's performance. This consists of three circles overlapping each other, each circle representing a team need:

Drawing upon the discipline of social psychology, John Adair developed and applied to training the functional view of leadership. The essence of this he distilled into the three interrelated but distinctive requirements of a leader. These are: to define and achieve the job or task [Task need], to build up and coordinate a team to do this [Team need], and to develop and satisfy the individuals within the team [Individual need] ... the team leader's or facilitator's task is to concentrate on the small central area where all three circles overlap....

This same approach can be used to measure an internal auditing team's performance in managing knowledge needed to contribute added-value to the organization – clearly define the task and performance measures; establish the right team; attend to individual needs of reinforcement and growth. Not always easy to achieve all three when the team crosses organization boundaries and goes out into the world of education. Yet, important to achieve all three if the internal auditing team is to be successful in managing and growing the knowledge it needs to complete the task set by its charter and professionalism.

The London Chapter of The IIA recognized in the early 1970s that teaching and research at universities are key to the improvement of internal auditing knowledge for its future. Professor Andrew Chambers (1976)[6] discussed progress in teaching at universities, commenting '... *the race has hardly begun*'. As the first Senior Research Fellow in Internal Auditing at the Graduate Business Centre, The City University, London, Chambers developed and taught a specialist option on its Management MSc courses in Administrative Sciences, which included internal auditing empirical research. This was possibly the first time internal auditing had featured as the principal element of any taught degree programme – '... *let alone a Masters degree.*'

At an early stage in its development contact had been made with the London Chapter of The IIA. A meeting with its Education Committee launched a working relationship, resulting in a strategy of '... *developing internal auditing as a taught subject for degree students and as a research discipline'*. An early recognition by Chambers and others that knowledge acquired and managed by internal auditing needed to be taught and researched at an academic level. At the time this was cutting edge. Chambers saw internal auditing integrating easily into existing, already flexible, management programmes at The City University. He predicted internal auditing research at the time as being the internal auditing course's main long-term objective, *'Perhaps the most long-term objective is to develop internal audit research, degree, and post-experience courses in other universities. At least in the UK, there is only one University heavily involved at the moment.'*

After 1976 there were more internal auditing academic developments in the United Kingdom and across the world. Other universities started to teach internal auditing vocational knowledge and encourage empirical internal auditing research by their students. Many of these university courses were recognized by The IIA and led into its certification and qualification programmes. Programmes were managed by The IIA, some by universities, and some by its affiliated National Institutes, including the IIA–UK & Ireland.

In the United Kingdom the then South Bank Polytechnic, London (now London South Bank University) assisted the IIA–UK & Ireland in the development of, and taught, an IIA–UK & Ireland Diploma in Internal Auditing, launched in the early 1980s. In 1991, it developed an internal auditing option unit in one of its undergraduate accounting programmes. Then, and possibly even today, the only university course world-wide teaching internal auditing as a separate course unit at undergraduate level. My inaugural address launching this course recognized other internal auditing academic developments around the world:

> Since the mid-1980s, there has also been a growth of graduate teaching in the United States, some sponsored by The IIA. There is also graduate teaching of internal auditing in France and Australia. Other countries are following and the weight of their contribution to research and the teaching of internal auditing will add to the value and importance of [internal auditing] qualification.
>
> This is all good news for Higher Education as it moves with a high growth rate towards the end of the century. The growth in the teaching of internal auditing, however, cannot be seen in isolation from other disciplines such as accounting and management. I see a need for more integration of the teaching and examination of internal auditing into other teaching programmes, allowing students and working internal auditors more choices in their career plans when they qualify. A higher profile for internal audit qualification links into management education and the teaching of corporate governance. Recognized links to MBA programmes, accounting, banking, legal, insurance and administration teaching and research will be essential by the year 2000.

A review of my 1991 address was published in the Institute of Chartered Secretaries and Administrators[7] journal, ending with:

> Professor Ridley stressed creativity, composition, perception and relationship skills as important for [internal] auditors. His view of world-class internal audit involves professionalism in training, quality in customer commitment and truly international and up to date standards.

Do you recognize the PQS's for world-class internal auditing, discussed in Chapter 3?

Not all my predictions have come true or challenges have been met in teaching internal auditing across many academic courses, but much has been achieved. This undergraduate course unit has been very successful with students. Many have moved on to internal auditing careers with organizations and professional accounting firms. This has been recognized formally by the Association of Chartered Certified Accountants, London, as an exemption for some of its professional examinations; and an updated version of the course unit is still taught today by the London South Bank University (LSBU) on professionally accredited courses. Its knowledge requirements have always been focused and assessed using The IIA statements on internal auditing responsibilities and then its *International Standards* and now *International Professional Practices Framework*.

In 2000 the London South Bank University validated a postgraduate course in corporate governance, in collaboration with the Institute of Chartered Secretaries and Administrators. This now offers direct entry to Master's level teaching for students with related professional qualifications.

In parallel with the City University and London South Bank University internal auditing postgraduate teaching and empirical research, the University of Central England, Birmingham, launched its own postgraduate and internal auditing certification programmes in auditing and risk management. These programmes of teaching and research attracted considerable support from overseas internal auditors, their employers and governments, quickly achieving recognition from The IIA and IIA–UK & Ireland, as well as other countries' National Institutes and Chapters, affiliated to The IIA. At the same time the UK Civil Service College started to teach the IIA–UK & Ireland diplomas. This college, now named the National School of Government, teaches a full range of courses leading to the IIA–UK & Ireland qualifications, including the Government Internal Audit Certificate.

The IIA–UK & Ireland qualifications were given considerable promotion and later developed into the qualification MIIA (Member of the Institute of Internal Auditors); then a new qualification for entry to the MIIA was launched – the PIIA (Practitioner in Internal Auditing). *[More recently both these qualifications have become the Diploma in Internal Auditing (was the PIIA) and the Advanced Diploma in Internal Auditing (was the MIIA). In each of the developments of these qualifications the syllabuses have been revised to reflect a widening scope of internal auditing responsibilities and today's nature of internal auditing in risk management, control and governance processes.]*

O'Regan (2001)[8] '. . . *studied the current professional status of internal auditing'* and recognized The IIA as '. . . *the driving force behind the increasing professionalization of internal auditing over the last half-century'*. A driving force of research that has developed, captured and communicated the body of knowledge we know today. He listed, among other attributes of The IIA, '. . . *a defined body of examined and certified knowledge. . . . This attribute, more than any other, has driven development of the profession and science of internal auditing as we know it today.'*

Article:
Wise Internal Auditors Manage Knowledge Well[9] (2001)

Those that study and advise on knowledge management have written well on this subject over the past few years. Both as a product of important management and as an learning and as an management tool to motivate vation. Knowledge management is a means of developing, capturing and communicating information.

> **'Knowledge management is a means of developing, capturing and communicating information.'**

information. It is also about searching information to improve strategic thinking and decision-making processes. Most good knowledge management processes now use electronic methods to ensure that all information available is being used to best advantage for the organization and its entire staff.

Bill Gates[a] (1999) of Microsoft discusses the value of the electronic library of knowledge in all organizations '. . . *to gather and organize information, disseminate the information to people who need it, and constantly refine the information through analysis and collaboration'*. His simplified definition of knowledge management is '. . . *nothing more than managing information flow'*. But is management of information enough and can it ever be simplified? In most organizations management of information is one of its most difficult tasks. Too often disorganized and not used wisely.

All organizations have seen explosions of information. Storing and searching that information to achieve an organization's two key objectives – its aims and improved performance – is not that easy. It requires good planning, efficient methods and a commitment to share knowledge. How often are all your information flows tested for the knowledge requirements of these two key objectives? Do you ever do this in your internal auditing function, your auditee's function or for the whole organization? Such tests are becoming more and more important as volumes of information continue to grow. Internal auditors must have a clear responsibility to address and evaluate knowledge management in their own functions and in all other areas of their organizations.

Auditing, as practised by internal auditors or any other type of auditor, is based on established principles that have been tested and developed over many years. It has its own *'scientists'* who have explored and developed better methods and opened up new boundaries of knowledge for those that practise its art. Committed practitioners have driven its development, either individually or in groups. Its principles have a universal acceptance. Its standards are continually being developed and revised to meet new demands by both practitioners and those who rely on its services. There is a continuous programme of research and development at academic and practitioner levels that documents and influences what is practised.

The IIA's 1941 Certificate of Incorporation sowed the seeds for a science of internal auditing. This stated that the IIA's then purpose as a profession was:

> To cultivate, promote and disseminate knowledge and information concerning internal auditing and subjects related thereto; to establish and maintain standards of integrity, honour and character among internal auditors; to furnish information regarding internal auditing and the practice and methods thereof to its members, and to other persons interested therein, and to the general public; to cause the publication of articles relating to internal auditing and practices and methods thereof; to establish and maintain a library and reading rooms, meeting rooms and social rooms for the use of its members; to promote social intercourse among its members; and to do any and all things which shall be lawful and appropriate in furtherance of any of the purposes hereinbefore expressed.

---

[a] *Business @ the Speed of Thought – Using a Digital Nervous System* (1999: p. 238), Bill Gates, Penguin Books Ltd, England.

The IIA has researched a common body of knowledge for internal auditing since the 1970s. Its knowledge framework, researched and published[b] in the early 1990s, has this to say about internal auditing knowledge:

> ... internal auditors must possess skills and knowledge from several different disciplines. They must be excellent communicators, both orally and in writing. They must be well versed in computers and technology to be proficient in the new Information age. They must be logical thinkers. They must possess accounting, economics, finance, and other types of management knowledge to understand business and the context in which organizations operate. They must also have numerous other types of support knowledge, such as human relations, sampling, quantitative methods, and fraud detection abilities. Indeed, it appears that the knowledge required to be an effective internal auditor almost demands that one be 'superhuman' – an expert in numerous disciplines.

Detail supporting this research was used to update the syllabus for The IIA Certified Internal Auditor (CIA®) examination programme as it is today. Further research by the IIA[c] in the late 1990s resulted in a new competency framework for internal auditing. Created from global research this framework identifies knowledge areas vital to internal auditing. Its guidance is now impacting much of the teaching and training in internal auditing today across the world. Its influence will grow, placing new demands on knowledge requirements for all internal auditors.

O'Regan[d] (2001) studied the current professional status of internal auditing and recognizes The IIA as '... the driving force behind the increasing professionalisation of internal auditing over the last half-century'. He lists among other attributes of The IIA '... a defined body of examined and certified knowledge...'. This attribute, more than any other, has driven development of the profession and science of internal auditing as we know it today. That defined body of knowledge is clearly stated in the current syllabi of the IIA Certified Internal Auditor (CIA) examination programme and new international standards for the professional practice of internal auditing. Both are available in electronic form and provide a bank of knowledge that will grow, adding significant value worldwide to all internal auditing functions. Good knowledge management skills will be needed by internal auditors for these to be used to create best professional internal auditing practices. They should impact all internal auditors and provide continuous opportunities for performance improvement.

This year has seen a number of case studies being published showing how internal auditors are contributing to knowledge management in the organizations they serve. Four such studies developed by the IIA–UK & Ireland (2001)[e] demonstrate how internal auditors in Lex Service, Bank of England, Central Bank of Ireland and HM Customs & Excise have embraced knowledge management.

---

[b] *A Common Body of Knowledge for the Practice of Internal Auditing* (1992), W. Steve Albrecht *et al.*, The IIA.
[c] *Competency Framework for Internal Auditing* (CFIA) (1999), William Birkett *et al.*, The IIA.
[d] 'Genesis of a Profession: Towards Professional Status for Internal Auditing', David O'Regan, *Managerial Auditing Journal*, 16.4 (2001: pp. 215–226).
[e] 'Knowledge and Power', Neil Hodge, *Internal Auditing & Business Risk*, February (2001: pp. 14–18), IIA–UK & Ireland.

Each using electronic methods to store, manage and spread knowledge about their internal auditing to all audit staff and others in their organizations. Each using their auditing to review how knowledge in their organizations is being managed.

A recent issue of The Institute of Internal Auditor's newsletter *Auditwire*[f] (2001) also outlines how other North American-based internal auditors are '... *getting involved and shaping key roles* ...' in effective knowledge management. The article demonstrates how internal auditors in General Motors Corporation, Ford Motor Company, Xerox Corporation and Tosco Corporation are developing their knowledge management strategies and skills, as well as contributing to the dissemination of knowledge about control and risk across their organizations. All use databases linked to electronic communication systems to communicate their knowledge, both globally within their internal auditing functions and across their organizations. Each sees this as an added value to the services they provide. It improves the quality of audits and increases management awareness of best practices. For those internal auditing functions with a high turnover rate, their planned and structured sharing of knowledge is seen to continuously improve the performance of all levels of staff, whether new or experienced, contributing to better teamwork, supervision and management of all resources.

It is not only large internal auditing functions that embrace the challenges of Intranet to spread knowledge throughout their services. The internal audit manager of Network Housing Association, London, has used her organization's Intranet to establish a 'home site' for internal auditing. This site spreads up-to-date knowledge of its staffing, charter, audit planning, risk assessments, auditing procedures and quality assurance measures for all the organizations it serves. Capturing such knowledge and keeping it up to date provides an important stimulus and challenge. For its internal auditing staff it is an excellent learning process.

But it is not just in-house Intranet knowledge that internal auditors should manage. Worldwide websites now provide large databases of knowledge with powerful search engines. There can be few internal auditing activities that could not benefit from knowledge freely available on websites set-up outside the organizations they serve. All internal audits, risk assessments and consultancy activities need to manage and search this external knowledge. Any internal auditors today that do not reference into Internet websites are weakened by lack of a full understanding of the knowledge available for the services they provide.

The IIA[g] has also published guidance on the use of the Internet by internal auditors. Written by an internal auditor this book provides '... *options for accessing the Internet, useful Internet tools and services for audit professionals, a comprehensive list of available resources, and case studies of how internal auditors use the Internet for audit-related work.*' The author, Jim Kaplan, has his own website, www.auditnet.org, providing useful references for all internal auditors seeking to increase their knowledge and the value of their services.

---

[f] 'Harnessing Knowledge', *Auditwire*, May 2001, The IIA.
[g] *The Auditor's Guide to Internet Resources*, 2nd edition (2000), Jim Kaplan, The IIA.

Creating frameworks for the implementation of good knowledge management practices has occupied many consultants over the past few years. Bain & Company[h] research lists knowledge management requirements as

- Catalogue and evaluate the organization's current knowledge base;
- Determine which competencies will be key to future success and what base of knowledge is needed to build a sustainable leadership position therein;
- Invest in systems and processes to accelerate the accumulation of knowledge;
- Assess the impact of such systems on leadership, culture, and hiring practices;
- Codify new knowledge and turn it into tools and information that will improve both product innovation and overall profitability.

Lloyd[i] sees '. . . *a close link among data, information, knowledge and wisdom . . .* '. He argues that '*. . . we start with wisdom and that provides the framework within which to manage knowledge . . .* ' His definition of wisdom is the combination of knowledge and values. It is the use to which knowledge is put that is critical in all knowledge management processes. Being wise after the event is frequent. The art of good internal auditing must always be to be wise before the event. Being wise about knowledge before the event is a key to success in all internal auditing services.

Knowledge management will always be key to innovation and creativity in all sciences. Whether you view internal auditing as a profession, science or art, or none of these, there is no doubt that it requires wisdom and well-managed knowledge to add value in all the services it provides – knowledge not just of the organization, but also knowledge that is available outside the organization. There are many roles for internal auditors to occupy in knowledge management, as a user, as a communicator and a provider of assurance. Roles that now require wise internal auditors to have the knowledge to be not only good auditors, but also to be good teachers and consultants.

CUTTING EDGE INTERNAL AUDITING MANAGES KNOWLEDGE WELL TODAY AND IN THE FUTURE

Today, with many more universities worldwide researching and teaching internal auditing knowledge: there are many good examples of pioneering internal auditing learning. This has established an internal auditing knowledge bank of hundreds, if not thousands worldwide, of projects researching internal auditing knowledge at postgraduate and doctorate levels. Many of which have taken that knowledge into the practices of internal auditing we know today. That transfer of knowledge will continue to grow as an important part of internal auditing's professional development.

The European Confederation of Institutes of Internal Auditing (ECIIA) promotes an annual conference on research into internal auditing knowledge. The Fifth Annual Conference in 2007 was held at the University of Pisa, Italy. (See Figure 15.1 for the programme of research

---

[h] *Management Tools – An Executive's Guide* (2001), Bain & Company, USA. www.bain.com
[i] 'The Wisdom of the World – Messages for the New Millennium', Professor Bruce Lloyd, article in *The Futurist*, USA. www.wfs.org

PhD Colloquium – Papers
- The Process of Consulting on Management Control
- Changes in the Culture of Control
- The Impact of Organizational Models to Prevent Corporate Misconduct, on Internal Control Systems. An Empirical Research on Italian Listed Companies
- Characteristics of a Central Change Programme within a Governmental Bureaucracy: A Grounded Theory Study
- The Information Security Governance on Italian Companies: An Interpretative Contingent Model
- Higher Education Governance – The Case of Australian Universities
- How Corporate Governance Mechanisms could Enhance the Financial Information
- The ERM in US Listed Firms' Disclosure and Value Implications
- First Serious Step in Workload Audit of Latvia
- What Does it Take for Internal Auditing to Become a Separate Profession? An Analysis of Danish Internal Auditing
- The Independence of The Internal Audit Departments in the Saving Banks: A Descriptive Study

Main Conference – Research Papers
- Innovative Practices in Today's Internal Auditing
- Internal Auditing and Communication: A South African Perspective
- The Influence of Principles and Guidelines on Corporate Governance and Internal Auditing Practices: A Comparison Between Australia and Belgium
- Explaining the Importance of Internal Auditing in Belgian Companies: Agency Model Versus Control Environment Model
- Internal Auditing and Consulting Practice: A Comparison between UK and Ireland and Italy
- Risk-Based Internal Auditing within Greek Banks – A Case Study Approach
- Effective Working Relationships between Audit Committees and Internal Audit – the Cornerstone of Corporate Governance in Local Authorities
- Internal Auditing in Large Italian Business Groups: the 'Delegation Model'
- The Internal Auditing Function in Italian Listed Companies: State of Art and Future Perspective: Results of an Empirical Research
- The Role of the Internal Audit Activity in Assessing the Ethical Culture of an Organization
- Stakeholder Involvement in Corporate Decision Making – Fantasy or Reality? An Opportunity for Internal Auditing
- Corporate Governance Ratings and Financial Restatements
- An Organizational Approach to Comparative Corporate Governance: Costs, Contingencies, and Complementarities
- The Corporate Governance (CG) in Italy after the Approval of Law 262/2005. The Impacts on Internal Control (IC) Systems and on Internal Auditing (IA) Function
- Corporate Governance and Codes of Conduct: How Italian Companies are Responding to the New Corporate Governance Code

Figure 15.1   Fifth European Academic Conference On Internal Audit And Corporate Governance: University Of Pisa, Italy – April 2007
Source: European Confederation of Institutes of Internal Auditing (2007)

papers presented.) This gives some understanding of the scope and depth of current research into internal auditing and related knowledge and practices today. It is only a snapshot of current research but represents the high interest in internal auditing at universities. This can only increase as the knowledge required by internal auditors expands.

Knowledge of internal auditing and its development through research continues to grow across the world at many universities and colleges. The Cass Business School in London still has a strong MSc Management course with an internal auditing option:[10]

The MSc in Management is an academically rigorous and highly practical programme offering graduates from a variety of backgrounds the opportunity to develop knowledge and skills in key areas of modern management. The course allows students to tailor their studies to suit their particular interests and ambitions. The first term focuses on foundation management tools, allowing students to identify areas of strength and interest. The second term allows students to specialize in either general management, internal auditing, marketing, film business or entrepreneurship. This follows through to electives and projects. The Internal Audit stream is for those who want to go into the area of corporate governance, a prominent feature of most large organizations.

The Birmingham City University[11] has widened the knowledge base from which it teaches and researches internal auditing:

Further, the MSc must enable students to develop an holistic perspective so that they are able to view their own organizations in the context of the global environment, and equip them with ethical, equity, environmental perspectives, so that they are able to ensure that those in management operate in an ethically responsible manner and produce goods and services needed in an environmentally friendly way: with proper regard for fairness, quality, health and safety and optimum use of resources. They also need to demonstrate through research and rational argument that the beneficial interest of the organization is connected with that of the global society, short-term and long-term. This is to promote an ethical culture in their organizations that is not just altruism, but self-interest of management to promote societal interest.

The aims of its postgraduate and diploma course programme in internal audit, risk management and governance are:

To equip students with the knowledge, skills and attitudes to enable them to carry out management, operational, financial, quality, ethical and environmental audits in accordance with accepted professional standards, provide solutions to business problems, undertake a consultancy and facilitator role to help promote the best business practice and manage audit teams, audit departments and organizations.

In addition to its postgraduate programme it also offers learning courses accredited by The IIA and IIA–UK & Ireland for their professional qualification programmes and the international Certified Information Systems Auditor and Certified Fraud Examiner qualifications.

The London South Bank University is now working in partnership with the IIA–UK & Ireland[12] in e-learning development and teaching of its Advanced Diploma learning programme.

. . . this includes access to internet-based learning resources, guidance for wider reading and study, dedicated tutor support, marked assignments and feedback, and on-line mock exams to prepare candidates for the Institute's professional examinations. As well as enrolling with London South Bank University, which provides access to a range of University learning resources including electronic library facilities and a wide range of on-line academic and professional journals.

It is also currently developing a Masters course in Internal Auditing, denominated MSc Management (Internal Auditing). With a syllabus developed to closely follow the subjects covered in the Professional Qualifications offered by both the IIA–UK and The IIA, the programme's aim is to provide an attractive opportunity for internal auditors, usually in full-time employment, to prepare for their professional examinations, while at the same time obtaining the fuller (more thoughtful and challenging) education that university courses can provide. Additionally, the programme aims to provide professionally qualified internal auditors with the opportunity for a 'fast track' to advanced study, by way of a 'top up' taught course comprising taught units on research methods and contemporary research issues, followed by a relevant dissertation. Designed to be delivered in e-learning format, students will be able to undertake the course wherever they are located with no need to physically attend classes. It is planned to launch the course in phases, initially as a top up for students who have achieved the IIA UK's Advanced Diploma in Internal Auditing and Management or The IIA's Certified Internal Auditor qualification, later as a fully developed MSc open to all graduate students.

These academic/professional institute partnered learning programmes in the United Kingdom are good examples of using teams of academics and practitioners to develop and manage internal auditing knowledge well. Such Partnerships are established globally in a number of countries. They are encouraged by The IIA's now Internal Auditing Education Partnership Program (IAEP). They are creating a good academic knowledge base for cutting edge internal auditing in the future.

Add to this base the research programmes promoted by The IIA Research Foundation and other members of The IIA's global network and the body of internal auditing knowledge will continue to grow as a science across all sectors in every country. The IIA is again researching that body of knowledge as I write this book. Details of this are in The IIA website and notices on the progress of this research will appear during 2007 onwards:

CBOK is a comprehensive survey that will capture the state of the internal auditing profession throughout the world, including:

- The knowledge and skills that internal auditors possess.
- The varying skill and organizational levels that practice internal auditing work.
- The actual duties performed by internal auditors.
- The structure of internal audit organizations.
- The types of industries that practice internal auditing.
- The regulatory environment of various countries.

CBOK will provide an understanding of the unique value-added role internal auditing has in organizations throughout the world. This understanding will enable us to better define the future of internal auditing and ensure that it remains a vibrant and relevant contribution to organizations.

The results of CBOK will drive many crucial aspects of The IIA for the next three years, including:

- Certifications and exams
- Standards
- Advocacy
- Practice Advisories
- Educational Programs
- Educational Products
- Publications

Today's CBOK survey has created a new global team that will have a significant impact on the management of knowledge for internal auditing, and how it will be practised in the future. That impact will be felt by thousands of internal auditing teams across the world – or at least it should be felt. It will need to be interpreted into risk management, control and governance processes at all levels across every organization with an internal auditing activity. Management of the future knowledge needed for internal auditing will always need cutting edge resources and practices, both academic and in the services internal auditors provide.

Successful management of knowledge by the internal auditor and internal audit team must always be at the cutting edge of learning. It must be to be successful. Today and tomorrow's demands on internal auditors and their organizations will place continuing pressure for individuals, teams and organizations to learn fast and widely. As mentioned earlier in my article of 2001, Bill Gates sums this up when defining knowledge management *'As a general concept – to gather and organize information, disseminate the information to the people who need it, and constantly refine the information through analysis and collaboration.'* When discussing knowledge management at Microsoft he goes on to say:

> So let's be clear on a couple of things first. Knowledge management as I use it here is not a software product or a software category. Knowledge management doesn't even start with technology. It starts with business objectives and processes and a recognition of the need to share information. Knowledge management is nothing more than managing information flows, getting the right information to the people who need it so that they can act quickly.

If internal auditing manages its own knowledge well it can add considerable value in an organization's management of information flows, including security... but that is another aspect of knowledge management. Security of information shared in and around an organization can be critical for its reputation and even survival. Managing knowledge well must always take into account how the information created from that knowledge is stored and retrieved. In today and tomorrow's operating environments and legal requirements information stored in organizations, in whatever form, will always need a level of protection appropriate to its confidentiality and sensitivity. This is not always easy to achieve,

CHAPTER SUMMARY

This chapter emphasizes the importance of internal auditors and internal audit teams managing well the body of knowledge they need to add-value in their planning and findings. Knowledge that sets the 'tone' of the services they offer, making the picture they are painting attractive to their customers. That management of knowledge requires personal continuing professional development planning and efficient teamworking: both within the internal audit activity and across their organizations into the world of education at universities and colleges. This has always been recognized by The IIA and membership as core to its professional status, in its *International Standards*, promotion of research, education partnerships and academic accreditations and awards. If the internal audit team manages its knowledge well this will provide a good benchmark and the right experiences to evaluate and contribute to the management of knowledge in the operations it reviews, including its security and protection.

Without exception managing knowledge well in internal auditing, as individuals and in teamworking, is needed for all the innovation Gray and Gray (1997) motivations, goals and categories, including the additions and changes already made in Chapters 2 to 14:

Motivations

1. Progress within the field of professional internal auditing.
2. Increasing competition leading to pressures to reduce costs and increase efficiency.
3. New challenges, such as increasing internal control risks due to staff reductions and restructuring.

4. Opportunities to increase efficiency and quality as a result of technological advances.
5. Changes in corporate management practices and philosophies, such as Total Quality Management, re-engineering, continuous quality improvement, or related approaches.
6. Challenges and opportunities of global issues and developments.
7. **Social and environmental issues, including health and safety, impacting all organizations.**
8. **Recognition that professionalism, quality and standards are essential attributes for world-class status in any internal auditing activity.**
9. **Importance of organizational governance to meet regulatory and stakeholders' needs.**
10. **A continuous search for good and evil in how organizations and all their operations are directed and controlled.**
11. **Recognition that all types of crime in and by an organization should be fought.**
12. **Encouragement to think creatively.**
13. **Commitment to the promotion of a good business plan.**

Goals

1. **Continuous** Improvement of the quality of internal auditing services.
2. **Achieve best practice by continuously benchmarking.**
3. Expansion of services to increase the value-added of internal auditing.
4. Boost staff skills, performance and morale.
5. **Sell internal auditing as future focused.**
6. **To reduce the opportunities for all types of crime in an organization.**
7. **Increase satisfaction from all our customers.**
8. **Add new skills in the art of questioning.**
9. **Sell internal auditing services as a contribution to the organization's good reputation.**

Categories

1. Changes in the way that internal auditors interact with the rest of their enterprises and **all those with a stakeholder interest.**
2. Internal restructuring and changes in the organization and management of internal auditing.
3. Creation of new audit services and methods.
4. Changes in the use of technology.
5. **Continuously improve knowledge and skills in the teams of staff who carry out internal auditing engagements.**
6. **New services to fight crime.**
7. **Assistance in evaluation of the board's performance.**
8. **Continuous improved satisfaction from all our customers.**
9. **Changes in the way internal auditing asks questions.**
10. **Contributions to the organization's good reputation.**

Goal 4 could be improved by deleting 'Boost staff' and adding '**Manage knowledge**' at the beginning, and '**well**' at the end.

In Chapter 16 the Gray and Gray research will finally be reviewed taking into account the additions and changes made in each of the previous chapters.

INTERNAL AUDITING MANAGING KNOWLEDGE PRINCIPIA 1998 AND 2008

My 1998 principia for internal auditing included the following, which can be related to managing knowledge (numbers refer to the list in Appendix A):

7. To be successful, internal auditing must attract and satisfy talented people.
31. Successful internal audit teams in an organization's web of teams are everything.
35. Audit recommendations are best when they are created by a successful team.

These are now changed to reflect the importance of internal audit managing knowledge well (see Appendix B):

23. Internal auditing must attract and encourage knowledgeable and talented people to be internal auditors and to be members of the internal audit team.
24. Internal auditors must manage their knowledge well, for their own continuous development and success of the teams in which they participate.
25. Knowledge in internal auditing needs to be maintained, developed and managed continuously, as a means to an end and not an end in itself.

A VISION FOR INTERNAL AUDITING MANAGING KNOWLEDGE WELL

> **Knowledge is our most important asset – we manage it well**

SYNOPSES OF CASE STUDIES

Case 15.1: Opportunities for Strategic Innovation – Examination Question

Synopsis

This case study examination question and model answer is from the IIA–UK & Ireland Advanced Diploma in Internal Auditing and Management, demonstrating the level of knowledge theory (management, marketing, agency, stakeholder, governance, social responsibility, environmental), as well as the importance of legal and regulatory requirements, required by its syllabus. While reading the question and model answer you should imagine the cutting edge internal auditing resources and practices needed in the scenario to improve the value that internal auditing can provide to the board, management and all stakeholders, during the implementation of the described strategy and future operations.

> This examination question and model answer are reproduced with permission from the Institute of Internal Auditors – UK & Ireland. The examination question was set in the M1 *Strategic Management* paper of the IIA Advanced Diploma in Internal Auditing and Management, in November 2006.

After Reading the Case Study Consider:

1. What knowledge would you need to manage in your engagement team to be able to add best value to the organization wearing an assurance hat?
2. What knowledge would you need to manage in your engagement team to be able to add best value to the organization wearing a consultant's hat?
3. What knowledge would you need to manage in your engagement team to be able to add best value to the organization wearing a teacher's hat?
4. What knowledge would you need to manage in your engagement team to be able to add best value to the organization wearing a facilitator's hat during the assessment of risks associated with the board's strategy?
5. How did the key observations you make when reading the case study compare with the model answer?
6. Did you imagine any cutting edge resources and practices that would improve the value of your services to the organization as the board's strategy is implemented and in future operations?

Case 15.2: Internal Audit Capabilities and Needs

Synopsis

'... the responsibilities of internal audit functions have increased substantially in scope and complexity, creating the need for a commensurate increase in the knowledge, skills and expertise of internal audit professionals.' Continuing professional development and the management of knowledge are key to the success of every internal auditor and internal auditing. Improvement of the internal auditing knowledge base will come from '... committing to the dynamic process of continual professional development', and well-managed knowledge delivered by cutting edge resources and practices.

Extract from the 'Introduction' and 'What's Next' in *Internal Audit Capabilities and Needs Survey – Assessing General Technical Knowledge, Audit Process Knowledge, and Personal Skills and Capabilities of Internal Auditors* (2006: pp. 1 and 12), Protiviti Inc., *USA* (www.protiviti.com). Reprinted with permission.

After Reading the Case Study Consider:

1. How good is your own and your internal auditing knowledge and experience in corporate governance, fraud risk management and Enterprise Risk Management? What actions are being taken to continuously improve this knowledge and experience at academic, training and skill levels?
2. How effective is your own and your internal auditing of information technology in your organization? Does your knowledge and experience of information technology include its development, operations and use as an auditing tool? What actions are being taken to continuously improve this knowledge and experience at academic, training and skill levels?
3. What '... other areas of expertise' do you expect to see needing improvement now and in the future for yourself and your internal auditing? What actions are being taken to continuously improve this knowledge and experience at academic, training and skill levels?

Case 15.3: The IIA Research Foundation Report – March 2007

Synopsis

'*Staying on the cutting edge of knowledge and understanding our profession is what The IIA Research Foundation is all about.*' So starts this 2007 open letter from the Vice Chairman of its board, introducing its new mission statement '*. . . to expand knowledge and understanding of internal auditing. . .*'. Research in internal auditing theory and practices will be the key to the success of its professionalism as a service to all organizations, nationally and globally. From this research '*. . . we endeavour to understand our profession today and what tomorrow may bring*'.

> This is the Foreword to the March 2007 Report. The full report is available on www.theiia.org Copyright 2007 by The Institute of Internal Auditors Research Foundation, 247 Maitland Avenue, Altamonte Springs, Florida 32710-4201, USA. Reprinted with permission.

After Reading the Case Study Consider:

1. Is your internal auditing '*Staying on the cutting edge of knowledge and understanding of our profession . . .*'?
2. Is your internal auditing contributing to the '*. . . Understanding, Guiding and Shaping. . .*' of internal auditing through research and use of educational products?
3. Does your internal auditing bookshelf contain all the research and educational material needed for its cutting edge resources and practices?
4. Is your internal auditing contributing in any way to the achievement of the IIARF mission?

Case 15.4: There Are No More Internal Audit Experts, Only *Communities of Practices* Experts

Synopsis

'*. . . what is needed now* [in internal auditing] *is empowerment of **communities of practices** that self-manage intellectual capital in order to respond flexibly to changes in the environment and stay competitive.*' How *communities of practices* can be developed to manage knowledge is discussed from research, both theoretical and empirical. How *communities of practices* can be developed by internal auditing to manage its own knowledge and contribute to the management of knowledge in an organization is also discussed. Cutting edge internal auditing resources and practices need *communities of practices* to motivate and drive their development.

> Contributed by Ronald Lackland, CIA, CGAP, CCSA, CFE, MIRM, MBA, MSc, PGCE, Senior Course Director in Audit Management and Consultancy and PhD Candidate, Centre for Internal Audit, Risk Management and Governance, Birmingham City University Business School, Birmingham, UK.

After Reading the Case Study Consider:

1. How many *communities of practice* can you identify in your internal auditing, and across your organization with internal auditing presence?
2. Can you recognize the *'... three domains of intellectual capital, namely: human, structural and relational...'* in your internal auditing knowledge management strategy? You should be able to and from that develop your management of knowledge.
3. Is your internal auditing *'... establishing communities of practices with members from across the organizations it serves...'* and does it use these to *'... assist senior management in keeping the organization in a sustainable advantageous "cutting edge" position'*?

Case 15.5: Teams and Work Groups – Working Across Networks

Synopsis

'The skills of working across boundaries that are increasingly required for successful team work are also important in networks, and other loose but important connections.' Successful teams in an organization are *'... responding to current challenges'* by managing their knowledge and experience well. How well they respond to today's and tomorrow's issues is fundamental to the learning programme in every organization. How well internal auditing teams manage their knowledge and experience is key to the development of their cutting edge resources and practices.

> From *In Business* (1997), A2, 1.6, published with permission from ICSA Publishing Limited, London, England and used as Case Study 4.1 in *Leading Edge Internal Auditing* (1998 and reprinted 2007), Jeffrey Ridley and Andrew Chambers, ICSA Publishing Limited, London, England.

After Reading the Case Study Consider:

1. How do these team principles operate in your own organization and internal auditing?
2. How do you *'... notice, review and record the learning that is taking place'* in your teams?

SELF-ASSESSMENT QUESTIONS

The following 20 multi-choice questions are reproduced with permission from The IIA. They represent knowledge currently required for its Certified Internal Auditor examinations, details of which and the syllabus are available on its website. Suggested answers are in Appendix C Readers should explore the knowledge that supports the suggested correct answer through internal auditing textbooks and The IIA *International Standards*, *Code of Ethics* and supporting guidance.

15.1 As part of a company-sponsored award programme, an internal auditor was offered an award of significant monetary value by a division in recognition of the cost savings that resulted from the auditor's recommendations. According to the *Professional Practices Framework*, what is the most appropriate action for the auditor to take?

    (a) Accept the gift since the engagement is already concluded and the report issued.

    (b) Accept the award under the condition that any proceeds go to charity.

    (c) Inform audit management and ask for direction on whether to accept the gift.

    (d) Decline the gift and advise the division manager's superior.

15.2 An internal auditor assigned to audit a vendor's compliance with product quality standards is the brother of the vendor's controller. The auditor should:

    (a) Accept the assignment, but avoid contact with the controller during fieldwork.

    (b) Accept the assignment, but disclose the relationship in the engagement final communication.

    (c) Notify the vendor of the potential conflict of interest.

    (d) Notify the chief audit executive of the potential conflict of interest.

15.3 The *Standards* require that internal auditors possess which of the following skills?

    I. Internal auditors should understand human relations and be skilled in dealing with people.

    II. Internal auditors should be able to recognize and evaluate the materiality and significance of deviations from good business practices.

    III. Internal auditors should be experts on subjects such as economics, commercial law, taxation, finance, and information technology.

    IV. Internal auditors should be skilled in oral and written communication.

    (a) II only.

    (b) I and III only.

    (c) III and IV only.

    (d) I, II, and IV only.

15.4 Using the internal audit department to coordinate regulatory examiners' efforts is beneficial to the organization because internal auditors can:

    (a) Influence the regulatory examiners' interpretation of law to match corporate practice.

    (b) Recommend changes in scope to limit bias by the regulatory examiners.

    (c) Perform fieldwork for the regulatory examiners and thus reduce the amount of time regulatory examiners are on-site.

    (d) Supply evidence of adequate compliance testing through internal audit workpapers and reports.

15.5 Which of the following activities undertaken by the internal auditor might be in conflict with the standard of independence?

    (a) Risk management consultant.

    (b) Product development team leader.

    (c) Ethics advocate.

    (d) External audit liaison.

15.6 The internal audit activity should contribute to the organization's governance process by evaluating the processes through which:

    I. Ethics and values are promoted.

    II. Effective organizational performance management and accountability are ensured.

      III. Risk and control information is communicated.

      IV. Activities of the external and internal auditors and management are coordinated.

(a) I only.

(b) IV only.

(c) II and III only.

(d) I, II, III, and IV.

15.7 Which statement most accurately describes how criteria are established for use by internal auditors in determining whether goals and objectives have been accomplished?

    (a) Management is responsible for establishing the criteria.

    (b) Internal auditors should use professional standards or government regulations to establish the criteria.

    (c) The industry in which a company operates establishes criteria for each member company through benchmarks and best practices for that industry.

    (d) Appropriate accounting or auditing standards, including international standards, should be used as the criteria.

15.8 Assessments of the independence of an organization's external auditors should:

    (a) Be carried out only when the external auditor is appointed.

    (b) Not include any participation by the internal audit activity.

    (c) Include the internal audit activity only when the external auditor is appointed.

    (d) Include the internal audit activity at the time of appointment and regularly thereafter.

15.9 The primary reason that a bank would maintain a separate compliance function is to:

    (a) Better manage perceived high risks.

    (b) Strengthen controls over the bank's investments.

    (c) Ensure the independence of line and senior management.

    (d) Better respond to shareholder expectations.

15.10 Which of the following statements regarding corporate governance is **not** correct?

    (a) Corporate control mechanisms include internal and external mechanisms.

    (b) The compensation scheme for management is part of the corporate control mechanisms.

    (c) The dilution of shareholders' wealth resulting from employee stock options or employee stock bonuses is an accounting issue rather than a corporate governance issue.

    (d) The internal auditor of a company has more responsibility than the board for the company's corporate governance.

15.11 An organization's management perceives the need to make significant changes. Which of the following factors is management **least** likely to be able to change?

    (a) The organization's members.

    (b) The organization's structure.

    (c) The organization's environment.

    (d) The organization's technology.

15.12 The control that would most likely ensure that payroll checks are written only for authorized amounts is to:

(a) Conduct periodic floor verification of employees on the payroll.

(b) Require the return of undelivered checks to the cashier.

(c) Require supervisory approval of employee time cards.

(d) Periodically witness the distribution of payroll checks.

15.13 During a preliminary survey, an auditor found that several accounts payable vouchers for major suppliers required adjustments for duplicate payment of prior invoices. This would indicate:

(a) A need for additional testing to determine related controls and the current exposure to duplicate payments made to suppliers.

(b) The possibility of unrecorded liabilities for the amount of the overpayments.

(c) Insufficient controls in the receiving area to ensure timely notice to the accounts payable area that goods have been received and inspected.

(d) The existence of a sophisticated accounts payable system that correlates overpayments to open invoices and therefore requires no further audit concern.

15.14 During an assessment of the risk associated with sales contracts and related commissions, which of the following factors would most likely result in an expansion of the engagement scope?

(a) An increase in product sales, along with an increase in commissions.

(b) An increase in sales returns, along with an increase in commissions.

(c) A decrease in sales commissions, along with a decrease in product sales.

(d) A decrease in sales returns, along with an increase in product sales.

15.15 An internal auditor plans to conduct an audit of the adequacy of controls over investments in new financial instruments. Which of the following would **not** be required as part of such an engagement?

(a) Determine if policies exist which describe the risks the treasurer may take and the types of instruments in which the treasurer may make investments.

(b) Determine the extent of management oversight over investments in sophisticated instruments.

(c) Determine whether the treasurer is getting higher or lower rates of return on investments than are treasurers in comparable organizations.

(d) Determine the nature of controls established by the treasurer to monitor the risks in the investments.

15.16 If an auditor's preliminary evaluation of internal controls results in an observation that controls may be inadequate, the next step would be to:

(a) Expand audit work prior to the preparation of an engagement final communication.

(b) Prepare a flowchart depicting the internal control system.

(c) Note an exception in the engagement final communication if losses have occurred.

(d) Implement the desired controls.

15.17 Divisional management stated that a recent gross margin increase was due to increased efficiency in manufacturing operations. Which of the following audit procedures would be most relevant to that assertion?

(a) Obtain a physical count of inventory.

  (b) Select a sample of products, then compare costs-per-unit this year to those of last year, test cost buildups, and analyse standard cost variances.

  (c) Take a physical inventory of equipment to determine if there were significant changes.

  (d) Select a sample of finished goods inventory and trace raw materials cost back to purchase prices in order to determine the accuracy of the recorded raw materials price.

Use the following information to answer questions 15.18 to 15.20:

A company maintains production data on personal computers, connected by a local area network (LAN), and uses the data to generate automatic purchases via electronic data interchange. Purchases are made from authorized vendors based on production plans for the next month and on an authorized materials requirements plan (MRP) which identifies the parts needed for each unit of production.

15.18 The production line has experienced shut-downs because needed production parts were not on hand. Which of the following audit procedures would best identify the cause of the parts shortages?

  (a) Determine if access controls are sufficient to restrict the input of incorrect data into the production database.

  (b) Use generalized audit software to develop a complete list of the parts shortages that caused each of the production shutdowns, and analyse this data.

  (c) Select a random sample of parts on hand per the personal computer databases and compare with actual parts on hand.

  (d) Select a random sample of production information for selected days and trace input into the production database maintained on the LAN.

15.19 Which of the following audit procedures would be most effective in determining if purchasing requirements have been updated for changes in production techniques?

  (a) Recalculate parts needed based on current production estimates and the MRP for the revised production techniques. Compare these needs with purchase orders generated from the system for the same period.

  (b) Develop test data to input into the LAN and compare purchase orders generated from test data with purchase orders generated from production data.

  (c) Use generalized audit software to develop a report of excess inventory. Compare the inventory with current production volume.

  (d) Select a sample of production estimates and MRPs for several periods and trace them into the system to determine that input is accurate.

15.20 Audit engagement programs testing internal controls should:

  (a) Be tailored for the audit of each operation.

  (b) Be generalized to fit all situations without regard to departmental lines.

  (c) Be generalized so as to be usable at various international locations of an organization.

  (d) Reduce costly duplication of effort by ensuring that every aspect of an operation is examined.

NOTES AND REFERENCES

1. Interview with Erroll J. Yates, Chairman and Managing Director, Kodak Limited, UK, 1990, as reported by Greg Norman in *The Edge*, Hemel Hempstead, Hertfordshire, England. See also the article 'Worth Repeating' in Chapter 16 of this book.
2. *The Fifth Discipline – The Art & Practice of The Learning Organization* (1990), Bantam Doubleday Dell Publishing Group Inc. USA.
3. *The Structure of Internal Audit* (1997), Ernst & Young, London, England.
4. *Total Organizational Excellence: Achieving World-class Performance* (1999), Professor John S. Oakland, Butterworth-Heinemann, Oxford, England.
5. *Effective Leadership*, 2nd edition (1998), John Adair, Pan Books, London, England.
6. *Recent Developments In Internal Auditing*, Conference, 24–25 February 1976: (pp. 108–109), Professor Andrew Chambers, The Graduate Business Centre of The City University, London, England.
7. *Internal Auditing: A Future Vision* (July 1992), James Harbord, Administrator, Institute of Chartered Secretaries and Administrators, London, England.
8. 'Genesis of a Profession: Towards Professional Status for Internal Auditing,' David O'Regan, *Managerial Auditing Journal*, 16/4 (2001: pp. 215–226).
9. Published in *Internal Control*, Issue 47 (December 2001), abg Professional Information, London.
10. Accessed from www.cass.city.ac.uk/masters, March 2007.
11. Ronald Lackland, CIA, CGAP, CFE, MIRM, MBA, MSC, PGCE, Senior Course Director, Centre for International Audit, Governance & Risk, University of Central England Business School, Perry Barr, Birmingham, England. [now the Birmingham City University – www.bcu.ac.uk]
12. 'E-learning Programme for Advanced Diploma,' Adrian Pulham, *Internal Auditing & Business Risk* (January 2006), IIA–UK & Ireland.

16

The Future Of Internal Auditing Is Yours

*'To be successful we must be sensitive to the problems of each day.
All can have an impact on our professional activities far beyond the
changes we may foresee at the present time.'*

Jeffrey Ridley 1975[1]

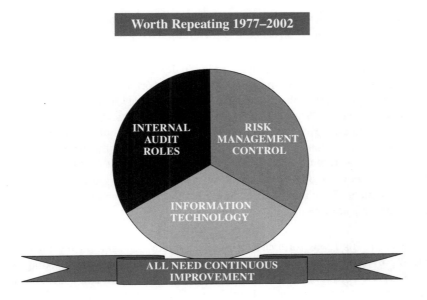

WORTH REPEATING AGAIN

There is never an end to any book on internal auditing just as there is never an end to the scope of its services in any organization. Problems and events that occur each day will always continue to open up new challenges and opportunities for the organization and internal auditing. Independence, objectivity and best practices of internal auditors will always be a needed service at board and operation levels. Internal auditors will wear new hats. Crime will always require organizations to have a high level of security and good understanding of law and regulations. How an organization conducts itself and its reputation will be even more critical for success in the future. Effectiveness and efficiency will always demand quality policies and programmes; right first time targets and measurements; and, a focus on customer satisfaction. Internal auditing will always need to promote its professionalism and continuously improve. Information and the technology used to create and communicate will become even faster, easier to use and abuse. Knowledge will explode, opening up new pathways for the fast internal auditors to walk and ask the right questions. Internal auditors will always need to think creatively and innovate.

My book has been about exploration in internal auditing and how this is a pathway into management cultures and practices at all levels, including strategy, policy and operation processes; embracing all an organization's stakeholders; spanning all its supply chains; and understanding the need to comply with laws, regulations, standards and principles. It has also been about imagination and creativity in internal auditing, what this has achieved in the past and is achieving in the present, and what it can and should achieve in the future. From this imagination and creativity best practices have emerged encouraging internal auditors to wear new hats, or wear their old hats at new angles and with feathers.

I started my book describing internal auditing as always an exploration requiring best practices and commitment, comparing it to travelling into space:

> I have always seen internal auditors, individually and as teams, following a similar strategic path of commitment, imagination and teamwork in the exploration of each audit engagement. They start with organization and auditing strategies and step along a path that is not familiar, with an achievement in mind. They do this with teamwork. They are trained to do this. They are taught to be good auditors: but they cannot be taught to be the best auditor. That depends on their commitment and imagination: how they can coordinate their work with others; how quickly they can react to the situations they find themselves in; how innovative they can be in their practices; how sensitive they are to their environment. They may not be aiming for the Moon, but at the beginning of every engagement they are looking into the unknown.

In the early 1970s I was fortunate to report to senior managers in my internal auditing career who provided support for my internal auditing explorations, who encouraged me to be imaginative and creative, and who widened my scope of auditing and audit objectives. The two who were most supportive were Errol Yates, Finance Director at Kodak Limited (later to be Chairman and Managing Director) and Harold Russell, General Auditor at Eastman Kodak Inc. Both also gave considerable support to The IIA in the United Kingdom, United States and globally.

During my year of office as President of the United Kingdom Chapter in 1975, Erroll gave a lunchtime address at one of the Chapter meetings in London, subsequently published in The IIA journal *Internal Auditor* with the title 'Internal Audit – A Managerial Control'.[2] After his death in 2000 I suggested to The IIA that his article be printed again, with added updates by myself. This repeated article was in the *Internal Auditor*, December 2001, with the title 'Worth Repeating'. In 2008 it is still worth repeating again. Its discussion is still relevant to professional internal auditing now and will continue to be so in the future. It can be seen in today's cutting edge internal auditing resources and practices.

Article:
Worth Repeating (2001)[3]

WORTH REPEATING

Sometimes, it's valuable to look at what
has been said in the past to get an idea of
just how far internal auditing has progressed.

ERROLL J. YATES, chairman and managing director of Kodak Limited, U.K., died in 2000. For most of my working internal audit from the 1960s to the and supported the fessional internal career with Erroll – 1990s – he promoted development of professional auditing. During the

> '*Internal auditing . . . an important part of the management team*'

12 years I was the manager of internal auditing for Kodak and reported directly to him, I found that his vision of internal auditing as a consultancy in business, and as a profession, was in advance of the practice in many organizations of the day. Even now, with a new definition of professional internal auditing, his thoughts still represent a paradigm shift for many practitioners.

In the June 1977 issue of *Internal Auditor*, Erroll wrote of the need for internal auditors to think like managers, to be '. . . an important part of the management team . . . to contribute to an organization's objectives, to focus attention on both efficiency and effectiveness'. His words are worth repeating as a tribute to his memory and forward thinking. They still have many years of life in 21st-century internal auditing.

On the following pages, is my article 'Worth Repeating', published in the December, 2001 issue of *Internal Auditor*. This includes a reprint of Erroll's 1977 article, along with some of my personal insights into the profession as it had evolved since then.

Readers should bring Erroll's article up to date with their own insights into how professional internal auditing has developed since 2001, and what they foresee happening to continuously improve the future services it provides.

INTERNAL AUDIT

A Managerial Control

ERROLL J. YATES

Erroll's choice of title, "A Managerial Control," came from The IIA's Statement of Responsibilities (SOR), which defined internal auditing as "... a constructive service to management ... a managerial control which functions by measuring and evaluating the effectiveness of other controls." He saw internal auditing as an important part of his control responsibilities as a manager: "Management needs to know that efficient controls are operating, helping to ensure that people and assets are safeguarded and well-directed." His emphasis on controls for safeguarding people and directing their performance predated much of today's thinking on people management. His understanding that learning is a prime support for effective control was an important part of the management program he set for himself and others and a major contributor to his success.

Statutory auditors are now more involved in reviewing published management statements on internal control linked to their audit of financial statements. The IIA has spent much time and effort developing international and national guidelines for the content of these statements and their review, which will need to be continuously improved if they are to serve their purpose.

Erroll's development of quality programs in the 1980s and early 1990s involved internal auditing. He saw a positive and proactive role for internal auditors in developing quality management and improvement programs. This was at a time when few internal audit departments had formal quality assurance programs in their own functions, and few were involved in their organization's programs. He encouraged registration of Kodak's internal audit processes to the international quality standard ISO 9000 and, as chairman and managing director of Kodak, celebrated this achievement. Today, many internal auditors are experienced in quality assurance and management. The IIA's recent statement that quality assurance programs must meet the requirements of the new IIA *Standards for the Professional Practice of Internal Auditing* is yet another step toward recognition of internal auditing as a self-regulating profession.

M ANAGEMENT TODAY HAS TO PAY increasing attention — and rightly so — to ever declining operating profit margins. These margins become even lower if measured by the more accurate current purchasing power accounting or current cost accounting methods recently put forth by the Sandilands Committee [the U.K. body that made recommendations on inflation accounting]. Internal audit is one tool which can, if used effectively, help management in its day-to-day control function.

Modern management needs something more than confirmation of the true and fair state of company business and the knowledge that money was spent as reported by statutory auditors. Management needs to know that efficient controls are operating, helping to ensure that people and assets are safeguarded and well-directed.

It is time for management to entrust independent appraisal activity to the internal auditor. The internal auditor should review managerial and other controls that relate to efficiency as well as to data. To review these efficiently, internal auditors must think like management. They must shake off the stereotyped image of the cash-counting, stamp-counting, or stock-checking role that, unfortunately, still lingers.

The Institute of Internal Auditors has published aims for the development of internal auditing. Its plans for education and research clearly demonstrate a growth in status. Considering its short life — some 35 years — and relatively small number of members. The Institute can be justly proud of the standard of its Code of Ethics and the vision behind the concepts in its Statement of Responsibilities of Internal Auditors.

All professions need such a foundation of technical excellence if they are to grow. But technical excellence is in itself not sufficient to guarantee growth. Those whom the profession serves must also support it. And that support should come from the highest level.

Internal auditing is no exception. While it takes time to develop the support necessary for growth, it is becoming obvious that there is an increasing acceptance of the internal auditor's role in most organizations. And this role is not merely part of the internal checking system but as an important part of the management team. Today's internal auditor appraises controls rather than acting as the control. I wonder if IIA members, as a body, have done all they can to ensure that the internal auditor's responsibilities are understood and practiced. Lip service to the modern concepts of internal audit is one thing. Putting it into practice is another.

My own company, Kodak Limited, has used internal auditing as an independent appraisal since the early 1930's. Active acceptance and support at the highest levels of the company have marked the transition from traditional internal check to the present accepted concepts of modern internal auditing. Such progress has, of course, also stemmed from the imaginative service of the auditors. No doubt similar patterns of progress are occurring in other organizations throughout the United Kingdom. Although management attitudes may differ, the fact that an internal audit department exists is proof that a growing and necessary service for management is developing.

The Institute's Statement of Responsibilities defines internal auditing as a managerial control, which functions by measuring and evaluating the effectiveness of other controls. To identify the challenges and opportunities available to internal auditors, one must first define control and examine how it fits into the key functions of management today.

Control, in this paper, concerns the managerial function of setting targets and plans and ensuring that performance conforms to them as nearly as possible. I presume this is what is meant in The Institute's Statement of Responsibilities when it refers to the measurement and evaluation of the effectiveness of controls, key management functions usually delegated to the internal auditor. In any company, management has the tasks of:

- forecasting the future, using all available modern techniques
- setting the organization and plans to meet those forecasts
- reviewing performance against forecast for the period under review

Internal audit, whether currently so used or not, can and should play a part in all three fields of management activity. Many companies set up special departments or alternatively engage outside consultants to forecast. This

The internal audit profession today, with its global strategies, new standards, and experienced research foundation, is a world of difference from internal auditing in the 1970s. These changes have come about through many voluntary contributions by members and the support of The IIA's staff worldwide. Erroll gave strong support for the development of the first United Kingdom Chapter, which subsequently became the IIA-UK. He also encouraged his management team to promote internal auditing as a service to the whole organization.

At the time, "participative" internal auditing was at the beginning of its development and not practiced by many. The IIA's *Standards* had defined one of the primary objectives of control as including the accomplishment of objectives. Today, internal auditors in many organizations are seen as members of the management team, contributing through audit, consultancy, and teaching to the achievement of organizational objectives.

Changes to The IIA's SOR in 1981 focused internal auditing away from just management, to being "a service to the organization ... a control which functions by examining and evaluating the adequacy and effectiveness of other controls." This significantly changed the customer base for internal auditing, from management to all levels of responsibility across the whole organization, including — most importantly — the board.

includes economic forecasts, financial forecasts, and any other type of forecast. Also, most companies have sophisticated corporate or lower level planning departments.

What is really needed is a periodic, independent appraisal of these forecasting and planning activities. Someone must have the responsibility to ask:

- Are the proper techniques being used?
- Are the various departments liaising with each other, or are forecasts made on an arbitrary basis?
- Are the planners relating their plans to management decisions, or are they building in their own safeguards?

Likewise, who in management has the time to review all stages ensuring that original sales estimates, stock norms, and order-lead times are being used and that insurance levels are not built in at various stages leading to inefficiencies?

The internal auditor should have this responsibility. But before he takes on these and similar reviews, he must prove himself capable. He has to be knowledgeable in these various fields. He must have practical experience as well as academic qualifications.

IIA members have a special role in this area. They must attract academically qualified people with practical experience to the internal audit profession. More importantly, they must then convince management that internal auditors are capable of carrying out this function.

The third management task — reviewing actual performance against plans and objectives — is the control function of management. It ensures that standards, database systems, information systems, and internal controls are established, reviewed, and monitored. Again, although internal auditors are extensively used in establishing, reviewing, and monitoring internal controls, other specialist professions are called upon in other areas. Yet, it is the internal auditor, by his very independence, who could be used in these other fields as well.

Management could delegate to internal auditors the examination of standards, database systems, and information systems to ensure that information being provided is relevant. Since management today has so much to occupy it without being burdened by excessive and/or useless information, the need-to-know rather than the nice-to-know attitude must come to the fore. And internal auditors can play a very active role here.

My company uses the internal audit function in three separate roles to provide a service to management and, at the same time, to develop the internal auditor.

First, using the word audit in its generally accepted sense, the auditor reviews all controls established by management.

At the beginning of each year, first-line management is made aware of the company's overall audit plan. We then involve management in audit plans through discussions immediately before audits and by participation during and after audits. We believe management involvement in

---

Erroll would have been pleased to see the current internal auditing involvement in risk assessment and management, through research and practice. The key to management success is to predict into the future as far as the eye can see. Erroll saw that the internal auditor could make a valuable contribution in this prediction process as long as he or she had a base of experience and knowledge from which to draw.

Promotion of internal auditing as a qualified profession has increased significantly since the 1970s. The IIA's Certified Internal Auditor education and examination program is now recognized worldwide by both internal auditors and employers, though there is still much to be achieved for this recognition to be universal.

Internal auditors' role in systems development and the audit of computer operations grew in the 1970s. In both roles, the auditor focused on control over technology and information. Erroll's view on the internal auditor's contribution to selection of the right information for decision-making is probably a forerunner to the need for internal auditing to be involved in the organization's knowledge management process.

the audit process widens the auditors' coverage and improves the service offered.

We expect our internal auditors to maintain a close, working relationship with our external auditors and to be aware of all other in-company and government audit and inspection activities. This again broadens the scope of the internal auditors' work and increases their awareness of current control needs.

Independence is essential to the effectiveness of internal auditing; a fact my company has long recognized. To promote such independence, we have an Audit Committee at Board level. Each Internal Audit Department, worldwide, has a reporting line through the corporate auditor.

The Audit Committee is responsible for reviewing the work of both internal and external auditors worldwide. This high level of independence is still a unique concept, I believe, outside of the United States.

Second, we believe that, to be really successful, modern internal auditing must move to the present. Management must encourage this. Internal auditors are often placed in the role of internal consultants, advising on changes to control. The internal auditors' work provides a breadth and depth of coverage, which, if developed properly, can provide a valuable control consultancy service for management.

There is the danger that in his consultant role an internal auditor might lose some — if not all — of the independence needed for control reviews. The enthusiastic internal auditor with ability and ambition might well take over where the manager fears to tread. But I believe this is a risk which, if recognized and watched, is well worth taking considering the benefits that can be achieved for both the internal auditor and the organization.

Third, probably one of the roles least recognized and developed in many companies is that of the internal auditor as a teacher. Many organizations use the Internal Audit Department as a training ground for management trainees. Because of the work auditors do, this must be expected. Today, more than ever before, many managers with auditing experience are moving into senior-line positions.

In using the term teacher, I refer to using the internal auditor's knowledge and experience to contribute to prevention rather than cure. Obviously, opportunities to teach do not exist in all organizations. But where they do exist, I strongly recommend that the internal auditor develop this role. In my company, internal auditors have taken the opportunity to teach the concepts of internal control by either lecture or workshop and case study techniques.

All levels of staff attend training courses run by the company training departments. At the request of divisional managers, the Internal Audit Department also conducts its own workshops both before and after audits. The internal auditor is, of course, in a unique position to teach not only by participating in training courses but

In 1975, few internal auditors reported directly to the board of directors. Throughout his career, Erroll insisted on an internal audit line of reporting to the board. Such reporting lines are now much more the norm and essential for internal auditor independence. Yet, there are still some internal audit activities that have little or no contact at board level.

Significant changes have been made in many corporate boards resulting from the studies and focus on corporate governance during the 1990s. The use of audit committees in the private, public, and voluntary sectors is now commonplace throughout many countries. However, too many annual reports still do not include a statement signed by the audit committee chairperson, as recommended by the 1987 Commission of Sponsoring Organizations of the Treadway Commission.

The 1980s saw an increasing role for internal auditors as consultants in their organizations, often related to information technology and systems but also in other operating functions. The increasing use by boards, and management, of risk assessment processes and their necessary understanding of governance issues has opened new doors for many consultant internal auditors. It will be important for the future of internal auditing that the independence and objectivity issues surrounding consultancy are clear and not overlooked.

also by representing in all that he personally practices, the standards and code of ethics of The Institute. By doing so, he leads by personal example. And by leading, he teaches others to follow.

We at Kodak Limited believe the internal auditor's role in management control can be achieved most successfully if he is allowed to develop the three roles I have mentioned:
- As an independent control auditor
- As an internal consultant
- As a teacher

His success in each of these roles increases his status and provides opportunity for considerable job satisfaction while contributing to effective managerial control.

I have outlined, rather generally, the important management functions internal auditors can perform and the part I believe internal auditors can and should play.

If internal auditors are to take their place in the top ranks of management universally, then they must show more forcibly that they are ready and willing to do so. One reads statements from professional bodies on various matters these days — statements of standard accounting practices, inflation accounting, taxation, the function of management audits, and so on. Yet I find it difficult to recall or find reference to any statement of authority by internal auditors.

Where does The Institute stand on inflation accounting? Are its members for current purchasing power accounting? or current cost accounting? or are they resigned to continue with historical cost? If IIA has definite views on inflation accounting, are they known to the Sandiland's Committee? What is IIA's official view on The Corporate Report, the paper published for comment by the Accounting Standards Steering Committee? If The Institute, as an official body, doesn't have any views on The Corporate Report, something is wrong somewhere. Although I have seen the list of IIA publications and research reports, is IIA, as a body, really known to the public at large?

How many academic instructors promote internal audit as a profession? If the answer is "not many," what is The Institute doing about it? The first seeds have been sown, but are they enough? As a manager, I see the need for a growing number of internal auditors to keep pace with the expanding technical and professional advances, which accompany progress. There is evidence that management in many organizations acknowledges this need. This is a sign that the standards internal auditors are setting for themselves are recognized by managers as necessary for the success of their enterprises and the general economy.

Effective managerial control is vital. I see the internal auditor's contribution to its effectiveness as a very important part of the management function. This allows the internal auditor to take his rightful place in management.

It was Erroll's early perception of internal auditors in three roles — as auditor, consultant, and teacher — that made him far ahead of his time. Even now, his advocacy for all these roles sets him apart from many managers. True, the new definition of internal auditing reflects two of the roles — assurance and consulting activity — but the third has not yet received the profile in professional internal auditing that it should.

Yet, in many organizations, internal auditors are teaching all levels of staff in a variety of ways: by example, by instruction, and through training courses. And in many organizations, internal auditing is seen at board and management level as an excellent training ground for future managers. This requires teaching skills from those who manage and work in internal auditing.

In the United Kingdom, the Sandilands Committee made recommendations in 1975 on current cost accounting methods of reporting in financial statements. If adopted, these methods would have had significantly impacted reported earnings. At the time Erroll wrote this article, this accounting issue was being debated across the world, resulting in changes to financial reporting. Erroll believed that the internal audit profession should contribute to this debate and publish a position statement. He later widened this to include other national and international management, accounting, and auditing issues. Yet, he saw little evidence of it happening. Although it's now happening at the international level, it is less clear whether or not it's happening at the chapter and national institute levels. Internal auditors need to ask themselves continually: Is enough being done to contribute publicly to the national and international debate in all the issues that impact our knowledge requirements for best practices in professional internal auditing? To be a true profession, our voice must be heard over and over again.

The IIA's influence in the academic field at the postgraduate level is now significant. Its Research Foundation provides a wealth of knowledge for the learning manager and internal auditor. There has been less penetration into the teaching of internal auditing at undergraduate levels, with few course units teaching internal auditing. Even in classes teaching internal auditing for accountancy and other professional examinations, the students' level of understanding about the profession upon graduation doesn't always meet the standards of The IIA.

THE FUTURE FOR INTERNAL AUDITING IN
A FLATTER WORLD

Thomas Friedman (2005)[4] in his prize-winning book demonstrates excellent insight into *'. . . a whole new age of globalization'* discussing new opportunities and challenges in today's and tomorrow's 'flattening world'. The last paragraph in his book contains this important sentence for every internal auditor today and in the future:

> You can flourish in this flat world, but it does take the right imagination and the right motivation.

My book has been about imagination and motivation in the flourishing world of professional internal auditing. It started with imagination and contains many motivating themes for internal auditing as one of the *'cornerstones of organizational governance'*. The strength of that cornerstone and its continuing improvement will depend on your imagination and motivation. Some of the challenges and opportunities you will face tomorrow are:

Accountability	Health	Professionalism
Continuous Improvement	Human Rights	Risk Management
Control	Innovation	Regulation
Creativity	Integrity	Safety
Crime	Knowledge	Security
Customer Focused	Laws	Skills
Data Protection	Openness	Social Responsibilities
Equality	Organization structures	Strategy
Environmental Management	Quality Management	Supply Chain Management
Globalization	Policies	Systems
Governance	Procedures	Technology

All apply to every organization. All apply to every internal audit activity. All apply to every internal auditor. All are discussed in this book. And there will always be others.

MOTIVATIONS, GOALS AND CATEGORIES FOR INNOVATION IN INTERNAL AUDITING 2008

Throughout my book I have referenced into the Gray and Gray (1997) research, their motivations, goals and categories for innovation in internal auditing. I am indebted to them for their insight. Their research has proved to be an invaluable guide to me in my teaching and research, and I am sure to others. Their analysis and understanding of how innovation is encouraged, achieved and monitored in internal auditing has stood the test of time well. In each chapter I have made my own additions and changes to these and invited readers to do the same. In Chapter 15 I concluded with the following:

Motivations

1. Progress within the field of professional internal auditing.
2. Increasing competition leading to pressures to reduce costs and increase efficiency.
3. New challenges, such as increasing internal control risks due to staff reductions and restructuring.
4. Opportunities to increase efficiency and quality as a result of technological advances.

5. Changes in corporate management practices and philosophies, such as Total Quality Management, re-engineering, continuous quality improvement, or related approaches.
6. Challenges and opportunities of global issues and developments.
7. **Social and environmental issues, including health and safety, impacting all organizations.**
8. **Recognition that professionalism, quality and standards are essential attributes for world-class status in any internal auditing activity.**
9. **Importance of organizational governance to meet regulatory and stakeholders' needs.**
10. **A continuous search for good and evil in how organizations and all their operations are directed and controlled.**
11. **Recognition that all types of crime in and by an organization should be fought.**
12. **Encouragement to think creatively.**
13. **Commitment to the promotion of a good business plan.**

Goals

1. **Continuous** Improvement of the quality of internal auditing services.
2. **Achieve best practice by continuously benchmarking.**
3. Expansion of services to increase the value-added of internal auditing.
4. **Manage knowledge**, skills, performance and morale **well**.
5. **Sell internal auditing as future focused.**
6. **To reduce the opportunities for all types of crime in an organization.**
7. **Increase satisfaction from all our customers.**
8. **Add new skills in the art of questioning.**
9. **Sell internal auditing services as a contribution to the organization's good reputation.**

Categories

1. Changes in the way that internal auditors interact with the rest of their enterprises **and all those with a stakeholder interest.**
2. Internal restructuring and changes in the organization and management of internal auditing.
3. Creation of new audit services and methods.
4. Changes in the use of technology.
5. **Continuously improve knowledge and skills in the teams of staff who carry out internal auditing engagements.**
6. **New services to fight crime.**
7. **Assistance in evaluation of the board's performance.**
8. **Continuous improved satisfaction from all our customers.**
9. **Changes in the way internal auditing asks questions.**
10. **Contributions to the organization's good reputation.**

I could shorten these lists but would prefer not to in case I lose the importance of each of the statements: they provide a good framework and summary for my book. They are all important for internal auditing in the future: for those who practice it; for their customers; and for those who teach it and research its principles and standards. I leave the shortening and any further changes or additions to you and future internal auditing.

VISIONS FOR CUTTING EDGE INTERNAL AUDITING 2008

I have suggested visions for cutting edge internal auditing, one in each chapter from Chapter 1. This has been more to emphasize the importance of having a vision that inspires, rather than just a direction. I am still pleased about the vision my internal audit team created in 1990 when we started our walk down the quality road – *Our Audits Are Plaudits*. It may not be a perfectly worded phrase but was intended to demonstrate that we were more interested in congratulating our customers on their risk, control and governance processes, rather than finding faults. To be in that situation we had to focus more of our planned time on wearing consulting and teaching hats. To do this we had to change and improve our knowledge, skills and processes. This led us down the ISO 9000 registration road and to new missions, key performance measures and rewards. It led us to formally having recognition at board level of our need to comply with The IIA *International Standards* and *Code of Ethics*: not just at board level but also with all our customers. For all internal auditing calling itself professional this recognition is a must.

The following are the visions from each chapter, in sentence form. Think hard about them. They all have deep messages and should inspire change and direction:

Chapter

2 To be seen as a professional service adding significant value with our high quality, independent and objective services.

3 We provide a service seen by all our customers and stakeholders as world-class.

4 We wear a variety of independent and objective hats to meet all our customers' needs.

5 We aim to add best value to good governance.

6 Our services include a fight against all types of crime.

7 Our independence, resources and professional practices assist board performance.

8 Our quality delights all our customers.

9 To continue to be the best supplier of professional internal auditing services.

10 We are committed to continuously improve.

11 We have no boundaries in our thinking.

12 We understand your business needs and ask the right questions to help you achieve these.

13 We add value to the organization's good reputation.

14 We promote our professional values at all times.

15 Knowledge is our most important asset – we manage it well.

All these visions can be used to motivate and achieve the goals listed above. Try this as an exercise – arrange the visions into three groups: (1) Internal Auditing Professionalism; (2) Creativity; (3) Governance. Now link the motivations listed above into these groups. You should now have the motivations needed in each group to achieve the visions. Now place the goals listed into their appropriate vision groups. Finally, place the categories into their appropriate group. You now have a cutting edge internal auditing plan. Check this plan with the chapters in this book and you will find that each chapter can be related to one of the groups. This interlocking picture of visions, motivations, goals, categories and my chapters should give you an interesting framework for imagining, planning and implementing your cutting edge resources and practices.

(Compare your finished framework with mine at Appendix C. We will not be exactly the same because our internal auditing experiences are different, though I hope we are close. Yours has to be right for you, your customers and your organization.)

PRINCIPIA FOR CUTTING EDGE INTERNAL AUDITING 2008

I believe Professor Andrew Chambers' and my 1998 principia for internal auditing, as listed in Appendix A, have stood the test of research and changes in internal auditing practices well since they were written – although the profession of internal auditing has continued to develop to meet the global and technological challenges and opportunities of risk, control and governance theory and processes since then. Nevertheless, there are improvements that can be made to these principia, and these have been discussed in each chapter. The new principia for 2008 listed in Appendix B are not rules but basic principles for cutting edge internal auditing. It is for internal auditors in the future to interpret and improve on these as they practise internal auditing in their organizations. It is for their customers to challenge internal auditors on their importance and understanding.

A CUTTING EDGE INTERNAL AUDITING MODEL FOR 2008

In Chapters 1 and 5 I discussed my model for cutting edge internal auditing resources and practices explaining the importance of each of the lines, circle and symbols. Other chapters have developed key parts of the model, referencing into the interactions between professional internal auditing, governance, quality and time, and importantly for today and tomorrow's change. These can be reflected in the model as now shown in Figure 16.1.

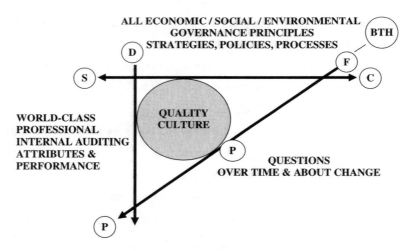

Figure 16.1   Cutting Edge Internal Auditing Model 2008
Source: J. Ridley (2008)

My belief is that time and change will have the greatest impact in the future. Time, because inevitably there will be new challenges and opportunities for internal auditing in the future. Change, because that is what internal auditing should be all about. Change, both by continuous improvement and change by re-engineering – starting afresh with new visions and missions, and new resources with better knowledge and skills. Change to meet today and tomorrow's risks, and those 'beyond the horizon'.

My hope is that the model will keep on being developed by the value of professional internal auditing as it is promoted and recognized in the future.

ARE THESE THE LAST WORDS?

There never will be last words for professional internal auditors. As a service to all levels in an organization the words will continue. The aim will always be to increase their global professional status and recognition by stakeholders, both inside and outside the organization in which they work. In all sectors, organizations can no longer consider themselves to be isolated or just regional or national, they will have to think global. There will be few, if any, exceptions. The world will continue to become flatter and organizations become less isolated. There will be more and more collaboration across supply chains of knowledge, research, people and materials. These continuing changes will require all organizations to have new structures: to recognize and control new global risks and opportunities with stronger governance processes. Internal auditing will have many 'field days' ahead. There will be many more words written and communicated to describe this as it happens. The body of knowledge[5] for professional internal auditing will continue to expand and challenge both internal auditors and their customers.

In the late 1960s, at a presentation to my then management, I listed the following strong influences on the development of internal auditing:

The IIA and its global structure and network of member groups
Management
Audit committees
Internal Auditors themselves
External Auditors
Shareholders
Regulators
Governments
Public

Add to this list now:

Consultants
Boards and Governing Bodies
Other Professional Institutes and their networks of member groups
Standard Setters
Global Institutions

Except for the Public they are all now active in influencing how internal auditing is established, its terms of reference and effectiveness. The public in their many roles as stakeholders have still to see the importance of internal auditing in organizations. The World Wide Web is starting to make this happen with more information concerning internal auditing freely available to download – and this flow of information about internal auditing will grow. First, whether internal auditing exists; next, how effective it is; then, what it is reporting. This is already happening in some parts of the public sector.

Some months ago I arrived at my golf club one evening to play a short game as a single. I met on the first tee a young man in his late teens. He had just finished his 'A' level education and was planning his entrance to a university. As we proceeded down the fairway he asked me what I had been when working. I told him I had been an internal auditor. 'What is that?' was his reply. He should never have asked! We went the next few fairways discussing the adventures and challenges of being an internal auditor rather than concentrating on the golf. He represented to me the public. Independent and objective internal auditing has still some way to go in its education of the public in what it does and what its *International Standards* mean to so many organizations, across all sectors and the globe. That time will come.

SYNOPSES OF CASE STUDIES

16.1: Issues that will Impact Internal Auditing in the 21st Century

Synopsis

The speed of change in the last 70 years has been fast: '. . . *imagine what further changes await us in the next 70.*' Cutting edge internal auditing must always look into the future. Discussed are a number of factors to be considered when doing so – perception, professionalism, the nature of its work, globalization, sustainability, social responsibility, risk management, multiculturalism, regulation, knowledge and technology. All are considered with their implications for future internal auditing.

Contributed by Lal Balkaran, MBA, FCMA, FCIS. CIA, CGA, based on his paper, delivered at The IIA–Toronto 60th Anniversary celebration at the Royal York Hotel, Toronto, Canada, on 19 May 2004. Lal Balkaran is a Past President of the Institute of Internal Auditors, Toronto and sits on the Board of Research and Education Advisers and the Editorial Advisory Board of the Global Institute of Internal Auditors in Orlando. He also sits on the Internal Audit Advisory Committee of the Government of Canada in Ottawa. Mr Balkaran has authored six reference books on business and five non-business books and has had articles published on internal auditing and on other subjects in various periodicals across the globe. He published the world's first dictionary of auditing titled *A Practical Guide to Auditing and Related Terms* (LexisNexis: Toronto, 2003).

After Reading the Case Study Consider:

1. How well do the 21st century predictions by Lal Balkaran relate to and support the cutting edge theme and chapter contents of this book?
2. Does the term 'value-added' used in the case study mean the same as 'cutting edge'?
3. Does your internal auditing '. . . *understand foreign languages, different cultures, political economies, and the nature of economic output. . .* ' across the world?
4. Are the qualifications and certifications you require your internal audit staff to achieve international and at the cutting edge of knowledge?

5. How well does your internal auditing understand the new International Financial Reporting Standards?
6. Is the focus, knowledge, perception and organization of your internal auditing at the cutting edge of adding value in your organization tomorrow?

Case 16.2: Internal Auditing in Europe

Synopsis

'The growth of the profession has been amazing.' In Europe the European Confederation of Institutes of Internal Auditing (ECIIA) has worked closely with the European Union, representing internal auditing across 30 countries, promoting the profession's *International Professional Practices Framework*. It sees the future of internal auditing at the '. . . *highest level in the organization. . .* ' focusing on and cutting the edge of *'governance, risk management expertise, business acumen, creative thinking and problem solving, communication skills and a strong ethical compass. . .* '.

Paper presented by Richard Nelson, President of the ECIIA 2005–06, at its annual conference, Helsinki, Finland, 2006.

After Reading the Case Study Consider:

1. Have you earned the right '. . . *to be involved at the highest level in the organization. . .* '?
2. How are the attributes '. . . *governance and risk management expertise, business acumen, creative thinking and problem solving, communication skills and a strong ethical compass. . .* ' being built into your internal auditing and its training and development programmes?

Case 16.3: The Finance Professional in 2020

Synopsis

This prediction of the financial professional in 2020 also has messages for internal auditing. Its challenges and opportunities pattern many of the current predictions for the internal auditor – *'enhanced globalization, changing demographics and significantly increased business complexity'*. It recognizes a future scenario of worldwide competition on '. . . *the basis of knowledge and innovation'*. It sees evolving roles for the finance professional driving as key *'The ability to exercise professional judgement based on a foundation of ethics, broad but deep technical excellence plus strategic awareness and communication'*: all attributes for cutting edge internal auditing resources and practices.

Contributed with permission from the Association of Chartered and Certified Accountants. The full report *Insights Series the Finance Professional in 2020* (2007) can be downloaded from its website www.accaglobal.com

---

After Reading the Case Study Consider:

1. Do you see any of the predictions in this research applying to internal auditing professional staff in your organization?
2. Are your internal auditing professionals contributing to development of '... *new and innovative means of measurement and reporting...* ' in your organization?
3. Which of the predicted roles for the finance professional would you expect to be seen evolving in your future internal auditing – navigator, centurion, entrepreneur, technical specialist, t-shaped professional and technician – any or possibly all?
4. Is the key '... *ability to exercise professional judgement based on a foundation of ethics, broad but deep technical excellence plus strategic awareness and communication*' being encouraged and developed in internal auditing in your organization?
5. Is your internal auditing focused '... *highly on knowledge...* '?

Case 16.4: Next Generation Accountant: A New Outlook on a Timeless Profession

Synopsis

This US-based research highlights similar predictions as in Case 16.3. Eight issues are addressed, each with important implications for accountants (and internal auditors). Looking ahead it predicts that '... *the most successful professionals will prepare for and remain open to continuing change... the ability to adapt may be the most timeless competency a professional can have*': an important attribute for cutting edge internal auditing resources and practices in the future.

> This case study is contributed with permission by Robert Half International Inc. (RHI). For more information, visit www.nextgeneration.com Next Generation Accountant, *A New Outlook on a Timeless Profession* (2005) is presented by Robert Half International Inc. (RHI). Founded in 1948, RHI is the world's leader in specialized consulting and staffing services and a member of Standard & Poor's widely tracked S&P 500 index. RHI's financial staffing divisions include Robert Half® Finance & Accounting, Accountemps® and Robert Half® Management Resources, for full-time, temporary and senior-level project professionals, respectively. [For more information about RHI's services, please visit roberthalf.com, accountemps.com and roberthalfmr.com] At the time of publication of this book Robert Half is recognized by The IIA as a Principal Partner in the development and promotion of professional internal auditing worldwide: it is also the parent company of Protiviti Inc. www.protiviti.com Protiviti® is a leading provider of independent internal audit and business technology risk consulting services.

After Reading the Case Study Consider:

1. How will the ideas, issues and trends affecting next generation accountants have an impact on and influence internal auditing in the future? Note how many of these link into themes discussed in this book.
2. How do these ideas, issues and trends offer opportunities for internal auditing? They should all influence the development of cutting edge internal auditing resources and practices!

Case 16.5: Internal Auditing Must Take a Lead in Meeting the Risks from Future Information and Communications Technology

Synopsis

Continuous research by the Audit Commission in the UK into public and private sector experience with information and communications technology (ICT) abuse, recognizes that '*... new technology continues to present an ever-increasing range of risks for users'*. Attitudes to this vary among users. Internal auditing will have opportunities in the future '*... to take the lead here, to influence and point people in the direction of* [security] *improvement...*'. Internal auditing should be '*... frightening people who have influence...*' into taking appropriate action. Listed are questions that should '*... raise the heckles of internal auditors, resulting in cutting edge resources and practices for the audit of IT security'*.

Contributed by Iain R. Brown, Technical Manager, Audit Commission, Visiting Senior Lecturer at the Birmingham City University and author of *As IT Is: A Taste of IT Security and Computer Audit*. This case study is based on a viewpoint article written by him and published in *Internal Auditing & Business Risk*, February 2005.

After Reading the Case Study Consider:

1. Is internal auditing in your organization taking a lead in facilitating and measuring the risks from future information and communications technology?
2. What recommendations can you take from this case study to create cutting edge internal auditing resources and practices in your organization's identification, measurement and monitoring of these risks?
3. Is your organization's control over information and communications technology best practice now and will it be in the future?

NOTES AND REFERENCES

1. From the author's Presidential Address, at the first meeting of the United Kingdom Chapter of The IIA, 1975. Repeated from Chapter 2 of this book.
2. 'Internal Auditing – A Managerial Control', *Internal Auditor*, Erroll J.Yates, (June 1977) The IIA.
3. 'Worth Repeating', *Internal Auditor* (December 2001: pp. 37–43), The IIA.
4. *The World is Flat – A Brief History of the Globalized World in the 21st Century* (2005), Thomas Friedman, Penguin Group, London, England.
5. As I finish my book this body of knowledge is being researched globally. The results of this research are now available from The IIA – *A Global Summary of the Common Body of Knowledge* (2006) [Also see articles on this research in The IIA *Internal Auditor*, December 2007]. This research will influence significantly the direction of professional internal auditing for many years to come, its examinations, research, seminars, publications, position statements, *International Standards*, *Code of Ethics* and the way it will promote itself. See also www.theiia.org for more information concerning this research and its findings.

Appendix A
Leading Edge Internal
Auditing – Principia 1998

(At the end of each principle the chapter in which it is discussed is shown in brackets)

1. Understanding the history and development of internal auditing is the foundation for creating a vision for its future. (3)
2. Internal auditing is developing as a spectrum of unrestricted traditional, new and leading edge activities across all organizations of all sizes, in all sectors. (4)
3. Best practice internal auditing and good management practices use the same quality measures of planning, doing, checking and action. (9)
4. Many of the attributes demonstrated by internal auditors, and valued most by management, are the same attributes recommended in codes of best practice for internal auditors. (14)
5. Seeking best practice internal auditing is a continuous learning process. (10)
6. Professional internal auditors critically understand today's and tomorrow's management principles and practices. (5)
7. To be successful, internal auditing must attract and satisfy talented people. (15)
8. Internal auditing objectivity and independence are its most important assets. (5)
9. Coordination of all audit work in an organization strengthens its objectivity and independence. (5)
10. Imagination and confidence are the keys to innovative internal auditing. (11)
11. Internal auditors should always be seen as control experts. (5)
12. Planning, organizing, directing and monitoring are essential parts of all control activities.(5)
13. Divisions of responsibilities are a key control mechanism. (5)
14. Financial, social, quality and environmental control objectives are international issues, across all supply chains, in all sectors. (5)
15. Control embraces all aspects of governance, including ethics, equality, honesty, caring and sustaining. (13)
16. Creating integrated control frameworks in an organization provides an understanding of their strengths and weaknesses. (5)
17. Understanding how fraud is perpetrated is key to its prevention and detection. (6)

18. The best internal auditors review control in the past and present, and accurately forecast the future. (12)
19. Internal auditing should contribute to the reliability and integrity of all management reports and statements on control. (5)
20. Control self-assessment by managers is essential for all aspects of management and auditing. (5)
21. Success of internal auditing lies in how it is researched and developed, and then promoted in the organization market place. (14)
22. Innovation and understanding its customers' needs are the keys to how internal auditing should be sold throughout the audit process. (14)
23. Internal auditing vision and mission statements must be exciting. (3)
24. Measures of internal auditing performance must be linked to its customers' and organization's objectives. (5)
25. Audit committees should strengthen internal auditing objectivity and independence. (7)
26. Internal audit charters must be based on professional standards and ethics. (3)
27. Use superlatives to reinforce internal audit staff and market their services. (14)
28. Internal auditing procedures and documents are an essential part of marketing internal auditing quality. (8)
29. Benchmark internal audit marketing with the marketing of other services, within and outside the organization it serves. (9)
30. Market internal auditing as a contribution to your organization's quality improvement programme. (14)
31. Successful internal audit teams in an organization's web of teams are everything. (15)
32. Look for features of excellence in internal audit teamwork. (3)
33. Use team concepts to encourage change, quality and innovation in the internal audit unit and organization it serves. (10)
34. Learn to recognize, applaud and reward achievement by internal audit teams. (8)
35. Audit recommendations are best when they are created by a successful team. (15)

Appendix B
Cutting Edge Internal
Auditing Principia 2008

(At the end of each principle the chapter in which it is discussed is shown in brackets)

1. World-class status for internal auditing requires a vision for its professionalism, quality and standards that meets the needs of all its customers, at all levels in an organization and those outside the organization. (3)
2. All internal audit teams should strive for a world-class status in their engagements and be appropriately rewarded when this is achieved. (3)
3. Internal auditing is developing as a spectrum of unrestricted traditional, new and cutting edge activities across all organizations of all sizes, in all sectors. (4)
4. Good governance is fundamental for all management practices, in all parts of an organization, at all levels and across all its supply chains and operating relationships: this includes the principles of integrity, openness and accountability in all transactions. (5)
5. Governance should be established as a framework of directing and controlling to encourage good performance and discourage evil in the achievement of economic, social and environmental objectives. (5)
6. Internal auditors should be trained and experienced to be able to promote themselves as experts in the practices and coordination of risk management, control and governance processes. (5)
7. Internal auditing performance should always be measured against the status and state of governance in an organization. (5)
8. Internal auditing should encourage and contribute to the self-assessment of risk management, control and governance by all employees at all levels in an organization: this contribution can be by teaching the principles on which these are based. (5)
9. Internal auditing should fight all types of crime at all levels in an organization at all levels, across all relationships with its stakeholders and the public. (6)
10. The primary role of internal auditing is to assist board performance in the achievement of the organization's vision and objectives, within a well governed, regulated and legitimate environment. (7)
11. A total commitment to quality principles, practices and customer delight in an internal audit activity is essential for its success, if not survival. (8)

12. Knowledge and experience of benchmarking are essential for internal auditing in the management of its performance, in the auditing/review processes in all its engagements, and the assurance/consulting services it provides. (9)
13. The focus of internal audit benchmarking should always be on the needs of its customers and stakeholders of the organizations it serves. (9)
14. Benchmarking should never be a 'one-off' activity. It is a continuous process for improvement. (9)
15. A commitment to continuous improvement in all the services provided by internal auditing is essential if the needs of all its customers and suppliers are to be satisfied now and in the future.
16. Creative thinking in internal auditing is essential and should be encouraged by experiment and development to support continuous improvement in all its resources and practices. (11)
17. Internal auditing should use its engagements to evaluate the creative thinking and processes in all the operations it reviews. (11)
18. It is essential for internal auditing to ask the right questions of the past, present, future and 'beyond the horizon', to the right people and from a good knowledge and understanding of risks, controls and governance.
19. Internal auditing has a responsibility to contribute to the processes of assessing reputation risks and advising at all levels in their organizations on how reputation can be managed and enhanced through good corporate responsibility practices. (13)
20. Success of internal auditing lies in how its professional best practices are researched, developed and promoted in its organization market place. (14)
21. Understanding its customers risk management, control and governance needs are the keys to how internal auditing should be sold throughout the audit process. (14)
22. Use superlatives to reinforce internal audit staff and promote their services. (14)
23. Internal auditing must attract and encourage knowledgeable and talented people to be internal auditors and to be members of the internal audit team. (15)
24. Internal auditors must manage their knowledge well, for their own continuous development and success of the teams in which they participate. (15)
25. Knowledge in internal auditing needs to be maintained, developed and managed continuously, as a means to an end and not an end in itself. (15)

Appendix C
Answers To Self-Assessment Questions

Chapter 4

4.1 My fifteen hats are:

Manager	Team Player	Auditor	Assurer	Consultant
Risk Adviser	Teacher	Researcher	Regulator	Networker
Communicator	Motivator	Ambassador	Diplomat	Innovator

Chapter 9

9.1 and 9.2 What score did you obtain?
32–48   You are ready for benchmarking
16–31   You need some preparation
0–15   You need some help!

Any difference between the two scores will require some analysis of why this exists, preferably by a team consisting of both management and internal auditors.

Chapter 15

15.1 Solution: (c)

(a) *Incorrect.* Audit management should always be informed concerning any such offers.
(b) *Incorrect.* Audit management should always be informed concerning any such offers.
(c) *Correct.* Audit management should be consulted for guidance.
(d) *Incorrect.* This could erode the audit function's relationship with the division in question. Audit management should first be informed and consulted for guidance.

15.2 Solution: (d)

(a) *Incorrect.* Even if the auditor avoided contact with the controller, there would still be the appearance of conflict of interest.
(b) *Incorrect.* Situations of potential conflict of interest or bias should be avoided, not merely disclosed.
(c) *Incorrect.* Conflicts of interest should be reported to the chief audit executive, not the vendor or engagement client.

(d) *Correct*. Practice Advisory 1130-1.1 states that internal auditors should report to the chief audit executive any situations in which a conflict of interest or bias is present or may reasonably be inferred.

15.3 Solution: (d) (I, II and IV only)

I, II, IV. *Correct*. Internal auditors are expected to be able to recognize good business practices, understand human relations, and be skilled in oral and written communications.

III. *Incorrect*. Internal auditors are not expected to be experts in a wide variety of fields related to their audit responsibilities.

15.4 Solution: (d)

(a) *Incorrect*. Internal auditors should not attempt to influence regulators' interpretations of law.

(b) *Incorrect*. Internal auditors should not attempt to influence the scope of work of the regulatory examiners. This would be unethical and a violation of the *IIA Code of Ethics*.

(c) *Incorrect*. Internal auditors should not perform fieldwork for regulatory examiners.

(d) *Correct*. Internal auditors have immediate access to workpapers and reports, which can supply evidence of compliance testing to the regulatory examiners.

15.5 Solution: (b)

(a) *Incorrect*. This does not conflict with the independence of the internal audit activity.

(b) *Correct*. In some circumstances, such as a product development team, the role of team leader or member may conflict with the independence attribute of the internal audit activity. The auditor can participate as a consultant to the team but should not participate as a team leader.

(c) *Incorrect*. To improve the ethical climate, the internal auditor should assume the role of ethics advocate, which therefore does not conflict with the independence of the internal audit activity.

(d) *Incorrect*. This does not conflict with the independence of the internal audit activity as the internal and external audit functions both share information and work collaboratively outside of the influence of management.

15.6 Solution: (d) (I, II, III, and IV)

I. *Correct*. Evaluating whether ethics and values are promoted would contribute to corporate governance, according to Standard 2130.

II. *Correct*. Evaluating the effectiveness of organizational performance management and accountability would contribute to corporate governance, according to Standard 2130.

III. *Correct*. Evaluating how risk and control information is communicated would contribute to corporate governance, according to Standard 2130.

IV. *Correct*. Evaluating the coordination of the external and internal auditors and management would contribute to corporate governance, according to Standard 2130.

15.7 Solution: (a)

(a) *Correct*. This is supported by Implementation Standard 2120.A4.

(b) *Incorrect*. In instances where management has not established the criteria, or if, in the auditor's opinion, the established criteria are judged less than adequate, the auditor should work with management to develop appropriate evaluation criteria.

(c) *Incorrect*. These are sources of information which will assist management in establishing goals and objective, relevant, meaningful criteria.

(d) *Incorrect*. Accounting or auditing standards would not be appropriate for this purpose.

15.8 Solution: (d)

    (a) *Incorrect*. This assessment should be carried out at least annually.
    (b) *Incorrect*. The board may request the chief audit executive (CAE) to participate in assessing the performance of the external auditors, and this may include assessment of independence.
    (c) *Incorrect*. See answers (a) and (b).
    (d) *Correct*. See answers (a) and (b).

15.9 Solution: (a)

    (a) *Correct*. Organizations such as brokers, banks, and insurance companies may view risks as sufficiently critical to warrant continuous oversight and monitoring.
    (b) *Incorrect*. A separate compliance function may have recommendations to help strengthen controls but this is not their primary purpose.
    (c) *Incorrect*. Management is not independent as risk management is their direct responsibility.
    (d) *Incorrect*. This will help respond to shareholder needs, but it is not the primary reason for establishing the compliance function.

15.10 Solution: (d)

    (a) *Incorrect*. Corporate control mechanisms do include internal and external mechanisms.
    (b) *Incorrect*. Management's compensation scheme is part of corporate control mechanisms.
    (c) *Incorrect*. The dilution of shareholder's wealth resulting from employee stock options or employee stock bonuses is an accounting issue rather than a corporate governance issue.
    (d) *Correct*. The board is ultimately responsible for the company's corporate governance, not the internal auditors.

15.11 Solution: (c)

    (a) *Incorrect*. Management is able to change the organization's members.
    (b) *Incorrect*. Management is able to change the organization's structure.
    (c) *Correct*. Environment is often determined by external forces, outside the direct control of the organization.
    (d) *Incorrect*. Management is able to change the organization's technology.

15.12 Solution: (c)

    (a) *Incorrect*. Employees may be properly included on payroll, but the amounts paid may be unauthorized.
    (b) *Incorrect*. Undelivered checks provide no evidence regarding the validity of the amounts.
    (c) *Correct*. The employee's supervisor would be in the best position to ensure payment of the proper amount.
    (d) *Incorrect*. Witnessing a payroll distribution would not assure that amounts paid are authorized.

15.13 Solution: (a)

    (a) *Correct*. This preliminary survey information should prompt the auditor to identify the magnitude of such duplicate payments.
    (b) *Incorrect*. Unrecorded liabilities would not result.
    (c) *Incorrect*. The existence of duplicate payments is not related to a problem in the receiving area.
    (d) *Incorrect*. Duplicate payments are not overpayments; they are exceptions and should be handled as such.

15.14 Solution: (b)

(a) *Incorrect*. These trends would not result in scope expansion, because they are compatible.
(b) *Correct*. These trends may indicate inflated sales figures.
(c) *Incorrect*. These trends would not result in scope expansion, because they are compatible.
(d) *Incorrect*. These trends would not result in scope expansion, because they are compatible.

15.15 Solution: (c)

(a) *Incorrect*. Since new financial instruments are very risky, the first step of such an engagement should be to determine the nature of policies established for the investments.
(b) *Incorrect*. Oversight by a management committee is an important control. Therefore, the auditor should determine the nature of the oversight set up to monitor and authorize such investments.
(c) *Correct*. Although this might be informational, there is no need to develop a comparison of investment returns with other organizations. Indeed, some financial investment scandals show that such comparisons can be highly misleading because high returns were due to taking on a high level of risk. Also, this is not a test of the adequacy of the controls.
(d) *Incorrect*. A fundamental control concept over cash-like assets is that someone establishes a mechanism to monitor the risks.

15.16 Solution: (a)

(a) *Correct*. If the preliminary evaluation indicates control problems, the auditor usually decides to perform some expanded testing.
(b) *Incorrect*. If a flowchart were necessary, the auditor would have prepared one during the preliminary evaluation.
(c) *Incorrect*. The auditor is not ready to make a report until more work has been performed.
(d) *Incorrect*. Auditors do not implement controls; that is a function of management.

15.17 Solution: (b)

(a) *Incorrect*. This procedure would be useful only to determine if the cause was due to overstated inventory.
(b) *Correct*. An analysis of operations would be relevant in determining the efficiency of operations.
(c) *Incorrect*. Changes in equipment may signal an improvement in efficiency, but this approach would not be as relevant as that in answer (b).
(d) *Incorrect*. This procedure would be relevant in determining the correctness of raw materials purchases, but would not provide any evidence regarding the efficiency of operations.

15.18 Solution: (b)

(a) *Incorrect*. Access controls are tangential to the issue. Authorized, but incorrect data, could also be the problem.
(b) *Correct*. This procedure would establish the cause of the problem.
(c) *Incorrect*. This would provide useful information, but it is not as comprehensive as answer (b). Further, answer (b) provides more information on the cause.
(d) *Incorrect*. This tests only one source of the data inaccuracy (that is, the input of production data); other sources of potential error are ignored.

15.19 Solution: (a)

(a) *Correct*. This is the most appropriate procedure because: (i) the auditor has already determined that there is a concern; and (ii) this procedure results in a direct comparison of current parts requirements with purchase orders being generated. Differences can be identified and corrective action taken.

(b) *Incorrect.* This procedure provides evidence that all items entered are processed. Comparison with currently generated purchase orders does not provide evidence on whether the correct parts are being ordered.

(c) *Incorrect.* Generalized audit software is a good method to identify an inventory problem. However, the excess inventory may not be the result of a revised production technique. Answer (a) more directly addresses the audit concern.

(d) *Incorrect.* This procedure provides evidence on the input of data into the system, but does not provide evidence on whether changes in the production process have been implemented.

15.20 Solution: (a)

(a) *Correct.* A tailored program will be more relevant to an operation than will a generalized program.

(b) *Incorrect.* A generalized program cannot take into account variations resulting from changing circumstances and varied conditions.

(c) *Incorrect.* A generalized program cannot take into account variations in circumstances and conditions.

(d) *Incorrect.* Every aspect of an operation need not be examined — only those likely to conceal problems and difficulties.

(Recommended solutions are provided by The IIA)

Chapter 16

Visions/Motivations/Goals/Categories/Chapter Framework

Vision Groups	Motivations	Goals	Categories	Chapters
Professionalism				
2	1	4	1	2
3	8	5	2	3
4	13	7	8	4
8		8	9	8
12		9		12
14				14
15				15
Creativity				
9	2	1	3	9
10	4	2	4	10
11	5	3	5	11
	6		6	
	12			
Governance				
5	3	6	7	5
6	7	*	10	6
7	9	*		7
13	10			13
	11			

* A fault in my framework is that only one goal of fighting crime appears in the Group *Governance*, though most of the visions of the Group *Professionalism* contribute to good

governance. On reflection I should have added new goals in Chapter 5 (good example of continuous improvement!). My following suggestions for new Governance Goals are taken from The IIA 2006 Position Paper on organizational governance, discussed in Chapter 5:

1. Provide independent, objective assessments on the appropriateness of the organization's governance, structure and the operating effectiveness of specific governance activities.
2. Act as catalysts for change, advising or advocating improvements to enhance the organization's governance structure and practices.

Bibliography

The bibliography for cutting edge internal auditing in the 21st century starts with the many references in and at the end of each chapter. The following bibliography does not contain all these references. Articles in professional journals, including my own, are excluded: my own are presented in a separate listing in date order of publication. Apart from a few exceptions, what I have listed here is material published since the beginning of this century, which I believe should be on all internal audit activity bookshelves and available to be read and referenced into by every internal auditor in their pursuit of cutting edge internal auditing resources and practices.

Against each of the publications listed is a 'tick' box ☐. Use this box to indicate those publications you have read, referenced into recently or have in your internal audit activity's library. My recommendation is that all should be ticked.

The future will create more research and published material to guide professional internal auditing in its resources and practices. That is the progress of creativity and innovation in all professions, if not life. Keep adding to this bibliography through your own searches for best practices, wearing the many hats available to you. Continuously seek out best practices in the opportunities, challenges and adventures internal auditing will always provide.

Anastasi, Joe, John Wiley & Sons, Inc., Hoboken, New Jersey, USA
☐ (2003) *The New Forensics – Investigating Corporate Fraud and the Theft of Intellectual Property*

Attorney General's Office, London, England
☐ (2006) *Fraud Review – Final Report*

Bain & Company, Boston, USA
☐ (2007) *Management Tools 2007: An Executive Guide*, Darrell K. Rigby

Business in the Community (BITC), London, England
☐ (2003) *The Business Case for Corporate Responsibility*, Arthur D. Little
☐ (2005) *Rewarding Virtue – Effective Board Action on Corporate Responsibility*

Cabinet Office, United Kingdom Government, London, England
☐ (2001) *Getting it together – A Guide to Quality Schemes and the Delivery of Public Services*, Quality Schemes Team

Chambers, Andrew D., Management Audit LLP, Lincolnshire, England
☐ (1997) *The Operational Auditing Handbook,* and Graham Rand, John Wiley & Sons Ltd, Chichester, England
☐ (2005) *Tottel's Corporate Governance Handbook*, 3rd edition (2005), Tottel's Publishing, Haywards Heath, England
☐ (2005) *Tolley's Internal Auditor's Handbook*, LexisNexis Group, Great Britain

Chartered Institute of Management Accountants, London, England
☐ (2004) *Enterprise Governance – Getting the Balance Right*, with International Federation of Accountants

Chartered Institute of Public Finance and Accountancy, London, England
☐ (2004) *Good Governance Standards for Public Services*, Sir Alan Langlands, Office for Public Management Ltd, supported by the Joseph Rowntree Foundation
☐ (2007) *Delivering Good Governance in Local Government Framework* and *Delivering Good Governance in Local Government: Guidance Note for English Authorities*, with the Society of Local Authority Chief Executives and Senior Managers (SOLACE), London, England.

Committee of Sponsoring Organizations of Treadway Commission, Institute of Certified Public Accountants, New Jersey, USA
☐ (2004) *Enterprise Risk Management – Integrated Framework* American

Committee on Standards in Public Life, London, England
☐ (2007) *Annual Report 2006*

Department for Environment Food and Rural Affairs, London, England
☐ (2006) *Environmental Key Performance Indicators – Reporting Guidelines for UK Businesses*

Department for Innovation, Universities & Skills, London, England
☐ (2008) *Innovation Nation – Unlocking talent*, White Paper Cm 7345

Department of Trade & Industry, London, England
☐ (2000) *From Quality to Excellence*
☐ (2003) *Global Economy: The Innovation Challenge*
☐ (2006) *Succeeding Through Innovation*

Drucker, Peter F., Butterworth–Heinemann, Oxford, England
☐ (1955 reissue 2006) *The Practice of Management*
☐ (1967 reissue 2006) *The Effective Executive*

European Confederation of Institutes of Internal Auditing, Brussels, Belgium
☐ (2005) Position Paper: *Internal Auditing in Europe*

European Foundation for Quality Management, Brussels, Belgium
☐ (1999) *EFQM Excellence Model*

Financial Reporting Council, London, England
☐ (2003) *Audit Committees Combined Code Guidance*, Sir Robert Smith
☐ (2005) *Internal Control: Revised Guidance for Directors on the Combined Code* (Flint report)
☐ (2006) *The Combined Code on Corporate Governance*

Fraud Advisory Panel, London, England
☐ (2007) *Which Way Now? Evaluating the Government's Fraud Review, Eighth Annual Report 2005–06*, London, England

Friedman, Thomas, Penguin, Penguin Books Ltd, London, England
☐ (2005) *The World is Flat – A Brief History of the Globalized World in the 21st Century*

Global Reporting Initiative, Amsterdam, The Netherlands
☐ (2000) *Sustainability Reporting Guidelines on Economic, Environmental and Social Performance*
☐ (2006) *Sustainability Reporting Guidelines*

HM Treasury, London, England
☐ (2001) *Holding to Account*, The Review of Audit and Accountability for Central Government, Lord Sharman of Redlynch

☐ (2002) *Government Internal Audit Standards – Quality Assurance Questionnaires*
☐ (2003) *Managing the Risk of Fraud – A Guide for Managers*

☐ (2004) *Good Practices Tackling External Fraud*, and National Audit Office
☐ (2004) *The Orange Book: Management of Risk – Principles and Concepts*
☐ (2004) *Building Effective Boards: Enhancing the Effectiveness of Independent Boards in Executive Non-Departmental Public Bodies* (2004), Lynton Barker
☐ (2005) Corporate Governance in Central Government Departments: *Code of Good Practice*, Professor Sir Andrew Likierman

Institute of Business Ethics, London, England
☐ (2001) *Risk Business – Towards Best Practices in Managing Reputation Risk*, Jenny Rayner
☐ (2005) *Setting the Tone – Ethical Business Leadership*, Philippa Foster Back OBE
☐ (2006) *Living Up to our Values – Developing Ethical Assurance* (2006), Nicole Dando and Walter Raven

Institute of Directors (2005), London, England
☐ (2005) *Director's Guide: Information Security*
☐ (2007) *Leading Health and Safety at Work* (2007), Consultation Draft, and Health and Safety Executive

Institute of Internal Auditors Inc.
☐ (1996) *Audit Customer Satisfaction: Marketing Added Value*, Cindy E. Cosmas
☐ (2000) *The Auditor's Guide to Internet Resources*, 2nd edition, Jim Kaplan
☐ (2003) *Sawyer's Internal Auditing – The Practice of Modern Internal Auditing*, 5th edition, Lawrence B. Sawyer, Mortimer A. Dittenhofer, James H. Scheiner
☐ (2004) Internal Auditing's Role in Sections 302 and 404 of the Sarbanes–Oxley Act
☐ (2005) *Global Technology Audit Guide (GTAG 1) – Information Technology Controls*
☐ (2006) *Organizational Governance: Guidance for Internal Auditors*
☐ (2006) *Quality Assessment Manual Fifth Edition*

Institute of Internal Auditors Research Foundation
☐ *(1995) Total Quality Improvement Process and The Internal Audit Function*
☐ (1996) *Enhancing Internal Auditing Through Innovative Practices*, Glen L. Gray and Maryann Jacobi Gray
☐ (1999) *Competency Framework for Internal Auditing (CFIA)*, Elaine R. McIntosh
☐ (2000) *Audit Committee Effectiveness – What Works Best*, 2nd edition, PricewaterhouseCoopers
☐ (2001) *Internal Audit Reengineering: Survey, Model, and Best Practices*, Parveen P. Gupta
☐ (2002) *Systems Assurance and Control* (SAC)
☐ (2002) *A Balanced Scorecard Framework for Internal Auditing Departments*, Mark L. Frigo
☐ (2003) *Continuous Auditing: Potential for Internal Auditors*, J. Donald Warren and Xenia Ley Parker
☐ (2004) *Sawyer's Words of Wisdom*, Lawrence B. Sawyer
☐ (2004) *Changing Internal Audit Practices in the New Paradigm: The Sarbanes–Oxley Environment*, G. Gray
☐ (2005) *Continuous Auditing: An Operational Model for Internal Auditors*, Mohammad J. Abdolmohammadi and Ahmad Sharbatouglie
☐ (2006) *Implementing the Professional Practices Framework*, 2nd edition, Urton Anderson and Andrew J. Dahie
☐ (2006) *Sustainability and Internal Auditing*, Hans Nieuwlands
☐ (2007) *Global Summary of the Common Body of Knowledge 2006*, Preview Edition
☐ (2007) *Four Approaches to Enterprise Risk Management. . . and Opportunities in Sarbanes–Oxley Compliance* (2007), James Roth, Donald Esperen, Daniel Swanson, Paul Sobel

Institute of Internal Auditors – UK & Ireland
☐ (1993) *Professional Briefing Note Two: Environmental Audit*
☐ (1999) *Professional Briefing Note Fifteen: Ethical and Social Responsibility*
☐ (2000) *Benchmarking Survey*

☐ (2000) *Effective Marketing: Guidance on Marketing your Internal Audit Function*
☐ (2000) *Learning for the Longer Term*
☐ (2000) *Audit Committees and Internal Auditors* – A Position Statement
☐ (2000) *Corporate Ethics and Social Responsibility*
☐ (2001) *Whistleblowing and the Internal Auditor* – A Position Statement
☐ (2003) *Risk Based Internal Auditing* – Position Paper
☐ (2003) *Ethical and Social Auditing and Reporting* – *The Challenge for the Internal Auditor*
☐ (2004) *Internal Auditing Standards* – *Why They Matter*
☐ (2007) *Meeting higher expectations*
☐ (2007) *Quality assurance and improvement programmes*

International Chambers of Commerce, Paris, France
☐ (2005) *Rules of Conduct and Recommendations*

Moeller, Robert, John Wiley & Sons Ltd, Chichester, England.
☐ (2005) *Brink's Modern Internal Auditing Sixth Edition*

National Council For Voluntary Organizations, London, England
☐ (2005) *Good Governance* – *A Code for the Voluntary and Community Sector*, developed with Association of Chief Executives of Voluntary Organizations (ACEVO), Charity Trustees Network (CTN) and Institute of Chartered Secretaries and Administrators (ICSA)

National Association of Pension Funds (NAPF) London, England
☐ (2005) *Pension Scheme Governance* – *Fit for the 21st Century?*

Oakland, John S., Butterworth–Heinemann, Oxford, England
☐ (2002) *Total Organizational Excellence* – *Achieving Worldclass Performance*

Organization for Economic and Cooperation Development, Paris, France.
☐ (2004) *Principles of Corporate Governance*

O'Regan, David, John Wiley & Sons, Hoboken, New Jersey, USA
☐ (2003) *International Auditing*
☐ (2004) *Auditor's Dictionary* – *Terms, Concepts, Processes, and Regulations*

Rayner, Jenny, John Wiley & Sons Ltd, Chichester, England
☐ (2003) *Managing Reputational Risk* – *Curbing Threats, Leveraging Opportunities*

Ridley, Jeffrey and Chambers, Andrew D., ICSA Publishing, London, England
☐ (1998 reissued 2007) *Leading Edge Internal Auditing*

Ridley, Jeffrey, John Wiley & Sons Ltd, Chichester, England
☐ (2008) *Cutting Edge Internal Auditing*

Spencer Pickett, K.H.
☐ (2002) *Financial Crime Investigation and Control*, John Wiley & Sons Inc., New York, USA
☐ (2003) *The Internal Auditing Handbook*, 2nd edition, John Wiley & Sons Ltd, Chichester, England

Treadway Commission, American Institute of Certified Public Accountants, New Jersey, USA
☐ (1987) *Report of the National Commission on Fraudulent Financial Reporting*

Tomorrow's Company, London, England
☐ (2006) *Tomorrow's Global Company* – *The Challenges and Choices: Climate change* – *the role of global companies*

Chronology Of Author's Articles And Research

Author's articles and research, published between 1975 and 2006, included in chapters

Chapter 13   *Quality and Environmental Auditing – A Time for Internal Auditors to be Involved* (1997)
'...few internal auditors have become involved in environmental auditing.'

Chapter 14   *All-Year Greetings from Internal Auditing* (1997)
'There are still too few good examples of internal auditing brochures, selling a leading edge service, linked to professional standards, ethics and delighted customers.'

Chapter 14   *Marketing Internal Auditing Starts with a Vision* (1998)
'The research showed that only a few internal auditing functions had approached the marketing of their internal auditing using a vision statement and business plan.'

Chapter 1   *We Should Have a Vision to be Innovators* (1998)
'Creativity, innovation and experimentation are now key to our professional success. They must be the vision of all internal auditing functions.'

Chapter 9   *Have a 'Best Value' Christmas and Prosperous 'Learning' New Year* (1998)
'Understanding and experience of best practice benchmarking is the key to best value.'

Chapter 3   *A New Internal Auditor for a New Century* (2000)
'In a competitive market place you also need to be a quality champion, self-assess the value of your quality initiatives and measure your customers' satisfaction.'

Chapter 4   *Internal Auditors are Ambassadors in the Commonwealth...Across the European Union, and Internationally Too!* (2000)
'I have always strongly believed that internal auditors are 'ambassadors' of good governance conduct and best practices, at all levels in their organizations, and in all their travels.'

Chapter 5   *Weak Links in the Supply Chain* (2000)
'Today's and tomorrow's internal auditors must also decorate their risk assessment, audit planning, working papers and audit reports with the many external supply chains in every audit.'

Chapter 5   *Risk Management, Control and Governance Challenges and Opportunities for Internal Auditors* (2000)
'Internal auditors will have to take the power of risk assessment to their elbows...'

Chapter 7   *How Effective is Your Audit Committee?* (2000)
'Only when all audit committees take seriously the importance of benchmarking themselves against worldwide best practices, will their contribution to good governance be at its best.'

Chapter 13   *Social Responsibility – A Challenge for Organizations and Internal Auditing* (2000)
'...social responsibility is now an important part of the principles of good corporate governance...'

Chapter 9   *Shout How Best You Are in All Your Internal Audit Market Places* (2001)
'When best practice is achieved it should be shouted to all customers.'

Chapter 13   *Skeletons in the Closet* (2001)
'What can be more important than health, safety and the environment?'

Chapter 8   *Quality Schemes and Best Value in the 21st Century* (2001)
'A successful internal auditing role requires all internal auditors to understand how quality schemes contribute to success.'

Chapter 12   *Mind Your Language* (2001)
'Popular words used in 1996 to describe internal auditor qualities were – rigorous, astute, self-starter, innovative, proactive, creative, leader. They are still used today. How do you use these terms in the questions you ask your auditees?'

Chapter 15   *Wise Internal Auditors Manage Knowledge Well* (2001)
'Knowledge management is a means of developing, capturing and communicating information.'

Chapter 16   *Worth Repeating* (2001)
'Internal auditing...an important part of the management team.'

Index

Index compiled by Annette Musker